Marguerite Patten

Cooking Today

in colour

Hamlyn

London · Sydney · New York · Toronto

© Copyright 1971 The Hamlyn Publishing Group Limited
Published by
THE HAMLYN PUBLISHING GROUP LIMITED
London · New York · Sydney · Toronto
Hamlyn House, Feltham, Middlesex, England
ISBN 0 600 36007 5

Reprinted 1972
Printed in Holland by Smeets, Weert.

The Publishers would like to thank

WRIGHTON INTERNATIONAL FURNITURE
for supplying the picture of Wrighton
kitchen units on the back cover

DOMESTIC APPLIANCE DIVISION OF
TUBE INVESTMENTS LTD.
for supplying two pictures of New
World Cookers on the front cover

Chocolate Almond Gâteau
Potato Soup
Pigeon and Mushroom Pie
PHOTOGRAPHS BY CHRISTIAN DELU

Turkey and accompaniments
PHOTOGRAPH BY JOHN LEE

Contents

Acknowledgments

These colour photographs are by the kind co-operation of:

AMERICAN RICE COUNCIL	Fish Goulash and Rice 7 Paprika Beef and Rice 12
AUSTRALIAN RECIPE SERVICE	Overlanders' Punch 48
BRITISH BACON CURERS' FEDERATION	Bacon Dishes 8
THE CHEESE BUREAU	Sole Mornay, Cheese Kedgeree 5
CHERRY VALLEY FARMS LTD.	Gosling and Spring Vegetables 19 Roast Duck and Salads 24
CHRISTIAN DELU	Potato Soup 1 Jellied Meat Mould 13 Roast Chicken 17 Chicken in Cider 21 Stuffed Red Peppers 22 Roast Venison 23 Party Quiche 28 Peach Meringue 30 Golden Orange Pudding 31 Chocolate Choux 32 Strawberry Milk Shake 34 Apricot Cream Diplomat 35 Pigeon and Mushroom Pie 37 Meringue Gâteau 44 Chocolate Almond Gâteau 47 Fudge 50
FLEETWAY STUDIOS	Stuffed Pancakes 14
FLOUR ADVISORY BUREAU	Open Sandwiches 27 Apricot and Walnut Bread Mixed Fruit Bread 38 Plaited Loaf and Rolls, etc. 39
FRUIT PRODUCERS' COUNCIL	Pear and Cheese Mousse 26
NEW ZEALAND LAMB INFORMATION BUREAU	Lamb Moussaka 11 Mixed Grill 20
PLUMROSE LTD.	Spice Cake 40 Danish Cornets 41
R. H. M. FOODS LTD.	Chicken and Vegetable Soup 2 Mediterranean Style Stuffed Herrings 3 Blackberry and Apple Pie 25 Scones 29 Swiss Roll 36 Butterfly Cakes 46 Birthday Cake 49
SYNDICATION INTERNATIONAL	Fish and Chips 6 Spaghetti Bolognese 9 Barbecued Steak 15 Stuffed Pork 16 Golden Fruit Pudding 33 Melon Supreme 42 Danish Apricot Crumble 43 Marmalade 45

Introduction

I have compiled this book to help make the metric system become more familiar and therefore easier to follow. In the future in Great Britain we shall purchase food and calculate ingredients in recipes by the metric system measurements of weight–that means in grammes, kilogrammes etc., rather than ounces and pounds.

Naturally this metric system can be confusing at first, but like everything new it will soon 'fit into place' and become acceptable.

The metric system (based on tens, like the decimal system) has advantages in that calculations are very easy to make; if you wish to prepare a smaller or larger quantity than in the recipe you can divide or multiply the ingredients very simply. You may have collected Continental recipes over the years–these can now be followed with less trouble, for in the future we shall use the same system of weighing and measuring as Continental countries.

Many of you will not wish to buy new weighing scales, so every recipe in this book, will give you *both* the old Imperial measurements (ounces etc.) *and* the new modern Metric measurements: in addition you will find guidance on American cup measurements in the table on page 11.

We live in a new and exciting world, with many wonderful inventions and developments–fortunately some of the most interesting work has been carried out in the field of kitchen appliances. Many homes today include one at least of these 'up to the minute' aids: I refer to articles such as automatic cookers, electric mixers, home freezers, etc. While manufacturers give excellent instructions on using the particular appliance, I feel it is also helpful to know just *how* you can make use of these when preparing a new recipe or an old favourite. You will, therefore, find that by each recipe I have given instructions as to whether it is suitable for an automatic oven, and if so, *how* to cook the dish and make it part of an automatic meal. You will also find general information on automatic cookers on page 12.

An electric mixer and liquidiser (often called a blender) is perhaps one of the most labour-saving of all kitchen appliances. It does enable one to prepare dishes that are normally complex and time-consuming in a relatively short time. Hints on the best use of your mixer and/or liquidiser are given where relevant, as well as on page 15.

In the past, one had no choice but to make every dish with basic fresh ingredients, but most of us who claim to be 'busy people' have discovered there are occasions when a convenience food may be incorporated in the recipe to save either preparation time or cooking time: so I have indicated just how this can be done.

Today there is a great deal of emphasis on 'keeping slim'–often it is because one wishes to wear clothes well, but more frequently it may be on medical advice, for doctors stress that a *fat* person is not necessarily a *fit* person and that one should establish a sensible weight and try to maintain this by correct diet. It is not easy when you are cooking for a family to have one menu for someone who wishes to lose weight and an entirely different menu for the rest of the family, so hints on making recipes less fattening are included. Sometimes, of course, this may not be possible– the recipe is just unsuitable for someone slimming; and where this is so it is stated. I must point out that this is *not* a slimmers book, it is *not* a book of special diets, *it is a book of food to be enjoyed*. If you have to go on a very strict diet you must follow a considerably more restricted menu specifically designed for weight reduction. Hints on slimming are given on page 17.

Over the years, refrigerators have *steadily* become an essential part of most homes; but the interest and rapid growth in the purchase and use of domestic freezers has been surprising to many people, until they have realised from their own experience, or that of close friends, the possibilities of a deep freezer in the home. It allows one to store food for a very much longer period than in a refrigerator. You can therefore prepare and cook dishes in larger quantities–and can freeze part of the food for other meals, so saving time in preparation *and* cooking. Like any new development though, *successful* home freezing depends on certain basic rules and you will find these outlined on page 19. I have, additionally included information for every recipe that is suitable for home freezing.

As you will see, this book contains a considerable amount of varied information; that is why it has been given the title of 'Cooking Today'. I hope you enjoy using this book, and that it will help you to produce interesting meals in the easiest manner.

Useful Facts and Figures

Oven temperatures

The following chart gives the conversions from degrees Fahrenheit to degrees Celsius (formerly known as Centigrade) recommended by the manufacturers of electric cookers.

Description	Electric Setting	Gas Mark
very cool	225° F.–110° C.	$\frac{1}{4}$
	250° F.–130° C.	$\frac{1}{2}$
cool	275° F.–140° C.	1
	300° F.–150° C.	2
very moderate	325° F.–170° C.	3
moderate	350° F.–180° C.	4
moderate to	375° F.–190° C.	5
moderately hot	400° F.–200° C.	6
hot	425° F.–220° C.	7
	450° F.–230° C.	8
very hot	475° F.–240° C.	9

NOTE: this table is an approximate guide only. Different makes of cooker vary and if you are in any doubt about the setting, it is as well to refer to the manufacturer's temperature chart.

Comparison of weights and measures

Imperial and Metric weights and measures have been used throughout this book. In addition it is useful to note that 3 teaspoons equal 1 tablespoon; the average English teacup is $\frac{1}{4}$ pint; the average English breakfast cup is $\frac{1}{2}$ pint; and when cups are mentioned in recipes they refer to a B.S.I. measuring cup of $\frac{1}{2}$ pint or 10 fluid ounces.

American equivalents are given in the conversion tables opposite for a variety of foodstuffs. It should be noted that the American pint is 16 fluid ounces, as opposed to the British Imperial and Canadian pints which are 20 fluid ounces. The American $\frac{1}{2}$-pint measuring cup is 8 fluid ounces and is therefore equivalent to $\frac{2}{5}$ British pint. In Australia the British Imperial pint, 20 fluid ounces, is used for liquid measures. Solid ingredients however are generally calculated in the American cup measure. In America, standard cup and spoon measurements are used.

Metrication

For quick and easy reference when buying food it should be remembered that 1 kilogramme (1000 grammes) equals 2·2 pounds (35$\frac{3}{4}$ ounces)– i.e. as a rough guide, $\frac{1}{2}$ kilogramme (500 grammes) is about 1 pound. In liquid measurements 1 litre (10 decilitres or 1000 millilitres) equals almost exactly 1$\frac{3}{4}$ pints (1·76), so $\frac{1}{2}$ litre is $\frac{7}{8}$ pint. As a rough guide, therefore, one can assume that the equivalent of 1 pint is a generous $\frac{1}{2}$ litre.

A simple method of converting recipe quantities is to use round figures instead of an exact conversion, and in this book a basic equivalent of 25 grammes to 1 ounce, and a generous $\frac{1}{2}$ litre to 1 pint has been used. Since 1 ounce is exactly 28·35 grammes and 1 pint is 568 millilitres it can be seen that these equivalents will give a slightly smaller finished dish, but the proportion of liquids to solids will remain the same and a satisfactory result will be produced.

The following tables show exact conversions to the nearest whole number and alongside the recommended amount.

Solid and dry ingredients

Imperial	Exact conversion to nearest whole number	Recommended equivalent*
Ounces	Grammes	Grammes
1	28	25
2	57	50
3	85	75
4	113	100
5	142	125
6	170	150
7	198	175
8	226	200

Liquids/fluids

Imperial	Exact conversion to nearest whole number	Recommended equivalent used only in some recipes*
Pints	Millilitres	Litres
1 pint (20 fl-oz)	568	$\frac{1}{2}$ litre–generous
$\frac{3}{4}$ pint	426	$\frac{3}{8}$ litre–generous
$\frac{1}{2}$ pint	284	$\frac{1}{4}$ litre–generous
$\frac{1}{4}$ pint	142	$\frac{1}{8}$ litre–generous
1 fl oz	28·4	25 ml
B.S.I. tablespoon		18 ml
B.S.I. teaspoon		5 ml

*see notes in each chapter.

BRITISH MEASURE	AMERICAN EQUIVALENT
FLOUR—PLAIN OR SELF-RAISING:	SIFTED FLOUR—ALL PURPOSE:
$\frac{1}{2}$ ounce ($1\frac{1}{2}$ level tablespoons, *BSI*)	3 tablespoons (*American*)
1 ounce (3 tablespoons, *BSI*)	$\frac{1}{4}$ cup (*American, measuring*)
4 ounces	1 cup
CORNFLOUR:	CORNSTARCH:
1 ounce	4 tablespoons (*American*)
$4\frac{1}{2}$ ounces	1 cup
ICING SUGAR:	SIFTED CONFECTIONERS' SUGAR:
7 ounces	1 cup
SOFT BROWN SUGAR:	LIGHT AND DARK BROWN SUGAR:
4 ounces	$\frac{1}{2}$ cup (firmly packed)
CASTOR OR GRANULATED SUGAR:	GRANULATED SUGAR:
4 ounces	$\frac{1}{2}$ cup
BUTTER, MARGARINE, COOKING FAT, LARD,	BUTTER, SHORTENING, LARD, DRIPPING,
DRIPPING:	SOLID OR MELTED:
1 ounce	2 tablespoons (*American*)
8 ounces	1 cup
GRATED CHEESE—CHEDDAR TYPE:	GRATED CHEESE—CHEDDAR TYPE:
4 ounces	1 cup
8 ounces grated Parmesan cheese	1 cup

CEREALS AND CEREAL FOODS	
8 ounces pearl barley/tapioca	1 cup
6 ounces semolina/ground rice	1 cup
3 ounces fresh soft breadcrumbs/cake crumbs	1 cup
2 ounces dried breadcrumbs	1 cup
2 ounces oatmeal	1 cup

VEGETABLES AND FRUITS	
4 ounces carrot	1 cup coarsely grated carrot
4 ounces cooked sweet corn	1 cup
4 sticks celery	1 cup chopped celery
7 ounces chopped tomatoes	1 cup
1 pound cooking apples	3 medium sized
1 pound eating apples	4 medium sized
3–4 ounces button mushrooms	1 cup
6 medium sized beetroot	1 cup diced beets
$\frac{1}{2}$ an average size cucumber	1 cup diced cucumber
6 ounces crushed strawberries	1 cup

PRESERVES	
12 ounces clear honey/golden syrup/ molasses/black treacle	1 cup
11 ounces maple syrup	1 cup
8 ounces jam/marmalade/jelly	1 cup

DRIED FRUITS, NUTS	
6 ounces currants/sultanas/raisins	1 cup
4 ounces mixed candied peel	1 cup
5 ounces whole shelled almonds	1 cup

Using an Automatic Cooker

A wide range of both gas and electric cookers are fitted with an automatic timing device. This means that uncooked food may be placed in the cold oven and the oven pre-set for the correct cooking time to produce a meal much later in the day. Using the cooker will entail firstly a thorough check to make certain you are familiar with the controls, then:

a) setting the time the oven should be turned or switched ON and also OFF,

b) ensuring that the gas setting or electric thermostat are at the correct position for the particular menu,

c) making certain that the main gas supply or electric main switch are on.

Foods that can be put in a cold oven and left to cook automatically are many – you can put breakfast in the oven overnight to be ready at the time you want, or – if you are out all day – you can put dishes or a complete menu in the oven and set the controls so that the oven switches on automatically at a pre-planned time. This will enable you to come home in the evening and find a meal ready-cooked.

MEAT, POULTRY AND FISH: cook as usual – do not over-time the cooking period for fish.

VEGETABLES: do not try and cook green vegetables this way.

PEAS, CARROTS, OTHER ROOT VEGETABLES: cook in a casserole, see below and full instructions on page 110.

CAKE AND SPONGE MIXTURES: excellent, except for a sponge where the eggs and sugar are whisked together.

PASTRY: shortcrust or flaky – excellent: not suitable for puff pastry.

YEAST COOKERY: excellent; make sure the dough is well proved and the oven set to switch on almost immediately the food is put into the oven.

BATTERS: a Yorkshire pudding batter can be left in a very well greased tin in the oven.

Manufacturers of the cookers give a great deal of information on suitable menus. In this book, therefore, I aim to extend this service and show how the majority of dishes may be cooked in an automatic oven. For example, many people do not realise you can –

1. *Cook most vegetables* (excluding green vegetables which lose their Vitamin C) in the oven.

Specific recommendations for vegetable cooking are given in that chapter, but all you need to do for 'boiled vegetables' is place the prepared vegetables in a casserole, *cover* with cold water, add seasoning and a small knob of butter or margarine (which helps to retain flavour and appearance) and *cover* the container very tightly. You may find a casserole lid is an insufficient covering, in which case, use foil and be sure to tuck the edges very tightly round the container.

2. *Steam the majority of puddings in an oven.* The first essential is to make certain that you have an outer container sufficiently large so that you have enough cold water around the pudding in its basin, to create the conditions of steaming. Cover the pudding in the usual way, but you then need a second cover which goes over the pudding *and* the container of water. This is to stop the water evaporating. You could use either foil or a casserole lid, (should you be using a casserole as the outside container) or even a cake tin (without a loose base), a bigger basin or an ovenproof mixing bowl. Naturally the oven temperature must be suitable for the particular pudding you are cooking. If you are reheating a Christmas pudding, for example, most temperatures are suitable. You would simply allow a long period of reheating in a cool oven, and a shorter period when reheating in a hotter oven. Should you use this oven 'steaming' method for cooking a sponge pudding, it is very important to have the oven *sufficiently hot* so that the uncooked pudding will rise properly. You could not put an uncooked sponge pudding into a very cool oven and expect a good result. Use a moderate oven, approximately 350–375°F. (180–190°C.) Gas Mark 4–5, and allow approximately 1¼ hours in the centre of the oven for a sponge

pudding made with 5–6 oz. flour, etc. If the oven is hotter, protect the outer container by wrapping in foil and try to shorten the cooking time to 1¼ hours. If the oven temperature is very moderate, 325–350°F. (190–200°C.) Gas Mark 3–4, allow about 1¾ hours, but do not use a lower setting for an uncooked pudding mixture.

3. *The rather surprising thing* about an automatic oven is that you can place most foods in a cold oven without harming them. People are generally very surprised that cake mixtures, yeast doughs, etc., are quite satisfactory. In my experience, the only foods that are a dismal failure when placed in a cold oven are:
a) puff pastry–other pastry is quite all right,
b) the type of sponge where you whisk the eggs and sugar (used for Swiss rolls, etc.)–a Victoria Sandwich mixture is quite successful,
c) scones are less good than when baked immediately.
Naturally, one needs to follow slightly different techniques on occasions, and specific information about each group of foods, i.e. pastry, vegetables, etc., will be found at the beginning of each chapter.

To use an automatic oven successfully:

1. Select the menu carefully–choose dishes that need approximately the same cooking time.

2. Place the prepared dishes in the correct position, i.e. those that need the hottest part of the oven towards the top of the oven, etc.

3. If you are afraid of the pudding or pie browning too much by the time the meat, etc., is cooked, put a double sheet of greaseproof paper or foil on

top, to hinder browning. You can adjust cooking times slightly by the position in which you place the food and by the container which you select, e.g. a sponge pudding that takes 1 hour in a 7-inch container would take 1¼ hours if cooked in a deep 6-inch container–so if necessary alter the size of the cooking container to suit your menu.

4. *Timing:* If you are sure you will be present to take the food out of the oven the *moment* it is ready and the oven turns itself off, allow just 5–10 minutes extra cooking time for the heating-up period. If you are *not sure* you will be present to take the food out of the oven the moment it is cooked, then allow normal cooking time, for the food will continue to cook in the warm oven and warm containers, even though the gas or electricity is switched off.

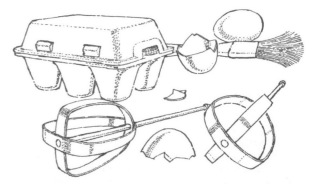

5. *Remember* to put plates and dishes to warm in the warming drawer if your cooker is equipped with one–failing this, put them into the oven for a short time.
You can also use the automatic timing device even if you are at home. You can place the food in the oven at the right setting and switch on–do not forget to set the cooker to the automatic position and the timer for the cooking period. This means that should you be busy in the house, in the garden or entertaining friends, you do not have to worry that the food cooking in the oven could be forgotten–the oven will switch off or turn off at the pre-determined hour.
When you have finished using the cooker on automatic timing, it is very *important* to check that you return this to the manual setting when controlling the oven yourself.

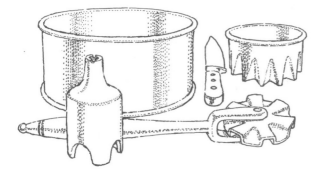

Producing Meals in a Shorter Time

I am always being asked how one can shorten time in either preparing or cooking food. Today many people *are* very short of time; possibly they run a home and have a job or career as well, and they need to produce appetising dishes with the minimum of delay. You will find, therefore, that where there is a 'short cut' I have mentioned this in both the introduction to the chapters and in the actual recipes. Some of the 'short cuts' you may care to try are:

1. Using a pressure cooker to shorten the actual cooking time; information on pressure cooking is given below.

2. Making use of convenience foods to save the preparation of fresh ingredients–convenience foods may be grouped as follows:
a) *Canned foods*–it is often possible to use a can of soup instead of making a sauce; to use canned vegetables instead of preparing fresh ones; to use canned fruits, etc., instead of cooking fresh fruit.
b) *Frozen foods*–these have become part of our everyday diet, and they enable one to have fruit and vegetables out of season in a very pleasant way: they can also save a great deal of time in the preparation of vegetables–so in many cases in a recipe you are given the choice of either fresh or frozen foods.
c) *Dried foods*–there have been great strides in commercial drying of foods. The modern method is known as A.F.D. (Accelerated Freeze Drying). Dehydrated soups are often an excellent way of producing a quick sauce or a flavouring in a stew or casserole dish. You can use stock cubes instead of home-made stock. Dehydrated herbs enable you to add flavouring when fresh herbs are difficult to obtain, and dehydrated vegetables such as peas, onions, celery, etc., may be used instead of the fresh vegetables.

3. Sometimes there is a quick 'cut' to a recipe, for example on page 146 you have the usual methods of making white sauce, but also tips on making it in an easier and quicker manner.
Very often it is possible to save time by preparing double quantities of pastry, etc. on one day, some of which can be stored in the refrigerator or freezer to use later, in another dish.
This book will give you time-saving hints wherever possible. One of the best ways of saving cooking time is by cooking food in a pressure cooker, often called a pressure pan.

Using a pressure cooker

Manufacturers of pressure cookers will give you detailed information for the particular model in their own instruction book. These are the points to remember:

1. The reason foods cook so quickly in a pressure cooker is because when the weight is placed in position you bring the temperature of water in this container far higher than boiling point (100°C., 212°F.). This means that all foods are being cooked at a very much higher temperature than usual, and so are tender within a much shorter period.

2. Many people are a little nervous about using a pressure cooker, but until the weight is put in position and the pressure built up inside, your pressure cooker is just an ordinary saucepan, and indeed can be treated as such. When pressure is built up inside, you will recognise this by the noise, and it is then important to reduce the heat so you maintain the pressure but do not increase it; experience will tell you how to deal with this.

3. Sometimes you will be told to allow the pressure to 'drop at room temperature'. This means you remove the cooker from the heat, and allow the pressure to drop without any further attention.

4. Sometimes you will be told to cool the cooker immediately or to 'reduce pressure instantly'. This means that you should lift the pressure cooker into the sink and either stand it in cold water or allow the cold water to run over the top of the cooker. The reason for this is to make certain the food does not over-cook in the hot container.

5. WHICHEVER METHOD OF COOLING YOU ARE USING, DO NOT PULL THE PRESSURE WEIGHT OFF THE TOP OF THE COOKER. IF YOU DO YOU WILL HAVE A SUDDEN 'BURST' OF STEAM WHICH COULD SCALD YOU: IF YOU HAVE SOUP OR OTHER LIQUID INSIDE THIS COULD SPURT OUT. IF YOU WANT TO TEST IF THE PRESSURE HAS DROPPED, TOUCH THE WEIGHT VERY GENTLY WITH A FORK AND IF THERE IS NO HISSING, TEST A SECOND TIME TO BE SURE. YOU MAY THEN REMOVE THE WEIGHT AND OPEN THE COOKER.

6. Because I believe a pressure cooker used wisely and selectively is ideal for saving time, I have given brief information in each chapter.

Using an Electric Mixer or Blender

The various models of electric mixers vary in price and size, they range from small portable hand mixers to large models on their own stand. When you buy an electric mixer, therefore, it is important to decide just how much you will be using it. If dealing with fairly small quantities of ingredients only, when making cakes, etc., undoubtedly a small hand mixer is adequate. Generally speaking, these are extremely efficient–the one attachment will be equally good at creaming fat and sugar, vegetables such as potatoes, whisking egg whites for meringues, or cream, etc. It is sometimes possible to get a stand and bowl for these small mixers, which makes them 'dual purpose'–they can be used as a portable mixer (which you hold), or the type of mixer where you leave the food in the bowl, switch on, and the mixer will do the work with little if any attention. Obviously if dealing with larger quantities of food, it is worth while investing in one of the larger electric mixers. In addition to creaming, whisking, beating, you will find that larger models have extra attachments that will mince, shred and do a great variety of other jobs in preparing food.

Do not confuse a liquidiser (often called a blender) with an electric mixer. Sometimes the liquidiser *is* an attachment that fits on to a mixer; often it is an entirely separate appliance. The purpose of a liquidiser is quite different from a mixer, for example you cannot use it to stiffly whisk egg whites, and it is not meant for creaming. The main uses are:

a) to give smooth purées of fruits, vegetables, ingredients for soups, etc.,

b) to prepare milk shakes and other drinks,

c) to prepare dry ingredients, e.g. many kinds of stuffing; make breadcrumbs; chop nuts, etc.

Obviously it is important to refer to the manufacturer's instructions as to what your particular liquidiser will do. Many people have spoiled the blades at the base of the liquidiser by expecting it to grind coffee and deal with other very hard substances. Some liquidisers may well do this, if they will, the manufacturer will tell you.

To get the best use from your mixer:

When creaming–modern margarine can often be used straight from the refrigerator, but it is unwise to make the initial creaming of fat of any kind too laboured for a mixer; if you do, you are inclined to over-heat the motor of the mixer. It is a mistake, of course, to melt fat when creaming (unless the recipe says so) for you exclude the air, and do not produce a really light mixture. It is far better just to warm the mixer bowl or basin before putting in the fat and sugar; in this way creaming is made simple. Where you have a choice of speeds on your mixer, it is a mistake to use a very fast one when creaming, for you throw the fat and sugar against the sides of the bowl or basin, and will need to stop and scrape this from time to time.

SPEED–always use a slow or steady speed when creaming fat and sugar, vegetables, etc.

When whisking–the basic rules you observe when

hand whisking apply when using a mixer. If whisking *egg whites* make absolutely certain that the bowl is cool and dry, with no specks of egg yolk or grease. *Cream* thickens very quickly with the help of an electric mixer–it is, therefore, unwise to leave this unattended, for over-whipped cream becomes 'buttery' and is spoiled. When making *mayonnaise*, this may be prepared with a mixer or liquidiser (see below). Follow the same rules for making mayonnaise as if you were doing it by hand, see recipe. You will find, however, that with the greater power of an electric mixer you can add the oil *slightly* quicker.

SPEED–maximum for egg whites; slower for cream, mayonnaise.

When beating–the term 'beating' is a fairly elastic one–you can use a mixer for beating the eggs for an omelette or the ingredients for a pancake batter.

SPEED–where the mixture is rather soft and liquid, use a low speed to prevent splashing. Many cake recipes talk about 'beating the ingredients together', here again you are well advised to use a low speed.

In making icings such as a Royal icing you beat the mixture; an electric mixer is admirable for this. *It is, however, very important that you do not over-beat a Royal icing, otherwise you incorporate too much air and cannot get a smooth coating on the cake, and also it will be very difficult to pipe as the captured air prevents a smooth flow of icing.* Therefore, beat only until the icing is shiny and white: again, a slow speed is better.

When folding–in many recipes you will find the term 'folding'. One folds the sugar into egg whites for some meringues. You can do this with an electric mixer using the *lowest speed.* In many cake recipes it is necessary to fold the flour into the rest of the ingredients. In my experience, a mixer is not a good idea for this particular purpose. It is virtually impossible to reduce the speed of the average mixer sufficiently, and there is a tendency to over-beat the flour–so impairing the texture of the cake. You can add the flour in a cake recipe where you are told to beat this in, but *not* where you are instructed to fold or blend gently.
SPEED–generally low, but see above.

To get the best use from your liquidiser when making purées:
It is important that a liquidiser goblet is warmed by holding it over the pan of steaming mixture before making a purée of *hot* fruit, vegetables, etc. Never leave the liquidiser running if the purée is so thick that the blades cannot revolve. Switch off, and add a little extra liquid. The blades should always be able to revolve freely. *Remember that when you switch on a liquidiser to make a purée you should not over-fill the goblet.*
SPEED–*it is advisable to start on a low speed to prevent the mixture rising in the container, for the force of the purée could dislodge the lid, and create a great deal of mess as well as a danger of scalding your hand.*

When making drinks–there are a great number of drinks one can make in a liquidiser, ranging from flavoured milk shakes to more sophisticated cocktails.
SPEED–where you wish the mixture to rise, as in a milk shake, use the highest speed and be careful not to over-fill the goblet.

When making stuffings–do not over-fill the goblet with the dry ingredients–it is better to add these slowly, see the chapter Stuffings and relishes.
SPEED–generally medium.

When making mayonnaise–there is a technique in making this in a liquidiser, as in a bowl–read the recipe carefully on page 154.
SPEED–slow, increasing slightly as the oil is added.

Care of your electric mixer

It is important to read the manufacturer's card or instruction book carefully, and to check if regular servicing is recommended. If so, then have this carried out at the specified periods.
NEVER use the mixer or any part of this when it seems to be running incorrectly, otherwise you might well cause more damage, which could be quite costly.
One of the most usual faults in using a mixer (or any part of this) is to put too much strain on the motor–if the machine seems unduly hot or smells of burning or runs badly, then switch OFF at once. It may just be you are overworking the machine and motor, and if you rectify this mistake all will be well; remove some of the food, start again, check carefully. Briefly these are the things that give a mixer too much effort:

1. Over-filling the goblet of the liquidiser (blender) –you strain both the motor and the blades, and get a poor result.

2. Trying to cream fat that is too hard, so making it impossible for the whisk or beater to turn properly–see recommendation on creaming.

3. Using an incorrect speed for the particular job– use slow speeds when handling heavy ingredients; quicker speed for light ingredients, or when the mixture has become softer.

4. Putting food into the liquidiser *too quickly* through the mincing or shredding attachment OR having pieces of food which are too large so the blades cannot cope. If this happens, SWITCH OFF, remove food, cut more finely, and start again– NEVER PUT YOUR FINGERS INTO THE GOBLET OR NEAR THE MINCER WHEN IN MOVEMENT; AND NEVER PUSH THE FOOD WITH A SHARP KNIFE.

Slimming in a Practical Way

As stressed in the introduction, this book is *not* a book for strict slimming diets. It is, however, a book which enables you to *adapt* recipes to be less fattening. In order to understand what happens to most people when they are over-weight one must realise that the amount of energy given by foods is measured in terms of a heat unit called a calorie. Just as a car engine needs fuel to enable it to work properly, so the body needs food to give it energy. This energy is used in working, for creating warmth, and even when sleeping it is needed for breathing and keeping the heart beating. A calorie is the amount of heat required to raise the temperature of 1,000 grammes (approximately 2 pints) of water by one degree centigrade. The amount of calories in foods varies a great deal. If more calories are eaten than are required for an individual's daily activity they will be converted into fat by the body. This means that when you need to lose weight you cut down on your calories. An ideal slimming diet, however, provides the essential foods—protein, vitamins, etc. *Any drastic slimming diet must be followed only under doctor's orders.*

Fats and carbohydrates (starches and sugars) are HIGH CALORIE FOODS. Green vegetables and certain fruits (particularly citrus fruits) are LOW CALORIE FOODS, and also provide essential Vitamin C.

If you wish to lose just a small amount of weight, it is possible to do this if you change and adapt family recipes by *omitting or reducing fats and carbohydrates.* If you need to lose a considerable amount of weight you require a 'long-term' slimming diet.

When you look at the calories for *meat* it may appear that this is high in calories. Obviously very fat meat will be more fattening than lean meat, but meat is an essential protein and as such has a very important place in a normal slimming diet. *Fish* is another excellent protein food, and much fish is low in calories too. *Cheese* is high in calories (with the exception of cottage cheese) but it provides not only protein but calcium as well, so in most diets a certain amount of cheese should be included. *Eggs and milk* are important foods—the former being relatively low in calories. You can reduce the calories in milk by having skimmed rather than creamy milk.

As the calorie content of food can be increased by the method of cooking—heated fat in frying for instance, being readily taken up by most foods—I have suggested alongside the recipes how this may be avoided.

Table of Calorie Values

Food	Amount	Calories
BEVERAGES		
Beer—ale, mild	½ pint	130
Beer—ale, strong	½ pint	210
Cider	½ pint	120
Chocolate	1 cup	180
Cocoa—½ milk	1 cup	110
Coffee—black	1 cup	0
Coffee—milk, no sugar	1 cup	30
Coffee—milk and sugar	1 cup	85
Malted drinks	1 cup	205
Mineral waters—artificial	1 glass	100
Spirits—brandy, gin, rum	1 oz.	75
Tea—milk, no sugar	1 cup	20
Tea—milk and sugar	1 cup	75
Wines—port, sherry	2 oz.	90
Wines—table, dry	4 oz.	70
BISCUITS		
Biscuits—plain	1 oz.	105–115
Biscuits—sweet	1 oz.	135–145
Crispbread—starch-reduced	1 oz.	110–120
BREAD		
Bread—wholemeal, brown or white, fresh or toasted	1 oz.	70
Starch-reduced roll	1 roll	18
CAKES		
Cakes—plain	1 slice: 2 oz.	150
Cakes—rich, iced	1 slice: 2 oz.	210
Doughnut	2 oz.	195
Fruit cake	1 slice: 2 oz.	180
CEREALS		
Barley—pearl, dry	1 oz.	95
Cornflour—custard powder	1 oz.	100
Cornflakes, breakfast cereals	1 oz.	106–110
Flour	1 oz.	100
Lentils—dried	1 oz.	164
Macaroni—uncooked	1 oz.	80–100
Oatmeal	1 oz.	110
Rice—dry	1 oz.	90
Soya flour—whole	1 oz.	120
Spaghetti—dry	1 oz.	80
CHEESE		
Cheese—Cheddar	1 oz.	120
Cheese—cottage	1 oz.	40–50
Cheese—cream	1 oz.	145
Cheese—Dutch	1 oz.	90
Processed	1 oz.	120
EGGS		
Eggs—raw	1: 2 oz.	80
Eggs—boiled	1	80
Eggs—poached with butter	1	120
Eggs—fried	1	140
Eggs—scrambled	1	140
Egg white	1	11
Egg yolk	1	69

Food	Amount	Calories	Food	Amount	Calories
FATS AND MILK			Ham—fat	4 oz.	375
Butter	¼ oz.	65	Heart	4 oz.	265
Lard	¼ oz.	60	Kidneys	4 oz.	145
Margarine	¼ oz.	55	Lamb—lean	4 oz.	230
Milk—whole	½ pint	166–180	Lamb—fat	4 oz.	375
Milk—skimmed	½ pint	70	Liver	4 oz.	160
Milk—condensed	1 oz.	100	Mutton—lean	4 oz.	230
Milk—evaporated	1 oz.	45	Mutton—fat	4 oz.	370
Cream—thin	1 oz.	55	Pork—lean	4 oz.	270
Cream—thick	1 oz.	100	Pork—fat	4 oz.	450
Yoghourt	¼ pint	100	Sausages—beef	2 oz.	120
FISH			Sausages—pork	2 oz.	145
Crab	2 oz.	75	Steak	4 oz.	300
Cod fillets	4 oz.	95	Tongue	4 oz.	290
Haddock—fresh	4 oz.	115	Veal—lean	4 oz.	145
Haddock—smoked	4 oz.	120	Sweetbreads	4 oz.	250
Halibut	4 oz.	140	**MISCELLANEOUS**		
Hake	4 oz.	90	Cocoa powder	¼ oz.	30
Herring	1 : 4 oz.	190	Honey	1 oz.	80
Lobster	4 oz.	65	Ice cream—vanilla	2 oz.	115
Mackerel	4 oz.	90	Jam, jellies, marmalade	½ oz.	35–60
Oysters	6 medium	65	Jelly—dessert	4 oz.	85–100
Plaice	4 oz.	90	Junket	(as milk)	
Salmon—fresh	4 oz.	155	Oils—salad	¼ oz.	60
Salmon—canned	4 oz.	190	Pickles—non thickened	1 spoon	5–10
Salmon—smoked	2 oz.	175	Soup—thin	4 oz.	20
Sardines	2 oz.	160	Soup—creamy	5 oz.	80+
Shrimps	4 oz.	55	**NUTS**		
Sole	4 oz.	90	Almond	1 oz.	170
FRUIT			Chestnuts	2 oz.	75
Apple—cooked	5 oz.	75	Peanuts	2 oz.	335
Apple—raw	1 : approx. 4 oz.	45	Walnuts	1 oz.	185
Apricots—fresh	4 oz.	30	**POULTRY**		
Apricots—canned	4 oz.	60	Chicken	4 oz.	165
Apricots—dried	1 oz.	50	Duck	4 oz.	190
Banana	1 average	80–100	Goose	4 oz.	355
Blackberries—fresh	2 oz.	15	Turkey	4 oz.	185
Blackberries—canned	4 oz.	75	**SUGAR AND SWEETS**		
Cherries—fresh	4 oz.	45	Sugar—white	½ oz.	55
Cherries—canned	4 oz.	95	Sugar—brown	½ oz.	50
Coconut—fresh	1 oz.	170	Boiled sweets	1 oz.	120
Coconut—desiccated	1 oz.	180	Chocolate—plain, milk	1 oz.	150
Dates—dried	1 oz.	85	**VEGETABLES**		
Figs—dried	2 oz.	115	Asparagus	6 stalks : 3 oz.	15
Gooseberries	4 oz.	40	Beans—baked	4 oz.	100
Grapefruit	4 oz.	25	Beans—broad	1 oz.	15
Grapes	4 oz.	60	Beans—haricot, dried	1 oz.	70
Lemon	1 : 3 oz.	30	Beans—French or runner	4 oz.	15
Loganberries	4 oz.	20	Beetroot	2 oz.	15
Melon	1 oz.	4	Broccoli	4 oz.	15
Olives	½ oz.	25	Brussels sprouts	4 oz.	20
Orange	1 : 6 oz.	40	Cabbage	4 oz.	20
Peaches—canned	4 oz.	64	Carrots	2 oz.	15
Pear—fresh	6 oz.	50	Cauliflower	4 oz.	20
Pear—canned	2 halves	75	Celery	2 oz.	5
Pineapple—fresh	6 oz.	65	Cucumber	2 oz.	10
Pineapple—canned	6 oz.	120	Leeks	4 oz.	15
Plums—fresh	4 oz.	30	Lettuce	2 oz.	10
Plums—canned	4 oz.	80	Marrow	4 oz.	10
Prunes—dried	2 oz.	75	Mushrooms	2 oz.	2
Raisins	2 oz.	125	Onions	4 oz.	25
Raspberries—fresh	4 oz.	25	Parsnips	4 oz.	55
Rhubarb	4 oz.	5	Peas—canned	4 oz.	25
Strawberries	4 oz.	30	Peas—fresh	4 oz.	75
MEATS			Peas—dried	1 oz.	85
Bacon—lean	2 oz.	175	Pepper—vegetable	1 oz.	10
Bacon—fat	2 oz.	260	Potatoes—boiled	2 medium : 4 oz.	95
Beef—corned	4 oz.	280	Potatoes—fried	4 oz.	270
Beef—roast, lean	4 oz.	210	Spinach	4 oz.	20
Ham—lean	4 oz.	265	Tomatoes—fresh	4 oz.	20

Using a Home Freezer

If you should be reading this before you have purchased a home freezer, remember there is a great variety of models from which to choose. You can have a deep freezing compartment combined with a domestic refrigerator, and this is an admirable choice if you have not much space, but at the same time are anxious to have facilities for home freezing. The freezing compartment is generally mounted above the refrigerator. Some modern refrigerators have a freezing compartment which is capable of storing an appreciable amount of ready-frozen food, or food you yourself may freeze.

Separate home freezers are obtainable in chest models (with a top opening lid) and upright models looking like an ordinary refrigerator. Obviously your choice of size, model, etc., depends on the space available and the amount of food you feel you would either store or freeze in it. It is possible to keep a home freezer in an outside garage if there is no room in the kitchen. Makers of freezers, usually called *home* freezers when sold to the domestic market, will give you basic instructions for use. *Follow their specific instructions carefully.*

These are the general points to remember:

a) FREEZING–in order to conserve moisture and flavour in the food, one should freeze *as quickly as possible*. It is, therefore, essential to learn about the control on your home freezer, to set this to the coldest position when freezing raw or cooked food and to keep it there for approximately 24 hours.

Cooked food must be cooled before freezing. The exception to this rule is when you are freezing cream or water ices, see page 185.

b) QUANTITY OF FOOD TO FREEZE–quick freezing is very important, as stated in a) above, and it is, therefore, essential that you do not attempt to freeze too much food at one time. Manufacturers recommend 10% of the total capacity, i.e. if you buy a deep freeze that will hold 200 lb. of frozen food, you can freeze 20 lb. at one time.

c) PACKAGING–when freezing food it should be wrapped. You will find recommendations for wrapping at the head of each chapter. The purpose of wrapping food is to retain moisture, texture and flavour. Do not imagine that packaging is very expensive; you will need to buy some containers, but these are the other things you could use:

1. *Aluminium foil*–there is a heavy duty foil which is stronger and therefore better for freezing.

2. *Waxed containers with lids*–you can buy these in special home freezer packs, but old yoghourt, ice cream or cream containers (if well washed and dried) may be used. Remember not to discard these after use–they can be cleaned, dried and used again. If the lid is damaged, then cover with foil.

3. *Sheets of polythene or polythene bags*–you should buy heavy duty polythene which is stronger.

4. *Polythene boxes and containers*–of the type you store food in in the refrigerator.

5. *Ovenproof basins, casseroles, oven-to-table ware*–these are particularly useful for stews and casserole dishes, and suggestions for lining the casserole or basin with foil are given under stews, page 76 and puddings, page 83.

6. *Foil dishes of various shapes*–excellent for pies, pasties, etc.

d) STORING–if you buy commercially frozen food there is no need to alter the control on your home freezer when putting this food in to store. When once fresh food is frozen return the cold control to recommended position for storage, see point a).

e) LENGTH OF TIME FOR STORAGE–the recommendations for the length of storage time are given at the head of each chapter, or under particular recipes. This is the length of time where the food remains in first class condition. If you store the food for a longer period than this, it is likely to deteriorate either in flavour, texture or in both.

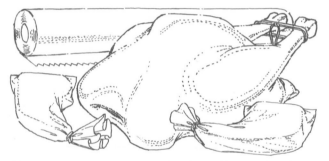

f) DEFROSTING THE FOOD–foods will vary in the preparation needed before they are served. You will find advice on this at the heading of each chapter, or under the particular recipe, see below, point 6.

g) DEFROSTING THE FREEZER–instructions will be given by the manufacturer on how often this should be done. It is wise to choose a time when the cabinet is fairly empty.

h) REHEATING FROZEN FOOD–recommendations for reheating are given where these are necessary.
Some important rules for freezing:
1. Use the freshest and best quality food available.
2. Freeze as soon as possible after buying, preparing, cooking (allow cooked dishes to become cold).
3. Remember to set home freezer to coldest position, see above.
4. Freeze in convenient sized portions, e.g. if you freeze a whole turkey you will have to let the whole bird defrost before using it: in the case of a small family, therefore, it may be better to joint the turkey before freezing.
5. Pay attention to recommendations about packaging and fast freezing, these will make certain that your frozen food is extremely good.

6. Many people are worried about re-freezing frozen food–here are the points to watch:
In the case of frozen *raw* food–vegetables, fish, meat, etc., you MUST NOT allow it to thaw out; use some, then re-freeze the remainder.
If when you use a frozen cooked dish (allowing it to defrost–or heating it) you have any left, you MUST NOT re-freeze what is left over.
If you allow frozen, raw food to defrost, then use it to make a cooked dish–it is absolutely safe to freeze this, as you have started a completely new cycle of freezing.
7. When freezing foods containing an appreciable amount of liquid (fruits, fruit juices, soups, etc.) allow 'head room', i.e. about $\frac{3}{4}$–1 inch at the top of the container. This allows for the expansion of the liquid content as it freezes.
8. When wrapping food in sheets of foil or polythene or putting into bags, make sure that the wrapping fits as tightly as possible round the food, expelling the air with your hands as you do so. Seal tightly according to manufacturer's instructions.
The reason for this is that the closer the food is wrapped the quicker it will freeze, and as I have mentioned, really fast freezing is one of the secrets of preserving flavour in frozen food.

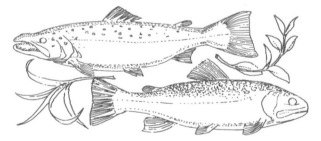

RE-USING WRAPPINGS–Clean the wrapping or container carefully; dry it thoroughly after wiping or washing. Obviously it is important that all containers are scrupulously clean when you re-use.
9. Label clearly–one always *thinks* one will remember what was in the packet–one may forget. For easy identification, use different coloured labels, e.g. all green labels for vegetables–blue for meat dishes, etc., or use particular containers –all square green for one group; round blue for others, etc.
10. Keep a record of what you have put in the home freezer.

Colourful Menus

A good menu should consist of dishes that are nutritious, in that it gives a good balance of food values, and the meal is pleasant and satisfying to eat. The food in the menu should be chosen to give variation in flavour, texture and also colour; for example, it is undesirable to have everything white—as could happen if you served a creamy chicken soup followed by creamed white fish with mashed potatoes and then a milk pudding.

The recipes and introductions that follow will help you to plan menus that save time and effort; you can make use of a refrigerator and/or home freezer to plan ahead; you can put the entire meal in an automatic oven so that it may be left without further attention. If you do not have an automatic timing device on your particular oven it may still be possible to place the complete meal in the oven and switch or turn on and leave it there to 'cook itself'.

Decorating and garnishing food

Having taken steps to plan a good menu, it is important to present it in such a way that it has the maximum of 'eye appeal'.

Garnishing hors d'oeuvre—Use lettuce, lemon, sliced tomatoes, etc., to give colour; the Prawn cocktail facing page 49 would look far less interesting if it were not topped with a slice of tomato, capers, and a generous piece of lemon surmounted by prawns.

Garnishing soups—If white, add parsley, chives or other herbs, or chopped pepper, or croûtons, see page 33, or browned blanched almonds. If red, use herbs, croûtons or cream. If brown, use herbs or cream or tiny pieces of carrot.

Garnishing fish—Lemon is an obvious choice with fish; cut into:
a) thick quarters (wedges); remove pips and excess pith;
b) thin slices; twist these as picture facing page 56, or divide in quarters as 'butterflies';
c) halves; you can cut in a Van-Dyke fashion, as the melon picture, facing page 185.
Use parsley and other herbs, etc.

Garnishing meat—Stews need little extra garnish as the vegetables provide colour. Roast potatoes or other vegetables can be arranged round the meat, the stuffed pork facing page 89 would look far less interesting if served by itself on the dish. Be more adventurous—in the chicken dish facing page 96, and the Crown of pork facing page 65 use fruit to give colour as well as flavour.

Garnishing vegetables and salads—Most root vegetables taste and look better if tossed in melted butter and chopped herbs. Parsley is the most usual and the 'safest' herb to use, since its flavour does not conflict or overpower, but try chives with carrots and turnips, mint *and* parsley with new potatoes, etc.
Green vegetables—Top with fried tiny or sliced onions, or a sprinkling of paprika, etc.
Salads contain interesting ingredients so additional garnish is rarely necessary. A salad dressing gives a pleasant 'shine' as well as a good flavour.

Garnishing savoury dishes—Egg dishes look best with green herbs like parsley; the golden topping of cheese contrasts with tomatoes, mushrooms, etc., so have the garnish all ready, and do not take too long in arranging this on the food as egg and cheese dishes spoil if kept waiting.

Decorating puddings and desserts—This will vary according to the type of pudding. You cannot decorate hot puddings with piped cream as this would become softened; often a dusting of sugar is adequate.
Cold desserts are decorated in many ways, e.g.
a) use piped cream as on pages 189 and 191. Never over-whip cream, if you do it will become 'buttery' and as you pipe the cream will separate.
b) cherries—Maraschino, glacé, fresh, etc., use small pieces on individual desserts.
c) crystallised fruit, flowers (colour can run, so add at last minute), see page 189.
d) canned or cooked fruits, as page 186.
e) a glaze—instructions for making, see page 182.

Decorating cakes—This is an art needing practice; it gives wonderful satisfaction, so it is worth taking time to perfect this.
Simple cakes are decorated with sugar, as Swiss roll, facing page 176, or Chocolate sweets, between pages 216/217.

Hors d'oeuvre and Appetisers

There are no very definite 'rules' as to the kind of foods one must serve at the beginning of a meal as an hors d'oeuvre. I think it is important that the food should be interesting and as imaginative as possible; so stimulating one's appetite for the more substantial dishes to follow. Obviously your choice of hors d'oeuvre depends upon the rest of the menu; most people would prefer NOT to eat fish as the first course if the main course is a fish dish. If the main course is very substantial, choose a light hors d'oeuvre and never let the flavour of this first course be so strong that it spoils one's palate for the food that will follow.

The term 'appetiser' covers not only hors d'oeuvre but all those delicious savouries served *with* drinks. When you are entertaining it is quite a good idea to serve an interesting tray of appetisers while your guests enjoy their 'pre-dinner' drink, instead of preparing a more formal hors d'oeuvre. The appetisers are planned to serve instead of an hors d'oeuvre; many more that could be used for this purpose, as well as for a cocktail or buffet party, are on pages 165 to 170.

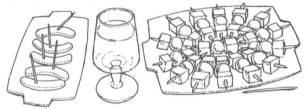

Metric Conversions

Many of the recipes in this chapter are so simple that the conversion from the Imperial to the Metric system cannot be a problem.
Where butter is added in cooking, the 25 grammes accepted as the equivalent of 1 oz., is quite adequate. If the recipe needs a sauce you will produce very slightly less with the metric quantities (see the comments under White sauce, page 146).

Drinks to serve with hors d'oeuvre

A dry sherry or dry white wine is a wise choice to accompany most hors d'oeuvre, especially those made with fish.
Obviously at a cocktail party a selection of drinks will be served. If you wish to restrict the choice of drinks, offer dry or medium sherry, vermouth, gin or whisky. You could add a wine cup, see page 242.

Saving time when making hors d'oeuvre and appetisers

You can produce interesting ideas for a first course or appetiser with little time and effort:

FRUIT
Fruit juices-serve fresh, canned or defrosted frozen orange juice, flavour with a little mint; blend with pineapple juice. Make tomato juice cocktails flavouring juice with seasoning, lemon juice or dry sherry, and Worcestershire sauce.
Avocado pears-halve ripe pears, remove the stones, sprinkle lightly with lemon juice to prevent flesh becoming dark. Fill centres with a) vinaigrette dressing, page 155, or b) shell fish in this dressing or cocktail sauce, page 26, or c) cottage cheese blended with dressing or mayonnaise and lemon juice, finely chopped red pepper and green olives, or d) arrange slices skinned avocado with segments of fresh grapefruit; serve on lettuce leaves.
Melon-serve with a) ginger and sugar, or b) cut into balls or diced and blended with fresh orange or canned mandarin orange segments, or c) with slices of Parma ham (this freezes well) or try sliced salami, for a change.
Cubes of melon can be combined with diced cheese, ham or prawns as cocktail snacks.
Grapefruit (canned or fresh)-serve with a) sugar and topped with cherries or flavoured with Kirsch or sherry, or b) blend segments with prawns or shrimps, serve on salad or a bed of shredded lettuce in glasses or halved grapefruit skins. Top with cocktail sauce, page 26, if wished.

VEGETABLES
Canned artichoke hearts, asparagus, sliced fresh tomatoes, etc., make interesting salads. Arrange on lettuce, top with herb flavoured dressing, page 155.

FISH AND MEAT
Smoked fish-serve smoked salmon, smoked eel (allow about 50 grammes per person), smoked trout (allow 1 per person) on lettuce with brown bread and butter and lemon segments. Serve paprika or cayenne with salmon; horseradish sauce with eel and trout. Scrambled egg is also often served with smoked eel.
Ready cooked meats, salami, smoked ham, as well as bought pâté, are always good as an hors d'oeuvre. Garnish with salad.

Cooking hors d'oeuvre and appetisers in the automatic oven

There are a number of dishes in this chapter that can be placed into the oven and left to cook without any attention. This enables a busy hostess to relax, knowing that these savoury dishes cannot be spoiled by over-cooking. In addition to the recipes shown as suitable for automatic cooking on the following pages, you can choose:

FRUIT HORS D'OEUVRE AND APPETISERS

Baked grapefruit-halve and prepare the grapefruit. Top with a little butter, brown sugar or honey, a sprinkling of powdered cinnamon or a small amount of sherry. Set the oven for 20 minutes cooking time at a moderately hot temperature.

Orange and bacon kebabs-choose really large oranges, cut away the peel and pith, divide the oranges into large segments. Wrap these in strips of bacon and secure with wooden cocktail sticks. Put into a shallow dish and set the oven for 20 minutes cooking time at a moderately hot temperature.

Pineapple cheese kebabs-drain cubes of canned pineapple and put on to wooden cocktail sticks with cubes of Cheddar or Gruyère (or other good cooking cheese). Set the oven for 10–15 minutes cooking at a moderately hot temperature; do not over-cook. Serve in the ovenproof cooking dish.

VEGETABLE HORS D'OEUVRE AND APPETISERS

Stuffed mushrooms-wash, but do not peel, perfect small mushrooms; take out stalks and use for soup. Place in a well-buttered shallow dish with the dark side uppermost. Blend a little grated Parmesan cheese with cream cheese, spoon into the 'cup' of each mushroom. Cover with buttered foil. Set the oven for 20 minutes cooking time at a moderately hot temperature. If serving as a cocktail savoury, place each mushroom on a round of fried bread (which crisps up well in the oven).

MEAT HORS D'OEUVRE AND APPETISERS

Sausage and bacon kebabs-sandwich halved cooked sausages with cheese, pâté or chutney, wrap in bacon, or wrap bacon round cooked prunes, or uncooked kidney, and bake for 20–25 minutes in a moderately hot oven.

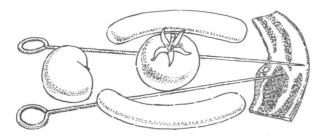

Home freezing of hors d'oeuvre and appetisers

It is possible to freeze many dishes prepared for hors d'oeuvre or appetisers. You will find details alongside the relevant recipes, and in addition the following simple suggestions freeze extremely well.

FRUIT

All fresh fruit juices and fresh tomato juice-press very ripe tomatoes through a sieve, strain juice, pack and freeze; add flavourings when thawed out. Keeps up to 1 year.

Segments of fresh grapefruit-do not add sugar (or use very little as this can be adjusted when serving). Better used within 3 months.

Melon balls-choose *firm* but ripe fruit, put balls in containers, cover with a sugar and water syrup (use 100 grammes (4 oz.) sugar to each 500 ml (1 pint) water). Flavour syrup with ginger or sherry or lemon juice. Use within 2–3 months as melon tends to become over-soft.

VEGETABLES

Fresh asparagus, corn on the cob and many other vegetables form perfect hors d'oeuvre, and most freeze well–see comments on page 111.

Ratatouille (and various adaptations of this) is another vegetable dish that could be served as a hot or cold hors d'oeuvre, see page 121.

FISH

Most fish freezes well, and you can save a lot of time if you prepare and freeze:

Smoked salmon, trout, eel, etc., with brown bread and butter. Cover fish before freezing; do not cover bread and butter until firm so the butter does not stick to the wrapping. Oily fish should be used within 3 months. Fish spreads (made by blending butter, etc., and flavourings with pounded freshly cooked fish–shell, white or oily) are an excellent topping for cocktail snacks–to each ½ kilo (1 lb.) fish use 75–100 grammes (3–4 oz.) butter, lemon juice, chopped herbs and/or spice and seasoning to give a piquant flavour. Use within 2–3 months.

MEAT

In addition to the pâté recipes on pages 30 and 31, most pâtés freeze well. They lose their moist texture though if stored in the freezer for longer than 6–8 weeks, so use within that time. Cooked meats such as salami freeze well. Buy ready sliced; if you are buying a large quantity it is wise to separate each few slices with squares of waxed or greaseproof paper so you can easily take off the amount required.

These highly spiced and often quite fat meats are best used within 3–4 months.

EGGS AND CHEESE
HORS D'OEUVRE

Eggs can form excellent hors d'oeuvre in salads and savoury dishes. In addition to recipes in this chapter, see page 167.

FRIED EGGS: fry in butter, then lift eggs on to a hot dish and allow the butter to turn dark brown, add lemon to taste and pour over. This simple but classic method of cooking may be varied by adding a) finely chopped ham to the browned butter, b) chopped herbs and finely diced onions and frying these first in the butter, then adding the eggs.

EGGS EN COCOTTE: in this dish eggs are baked in small cocotte dishes. Put a little cream at the bottom of each dish, break an egg on top, season lightly, then cover with more cream and bake for about 15 minutes towards the top of a moderately hot oven. The basic dish can be made more interesting by adding: a) chopped cooked mushrooms or asparagus to the cream, b) finely diced ham or shell fish, c) topping the eggs with grated cheese. Serve to be eaten with a teaspoon.

OMELETTES: there are many omelettes on pages 158 to 159 and small portions make an excellent hors d'oeuvre. Of course, they are not a good choice when entertaining–since you must cook and serve immediately–with the exception of oven cooked omelettes, see page 159.

POACHED EGGS: serve poached eggs topped with cheese sauce as a first course, see page 157, or on a bed of cooked spinach or other vegetables.

SCRAMBLED EGGS are rarely served as hors d'oeuvre, but the French piperade is excellent. Details are on page 158.

CHEESE in hors d'oeuvre: cheese in a sauce, as a filling in Canneloni or other pancakes or a topping for eggs, is one of the most usual and popular ways of flavouring the first course of the meal. Recipes are on pages 162 to 164.

Automatic Oven
If the oven is set for a short cooking period you may be able to cook eggs en cocotte or some of the dishes such as poached eggs with a cheese sauce, page 146; but care must be taken to time correctly–if over-cooked, eggs are spoiled, and cheese becomes very tough.

Speedy Meal
Fortunately most egg dishes cook very quickly so they are an ideal choice when in a hurry, also egg dishes need very little preparation.

Slimming Tips
Eggs are low in calories so make the ideal hors d'oeuvre. Cheese is often omitted from slimming diets, but a little cheese is important since it provides not only protein but calcium. In some recipes you may be able to substitute cottage cheese for the variety given.

Home Freezing
Comments about freezing egg and cheese dishes are on page 156.

Eggs Flamenco

Serves 2–4*
Cooking time 15–20 minutes
Oven temperature 400°F. (200°C.), Gas Mark 5–6

Ingredients	Metric	Imperial
butter	25 grammes	1 oz.
clove garlic (optional)	1	1
eggs	4	4
cooked *or* canned peas	3 tablespoons	3 tablespoons
cooked ham	25 grammes	1 oz.
sliced salami	25 grammes	1 oz.
canned red pepper	1–2	1–2
canned asparagus tips	4	4
seasoning	to taste	to taste

1 *Choose 2 ovenproof dishes for a light main dish or 4 individual dishes for an hors d'oeuvre.
2 Spread the dishes with butter, then rub the cut clove of garlic round these.
3 Break the eggs into the dishes, then arrange all the other ingredients round the eggs to give a colourful effect. The ham, salami and red pepper should be cut into strips.
4 Season very generously and bake above the centre of a moderately hot oven until the eggs are set. Serve at once.

Automatic Oven
This could be cooked in an automatic oven, but cover the eggs with a very little milk and each dish with foil, so the eggs do not harden with standing.

Slimming Tips
Excellent for slimmers; omit peas and use rather more red pepper and a skinned sliced tomato. To give a green colour use diced green pepper or chopped parsley. Reduce the amount of butter slightly.

Home Freezing
The uncooked eggs do not freeze well in this recipe, but it is an excellent idea to freeze the other ingredients in the containers (this is a very good way of using small quantities of left-over foods). Allow to defrost (about 2 hours at room temperature), top with the eggs and continue as recipe.

Curried Hard-Boiled Eggs

Serves 4–8*
Cooking time 30 minutes

Ingredients	Metric	Imperial
FOR THE CURRY SAUCE:		
butter	25 grammes	1 oz.
oil	1 tablespoon	1 tablespoon
onion	1 large	1 large
cornflour	2 teaspoons	2 teaspoons
curry powder	2–3 teaspoons	2–3 teaspoons
chicken stock	284 ml	½ pint
milk	142 ml	¼ pint
chutney	2–3 teaspoons	2–3 teaspoons
freshly grated coconut	1 tablespoon	1 tablespoon
seasoning	to taste	to taste
eggs	8	8
TO SERVE:		
long grain rice	4 tablespoons	4 tablespoons
water	see stage 6	see stage 6
TO ACCOMPANY CURRY:		
chutney	to taste	to taste
bananas	2–3	2–3
green pepper	1	1
tomatoes	2	2
salted nuts	50–75 grammes	2–3 oz.

**4 for light main dish or an excellent hors d'oeuvre for 8.

1 Heat the butter in a pan with the oil.
2 Fry the finely chopped onion until tender, then stir in the cornflour and curry powder, cook for a few minutes.
3 Gradually add the stock, milk and other ingredients except the eggs.
4 Simmer gently for about 20 minutes adding seasoning to taste – remember this is a mild curry.
5 Meanwhile hard boil the eggs, crack and shell.
6 Cook the rice: the best way to do this is to use double the amount of water, i.e. if using 4 tablespoons rice you need 8 tablespoons water.
7 Put the rice and water in the pan with a good pinch salt. Bring to the boil, stir with a fork, lower the heat, cover the pan and simmer for 15 minutes; by this time the water should be absorbed.
8 Arrange the rice on a hot dish.
9 Top with the eggs and sauce, serve with chutney, sliced bananas, sliced green pepper and tomatoes and salted nuts.

Speedy Meal
Using a can of Mulligatawny soup and adding curry powder is an excellent and quick way of producing a curry sauce. Stir a little chutney and other flavourings in as you heat. This particular soup is less successful for a Devilled sauce, so choose a Cream of onion or Chicken soup and add mustard and other flavourings.

Slimming Tips
The amount of thickening in this curry sauce is very small so you could include this in a fairly 'Lenient' slimming diet. Be sparing with sweet things like the chutney, omit bananas but serve more tomatoes and green pepper. You can also serve the Devilled and Mexican sauces, omitting the high calorie ingredients where necessary.

Home Freezing
Curry sauces freeze very well; it is possible to freeze complete curries containing fish or meat but *not* eggs. Both the Devilled sauce and the Mexican style sauces will also freeze well.

Eggs in Devilled Sauce

1 Choose the ingredients for this dish as recipe above, but substitute from 2–4 teaspoons made-mustard (French or English) for the curry powder.
2 Prepare the sauce, adding the mustard at stage 2; when the sauce has thickened, taste and gradually stir in a few drops Worcestershire sauce and a shake of cayenne pepper.
3 Arrange the eggs on rice *or* this is quicker to prepare and very pleasant if the eggs are put on to crisp toast or fried bread, and coated with the sauce at the last minute.

Eggs Mexican Style

1 Use the recipe for curried eggs, but omit the curry powder.
2 Add Tabasco sauce to taste (remember it is very strong) and a chopped green and chopped red pepper at stage 3.

FISH AS AN HORS D'OEUVRE

Most fish dishes are excellent as the 'starter' to a meal. Use the recipes on the following pages and the chapter on fish dishes, page 42. Obviously you will make smaller portions or use the recipe to provide a dish for more people, since the recipes are intended for main meals.

Fish omelettes and fish-filled pancakes are excellent. Make plain or soufflé omelettes and fill with shell or cooked or canned fish, heated either in butter or a sauce. Fill pancakes with a similar mixture, roll and top with sauce or grated cheese; brown in the oven or under the grill.

Home Freezing

Details of freezing are given under the various recipes. Fish filled pancakes, mentioned opposite, freeze excellently. Use within 2 months, and it is advisable to allow them to defrost before reheating—this takes about 2–3 hours at room temperature.

Fish Mayonnaise

Serves 4–8*
Cooking time 10–15 minutes

Ingredients	Metric	Imperial
white fish—preferably turbot, halibut, skate *or* very fresh cod	¾ kilo (weight free of bone and skin— so buy almost double this amount with skate)	1½ lb. (weight free of bone and skin— so buy almost double this amount with skate)
water	to cover	to cover
bay leaf	1	1
parsley	sprig	sprig
lemon rind (optional)	small piece	small piece
seasoning	to taste	to taste
FOR THE DRESSING:		
mayonnaise	142 ml	¼ pint
ripe tomatoes	2 large	2 large
thick *or* thin cream	2 tablespoons	2 tablespoons
Worcestershire sauce	few drops	few drops
Chilli *or* Tabasco sauce	few drops	few drops
FOR THE SALAD:		
lettuce	1	1
cucumber	½ small	½ small
lemon	1	1
hard-boiled eggs	1 or 2	1 or 2

*4 as light main course, 8 as hors d'oeuvre.

1 Simmer the fish with the water, herbs, lemon and seasoning until just tender, but unbroken. Lift out and drain well.
2 Put mayonnaise into a basin, rub tomatoes through a sieve, add to the mayonnaise with all the other dressing ingredients.
3 Arrange the flaked fish on the bed of lettuce, top with the sliced cucumber, lemon wedges and sliced or chopped hard-boiled egg. Pour mayonnaise over or serve separately.

Speedy Meal

If you use canned fish, such as tuna or salmon, you save time cooking the fish. The dressing is quickly made by using ready-prepared mayonnaise, tomato ketchup or concentrated tomato purée (use the latter very sparingly) in place of fresh tomatoes.

Slimming Tips

Choose white fish as recipe, rather than oily canned fish suggested above. Make a low calorie salad dressing as page 43 and flavour this with fresh tomato purée and the other ingredients in the dressing.

Mixer

The liquidiser is ideal for making mayonnaise, see page 154. Keep sufficient mayonnaise in the goblet for the dressing, add the skinned tomatoes and other ingredients and emulsify.

Fish Cocktails

These are not only delicious to eat but very practical, since you need relatively small amounts of fish, so even expensive shell fish serves quite a number of people. Fish cocktails should be served in glasses over ice, but they look equally pleasant and attractive if served in small dishes, see picture facing page 49.
To make a fish cocktail: put a layer of finely shredded lettuce at the bottom of the dish or glass; make the *Cocktail sauce*—which is just the same as the dressing in the recipe above. Toss shelled shrimps or prawns or other fish in this, pile on to the lettuce and garnish with lemon and parsley.

Slimming Tips

You can make a very slimming and interesting fish cocktail by blending cooked shell fish, white fish, segments of tomato, cucumber and chopped green pepper. Put on a bed of shredded lettuce, then top with a low calorie cocktail dressing made by blending a few drops of lemon juice, concentrated tomato purée and Worcestershire sauce into a small carton of yoghourt.

Rollmops in Mustard Mayonnaise

Serves 4–8*
Cooking time – no cooking

Ingredients	Metric	Imperial
rollmop herrings	8 rolls	8 rolls
FOR THE SAUCE:		
mayonnaise	142 ml	¼ pint
natural yoghourt	142 ml	¼ pint
made-mustard		
(English *or* French)	3 teaspoons	3 teaspoons
sugar	good pinch	good pinch
celery	1–2 sticks	1–2 sticks
chopped parsley *or* chives	2 teaspoons	2 teaspoons
TO GARNISH:		
cucumber	small piece	small piece
tomatoes	3–4	3–4
watercress *or*	1 bunch	1 bunch
lettuce	few leaves	few leaves

*4 as light main course, 8 as hors d'oeuvre.

1 Lift the herrings from the jar, drain and put aside. Keep the liquid–see stage 2.
2 Blend all the ingredients for the sauce, chopping the celery very finely. Taste, and if wished add a little liquid from the herrings to give a sharper flavour.
3 Arrange the herrings on the serving dish. Coat with the sauce and garnish with the sliced cucumber, tomatoes and watercress.

Note: this is very good served with rye bread or crispbread.

TO MAKE ROLLMOPS–divide 8 herrings into fillets, soak for 2 hours in brine made from 50 grammes (2 oz.) salt and 284 ml (½ pint) water. Drain, put in dish, cover with cold vinegar, leave for 4 hours, lift out, roll round thinly sliced onions. Pack into jars with a few gherkins, 1–2 bay leaves, 1 chilli pepper per jar. Boil 568 ml (1 pint) malt vinegar with 1 tablespoon pickling spices for 10 minutes, cool, strain over herrings and seal down. Store for 3–4 weeks in a cool place before using. Allow 1–2 fillets per person.

Automatic Oven

In place of rollmop herrings you can substitute soused herrings. These can be cooked in an automatic oven–see recipe, page 53.

Slimming Tips

Rollmop herrings and soused fish are both a wise choice, for the method of preparing and cooking uses no fat. Of course some slimming diets do not recommend oily fish such as herrings, so be guided by this.

Home Freezing

Rollmop herrings keep well without freezing and those you buy are in hermetically sealed jars, so freezing is unnecessary. Soused herrings can be frozen, see recipe, page 53.

Home Freezing

To store rollmops for longer, freeze *after* storing as recipe for 2–3 weeks; this time of storage is necessary for good flavour. Lift out of jars, pack in waxed containers, allow 1·5 cm (½ inch) headroom, freeze, store for a maximum of 6 weeks, defrost at room temperature–takes about 2–3 hours.

Devilled Crab

Serves 2–4*
Cooking time 10 minutes

Ingredients	Metric	Imperial
crab *or*	1 medium	1 medium
canned crab meat	200 grammes approx.	8 oz. approx.
butter *or* margarine	75 grammes	3 oz.
curry powder	good pinch	good pinch
cayenne pepper	good pinch	good pinch
mayonnaise	2 tablespoons	2 tablespoons
Worcestershire sauce	1 teaspoon	1 teaspoon
soft breadcrumbs	4 tablespoons	4 tablespoons

*2 for a light main meal or 4 as an hors d'oeuvre.

1 Prepare the crab, cracking body and claws and removing the flesh; if using canned crab meat, open can and flake the crab meat.
2 Blend with 50 grammes (2 oz.) of the melted butter and other ingredients except the crumbs.
3 Either put back into the crab shell or in 2–4 individual dishes or scallop shells.
4 Top with the crumbs and the rest of the melted butter and brown under a hot grill. Serve very hot.

Speedy Meal

Buy ready 'dressed' crab from the fishmonger. Check before buying that the crab meat does not look dry or smell too strong, indicating it is not very fresh. You can choose canned crab to save time.

Mixer

Use the liquidiser to make home-made mayonnaise and also to make the breadcrumbs (use 2 medium slices, without crusts, to give 4 tablespoons). You cannot *add* the bread to the mayonnaise in the goblet, this makes a sticky mixture.

Home Freezing

Crab meat freezes well, so prepare the crab and freeze, or buy ready frozen and store.

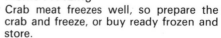

White Fish Mousse

Serves 4–8*
Cooking time 15 minutes

Ingredients	Metric	Imperial
white fish–	½ kilo	1 lb.
halibut *or* fresh	(weight when	(weight when
haddock, excellent	free of bone, etc.)	free of bone, etc.)
water	142 ml	¼ pint
dry white wine	142 ml	¼ pint
onion	1 small	1 small
seasoning	to taste	to taste
powder gelatine	1 level tablespoon	1 level tablespoon
mayonnaise	3 tablespoons	3 tablespoons
horseradish cream	1 teaspoon	1 teaspoon
eggs	2	2
thick cream	4 tablespoons	4 tablespoons
TO GARNISH:		
lettuce	few leaves	few leaves
lemon	1	1
mayonnaise	to taste	to taste
paprika	to taste	to taste

*4 for light main dish, 8 as hors d'oeuvre.

1 Put the fish into the water, add most of the wine, the whole onion and seasoning.
2 Simmer very gently for about 10 minutes until just tender but not overcooked.
3 Lift out the fish, put into a basin and flake carefully.
4 Soften the gelatine in the remaining wine, stir into the hot liquid and make sure it is thoroughly dissolved.
5 Blend the mayonnaise, horseradish, egg yolks and whipped cream.
6 Strain the gelatine mixture on to this, add to fish and mix well.
7 Allow to cool and begin to stiffen slightly, then fold in the stiffly beaten egg whites.
8 Allow to set, then unmould on to a bed of lettuce, garnish with lemon slices and mayonnaise, top with paprika.

Automatic Oven
The fish may be cooked for this dish when the oven is in use. Allow about 20 minutes in the centre of a moderate oven, adding the ingredients mentioned in stage 1. Cover the dish tightly.

Speedy Meal
Use canned fish instead of cooking white fish, or use left-over cooked white fish, or cooked salmon. To speed the setting, stand the basin on ice at stage 8, or put into freezing compartment, or freezer.

Mixer
Use the mixer for whisking the egg whites; make sure they are very stiff.

Slimming Tips
Substitute yoghourt for mayonnaise and cream, but as this does not whip and gives a thinner mixture, use 2 tablespoons *less* water in cooking the fish, and to compensate for the lack of flavourings (which would have been incorporated in mayonnaise) be rather more generous with seasoning.

Home Freezing
This recipe is *not* successful when frozen, due to the mayonnaise content in the recipe, but you *could* freeze the slimming version, or substitute very well-seasoned cream.

Cod's Roe Pâté

Serves 8
Cooking time – no cooking

Ingredients	Metric	Imperial
smoked cod's roe	½ kilo	1 lb.
fresh butter	50–75 grammes	2–3 oz.
lemons	1–2	1–2
pepper	to taste	to taste
garlic (optional)	1 clove	1 clove
thick cream (optional)	2–3 tablespoons	2–3 tablespoons

1 Slit the skin and scrape away the soft roe, do this carefully so none of the mixture is wasted.
2 Put into a basin and cream with the butter, use only 50 grammes (2 oz.) if you intend adding cream.
3 Beat well, blend in cream: begin flavouring by adding the juice of 1 lemon only, taste, add seasoning and very finely grated lemon rind, if wished. Continue like this, crushing the clove of garlic.
4 Serve with hot toast and butter.

Speedy Meal
Use a jar of smoked cod's roe, which is smooth and needs just extra seasoning, etc. Use ready-prepared fish for potted fish.

Home Freezing
Both the cod's roe pâté and the potted fish freeze well, but I find it best to use within a month, otherwise the texture and flavour begin to be lost.

POTTED FISH: use ½ kilo (good 1 lb.) boneless weight cooked salmon. white or shell fish. Flake, pound until smooth, blend with 75 grammes (3 oz.) butter, seasoning, ground mace or nutmeg, lemon juice or crushed garlic, to taste. Pot with 50 grammes (2 oz.) melted butter. Serves 6–8.

Prawn Moulds

Serves 4–6*
Cooking time 10 minutes

Ingredients	Metric	Imperial
eggs	2	2
shelled prawns	75 grammes	3 oz.
tomato juice	12 tablespoons	12 tablespoons
powder gelatine	2 level teaspoons	2 level teaspoons
small green pepper	1	1
small gherkins	2	2
mayonnaise	1 tablespoon	1 tablespoon
TO GARNISH:		
lemon	1	1
lettuce	few leaves	few leaves

*4 as light main meal, 6 or even 8 as hors d'oeuvre.

1 Hard boil the eggs until just firm; crack the shells, plunge into cold water.
2 Shell and chop coarsely.
3 Cut large prawns into small pieces.
4 Heat all the tomato juice except 1 tablespoon.
5 Soften the gelatine in the remaining tablespoon of cold tomato juice.
6 Stir into the hot liquid and continue stirring until dissolved.
7 Allow the tomato gelatine liquid to cool, then add the eggs and prawns.
8 Cut the pulp of the green pepper and the gherkins in small pieces.
9 Add to the prawn mixture then finally add the mayonnaise.
10 Put into prepared* individual moulds and allow to set.
11 Turn out and garnish with lemon and lettuce leaves.

*to prepare jelly moulds so the mixture comes out easily–rinse in cold water or brush very lightly with oil.

TO TURN OUT: dip in hot water for a few seconds only.

Speedy Meal

If you stand the moulds either in a dish full of ice, or in the freezing compartment of a refrigerator, or in the freezer for a short time you hasten setting.

Slimming Tips

These moulds, like many fish moulds, are ideal when slimming for they *look* interesting and the drawback with so many slimming dishes is their dull appearance. Where a mould contains cream or other rather high calorie ingredients you can always replace this with skimmed milk. Shell fish is particularly good for 'slimmers' as it is satisfying *and* interesting.

Home Freezing

Cover the moulds carefully when set; if left uncovered the jelly would crack rather badly due to excess evaporation. Use within 3–4 weeks and defrost for several hours in room temperature. To hasten defrosting stand in *cold* water. See comments on jellies, page 128.
The small amount of mayonnaise could cause a poor result, so substitute well-seasoned cream.

More Fish Hors d'oeuvre and Appetisers

BAKED STUFFED AVOCADO PEARS: cut ripe avocados lengthways, remove the stones, brush with olive oil and sprinkle with lemon juice. Blend a) flaked crab, b) chopped prawns, c) flaked cooked or canned salmon with either mayonnaise or a thick very well seasoned white or Hollandaise sauce, page 152. Put into pear, top with finely grated cheese and heat for 20 minutes in a moderate oven.
Serve as a formal hors d'oeuvre to be eaten with a teaspoon.
To serve as an appetiser. Remove avocado pulp carefully from the skin, mash with seasoning, little oil and lemon juice, put back into the skin, top with fish, as above. Heat then serve as a hot 'dip' before the meal.

FRIED PRAWNS OR SCAMPI: both cooked prawns (of all sizes) and the frozen uncooked scampi can be fried. Allow frozen fish to defrost and drain, remove shells–this is easy if you drop prawns into hot water for a minute. Dry, then coat in egg and crumbs, fry in deep or shallow fat until crisp and brown.
To serve as a formal hors d'oeuvre arrange on lettuce, garnish with lemon and serve with tartare sauce, see page 146.
To serve as an appetiser. Put cocktail sticks in the prawns (halve if too big) and arrange on hot dish with the sauce in a bowl in the centre as a 'dip'.

BUTTERFLY PRAWNS–choose large prawns, shell if necessary. Make a 2-cm (1-inch) cut up centre of tail end, coat in thin batter, page 46, fry until crisp and brown, serve as above.

Automatic Oven

If the avocado is well sprinkled with lemon it would stand for a very short time before being cooked.
The fried dishes may be cooked, drained and cooled. Reheat for about 10 minutes on flat trays.

Mixer

Use the liquidiser for making Tartare sauce and fritter batters.

Home Freezing

Avocado pears *do* freeze and keep well for the same time as other fruit. Buy when ready to serve but check they are not over-ripe. Freeze, then wrap after 24 hours. Defrost in the cabinet of the refrigerator or at room temperature, they take about 6–7 hours or longer if put high up in a refrigerator. Use as soon as possible after defrosting as flavour and texture begin to spoil quickly. Coated or even fried scampi or prawns can be frozen, the former is better. Use as shell fish.
Batters freeze excellently. Use after about 6 weeks.

MEAT AS AN HORS D'OEUVRE

In addition to ideas given on page 167 various kinds of meat can be served as an hors d'oeuvre. One of the most popular is pâté, and several recipes follow for making your own pâté.

A terrine, which can also be served as a main dish, is equally suitable for a first course, see page 87, and so is the *Liver soufflé* on page 162.

CHOPPED LIVER–a Jewish delicacy, is very simple to prepare. Choose chickens' or calves liver (lambs or pigs liver is too strong in flavour). To 200 grammes (8 oz.) liver allow a small onion and approximately 40 grammes (1½ oz.) chicken fat. Cut the liver into thin slices so it cooks quickly and chop onion finely, then fry together in the hot fat for about 3 minutes. Remove from the pan, chop again or mince, blend with any chicken fat and garnish with chopped hard-boiled egg.

Speedy Meal
A very easy form of chopped liver is made by heating sliced liver sausage in a little butter or chicken fat, then blending it with chopped chives or spring onion and hard-boiled egg.

Slimming Tips
Chopped liver is an excellent dish either as an hors d'oeuvre or light main dish. If you use a 'non-stick' pan you can reduce the amount of fat. Liver provides valuable iron as well as protein.

Home Freezing
Not satisfactory cooked, but you can freeze uncooked.

Liver Pâté No. 1

Serves 6–8
Cooking time 1¼ hours
Oven temperature 325–350° F. (170–180°C.), Gas Mark 3–4

Ingredients	Metric	Imperial
liver*	¼ kilo	1 lb.
	(poor weight)	(good weight)
bacon rashers	200–225 grammes	8 oz.
	(cut thinly)	(cut thinly)
onion (optional)	1 small	1 small
butter	75–100 grammes	3–4 oz.
flour	25 grammes	1 oz.
milk *or* milk and thin cream *or* stock *or* red wine	142 ml	¼ pint
brandy *or* extra liquid	2 tablespoons	2 tablespoons
eggs	2	2
seasoning	to taste	to taste

*all chicken or other poultry liver or tender calf's liver, etc.

1 Mince, finely, the liver and nearly half the bacon rashers, adding the onion if wished.
2 Make a thick sauce of 25 grammes (1 oz.) of the butter, the flour and liquid, then add the minced liver and bacon and rest of the ingredients.
3 Line sides and base of a 1 kilo (2 lb.) loaf tin with rest of bacon rashers, remove rinds, put in the mixture.
4 Cover with greased foil, stand in a tin of water and cook in the centre of a very moderate oven.
5 Put small weights on this as it cools (this makes it easier to cut), cover with rest of the butter which should be melted.
6 Serve as pâté.

Note: herbs, particularly parsley, may be minced with the liver, and the sauce flavoured with a pinch of powered ginger and/or nutmeg.

Automatic Oven
You will often find you can leave a pâté in the oven as the slow cooking needed in most recipes means it will be quite successful even if you are not in the house to take it out of the oven. Protect the mixture from hardening as it cooks by standing the dish in a tin of cold water. In order to ensure this water does not evaporate too early in cooking, cover the top of both the dish containing the pâté and the outer container with foil.

Speedy Meal
The recipes that can be put into a liquidiser are quick; if the butcher minces the liver for you that will help. Many bought pâtés are excellent but sometimes you can improve them by a) beating with a little whipped cream to give softer mixture and b) adding extra seasoning, flavouring or a little brandy. If you make the pâté rather soft by this method, spoon neatly in portions using a soup spoon dipped in hot water.

Mixer
A liquidiser can produce a pâté within a minute or two. Be careful you do not over-fill the goblet otherwise the blades cannot revolve. Melt the butter if it has hardened slightly.

Home Freezing
All the pâtés on this page freeze well. Wrap very well indeed, as pâté does dry out easily. Do not keep longer than time recommended on page 23.

Cheese and Liver Pâté

Follow the directions for Pâté No. 2, but use half the butter only, and preferably choose poultry livers. When cooked, put 2–3 hard-boiled eggs through the mincer or in the liquidiser with the liver, etc. When minced or emulsified, gradually beat well into 100–150 grammes (4–6 oz.) cream cheese. This is a delicious pâté. If ever you can add 1 or 2 chopped truffles, plus the brandy, it becomes highly luxurious. Serve as pâté.

Liver Pâté No. 2

Serves 6–8
Cooking time 10 minutes

Ingredients	Metric	Imperial
liver*	250–300 grammes	10–12 oz.
butter	75–100 grammes	3–4 oz.
onion (optional)	1	1
bacon rashers (optional)	1–2	1–2
cloves of garlic (optional)	1–2	1–2
thick cream** *or* good stock *or* brandy**	1–3 tablespoons	1–3 tablespoons
seasoning	to taste	to taste
TO GARNISH:		
lettuce	few leaves	few leaves
lemon	1–2	1–2

*this can be all poultry liver (you can buy frozen chickens' livers); it can be all calf's, lamb's or pig's liver, but a mixture gives a most interesting flavour.
**the amount depends both on the moisture in the liver and your choice on whether you want a creamy pâté or not.

1 Cut the liver into thin strips so it cooks quickly without hardening.
2 Heat the butter, take care it does not brown. Cook sliced onion for 1 minute with bacon rashers and crushed garlic.
3 Add the liver and continue cooking until just tender.
4 If using a mincer, put liver and bacon (if wished) through this, gradually work in liquid, seasoning and butter left in the pan, with the garlic, but not the onion. If not using a mincer, put on to a plate or in a bowl (not a chopping board as you waste meat juices), chop very finely, then pound with ingredients above. If using a liquidiser, put part of the liver, bacon and liquid, plus butter from the pan, into the goblet–see opposite. When smooth, repeat with remaining ingredients. Put into a dish and season.
5 Either put into dish, then top with melted butter and chill, or, like the original pâtés served in a dough crust, cut crust from one end of a small loaf, remove nearly all the crumbs (use for breadcrumbs or in cooking) and pack the pâté into this. Press crust back in position, then chill.
6 TO SERVE: if in a dish–either cut in slices or scoop out, garnish with lettuce and lemon, serve with hot toast and butter; if in a bread case–slice with a sharp knife, serve on a bed of lettuce or mixed salad, with wedges of lemon.

Note: this pâté can be varied a great deal, e.g. blend 50–75 grammes (2–3 oz.) cooked tongue or ham, and/or diced gherkins or chopped herbs at stage 4.
Truffles have become rare and expensive so are not usually put in pâté; neatly sliced mushrooms, lightly cooked in butter, could be added to the prepared pâté at the end of stage 4.

Speedy Meal

This *is* a quick and easy recipe, but if you mince the liver *before* cooking it at stage 3 it takes approximately 1 minute only. The garlic and bacon may be minced *with* the liver, but do *not* mince the onion; use to flavour as suggested in the recipe. If this method of preparation is used then further mincing is unnecessary.

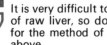

Mixer

It is very difficult to make a smooth purée of raw liver, so do not use the liquidiser for the method of preparation suggested above.

Home Freezing

The comments made on page 30 about freezing pâté apply here. If you are making the pâté especially for freezing, you will find it very satisfactory if you use 2 tablespoons red wine and 1 tablespoon brandy. This gives a stronger flavour. Naturally you can use wine and brandy even when you do not intend to freeze the mixture.

Rillette

Serves 2–6
Cooking time 30–45 minutes

1 Use giblets of any poultry, plus flavourings as in Pâté No. 2. Giblets from chicken or duck serve 2–3 only, but those from turkey or goose give a large amount of meat.
2 Simmer giblets with just enough water to cover, onion, garlic, bacon and seasoning, until tender but not over-cooked.
3 Cool enough to handle, then remove bones and gristle and proceed as Pâté No. 2, stage 4, melting the butter to blend. You will need extra seasoning as the meat is not so full of flavour. Serve as pâté.

Automatic Oven

If roasting poultry, also cook the giblets in a covered dish. Add enough liquid to cover. The liquid left can be used in a gravy. Put in the coolest part of the oven and wrap the outside of the dish in foil. Cook for same time as the poultry, but if you can remove a little earlier you will keep a firmer texture to the meat.

Home Freezing

Can be frozen as pâté, but retains flavour less well.

Making Soups

There is such a variety of soups you may make at home that I have concentrated on original and particularly easy recipes and avoided many of the classic soups which you find in other books. These are points to remember about all soups, whether in this or other books:

A SOUP IS VERY FILLING–it gives one a sense of warmth and well-being and should be chosen with the rest of the menu in mind, i.e. if you plan a really substantial main course choose a clear or low calorie soup.

AVOID A REPETITION OF FLAVOURS–if your main dish contains tomatoes then avoid a tomato flavouring in the soup; if the main course is a 'creamy' type of dish your soup should be clear, without cream or creamy sauce added.

SOUPS MAY BE ADAPTED almost more than any dish; you can add flavourings and thickenings as *you wish* rather than following a standard recipe.

Metric Conversions

There are very few soups that need a completely accurate measurement, for if the consistency is a little thicker than you personally like, it can always be made thinner with stock, cream or milk. This means that where the Imperial measurement is 2 pints you can happily measure a litre of liquid and adjust as you wish. As a litre is LESS than 2 pints, the soup will tend to be thick, so when ready to serve add extra stock, milk or cream; heat gently.

Drinks to serve with soup and add to soup

A dry or medium dry sherry is an ideal wine to serve with soup or you can have a well-chilled white wine, preferably a dry one (Chablis is particularly good with white soups). If having strongly flavoured soups like game, then a medium sherry or even a red wine might be preferred.

Many soups are improved by adding a little wine when cooked and ready to serve. There are many recipes where wine is not mentioned, but if you taste the soup and add a little wine you will find it gives additional interest. Obviously you must allow less stock or other liquid if you intend using some wine. Where a recipe contains cream and/or egg, great care must be taken that the soup is not boiling when wine is added, also that it does not boil after adding the wine (otherwise it may curdle).

Cooking soups in the automatic oven

Any dish with a fairly large amount of liquid can be troublesome if left in an oven for any length of time; you *can* cook many soups as part of an automatic meal in the oven but make sure that:
a) the oven temperature is not so hot that the soup could boil over;
b) the container is well covered so the soup liquid does not evaporate too much;
c) the container is not over-filled.

Saving time when making soups

a) use a stock cube and water rather than boiling bones to make stock;
b) use a pressure cooker for stock, or for making the soup itself, see below;
c) use dehydrated onions or other dehydrated vegetables, frozen or canned ingredients; add to a basic stock to give an interesting soup in a short time;
d) make full use of the liquidiser for a purée of vegetables, chicken, etc., see below.
REMEMBER A PRESSURE COOKER is ideal for making stock from bones. Cover bones with cold water and seasoning, allow approximately 45 minutes–1 hour at 15 lb. pressure; you will produce a stock comparable with one normally simmered for several hours in a saucepan. Use about half to two-thirds usual amount of liquid.
When using the pressure cooker–
1. Remove the rack for soups or stock.
2. Never more than half fill the cooker.
3. In soup recipes where total cooking time in a saucepan is under 15 minutes, use two-thirds the amount of liquid; where cooking time is longer than this, use half the amount of liquid.
4. As you have less liquid and retain more mineral salts in vegetables, use less seasoning.
5. Allow pressure to drop at room temperature.

Note: never lift pressure weight while soup is still under pressure in the pan–this could scald you.

1. Potato soup, see page 35

Making stock

Stock is mentioned in recipes for soups, stews and even some sauces. Instructions for making meat stock in a pressure cooker are given on the previous page; to make stock in a saucepan, cover bones with cold water, add seasoning, bunch of herbs if wished, vegetables to taste (omit if you wish stock to keep well), cover pan and simmer for several hours.

Brown stock is made from beef bones (a marrow bone is best), mutton bones, or use cheap shin of beef and bones of game or duck or goose carcass.

White stock is made from veal bones or the carcass of chicken or turkey.

Fish stock is made by simmering fish bones, skin, plus a fish head if wished, for about 45 minutes. You can use a little wine instead of all water.

All stocks freeze well, so make large quantities at one time.

Using a mixer when making soups

The development of liquidisers has probably done more than anything else to make home-made soups popular during the past years, as the effort of sieving vegetables, or chopping them very finely, precluded many busy housewives from having a home-made soup as often as they would wish. Remember liquidisers will deal with all vegetables, but will not remove pips and skin from tomatoes.

a) *If you want a smooth purée soup*, cook vegetables until tender, put into WARMED liquidiser goblet (take care this is not over-filled, see page 15) switch on until smooth, return to pan and reheat if necessary.

b) *If you want tiny pieces of vegetable in soup* put liquid into liquidiser goblet (with a lid which has a removable cap, take this out), switch on to steady speed, feed pieces of vegetable gradually through cap. If you do not have a cap in the lid, then tilt lid slightly to avoid splashing, feed vegetables from side of goblet. *This method is suitable for all vegetables except onions* which have a very strong flavour even when cooked. It is advisable to partially cook onions, then put into the stock with other raw vegetables. The great advantage of this method is that vegetables need very short cooking only, and in consequence tend to retain much more of their vitamins.

The fashion for chilled, frosted or cold soups is growing in this country, and in some cases you can prepare a purée without any previous cooking at all. Good examples are Spanish Gazpacho and a Cucumber cream soup, page 41.

Home freezing of soups

Basically follow the rules for making soups to freeze as when making stews:

a) *It is better to thicken a soup with cornflour* rather than flour. This may sound unusual, but cornflour presents less problems providing you remember you need half the quantity only and *cook very lightly*–or use potato flour, see page 145, point 2). If you have made a large amount of soup thickened with ordinary flour and you wish to freeze some, it may be that when you reheat this it will become thin instead of its original thicker consistency. All you need to do when reheating is thicken again with more cornflour or flour blended with liquid.

b) *You should avoid mixtures that might curdle* when being reheated. If the soup looks slightly curdled, put into a liquidiser, switch on until smooth again, reheat with great care. If you have no liquidiser, whisk defrosted soup sharply as it heats and that should be satisfactory, or sieve and reheat with care.

c) *As soup contains a high percentage of liquid* and expands as it freezes, allow at least 2 cm (¾ inch) at top of container in which it is being frozen.

d) *To defrost soups* in a waxed container, speed defrosting by standing container in cold or warm water. When the outside of the block of frozen soup begins to thaw, tip into a saucepan for reheating.

e) *Length of time for storing soup*–this varies a great deal according to the soup. Vegetable soups store longer than any other.

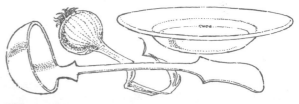

Slimming

One often reads that soups 'are fattening'. This is quite wrong. Some soups contain virtually no calories at all or are very low in calories. There are diets which restrict liquid intake and if you are following one of these, each cup of soup (however low in calories) must be counted as liquid. I am a great believer in serving low calorie soups on a diet, for they mean you have more interesting meals, and lack of interest is often the main criticism of slimming diets.

Some garnishes for soup

Use chopped parsley and other herbs, paprika, blanched almonds, diced crisp toast.

Croûtons: are made by frying tiny dice of bread in deep fat or hot butter.

Garlic croûtons: either fry as above, toss in plenty of garlic salt; or add crushed garlic to butter when frying. Drain croûtons well.

FAMILY SOUPS

The soups in the first part of this chapter are easy to make, use readily available ingredients and are quite inexpensive. Here are other quick suggestions for family soups:

QUICK VEGETABLE SOUPS—as many vegetables have strong flavours you do not need chicken or other stock; if used this would provide a more interesting flavour, but in a true vegetable soup the flavour of stock should not predominate. Use 852 ml (1½ pints) liquid—water or milk and water or white stock. Put into saucepan, add about ½ kilo (1 lb.) mixed diced vegetables (as picture opposite) or cut into matchsticks. Season to taste, simmer steadily until tender (with most root vegetables cut into reasonably small pieces this would take about 20–30 minutes). Season again, if liked serve topped with chopped parsley or parsley and cheese. It is not essential to thicken this soup, but below are creamier thick soups. Serves 4–5.

VEGETABLE PURÉE SOUPS—follow proportions above, although amount of vegetables could be reduced slightly if you do not wish too thick a purée. Cook until tender, sieve and reheat, adding a little milk or cream if wished.

CREAM OF VEGETABLE SOUPS—the simplest way to make creamed soup is to prepare as vegetable or vegetable purée soup, then blend in cream, top with thick or thin cream before serving; or use less stock or water in cooking vegetables, then blend with a thin white sauce, as page 146; or as follows: prepare as quick vegetable soup above then blend either 25 grammes (1 oz.) flour or 15 grammes (½ oz.) cornflour or 25 grammes (1 oz.) potato flour (dehydrated potato will do) or 25 grammes (1 oz.) semolina (this gives an excellent flavour) with 284 ml (½ pint) milk or, better still, half milk and half thin cream. Stir into the soup and cook until thickened. This soup can be topped with cream or yoghourt before serving.

Automatic Oven

One often has space in the oven when cooking a meal, and it is an excellent idea to cook a soup in a covered casserole for another meal. The quick vegetable soup opposite can be adapted according to the time the oven is set—use slightly larger pieces of vegetables and cook for 1½–2 hours in a very moderate oven. Grated or finely chopped vegetables would take about 1 hour.

Speedy Meal

Make the soup with a packet of mixed frozen vegetables, or grate the vegetables instead of chopping; this is quicker to prepare and will cook in about 10 minutes —use a little less liquid as cooking time is shorter.

Home Freezing

Cooked diced root vegetables can be disappointing in a soup as they tend to go 'mushy'. Ideally I would freeze the diced vegetables (not potatoes) as mixed vegetables page 111, then make this soup. The purée soup will freeze well; if the purée 'separates out' simply stir briskly when reheating. Use within 2–3 months.

Soup Paysanne

Serves 4–6
Cooking time 40–45 minutes

Ingredients	Metric	Imperial
margarine or bacon fat	50 grammes	2 oz.
onions	2 large	2 large
potatoes	2 medium	2 medium
turnip	1 small	1 small
carrots	3 large	3 large
water or ham or	1 litre	2 pints
chicken stock	(good measure)	
bouquet garni	spray	spray
tomatoes	3–4 medium	3–4 medium
seasoning	to taste	to taste
TO GARNISH:		
chopped parsley	2 tablespoons	2 tablespoons

1 Heat the margarine or bacon fat in the pan, then toss the finely chopped onions in this for several minutes.
2 Dice all the other vegetables, except the tomatoes, mix with the onions, add the water or stock and the *bouquet garni*.
3 Bring just to the boil, cover the pan tightly, then simmer for 30 minutes.
4 Skin tomatoes by dipping into boiling water for a minute, then into cold water, or by inserting a fine skewer into the tomato and turning it over a lighted flame of the gas ring until the skin pops.
5 Slice tomatoes neatly and thinly, add to the soup, season well, remove the *bouquet garni* before serving and top with chopped parsley.

Automatic Oven

As this soup takes a reasonable time to cook it could be completed in a very moderate oven. Complete stages 1 and 2, put into a very moderate oven and cook for about 1 hour; you can add the tomatoes, see stage 5, just before serving.

Speedy Meal

Take canned or dehydrated mixed vegetable soup, heat with mixed herbs to flavour and add the sliced tomatoes just before serving or use a pressure cooker for stage 3, allow 5 minutes at 15 lb. pressure instead of 30 minutes simmering.

Mixer

Read the directions on page 33, point b) on using a liquidiser to give finely chopped vegetables, or use shredding attachment.

Home Freezing

Prepare the soup to the point of adding the tomatoes. Freeze and add the tomatoes when reheating. This type of soup, and all vegetable soups in this chapter, may be stored for 3–4 months.

Golden Potato Soup

Serves 4–6
Cooking time 20 minutes

Ingredients	Metric	Imperial
cloves of garlic (optional)	1 or 2	1 or 2
salt	pinch	pinch
old potatoes	about 300	about 11–12
(peeled weight)	grammes	oz.
onions	2 large	2 large
butter	50 grammes	2 oz.
olive oil	2 tablespoons	2 tablespoons
chicken stock	852 ml	1½ pints
bouquet garni	spray	spray
seasoning	to taste	to taste
TO GARNISH:		
chopped watercress	2 tablespoons	2 tablespoons
grated cheese	2 tablespoons	2 tablespoons

1 If you like garlic, peel and crush the cloves with the point of a knife (a good pinch of salt helps to do this); if you wish a more delicate garlic flavour, either rub round the saucepan with 1 cut clove, or put the cloves into the chicken stock and allow to stand for a while, then remove.
2 Cut potatoes and onions into matchstick lengths, toss in hot butter and oil until beginning to change to a golden colour.
3 Add stock, herbs, garlic, seasoning; simmer for 10 minutes, then serve topped with watercress and cheese.

Variation: use diced or cubed potatoes and add a little chicken meat and one or two bay leaves.

Speedy Meal
To save time in preparation use frozen potato chips in place of potatoes given in this recipe and cut these into quarters; substitute garlic salt, which will impart a more delicate flavour.

Home Freezing
A very satisfactory soup to freeze. Naturally you will freeze without the garnishes and add these when the soup is defrosted, heated through, and ready to serve. The rather high percentage of fat (butter and oil) means this soup is better used within 2 months.

Onion Soup

Serves 4–5
Cooking time 3–5 minutes

Ingredients	Metric	Imperial
onions	3 large	3 large
butter	50 grammes	2 oz.
brown stock*	1 litre	2 pints
seasoning	to taste	to taste
TO GARNISH:		
chopped parsley	1–2 tablespoons	1–2 tablespoons

*really good flavoured stock or add beef cubes.

1 Peel, slice onions thinly, cut into little pieces.
2 Cook for about 10 minutes in hot butter until golden.
3 Add stock and seasoning, simmer until onions are tender.
4 Top with parsley, or grated cheese, or cheese on rounds of toast or bread, and brown under the grill.

Speedy Meal
Use canned consommé and grated or dehydrated onions.

Slimming Tips
An excellent soup on a slimming diet, but omit the bread *and* the cheese. This type of clear soup can be varied by simmering mushrooms, tomatoes, diced cucumber, or a mixture of low calorie vegetables in the strong brown stock.

Home Freezing
Use within 3 months. Do not add bread or cheese until reheating.

Tomato soups ARE A FAVOURITE WITH MOST PEOPLE.

TOMATO PURÉE SOUP–chop 1 onion, 2 rashers bacon, toss in 50 grammes (2 oz.) butter for 5 minutes. Add 1 kilo (2 lb.) tomatoes and 568 ml (1 pint) white stock. Season, add herbs to taste, simmer until tender. Sieve and reheat, or blend pulp with 1 tablespoon cornflour before reheating. Serves 4–5.

CREAM OF TOMATO SOUP–prepare purée as above, also make White sauce as page 146, with 284 ml (½ pint) milk. Whisk very hot purée and very hot sauce together, serve at once to prevent curdling. Serves 5–6.

CHILLED TOMATO CUCUMBER SOUP–simmer 1 small peeled cucumber, grated, with tomato purée above, sieve. Make thinner with 284 ml (½ pint) thin cream or more stock. Add several spoonfuls chopped pickled cucumber and shrimps. Serves 7–8.

Automatic Oven
Tomato soups are better cooked in a saucepan rather than in the oven.

Mixer
Make a purée of the tomatoes with liquidiser *before* cooking, so shortening the cooking time and retaining more flavour. Simmer for a very short time only, then sieve or strain to remove the pips. In the Cream of tomato soup the liquidiser will emulsify the hot purée and hot sauce to a *very* smooth texture.

Home Freezing
It is best to freeze the tomato purée and add sauce, etc. when defrosted.

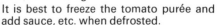

Scotch Broth

Serves 4
Cooking time nearly 3 hours

Ingredients	Metric	Imperial
pearl barley	25 grammes	1 oz.
stewing beef *or* mutton	200 grammes	8 oz.
water	1 litre	2 pints
leaks *or* onions	75 grammes	3 oz.
sliced carrots	200 grammes	8 oz.
diced swede	200 grammes	8 oz.
seasoning	to taste	to taste
sliced cabbage	50 grammes	2 oz.
TO GARNISH:		
chopped parsley	1 tablespoon	1 tablespoon
cooked prunes (optional)	a few	a few

1 Blanch the barley by putting into cold water, bringing to the boil, then pouring the water away.
2 Put barley, diced beef and water into a pan, bring to the boil, skim and simmer gently for 1 hour.
3 Slice the leeks or onions finely, prepare carrots and swede.
4 Add all the vegetables, except the cabbage, plenty of seasoning and cook for a further 1½ hours; add the sliced cabbage and allow another 15 minutes cooking.
5 Skim off any superfluous fat from broth, then pour into a hot bowl or cups, garnish with parsley and prunes (cut into neat strips). The meat can be used as a separate dish or chopped and added to the soup.

Note: this is a very good basis for all meat broths; you could use diced ox kidney instead of beef or mutton.

OX-TAIL SOUP–use proportions as Scotch broth, but as bones of ox-tail are heavy, use ½ kilo (1 lb.) jointed ox-tail, omit barley and use 50 grammes (2 oz.) dried haricot beans. Cook the beans as page 112, add to the soup at stage 4.

Automatic Oven

The barley must be blanched for Scotch broth then the soup could be prepared to stage 4, placed in a casserole, covered well, and cooked for several hours in the centre of a very moderate oven, so saving the fuel used by a gas or electric boiling ring. One can often put a casserole of soup in the oven, but do read the instructions on page 32 about cooking soups in an oven.

Home Freezing

This soup is disappointing when frozen. The barley looses its texture and taste. You could freeze the soup without the barley and add this when reheating, if wished. Use the soup within 2–3 months.

Chicken Broth

Serves 4–6
Cooking time 1½–2 hours

Ingredients	Metric	Imperial
carcass of chicken	1	1
water	1½ litres (good measure)	3 pints
bouquet garni	spray	spray
bay leaf	1	1
seasoning	to taste	to taste
onions	2–3	2–3
carrots	2–3	2–3
long *or* medium grain rice	50 grammes	2 oz.
TO GARNISH:		
chopped parsley	1 tablespoon	1 tablespoon
chopped rosemary	1 teaspoon	1 teaspoon

1 Cover the carcass of chicken with the water, add *bouquet garni*, bay leaf and a little seasoning, then simmer steadily for 1–1½ hours.
2 Remove carcass from the liquid, allow to cool slightly; add diced onions and carrots and simmer for 10 minutes.
3 Add the rice and continue cooking for 10 minutes, then add any tiny pieces of chicken left on the carcass, chopped, and heat for a further 10 minutes.
4 Top with the chopped herbs.

Automatic Oven

Cook the soup to stage 3 in a covered casserole in a very moderate oven for 2½–3 hours. You will then need to continue as stage 3, using a saucepan.

Speedy Meal

Use a pressure cooker for stage 1, cooking carcass for about 20–30 minutes at 15 lb. pressure, after which use the cooker like an ordinary saucepan.

Slimming Tips

Chicken and meat clear broths are extremely good on any slimming diet; they are very satisfying and have a strong flavour which many dishes lack. As chicken is low in calories this is a good soup, although you should be sparing with the carrots (use sliced mushrooms instead) and omit the rice from your portion.

Home Freezing

Prepare to the end of stage 2. Prepare pieces of chicken, put into soup and cool, then freeze. Add the rice when reheating the soup. Use within 3 months.

SOUPS FOR SPECIAL OCCASIONS

These soups are ideal when you wish a change of flavour.

CUCUMBER PURÉE SOUP–remove most of the peel from a large cucumber, leave on a little for colour. Chop and simmer with 1 chopped onion, 568 ml (1 pint) chicken stock and seasoning until tender. Sieve, then reheat with 284 ml (½ pint) thin cream or blend with cream and little lemon juice, and chill.

AVOCADO PURÉE SOUP–sieve pulp from 3 *ripe* avocado pears, mix with lemon juice, proceed as above; serve hot or cold.

Curry Soup

Serves 4
Cooking time 30–35 minutes

Ingredients	Metric	Imperial
onion *or* leek	1 large	1 large
margarine *or* butter	25 grammes	1 oz.
tomatoes	2 medium	2 medium
chicken *or* beef stock *or* water and stock cubes	¾ litre (generous measure)	1½ pints
curry paste	1 teaspoon	1 teaspoon
chilli sauce	few drops	few drops
seasoning	to taste	to taste
lemon juice	squeeze	squeeze
long grain rice	25 grammes	1 oz.

1 Peel and chop onion or leek, toss in hot margarine or butter but do not allow to discolour.
2 Skin, halve and de-seed the tomatoes.
3 Add to onion, stir in stock blended with curry paste.
4 Bring to the boil, add chilli sauce, seasoning and squeeze lemon juice.
5 Simmer for 10 minutes. Sieve if required, and pour back into the saucepan.
6 Add the rice and with the lid on the pan, so the liquid does not evaporate, continue cooking for a further 15 minutes, or until the rice is tender.

Tomato Chilli Soup

Serves 4
Cooking time 20–25 minutes

Ingredients	Metric	Imperial
onion	1 medium	1 medium
tomatoes	½ kilo (poor weight)	1 lb. (good weight)
beef stock *or* water and 1–2 beef stock cubes	¾ litre (generous measure)	1½ pints
seasoning	to taste	to taste
chilli sauce*	to taste	to taste

*chilli sauce is very hot, but if you are fond of hot things you can take quite an amount, but do add it gradually.

1 Chop the onion, skin and chop the tomatoes.
2 Simmer in the stock for approximately 15 minutes, then sieve or stir vigorously to give a smooth texture.
3 Add the seasoning and chilli sauce, tasting as you add.

TO VARY:
Omit chilli sauce, add a little Worcestershire sauce or a pinch curry powder.

Mixer
The liquidiser is ideal for both the cucumber and avocado soups (remember the lemon juice with the latter). Emulsify the vegetable or fruit, add the cream, etc., then heat gently and emulsify again.

Home Freezing
Do not attempt to freeze the soups *with* the cream; freeze the purée; defrost, emulsify or beat if not quite smooth, then *add* the cream. Use within about 3 months.

Speedy Meal
Use either dehydrated onion or a packet of onion soup and water in place of fresh vegetable and stock.

Mixer
Put the partially cooked onions, tomatoes and stock into a blender and emulsify to give a smooth thin purée.

Slimming Tips
Omit the margarine and the rice. This makes a well-seasoned and highly flavoured soup, low in calories.

Home Freezing
This soup freezes well, but it is more satisfactory if the rice is only half cooked before freezing.

Mixer
Chop the onion and simmer in the stock for 10 minutes, liquidise the tomatoes, add to the stock, heat, flavour and serve.

Slimming Tips
This is created to be a particularly slimming soup; none of the ingredients is high in calories. It is an excellent soup in cold weather for it is warming and very pleasant. You can vary it if you do not like chilli sauce, either as suggested in the recipe, or by adding very finely chopped gherkins, olives and pickled cucumber.

Home Freezing
The basic recipe is first-class when frozen; be careful about the amount of chilli sauce, this is a flavouring that does seem to become stronger in freezing. Use within 3–4 months.

Consommé plus

Consommé is made by simmering shin of beef until a good brown stock is obtained, which is then strained, flavoured and cleared. This takes time, and many people will not think it worth while, so you may prefer to use stock cubes with ordinary stock or water (to give a stronger taste and better colour), or you can use canned consommé. To add interest it can be garnished with diced vegetables (jardinière) or with cooked noodles; it may be topped with tiny strips of cooked pancake, cooked rice or noodles. Flavour consommé with sherry or concentrated tomato purée for a change (the latter spoils the clarity of consommé, but gives a good taste).

Slimming Tips
Consommé, whether home-made or canned, is an excellent choice on any diet, providing the garnishes are wisely chosen, i.e. a very few vegetables, but *not* pasta in any form. Serve the consommé iced or jellied in summer time. Sherry is often excluded from slimming diets, so flavour with lemon instead.

Home Freezing
Consommé, like stock, freezes very well indeed. It is wise to remove surplus fat before freezing. To serve iced, bring out of the freezer in good time; it should not be solid.

Low Calorie Mushroom Soup

Serves 4
Cooking time 10–15 minutes

Ingredients	Metric	Imperial
onions	2 medium	2 medium
mushrooms	¼ kilo	8 oz.
beef stock*	¾ litre	1½ pints
parsley	small bunch	small bunch
yeast extract	½–1 teaspoon	½–1 teaspoon
seasoning	to taste	to taste

*it is absolutely essential to have a very good beef stock for this soup to make it really palatable. You could use stock cubes and water, but this tends to make too salty a flavour, so it is worth while boiling bones.

1 Chop the onions and mushrooms finely.
2 Put into the stock and simmer until vegetables are tender.
3 Add the chopped parsley, yeast extract and seasoning to taste. Serve very hot.

Automatic Oven
Cook in a covered casserole for about 1 hour in a very moderate oven.

Speedy Meal
Use dehydrated onions instead of fresh. Follow directions on the packet.

Mixer
The onions may be chopped coarsely, simmered for 10–15 minutes in the stock, then put into the warmed blender with the uncooked mushrooms. Switch on until finely chopped; return to pan and complete.

Duck and Orange Soup

Serves 4–6
Cooking time 1½ hours

Ingredients	Metric	Imperial
duck carcass	1	1
water	568 ml	1 pint
onion	1	1
seasoning	to taste	to taste
oranges	2	2
dry sherry	2–3 tablespoons	2–3 tablespoons
cornflour	2 *level* tablespoons	2 *level* tablespoons
TO GARNISH:		
orange	1	1

1 Break the duck carcass into pieces, put into a saucepan, add the giblets too, if available.
2 Add the water, whole peeled onion, a little seasoning and the thinly pared rind from all the oranges.
3 Cover the pan tightly and simmer for 1 hour.
4 As duck is so fat, allow the stock to become quite cold, then remove excess fat.
5 Warm the stock again, strain carefully, then return to the saucepan.
6 Blend juice of two oranges and dry sherry with the cornflour and stir into the stock.
7 Bring to the boil and cook until thickened.
8 Meanwhile, cut away pith and skin from third orange, cut pulp into tiny pieces. Stir into the soup and serve.

Automatic Oven
Cook the soup to the end of stage 3 in a covered casserole in a very moderate oven, allowing about 1½ hours, then complete in a saucepan.

Home Freezing
This is a good soup to freeze, but you will get a better result if you prepare only to the end of stage 5. When reheating continue as stage 6 onwards. Use within 3 months.

Sea-food Soup

Serves 6
Cooking time 45 minutes

Ingredients	Metric	Imperial
white fish	½ kilo	1 lb.
(use cheap cod, rock	(poor weight)	(good weight)
salmon, etc., with skin)		
shrimps *or* prawns	284 ml	½ pint
(in shells)		
water	1 litre	2 pints
saffron*	pinch	pinch
onions	2 medium	2 medium
tomatoes	2 medium	2 medium
seasoning	pinch	pinch
margarine *or* butter	50 grammes	2 oz.
TO GARNISH:		
white *or* brown	2–4 tablespoons	2–4 tablespoons
breadcrumbs		
chopped parsley	1 tablespoon	1 tablespoon

*or use few strands saffron.

1 Skin fish, shell prawns or shrimps–put skin and shells in the water, with saffron, peeled chopped onions, and chopped tomatoes.
2 Season, simmer steadily in covered pan for 30–35 minutes.
3 Strain liquid; onions and tomatoes may be left out after stage 2, or rubbed through a sieve then added to the liquid.
4 Meanwhile, cut fish into strips, halve large prawns; toss fish in the hot margarine or butter until golden.
5 Add stock, shell fish, more seasoning, and heat thoroughly.
6 Serve soup topped with breadcrumbs and chopped parsley.

Sea-food Chowder

1 Use ingredients for Sea-food soup, but add *bouquet garni* of fresh herbs, 2 medium sized old potatoes or about 6 small new potatoes, and 2 rashers of back or lean streaky bacon.
2 Make stock as basic recipe with skin and shells, but add the *bouquet garni*; simmer for 30 minutes then strain.
3 Meanwhile, dice peeled onions and potatoes, skinned tomatoes and bacon and toss in the hot margarine or butter.
4 Add stock, bring to the boil, then simmer for 10 minutes.
5 Add pieces of fish, simmer for 5–10 minutes, put in shrimps or prawns and garnish as the basic soup.

Creamed Sea-food Soup

1 Use basic recipe, but 568 ml (1 pint) water; strain the stock as stage 3; do not sieve the onions and tomatoes.
2 Toss the fish in fat as stage 5, be extra careful not to brown; stir in 25 grammes (1 oz.) cornflour or 50 grammes (2 oz.) flour, blended with 284 ml (½ pint) milk. Pour in the stock, bring to the boil, cook until thickened.
3 Add the prawns and 142 ml (¼ pint) thin cream, with any extra seasoning required, then heat gently.
4 Garnish with chopped parsley and paprika.

Spiced Sea-food Soup

1 Ingredients as basic soup; add pinch curry powder, cayenne, *bouquet garni*, crushed clove of garlic.
2 Serve with garlic croûtons, page 33, and with finely chopped parsley and chopped chives or spring onion tops.

Automatic Oven

The basic Sea-food soup could be put into an automatic oven in a covered dish if prepared up to stage 5. It would take about 40–45 minutes to heat through in the coolest part of a very moderate oven. The Sea-food chowder could be prepared to stage 6 and put into the oven to cook the potatoes, etc. The fish should be cut into large pieces in this case and added at the same time as the potatoes. Add shell fish at the last minute.

Note: be careful about leaving fish soups in the oven for any length of time.

Speedy Meal

Use water, about 1 chicken stock cube and a little anchovy essence instead of fish bones, etc., omitting the long simmering. Dehydrated onions and about 1 tablespoon concentrated tomato purée can be used to flavour instead of fresh onions and tomatoes, or use a pressure cooker and allow 5 minutes at 15 lb. pressure for stages 1–3; after this use the pressure cooker as an ordinary saucepan to complete the soup.

Mixer

Use the liquidiser for emulsifying the ingredients in any of the recipes to give a Fish purée soup. Also use the liquidiser to:
a) make a purée of the onions and tomatoes (basic soup, stage 3);
b) make crumbs from bread;
c) chop the parsley.

Slimming Tips

All the fish soups on this page are excellent when slimming, except the creamed version and the chowder. If you wish to make a chowder that is lower in calories increase the amount of onions and decrease the amount of potatoes; also use all lean bacon.

Home Freezing

The basic recipe and variations are excellent soups to freeze. Prepare to the end of the recipe, but shorten the simmering time so the fish is not over-cooked. Do not add the garnish until the soup is reheated. Store for about 6 weeks only. There is no need to defrost the soup; tip into a pan and heat. The Creamed sea-food soup is really better if no cream is added (see stage 3) before freezing; add when reheating.

Chicken and Corn Soup

Serves 4–6
Cooking time 1¼–2¼ hours

Ingredients	Metric	Imperial
chicken carcass	1	1
or frozen chicken joints	2	2
water	1 litre (generous measure)	2 pints
bacon rashers	2	2
or ham bone	1	1
bay leaf	1	1
bouquet garni	spray	spray
onions	2	2
seasoning	to taste	to taste
corn cobs	2	2
thin cream	142 ml	¼ pint
eggs	2	2

1 Put chicken carcass or defrosted chicken joints into the pan with the water, bacon rashers or bone, herbs, whole onions and seasoning. Simmer for at least 1 hour and preferably up to 2 hours.
2 Cook corn cobs in a separate pan, strip off kernels.
3 Lift herbs, chicken and bacon or bone out of liquid; cut meat into neat pieces, return to liquid with the corn.
4 Blend cream and eggs, whisk into the hot but not boiling soup–heat gently *without* boiling, stirring or whisking well to prevent curdling, taste, re-season if necessary and serve.

CHILLED CHICKEN AND CORN SOUP–the soups that follow and the chicken soup above are excellent chilled. When making the chicken soup, proceed to stage 3 (remove chicken; use in salads or Chicken croquettes, page 134). Follow stage 4, chill, add corn, chopped pickled cucumber and diced green pepper. A little cream cheese may be added before serving.

Automatic Oven

Stage 1 could be prepared in a covered casserole in a cool to very moderate oven, allowing about 2 hours. Do this when cooking a meal to save gas or electricity.

Speedy Meal

Use a pressure cooker for stage 1, allowing 25–40 minutes at 15 lb., pressure, and use canned corn (creamed corn or the kernels), or buy cream of chicken soup and just heat the corn in this.

Mixer

If you wish a purée of chicken instead of pieces of chicken, put the meat *free from bone* plus liquid into the warmed goblet, then continue as stage 4.

Home Freezing

The completed soup could be frozen, but this causes complications as you try to reheat a mixture containing cream and eggs, so prepare to the end of stage 3 and freeze. This should be used within 2–3 months–then just heat and continue as stage 4.

Vichyssoise

Serves 4–6
Cooking time 40 minutes

Ingredients	Metric	Imperial
leeks	6 medium	6 medium
butter	50 grammes	2 oz.
chicken stock	852 ml	1½ pints
or chicken stock	568 ml	1 pint
and white wine	284 ml	½ pint
potatoes	2 medium	2 medium
chopped parsley	1 tablespoon	1 tablespoon
chopped chives	2 tablespoons	2 tablespoons
seasoning	to taste	to taste
thin *or* thick cream	142 ml	¼ pint
TO GARNISH:		
chopped chives	1 tablespoon	1 tablespoon

1 Prepare the leeks, chop, then toss in melted butter until pale golden, but do not brown.
2 Add stock or stock and wine, peeled chopped potatoes, parsley and half the chopped chives. Season well and simmer gently for 30 minutes.
3 Rub through a fine sieve; when cool gradually add cream.
4 Season to taste when quite cold.
5 Serve very cold, garnished with chopped chives.

Automatic Oven

The soup can be simmered in a well-covered casserole for about 1 hour in a very moderate oven.

Speedy Meal

Use a pressure cooker and allow 10–15 minutes at 15 lb. pressure, or buy canned Vichyssoise soup and add white wine, cream and chives to flavour.

Mixer

A liquidiser is excellent for this soup. There is no need to chop the herbs–simply add sprigs of parsley and blades of chives to the soup in the goblet with the cream, and emulsify until smooth.

Home Freezing

The best result is obtained by freezing the smooth leek and potato purée *without* the wine and cream. This keeps for several months. Allow to defrost–the flavour is excellent, but the purée does not look very smooth, so beat hard or emulsify again, then add wine, cream, herbs.

Crab Vichyssoise

1 Use the same method as Vichyssoise soup, but only 2 leeks, 3 potatoes and a small cooked crab or equivalent in canned crab.
2 Continue as basic recipe until ready to add cream, stage 3.
3 Put in the cream and flaked crab meat, beat well or emulsify in the liquidiser.
4 Season well, add flavour with lemon juice if desired.

Home Freezing
This soup freezes excellently—follow the directions for Vichyssoise. You can freeze the crab with the vegetable purée, but this means you must use the soup within 5–6 weeks.

Gazpacho

Serves 4
Cooking time – none

Ingredients	Metric	Imperial
water	568 ml	1 pint
tomatoes	½ kilo	1 lb.
	(poor weight)	
cucumber	1 medium	1 medium
onion *or*	1	1
several spring onions		
cloves of garlic	1–2	1–2
green pepper	1 small	1 small
seasoning	to taste	to taste
olive oil	little	little
lemon juice *or*		
white wine vinegar	little	little
TO SERVE:		
croûtons (see page 33)	4–6 tablespoons	4–6 tablespoons
extra cucumber	small piece	small piece
green and/or red pepper	1	1
spring onions	3–4	3–4

1 Put the water into the refrigerator to become very cold.
2 Skin tomatoes if liked–this helps when sieving the mixture, and gives a particularly smooth mixture if using an electric blender or liquidiser.
3 Peel cucumber, cut into very small dice.
4 Chop tomatoes, onion, garlic and add to the cucumber.
5 Either pound until smooth or rub through a sieve. The pepper can also be sieved or chopped very finely once all the seeds and core have been removed.
6 If using an electric liquidiser you will need to add a little water so that none of the thick mixture is wasted.
7 Put the purée into a basin, gradually beat in seasoning, olive oil and enough cold water to give a flowing consistency.
8 Taste and re-season and add lemon juice.
9 To make the garnishes–prepare the tiny croûtons as page 33, peel and dice cucumber, pepper and onions very finely.
10 Chill the soup thoroughly, serve in cold soup cups topped with the garnishes.

Speedy Meal
Omit water and tomato purée and use up to approximately 850 ml (1½ pints) bottled or canned tomato juice. Chill, then add the vegetables as recipe to *part* of the juice, then 'thin down' with the juice instead of water.

Mixer
As detailed in the recipe; you do not remove the seeds of the tomatoes. The liquidiser can also 'chop' the green pepper, cucumber and onions if you add to the tomato purée and switch on for a limited period.

Slimming Tips
This is an ideal soup if you are on a diet for every vegetable is low in calories. You can keep the amount of olive oil to a minimum so that it is less rich in fat than usual. The soup has the advantage that it is refreshing yet filling.

Home Freezing
This soup may be completed and frozen and is very good, but the cucumber tends to become 'watery' with storage, so compensate for this by making a thicker soup than usual before freezing. The garnishes (with the exception of the croûtons) should not be frozen as they lose their crispness when thawed out.

Cucumber Cream Soup

1 Chop a large peeled cucumber very finely.
2 Put into a basin with 2 tablespoons finely chopped chives or 1 tablespoon finely chopped spring onion.
3 Add plenty of seasoning, good squeeze lemon juice, and 284 ml (½ pint) yoghourt; leave to stand for 1 hour.
4 Gradually blend in 142 ml (¼ pint) thin cream, then taste and add more seasoning and lemon juice.
5 Chill thoroughly, and serve topped with tiny croûtons. Serves 5–6.

Speedy Meal
Adapt this recipe for a very quick soup by adding grated raw cucumber to a can of chicken soup and diluting with a little cream.

Mixer
A purée of cucumber soup is produced in the liquidiser within seconds almost, and you have a wonderful smoothness.

Home Freezing
Although cucumber does not freeze well, the purée of cucumber does. Add cream, etc., after defrosting. Use within 2 months.

Cooking Fish

The fish dishes in this chapter give a wide choice of recipes. While I have indicated the particular kind of fish I would prefer to use, there are generally ideas given for alternative fish in each recipe, so you can make the dish throughout most of the year. I have also given a section on dishes that are equally suitable for hors d'oeuvre or a main dish.

FISH IS A HIGHLY PERISHABLE FOOD so choose it carefully. Fresh fish never has a smell of ammonia; the scales and flesh should be firm and bright. If you have any cooked fish left, do store with the same care given to keeping uncooked fish.

WHEN COOKING FISH time this carefully, for overcooked fish loses both texture and flavour. Select flavourings with discretion so the delicate taste of the fish is not spoilt. White fish in particular needs discreet, rather than generous, flavourings. Grilled fish can become very dry as it cooks, unless 'basted' with butter.

Metric Conversions

As fish is an important protein food you should not 'cut down' on this. You will, therefore, sometimes find that quantities under the metric system generally are inclined to be generous. As you know, 1 kilogram is 2·205 lb., but I often give 1 kilo of fish as the amount to buy in place of 2 lb. fish. You will obviously give the family slightly larger portions than usual. Fish can dry easily in cooking, and therefore one needs to be generous when using butter or other fat; this is why I sometimes give 25–30 grammes as the equivalent of 1 oz.

Drinks to serve with fish

When serving fish as a first or main course, most people would prefer to choose either a dry sherry or white wine; neither of which would 'overshadow' the flavour of the fish as red wine is likely to do. Sherry is generally served at room temperature, but a dry sherry is very pleasant when lightly chilled. A white wine is best when chilled before serving, but do not serve at too cold a temperature. Another type of wine that blends with fish is a chilled vin rosé.

Home freezing of fish

If you intend to freeze *uncooked* fish, make sure it is very fresh. If you catch fish yourself, or are sure you can buy *absolutely fresh fish*, it is safe to freeze this.

Prepare the fish ready for serving; obviously you should clean it well and cut into convenient-sized portions. If freezing whole salmon, many people prefer the flavour of the fish if left 'ungutted' and *not* cleaned, but personally I clean salmon and remove the intestines. Remember if you freeze salmon whole you must either defrost the whole fish before cooking, or saw or cut into convenient-sized pieces, then allow these to defrost. If the slices of salmon are small you need *not* defrost. Other ways to make sure fish keeps particularly well in the freezer are to:

a) freeze the fish without wrapping, when very frozen dip in very cold aspic jelly liquid to give a coating, freeze again and wrap–this is excellent for salmon trout.

b) freeze the fish in a layer of ice cold water. When solid, dip quickly into warm water to melt away excess ice. Put back in the freezer again to make certain the very thin coating of ice is solid, then wrap. This method is particularly good for scallops. The extra layer of frozen jelly or water helps to keep the fish a firm texture.

Raw white or freshwater fish keeps up to 6–8 months.

Oily fish, like salmon and trout, keeps 3–4 months.

Raw shell fish or dishes containing cooked shell fish keep up to 4–6 weeks.

Times for keeping cooked fish dishes in the home freezer are given under recipes.

Most white, freshwater and oily fish can be cooked from the frozen state, but it is advisable to allow shell fish and salmon trout to defrost before cooking, see also above.

Using a mixer for fish dishes

A mixer is not as useful for preparing fish dishes as for other kinds of food. If you have a mincing attachment, use this for mincing *uncooked* fish in Fish creams, see page 54. Use a steady speed and push well so the fish does not 'clog' the mincer. A liquidiser can be used for some of the sauces and many stuffings served with fish, and also for preparing ingredients.

Saving time when cooking fish

a) fish is a quickly cooked food, so is a wise choice when time is limited.

b) choose ready-coated frozen fish where suitable; this saves preparation time–cook fish where possible from frozen state. This does not apply to shell fish, which are better defrosted before cooking.

c) remember wine and cream used together make a wonderful sauce for fish, with little effort, see recipe page 152.

d) herbs and spices often add the necessary flavour to fish with the minimum of time and effort, see recipe page 46.

A PRESSURE COOKER is really unnecessary as a method of saving time, as fish is easily over-cooked. There is, however, an entirely different advantage given by a pressure cooker for fish cookery: you have far less smell than when using an ordinary saucepan. When cooking in a pressure cooker, do not use the rack, put the fish into the cooker with cold salted water (amount given in manufacturer's book) and any other flavourings you wish; put on the lid, bring up to 15 lb. pressure, allow approximately 3 minutes per lb., cool rapidly. If you wish to keep the fish rather drier in texture, put it in a heat resistant container on the rack in the pressure cooker, add any seasonings or flavourings required, have sufficient water in the pressure cooker to come half way up the container, put on lid, bring to 15 lb., pressure, cook as above. If the heat-resistant container is of the type that could crack easily be careful *you do not cool the pressure too rapidly* under the cold tap, but allow to drop at room temperature. In this case, shorten the cooking time to 2 minutes per lb.

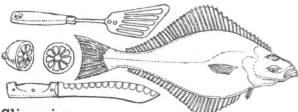

Slimming

Fish is a low calorie protein food; this applies especially to white, shell or some freshwater fish, so is an excellent choice for a slimming diet. The only problem is how to cook fish so you do not add an appreciable amount of fat or rich sauces. Two of the best ways are by poaching, page 50 or wrapped in foil, page 45. Fish salads are also a low calorie and palatable way of serving fish. Flavour poached or grilled fish with plenty of lemon rind and juice, seasonings and herbs.

A low calorie salad dressing is made by blending 125 grammes (5 oz.) natural yoghourt with 2 teaspoons lemon juice, seasoning and 1 teaspoon made-mustard and finely chopped fresh herbs. This can be varied with tomato purée, pinch curry powder, mixed herbs or spices to taste.

Cooking fish in the automatic oven

It is very unwise to leave uncooked fish for any length of time in the cold oven, especially in hot weather. If you leave it in the oven for a short time only there is no reason why fish dishes cannot form part of an automatic meal. It would be wiser to use frozen fish if you have to pre-set the oven beforehand, for fish cannot spoil while it is frozen and naturally as it takes time to thaw out in a cold oven harmful bacteria will not develop. Make certain you do not allow too long a time for cooking, as fish could spoil if left in the oven and if by chance the family are a little late coming in for their meal. This would occur even if the cooking period was over and the oven has automatically switched off, for fish over-cooks so readily that the heat left in the oven is sufficient to dry the flesh.

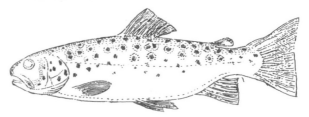

Easy dishes for the automatic oven

BAKED FISH IN EGG SAUCE: put 4 portions of well-dried, seasoned white fish in a buttered oven-proof dish. Beat 2 eggs with a little seasoning and 284 ml ($\frac{1}{2}$ pint) milk. Pour over fish; cover dish with greased foil or a well fitting lid. Place in centre of oven, set to give 1 hour's cooking at very moderate. Casserole of carrots, page 114, and small Jacket potatoes (placed in hottest position) and Orange crumble, see page 206, (in centre of oven) could form a complete meal. This dish freezes well *before* being cooked. Vary by adding grated lemon rind or grated onion and herbs to custard.

FISH AND POTATO BAKE: put a layer of thinly sliced potatoes at bottom of a buttered oven-proof dish. Top with portions of well seasoned white fish (add a little grated onion to flavour if wished, or chopped herbs). Add another layer of thinly sliced and well seasoned potatoes, plus small knobs of butter or margarine. Pour enough milk over the dish to cover top layer of potatoes, to prevent them becoming discoloured as they stand in the oven. Stand in the centre of the oven (it may be worth while putting the dish in a tin just in case the milk boils over at the beginning of cooking). Set the oven to give $1\frac{1}{4}$–$1\frac{1}{2}$ hours cooking (depending on thickness of potatoes) at a very moderate to moderate heat. Macedoine of vegetables, page 114, and Upside down pudding page 204, complete the meal.

This fish dish *does not* freeze well before cooking, but you could prepare the dish, cook lightly, then freeze: defrost and reheat again when serving.

BASIC WAYS TO COOK FISH
FAMILY DISHES

The following are the 5 basic ways to cook fish:

To bake fish

The simplest way to bake fish is to put it into a greased shallow ovenproof dish, season, add a squeeze of lemon juice. Thin fillets may be rolled or folded; bake in the centre of a moderate oven 350–375°F. (180–190°C.), Gas Mark 4–5, allow the following times:

12–15 minutes–thin fillets of fish;
15–20 minutes–rolled, folded or thick fillets of fish;
20–25 minutes–whole small fish or thick slices or steaks.

If you wish the fish to remain rather soft and not brown on top, cover with a little milk and white wine, then cover dish with greased foil or greaseproof paper.

Stuffed baked fish

Split whole fish, bone and fill with any favourite stuffing; parsley and thyme (often called veal stuffing) is a wise choice for most fish, particularly if very well flavoured with lemon. The amount of stuffing on page 142 is enough to stuff 4 herrings, whiting or 1 cod (large enough for 4–5 people). If wishing to cook cutlets (or steaks) of cod or other fish, press stuffing against the slice of fish, tie into position. Spread the stuffing on fillets of fish, roll firmly. Follow basic times for baking above, but allow an extra 5 minutes cooking time for fillets or steaks, or 10 minutes additional for whole fish.

Baked fish provençal

Put a layer of *thickly* sliced well seasoned tomatoes and thinly sliced onions under and over the fish. Add 2–3 tablespoons white wine if wished. Bake as the times at top of the page adding an extra 10 minutes for fillets or cutlets, and 15–20 minutes for whole fish.

Baked fish en cocotte

Put tiny skinned rolled fillets of plaice, or sole, or large shelled prawns into small buttered ovenproof dishes. Season lightly. Cover with a little thick cream (you will need about 8 tablespoons cream for 4 small dishes, and 4 fillets fish or about 16 large prawns). Top with about 4 teaspoons melted butter, bake for 15–20 minutes in the centre of a moderate oven.

Fish and potato bake

Put a layer of very thinly sliced raw potatoes at the bottom of a buttered dish, top with cutlets of white fish, season well and cover with milk. Spread another layer of very thinly sliced potatoes over the top and about 25 grammes (1 oz.) melted margarine or butter. Bake in the centre of a moderate oven for about 45 minutes–1 hour (depending upon the depth of potatoes). This recipe can be varied quite a lot: add finely chopped or grated onions to the potatoes; put layers of grated cheese with the potatoes; omit the milk, top the fish with thick slices of skinned tomatoes.

Fish in egg custard sauce

The easiest way to bake fish is in a savoury egg custard. Put 4 prepared portions of white fish (skinned if possible) into an ovenproof dish, season lightly. Beat 1 large egg (or 2 egg yolks), into 284 ml (½ pint) milk, pour over fish, bake as recipe above.

Automatic Oven
Fish may be left in the oven, but see the comments on page 43, for it is very important that fish, which is such a highly perishable food, should not be left exposed for too long a period to the air. For a complete automatic meal choose: Stuffed baked fish with oven 'fried' potatoes, page 115, Peas à la française, page 120 and an Apple Charlotte, page 206.

Speedy Meal
One of the quickest ways to prepare an interesting fish dish is to top with a concentrated soup, and bake as directions for the first recipe opposite. Allow 10 minutes additional cooking time to ensure that the soup is thoroughly heated.

Mixer
The liquidiser can be extremely useful in preparing herbs, cheese, etc., as toppings for baked fish.

Slimming Tips
One of the easiest and best methods of baking fish is in foil (see opposite). If you wish to lose weight, then use this method as often as possible. Spread the piece of foil with thickly sliced seasoned tomatoes, put the piece of fish on top, season and flavour with lemon juice. Close the foil package and bake, see timing opposite.

Home Freezing
Most baked fish dishes can be frozen if wished, but do not over-cook, otherwise the fish will be disappointingly dry when reheated. Use any of these dishes within 2 months for the best result.
To prepare complete frozen meals using baked fish:
put lightly cooked stuffed fish into aluminium foil containers, add cooked mixed vegetables. Cover and freeze. Reheat without defrosting in a moderate oven for about 40 minutes. Cook Baked fish Provençal in the type of dish that can be transferred to the freezer. Freeze Duchesse potatoes, page 120, and cooked carrots in another container, but pack the covered dishes together so they can both be 'located' easily when you wish to reheat, see timing above.
The automatic menu above, also freezes well.

To steam fish

Steamed fish, generally considered an invalid dish, is probably one of the most easily digested methods of cooking fish; particularly if used for fillets of sole, plaice, whiting or portions of fresh haddock. The simple method of steaming is as follows:

1 Put fish on to a buttered ovenproof plate large enough to fit over the top of a saucepan.
2 Half fill the saucepan with water and bring to the boil.
3 Season the fish, add a small knob of butter or margarine and 1–2 tablespoons milk; cover with a second plate, the lid of the saucepan or greased foil.
4 Lift over the boiling water and cook for:
   8–10 minutes–thin fillets of fish;
   10–12 minutes–folded, rolled or thicker fillets;
   12–15 minutes–whole fish.
5 Lift the fish from the plate on to a hot serving dish, garnish with parsley and lemon, or serve with a sauce.

MORE INTERESTING WAYS OF STEAMING FISH
If cooking for 1 or 2 people you may find steaming is the easiest method, try these ways of flavouring the fish:

WITH TOMATOES–skin tomatoes, put a thickly sliced layer on the well-buttered plate. Lay fish on top, season, add a little chopped parsley, chopped chives, a topping of sliced seasoned tomatoes and a little butter. Do *not* add milk. Cover, steam as above, allow an extra 5–10 minutes to cook tomatoes as well as fish. If you like to add 1–2 tablespoons white wine, you will find it gives an excellent flavour.

WITH MUSHROOMS–use butter and milk as basic recipe, but add a few small *sliced* mushrooms; allow an extra 5–10 minutes.

Automatic Oven
The method of cooking fish in foil, point a) is ideal for oven cooking, but the tightly wrapped fish does become extra warm when left in the oven for any length of time before cooking begins, so read comments on page 43, about the advantage of using frozen fish.

Speedy Meal
Both steaming and cooking in foil are among the quickest ways of preparing fish for a meal.

Slimming Tips
Steaming fish, providing a small amount of butter only and skimmed milk are used (unless on a high fat diet, see page 43 slimming note regarding this) is a sensible method to employ, for many people dislike the dry texture of fish without a sauce and this gives you rather the same result as a sauce. Mention is made opposite about foil cooking as ideal for slimming.

Home Freezing
Cooked steamed fish is not the best form of fish to freeze; but you could freeze the *raw* fish with the flavourings, etc. suggested opposite on a covered tin or plate or thick foil then it is all ready to cook as required.
The 'parcels' of fish in foil could be prepared, labelled carefully to prevent confusion, then frozen. Store for times given, page 42.

To cook fish in foil

One of the most successful ways of retaining the flavour of fish is to cook it in aluminium foil. This has the effect of steaming fish but you have a more pronounced flavour. The wrapped fish can be: (a) cooked in the oven as baked fish–but work out the cooking time, as table opposite, then add an extra 10 minutes to compensate for the time it takes for the heat to penetrate the foil; (b) cooked in a saucepan of water as for poaching, page 50, but add a generous 5 minutes extra cooking time when using this method for the heat of the water to penetrate–make a tight parcel so the flavour and moistness of the fish is retained; (c) placed on a tin *over* boiling water as steamed fish–allow a generous 10 minutes extra cooking time for the heat to penetrate.

When slimming use this method of cooking fish, so little if any fat is necessary. If using no fat, lay the fish on the foil with a very little moisture (skimmed milk or lemon juice or white wine) to prevent it 'sticking' to the foil. Season well, add any flavouring you wish such as sliced raw mushrooms, skinned sliced tomatoes, finely chopped mixed herbs, grated onion or chopped chives. Wrap in the foil and cook.

WINE COOKED FISH: spoon several tablespoons vin rosé over the fish, add butter to taste, seasoning and sliced mushrooms; wrap and cook by whichever method you prefer.

ANCHOVY FILLETS: lay fillets of fish on to oiled foil (use oil from can of anchovies), add a little pepper and chopped parsley, wrap and cook. When cooked, unwrap, sprinkle grated cheese over the fish, then brown under a hot grill and serve.

To fry fish

Fish can be fried in 2 ways; in a little fat (shallow frying) or in deep fat or oil. Before frying coat the fish–choose one of the following:
a) SEASONED FLOUR–allow about 25 grammes (1 oz.) flour and salt and pepper to taste, to 4 large or 8 small fillets or portions of fish;
b) EGG AND CRUMBS–see Rolled fried fillets for method of coating. Allow about 1 level tablespoon seasoned flour as first coating, then 1 egg and 3–4 tablespoons crisp breadcrumbs to 4 large or 8 small fillets or portions of fish, or about 16 large scampi;
c) BATTER–to coat 4 large or 8 small fillets or portions of fish proceed as follows:
1 Sieve 100 grammes (4 oz.) flour with pinch salt, add 1 egg, beat well, gradually beat in 142 ml (¼ pint) plus 4 tablespoons milk.
2 For a thinner coating, use 6 tablespoons milk, or use milk and water for a more economical batter.
3 Coat fish in seasoned flour (15 grammes (½ oz.) flour, shake pepper, pinch salt), then dip into the batter.
4 Lift out with a fork and spoon, hold over batter so surplus may drip back into the bowl. This saves any mess as fish is put into the fat, and also avoids too thick a coating.
5 Use smaller amount of milk for rather solid pieces of fish such as cod, and thinner batter, i.e. larger quantity of milk, for thinner pieces of fish.
d) OATMEAL–is another excellent coating; this is used for oily fish like herrings (it is equally suitable for mackerel) but is rarely used as a coating for white fish.

Fish can be fried very well without coating, especially when you wish to serve with brown butter, see Fish meunière below.

Timing for frying

SHALLOW FRYING

1 Coat fish in flour or egg and crumbs (batter is unsuitable for this method).
2 Heat approximately 50 grammes (2 oz.) fat for thin fish or about 75 grammes (3 oz.) for thicker pieces of fish. Test temperature of fat (see under deep frying), put in coated fish, and cook for:
4 minutes–thin fillets of fish (turn after 2 minutes and cook for the same time on the second side);
5–6 minutes–thicker fillets (cook as above, lower heat for final 1–2 minutes);
7–9 minutes–thick pieces or whole fish (cook as thin fillets, then lower heat for the final 3–5 minutes).
3 Drain on absorbent paper (see under deep frying) and serve garnished with lemon and parsley.

Fish Meunière

This classic French way of cooking fish is simple; use for sole, or other white fish, and trout. If frying enough fish for 4 portions, put approximately 75 grammes (3 oz.) butter in a large frying pan. Prepare fish (skin white fish if wished, clean trout), season. Some recipes coat fish in flour, but do this very lightly so it absorbs the butter taste. Heat butter, fry the fish, see times above. When cooked, lift out of pan, put on a very hot dish. If the fish has absorbed most of the butter, add a little more and melt. Add ½–1 tablespoon lemon juice or vinegar, 1–2 teaspoons chopped parsley, 1–2 teaspoons capers: heat until butter turns dark brown, remove from heat, pour over fish and serve. Garnish with lemon and parsley.

Speedy Meal
Fish is a natural choice when you wish to prepare a quick meal, for it does cook quickly. Choose ready-coated frozen fish (of which there is a very good selection) to save time coating in egg and crumbs or batter. If you have a home freezer, coat raw *fresh* fish when you have time, freeze and use as required. Fry fish as Sole meunière without the trouble of coating the fish.

Mixer
The liquidiser can be used for making soft crumbs, which can be dried in a slow oven until crisp and brown, then rolled until fine. In this way you use up left-over bread and save the expense of buying browned crumbs (raspings). You can also use the liquidiser for making the batter for coating fish, see opposite.

Home Freezing
Mention has already been made of preparing and storing ready-coated uncooked fish in the freezer, or storing commercially coated fish. It is also possible to freeze ready-fried fish, see under Rolled fried fillets and fried fish in butter, etc., page 50. The full directions for covering frozen fish to freeze are on page 50. If you wish to make fried fish the basis of a complete frozen meal then buy deep foil dishes and put the fried well drained fish in these, add fried chips or creamed potatoes, cooked peas or other vegetables. Cover the dish with foil and freeze.
To reheat: if you have both fried fish and fried potatoes, remove the foil covering completely (so the food will crisp again) then put a small piece back over the other vegetables so they do not dry. Do not defrost, but put immediately into a moderate oven and heat for about 30 minutes.

Home Freezing
Fish meunière freezes very well for a limited period of about 1 month. Cook as recipe opposite making sure the fish is not over-cooked. Put into suitable container, cover, freeze; reheat as above, allowing about 20–25 minutes for small fillets. Do not unwrap the container when you reheat.

DEEP FRYING

1 Coat fish in egg and crumbs or batter (flour alone is unsuitable for this method).
2 Heat pan of deep fat with frying basket in position.
3 Test to see if fat or oil is hot enough; a cube of bread should turn golden brown within 1 minute in fat; oil takes slightly under 1 minute to brown the bread.
4 If the bread shows no signs of browning in this time, heat fat or oil longer, test again. If the bread browns very much more quickly, the fat or oil is *too hot*. Remove pan from heat and cool–remember over-heated fat or oil can give an unpleasant taste to food.
5 Lower fish carefully into frying basket; never bend over the pan of hot fat in case it splutters.
6 Reduce heat slightly so fat does not continue to become hotter–cook for:
3 minutes–thin fillets of fish;
4 minutes–thicker fillets of fish;
5 minutes–thick pieces or steaks of fish.
7 Lift fish in frying basket out of pan, hold basket over the pan for a few seconds so that surplus fat drains back into it.
8 Tip fish on to crumpled tissue or kitchen paper on a hot plate or tin; this drains excess fat and makes sure the fish is really crisp. Serve garnished with lemon and parsley.

CHOOSING THE METHOD OF FRYING

WHITE FISH–fillets and steaks can be shallow *or* deep fried, but you produce a more even browning, without turning the fish, if you deep rather than shallow fry.

SCAMPI (LARGE PRAWNS) coated with egg and crumbs or batter should be deep fried where possible, as this gives a better brown coating on the outside. If you want to cook without coating they are very delicious à la meunière, see page 46.

SALMON is a fish rarely fried, but it is excellent. The contrast between the crisp, dry outside and the moist flesh is more successful if you choose a very light batter coating and deep fry. Follow directions for making batter, see page 46, but separate the white from the yolk of egg. Prepare batter with yolk only, then fold in stiffly beaten white at last minute. Dip lightly floured fish in this and fry–drain very well. Shallow frying can make salmon almost *too* rich.

HERRINGS AND TROUT are usually shallow fried, although fillets of herring could be rolled and deep fried.

FISH FRITTERS–make a fritter batter as page 46, using 100 grammes (4 oz.) flour, etc., add 200 grammes (8 oz.) prepared fish, this can be a) flaked crab or other shell fish, b) a mixture of cooked shell fish (crab, mussels, prawns, etc.) or c) cooked white fish. Flavour with chopped chives, chopped parsley, grated lemon rind, and a few drops Tabasco sauce. Fry in hot oil, drain well on absorbent paper.

FISH CAKES–blend ¼ kilo (½ lb. approximately) cooked flaked white fish (this can be poached, steamed or baked) with an equal amount of smooth mashed potatoes. Bind with an egg, season well and form into flat round cakes. Coat in seasoned flour, egg and crisp breadcrumbs. Fry in shallow fat until crisp and brown. Drain on absorbent paper, serve.

 ### Automatic Oven
Although it really cannot be said to be true 'frying', one can 'fry' fish in an oven. Coat the fish in egg and crumbs, grease the baking sheet or tin under each piece of fish thoroughly–do not grease the whole sheet, or you will have fat 'fumes' that are not necessary. Spoon a little oil or melted fat carefully over each piece of fish and cook fillets for 15 minutes, thicker pieces of fish for 20–25 minutes, towards the top of a moderately hot oven, or a little longer at a cooler temperature.

Rolled Fried Fillets

Serves 4
Cooking time 6–7 minutes

Ingredients	Metric	Imperial
fillets of plaice,	4 large *or*	4 large *or*
sole *or* whiting	8 small	8 small
flour	1 level tablespoon	1 level tablespoon
seasoning	to taste	to taste
TO COAT:		
egg	1	1
crisp breadcrumbs	3–4 tablespoons	3–4 tablespoons
(raspings)		
TO FRY:		
deep oil *or* fat		
TO SERVE:		
chipped potatoes, see page 115		
TO GARNISH:		
lemon	1	1
parsley	few sprigs	few sprigs

1 Skin the fish if the fishmonger has not already done so; to do this, dip tip of a sharp knife in a little salt, make a cut at tail end of each fillet, gently cut flesh away from skin.
2 If you find it difficult to do, dip blade of knife again in the salt.
3 Roll fillets firmly from tail end, secure with wooden cocktail sticks.
4 Mix flour and seasoning on a plate, turn fillets in this.
5 Beat egg, add 1 tablespoon water if wished, brush fillets with this.
6 Put crumbs into a paper bag, drop fillets into this, shake gently until evenly coated, or put crumbs on a flat plate or on to a piece of greaseproof paper, turn fillets in this.
7 Pat crumbs firmly into the fish with a flat bladed knife.
8 Meanwhile, heat oil or fat (to test, drop in a cube of day-old bread and it should turn golden brown within 1 minute).
9 Lower the basket into the fat for a moment so this becomes hot (it prevents the fish sticking to the basket).
10 Bring out basket, hold above fat, put in rolls of coated fish.
11 Lower into the hot fat and fry for 6–7 minutes until golden brown.
12 Lift out, and drain on absorbent paper.
13 Serve with chipped potatoes, and garnish with quarters of lemon and parsley.
14 The parsley could be fried if wished–wash and dry, then plunge into the very hot oil or fat. Lift out and serve at once while crisp and still green.

Note: fillets that are not rolled like this would cook in a slightly shorter time. You would, however, need rather more egg and crumbs to coat 8 flat fillets.

Speedy Meal

Buy frozen ready-coated fish which can be deep or shallow fried from the frozen state.

Slimming Tips

Some very authoritative slimming diets recommend eating fairly large quantities of fat; if you are following such a diet you could fry fish, although it is better to dispense with the crumb coating. Most diets, however, suggest that fish is grilled (with the minimum of fat) instead of being fried.

Home Freezing

Coated fish can be frozen. Wash, dry and coat the *very fresh* fish as stages 1–2 and 4–7 (there is no need to roll the fish). Freeze then wrap; if you wrap before freezing the crumbs could stick to the wrapping. For length of time to keep the fish, see page 42.
Very few people think of freezing ready-fried fish, but this is extremely sensible, for frying is a hot job and produces an unpleasant smell. Cook the fish lightly–do not over-cook. Drain on absorbent paper and when cold put on to double thicknesses of heavy foil, wrap tightly then freeze. To reheat, open out the foil and heat through in a moderately hot oven. Ready-fried fish should be used within 6–8 weeks.

Freezing complete meals with fish

One helpful aspect of home freezing is that one can freeze a complete meal ready for reheating later. You can prepare and serve a meal, but put complete portions of all food on plates to freeze. The plates used must be strong enough to withstand the extreme cold of the freezer and the heat of the oven. Even ovenproof plates must stand for a while before going from the freezer to be heated; this is why foil plates and dishes are so useful. Fish dishes cooked in a lot of butter, as Fish meunière page 46, should be used within about a month, other fish meals within 6–8 weeks.

Home Freezing

Points to remember when freezing complete meals:
a) choose foil plates or 'tough' plates or dishes, see opposite;
b) plan a meal so reheating of *all* ingredients takes the same time;
c) when you plan a complete meal you will combine foods that can be kept for varying times, so always plan storage time as for the food requiring the minimum of time–in this chapter it will be the fish.

3. Mediterranean style stuffed herrings, see page 133

To grill fish

Fish is rarely coated when grilled, but it can be flavoured, see below. The method of grilling is simple:
1 Pre-heat the grill *before* cooking the fish.
2 Brush the grid of grill with melted butter or margarine to prevent fish sticking, *or* place fish on a piece of greased foil on the grid or rack of the pan.
3 Brush fish with melted butter or margarine, season lightly and add a little lemon juice. Grill for:
2–3 minutes–thin fillets of fish (do not turn);
5 minutes–thicker fillets (do not turn, but lower heat for last few minutes of cooking time);
9–10 minutes–thick slices or steaks (turn fish during cooking and brush second side with melted butter or margarine).

LEMON BUTTER–blend grated rind and juice of 1 lemon with 25–50 grammes (1–2 oz.) butter, and brush the fish with this as it cooks. Excellent for white fish.

MUSTARD BUTTER–blend 1–2 teaspoons made-mustard and squeeze lemon juice with 25–50 grammes (1–2 oz.) butter, and brush the fish with this as it cooks. Ideal flavouring for herrings and for white fish.

GRILLED CURRIED FISH–sprinkle uncooked fish with a light dusting of curry powder as well as salt and pepper. If you like a strong curry taste, blend more curry powder or curry paste with the melted butter and 'baste' as the fish cooks. This is suitable for most fish.

BARBECUED FISH–although instructions for cooking this are on page 132, you can have much the effect of a barbecue if you 'baste' the fish with this *Barbecue sauce* (this is enough for 4 large or 8 small portions)–chop 1 small onion finely, blend with 1–2 teaspoons Worcestershire sauce, 2 tablespoons olive oil or melted margarine or butter, 1 tablespoon tomato ketchup, seasoning and a few drops Chilli or Tabasco sauce (there is no need to use butter, etc., when cooking the fish). If any sauce is left when the fish is cooked, warm and pour over the fish just before serving. Use firm fleshed white fish–cod, fresh haddock or hake–for this.

MARINATED FISH–skin the fish so it absorbs the marinade better. For 4 large or 8 small fillets, blend 1 small chopped onion, 1 crushed clove garlic (optional), 1 tablespoon freshly chopped herbs (parsley, lemon thyme, fennel–when available–*very little* marjoram and rosemary) or use all parsley with 2 tablespoons olive oil and 2 tablespoons white wine or dry cider. Season well and pour the marinade on to a flat dish. Put the fish in this, turn several times and leave for about 1 hour. Grill as usual, but there is no need to use butter, etc., when cooking.

Speedy Meal

A grill is one of the most useful parts of the cooker when you are short of time. Pre-heat the grill while preparing the fish or use ready-frozen fish. The very hot grill not only shortens cooking time but gives a better result as you 'seal in' the flavour of the fish almost immediately.

Slimming Tips

Grilling is always recommended as an ideal method of cooking when on a slimming diet, but most grilled fish *needs* a generous amount of butter to keep it moist, so this must be considered when choosing the way of cooking the fish.

Home Freezing

To prevent over-cooking it is better to freeze the uncooked fish, then grill to serve, rather than freeze *cooked* grilled fish (frozen fish does not need defrosting before being cooked under the grill) unless you are freezing a complete meal for reheating, in which case:
grill fillets or portions of fish *lightly*. Put on a plate or in a foil freezer dish, add grilled mushrooms, creamed potatoes, peas or other vegetable. Cover tightly, freeze. Use within 2 months and heat gently in a moderate oven.

Fish au Gratin

Serves 4
Cooking time as grilled fish

Ingredients	Metric	Imperial
white fish	4 portions	4 portions
butter	25–50 grammes	1–2 oz.
seasoning	to taste	to taste
Cheddar cheese	50 grammes	2 oz.
breadcrumbs	25 grammes	1 oz.

1 Grill fish as stages 1–3 above.
2 When nearly cooked top with the grated cheese and crumbs, return to hot grill and cook until crisp and brown.
3 Serve with cooked vegetables or a green salad.

4. Prawn cocktail, see page 26

To poach fish

The term 'poach' should be used instead of boiling to describe cooking fish in liquid, for 'boiling' means the liquid is so hot that the fish is very likely to break–poaching means cooking in liquid that barely simmers. You can 'poach' fish in water and seasoning, except for smoked salted fish when no salt is required; or in milk or milk and water; fish stock, see page 33; or in wine or a mixture of wine and water. Add herbs if wished, a sliced onion and/or carrot for flavour. The basic method of poaching is as follows:

Allow 284 ml ($\frac{1}{2}$ pint) liquid and $\frac{1}{2}$ level teaspoon salt to each portion of fish–if cooking several pieces of fish do not increase the amount of liquid a great deal; allow sufficient to cover fish. Put fish into *cold* salted liquid, bring just to boiling point, lower heat then simmer for:
3 minutes–thin fillets of fish;
5 minutes–thicker fillets;
7 minutes–thick slices or steaks.
Lift fish from liquid, drain on fish-slice, serve as follows:

WHITE FISH of all kinds can be poached and served with melted butter or a sauce.

SHELL FISH–lobsters, crab, prawns, shrimps–are cooked in salted water after buying or catching; mussels are 'poached' in liquid and prepared in various ways, see Moules marinière on page 56.

SMOKED HADDOCK OR COD, poach in water or milk, top with butter and a poached egg if wished. An excellent way to cook kippers is either to poach for a short time in water, or cover with boiling water and leave to stand about 5 minutes.

OILY fish of all kinds can be poached, but salmon does give problems in cooking, for if over-cooked it loses the moist 'oily' texture that is so much a part of its appeal.

TO COOK CUTLETS OF SALMON–season each cutlet lightly, add a squeeze lemon juice and wrap in *well* buttered greaseproof paper. Tie the 'parcels' lightly, put into a pan of cold water, then bring water steadily to boiling point. If you intend to serve the salmon cold, immediately remove pan from the heat, cover tightly, allow to cool in the water. If you intend to serve the salmon hot, it is wise to allow the water to simmer for a few minutes; remove fish to a large dish and unwrap the 'parcels'. Serve with Hollandaise or Tartare sauces, pages 152 and 146.

TO COOK LARGER PIECES OF SALMON–wrap as above (if wished); time as table for poaching, or you can cook the *unwrapped* salmon in water with a little white wine and/or lemon juice to flavour, seasoning, several slices of lemon and 1–2 tablespoons olive oil to help retain the 'oily' flavour.

TO SERVE WITH POACHED FISH

Poaching is a simple way to cook fish, and it can be a little dull unless served with an interesting garnish or sauce. Pour really hot melted butter, flavoured with chopped herbs and lemon juice, over white fish or salmon, or top with pats of 'Maître d'hotel' (parsley) butter, or serve with either Béchamel sauce, or White sauce, page 146, flavoured with little lemon and/or parsley, but add colourful garnishes, e.g. slices cooked carrot, parsley, tomato, etc., unless giving to someone on a strict diet. To make '*mock Hollandaise*' sauce, blend a beaten egg and little lemon juice or white wine vinegar into very hot, but not boiling, white sauce. *Cucumber butter* or *Cucumber sauce*, page 168, are ideal to serve with fish–to make Cucumber butter, peel $\frac{1}{4}$ small to medium cucumber, cut flesh into matchstick pieces. Stir into 75–100 grammes (3–4 oz.) melted butter, season well, add a good shake cayenne pepper and squeeze of lemon juice.

Automatic Oven

While one usually poaches fish in a pan it is useful to be able to cook smoked haddock in an uncovered *deep* oven-proof dish in the oven as a breakfast dish. Cut the fish in half or portions as for cooking in a saucepan, remove the fins and tails. Cover with water, milk or milk and water and cook for about 25–30 minutes in the centre of a moderate oven.

Home Freezing

Cooked poached fish can be frozen as part of a complete meal to take from the freezer as required, then to serve cold or to reheat. Some interesting but easy menus would be:
Poached salmon, mixed vegetables (all you need to do is defrost, add salad and salad dressing).
Poached salmon, topped with *Parsley butter* (made by creaming chopped parsley and little lemon juice into butter and forming into neat pats), either fried potatoes or cooked new potatoes and peas. Pack into a fairly deep foil dish or on to a large plate (strong enough to withstand the cold of the freezer) or arrange on a double thickness of foil. Wrap firmly and freeze. To use: heat through in a very moderate oven, or over a pan of hot water for about 25 minutes, and serve.

FAMILY DISHES

There are many economical and interesting fish dishes that all the family will enjoy, for example:

STUFFED JACKET POTATOES—cook large potatoes in their jackets. Halve, then mash the potato pulp with a little milk and butter and seasoning. Put a tiny rolled fillet of white fish or small portion white fish at the bottom of each potato case. Season and add either a) a little cream, b) thinly sliced tomatoes or c) sliced mushrooms. Pile the potato pulp over the fish then return to the centre of a moderate oven and cook for 30–35 minutes.

FISH PIE—cook and flake approximately ¾ kilo (1½ lb.) white fish. Blend with a white or parsley or cheese sauce made as page 146, with 284 ml (½ pint) milk and put into a pie dish. (Little snippets of crisply fried bacon, chopped parsley, capers, etc., may be added to the fish.) Add a layer of sliced hard-boiled eggs on top of the fish mixture, if wished, and top with creamed potatoes, then bake for about 35 minutes in the centre of a moderate oven. Serves 5–6.

Automatic Oven
Potatoes, stuffed as the recipe opposite, can be put into the automatic oven and left to heat through for a supper meal. As a change from the fish filling, you can use chopped bacon and tomato purée.

Home Freezing
The type of savoury dish that freezes well. Do not wrap until the potatoes are very hard. Use within 6–8 weeks.

Lemon Stuffed Herrings with Mushroom Sauce

Serves 4
Cooking time 40–45 minutes
Oven temperature 400° F. (200° C.), Gas Mark 5–6

Ingredients	Metric	Imperial
fresh herrings	4	4
seasoning	to taste	to taste
lemon stuffing	as page 142	as page 142
margarine *or* butter	25 grammes	1 oz.
FOR THE SAUCE:		
mushrooms	50 grammes	2 oz.
water	2 tablespoons	2 tablespoons
soured cream*	125 or 140 gramme carton	5 oz. carton

*or thin fresh cream soured with the juice of ½ lemon.

1 Remove heads from herrings, split, take out roes (put on one side) and the backbones (see page 53).
2 Season herrings and fill with lemon stuffing and chopped roes; fold fish to cover stuffing.
3 Grease an ovenproof dish with half the margarine or butter.
4 Put in the herrings, cover with sliced mushrooms, the rest of the margarine or butter, and the 2 tablespoons water.
5 Put a lid, or foil, on the dish and bake for 25–30 minutes towards the top of a moderately hot oven.
6 Remove the lid or foil, then add soured cream, and cook for a further 5 minutes.

Note: other stuffings to choose are—Parsley and thyme; Sage and onion; or Savoury rice, see pages 139 to 142.

Automatic Oven
Excellent, providing the time the fish, etc., is kept waiting in the oven is not too long.

Speedy Meal
See remarks about saving time under stuffings, page 138. Ask the fishmonger to prepare the herrings, i.e. bone them for you, so you then omit stage 1.

Mixer
The stuffing can be prepared in the liquidiser.

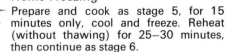

Slimming Tips
Herrings are an excellent protein food, although higher in calories than white fish. If you want a lower calorie stuffing than that suggested, then use sliced well seasoned tomatoes and sliced mushrooms.

Home Freezing
Prepare and cook as stage 5, for 15 minutes only, cool and freeze. Reheat (without thawing) for 25–30 minutes, then continue as stage 6.

Cod in Mushroom Sauce

1 Spread cutlets of cod (or other white fish) with lemon stuffing and sliced mushrooms.
2 Add cider or white wine in place of water.
3 Cook as recipe above, but reduce cooking time to 20–25 minutes.
4 Add the soured cream as stage 6 above.

Cheese Kedgeree

Serves 4–5
Cooking time 15 minutes

Ingredients	Metric	Imperial
eggs	2	2
butter	50–75 grammes	2–3 oz.
cooked smoked haddock	300 grammes	12 oz.
cooked long grain rice*	300 grammes	12 oz.
Cheddar cheese	200 grammes	8 oz.
seasoning	to taste	to taste
TO GARNISH:		
egg yolks	2	2
chopped parsley	2–3 tablespoons	2–3 tablespoons

*this refers to the cooked weight, you need 125–150 grammes (5–6 oz.) when uncooked, as the rice absorbs the water and becomes heavier in cooking.

1 Put the eggs to hard boil; crack the shells, cool rapidly, then remove the shells and chop the whites of the eggs.
2 Melt the butter, stir in the cooked flaked fish and cooked rice and heat quickly, tossing with a fork.
3 Add the grated cheese, the chopped egg whites and plenty of seasoning (remember smoked haddock can be rather salt so it is advisable to taste the mixture).
4 Pile into a shallow casserole or on to a hot dish.
5 Garnish with the sieved egg yolks and chopped parsley, as the picture facing page 56.

Speedy Meal

An excellent quick dish for breakfast or supper. Have the ingredients all ready to put together; remember that left-over cooked rice can always be used in savoury dishes if you put it into a pan of boiling water, just bring it to the boil, then strain and use. There is also very quick-cooking rice available that cooks within a few minutes.

Home Freezing

Not a good dish to freeze, as the rice loses its firm texture and the hard-boiled eggs become 'leathery'.

Macaroni Fish Pie

Serves 4
Cooking time 15–25 minutes

Ingredients	Metric	Imperial
macaroni	75 grammes	3 oz.
water	1 litre	2 pints
salt	a little	a little
white fish	½ kilo (poor weight)	1 lb.
FOR CHEESE SAUCE:		
butter *or* margarine	25 grammes	1 oz.
flour	25 grammes	1 oz.
milk	284 ml	½ pint
seasoning	to taste	to taste
dry mustard	pinch	pinch
grated Cheddar cheese	75 grammes	3 oz.
TO GARNISH:		
parsley	few sprigs	few sprigs

1 If using long marcaroni, break into small pieces, cook in nearly all the boiling salted water until tender. If using elbow length macaroni. cook as directed on the packet.
2 Meanwhile, simmer fish in little salted water until tender but not too soft.
3 Lift fish out and break into fairly big flakes.
4 Heat butter or margarine in pan, stir in flour, cook 'roux' for 2–3 minutes over low heat. Remove from heat, gradually add the milk and seasoning.
5 Bring to the boil, cook until thickened then add grated cheese, but do not boil after this.
6 Put drained macaroni and fish into a hot dish, top with cheese sauce.
7 Put for 2–3 minutes under a hot grill until the top is bubbly. Garnish with parsley, and serve with a green vegetable such as broccoli or a green salad. Potatoes are not necessary.

Automatic Oven

This can be prepared earlier, put into the oven and left to heat and brown. As the macaroni absorbs liquid as it stands, it is advisable to use 142 ml (¼ pint) extra milk in the cheese sauce, and also to rinse the macaroni in cold water after cooking at stage 1. Allow approximately 40 minutes in the centre of a very moderate oven.

Mixer

Use the liquidiser to prepare the cheese or to make a very smooth cheese sauce.

Home Freezing

Macaroni can be frozen, but tends to soften and lose its texture, so do *not* over-cook at stage 1. Cheese sauces *can* curdle with storage, even if you use cornflour instead of flour (use half quantity of cornflour) so this is *not* one of the best dishes to freeze, unless you accept the fact that the sauce may become a little thin when reheating. Store for 2–3 weeks only.

Fish and Mushroom Loaf

Serves 5–6
Cooking time 1 hour
Oven temperature 350–375° F. (180–190° C.), Gas Mark 4–5

Ingredients	Metric	Imperial
white fish*	½ kilo (very	1¼ lb.
weight (without bones)	good weight)	(poor weight)
bread (without crusts)	75 grammes	3 oz.
onion	1 small	1 small
parsley	good sprig	good sprig
mushrooms	50–75 grammes	2–3 oz.
eggs	2	2
seasoning	to taste	to taste
TO GREASE TIN:		
butter *or* margarine	25 grammes	1 oz.

*use cod or fresh haddock.

1 Put the fish through a mincer or cut into pieces, then chop until very fine.
2 Put the bread through the mincer or make into fine crumbs, also mince or chop the onion finely.
3 If possible mince the parsley or chop this; you need 2 teaspoons.
4 Wash and dry the mushrooms thoroughly and cut into neat slices.
5 Stir into the fish mixture with the beaten eggs and season well.
6 Grease the tin thoroughly, put in the mixture, cover with greased foil and bake for 1 hour in the centre of a moderate oven.
7 Turn out and serve hot with Mushroom or Tomato sauce, pages 51 and 150, or melted butter to which is added a little chopped parsley.

Automatic Oven

This can be the basis of a very interesting menu. Put a dish with 50–75 grammes (2–3 oz.) butter and a little chopped parsley in a covered dish in the warming drawer or somewhere near the oven so it will melt to serve with the fish loaf. Cook a shallow dish of Scalloped potatoes, page 114, in the centre of the oven (a deep dish would not allow potatoes in centre to be soft)—cook *small* onions or leeks in a casserole and Stuffed small baked apples in coolest part of oven.

Mixer

See comments in the Fish cream recipe about using the mincing attachment.

Home Freezing

This dish freezes well before cooking or when cooked. If freezing after cooking, make a little softer by adding about 1 tablespoon milk, as reheating would give too dry a texture. Use within 5–6 weeks.

Soused Herrings

Serves 4
Cooking time 1 hour
Oven temperature 300–325° F. (150–170° C.), Gas Mark 2–3

Ingredients	Metric	Imperial
herrings	8 small to	8 small to
	medium	medium
onion	1 small	1 small
pickling spice	1–2 teaspoons	1–2 teaspoons
sugar	1 teaspoon	1 teaspoon
bay leaves	2	2
water	142 ml	¼ pint
salt	½ teaspoon	½ teaspoon
mixed spice	½–1 teaspoon	½–1 teaspoon
vinegar	142 ml	¼ pint

1 Remove heads from the herrings, split along stomachs so the fish can be opened out flat.
2 Lay on a board with cut side down, run your fingers along the backbone very firmly, turn over, remove backbones.
3 Roll the fish and put into a covered casserole with all the other ingredients.
4 Cook in the centre of a slow to very moderate oven.
5 Leave until quite cold—the liquid in which the fish was cooked can be served with the fish, or strained and added to a salad dressing.

SOUSED MACKEREL—mackerel are equally as good soused as herrings. To vary, add slices of apple to the vinegar, etc., or serve with a gooseberry sauce, as with grilled mackerel.

Automatic Oven

This dish is cooked slowly, and it is an excellent idea to cook it in a tightly covered dish when the oven is in use.

Speedy Meal

Use tiny cocktail onions from a jar to save peeling a fresh onion.

Home Freezing

Cook the herrings as recipe—*do not overcook.* Allow the herrings and liquid to cool, then pack, allowing 1·5 cm (½ inch) headroom, as the liquid expands as it freezes. When frozen use within 6 weeks; allow to defrost at room temperature—this takes 2–3 hours.

FISH DISHES FOR SPECIAL OCCASIONS

Much of the fish one buys is expensive, particularly salmon, shell fish, sole, etc., so it will be served only on special occasions. More 'humble' fish can be made so interesting by good sauces that it too can be considered for important meals:

SALMON–cook, serve with mayonnaise and salad or Hollandaise sauce, page 152, or serve hot (poach as page 50, or grill as page 49, or fry as pages 46 and 47)–the fish can then be topped with lemon flavoured melted butter or Hollandaise sauce or a *Sauce Waleska*–to make this, add pieces of shell fish to either a Hollandaise or Béchamel sauce, page 146.

LOBSTER OR OTHER SHELL FISH–serve cold in salads or heat the flesh in a Béchamel or Cheese sauce, page 55, or in a very little cream, seasoning and wine, see page 56.

SOLE AND OTHER WHITE FISH–poach in wine or milk or fish stock, then top with various sauces–some of the most popular are Sauce Waleska, see above, Sauce Mornay, see page 55, or as Sole Veronique (this sauce is made by adding de-seeded grapes to a wine sauce, see page 152). If you wish a change from fried fillets or whole fried sole or other white fish, cut into 3-cm (1¼-inch) 'ribbons'–coat and fry. The correct name for this is Sole (or other fish) Goujons.

Home Freezing

As fish deteriorates so quickly it is often better to freeze the dish and reheat, rather than prepare the food a day beforehand and store it in a refrigerator. As no-one likes to be worried about the success of recipes though, here are points to remember.

Cooked salmon does lose some of its delicious 'oily' moist taste when frozen; it *is* better if frozen uncooked or bought fresh.

Shell fish can be a *little* tougher if cooked and frozen, although if you can buy *very* freshly boiled lobsters, etc., then freeze—they are much better than when the lobster has been allowed to stand some hours before freezing. Always thaw slowly. Read the comments about freezing sauces on page 145 and choose those (e.g. Hollandaise) that freeze without the possibility of any complications.

Fish Cream

Serves 6–8
Cooking time 1¼ hours
Oven temperature 325–350° F. (170–180° C.), Gas Mark 3–4

Ingredients	Metric	Imperial
white fish*, free from bones	¾ kilo (poor weight)	1½ lb.
butter	50 grammes	2 oz.
anchovy essence	1–2 teaspoons	1–2 teaspoons
flour	25 grammes	1 oz.
eggs	3	3
thick cream	142 ml	¼ pint
seasoning	to taste	to taste
breadcrumbs	50 grammes	2 oz.

*hake, turbot or halibut for luxury occasion; cod or fresh haddock for a more economical dish.

1 Either mince the raw fish or cut into small pieces, then chop until quite fine.
2 Put into a basin, add 25 grammes (1 oz.) of the melted butter and anchovy essence and mix well with the flour and egg yolks.
3 Whip the cream until it just holds its shape, and fold into the fish mixture.
4 Whisk the egg whites stiffly, add gently to the fish and season to taste.
5 Coat a 1½-litre (poor 3-pint) ovenproof dish with the rest of the melted butter and crumbs, put in the mixture.
6 Stand in a dish of cold water and bake in the centre of a very moderate oven until just firm.
7 Turn out carefully and serve hot with a Mushroom, Prawn or Hollandaise sauce, pages 51 and 152.

Automatic Oven

This makes an excellent main dish, choose Macedoine of vegetables, page 114, Jacket potatoes (baked in the hottest part of the oven), page 51, and Ginger pear upside down pudding, page 204, to complete the menu.

Speedy Meal

Use all canned pink salmon to save mincing fish, and cook in 6–8 small individual dishes for approximately 20–25 minutes in moderate oven.

Mixer

The mincing attachment of an electric mixer deals with raw fish very well. Feed through steadily and help through the mincer with the proper attachment.

Home Freezing

This fish cream freezes reasonably well for a limited period of 3–4 weeks. After this it tends to lose its very moist texture.

Sea-food Cream

1 Ingredients as fish cream but instead of all white fish use 50 per cent white fish, 25 per cent shell fish (flaked crab meat, chopped prawns, etc.) and 25 per cent flaked cooked or well drained canned salmon, or tuna fish.

Sole Mornay

Serves 4–8*
Cooking time 30 minutes
Oven temperature 375–400° F. (190–200° C.), Gas Mark 5–6

Ingredients	Metric	Imperial
fillets of sole	8 small	8 small
white wine or milk	142 ml	¼ pint
seasoning	to taste	to taste
FOR THE SAUCE:		
butter	25 grammes	1 oz.
flour	25 grammes	1 oz.
milk	284 ml	½ pint
seasoning	to taste	to taste
made-mustard	½–1 teaspoon	½–1 teaspoon
Cheddar cheese	75 grammes	3 oz.
TO GARNISH:		
mushrooms	50 grammes	2 oz.
butter	25 grammes	1 oz.
Cheddar cheese	25–50 grammes	1–2 oz.
lemon	1	1

*4 as a main dish or 8 as an hors d'oeuvre.

1 Fold or roll the fillets of sole, put into an ovenproof dish and cover with the wine or milk, season lightly.
2 Cook for approximately 15 minutes in a moderate to moderately hot oven–do not over-cook.
3 Lift out the fish and transfer to another hot dish.
4 Meanwhile make the cheese sauce with the butter, flour and milk; when thickened, add the strained liquid from cooking the fish, season lightly and add the made-mustard and grated Cheddar cheese.
5 Fry the mushrooms in the butter.
6 Top the sauce with the rest of the cheese (do not exceed this amount unless you add about 25–50 grammes (1–2 oz.) breadcrumbs); either brown for about 10 minutes in the oven or 3–4 minutes under the grill.
7 Top with a twisted slice of lemon and the mushrooms as the picture facing page 56. Serve sliced lemon with portions.

Automatic Oven
If this dish is prepared to stage 6 then put into the oven, it is quite satisfactory to leave it for a limited period before heating. As the fish and sauce will then be cold, allow about 25–30 minutes heating time above the centre of a moderate to moderately hot oven. When a cheese sauce has to stand like this, and then be reheated, you have a smoother sauce if you use 15 grammes (½ oz.) cornflour instead of 25 grammes (1 oz.) flour.
To make a complete meal, serve with Duchesse potatoes, page 120, Courgettes Provençal, page 121 and a Compôte of fruit, page 135.

Speedy Meal
Omit the cheese sauce, simply top the fish with a little full cream evaporated milk or thin cream and grated cheese, then proceed as stage 7.

Slimming Tips
Use an egg sauce as page 152, rather than thickening with a carbohydrate (cornflour or flour), then top with the grated cheese. Another low calorie adaptation could be made as follows–poach the fish in seasoned water, drain, put into a dish, top with yoghourt and a layer of cottage cheese, and brown.

Home Freezing
Prepare and cover, then freeze. Read the comments about freezing sauces on page 145. Use within about 6 weeks.

Parisienne Scallops

Serves 4
Cooking time 20 minutes

Ingredients	Metric	Imperial
scallops	4	4
milk	284 ml	½ pint
seasoning	to taste	to taste
butter	50 grammes	2 oz.
flour	25 grammes	1 oz.
thick cream	2 tablespoons	2 tablespoons
mushrooms	50 grammes	2 oz.
onions	2 small	2 small
breadcrumbs	2–3 tablespoons	2–3 tablespoons

1 Slice the scallops and put in a saucepan with the milk and seasoning and simmer gently for about 5 minutes.
2 Lift out and put on one side, then make a white sauce with half the butter, the flour and milk; when thickened add the cream.
3 Meanwhile fry the sliced mushrooms and very finely chopped onions in the remaining butter; when cooked mix with the sliced scallops.
4 Put into 4 scallop shells or individual dishes, coat with the sauce and crumbs, and brown under a hot grill.

Automatic Oven
This dish can be prepared, put into the oven and reheated at a later time, but as scallops, like all other shell fish, are easily spoiled by over-cooking, care must be taken in timing. Allow no more than 15 minutes, towards the top of a moderate to moderately hot oven. Read the comments about using cornflour instead of flour in the information given above. Serve with Baked tomatoes, Potato croquettes, page 115, and Bananas au rhum, page 135.

Mixer
The liquidiser will be useful in preparing a perfectly smooth sauce, see comments on page 146, and/or 'grating' the cheese and making the crumbs.

Home Freezing
See comments above. Substitute milk for cream to aid in producing a sauce that will not curdle when frozen and reheated. See comments about freezing uncooked scallops, page 42. Store 4–6 weeks only.

Moules Marinière

1 Scrub 1 litre–generous measure (2 pints) mussels well, discard any that are open and will not close when sharply tapped. The reason for this is that if the mussel remains open and does not close, the fish could have been dead inside for a considerable period, and therefore be dangerous to eat.
2 Put into a large pan, cover with water, add 1 small onion, 2 or 3 pieces celery (when available), seasoning and 1 bunch parsley; heat slowly until mussels open, approximately 5 minutes.
3 Remove beards from mussels. Sometimes you will find a small growth looking like a weed; this must be taken out.
4 Leave mussels on half the shell.
5 Re-boil liquid with 1 tablespoon tarragon vinegar and strain over them, add little white wine if wished. Serves 4.

Note: often the liquid is thickened by blending a little flour or corn-flour with thin cream, stirred into sauce and simmered gently.

Speedy Meal

It is possible to buy very good cans and jars of mussels. Make a wine sauce as page 152, add chopped parsley and a little liquid from the can or jar, and heat the mussels in this.

Slimming Tips

Mussels themselves are low in calories, and if you do not use a rich sauce they are a very wise and interesting choice. Open the mussels as recipe opposite, but do not thicken the liquid—use the recipe exactly as given.

Home Freezing

See shell fish, page 42. It is better to freeze mussels when opened at stage 2, rather than the mussels in a sauce.

Lobster in Whisky Sauce

Serves 4
Cooking time 20 minutes

Ingredients	Metric	Imperial
lobsters–		
small to medium*	2	2
tiny button mushrooms	50–60 grammes	2 oz.
butter	50–60 grammes	2 oz.
whisky**	3 tablespoons	3 tablespoons
thick cream	142 ml	¼ pint
seasoning	to taste	to taste
FOR THE TOPPING:		
grated Gruyère cheese	25 grammes	1 oz.

*use small lobsters for first course of a meal, but medium sized for main course.
**an unusual flavouring, but delicious; if wished use dry sherry instead.

1 Pull claws from the lobster, crack carefully. Split the body, remove and discard intestinal vein and stomach bag.
2 Take the meat from the body and claws and dice neatly.
3 Wash, dry and slice the mushrooms.
4 Toss mushrooms in the hot butter for about 3 minutes, add the whisky and cream then simmer for 1–2 minutes.
5 Add lobster flesh, heat for 2–3 minutes—*no more* otherwise you toughen the flesh—season lightly.
6 Spoon into halved lobster shells, top with finely grated cheese and brown under the grill.

Automatic Oven

Since shell fish is highly perishable, this dish is suitable for placing in the oven only a short time before being required. Heat for 15–20 minutes in a moderate to moderately hot oven.

Speedy Meal

Use canned lobster meat and serve in an ovenproof dish, not in the shell.

Slimming Tips

This is comparatively low in calories, as is all shell fish. However, a better way to make this when on a diet is to prepare the lobster, etc., as stages 1–4, but do not use cream. Simply mix the lobster with the cooked mushrooms and whisky and serve at once, or top with the cheese.

In a cream sauce

Instead of the thick cream, make a white sauce with 25 grammes (1 oz.) butter, 25 grammes (1 oz.) flour, generous 142 ml (¼ pint) milk and 4–5 tablespoons thin cream; season well.

Home Freezing

The version with cream freezes better than the one with cream sauce—proceed to stage 5, but do not heat lobster; freeze, then cover. Defrost and heat for 15–20 minutes in a moderate to moderately hot oven adding seasoning and cheese.

Shell fish in whisky sauce

Lobsters are very expensive, but shelled prawns, shrimps or sliced scallops can be used instead. If using scallops, cut into slices, simmer gently for 5–6 minutes in boiling salted water, drain and use as above.

5. Sole Mornay, see page 55. Cheese Kedgeree, see page 52

6. Fish and chips, see pages 46 and 116
7. Fish goulash and green rice, see page 57

Fish Goulash and Green Rice

Serves 6
Cooking time 40 minutes

Ingredients	Metric	Imperial
white fish–plaice, cod, (weight without skin or bone)	¾ kilo	1½ lb.
seasoning	to taste	to taste
lemon	1	1
celery salt	¼–½ teaspoon	¼–½ teaspoon
red pepper	1	1
tomatoes	8 large	8 large
chopped chives	1 tablespoon	1 tablespoon
butter	50 grammes	2 oz.
white wine	284 ml	½ pint
powdered cinnamon	½–1 teaspoon	½–1 teaspoon
paprika	1–2 teaspoons	1–2 teaspoons
FOR THE GREEN RICE:		
long grain rice*	200 grammes	8 oz.
water*	568 ml	1 pint
salt	1 *level* teaspoon	1 *level* teaspoon
butter	25 grammes	1 oz.
chopped chives	½–1 tablespoon	½–1 tablespoon
chopped parsley	½–1 tablespoon	½–1 tablespoon
chopped dill	1 teaspoon	1 teaspoon

*or instead of weighing, use 1 large cup rice and 2 large cups (same measure) of water.

1 Wash fish, cut into large squares, sprinkle with seasoning, lemon juice and celery salt.
2 Cut top from pepper, remove core and seeds. cut flesh into cubes.
3 Put tomatoes into boiling water for 1 minute, cool, skin.
4 Put pepper, chopped tomatoes and chives in the butter, cook gently for 5 minutes.
5 Add wine, cinnamon, paprika; simmer on a very low heat for 10 minutes.
6 Add fish squares to sauce, continue cooking for 15 minutes.
7 Meanwhile, put rice, water and salt into a saucepan, bring to the boil and stir once with a fork.
8 Lower heat to simmering, cover pan tightly, cook for about 15 minutes, then stir in butter and herbs (the rice will have absorbed the liquid).
9 Stir rice to blend in herbs, pile on to hot dish, top with the Goulash. Serve at once, see picture between pages 56/57.

Automatic Oven
Prepare the dish to stage 6, use a little less liquid as this does not evaporate so much in the oven. Put into a tightly covered casserole and heat for about 25–30 minutes in a moderate oven. Cook rice separately: put into a large casserole, cover with *boiling* water (quantity as in recipe), add salt, then stir briskly and cover the casserole. It will cook in the same time as the fish. Cook a dish of peas, also fruit, to complete the meal.

Speedy Meal
Use concentrated tomato soup to save preparing fresh tomatoes—flavour in stages 4 and 5 and heat for 5 minutes—omit any flavourings not available as the soup is well-seasoned. Pour over diced white fish and continue as stage 6.

Slimming Tips
Follow this recipe, but omit the butter from the ingredients and stage 4 from the method. Simmer the pepper, tomatoes and chives with the wine, etc., as stage 5, then continue as the recipe but do not serve with rice—instead have a green salad. Rice is a carbohydrate food, high in calories, and should not be eaten while trying to lose weight.

Home Freezing
Freezes very well; do not over-season when making this to freeze, see comments on page 42, as these seasonings may seem too strong when the dish is re-heated. Do not freeze the rice, but as explained on page 112, chopped herbs freeze excellently.

Fish Curry

Serves 6
Cooking time 40 minutes

Ingredients	Metric	Imperial
white fish–as above	as above	as above
seasoning	to taste	to taste
lemon	1	1
onions	1–2	1–2
butter	50 grammes	2 oz.
curry powder	½–1 tablespoon	½–1 tablespoon
white wine *or* fish stock	284 ml	½ pint
long grain rice	200 grammes	8 oz.

1 Prepare fish as above, sprinkle with seasoning, lemon juice.
2 Chop onions, fry in butter, then add curry powder and wine. Simmer for 10 minutes, continue as stage 6 above to end; omit butter and herbs in rice if wished.

Speedy Meal
Follow suggestion above, but use Mulligatawny soup instead of tomato.

Home Freezing
All curries freeze well, and this particular recipe is very good for this purpose as there is no flour or cornflour.

Note: all comments above apply to this recipe as well.

8. Glazed apricot gammon, page 69; Banana and bacon rolls, pages 75, 95; Cornish bacon pasties, see page 180; Sliced forehock with coleslaw, page 62; Gammon and vegetable risotto, page 119; Bacon kebabs, page 75; Bacon toasts, page 164; Collar of bacon hot pot, page 64

Cooking Meat

Meat is one of the most expensive foods in any housekeeping budget, and so in this chapter many dishes are planned to make use of cheaper cuts, or to use more expensive meats in economical ways.

CUTS OF MEAT–take time and trouble to learn about cuts of meat; find a helpful butcher if possible, who will give good advice where needed. Often a dish is less good than it should be because the joint of meat chosen is not quite right for the particular method of cooking. Remember, good quality meat should have some fat; many people try to buy completely lean meat, and are then disappointed because it is less moist than they had hoped.

WHEN COOKING MEAT remember that over-cooking often causes it to become dry and tough; this applies to liver in particular. Make judicious use of herbs, spices and vegetables with meat. If you do not wish to use wine in cooking meat, a little lemon juice or vinegar has the same effect in tenderising meat, see recipes page 72.

Metric Conversions

In many cases one buys chops etc., by number rather than weight, so metric calculations are only important to work out if the cost of meat is high or low. When buying meat by weight, it is easier to remember that the equivalent of 1 kilo (in round figures) is 2.2 lb., so if you usually buy 1 lb., of a certain meat, ask for 'barely' ½ kilo. Meat is a valuable protein food, so do not buy less quantity as all the family need adequate supplies of this essential food. *In the calculations of timing in order to be less cumbersome the term 1 lb., is used –naturally this also means ½ kilo (poor weight).*

Drinks to serve with meat and in meat dishes

When having an inexpensive meal try to find low-priced wines; you will be pleasantly surprised to find many are very good. As mentioned before, I think it is important to choose the wine YOU like (not necessarily what is considered 'right') but red wines do blend well with dark meat, and rich stews of beef, etc., and white or rosé with veal and more delicate dishes. Wine in cooking helps to tenderise the meat as well as give flavour.

Cooking meat in the automatic oven

Most cuts of meat, or meat dishes, are suitable for cooking in the oven. It is often the size of a joint that will determine the timing of the complete meal. When calculating cooking time of stuffed joints, weigh after stuffing. In very hot weather it is advisable to leave meat in the oven for only a limited period; avoid the more highly perishable veal and pork.

Saving time when cooking meat

Prime cuts of meat–steaks, chops, etc., are excellent as they cook quickly, but they are expensive. Prepared soups and sauces often enable you to produce an excellent stew with the minimum of preparation.

A PRESSURE COOKER is useful for cooking many meat dishes.

ROASTING MEAT–brown in fat as poultry, page 97. Add the water etc., bring to 15 lb. pressure, lower the heat; time carefully as in recipe. When cooking meat it is better to let the pressure drop at room temperature. With any pressure cooker you will find the joint is not as crisp as oven roasting, but you can crisp the outside under a hot grill.

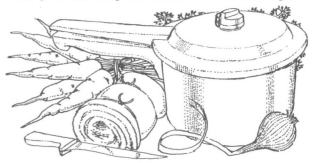

STEWING MEAT–do not use rack. In a recipe where the meat is first fried with vegetables, you do this in the pressure cooker, i.e. using it at this stage as an ordinary saucepan. You then add liquid, but because there is little evaporation in a pressure cooker, reduce the amount to half. Cooking times etc., are given in the recipes. A stew should be cooled rapidly, see page 61, unless stated to the contrary.

BOILING MEAT–the pressure cooker is particularly useful for meats that normally take a very long time, i.e. ox tongue. When boiling meat allow the pressure to drop at room temperature.

Using a mixer for meat dishes

A liquidiser will often be very valuable for producing an interesting (and low calorie) sauce to serve with meat dishes. A mincing attachment for the mixer can be used for mincing raw or cooked meats to give a variety of meat galantines etc., see page 87.

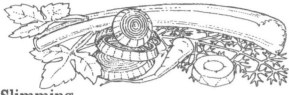

Slimming

Choose lean lamb and beef. Pork, which always has a fair amount of fat, is higher in calories, and veal needs fat in cooking to make it palatable. The basic method of grilling is ideal, and many stews also can be adapted to make them less fattening.

Home freezing of meat

RAW MEAT—do not freeze too freshly killed meat; it should be hung for the required length of time before freezing. Explore the possibilities of bulk buying of meat to save money. Cut, or ask the butcher to cut, into convenient-sized joints *before* freezing. Always wrap well to keep meat moist and ensure fastest freezing. Polythene wrapping or thick aluminium foil are ideal for wrapping; wrap firmly round the food and expel air as you do so. Wrap individual chops, steaks etc., with pieces of polythene paper between them, so you can 'peel off" the required number of chops at one time.

ROASTED OR BOILED JOINTS OF MEAT—either freeze as a joint (but remember this means you will have to thaw out the *whole* joint before you can use it), or carve and pack with pieces of polythene separating the slices and store.

TO COOK FROZEN MEAT—small pieces of meat, steaks, chops, etc., can be cooked from the frozen state. *Large joints of meat should be allowed to defrost before cooking*—to do this allow the meat to stand for about 24 hours in the cabinet of the refrigerator; a very large joint may take longer. If preferred, stand for several hours at room temperature. *Remember* when once the meat has thawed out it will be as highly perishable as fresh meat.

COOKED MEAT DISHES—one of the great advantages of home freezing is that you can make large quantities of stews, curries, etc., and freeze them for future meals. Remember:
a) choose a recipe where *all* the ingredients freeze well.
b) if the liquid is to be thickened, choose cornflour rather than flour (allow half the amount of cornflour to that of flour) and remove the stew from the heat immediately after thickening; this may well avoid the possibility of the liquid becoming thin during storage in the home freezer. Instead of cornflour you could use potato flour (rather difficult to obtain, but there is no fear of 'thinning out'—use the same amount as for cornflour) or see the recipe thickened with bread, page 76. People tend to make a great deal of unnecessary fuss about this 'thinning out' process; in practice it is very little trouble to thicken as you reheat.
c) if you freeze in a heatproof dish you can reheat the stew or casserole in this. *Never place the dish over heat immediately you take it from the freezer*—even if the type that *can* be carried from freezer to hot cooker. The solid mass of frozen food takes so long to defrost you will burn the bottom of the dish badly. Put in a slow oven until some of the outside of the food thaws, then place on top of cooker or raise the heat. If using ovenproof ware, allow mixture to thaw out slightly and dish to become warmed through at room temperature before reheating, otherwise you will break the dish.
d) if you *do not wish to have the dish* in the freezer, then line it with a double thickness of foil before cooking the food. Freeze in the foil-lined dish and when solid lift the foil and food out of dish, label, but add the name of the dish in which the food was frozen. Reheat in original dish.
e) with stews etc., you will probably have to cover the top *after* freezing, unless putting into waxed containers.
f) seasoning and flavouring tend to deteriorate during freezing. This point appears to be stressed a great deal—personally I do not find it much of a problem. I simply add an adequate amount of seasoning and flavouring before freezing and make certain I taste the dish when it is being reheated, then add any more if I feel it necessary.
Times for storing various casserole dishes are given under the recipes.

MEAT PIES AND PUDDINGS—all comments about thickening liquids as b) above apply. Lining basins with foil, as casserole dishes, are the same —see c) and d) above.
The pastry may either be frozen *with* the meat, etc., or separately as fruit pies, page 171.

Keeping frozen meats

The following maximum times ensure meat is at its best when brought out of the freezer:
BEEF—raw uncooked meat store up to 12 months; if salted or cooked up to 2 months.
LAMB AND MUTTON—as beef, although I find it best to use within 9 months.
PORK AND VEAL—use within 8 months if raw; as beef if cooked. Personally I am always disappointed in cooked frozen veal dishes.
HAM—uncooked, use within 3 months; if cooked as above; bacon rashers only 1 month.
OFFAL—use within 3 months.
STEWS AND CASSEROLE DISHES—any type of meat (including curries)—use within 2 months. They are excellent, but do not over-cook before freezing.

TO BOIL MEAT

Many meats are boiled, in particular bacon or ham, salted joints of beef (silverside or brisket), salted or fresh tongue, etc. The liquid in the pan should *not* boil rapidly; if you do this, the outside of the meat tends to become over-soft and difficult to carve while the inside will be under-cooked. It is important to see that the water *simmers* gently. When boiling meat, you put it into a pan of cold water and add any flavouring you wish. Bring the water to the boil, remove any grey scum from the top, cover the pan with a well fitting lid and *simmer* for the following times–calculate this from when you see the water just reach boiling point. Naturally salted meats should be soaked over-night, or for some hours before cooking, and they are cooked in *fresh* water, not the water in which they were soaked.

Cooking times, etc., for boiling meat

BACON, HAM
CHOOSE–forehock, collar, gammon, etc.
COOK FOR–25–30 minutes per lb., 25–30 minutes over. Shorter time for gammon and thinner joints.
USUAL ACCOMPANIMENTS–often served with parsley sauce.

BEEF
CHOOSE–fresh brisket or silverside or salt brisket or silverside.
COOK FOR–30 minutes per lb., 30 minutes over.
USUAL ACCOMPANIMENTS–dumplings, vegetables and a little of the liquid in which the meat was cooked.

LAMB, MUTTON
CHOOSE–breast, boned and rolled (could be stuffed), middle or scrag end of neck.
COOK FOR–1½ hours lamb; 2 hours mutton.
USUAL ACCOMPANIMENTS–mixed vegetables and caper sauce.

PORK (rarely cooked by boiling, except the head)
CHOOSE–head, belly, loin and spare rib.
COOK FOR–30 minutes per lb., 30 minutes over.
USUAL ACCOMPANIMENTS–vegetables and unthickened gravy.

TONGUE–generally pressed, see recipe below.
USUAL ACCOMPANIMENTS–cold with salad; hot with Madeira sauce, see page 147.

VEAL (rarely cooked by boiling, except the head)
CHOOSE–breast, boned and rolled (could be stuffed), head.
COOK FOR–30 minutes per lb., 30 minutes over.
USUAL ACCOMPANIMENTS–as for pork.

Flavourings to add to boiled meat

SEASONING–add little mustard to liquid for beef or bacon; peppercorns only or shake of pepper if the meat is salted.
HERBS OR SPICES–add a *bouquet garni* to all boiled meats.
VEGETABLES–add carrots, onions and other vegetables to the liquid at beginning of cooking time. If the meat has to be cooked for a long period and you wish vegetables to garnish the dish, it is better to add these approximately 45 minutes to 1 hour before the end of the cooking time.

Keeping boiled meats moist

If you intend to serve the meat hot, you will need to lift this from the pan when cooked and ready to serve; but if you intend to serve the boiled bacon, beef, etc., cold, and it is not pressed (as tongue) then either allow the meat to cool in the cooking liquid or remove from the stock, wrap immediately in foil. This ensures the outside does not dry.

Automatic Oven
As the cooking time of boiled meat is often very long, it is generally cooked in a saucepan. However, if you have a container so large that it will enable you to cover the meat with water (so that there is no fear of the liquid boiling over) there is no reason why you cannot 'boil' meat in a deep covered dish in the oven. Allow cooking time as opposite, but add an extra 45 minutes and use a very moderate heat. In order to assess the correct cooking time it is advisable to bring the meat in the liquid to the boil on top of the cooker, transfer to the casserole, and then time the cooking.

Slimming Tips
Boiled meats are excellent to include on a slimming diet, although bacon and ham are higher in calories than some other meats. This method of cooking meat means you are not adding extra fat, and you need not serve it in a thickened sauce for it will have a very moist texture. If your diet restricts the amount of fat you can eat, you will need to cut away any surplus fat before serving.

Home Freezing
Most of the points concerned with meat are covered in the introduction, page 58, and boiled meats are no different from any other. In order to keep the meat moist, allow it to cool if possible in the cooking liquid. When cold and still soft from the liquid, wrap and freeze. This prevents the outside becoming rather dry and unappetising. If you intend to serve cold, then allow to defrost at room temperature. Boiled lamb or mutton tends to soften rather during storage in a freezer, so make sure it is not over-cooked, if you intend to freeze after cooking. These meats are generally served hot and there is no need to defrost before reheating.
Bacon and ham keep less well than many other meats in a freezer–even so it is wise to freeze them rather than waste them, but use within time given on page 59.

Using a Pressure Cooker to 'boil' meats

A pressure cooker is excellent for cooking those meats that are normally simmered for the times on the previous page. The method used in a pressure cooker is as follows:
Soak the meat if it has been salted (see introduction on the previous page) then put the meat into the cooker without a rack. *Cover* with cold water if possible: this is very important with salted meats, for if the top surface of the meat is not covered it tends to remain over-salted and becomes hard. Add flavourings as suggested on the previous page. Put on the lid, bring to 15 lb. pressure, lower heat so it just maintains the pressure, and cook either as instructions in the particular recipe, or allow approximately 10 minutes per lb., and 10 minutes over. Allow pressure to drop gradually. If you wish to add vegetables (e.g. carrots, onions, etc.) remember they will become very over-cooked if left longer than 10 or 15 minutes, so cook the meat for the total time *less* 10 or 15 minutes (depending on size of vegetables). Allow pressure to drop gradually, put in vegetables, replace lid, bring cooker once again to 15 lb., pressure, lower heat to maintain this, and cook for the remainder of the time.

Speedy Meal

The pressure cooker ensures the minimum cooking time, but most meats that are usually boiled, i.e. ham, tongue, salt beef, etc., can be purchased ready-cooked. If you wish to serve the cooked meat for a hot meal—ensure that it is absolutely fresh (it would be dangerous otherwise)—heat a little home-made stock or tomato juice and heat the sliced meat in this. (Unfortunately most stock cubes are very salt, so would make already salted meat very unpalatable.) For special occasions, heat in a Cumberland sauce, page 150 or a Madeira sauce, page 147. You could also heat prepared vegetables in the stock.

To cook an Ox-tongue

Serves 8–10
Cooking time see stage 3

Ingredients	Metric	Imperial
salted ox-tongue	1	1
pepper *or* peppercorns	to taste	to taste
bouquet garni	spray	spray
powder gelatine	see stage 7	see stage 7

1 Soak the ox-tongue overnight in water to cover.
2 The next day, put into saucepan with fresh water the pepper and herbs; bring to the boil and remove any 'scum'–see introduction to boiling on previous page. Cover the pan, lower the heat and simmer gently.
3 Allow to cook gently for approximately 2½–3 hours; this is about 25–30 minutes per lb., and 25–30 minutes over.
4 Let the tongue cool sufficiently to handle, then remove from the stock.
5 Leave the lid off the saucepan and let the stock boil very quickly so it evaporates until approximately ½ litre (generous measure), or 1 pint, remains.
6 Meanwhile, remove skin and any bones from the tongue, roll this and place in either a 20-cm (8-inch) saucepan or other container. It is not particularly good for cake tins to be used for moist ingredients like this but if you have no other suitable tin you can use a cake tin (without a loose base).
7 Allow approximately 2 level teaspoons powder gelatine to each ½ litre (1 pint) liquid; there is a certain limited amount of natural setting substance in the stock.
8 Soften the gelatine in about 2 tablespoons cold liquid; add to hot stock, then stir until thoroughly dissolved.
9 Strain this prepared stock over the tongue–you should have plenty of liquid to cover the meat.
10 Cool, and when cool place an old saucer over the meat with a weight on top, leave until the jelly is firm and the meat cold.
11 Turn out and slice, to serve hot or cold.

Note: if you add a pig's trotter or calf's foot to liquid when boiling the tongue, you will need no gelatine.

Automatic Oven

Tongue could be cooked in a deep covered container in the oven if wished. Allow about 3½–4 hours at a very moderate heat.

Speedy Meal

Tongue is excellent in a pressure cooker. Allow about 25–30 minutes at 15 lb., pressure for an ox-tongue, and approximately 15 minutes for smaller tongues.

Slimming Tips

Tongue is an interesting and wise choice of meat on a slimming diet. It has sufficient natural flavour to make elaborate salad dressings and sauces superfluous, but if you wish to serve sliced tongue as a hot meal, try heating it in an *Orange mustard sauce*. For about 4 slices tongue, blend ½–1 teaspoon *French* mustard with 2 tablespoons orange juice and the same amount of stock. Put into a shallow pan, heat, add the slices of tongue (ham is also good in this) and heat gently for 15–20 minutes.

Home Freezing

The points about freezing boiled meats on the previous page also apply to tongue.

LAMBS OR CALVES TONGUES—either of these smaller tongues may be cooked and served hot or cold. Allow 1–1½ hours simmering, or approximately 15 minutes at 15 lb. pressure.

Collared Beef with Dumplings

Serves 7–8
Cooking time see stage 1

Ingredients	Metric	Imperial
fresh *or* salted brisket of beef	2 kilos	4 lb.
seasoning	to taste	to taste
allspice	2 teaspoons	2 teaspoons
bouquet garni	spray	spray
FOR THE DUMPLINGS:		
self-raising flour	100 grammes	4 oz.
seasoning	to taste	to taste
shredded suet	50 grammes	2 oz.
water	to mix	to mix

1 Tie meat into neat round (this gives name to dish). Soak salted meat over-night; cook fresh or salted meat as table, page 60, add seasoning, spice, herbs, and water to cover.
2 Blend flour, seasoning, suet, water to give sticky dough.
3 Roll in balls, drop into the boiling stock, cook for 20 minutes.

Note: the traditional Collared beef also includes powdered ginger, cloves and garlic to taste.

Speedy Meal
If you buy ready-cooked salted beef, you can give it an interesting flavour by heating for a short time in well-flavoured stock, then add the dumplings.

Home Freezing
Cooked dumplings, like all suet pastry, freeze excellently. They can either be frozen *in* a stew or *in* the stock or lifted from the stock, cooled, packed and frozen dry. To reheat you can either drop the frozen dumplings into hot liquid, reheating and thawing out simultaneously; heat with the stew; or you can defrost at room temperature, then reheat.

Sliced Forehock with Coleslaw

Serves 8
Cooking time see stage 2

Ingredients	Metric	Imperial
joint forehock bacon	1½–2 kilos	3–4 lb.
crisp breadcrumbs (raspings)	3 tablespoons	3 tablespoons
small white cabbage	½–1	½–1
onion	1	1
carrots	4 large	4 large
sultanas	50 grammes	2 oz.
pineapple cubes	small can	small can
mayonnaise	142–284 ml	¼–½ pint
lemon juice	1 tablespoon	1 tablespoon
seasoning	to taste	to taste
TO GARNISH:		
red pepper	½	½
parsley	few sprigs	few sprigs
cucumber	¼ medium	¼ medium

1 Have the joint boned and rolled, and soak overnight in cold water, unless it is a sweet cure which means it does not require soaking.
2 Place in a saucepan, cover with fresh cold water and simmer. Allow 30 minutes per lb. and 30 minutes over, so if the joint weighs 1½–2 kilos (just over 3–4 lb.) you calculate four times 30 minutes plus an extra 5 minutes to allow for the grammes over, i.e. 2 hours 5 minutes for 1½ kilos (just over 3 lb.) and for 2 kilos (just over 4 lb.) five times 30 minutes plus an extra 5 minutes to allow for grammes over, i.e. 2 hours 35 minutes.
3 Remove from liquor, cool enough to handle then skin and press the crisp breadcrumbs into the fat.
4 Shred washed and dried cabbage and mix with the finely chopped onion, grated raw carrots, sultanas and well drained pineapple.
5 Combine mayonnaise with lemon juice and seasoning.
6 Toss salad in mayonnaise until well coated.
7 Slice joint and arrange on a platter with the coleslaw piled in the centre.
8 Garnish with red pepper rings, parsley and sliced cucumber as picture facing page 57.

Automatic Oven
The forehock of bacon is very satisfactory if cooked in a covered container in the oven. This must be sufficiently deep to enable the bacon to be *completely* covered with liquid without any possibility of the liquid boiling over. Allow approximately 45 minutes per ½ kilo (1 lb.) and 45 minutes over in a very moderate oven. To make a complete menu (if serving the bacon hot), boil onions in a casserole, cook large jacket potatoes and bake a fruit layer pudding, rather than steam this.

Speedy Meal
Make use of the pressure cooker if you have one, see comments on page 61. Allow pressure to drop at room temperature before removing the lid. The extra time as the pressure inside the cooker drops is necessary for correct cooking.

Home Freezing
Store uncooked or cooked bacon for a limited time *only* in the freezer, see page 59. It is the combination of a high fat content and the fact the meat is cured, and therefore salted, which makes it less successful than other meats.

TO BRAISE MEAT

This is a more complicated form of cooking, for you combine two processes. Firstly you need to brown the meat in fat as though frying, then you lift the meat on to a layer of vegetables, etc., known as a '*mirepoix*'. The meat is then cooked very slowly as though for a casserole or stew; the braised beef on this page is a good basic recipe to use.

MEATS TO BRAISE–BEEF is ideal for braising and as you will see from the recipe below, reasonably tender cuts are used.
VEAL (cutlets, chops or fillet)–follow the directions for beef, below, but add finely grated lemon rind to the *mirepoix*.
SWEETBREADS–'blanch' as page 71, then continue as beef.
KIDNEYS–use lamb's or pig's–skin, leave whole (but remove gristle), proceed as beef, but cook for 45 minutes at stage 7.
PORK AND LAMB, which contain a high percentage of fat are less successful braised.

Braised Beef

Serves 4–6
Cooking time 1¼–1½ hours

Ingredients	Metric	Imperial
topside of beef *or* chuck steak *or* fresh brisket beef	1 kilo	2 lb.
fat bacon (cut in 1 thick slice if possible)	50 grammes	2 oz.
butter	25 grammes	1 oz.
FOR THE MIREPOIX:		
onions	2	2
carrots	2	2
bacon	25 grammes	1 oz.
butter	25 grammes	1 oz.
celery	few sticks	few sticks
bouquet garni	spray	spray
brown stock	284 ml	½ pint
red wine	284 ml	½ pint
seasoning	to taste	to taste

1 In braising one generally keeps the meat in a large piece, but if preferred you can cut it into thick 'fingers' to make it easier to serve, in which case reduce the cooking time to about 40–45 minutes at stage 7.
2 Dice the bacon neatly and put into the pan with the butter and cook for several minutes until an appreciable amount of fat is available.
3 Add the piece or pieces of meat, fry for several minutes on either side until golden brown.
4 Lift meat and bacon out of the pan on to a plate, but keep any fat left in the pan. If there is plenty of fat left, you could omit the butter from the ingredients for the *mirepoix*.
5 Peel and chop the onions and carrots finely, dice the bacon; toss in the hot fat remaining in the pan, or in the butter. When nearly tender, add the chopped celery.
6 Continue to cook for 2–3 minutes, then add the stock, wine, *bouquet garni*, and a generous amount of seasoning.
7 Replace the meat and chopped bacon from stage 4, cover the pan with a *very tightly* fitting lid (if the lid fits badly, put a piece of foil underneath) and cook gently until tender. Rump steak in one piece would need about 1 hour's very gentle simmering, but brisket or topside would need about 1¼ hours.
8 When the meat is cooked, lift on to a hot serving dish, either add the *mirepoix* to the dish, or, better still, rub through a sieve and heat again with the juices, as a very thick rich sauce.

Automatic Oven

Braised meat can be left in the oven if you do not allow too long a period before cooking, particularly in hot weather. Partially cooked meat, as this would be, is very susceptible to the development of harmful bacteria and you must complete stages 1–6 before putting the food in the oven. Proceed as stages 1–6, but transfer the *mirepoix* to a casserole, then put the beef on top and cover. Allow approximately 1¼ hours for rump steak and 1½ hours for other cuts of beef at a very moderate heat, and make sure the casserole has a well-fitting lid. It is also quite a good idea to lay a piece of buttered foil lightly over the meat to prevent the top becoming dry.
To make a complete menu with braised beef, have fairly plainly cooked vegetables, such as Jacket potatoes and a Casserole of peas. Follow with a Compôte of figs, see page 135 or a French rice pudding, page 201.

Mixer

The liquidiser makes the *mirepoix* into a smooth sauce within a matter of minutes. You may find the mixture is a rather thick sauce, so dilute with a little extra wine or stock before reheating.

Slimming Tips

Braising is a rich form of cooking meat, but has no flour or other carbohydrate ingredients, so if braising meat for the family you could have the meat without the rather rich sauce. Simply serve a portion of meat and, as a thin sauce, take a little liquid from the vegetables, etc., before you sieve or emulsify the rest to make the rich sauce.

Home Freezing

Braised meats freeze very well. I find I get the best result if I emulsify or sieve the sauce and pour this over the braised meat in the container used for freezing. When thawed you may find this appears to separate out slightly, but a brisk stir soon makes a smooth purée.

Making a Hot-Pot

The picture facing page 57 shows the Collar of bacon hot-pot given below. This is not really the most traditional type of casserole, for the true 'hot-pot' is prepared, cooked and served in the same dish, and the meat and other vegetables are topped with a layer of crisp brown potatoes, as the York hot-pot on page 82.

FLAVOURINGS TO ADD TO HOT-POTS
SEASONING—naturally you will season the layers of vegetables, meat, etc., but try adding paprika to the meat, so giving a slightly different colour and semi-sweet flavour.
HERBS OR SPICES—since there is a small amount of liquid in a hot-pot all flavourings are fairly concentrated, so use herbs and spices very carefully. Try fresh or powdered sage and thyme together; use fresh chopped mint or savory (very good with lamb); a pinch of ginger or powdered cinnamon—mix with seasoning to give even distribution—this is extremely good with bacon or beef.
VEGETABLES—add sliced, skinned tomatoes to the onions (use less stock than usual as tomatoes provide their own juice). Sliced swedes or parsnips can be used with potatoes in the traditional hot-pot, or use by themselves. Parsnips are better if parboiled before slicing.

Collar Bacon Hot-Pot

Serves 8
Cooking time see stage 3
Oven temperature 325–350° F. (170–180° C.), Gas Mark 3–4, then 425° F. (220° C.), Gas Mark 6–7

Ingredients	Metric	Imperial
collar joint bacon*	1½–2 kilos	3–4 lb.
dripping *or* fat	40 grammes	1½ oz.
onions	12 button	12 button
carrots	12 small	12 small
leeks	4	4
stock *or* beer	to cover (approx. 284 ml)	to cover (approx. ½ pint)
bouquet garni	spray	spray
bay leaves	2	2

*collar is a firm piece of bacon that becomes tender and remains moist with gentle cooking.

1 Have the bacon boned and rolled to make a neat joint. Soak in cold water overnight.
2 Place in a saucepan, cover with fresh cold water.
3 Bring to boil and simmer for half the cooking time, allowing 35–40 minutes per lb. and 40 minutes over; see calculation page 60.
4 Remove joint, cool enough to handle then skin and score the fat into squares.
5 Melt dripping in a large fireproof casserole and fry peeled vegetables until lightly browned. Add sufficient stock or beer to cover.
6 Place the joint in the casserole on the vegetables. Add *bouquet garni* and 2 bayleaves.
7 Cover and cook in the centre of a very moderate oven for remaining cooking time. Ten minutes before ready, remove lid and increase oven temperature to hot, to brown.
8 Serve, if liked, with Parsley sauce made with some of the stock from the vegetables, see recipe page 146.
9 Serve in the casserole as picture facing page 57, or on a flat dish, which makes it easier to carve.

Automatic Oven
The recipe opposite would need to be prepared to stage 6, then placed in the oven. If all the ingredients will become quite cold before the oven is set to switch on (stage 7) then add another 30 minutes to the cooking time. You will need to remove the lid for 10 minutes before serving.

Slimming Tips
Be sparing with the carrots in your serving, otherwise this recipe is quite suitable. Unfortunately beer is very high in calories, so it is advisable to use stock or a dry white wine instead. Bacon is a meat that is also of high calorific value, so a reasonably small portion should be served.

Home Freezing
Freezes well, but see comments on page 59 regarding times for successful storage in the freezer.

9. Spaghetti bolognese, see page 85

TO ROAST MEAT

This is one of the easiest methods of cooking meat; you can roast on a spit (many modern cookers have this either under the grill or in the oven) or in the more usual way in a tin. Some people think the latter way is baking rather than roasting, but the effect is very similar. There are two speeds:

QUICK–425–450°F. (220–230°C.), Gas Mark 7 (reduce heat to 375–400°F. (190–200°C.), Gas Mark 5–6 after first 15 minutes, or see under Automatic Oven opposite):
SLOW–350°F. (180°C.), Gas Mark 3–4.

Quick roasting is suitable for very good quality meat, but if meat has been chilled or frozen, I think it is better to use the slower method. Below you will find the roasting times in an open tin, plus cuts of meat to choose, etc.

Cooking times, etc., for roasting meat

BACON, HAM
CHOOSE–gammon slipper, middle gammon, back and ribs, top streaky, etc., (you need to soak the meat and partly cook by simmering, see page 69, Glazed apricot gammon. If you have 'sweet cure' bacon you can roast for the whole time, but the meat is more moist if simmered for part of the time). COOK FOR:

QUICK ROASTING–20–25 minutes per lb., 20–25 minutes over, or 25–30 minutes per lb., 25–30 minutes over. The difference in time allows for the shape of the joint; if a thin cut with a large diameter, choose shorter time; if a thick solid piece, choose longer period so that heat penetrates.
SLOW ROASTING–30–35 minutes per lb., 30–35 minutes over.
USUAL ACCOMPANIMENTS–roast vegetables, and as the bacon is often glazed, there is no need to make a sauce.

BEEF
CHOOSE–good quality aitchbone, fillet, rump (expensive but good for small joint), sirloin, good quality topside, good quality fresh brisket (for slow roasting). COOK FOR:

QUICK ROASTING–15 minutes per lb., 15 minutes over (underdone). 20 minutes per lb., 20 minutes over (medium).
SLOW ROASTING–25–35 minutes per lb., plus 25–35 minutes.
USUAL ACCOMPANIMENTS–Yorkshire pudding, horseradish cream or sauce, see page 151.

LAMB, MUTTON
CHOOSE–lamb or young mutton breast (boned and rolled), whole or half leg, loin, best end neck, saddle. COOK FOR:

QUICK ROASTING–20–25 minutes per lb., 20–25 minutes over.
SLOW ROASTING–35 minutes per lb., 35 minutes over.
USUAL ACCOMPANIMENTS–Lamb with Mint sauce, see page 153, thin gravy; Mutton with Onion sauce, see page 146, or redcurrant jelly, thick gravy.

PORK
CHOOSE–loin, whole or half leg, spare rib. COOK FOR:

QUICK ROASTING–25 minutes per lb., 25 minutes over.
SLOW ROASTING–35 minutes per lb., 35 minutes over.
USUAL ACCOMPANIMENTS–Sage and onion stuffing, see page 139, Apple sauce, see page 148.

VEAL
CHOOSE–breast (boned and rolled), loin or chump end of loin, piece of fillet (expensive but a good small joint), whole or half a leg, best end of neck. COOK FOR:
QUICK ROASTING–25 minutes per lb., 25 minutes over.
SLOW ROASTING–35–40 minutes per lb., plus 35–40 minutes.
USUAL ACCOMPANIMENTS–Veal stuffing, see page 139, Bacon rolls (sausages may also be added during cooking).

Automatic Oven
As explained on page 58, the size of your joint for roasting will determine the total cooking time. In an automatic oven, therefore, the meat is the most important food, and you plan your other dishes to fit in with the time for the particular joint. Below are automatic menus using roast meat:

Roast beef (if the cooking time does not exceed an hour you can leave a Yorkshire pudding in the oven, see page 160), roast potatoes, see page 116, Casserole of mixed vegetables, see page 114, Fruit pie, see page 184.

Roast lamb with roast onions and roast parsnips, Vichy carrots, see page 114, oven-cooked Cabinet pudding, see page 203.

Roast pork with sage and onion stuffing (cover the dish containing this with plenty of foil to keep it moist, unless the joint itself is being stuffed, as picture facing page 89), Potatoes Anna, Peas à la Française, see page 120, Fruit tart, see page 183.

The above menus naturally are for *quick roasting,* but as you will see opposite, it is suggested that after the first 15 minutes the heat is re-set. This is quite *impossible* if you are leaving the meal to cook by itself, so it is advisable to use the lower temperature and add a little extra cooking time.

Flavourings to add to roast meat

SEASONING—you can season the meat before cooking, but this is not essential.

HERBS OR SPICES—press 1 or 2 sage leaves on pork, or sprinkle with dried sage, see picture facing page 89; press a few mint leaves against young lamb, or make several little cuts in the flesh and press a thin slice of garlic into these; finely grated lemon rind can be sprinkled over veal, or lemon rind mixed with a little dried or finely chopped rosemary or lemon thyme.

VEGETABLES—most roast meats are excellent served with roast potatoes, parsnips, onions, etc.

GRAVY—it is traditional to serve beef with a thin gravy and other meats (particularly when stuffed) with a thick gravy.

Using fat when roasting

In the past it was considered important to use a generous amount of clarified dripping or fat when roasting meat, but over the years this practice has been largely discontinued. Obviously if you intend to roast potatoes round the joint you must use enough fat to roast these properly, but an excess of fat not only makes the oven unnecessarily dirty but also helps to harden the outside of the meat. That is why the minimum of fat should be used, in my opinion, for good roasting.

BACON AND HAM will need little if any fat, unless roasting very lean gammon, in which case spread the lean with a light coating of butter or other fat.

BEEF—good quality beef should have a generous amount of fat, except for topside, which is a naturally lean joint. If you have a reasonably fat sirloin and are not roasting potatoes, there is no need to add any extra fat at all. With topside, however, spread a little fat over the top of the meat before roasting.

LAMB, MUTTON—both have enough fat to 'baste' the meat without adding any extra.

PORK—although this is a very fat meat, you do add a little extra fat to crisp the skin and form crackling, see separate paragraph.

VEAL—this is so lean that fat must be used. If you spread the fat over the meat you keep the outside moist, but not the inside of the meat; this is why the French method of 'larding' veal is so good. Buy very fat bacon, or, to be more economical, cut narrow strips of fat from rashers of bacon you already have, and thread these through a larding (or clean carpet) needle, and insert into the meat. This means you have strips of fat running right the way through the meat as it cooks.

Using a covered roasting tin or foil

Have a covered roasting tin sufficiently large to allow fat to splash and drip from the top (as moisture evaporates) and brown outside of the meat. If the meat fits tightly into the tin, the outside will not brown or crisp. Remove the lid for the last 30 minutes for extra crispness. The advantage is that the oven keeps cleaner, but potatoes *cannot* be roasted round the meat.

With foil, either cover the top of the tin, or completely wrap the meat. This keeps the food moister, but if you want it brown and crisp, open the foil for the last 30 minutes of cooking time

With either a covered roasting tin or foil *you must allow a longer cooking time* or *increase the temperature* 25° F. (10°C.) with electricity, and 1 mark higher with gas.

Automatic Oven

If using slow roasting you can include Jacket potatoes (the heat is too low to roast vegetables and to cook Yorkshire pudding or pastry), Casserole of vegetables, see page 114, 'braised' vegetables, see page 113, reheated Sponge and other puddings, milk puddings.

Home Freezing

A roast dinner is a very popular one to freeze on individual plates or dishes. You can freeze: *sliced beef* in thin gravy, Yorkshire pudding, roast potatoes (take care they are well away from the gravy) and other vegetables. You will need to cover the beef and vegetables while reheating to prevent drying, but leave potatoes and Yorkshire pudding uncovered so as to become *reasonably* crisp again.

Roast lamb with mint sauce and vegetables. Unless including roast potatoes, see above, keep covered and reheat either over hot water or in the oven.

Roast pork (the crackling will stay crisp unless frozen *with* gravy to cover) with stuffing, apple sauce and vegetables. Remove covering from crackling *only* before reheating.

Roast veal (less satisfactory than other meats) with accompaniments as given.

To make pork crackling crisp

There are many theories on *how* you should produce a really crisp 'crackling' on the fat of pork. Some people like melted fat and salt; personally I dislike salt sprinkled on the meat and just use a very light brushing of melted fat, or better still olive oil, and roast in an uncovered roasting tin the whole of the cooking time. This is one occasion when I would not use foil or a covered roasting tin, but if you prefer to use either of these, remember the foil or lid must be removed for the last 30 minutes to encourage the skin to become crisp, but you will not have as good a result as when the meat is cooked uncovered for the whole period. The picture facing page 89 shows a really crisp outside to a stuffed rolled joint of pork, and this has been given extra flavour by a light sprinkling of dried sage before cooking.

Automatic Oven
Pork fat crisps excellently from a cold start in an automatic oven – indeed the fat seems to form a particularly crisp crackling.

Home Freezing
Although a generous amount of fat on a pork joint means that pork should be removed from the freezer within the time given on page 59, the crackling on cooked pork remains reasonably crisp.

To stuff meat

If you insert stuffing into meat, rather than cooking it separately, you give a better flavour to both meat *and* stuffing. Some joints will need the bones removed to stuff satisfactorily, but most butchers will do this if you ask. Should you buy meat with the bones still in, then cut these away from the flesh using a sharp flexible knife. Loin, breast, etc., when boned, give a flat piece of meat, and you simply cover this with stuffing, roll, then tie firmly to hold the stuffing in position, see picture facing page 89. It is also possible to have bones taken out of shoulder or leg, so you can put stuffing into the 'cavity' which remains. You may, however, prefer just to cut the flesh to make a 'pocket' and insert the stuffing into this. Remember you should calculate the weight of the joint, and therefore the cooking time, *after* putting in the stuffing.

Mixer
The liquidiser of an electric mixer is invaluable in making practically every stuffing quickly and easily, see page 139.

Home Freezing
Although stuffings freeze excellently, stuffed meat (as stuffed poultry) keeps perfectly for a *shorter* time in a freezer than meat which is *not* stuffed. The reason is that when stuffed the meat is made slightly softer and more moist in texture when frozen for a long period, and later defrosted; this impairs the flavour a little.

Roast chops, cutlets, etc.

It is possible to cook chops, etc., in the oven; the cooking time is longer this way, but the meat needs no attention as it browns evenly on both sides. Grease a roasting tin lightly and warm to ensure the meat will cook quickly; this is not possible when using the automatic oven. Put fat on lean gammon, steak or veal, and add to liver and kidneys. No fat is necessary with pork or pork sausages, with lamb (unless very lean) or young mutton (do not try to cook older mutton this way). Use nearly twice the cooking time allowed when frying or grilling, see pages 70 and 74, and cook towards top of a moderately hot to hot oven. Leave uncovered for a brown appearance, to look like grilling.

Automatic Oven
To make a complete meal choose a Casserole of frozen mixed vegetables, Duchesse potatoes, page 120, or heat canned new potatoes in a covered dish. Put tomatoes and/or mushrooms in a well-greased dish, cover mushrooms with a generous amount of margarine and season lightly. A Fruit Charlotte, see page 206, could be put into the coolest part of the oven, and the heat reduced when dishing up the main course, or choose *small* Stuffed baked apples, page 199.

Home Freezing
You can take frozen chops, steaks, sausages, etc., and cook them in this way, or in foil, without defrosting.

Foil wrapped meat

Although it really cannot be termed roasting, it is possible to cook chops, steak, etc., wrapped in foil in the oven. You should allow just over twice the cooking time needed when frying or grilling the meat, see pages 70 and 74, and have the oven moderately hot to hot. If slimming, use no fat, see comments opposite, but this method enables you to add a great deal of interest to the meat – for example:
a) grease the foil well, add thinly sliced seasoned mushrooms and other vegetables;
b) put interesting stuffings (see chapter on this, beginning page 137) over the meat;
c) spoon a little wine and chopped herbs over the meat, wrap the foil parcel tightly and cook as above.

Automatic Oven
An excellent way to leave meat in the oven as it does not dry while waiting for the oven to begin heating.

Slimming Tips
Foil cooking is quite the best method to use when you wish to lose weight, for to grill steak without fat spoils it, and even in a silicone frying pan you need a *very little* fat. Add herbs, dry wine, sliced tomatoes, seasoning of all kinds, to give additional flavour.

Making a Crown Roast

A Crown roast is an impressive joint and can be made with lamb, veal or pork with various fillings.

TO GARNISH AND SERVE THE CROWN—remove foil from bones, top with cutlet frills or with stoned olives, grapes or cherries. Cut Crown between the bones to serve.

WITH LAMB—choose loin or 2 joints of best end of neck (enough meat to form a Crown as picture facing page 65). Use the same stuffing as for pork (add this when lamb is cooked), or a sage and onion stuffing (put in before cooking the lamb), or cook the meat without stuffing and fill with a mixture of diced cooked vegetables just before serving. Another good stuffing for lamb is the *Sausage and kidney stuffing* on page 143.
WITH VEAL—choose loin, fill with parsley and thyme (veal) stuffing (cook with meat) or use recipe below, as pork.
WITH PORK—choose loin, fill with sage and onion stuffing, (which should be cooked with the meat) or any other fruit stuffings.

Automatic Oven
A crown roast is no more difficult to leave in the oven than any other roasted joint, and it can be prepared as suggestions opposite.

Speedy Meal
Use packet stuffings in place of the suggestions opposite.

Home Freezing
A stuffed, uncooked joint does not keep for as long a period as one without stuffing, but it is very convenient to have this all ready to cook.

Crown Pork Chops with Orange Rice

Serves 6–8
Cooking time see stage 3
Oven temperature 400–425° F. (200–220° C.), Gas Mark 6–7

Ingredients	Metric	Imperial
joint of pork chops*	12 chops	12 chops
seasoning	to taste	to taste
FOR STUFFING:		
butter	50 grammes	2 oz.
celery	approx. 200 grammes	8 oz.
onions	2–3	2–3
long grain rice	½ kilo (poor weight)	1 lb.
salt	1 teaspoon	1 teaspoon
chicken stock	850 ml	1½ pints
orange juice (fresh *or* canned)	284 ml	½ pint
seedless raisins	100 grammes	4 oz.
grated orange rind	½ tablespoon	½ tablespoon
TO GARNISH:		
oranges	1–2	1–2

*this is loin of pork.

1 Ask the butcher to partially chop the cutlets so they can be formed into a circle (crown roast) and tie twice. See picture facing page 65.
2 Season well and protect the tips of the bones with foil so they do not burn.
3 Roast the meat as the table page 65, allowing 25 minutes per lb. and 25 minutes over in a moderately hot to hot oven, then reduce the heat slightly as in the instructions on page 65; a crown roast always seems to take a little longer than other joints so add another 15 minutes.
4 To make the orange rice stuffing, allow the butter to melt in a saucepan, add the finely chopped celery and onions, then the rice and salt; mix well.
5 Pour the chicken stock and orange juice over the mixture.
6 Bring to the boil, stir once, lower heat to simmer and cook for 15 minutes in an uncovered pan.
7 Five minutes before serving, mix in the raisins and orange rind.
8 Serve the crown of pork filled with some of the orange rice; put the rest of the rice round the meat and garnish with orange segments.

Automatic Oven
The Pork crown roast opposite is less suitable than some recipes for a completely automatic meal, as the stuffing is added just before serving. You could pre-cook the stuffing and reheat this (with a little extra liquid) before serving.

Speedy Meal
Choose quick-cooking rice, dehydrated onions and canned orange juice.

Home Freezing
Rice is not a satisfactory food to freeze for any length of time: it loses its firm texture and becomes over-soft.

Crumbed Veal

Serves 7–8
Cooking time see stage 2
Oven temperature see stage 2

Ingredients	Metric	Imperial
leg of veal	1	1
fat bacon to lard	100–150 grammes	4–6 oz.
FOR THE COATING:		
butter	50 grammes	2 oz.
mushrooms	100 grammes	4 oz.
brown bread	150 grammes	6 oz.
(without crusts)		
seasoning	to taste	to taste

1 Prepare the veal for roasting by 'larding' with fat bacon, as suggested on page 66.
2 Calculate the roasting time as the table on page 65, i.e. 25 minutes per ½ kilo, poor weight, (1 lb.) and 25 minutes over if using quick roasting–read page 65 for temperatures, or 35–40 minutes per ½ kilo, poor weight, (1 lb.) for the slower method–temperatures also given on page 65.
3 Heat the butter, fry the *very* finely chopped mushrooms in this until soft, add crumbs made of the brown bread, season well. Add crushed peppercorns, not a shake pepper.
4 Spread thinly over top of the joint, cover with foil or greased greaseproof paper, and cook as usual.

Automatic Oven
The crumbed joint can be left just as any 'normal' joint. If using the quicker method of roasting you could have a separate dish of large roasted potatoes to serve *with* the meat. To prevent the potatoes becoming blackened while standing in the oven, either brush them with melted fat or turn in hot fat for a few minutes. This makes certain the air is excluded and so stops discolouring.

Mixer
Use the liquidiser to make the crumbs, and also to chop the mushrooms finely.

Home Freezing
Uncooked veal is reasonably successful to freeze, but I am always disappointed in the flavour of frozen cooked veal when reheated.

Glazed Apricot Gammon with Peaches

Serves 8
Cooking time see stages 2, 5 and 8
Oven temperature 350–375° F. (180–190° C.), Gas Mark 4–5

Ingredients	Metric	Imperial
joint middle gammon	2 kilos (approx.)	4 lb. (approx.)
apricot jam	4 tablespoons	4 tablespoons
cloves	to taste	to taste
demerara sugar	100 grammes	4 oz.
peach halves	large can	large can

1 Have the bacon boned and rolled. Soak in cold water overnight (unless it is sweet cure bacon which means it does not require soaking).
2 Place in saucepan, cover with fresh cold water and simmer for half the cooking time, allowing a total of 25 minutes per lb. and 25 minutes over, so if the joint weighs exactly 2 kilos (just over 4 lb.) you calculate five times 25 minutes plus an extra 5 minutes to allow for the grammes over, i.e. 2 hours 10 minutes.
3 After simmering for approximately 1 hour 5 minutes, lift out, cool enough to handle then remove the skin and lift on to a piece of foil.
4 Spread the fat with the apricot jam and bring the foil loosely over the top then put into a roasting tin.
5 Cook in the centre of a very moderate to moderate oven for half the remaining cooking time; approximately 35 minutes.
6 Uncover the bacon, stud with cloves (remember these are very strong, so do not add too many).
7 Sprinkle with brown sugar and arrange the drained peaches (not too well dried) in the roasting tin.
8 Spoon 2–3 tablespoons of the syrup from the canned peaches over the joint and bake uncovered for the remainder of the cooking time, approximately 30 minutes.
9 Serve the joint with the peaches round–you will notice in the picture facing page 57 that some of the peaches have also been 'studded' with cloves, this is not essential.

Automatic Oven
Obviously this bacon dish is not the ideal one for an automatic meal since there are various stages, i.e. simmering, stages 1–3, then roasting covered with foil, stages 4 and 5, and the final stages, 6–9, when the *uncovered* bacon is roasted.
The final stage could form the basis of an automatic meal, but of course the gammon will have become cold as it stands in the oven, so the cooking time at stage 8 would need to be about 45–50 minutes.

Speedy Meal
You can buy a ready-cooked joint of bacon or ham–make the coating as the recipe and just heat through in the oven.

Home Freezing
As already pointed out, bacon and ham are not among the most successful meats to freeze.

TO FRY MEAT

Frying meat is both quick and satisfactory providing correct types of meat are chosen. As frying is a quick way of cooking, you must be certain that the meat is tender enough to cook within a limited time. There are 3 methods of frying:

DRY FRYING in which meat cooks in its own fat; rashers of bacon are usually cooked this way, but you will need to add extra fat if cooking eggs, tomatoes, etc., in the same pan.

SHALLOW FRYING is used for steaks, chops, etc., where a small amount of fat is put into the pan. The secret when shallow frying is to ensure the fat is hot before the meat goes in, and to seal both sides of the meat over a high heat, thereby sealing in the juices and keeping it moist. After this, reduce heat so that meat cooks through to the centre.

DEEP FRYING is a way of cooking used chiefly for 'made up' meat dishes, some of which will be found in this chapter.

Cooking times, etc., for frying meat

BACON, HAM
CHOOSE–rashers of bacon of all kinds including thick gammon.

COOK FOR–DRY FRYING (most usual for thin bacon rashers)–cut away rinds from bacon; do not waste these, put into the pan, fry with the bacon, or fry before the bacon to give a little extra fat. This will be very important when frying eggs, tomatoes, etc., which need more fat. Arrange rashers so that the lean of the second rasher is *on top of the fat of the first rasher*; this prevents the bacon becoming hard and dry during cooking. Allow 3–5 minutes for thin rashers, which will not need turning; 12 minutes for thick rashers (turn after first 3–4 minutes then reduce heat when bacon begins to crisp).

SHALLOW FRYING (used for gammon)–put approximately 25 grammes (1 oz.) fat or dripping into frying pan. Heat until a faint haze is seen or a cube of bread turns golden brown in 1 minute. Do not over-heat or the outside of the meat will brown too quickly, but if the fat is not hot enough, the outside may be greasy, which is both unpalatable and indigestible. Allow 3–4 minutes on high heat; 6–8 minutes if very thick.

USUAL ACCOMPANIMENTS–fried eggs, fried tomatoes and mushrooms, etc., as steak, or with rings of pineapple, peaches, other fruit. Add the fruit to the hot fat just before bacon or ham is cooked, and heat through.

BEEF (generally bought as steak)
CHOOSE–fillet, rump, sirloin, minute steaks (thin slices sirloin or rump), porterhouse, entrecôte.

COOK FOR–SHALLOW FRYING–underdone ('rare') 2–3 minutes on high heat; medium rare, as above plus 4–6 minutes, heat turned low; well done, as rare, plus 6–10 minutes, heat turned low. Minute steak, 1 minute on either side.

USUAL ACCOMPANIMENTS–fried tomatoes, mushrooms or onion rings, garnish with watercress.

KIDNEY
CHOOSE–lamb's, calf's, pig's.

COOK FOR–SHALLOW FRYING–2–3 minutes on high heat plus 3–4 minutes, heat turned low. Remove skin and gristle, halve if wished, coat lightly with seasoned flour.

USUAL ACCOMPANIMENTS–as steak.

LAMB (or very young mutton)
CHOOSE–cutlets, chops (from loin), chops (from best end of neck).

COOK FOR–SHALLOW FRYING–3–4 minutes on either side on high heat, plus 6–8 minutes, heat turned low.

DEEP FRYING–coat chops with seasoned flour then egg and crumbs, fry in hot oil or fat. Reduce the heat as soon as the chops are put

Speedy Meal
Frying is one of the quickest methods of cooking meat, so it is ideal when you are short of time. A thin frying pan gives quicker cooking, but take care that the food does not burn.

Slimming Tips
It is difficult to be too dogmatic about frying foods, for some diets stress that fat is to be included; these are, however, very exceptional. Most people avoid fat therefore on slimming diets. If you have a non-stick pan you can cook most meats without adding fat at all. When cooking lean steak in a non-stick pan just brush the pan with a little oil before you start frying.

Home Freezing
There is no need to allow the meats given opposite, i.e. bacon, beef (steak) or lamb to thaw out before cooking. Kidneys may also be cooked from the frozen state although I prefer these defrosted at room temperature before frying. It is difficult to skin kidney and remove gristle if still frozen.

into the fat to prevent outside coating becoming too dark. Total cooking time about 10–12 minutes.

USUAL ACCOMPANIMENTS–fried tomatoes, mushrooms, garnish with parsley or watercress.

LIVER

CHOOSE–lamb's, calf's, pig's.

COOK FOR–SHALLOW FRYING–2–3 minutes on either side on high heat plus 4–6 minutes, heat turned low. Slice ½-cm (¼-inch) thick, coat lightly in seasoned flour.

USUAL ACCOMPANIMENTS–as steak.

PORK

CHOOSE–cutlets, chops (from loin or spare rib).

COOK FOR–SHALLOW FRYING–snip fat to crisp, allow 4–5 minutes on either side on high heat, plus 10–12 minutes with heat turned low.

USUAL ACCOMPANIMENTS–fried tomatoes or heated rings canned pineapple, garnish with watercress.

SAUSAGES

CHOOSE–large or small (chipolata).

COOK FOR–SHALLOW FRYING–prick before putting into frying pan to prevent skin from breaking. Cook over a slow heat for 2–3 minutes to make fat flow from the sausages. Allow 13 minutes total cooking time for large sausages; 9–10 minutes for smaller ones. Brown on both sides, then turn down heat to ensure they are cooked through to the centre.

USUAL ACCOMPANIMENTS–mustard, creamed (mashed) potatoes, tomatoes, mushrooms, etc.

SWEETBREADS

CHOOSE–lamb's or calf's.

PRE-PREPARATION–'blanch' sweetbreads by putting into cold water, bring to the boil and then throw away the water.

COOK FOR–about 25 minutes simmering (this gives a better result than long frying) in fresh water or white stock, with seasoning, and *bouquet garni*. Cool, skin, coat in seasoned flour, egg and crumbs.

SHALLOW FRYING–2–3 minutes on either side on high heat plus 4–6 minutes with heat turned low.

DEEP FRYING–a total of 3–4 minutes.

USUAL ACCOMPANIMENTS–as steak, or with Tomato sauce, page 150.

VEAL

CHOOSE–cutlets, chops (from loin, best end of neck), slices from fillet (top of leg, escalopes).

COOK FOR–SHALLOW FRYING–5 minutes on either side on high heat, plus 10–15 minutes with heat turned low, in 50 grammes (2 oz.) butter. First coat with seasoned flour, or flour then egg and crumbs.

USUAL ACCOMPANIMENTS–rings of lemon.

Tournedos of Beef

Serves 4
Cooking time see stage 2

Ingredients	Metric	Imperial
fillet steaks	4	4
bread	4 rounds	4 rounds
butter	75–100 grammes	3–4 oz.
TO FLAVOUR:		
chopped parsley	2 teaspoons	2 teaspoons
seasoning	to taste	to taste
brandy	1–2 tablespoons	1–2 tablespoons

1 If the butcher has not tied the fillet steaks to make rounds (tournedos), then form neatly into rounds and tie, using very fine string.
2 Cut rounds of bread, fry in the butter *with* the meat if using a large pan, or before if a smaller pan, see page 70 for frying time.
3 Serve the meat on fried bread; add the flavourings to the butter in the pan, pour over the meat.

Slimming Tips

Liver is such an important meat since it provides iron as well as protein, that this should be included in a slimming diet even if it means using a little fat—see comments on page 70 about non-stick pans. You could, however, simmer the liver in a very little stock, flavoured with mustard and herbs, or in stock with a little orange juice to give a new taste.

Home Freezing

Mushrooms, often mentioned as a garnish to fried foods, freeze excellently, for details see page 112, but whole or halved tomatoes are spoiled by freezing.

Allow liver to defrost before frying if possible. You *can* cook this from the frozen state, but it tends to produce an excessive amount of moisture. If defrosted drain and dry before cooking.

Speedy Meal

If preparing tournedos for a number of people, cut the loaf of bread lengthways so you have longer slices, and from these can cut more rounds of bread for frying. Use a sharp pastry cutter.

Home Freezing

The rounds of uncooked bread may be packed and frozen ready to fry when required. There is no need to defrost these. You may also freeze ready-fried bread and heat this through in the oven, rather than fry it. Although you could heat the ready-fried and frozen tournedos of steak, it *does* spoil the meat to cook it twice.

GARNISHES FOR TOURNEDOS

The garnishes on cooked steak give the name to the dish, e.g.

BARONNE–top grilled or fried steak with cooked mushrooms, serve with thick tomato purée and Béarnaise sauce, page 152.

BELLE-HÉLÈNE–top fried steak with asparagus tips and cooked button mushrooms or truffles.

DUMAS–top grilled steak with a thick slice of ham, Onion sauce, page 146, and grated cheese–melt under the grill.

MÉNAGÈRE–serve steaks in a border of Duchesse potatoes, page 120, topped with cooked Macedoine of vegetables, page 114 and Espagnole sauce, page 147.

MONÉGASQUE–top fried steak with fried sliced aubergine and thick tomato purée, garnish with olives.

Flavourings to add to fried meat

SEASONING–you can season meat before frying, but this is not essential. However, you can turn a very usual fried chop or steak into something rather unusual by your choice of seasoning–for example, Steak au poivre (or peppered steak) is made by shaking a liberal amount of black pepper over the meat or by pressing crushed peppercorns on to both sides of the steak before cooking. Lamb chops are delicious if seasoned with celery salt or paprika pepper before cooking.

HERBS OR SPICES–most herbs blend with meat, and very finely chopped herbs can be pressed into uncooked meat. A better way to introduce herbs into meat though is as follows:

MARINADES FOR MEAT–if you have any doubts as to whether meat for frying is likely to be tasteless or tough, it is an excellent idea to marinate it. This means putting it into a mixture of oil (which gives a moist texture) and either vinegar, lemon juice or wine (which breaks down the tissues of meat and makes it more tender), plus seasoning and herbs to flavour. Here are some suggestions you may care to try:

a) GARLIC MARINADE–sufficient for 4 large or 8 small chops or 4 steaks: crush 1–2 cloves garlic with tip of knife, blend with 4 table-spoons olive oil, 3 tablespoons red wine, and add plenty of seasoning. Put in a shallow dish, stand the meat in this for at least 1 hour, turn once or twice during this time. Fry as usual, but because of the oil content reduce the amount of fat used. This is a fairly generous amount of marinade and any left may be stored in a screw-topped jar for another occasion, or can be heated and poured over the meat, if wished.

b) LEMON AND ONION MARINADE–chop an onion very finely, blend with 2 tablespoons oil, 1 tablespoon lemon juice, finely grated lemon rind and seasoning. Proceed as above, but as the quantities are smaller the meat will absorb most of this.

c) HERB MARINADE–blend a tablespoon chopped herbs (include chopped chives if possible) with 2 tablespoons olive oil and 2 table-spoons white or wine vinegar, season very well then proceed as above.

VEGETABLES–most fried meats are served with fried vegetables, and these are either cooked in a separate pan or in the same pan while the meat is kept hot on a dish in a low oven, or on a hot plate, etc. *Tomatoes*–halve, season, cook for several minutes in the fat left in the pan. *Mushrooms*–wash, dry, trim but do not peel if good quality. These always need a fair amount of fat, so I always add a little extra to the pan before frying. *Fried onion rings and fried potatoes* are given on page 115.

GRAVY AND SAUCES–most fried meats are served without a gravy or sauce, but where these are necessary or give added flavour, it will be stressed in the recipe. Naturally, if you like gravy with fried meats you will prepare this, and it is wise to make this in the frying pan so that it absorbs any juices from the meat.

Speedy Meal

Many of the garnishes mentioned oppo-site are quick to prepare, but you can also make tournedos look more interesting by topping with sliced canned pâté (this is called Tournedos Rossini); with heated canned asparagus tips; with heated arti-choke hearts, etc.

Slimming Tips

This is the interesting type of steak dish you can eat on special occasions, even on a slimming diet, for the fried croûtons can be omitted if wished. The small number of extra calories in the garnish can be forgotten (as long as they are not included as a regular habit for the few odd calories can, and do, 'mount up' to an appreciable number in a week).

Home Freezing

Freeze the wrapped garnishes but store with the fillet steak so that you can pre-pare the tournedos without having to spend time 'searching' for them in the freezer.

Speedy Meal

Although frying *is* naturally a speedy way of cooking it can be made even quicker if you choose very thin slices of steak (minute steaks), or ask for thin slices of veal or pork cut from the leg joint. These are generally called escalopes and are described on page 73. If the bones of lamb chops are removed and the meat rolled and tied to form a 'noisette' of lamb, the meat cooks more quickly.

Slimming Tips

Use a non-stick pan and the very minimum of fat for steak; no fat for meat with its own fat. Adapt the marinade recipes opposite by decreasing the amount of oil used to half that given. Naturally, this gives a 'sharper' flavour to the marinade.

Veal Cordon Bleu

Serves 4
Cooking time 12–14 minutes

Ingredients	Metric	Imperial
thin fillets veal	4 large	4 large
cooked ham	4 slices	4 slices
(half the size of the veal)		
Gruyère cheese	4 slices	4 slices
(half the size of the veal)		
TO COAT:		
egg	1	1
water	1 tablespoon	1 tablespoon
fine soft breadcrumbs	50 grammes	2 oz.
TO FRY:		
butter	75 grammes	3 oz.
TO GARNISH:		
lemon	1	1
parsley	few sprigs	few sprigs

1 Put the veal on to a board, flatten well.
2 Lay the ham and cheese on top of half the meat, then fold like a sandwich.
3 Coat in the beaten egg, diluted with the water, then in the crumbs.
4 Heat the butter and fry until golden brown, then lower the heat; careful cooking is essential for the meat must be adequately cooked, but over-cooking spoils the cheese.
5 Garnish with lemon slices and parsley.

Mixer

Use the liquidiser for making the soft crumbs for coating the veal or for preparing crisp crumbs (do read the manufacturer's instructions and check whether the blades in *your* particular goblet are strong enough to grind the crumbs).

Home Freezing

The coated uncooked veal, whether plain, or filled with ham and cheese as the Veal Cordon Bleu, may be frozen; cook from the frozen state. It is also an excellent idea to freeze bags of soft crumbs; crisp breadcrumbs (raspings) will keep in tins, jars or packets *without* freezing. You can quite easily remove the amount of frozen crumbs you need, and it is very satisfactory to coat food with *frozen* crumbs; you get a very smooth even layer over the meat or fish.

Escalopes of Veal

Serves 4–6
Cooking time 10–12 minutes

Ingredients	Metric	Imperial
fillet of veal	¾ kilo	1½ lb.
(cut from leg)	(poor weight)	
seasoning	to taste	to taste
flour	25 grammes	1 oz.
TO COAT:		
egg	1	1
water	1–2 tablespoons	1–2 tablespoons
crisped *or* soft	about 3 good	about 3 good
breadcrumbs	tablespoons	tablespoons
TO FRY:		
fat *or* butter	75 grammes	3 oz.
TO GARNISH:		
lemon	1	1
watercress	few sprigs	few sprigs

1 Cut the fillet into 4–6 neat pieces, beat until very thin.
2 Coat each piece in seasoned flour, then dip in the egg mixed with the water.
3 Coat with breadcrumbs; press firmly on to the veal, shake off any surplus.
4 Fry in hot fat or butter until golden brown on both sides, then reduce heat and cook gently until tender; naturally soft breadcrumbs give a lighter colouring.
5 Garnish with lemon slices and sprigs of watercress.

Note: a more elaborate garnish is to top the lemon slices with chopped hard-boiled egg. chopped parsley and/or a few capers and anchovy fillets.

The veal fillets may also be served the Italian way with a *Tuna sauce* made by blending a small can of flaked tuna fish into about 142 ml (¼ pint) home-made mayonnaise.

Speedy Meal

If you do not wish to spend time coating the veal, fry in the hot butter then lift out, add a few capers to remaining butter, pour over the veal and serve.
Another speedy dish is to fry without coating the meat, lift on to a hot dish, then stir a few tablespoons of thick cream blended with a little paprika into the pan, heat gently and pour over the veal.
A more elaborate version of this is to fry fresh sliced mushrooms or heat well-drained canned mushrooms in the hot butter with the veal. Dish up the meat, but leave the mushrooms in the pan. Add the cream and paprika, stir and heat, then spoon over the meat.

TO GRILL MEAT

Grilling is a method of cooking that is extremely popular today for a variety of reasons. Firstly, it is quick; secondly it retains the maximum of flavour in good quality meat; thirdly it is considered that the meat is more easily digested and less fattening than when it is fried. In order to grill meat well you must select the right cuts of meat (the same as for frying), and you should also make certain the grill is very hot before the meat is put underneath. In this way you seal in the juices by quick cooking on either side of the meat. After this, reduce the heat and lower the position of the grill pan, where necessary, so that the heat penetrates very slowly to the centre of the meat. The one exception to the rule of putting meat under a pre-heated grill is when grilling bacon. If the grill is very hot, the fat of the bacon curls so quickly that it is inclined to burn. It is, therefore, wise to light or switch on the grill *as* the bacon is placed under it.

In order to keep grilled meat moist, it should be basted with melted butter or other fat during cooking; this is particularly important in the case of lean gammon and veal. Brush the meat with melted fat before it starts to cook, when you turn it on to the second side, and once or twice during the slower cooking period if you feel it necessary.

Cooking times, etc., for grilling meat

Cooking times are the same as for frying, so I will not repeat them. Choose the same cuts of meat as for frying and serve with the same accompaniments, although the recipes that follow do give special garnishes, etc., for grilled meat. Another usual accompaniment is Maître d'hôtel (parsley) butter, see page 50, or Béarnaise sauce, on page 152, for steaks which are served on special occasions.

Flavourings to add to grilled meat

SEASONING–many people consider seasoning is essential before grilling meat, but this is purely a matter of personal taste.
HERBS OR SPICES–you can use the same flavourings as for frying, see page 72, and you can also add other spices as required. For example, blend a little curry powder with the butter used for basting grilled meat, or a pinch of ginger–which is particularly good with grilled gammon.
MARINADES–these are the same as for frying, and after removing the meat from the marinade use this, rather than extra fat, to baste the meat during cooking.
VEGETABLES–grilled mushrooms and tomatoes are the usual accompaniment to grilled meat. The method of cooking these rather depends on the type of grill pan supplied with your cooker. If this has a wire mesh grid, this enables the heat to penetrate through to the pan itself and the vegetables will cook simultaneously in the pan with the meat. Many modern grill pans, however, have a rather solid grid–this is easier to keep clean, but prevents heat reaching the pan. With this type of grill pan, melt a little fat in the pan, put in the tomatoes (whole or halved) and/or prepared mushrooms, turn in the hot fat, season lightly and cook for about 5 minutes under the grill. Put the meat on the grid over the tomatoes, etc., and continue cooking. Or, cook tomatoes and mushrooms on the grid *with* the meat, take care they do not become over-cooked or dry. Fruit is a usual accompaniment to grilled meats, particularly bacon; brush with butter either rings of pineapple, halved peaches or prunes, etc., and put on grid towards end of cooking time. Sprinkle with sugar if required to give a shiny glaze, and heat carefully.

Speedy Meal
If you switch on or light the grill in plenty of time while preparing the meat for grilling, it is surprising how much more quickly it will start to cook. For very quick grilling choose minute steaks and grill for 1 minute on either side; or choose small cutlets rather than thicker chops.

Slimming Tips
Grilling is accepted as one of the best ways of cooking meat if you are on a slimming diet. If the diet is very strict, you must cook *all* meat, even steak, using no fat at all: so choose steak that has a little natural fat, keep this on while you cook the meat, and then cut away before serving. If you are allowed a very small amount of butter or other fat in the diet, it is wise to use this in basting the steak as it cooks. Chops have sufficient fat to present no problem. If the particular diet being followed stresses that all meat should be lean, it is better to leave any fat on the chop or cutlet during cooking, and remove afterwards.

Home Freezing
Never freeze cooked grilled meat, as it would be completely dry and unpalatable. You can, however, put frozen uncooked meat straight from the freezer to cook under the hot grill. You will find the cooking time is not very much longer than when the meat is fresh.

Kebabs

This term describes pieces of meat, etc., that are 'threaded' on to strong metal skewers and cooked under the grill. The bacon kebabs shown in the picture facing page 57 are a delicious 'modern' version of this traditional Mediterranean dish. Use diced steak, lamb, sausages, diced green and red peppers, sliced aubergines, small onions (parboiled if possible), tomatoes and mushrooms. Cook under the grill, see page 74, turning the skewers and 'basting' the meat, etc., with plenty of melted butter; flavour with seasoning, chopped herbs and a pinch of mixed spice.

Bacon Kebabs

Serves 4
Cooking time 8–10 minutes

Ingredients	Metric	Imperial
green pepper	1 small	1 small
streaky bacon rashers	16 small	16 small
tomatoes	4 large *or* 8 small	4 large *or* 8 small
oil	to baste	to baste
TO GARNISH:		
watercress	few sprigs	few sprigs
parsley	few sprigs	few sprigs

1 De-seed the pepper and cut into quarters or smaller pieces.
2 Blanch in boiling water for 5 minutes.
3 De-rind the rashers of bacon and stretch lightly with the back of a knife (this makes them easier to roll) then form into rolls.
4 Cut large tomatoes in half, but use small tomatoes whole.
5 Use 4 skewers and thread on each alternately, bacon rolls, tomato and pepper pieces; brush tomatoes and pepper with oil then grill until bacon is cooked through.
6 Serve on hot dish garnished with watercress and parsley as picture facing page 57.

Banana and Bacon Rolls

Serves 4–8*
Cooking time 6–8 minutes

Ingredients	Metric	Imperial
small bananas	8	8
lemons	2	2
streaky bacon rashers	8	8
pineapple jam	5–6 tablespoons	5–6 tablespoons
TO GARNISH:		
watercress	few sprigs	few sprigs

*4 as a light main dish, 8 as a buffet snack.

1 Peel bananas and dip in the juice from 1 lemon to prevent discolouring.
2 Remove rinds from bacon and carefully stretch each rasher with the back of a knife.
3 Wrap a piece of bacon round each banana and secure with wooden cocktail sticks.
4 Place under a moderately hot grill until light golden brown and crisp, turn round as necessary.
5 Heat pineapple jam with the juice from the remaining lemon and serve in a small jug or poured over the rolls.
6 Garnish with watercress.

If serving these as a cocktail party snack, do not leave the bananas whole as picture facing page 57, halve or even quarter the bananas and the rashers of bacon. Cook as above, and serve the sauce as a dip in the centre.

Speedy Meal
Cocktail onions, gherkins and canned well drained mushrooms can all be used on skewers for kebabs.

Home Freezer
If you care to fill skewers with diced uncooked steak, sausages, pieces of lamb, these can be wrapped and frozen. Do not defrost, simply brush with melted butter and cook under the grill. You can add small tomatoes, mushrooms and onions when ready to cook the kebabs, but do not freeze these (unless you cook the mushrooms lightly *before* freezing). Tomatoes and onions would not retain their texture.

Speedy Meal
These kebabs are very quick to prepare, as bacon cooks so speedily. To complete a speedy menu, serve on heated canned spaghetti.

Slimming Tips
Kebabs can be made so that they are 'low calorie'. Avoid the sausages and don't use too much fat in basting. Choose lean bacon in making the kebabs, opposite.

Home Freezing
Bacon kebabs are less suitable for freezing than if you use steak, etc.

Automatic Oven
This is a dish that could be served for breakfast as well as a main meal, and could be placed in the oven over-night to cook ready for breakfast the next morning. Make sure the bananas are very well coated in lemon juice, to keep them a good colour; also that each rasher of bacon completely covers each banana. Set the oven to a moderately hot temperature and for 25–30 minutes cooking time, and place the Banana and bacon rolls towards the top of the oven. If you like crisp bacon keep the rolls uncovered, but if you prefer the bacon more lightly cooked, cover the dish with foil and increase the cooking time by 5–10 minutes.

STEWS AND CASSEROLE DISHES

There are a variety of these dishes on the following pages, but remember cooking time depends on the cuts of meat used. When meat is young, as lamb cut from the leg in the recipe on page 78, cooking time can be short. Indeed you would lose flavour in this dish if cooked too slowly for too long a time. When meat is less tender (because it is a cheaper cut), use long slow cooking.

Flavourings for Stews and Casserole Dishes

SEASONING—be generous with all seasonings, use celery salt, crushed peppercorns and mustard of various kinds.

HERBS OR SPICES—nearly all herbs can be used—if fresh herbs are not available, use dried herbs sparingly.

THICKENING STEWS, ETC.—use flour, about 25 grammes, (1 oz.) to each 426 ml ($\frac{3}{4}$ pint) liquid for a reasonably thick stew, or half that quantity of cornflour, or try this *Bread thickening:* spread thick slice of crustless bread with French or English mustard, sprinkle with herbs, drop into the liquid 10 minutes before stew is ready to serve. Heat gently, then beat hard; the bread will thicken and give a smooth sauce.

Automatic Oven

Practically every stew *can* be cooked in the oven in a covered casserole instead of in a saucepan. The cooking time should be *increased* slightly, but the liquid should be decreased a little as you do not lose as much by evaporation as when cooking in a saucepan.

Speedy Meal

Use a pressure cooker, as instructions in the various recipes.

Home Freezing

Most stews *can* be frozen, read the comments in the introduction page 59, and by each recipe.

Paprika Beef

Serves 4–6
Cooking time 1 hour OR 2 hours

Ingredients	Metric	Imperial
topside beef *or* stewing steak	$\frac{1}{2}$–$\frac{3}{4}$ kilo	1$\frac{1}{4}$–1$\frac{1}{2}$ lb.
seasoning	to taste	to taste
onions	2 large	2 large
cooking fat	50 grammes	2 oz.
tomatoes	$\frac{1}{2}$ kilo (poor weight)	1 lb. (good weight)
brown stock	284 ml*	$\frac{1}{2}$ pint*
paprika**	$\frac{1}{2}$–1 tablespoon	$\frac{1}{2}$–1 tablespoon
bay leaves	2	2
bouquet garni	spray	spray
TO SERVE:		
long grain rice	8 tablespoons	8 tablespoons
salt	to taste	to taste
water	see stage 6	see stage 6

*a little more with stewing steak because of longer cooking time.
**this is a sweet, not hot, flavouring.

1 Cut meat into narrow strips as shown in the picture facing page 81, and season well.
2 Peel and chop onions finely, fry meat and onions gently in the hot fat until the meat is slightly browned.
3 Skin and chop tomatoes finely, add to meat with the stock (blended with paprika) bay leaves and *bouquet garni*.
4 Simmer steadily: allow approximately 45–50 minutes for topside of beef; about 1 hour 45–50 minutes for stewing steak.
5 By the time the meat is tender, the sauce will be reasonably thick; remove bay leaves and *bouquet garni*.
6 Meanwhile, prepare rice—either cook by method of using 16 tablespoons of water, with salt to taste, or more water. If using smaller quantity, put rice, salt and cold water into pan, bring to boil, stir briskly, cover and simmer steadily for 15 minutes, when liquid will have evaporated—or boil in about 3 pints salted water until tender, then strain, rinse with boiling water and dry for few minutes.
7 Put the rice on a dish and top with the paprika beef.

Automatic Oven

To cook in the oven, proceed as stages 1–3; transfer to a casserole, cover tightly and cook for 1–1$\frac{1}{4}$ hours if using topside of beef, or 2$\frac{1}{4}$ hours if using stewing steak. The heat should be very moderate. Obviously the choice of vegetables, etc., will vary according to the cooking time, but Jacket potatoes can be cooked for each occasion—choose *small* potatoes for 1–1$\frac{1}{4}$ hours; really big ones for 2$\frac{1}{4}$ hours, and wrap in foil.

Speedy Meal

Prepare sauce using canned tomatoes and heat fingers of cooked meat in this. Use a pressure cooker to save time, and allow 8–10 minutes for good quality meat, with slightly less stock, or 18–20 minutes for stewing steak at 15 lb. pressure. Allow pressure to drop gradually—to do this, remove cooker from the heat but do *not* cool under water. Wait until pressure drops before lifting lid.

Slimming Tips

A paprika sauce of this kind made without any thickening is ideal to include in a slimming menu. Rice is high in calories, so must be eaten in moderation, but if you boil the rice in salted water, strain and rinse in fresh boiling water, you do wash away some surplus starch.

Home Freezing

An excellent dish to freeze, but do not over-cook as the meat needs to be tender, but reasonably firm-textured.

Liver à l'Italienne

Serves 4–5
Cooking time 45 minutes

Ingredients	Metric	Imperial
small onions *or* shallots	4	4
mushrooms	50 grammes	2 oz.
oil	2 tablespoons	2 tablespoons
flour*	25 grammes	1 oz.
white wine	284 ml	½ pint
brown stock	6 tablespoons	6 tablespoons
seasoning	to taste	to taste
chopped parsley	1 tablespoon	1 tablespoon
calves liver	½ kilo	1–1¼ lb.

*or half the quantity of cornflour.

1 Chop peeled onions or shallots and mushrooms, and fry in the hot oil for a few minutes.
2 Add the flour, stir over a gentle heat for 2–3 minutes, gradually blend in wine and stock, cook until thickened.
3 Add seasoning, half the parsley and the thickly sliced liver; cover pan, simmer gently for 30–35 minutes.
4 Serve topped with the rest of the parsley, and with macaroni or noodles.

Automatic Oven
Make the sauce up to stage 3, adding the liver. Put into a casserole; make sure the liver is covered with liquid so it will not dry.
Cook for about 1 hour in the centre of a very moderate oven. Serve with a casserole of mixed frozen vegetables, canned spaghetti (add a little stock to this and wrap over outside of the casserole so it does not dry), and a Compôte of dried fruit.

Slimming Tips
This dish could be served on a slimming diet, for liver is an extremely valuable food which provides both protein and calcium. The amount of oil could be reduced, if wished.

Home Freezing
The flavour of this dish if frozen is disappointing. It is better to freeze the raw liver rather than the cooked dish.

Fricandeau of Veal

Serves 4–5
Cooking time 1½ hours

Ingredients	Metric	Imperial
fat bacon in one piece	100 grammes	4 oz.
stewing veal	½ kilo	1¼ lb.
	(good weight)	(poor weight)
onions	2	2
carrots	2	2
tomatoes	4	4
white stock	284 ml	½ pint
bouquet garni	spray	spray
bay leaf	1	1
cloves	2	2
seasoning	to taste	to taste
thick cream	4–6 tablespoons	4–6 tablespoons
TO GARNISH:		
paprika	1 tablespoon	1 tablespoon
chopped parsley	1 tablespoon	1 tablespoon

1 Dice the bacon, removing the rind, and the veal, then peel and cut onions, carrots and tomatoes into small pieces.
2 Fry the bacon for a few minutes, then add the meat and toss in the bacon fat.
3 Stir in the vegetables, stock, herbs, cloves and seasoning, and cover the pan; simmer for about 1–1¼ hours.
4 Lift the meat out of the sauce, discard cloves and bay leaf, then sieve the sauce, return to the pan with the meat and heat gently with the cream.
5 Serve topped with paprika and parsley.

Note: instead of sieving the sauce, serve as an ordinary stew, top with soured cream or yoghourt and the garnishes. If wished, you can blend 25 grammes (1 oz.) flour, or half this amount of cornflour, with 142 ml (¼ pint) milk or thin cream; stir into the sauce at stage 4 and cook steadily, without boiling, until thickened. Garnish at stage 5.

Automatic Oven
Prepare to stage 3, transfer to casserole and cover lightly. Allow about 1¾ hours in the centre of a very moderate oven, then either serve without sieving the sauce or sieve as stage 4. Serve with Potatoes Anna, page 120, broad beans cooked in a casserole and Caramel crumb pudding, see page 188, cooked in a dish of water in the coolest part of the oven.

Speedy Meal
Fry the chopped bacon and the veal as first part of stage 1. Add a can of creamed chicken soup and a little extra milk or water or stock. Simmer until tender and garnish.

Mixer
The liquidiser is excellent for emulsifying the ingredients at stage 4.

Home Freezing
I feel that veal is the least satisfactory meat to freeze, but *if* you wish to freeze this continue to stage 3; only then emulsify or sieve the sauce when reheating.

Chinese Style Sweet-Sour Lamb

Serves 4
Cooking time 1 hour

Ingredients	Metric	Imperial
salad oil	2 tablespoons	2 tablespoons
onion	1 medium	1 medium
lamb fillet (cut from leg)	½–⅝ kilo	1–1¼ lb.
cornflour	2 level tablespoons	2 level tablespoons
meat stock–*or* use ½ stock cube and water	284 ml	½ pint
green pepper	1	1
apricot halves	1 medium can	1 medium can
apricot liquor	5 tablespoons (taken from can)	5 tablespoons (taken from can)
sultanas	50 grammes	2 oz.
honey	1 tablespoon	1 tablespoon
wine vinegar	5 tablespoons	5 tablespoons
salt	½ level teaspoon	½ level teaspoon
powdered ginger	¼ level teaspoon	¼ level teaspoon
TO SERVE:		
noodles	100–150 grammes	4–6 oz.
butter	25 grammes	1 oz.
green salad		

1 Pour oil into a good sized saucepan and stand over a medium heat until oil sizzles.
2 Reduce heat to low, add grated onion and fry until pale gold.
3 Add lamb–cut into 2 cm (1 inch) cubes–and fry until all the cut sides are crisp and brown.
4 Stir in the cornflour, gradually blend in the stock and cook gently, stirring from time to time until a thick sauce.
5 Cut the pepper pulp into strips, discard core and seeds. Reserve a quarter of the strips and four apricot halves for garnish.
6 Add the rest of the pepper strips and coarsely chopped apricot halves to the meat in pan, together with the apricot liquor, sultanas, honey, vinegar, salt and ginger.
7 Cover pan with lid and simmer very gently for approximately 40 minutes or until meat is tender.
8 Remove lid and garnish with rest of uncooked pepper and apricot halves.
9 Serve with freshly cooked flat noodles, first tossed with butter, and a crisp green salad.

Automatic Oven

This dish could be prepared to the end of stage 6, then transferred to a casserole, covered tightly, and cooked for about 1 hour in the centre of a very moderate to moderate oven (or a slightly shorter time if the ingredients are still very hot). Obviously the noodles could not be cooked at the same time, so serve with oven-cooked tiny potatoes instead and a green salad.

Home Freezing

This dish freezes very well indeed.
Omit the green pepper used for garnish at stage 8, and add this when the dish is reheated.
There is a possibility that the sauce could become thin when reheating, in which case blend in a little more cornflour at that time.

More sweet-sour dishes

The combination of sweet and sharp flavours has become very popular during the past years, and the mixture of flavourings blends well with meats other than young lamb as in the recipe above–for example:

MUTTON–cook for about 1¼ hours at stage 7, less tender meat could be used–you may need to add a little extra stock at stage 6 to prevent the mixture becoming too dry.
LEAN PORK (cut from leg)–apricots could be used with pork, but canned pineapple is a better combination. Cook for 50 minutes at stage 7, as pork needs to be very tender.
DICED CHICKEN, which blends well with the apricot flavouring, is another food that is enhanced by the piquant taste of sweet and sour sauce. To give an interesting texture, add a few blanched almonds at stage 8.
For another sweet-sour sauce that is suitable for all types of food, see page 153.

Speedy Meal

The ideas opposite on sweet and sour dishes can be adapted when heating canned ham, etc. Prepare the sweet and sour mixture then add diced ham or luncheon meat, etc., and heat.

Slimming Tips

Obviously the sweet ingredients incorporated opposite are not ideal on any slimming diet, so here is a *'low calorie' sweet-sour sauce:*
blend 2 tablespoons vinegar with 2 tablespoons finely chopped mustard pickle, also blend 3 tablespoons orange juice with 1 or 2 average strength sugar substitute tablets, or equivalent in liquid sugar substitute. Heat together, add a few cocktail onions if wished, and/or a little well drained chopped canned pineapple.

Honey Crumbed Ham

Serves 12–15
Cooking time 3½–4 hours, see stage 2

Ingredients	Metric	Imperial
forehock ham	3 kilos	6–6½ lb.
peppercorns	2 teaspoons	2 teaspoons
bay leaf	1	1
TO COAT:		
thin honey	4–5 tablespoons	4–5 tablespoons
lemon juice	1–2 tablespoons	1–2 tablespoons
crisp breadcrumbs (raspings)	6–8 tablespoons	6–8 tablespoons

1 Soak the forehock of ham overnight, then drain well.
2 Put into a pan, cover completely with cold water, add the peppercorns and bay leaf; simmer steadily after the liquid comes to the boil, allowing 30 minutes per lb. (1 hour per kilo) and 30 minutes over.
3 When cooked, allow to cool slightly in the liquid, then cut off the skin; return to the liquid if serving cold, as this helps the ham to remain moist.
4 Blend the honey with the lemon juice and brush this over the fat, to give a thin coating.
5 Press the raspings on top of this to give a smooth coating; do this with a palette knife so they do not 'drop off' when the ham is carved.
6 Serve with a pineapple and lettuce salad, see below.

Pineapple and lettuce salad

Choose fresh pineapple when good and inexpensive, or substitute canned pineapple rings or fingers (not chunks). Wash and dry the lettuce, arrange in a bowl, then top with the skinned sliced pineapple. Add a little French dressing, page 155, just before serving.

Terrine of Ham and Veal

Serves 8–14*
Cooking time 2 hours

Ingredients	Metric	Imperial
fillet of veal	1 kilo	2 lb.
uncooked ham	1 kilo	2 lb.
streaky bacon	½ kilo	1 lb.
chopped thyme	1 teaspoon	1 teaspoon
powdered cinnamon	¼–½ teaspoon	¼–½ teaspoon
seasoning	to taste	to taste
eggs	2	2
sherry *or* brandy	1 wineglass	1 wineglass
bay leaf	1 or 2	1 or 2

*8 as main dish, 14 as hors d'oeuvre.

1 Cut the veal and half the ham in pieces; mince finely.
2 Slice the rest of the ham; remove bacon rinds.
3 Mix the thyme with the minced meat, add cinnamon, seasoning, beaten eggs and sherry or brandy (or a mixture).
4 Use about two-thirds of the bacon rashers to line the bottom and sides of a 1½–2-litre (3–4-pint) ovenproof dish.
5 Put in one-third of the minced mixture and a bay leaf, half the ham, more minced meat, the rest of the ham, then the remainder of the minced meat and a topping of the bacon rashers.
6 Steam for about 2 hours, or bake for the same time in a slow to very moderate oven, standing in a dish of water.
7 Put a plate and weight on top, allow to cool; remove any surplus fat. Serve cold with salad.

Automatic Oven

The hock of ham may be cooked as 'boiled' bacon in the oven, see the comments on page 62.

Speedy Meal

Buy a joint of boiled ham and coat in the same way; the combination of honey, lemon and crumbs is very pleasant.
If using canned pineapple in the salad use pineapple syrup in place of lemon, if wished.
See page 61 for hints on cooking bacon (or ham) in a pressure cooker.

Slimming Tips

While ham is fairly high in calories, (because of the generous amount of fat found in most hams) if you serve just the lean part with the minimum of fat you can include this in most slimming diets. Obviously you would avoid the honey and crumb coating.
Fresh pineapple is excellent on a low calorie diet.

Home Freezing

See comments on page 59.
Pineapple is *not* a good fruit to freeze.

Automatic Oven

This can be prepared and left to cook in an automatic oven. Cover both the terrine and the dish of water with foil so the water does not evaporate, for it is important that the sides of the terrine do not become dry.
Use the recipe opposite for other terrines that may be cooked in an automatic oven; choose chicken or pheasant in place of veal; mince the uncooked meat from the legs with half the ham, stage 1, and slice the breast meat and use with the sliced ham, stage 5.

Home Freezing

If wishing to freeze a terrine it is better to choose chicken or game rather than veal, for the meat retains flavour and texture better.
The ham and veal terrine will freeze for a short time (not more than 2–3 weeks) after that it does become rather flavourless.

Moussaka

Serves 4–6
Cooking time 1¾–2¼ hours
Oven temperature 325–350° F. (170–180° C.), Gas Mark 3–4

Ingredients	Metric	Imperial
margarine *or* fat	75–100 grammes	3–4 oz.
onions	2 large	2 large
aubergines	1–2	1–2
peeled potatoes	½ kilo	1 lb.
seasoning	to taste	to taste
minced lamb	¾ kilo	1½ lb.
tomatoes	4	4
FOR THE SAUCE:		
margarine *or* butter	50 grammes	2 oz.
flour *or*	50 grames	2 oz.
cornflour	25 grammes	1 oz.
milk	568 ml	1 pint
seasoning	to taste	to taste
Cheddar cheese	100 grammes	4 oz.
eggs	1–2	1–2
grated nutmeg	pinch	pinch
TO GARNISH:		
parsley	1 sprig	1 sprig

1 Heat the margarine, fry the thinly sliced onions for a few minutes, lift on to a plate; toss the sliced aubergines and potatoes in any fat remaining in the pan, for about 10 minutes. If you dislike the slightly bitter taste of the skin of aubergines, either peel these, or score the skin and sprinkle with salt then leave for 20 minutes *before* slicing. Season the vegetables well.
2 Mix the fried onions with the minced lamb and the skinned sliced tomatoes, season this mixture.
3 Melt the margarine in a saucepan (the pan used for frying onions, etc., is ideal as it gives flavour to the sauce).
4 Stir in the flour or cornflour, cook for several minutes, then gradually blend in the milk.
5 Bring to the boil and cook until thickened enough to coat the back of a wooden spoon.
6 Season well, add the grated cheese and the beaten egg or eggs and nutmeg, but do not cook again.
7 Put a potato and aubergine layer into the bottom of the dish, then a thin layer of sauce.
8 Follow with a meat layer, then a little more sauce; continue to fill the dish like this ending with potatoes and sauce.
9 Cover the dish, and bake for 1½–2 hours in the centre of a very moderate oven; the cooking time depends upon the depth of the dish; when cooked in a shallow dish as shown in the picture opposite, allow about 1½ hours.
10 Lift the lid of the casserole towards the end of the cooking period to brown the sauce, or keep back half the sauce, heat this *gently* without boiling and pour over the Moussaka just before serving.
11 Garnish with parsley as in the picture.

Automatic Oven

This dish is ideal to leave in the oven, for the potatoes are covered with sauce and also have had a thin coating of fat at stage 1, so will not discolour. The dish is so satisfying that other vegetables are not necessary; it is better served with a salad.

Cook a baked custard, page 187, or milk pudding, page 201, with this.

Speedy Meal

A 'mock' Moussaka can be made by topping layers of hot sliced potatoes and cooked or canned meat with a cheese sauce, and heating through in the oven.

Home Freezing

This freezes well for a short period. The sauce may separate, especially if made with flour, but this does not matter for it becomes 'part' of the complete dish. Cook, but do not over-cook before freezing, so that it is not dried and spoiled when reheated. It is better to allow the Moussaka to thaw out before reheating.

Do *not* freeze uncooked.

Variations on Moussaka

USING COOKED LAMB: fry the onions and the other vegetables a little longer until becoming soft, then shorten the cooking time by 30–40 minutes.

WITHOUT AUBERGINES: increase the potatoes to about ¾ kilo (1½ lb.) to compensate for the aubergines.

VEGETARIAN MOUSSAKA: instead of minced raw meat use 200–250 grammes (8–10 oz.) lentils. Soak in water to cover, simmer until a fairly soft purée, mix with onions, etc., and proceed as before.

Creamed Kidneys

Serves 4
Cooking time 20 minutes

Ingredients	Metric	Imperial
bacon	4–6 rashers	4–6 rashers
butter	25 grammes	1 oz.
lamb's *or* pig's kidneys	6–8	6–8
mushrooms	50 grammes	2 oz.
brown stock	6 tablespoons	6 tablespoons
thick cream	142 ml	¼ pint
seasoning	to taste	to taste
TO GARNISH:		
chopped chives	1 tablespoon	1 tablespoon

1 Remove rind from the rashers, chop bacon, then fry rinds for a few minutes with the butter.
2 Remove rinds from pan, heat the butter with the bacon fat, then add diced bacon, sliced skinned kidneys and sliced mushrooms.
3 Fry gently for 10 minutes, then add rest of ingredients and simmer for 5 minutes. Top with the chives.

Speedy Meal

This dish may be made with canned kidneys. Chop a little bacon, fry for a few minutes with mushrooms if wished, add the canned kidneys and heat thoroughly; stir in the cream and serve.

Home Freezing

Kidneys (like all offal) freeze well for a limited period—read the paragraph on storage times on page 59. If you wish to freeze complete dish, proceed to stage 2 then fry for 5 minutes only, add the stock, but *not* the cream. Reheat from the frozen state, and when thawed out, check that kidneys are tender, *then* add the cream and simmer gently.

Beef Olives

Serves 4
Cooking time 2–2½ hours
Oven temperature 300–325° F. (150–170° C.), Gas Mark 2–3

Ingredients	Metric	Imperial
stewing beef *or* topside	½–¾ kilo	1–1¼ lb.
onion	1	1
carrot	1	1
fat	50 grammes	2 oz.
seasoning	to taste	to taste
bay leaf	1	1
stock	426 ml	¾ pint
flour	25 grammes	1 oz.
FOR THE STUFFING:		
breadcrumbs	50 grammes	2 oz.
suet *or* margarine	25–50 grammes	1–2 oz.
chopped parsley	1 tablespoon	1 tablespoon
dried thyme *or* savory	1 teaspoon	1 teaspoon
grated lemon rind	1 teaspoon	1 teaspoon
seasoning	to taste	to taste
egg	1	1
milk	to mix	to mix

1 Ask your butcher to thinly slice topside or chuck steak into pieces 10 by 7·5 cm (4 by 3 inches).
2 Prepare the stuffing by combining all ingredients; the margarine should be melted.
3 Spread some of the stuffing on each piece of flattened, beaten meat, roll up, or form into a round like an olive, and secure with thick white cotton or very fine string.
4 Peel and slice the onion and carrot.
5 Heat the fat, fry the onion and beef olives; add the carrot, seasoning, bay leaf, and stock blended with the flour, cook until thickened.
6 Cover and simmer until tender, or transfer to covered casserole for about 2½ hours in a slow to very moderate oven. Remove the string before serving.
7 Arrange the beef olives and sauce in the centre of the dish, with cooked mixed vegetables (macedoine), and a border of piped or neatly forked creamed potatoes.

Automatic Oven

Use the centre position. Complete the menu with Scalloped potatoes, Macedoine vegetables, page 114, Apple Brown Betty, page 206.

Speedy Meal

Cook in a pressure cooker for 15 minutes at 15 lb. pressure; allow pressure to drop at room temperature.
a) use a packet stuffing,
b) use canned tomato or mulligatawny soup in place of stages 4–5; omit the vegetables.

Mixer

Make the stuffing in the blender as recipe on page 138.

Slimming Tips

Use unthickened stock or tomato juice in place of thickened sauce, or select one of the low calorie stuffings which you will find on page 90. Or, simply blend chopped mushrooms and skinned chopped tomatoes together and season—use in place of a stuffing.

Home Freezing

Make the sauce with 15 grammes (½ oz.) cornflour instead of 25 grammes (1 oz.) flour. Reduce the cooking time to 1–1½ hours to allow for reheating without over-cooking.

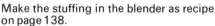

12. Paprika beef and rice, see page 76

Stewed Steak and Kidney

Serves 4–5
Cooking time 2 hours*

Ingredients	Metric	Imperial
stewing steak	½–¾ kilo	1¼–1½ lb.
lamb's kidneys	2–3	2–3
or ox kidney	100–150 grammes	4–6 oz.
seasoning	to taste	to taste
fat	25–50 grammes	1–2 oz.
water** *or* brown stock	568 ml	1 pint
flour *or*	25 grammes	1 oz.
cornflour	1 tablespoon	½ oz.

*naturally this varies according to the tenderness of the steak and size of pieces. The time given should be treated as minimum cooking time.

**there is really no need to add a stock cube since the kidney gives a strong flavour.

1 Cut the meat into neat pieces and season well.
2 Heat the fat in the bottom of a strong saucepan, and turn the meat in this until lightly browned.
3 Add most of cold liquid, bring to boiling point, cover pan, lower heat, and simmer until meat is tender.
4 Blend the flour or cornflour with the remaining cold liquid, stir into the stock and continue stirring until the sauce thickens.

TO ADD EXTRA FLAVOURING–add fried sliced onions after stage 3; put in approximately 100 grammes (4 oz.) small button mushrooms about 20 minutes before meat is cooked; if you are rather short of meat, add canned haricot beans towards the end of cooking time, or use fresh cooked haricot beans instead; use less stock and substitute tomato purée or tomato juice or red wine.

Automatic Oven

Prepare to stage 3, but put into a covered casserole and cook for about 2–2½ hours in the centre of a slow to very moderate oven.

Speedy Meal

Mix a can of stewed steak and a can of kidneys and heat gently. A pressure cooker is also excellent for this type of stew. Toss the meat in the hot fat as stage 2. Add *half* the amount of liquid given in the recipe, then cook at 15 lb. pressure for 15 minutes. *To cool rapidly:* make sure the stew does not over-cook, take the cooker to the sink, *do not remove* pressure weight. Either allow the cold water from the tap to flow over the top of the cooker until the pressure drops or stand the cooker in a little cold water. Remove lid, blend the flour or cornflour with a little cold liquid, stir into the pressure cooker and cook steadily until you have a thickened gravy.

Home Freezing

Either freeze meats *before* cooking; or cook as recipe (but for a slightly shorter period) then freeze. You can line a casserole or dish with foil, put in mixture and freeze this, then lift from container to store. Use cornflour to thicken, or *thicken after* reheating.

York Hot-Pot

Serves 4–5
Cooking time 2¼ hours
Oven temperature 300–325° F. (150–170° C.), Gas Mark 2–3

Ingredients	Metric	Imperial
peeled potatoes	½ kilo	1 lb.
peeled onions	½ kilo	1 lb.
seasoning	to taste	to taste
cooked ham	100 grammes	4 oz.
stewing veal	½ kilo	1 lb.
white *or* brown stock	284 ml	½ pint
margarine *or* dripping	25 grammes	1 oz.
TO GARNISH:		
chopped parsley	1 tablespoon	1 tablespoon

1 Cut potatoes and onions into thin slices.
2 Put about a third of potatoes at bottom of casserole, season lightly.
3 Blend onions with chopped cooked ham and diced stewing veal.
4 Put half meat mixture into casserole, add seasoning, then a layer of potatoes; put remainder of meat and onion mixture into casserole, season and add the liquid.
5 Cover with sliced seasoned potatoes and lid of casserole.
6 Cook for 1¾ hours in the centre of a slow to very moderate oven.
7 Lift lid off casserole, spread 25 grammes (1 oz.) margarine or dripping over potatoes, then leave uncovered so they brown well and continue cooking for a further 30 minutes.
8 Top with chopped parsley before serving.

Automatic Oven

A typical 'hot-pot', as the recipe opposite, is ideal for cooking in an automatic oven, although you must vary the method slightly. Fill the dish to the end of stage 4, then melt the margarine or dripping in a large saucepan and toss remaining potatoes in this. When coated with fat and beginning to change colour, put over top of the meat mixture and leave the casserole uncovered. In this way you prevent the potatoes discolouring.

Mixer

The slicer attachment on a mixer is ideal for slicing potatoes for a hot-pot, but as they will be rather thin they will become softer than usual.

Home Freezing

Do not over-cook the hot-pot, otherwise the potatoes tend to become over-soft when stored and then reheated. Not the most successful of dishes for freezing, as one seems to lose some of the flavour of the meat, etc.

MEAT PIES AND PUDDINGS

The recipes on this, and the next page, for steak and kidney pudding and pie are basic ones that can be varied by using different meats or a combination of meat and vegetables. You will find more savoury pastry dishes in the section that begins on page 177.

Steak and Kidney Pudding

Serves 4–6
Cooking time minimum of 3½–4 hours

Ingredients	Metric	Imperial
FOR SUET CRUST PASTRY:		
preferably self-raising flour	200–250 grammes*	8–10 oz.*
salt	good pinch	good pinch
suet	100–125 grammes*	4–5 oz.*
water	to mix	to mix
FOR THE FILLING:		
stewing steak	½–¾ kilo	1¼–1½ lb.
ox kidney	100–150 grammes	4–6 oz.
flour	25 grammes	1 oz.
seasoning	to taste	to taste
stock *or* water	2–3 tablespoons	2–3 tablespoons

*the thickness of the pastry depends upon personal taste. Allow half suet to flour, see page 174.

1 Prepare steamer. Make pastry as page 174. Turn pastry on to a lightly floured board; roll out two-thirds *thinly*, as this pastry rises if self-raising flour is used.
2 Line a well-greased ¾–1-litre (1½–2-pint) pudding basin with the pastry.
3 Either dice the steak and kidney, or prepare in the traditional way, i.e. cut narrow strips of steak, place a tiny piece of kidney on each strip, then roll neatly.
4 Mix the flour and seasoning on a plate and roll the meat in this.
5 Put steak and kidney into basin, add cold stock or water.
6 Roll out remaining pastry to form the lid.
7 Brush the edges with cold water, cover the pudding and press together to seal.
8 Cover with greased paper or foil and steam for 3½–4 hours; longer if you like rather large pieces of meat.
9 For a good result, make sure the water is boiling rapidly when the pudding goes on and always replenish with boiling water.
10 The heat may be reduced after the first 1½ hours when the crust will have risen.
11 To serve: the pudding should be lifted from the steamer, and if it is a plain white basin, wrap a folded serviette round this; with modern glassware this is not necessary.
12 It is wise to have a sauceboat of hot stock ready so that when the first slice of pudding is cut, you can 'fill up' with hot stock. If preferred, use a reasonably thin gravy.

Automatic Oven

It is *better* to steam a steak and kidney pudding on top of the cooker, but if you have to leave the pudding 'unattended' and are afraid of the pan boiling dry, it is a good idea to put it into the oven: switch on or light the gas and commence cooking at once.

Prepare and cover the pudding as the recipe opposite; stand in a container of boiling water, then cover both the pudding *and* the container with foil, so that little water evaporates during cooking. Cook for a minumum of 4½–5 hours in centre of a very moderate to moderate oven.

Speedy Meal

Cooking time is saved if the steak and kidney is cooked in a pressure pan for about 10 minutes at 15 lb. pressure. Cool rapidly, then put the meat and a little unthickened liquid into basin lined with suet crust and steam for 2 hours. You could also use canned stewing steak, but this does become very overdone by the time it has been cooked in suet crust.

Home Freezing

Steak and kidney puddings or any other meat puddings are some of the most successful meat dishes to freeze. The pudding can be prepared and frozen *uncooked*: but I find the best result is obtained by cooking the pudding for about 3 hours; cooling, then freezing it. When ready to reheat you must bring the ovenproof basin out of the freezer for 1½–2 hours before reheating, otherwise the basin will crack. However, if you cook the pudding in a foil basin or line a breakable basin in foil before making the pudding, you can remove the foil-wrapped pudding from the basin when it is frozen. This means you can bring the steak and kidney pudding straight from the freezer, put into the steamer and thaw out and complete cooking at *same time*.

Allow about 2 hours cooking.

More meat puddings

LAMB AND MUSHROOM PUDDING—use diced lean lamb instead of steak, and button mushrooms instead of diced kidney, add 12 small onions or shallots; reduce cooking time to 2¼ hours.
KENT PORK PUDDING—use diced fillet of pork instead of steak, mix with diced kidney, 2 peeled diced dessert apples, 2 chopped onions; season and flavour with chopped sage.
LIVER AND VEGETABLE PUDDING—use diced pig's liver and mixed vegetables in place of steak and kidney.

Steak and Kidney Pie

Serves 4–6
Cooking time 2 hours
Oven temperature 450–475° F. (230–240° C.), Gas Mark 8, then 325–350° F. (170–180° C.), Gas Mark 3

Ingredients	Metric	Imperial
FOR FLAKY PASTRY:		
preferably plain flour	150 or 170 grammes*	6 oz.*
salt	pinch	pinch
fat	100 or 115 grammes*	4½ oz.*
cold water	to mix	to mix
FOR THE FILLING:		
stewing steak	½–¾ kilo	1–1½ lb.
lamb's *or* sheep's kidneys	2	2
or ox kidney	about 100 grammes	about 4 oz.
seasoning	to taste	to taste
flour	15–25 grammes**	½–1 oz.**
beef stock	284 ml	½ pint
TO GLAZE:		
egg	1	1
milk *or* water	1 tablespoon	1 tablespoon

*see comments about metric conversion on page 171.
**depending on thickness, or use half quantity of cornflour.

1 Make pastry as page 175, keep in a cool place until ready to use.
2 Cut steak and kidney into small pieces and roll in seasoned flour or cut thin narrow strips of stewing steak and cut kidney into tiny pieces. Put a piece of kidney on each strip of stewing steak and roll firmly, then toss in seasoned flour.
3 Stand a pie support or egg cup in the centre of the dish to support the pastry, and then put in meat.
4 Pour over enough stock to come half-way over the meat.
5 Do not put more, otherwise the liquid may boil out in cooking (you can make extra gravy if required).
6 Roll out the pastry and cover the pie.
7 Use any scraps of pastry to form into 'leaves' and a 'rose' or 'tassel' to decorate the pie.
8 Brush the top of the pie with beaten egg mixed with milk or water, pressing the rose and leaves in position.
9 Make a tiny slit in the pastry over the pie support or egg cup to allow the steam to escape, and stand the pie dish on a baking tray.
10 Bake in the centre of a hot oven for about 15 minutes, to give the pastry a chance to rise. Put a piece of paper over the top of the pie, and lower the heat to very moderate to make sure the meat is cooked. Allow about a further 1½ hours.

Note: if preferred, the steak and kidney may be cooked almost entirely as the recipe on page 82. The cooked meat should then be placed in the pie dish and allowed to cool; (if steaming, it is difficult to keep the pastry cool and a good shape). Roll out pastry and continue as stages 7–9. Bake for approximately 15 minutes in a hot oven, then 25–30 minutes at a very moderate heat.

MUSHROOM AND STEAK PIE–add about 100 grammes (4 oz.) button mushrooms to the steak.

VEAL AND HAM PIE–use diced stewing veal instead of steak, and diced ham instead of kidney; flavour the flour with a little grated lemon rind and pinch dried lemon thyme.

Automatic Oven

To cook a steak and kidney pie in an automatic oven, you will be wise to pre-cook the meat as stewed steak and kidney, page 82, and to use either flaky pastry, as the recipe opposite, or, better still, short crust pastry. This means the pastry cannot be over-cooked. Set the oven for only *1 hour* cooking time and set the oven to moderately hot only, as you cannot reduce the heat if the meal is left 'unattended'. Naturally, you would not have such a good result with flaky pastry as when using the temperature opposite, that is why short crust is a wiser choice.

Include a casserole of frozen vegetables and *small* potatoes and a Compôte of fruit in the coolest part of the oven.

Speedy Meal

Pre-cook the meat in a pressure cooker for about 15 minutes at 15 lb. pressure, reduce the pressure rapidly, and thicken the gravy. Put into pie dish, allow to cool, then cover with pastry and bake until crisp and golden brown.

Home Freezing

There are various ways of freezing steak and kidney pies—

a) you can make but *not* cook the pie and freeze this, then cook from the frozen state. This is very satisfactory.
b) you can cook the pie as the recipe opposite, and freeze it. If you do this, thaw out before reheating, as the pastry becomes *too* brown before the meat is hot.
c) Cook the meat in a pie dish or a foil-lined pie dish and freeze; roll the pastry to a shape to fit over the pie dish, but freeze on a baking tray—when firm you can lift this off the tray and wrap well. To reheat: thaw out the meat sufficiently so the pie dish will not crack (unless you have frozen in foil; in this case put back into pie dish). Heat through the meat; bake the pastry separately and lift on to the pie dish when cooked. This sounds more troublesome but is on the whole better than b) where the pastry can sometimes become rather 'soft' as it thaws out and bakes; or can, on the other hand, crack a little—see under freezing pastry page 171.

USING MINCED BEEF: minced beef is economical as it can be used as the basis for a complete meal or as a sauce, see below. This sauce is extravagant for a family meal, but could be made more economical by leaving out the mushrooms and the red wine. In order to make a really good minced meat mixture, break up the lumps of meat as they start to form, do this either with a fork or with a wooden spoon. Use minced beef soon after buying, or store with care.

Spaghetti Bolognese

Serves 4
Cooking time 1 hour

Ingredients	Metric	Imperial
FOR THE SAUCE:		
butter	25 grammes	1 oz.
olive oil	1 tablespoon	1 tablespoon
finely chopped mushrooms	50 grammes	2 oz.
shredded onion	1	1
shredded carrot	1	1
minced raw beef	100–150 grammes	4–6 oz.
small can *or* tube	1	1
concentrated tomato		
purée, *or* small can		
Italian tomatoes	1	1
seasoning	to taste	to taste
good stock if using	284 ml	½ pint
canned tomatoes*		
red wine	142 ml	¼ pint
spaghetti	150–200 grammes	6–8 oz.
Parmesan cheese	50–75 grammes	2–3 oz.

*slightly more if using tomato purée.

1 First make the sauce; heat the butter and oil.
2 Fry mushrooms, onion and carrot.
3 Stir in the meat, simmer, then add remaining ingredients and cook until thickened, stirring occasionally.
4 While sauce is simmering, cook the spaghetti in plenty of boiling salted water until *just* tender (10–12 minutes).
5 Strain, put on to hot serving plates or dishes.
6 Top with the sauce and serve with grated Parmesan cheese.

To give a change of flavour, omit the red wine and stir a little cream into the sauce just before serving. See picture facing page 64.

Speedy Meal
Make the sauce with minced *cooked* meat and half the quantity of stock and cook for 20–30 minutes only.

Mixer
The raw or cooked meat may be put through the mincing attachment of the mixer. Use a medium speed and 'feed' the meat through steadily, pushing this down with the utensil supplied for this purpose.

Slimming Tips
This Bolognese sauce is quite suitable for a slimming diet (without the spaghetti of course); since this thickens with evaporation rather than by using flour or cornflour. Serve as a sauce over cooked marrow or courgettes, or other low calorie vegetables.

Home Freezing
It is convenient to store uncooked minced beef to use for sauces, etc. but even in a freezer the storage time must be relatively short, since there are so many exposed cut surfaces in minced beef.
The Bolognese sauce freezes extremely well; cook as recipe then freeze, and re-heat just before required. There is no need to defrost before cooking.

Hamburgers

Serves 4
Cooking time 25–30 minutes

Ingredients	Metric	Imperial
minced beef	½ kilo	1 lb.
onions	1 large *or*	1 large *or*
	2 medium	2 medium
seasoning	to taste	to taste
mixed herbs	½ teaspoon	½ teaspoon
chopped parsley	1 heaped	1 heaped
	teaspoon	teaspoon
Worcestershire sauce	1 teaspoon	1 teaspoon
TO FRY:		
fat	25 grammes	1 oz.

1 Put meat into a basin, add grated onion, seasoning, herbs, parsley and sauce; mix thoroughly together.
2 Form into large flat cakes and fry steadily in hot fat.
3 Serve on buttered hamburger rolls or with vegetables.

Mixer
Put the raw meat through the mincing attachment of the mixer. To make a more economical Hamburger put a medium sized raw potato through the mincer as well; drain this well and mix with the meat before forming into cakes.

Slimming Tips
Hamburgers are a low calorie form of meat cake. Bake or place on foil on the grill pan and cook on either side without using fat.

Home Freezing
Freeze uncooked cakes on flat trays; lift off and pack with a square of waxed or greaseproof paper between each. Fry bake or grill from the frozen state.

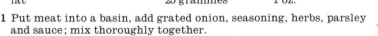

Meat Balls

Serves 4–5
Cooking time 10–15 minutes

Ingredients	Metric	Imperial
onion	1 medium	1 medium
butter *or* fat	25 grammes	1 oz.
breadcrumbs	50 grammes	2 oz.
milk *or* stock	6 tablespoons	6 tablespoons
minced beef	300–325 grammes	12 oz.
minced bacon *or* pork	100 grammes	4 oz.
egg	1	1
cornflour	1 *level* tablespoon	1 *level* tablespoon
seasoning	to taste	to taste
chopped herbs	to taste	to taste
TO FRY:		
fat *or* butter	50–75 grammes	2–3 oz.

1 Chop the onion finely, or grate this, and fry in hot butter or fat until tender, but not brown.
2 Put the crumbs into a basin, add the milk or stock, leave for about 15 minutes until the bread is soft.
3 Mix the onion and any fat in the pan with the bread and rest of the ingredients.
4 Form into small balls, using a spoon and your hands to shape them.
5 Heat half the fat, fry as many meat balls as you can get into the pan, turn over gently and cook until brown.
6 Repeat with the rest of the meat mixture; serve hot or cold. Gravy can be made in the frying pan, if wished.

Speedy Meal

Buy ready-minced beef and omit the bacon or pork; or omit crumbs and stock *and* minced bacon or pork, and substitute 150–200 grammes (6–8 oz.) sausagemeat.

Mixer

Use the mincing attachment for mincing (a) the onion and (b) the beef and bacon or pork, and use the liquidiser for making the crumbs.

Slimming Tips

If the balls are poached in very hot beef stock rather than fried in fat, they are far less fattening, and are very delicious. Use low calorie bread for breadcrumbs or make crumbs from 'slimming crispbread' or rolls.

Home Freezing

Freeze the mixture *after* cooking; it is difficult to keep them a good shape if you freeze before cooking.

Burgundy Meat Loaf

Serves 6–8
Cooking time 1¾ hours
Oven temperature 325–350° F. (170–180° C.), Gas Mark 3–4

Ingredients	Metric	Imperial
onions	2 medium	2 medium
garlic (optional)	1 clove	1 clove
butter *or* margarine	50 grammes	2 oz.
Red Burgundy	5 tablespoons	5 tablespoons
slice of bread (without crust)	50 grammes	2 oz.
fresh brisket *or* topside	½ kilo	1 lb.
pork sausagemeat	¼ kilo	½ lb.
eggs	2	2
seasoning	to taste	to taste
dried mixed herbs	pinch	pinch

1 Chop the peeled onions finely, and crush the clove of garlic.
2 Heat most of the butter and cook the onion until transparent, then add the wine and simmer for a few minutes.
3 Add the bread and beat into the onion mixture until smooth.
4 Mince the meat then blend with the onion mixture, sausagemeat and eggs.
5 Taste the mixture and add seasoning and herbs.
6 With the remaining butter, grease a 1–1½-kilo (2–3-lb.) loaf tin and piece of foil and press the mixture into tin.
7 Cover with greased foil, stand in a dish of cold water and bake for 1½ hours.
8 Turn out and serve hot with an Espagnole sauce and vegetables, or cold with salad. If serving cold it is a good idea to put weights on top of loaf as it cools so that it becomes firmer in texture and easier to slice.

Automatic Oven

The meat loaf can be cooked in an automatic oven; there is little fear of the water (see stage 7) evaporating during cooking, but to be absolutely sure this does not happen cover both the loaf *and* the dish of water with foil. To make a complete meal cook Carrots Vichy, page 114, Jacket potatoes, and a Caramel custard, page 187 in the coolest part of the oven (also in a dish of water). If you think the oven is too warm for this, cook a 'steamed' pudding instead, see recipes on page 202.

Mixer

Most of the ingredients can be put through the mincing attachment of the mixer; but do them in the following order so you have the best result: 1) mince the meat, then 2) the onion, and 3) finally, put the slice of bread through the mincer to make sure no onion is wasted. This saves beating the bread as stage 3.

Home Freezing

This meat loaf and most meat loaves freeze extremely well. Wrap very carefully. Allow to defrost before reheating gently, or serving cold. Use within 6 weeks to 2 months.

COLD MEAT DISHES AND MOULDS

The recipes that follow are for jellied meat moulds, etc., that are ideal to serve for cold meals. The dishes can be considered basic recipes and can be varied in many ways, i.e. add extra herbs, different vegetables or use a mixture of meats.

Remember, it is only the head of veal or pork, or pig's trotters, or calf's foot that contain enough natural gelatine to set a mould or brawn. If using other meats, you must *add* a trotter or foot, or use powder gelatine. When making a galantine (as recipe below) remember that to keep a moist texture to the meat it needs careful cooking in the oven.

Beef Galantine

Serves 6
Cooking time 1½–2 hours, see stage 3

Ingredients	Metric	Imperial
topside of beef	½ kilo	1 lb.
fat bacon	100 grammes	4 oz.
pork sausagemeat	200 grammes	8 oz.
mushrooms	50 grammes	2 oz.
onions	50 grammes	2 oz.
oatmeal *or* breadcrumbs	50 grammes	2 oz.
chopped herbs	to taste	to taste
seasoning	to taste	to taste
stock *or* tomato juice	5 tablespoons	5 tablespoons
eggs	2 small	2 large

1 Mince raw beef and bacon together, blend with rest of the ingredients–the mushrooms and onions must be very finely chopped–mix very thoroughly.
2 Put into a greased 1-kilo (2-lb.) loaf tin and cover with greased foil.
3 Stand in a large pan with water coming half way up the tin and steam gently for 1½ hours, or cook for about 2 hours in the centre of a very moderate oven. If baking, also stand tin in a dish containing water to keep sides moist.
4 Turn out and serve hot with vegetables and a brown or tomato sauce, or serve cold with salad.

Automatic Oven
The galantine should be cooked as timing, etc. in stages 3 and 4 opposite. Cook a milk pudding or baked egg custard in the coolest part of the oven, large Jacket potatoes and a casserole of whole carrots could complete the meal. (The Jacket potatoes may be topped with chive and parsley butter, i.e. blend generous amounts of the chopped herbs with the butter.)

Speedy Meal
If the galantine mixture is cooked in 6 small individual dishes they will take about 35–40 minutes steaming or 45–50 minutes baking.

Slimming Tips
In order to make the galantine less fattening, you could omit the oatmeal or breadcrumbs from the recipe. The amount of liquid could also be reduced to 2 tablespoons only.

Home Freezing
Freezes excellently either cooked or uncooked. If freezing before or after cooking use an extra tablespoon of liquid as the mixture tends to dry out. Naturally, if you have made the galantine and are freezing a portion you cannot adapt liquid, so wrap very well. Defrost for several hours at room temperature before cooking, reheating or serving cold.

Savoury Meat Shape

Serves 4–5
Cooking time 40 minutes

Ingredients	Metric	Imperial
cooked meats–use beef, lamb, pork, veal *or* any poultry	approx. ½ kilo	1 lb.
slice of bread (without crust)	50–75 grammes	2–3 oz.
milk	4 tablespoons	4 tablespoons
seasoning	to taste	to taste
chutney	2 tablespoons	2 tablespoons
chopped herbs	to taste	to taste
stock	2 tablespoons	2 tablespoons

1 Mince the various meats, put into a saucepan (the greater the mixture of meat the better).
2 Put bread and milk in a basin, leave for about 15 minutes, then tip soft bread and any milk left into the saucepan.
3 Add rest of ingredients, heat together until the bread has thickened the mixture.
4 Transfer to a greased basin, cover with foil, steam for 30 minutes. Serve hot or cold.

Automatic Oven
This could be cooked for approximately 35–40 minutes in a moderate oven. To complete menu, cook Peas â la française, page 120, *Potato soufflé* (to make this blend 2 eggs with just about ½ kilo (1 lb.) creamy mashed potatoes, and put into a soufflé dish), and *Fruit sponge*–cook sponge pudding (follow recipe for Victoria Sandwich with 2 eggs etc.) over the top of a fruit pie filling, in the centre of the oven; you may need to lower the heat when removing the Meat mould.

Home Freezing
This mould freezes well for a limited period of about 6 weeks–after this time it tends to lose flavour.

Pork Brawn

Serves 5–6
Cooking time 2½–3 hours

Ingredients	Metric	Imperial
pig's head	½ large	½ large
water	to cover	to cover
seasoning	to taste	to taste
bouquet garni	spray	spray
stewing steak	200 grammes	8 oz.

1 Wash the pig's head thoroughly in cold water.
2 Put into a large saucepan with water to cover, seasoning and the herbs.
3 Simmer very gently for 1½ hours in a covered pan, then add the diced stewing steak and simmer for a further 1–1½ hours or until the steak and head are very tender.
4 Cool enough to handle, then lift the head on to a dish and cut all the meat away, then cut this into neat dice.
5 Put into a basin or plain mould with the well drained steak (mix fat and lean meat together); cover with foil or a plate so that it does not dry while the stock is simmering.
6 Boil the stock rapidly in an open pan until reduced to just *under* 426 ml (approximately ¾ pint).
7 Strain over the meat and leave to set.

Pork and Tongue Brawn

If you use a whole pig's head and make a larger brawn you will naturally have the tongue, but an even better brawn is produced if you use 3 extra small lambs' or 2 pigs' tongues, or 1 calf's tongue. Add these at stage 3 if using tiny tender lambs' tongues, but at stage 2 with the larger tongues.

Pork and Carrot Brawn

Carrots add colour and absorb some of the rich flavour of the pork. Use same proportions and method as the brawn above, but add ½ kilo (1 lb.) peeled diced carrots 30 minutes before the end of cooking, this makes sure the carrots are cooked but retain their firm texture.
Pack the carrots and meat into the basin as stage 5, then continue as the basic recipe. Serve with pickled gherkins or cucumber and green salad. Serves 6–8.

Aspic Meat Mould

Serves 5–6
Cooking time 1½ hours

Ingredients	Metric	Imperial
stewing veal	½–¾ kilo	1¼–1½ lb.
white stock	568 ml	1 pint
onions	2	2
bouquet garni	spray	spray
seasoning	to taste	to taste
carrots	5–6 large	5–6 large
aspic jelly	1 packet	1 packet
TO GARNISH:		
parsley	1 sprig	1 sprig
tomatoes	3–4	3–4

1 Dice meat, simmer in stock with whole onions, herbs and seasoning for 1 hour; add carrots, finish cooking.
2 Make up aspic jelly with 426 ml (¾ pint) strained veal stock; pour a little into a plain mould. Make a design of sliced carrots on this, allow to set.
3 Add meat, diced carrots and rest of the liquid aspic jelly; when set, garnish with parsley and tomatoes.

Speedy Meal

A pressure cooker is excellent for cooking a pig's head (or a calf's or sheep's head which are also used in brawns). Prepare the head as stage 1 in the recipe opposite. Put into the pressure cooker (you may need to halve the head or ask the butcher to do this for you so it fits into the pressure cooker). Put in enough water to half-fill the pressure cooker, add seasoning and herbs. Put on the lid, bring up pressure to 15 lb. and lower the heat. If cooking pig's head brawn, as the recipe, allow approximately 25 minutes cooking time, then reduce the pressure under cold water, add the diced stewing steak, bring to pressure once more, and continue cooking for a further 15 minutes at 15 lb. pressure. Cool rapidly and continue then as stage 4 onwards. Use the pressure cooker as an ordinary saucepan *without* the lid, as stage 6.

Home Freezing

A brawn freezes perfectly; there is no loss of flavour or texture and the jellied stock both looks and tastes excellent. Allow several hours at room temperature for the brawn to thaw out properly.

Slimming Tips

Aspic moulds filled with lean meat are extremely good on a slimming diet, for the aspic itself contains no high calorie ingredients and it does lend a piquant flavour to cooked meat. Carrots are not a particularly low calorie vegetable, so reduce the amount of these if necessary, and use cucumber or tomatoes instead.

Home Freezing

This mould will freeze quite well. As explained under jellies, you do sometimes have a crystalline effect when the jelly thaws out. This does not affect the flavour; simply the appearance. As pointed out elsewhere in the book, however, veal is one of the least successful meats to freeze, and you may care to substitute beef or chicken.

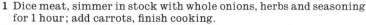

13. Jellied meat mould

16. Stuffed pork, see page 67

17. Roast chicken, see page 97

Cooking Poultry

One of the most economical foods today is chicken: it can be purchased ready-jointed to grill or fry, etc., so when cooking for only one or two people there is no need to buy a whole chicken; buy just the number of joints required. You will find several dishes in this chapter where ideas are given for adapting chicken dishes as a meal for one. At the present time, ready-jointed duck and other poultry are not easily obtainable.

POULTRY NEEDS CAREFUL BUYING–to judge the quality, check the bird has no excess fat or large bones covered with little flesh. The breast of chicken should be plump and firm (not limp or slightly damp in appearance). The legs should be plump and not feel sinewy. A small amount of pale yellow fat is *not* a bad thing (you often find this on farm birds) for it indicates it will have a moist flavour. You can judge the quality of turkey in exactly the same way. The most common faults in duck and goose are *too much* fat and *too little* meat on the breast; you should feel a layer of meat over the breast bones. Game birds can be judged like chicken and turkey.

FROZEN CHICKENS AND DUCKS are difficult to assess as they are generally packaged and one cannot easily tell their quality; you can experiment by buying different brands until completely satisfied, then buy this kind regularly, as frozen food manufacturers generally have consistent quality.

WHEN COOKING POULTRY OR GAME you naturally time according to the particular method of cooking, i.e. grilling or frying needs quick cooking. When roasting a fresh bird or well-hung game, you can cook quickly; if roasting frozen poultry or game you must defrost, and I find I get a better result if I cook slightly more slowly than with fresh birds. Casseroles and stews, of course, need slow cooking, particularly when using older boiling fowls. Good accompaniments (to give extra flavour) are important.

Do not over-cook chicken and turkey as they dry very easily. Duck and goose should never be under-cooked.

Metric Conversions

Poultry is a good source of protein, so do not allow less generous portions than usual. Conversion from Imperial to Metric means you cannot have exactly the same amount, so it is better to err on the side of larger amounts.

Drinks to serve with poultry

Obviously one will select wine that gives the most pleasure; whether white, red or rosé. Unless you have definite ideas on wine it is a good idea to try white or rosé with chicken or turkey, and more robust red wines with duck and goose. Poultry is often served for special occasions, so remember that a sparkling Burgundy is delicious with duck and goose (or any poultry) and champagne is perfect for the Christmas turkey.

Cooking poultry in the automatic oven

See comments about meat in an automatic oven. There are no complications about putting poultry or game into an automatic oven; put plenty of fat over the breast, or wrap in greased foil to prevent drying, see comments alongside recipes.

Saving time when cooking poultry

Modern breeding of very young chickens for frying and grilling means that you can prepare a meal in a very short time. The joints may be used equally well in quick-cooking casserole dishes.

A PRESSURE COOKER is excellent for producing a first class white stock from the carcass of chicken or turkey; or a brown stock from the carcass of duck, goose or game.

To 'roast' young poultry or game in a pressure cooker–allow 5 minutes per lb., weight *after* stuffing. Flour well, turn in a little hot fat in bottom of pressure cooker until brown, lift out, put in the rack, add approximately 4 tablespoons water (or as recommended by the manufacturer), stand the bird on the rack, put on lid, bring to 15 lb., pressure and cook according to weight. Allow pressure to drop at room temperature, lift out the bird, use some of the fat and liquid to make gravy. However, poultry, etc., in my opinion, is better cooked in a pressure cooker *if it is jointed* (and duck and goose are not very suitable).

If cooking whole birds there is a tendency for the breast to be over-cooked before the legs are tender.

Casserole dishes made with poultry and game cook well in a pressure cooker; an indication of time, etc., is given in each recipe. As there is little evaporation during cooking, reduce the liquid to half.

Using a mixer for poultry dishes

This is ideal for making stuffings and certain sauces; you can produce a variety of interesting accompaniments with the minimum of effort, see the recipes.

Slimming

Chicken, turkey and game may be included in a slimming diet, providing you do not ruin the effect with high calorie stuffings and rich sauces. Duck and goose are high in calories and best avoided; if you have to join friends in eating them, try to avoid the rather crisp rich skin and any pieces of fat. You save calories by wrapping chicken joints in foil, and using little fat in cooking.

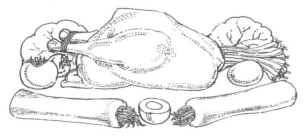

Slimming sauces and stuffings

All recipes are enough for 4–5 people.

FRUIT SAUCES–simmer fruits in a little water until tender. Apple, cherries, damsons, sharp plums and gooseberries are excellent with duck and goose; cranberries (which need more water) and apricots with chicken or turkey. When soft, either sieve, beat until smooth, or put into the liquidiser–*always remove stones*. Add sugar substitute to taste. Fruit sauces freeze well.
STROGANOFF SAUCE–slice 50 grammes (2 oz.) mushrooms, simmer for 10 minutes in 284 ml ($\frac{1}{2}$ pint) chicken stock with a chopped or grated onion, 2 teaspoons chopped parsley, a shake of garlic salt and seasoning. Blend in a good 142 ml ($\frac{1}{4}$ pint) natural yoghourt, and heat without boiling. Serve with chicken and turkey.
VEGETABLE SAUCE–simmer 3 tomatoes, 3 onions, and a bunch mixed fresh herbs in about 284 ml ($\frac{1}{2}$ pint) duck, chicken or other stock, or use half stock and half wine. Sieve or put in the liquidiser. Reheat, adding chopped green pepper and a few thinly sliced mushrooms. Excellent with any poultry, and freezes well.
MUSHROOM AND HERB STUFFING–slice about 200 grammes (4 oz.) mushrooms, mix with 4 large skinned tomatoes, 1 tablespoon chopped parsley, 1–2 teaspoons chopped fresh herbs, 2 tablespoons grated or chopped onion. Season well, cook inside turkey or chicken.
COTTAGE CHEESE AND OLIVE STUFFING–blend about 200 grammes (8 oz.) cottage cheese with 2–3 tablespoons sliced olives and plenty of pepper. Ideal for chicken, and good for game too.

APPLE AND ONION STUFFING–peel and chop 2–3 dessert apples, 2–3 onions, mix with seasoning, little powdered or fresh sage. Ideal for duck.

Home freezing of poultry and game

Before discussing home freezing of poultry and game, there is one point that is *very important*. *Where you intend to cook home frozen uncooked or commercially frozen uncooked poultry and game, it is advisable to allow the birds to defrost thoroughly*. It is surprising how long this takes, for example a 16–18 lb. frozen turkey could take as long as 48 hours.
TO FREEZE POULTRY AND GAME–draw and truss the bird. If you feel it is rather large for your family, it may be advisable to joint before freezing.
ALWAYS WRAP THE GIBLETS SEPARATELY–they may be put in a bag inside or beside the bird and the two wrapped together. Read comments about tight wrapping on page 20 as this makes a great deal of difference to the speed of freezing. If you stuff the bird before you freeze, this saves bother before cooking but has the disadvantage that it will keep for a shorter time.
Chicken, game and other poultry *without stuffing* keep for up to 12 months.
If stuffed you shorten the period to *approximately 6–8 months*. It is, therefore, a good idea to freeze the stuffing in a separate container.
The giblets of poultry keep for only up to 3 months; this is why if you place them inside poultry the bird and giblets should be used within 3 months. Cooked poultry or game dishes should be kept for a period of 2–3 months only.
Roasted birds can be frozen; it may be better to

joint or carve before freezing to save defrosting the whole bird, and you will need to dry the flesh on kitchen paper after defrosting and before reheating.

New ways to cook chicken

The following pages give a number of recipes you may not have tried before; below are easy ideas for interesting ways to cook chicken.
WHEN FRYING–fry sliced onion in shallow fat with joints of chicken; or coat chicken in crumbs *and* finely grated cheese before cooking.
WHEN GRILLING–blend grated lemon or orange rind and juice with butter or oil used in basting chicken joints; or add curry powder and little Worcestershire sauce to butter or oil.
WHEN ROASTING–use more fat than usual, add tiny onions and new potatoes during cooking period, turn in fat until brown. Put a sprig of rosemary in the chicken.

ECONOMY DISHES WITH CHICKEN

One of the most economical ways of cooking a chicken is to simmer this in water to cover until tender. Add seasoning, a *bouquet garni* of mixed herbs and vegetables to taste. The chicken giblets may be added but many people feel the liver gives a slightly bitter taste to the stock, so this may be omitted if wished.

Young chickens about 2 kilos (4 lb.) in weight when trussed will take about 1¼ hours of gentle simmering.

An older boiling fowl of the same weight will take about 2 hours or even a little longer, although fowls today are rarely old and tough. The boiled chicken will provide one substantial dish for a number of people. Several meals and suggestions are below and on page 92. The stock could be the basis of a good chicken and vegetable soup.

To serve boiled chicken

Take the cooked chicken out of the hot stock and either place it on a dish with cooked vegetables around and serve the sauce separately, or carve the chicken and arrange on a dish, then coat with the sauce. If vegetables have been cooked with the chicken they can be served round it.

SAUCES TO SERVE WITH BOILED CHICKEN

The sauce to serve with chicken should be made as White sauce, page 146, with all milk, or as the sauce in Chicken supreme, see page 93, i.e. using partly milk and partly stock. The latter has a much better flavour.

PARSLEY SAUCE–(made by adding finely chopped parsley to a White sauce, see page 146.)

PAPRIKA SAUCE–blend 1–2 teaspoons paprika with a little of the liquid when making a white sauce.

HARD-BOILED EGG SAUCE–add the chopped white of hard-boiled eggs to the sauce and coat the chicken with this. Garnish with the chopped or sieved egg yolks and chopped parsley.

WAYS TO USE COOKED POULTRY

The recipes on this and the following pages give suggestions for using ready-cooked chicken and other poultry.

RISSOLES

1 Mince or chop approximately 300–350 grammes (12 oz.) cooked poultry; if using a mincer you can put small particles of skin with the meat.
2 Heat 50 grammes (2 oz.) of fat or margarine in a saucepan and fry a medium-sized chopped onion in this.
3 Add 25 grammes (1 oz.) flour and stir well; gradually blend in approximately 8 tablespoons brown stock or milk. Stock is better with duck and goose, and milk *or* stock equally good with chicken and turkey.
4 Bring the sauce to the boil, cook until thickened, add minced poultry, 50 grammes (2 oz.) soft breadcrumbs or rolled oats, season well and flavour with herbs to taste.
5 Allow mixture to cool; form into round cakes or cutlet shapes, coat in 1 tablespoon seasoned flour, then beaten egg and crisp breadcrumbs and fry in a little hot fat, or in deep fat, until crisp and golden brown. Drain and serve hot or cold.

KROMESKIES

Make the mixture as above, but form in finger shapes. Wrap each finger in a rasher of bacon then dip in seasoned flour and then in batter, see page 160, fry in deep fat until crisp and brown.

Automatic Oven

If more convenient, cook the chicken or boiling fowl in a very moderate oven. Allow nearly 50 per cent longer cooking period than given in the recipe opposite.

Mixer

Remove any meat from the giblet bones, put into the warmed liquidiser goblet with the vegetables and chicken stock. Emulsify until a smooth purée, heat and serve as chicken and vegetable soup.

Home Freezing

The chicken stock and the chicken freeze well, see comments about freezing poultry on page 90.

Speedy Meal

A pressure cooker can be used.

Cook the chicken whole and allow 7 minutes per lb. at 15 lb. pressure, cool rapidly–if a tender bird you should find it is cooked–if an older bird, allow 7–10 minutes per lb. and 7–10 minutes over. There is a tendency though for the breast to be over-cooked this way before the legs are tender, so I like to joint a boiling fowl.

Give the legs 7–10 minutes at 15 lb. pressure, reduce the pressure rapidly and then add the chicken breasts, bring once again to pressure and cook for 10 minutes, or if a rather old fowl, allow an additonal 12–15 minutes to cook breasts.

Speedy Meal

Instead of frying the onion, and making the sauce, add, to bind, 6 tablespoons condensed tomato or other soup.

Slimming Tips

Omit both the thickened sauce and crumbs. Fry the onion in 25 grammes (1 oz.) fat then add to meat with seasoning and herbs to flavour, and bind with the egg yolk only. Coat in egg white and the minimum of crumbs, then bake the rissoles in the oven instead of frying.

Home Freezing

Both the cooked rissoles and kromeskies freeze well for a limited period, up to 1 month or 6 weeks. Rissoles are equally satisfactory frozen uncooked or cooked. To freeze when cooked, fry lightly, drain well on absorbent paper, wrap and then freeze. The kromeskies can only be frozen when cooked. Fry until the batter is pale in colour, drain well, cool, then wrap when quite hard, and freeze.

Chicken Stroganoff

Serves 4
Cooking time 20 minutes

Ingredients	Metric	Imperial
onion	1 medium	1 medium
mushrooms	100 grammes	4 oz.
butter	50–75 grammes	2–3 oz.
diced cooked chicken—	½ kilo	1 lb.
leg *or* breast *or* mixture	(poor weight)	(generous weight)
soured cream*	284 ml	½ pint
seasoning	to taste	to taste
paprika	½–1 teaspoon	½–1 teaspoon
TO SERVE:		
rice	100–125 grammes	4 oz.
salt	½ teaspoon	½ teaspoon
water	284 ml	½ pint
TO GARNISH:		
paprika	pinch	pinch
parsley	few sprigs	few sprigs

*or use fresh thick cream and the juice of 1 large lemon.

1 Peel and chop the onion very finely, and wash and slice the mushrooms.
2 Cook these in the hot butter until just soft, but do not allow the onion to brown.
3 Add diced chicken, cream, etc., and heat gently. Do *not* allow to boil or the sauce can 'separate' and give rather hard curds and a 'watery' liquid.
4 While the vegetables cook at stage 2, prepare the rice: put rice, salt and cold water into a saucepan, bring to the boil, stir briskly with a fork.
5 Lower the heat, cover the pan and simmer for 15 minutes.
6 Serve chicken mixture on the bed of rice, and garnish with paprika and chopped parsley.

Mixer
The sauce in the recipe opposite *must* be simmered gently and carefully. If it separates at all, which if cooked too quickly, it will, then lift the chicken out with a perforated spoon and arrange on bed of rice: put the very hot sauce into the warmed liquidiser goblet and emulsify for a few seconds, then pour over the chicken, garnish and serve.

Home Freezing
This dish does not freeze well, but it is a good way to use frozen chicken. Allow the chicken to defrost before using in the sauce.

Chicken in Cider

Serves 6–8
*Cooking time 1½–2½ hours**

Ingredients	Metric	Imperial
large roasting *or* boiling fowl*	2½–3 kilos	5–6 lb.
butter	50–75 grammes approx	2–3 oz. approx
mixture of vegetables in season	1 kilo	2 lb.
bouquet garni	spray	spray
seasoning	to taste	to taste
dry cider	1 litre (generous measure)	2 pints

*see stage 2.

1 Truss the chicken, brown lightly in butter in a strong pan or flame-proof casserole; lift out, add vegetables, heat in the butter, then remove.
2 Replace chicken and other ingredients, apart from the vegetables, with the cider, simmer until tender*, or place in the oven (see also Automatic Oven). Naturally cooking time will vary according to the age of the chicken.
3 The vegetables may be cooked *with* the chicken, or added *during* cooking to ensure they are not over-cooked, see picture facing page 113. Thicken sauce if required, with flour or cornflour, and add a little cream to flavour.

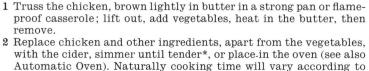

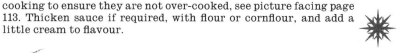

Automatic Oven
Proceed as stages 1 and 2 then cook the chicken, etc. in a deep covered casserole. Choose large vegetables which will not over-cook. Allow about 1¾–2¾ hours, depending upon the tenderness of the chicken or fowl.

Speedy Meal
Could be prepared in a pressure cooker see page 91, under 'Speedy Meal'. Turn the chicken and vegetables in the hot butter in the pressure cooker, then add about 568 ml (1 pint) cider, etc., bring to 15 lb. pressure and cook as timing on page 91, or joint the bird and cook as recommended on that page.

Slimming Tips
Dry cider could be used for cooking this chicken dish for a slimming diet, providing you avoid vegetables high in calories. Do not serve the sauce.

Home Freezing
I find that it is better to defrost a frozen chicken and cook in this manner. The cider then plays a very important part in both tenderising and giving extra flavour.

Chicken Supreme

Serves 4
Cooking time 15–20 minutes

Ingredients	Metric	Imperial
cooked chicken breasts and wings	2	2
chicken stock	284 ml	½ pint
butter	25 grammes	1 oz.
flour	25 grammes	1 oz.
or cornflour	1 tablespoon	½ oz.
milk	142 ml	¼ pint
seasoning	to taste	to taste
grated nutmeg	pinch	pinch
thick cream	3–4 tablespoons	3–4 tablespoons
dry sherry	1–2 tablespoons	1–2 tablespoons
TO GARNISH:		
parsley	few sprigs	few sprigs
paprika	pinch	pinch

1 Cut chicken breasts into neat slices, and divide wing joints into two pieces.
2 Simmer in half the stock until really hot.
3 Make a coating sauce of the butter, flour or cornflour, milk and the remainder of the chicken stock.
4 Season the sauce and stir in the nutmeg, cream and sherry, and add a little extra chicken stock if the sauce is too thick; heat gently and *do not* boil.
5 Lift the chicken meat on to a hot dish with a fish slice or perforated spoon, coat with the sauce and garnish with chopped parsley and paprika.
6 Serve with boiled rice, or with triangles of toast, or mixed vegetables.

Speedy Meal

A can of Cream of chicken soup could be used to coat ready-cooked chicken joints purchased from a supermarket or store. Remove the skin from the chicken, dilute the soup with milk or water, and heat the chicken joints in this, add the sherry, if wished.

Mixer

The sauce should be very creamy; if put into the warmed liquidiser goblet before coating the chicken, you will have an exceptionally smooth sauce.

Home Freezing

This dish can be frozen; choose corn-flour for thickening the sauce and omit both the cream and the sherry. When you wish to serve the dish, heat gently, and then when hot stir in the cream and sherry. Do not store longer than 6–8 weeks in the freezer.

TO BRAISE POULTRY

Chicken or duck are the most suitable poultry to braise, for they are sufficiently small and compact to fit into a large pan. If you wish to braise turkey or goose, then you will need to joint these to fit into the pan.

Duck and goose are both very rich-fleshed and 'fatty' poultry and it is therefore important to braise these, then allow the 'mirepoix' to cool so you may remove the layer of fat before proceeding further. The recipe on page 63 for Braised beef can be followed for poultry, with the following modifications.

CHICKEN: use either white or red wine, and if the chicken is young and tender allow about 1¼ hours cooking time.
DUCK: add about 200 grammes (8 oz.) shelled chestnuts to the onions at stage 5 of Braised beef, page 63. The celery and carrots can be omitted if wished. A young duckling will take about 1¼ hours; but an older duck, about 2 hours cooking. This is an excellent way of cooking older poultry. Use red wine.
GOOSE: jointed goose will take about 2 hours cooking and chestnuts can be added as for duck, above. It is quite a good idea to braise goose legs only, and to roast the breast of goose, so giving two entirely different meals. Use red wine as Braised beef.
TURKEY: braise the turkey legs for about 2–2¼ hours (depending on the size of the turkey), and roast the breast of turkey, so giving two entirely different meals. Use either red or white wine.

Automatic Oven

Braised poultry can be cooked in the oven, rather than in a saucepan, if more convenient—read the information on braised meat on page 63.

Home Freezing

Braised poultry freezes well, particularly duck; do not over-cook the poultry before freezing so that it will retain texture and flavour when reheated.

TO FRY POULTRY

Although young frying chickens are the most usual poultry to fry, you can reheat pieces of cooked turkey, duck and goose in the frying pan (see below) or fry 'made-up' dishes using poultry. Choose the method of frying as under:

SHALLOW FRYING: for heating pieces of meat and for the coated rissoles, etc., this is ideal.

DEEP FRYING: use this for coated rissoles, etc., but not for reheating *uncoated* poultry as the intense heat would give too hard a layer of outside flesh. The crumb coating is better in deep fat; you get a more crisp brown covering.

Fried Chicken Joints

CHOOSE—fresh jointed spring chicken or frozen chicken joints. If using frozen chicken joints you can cook from the frozen state, but it is better to allow these to defrost then to dry them well on kitchen paper before cooking.

TO PREPARE: either flour the chicken joints or coat in seasoned flour, then egg and crumbs or batter, or fry as the special suggestions. COOK FOR:

SHALLOW FRYING—put approximately 50 grammes (2 oz.) fat or butter, or 2–3 tablespoons oil, into the frying pan. This is enough for 4 joints of chicken. Heat as directions under frying meat, page 70. Put in the chicken joints and fry quickly on one side, then turn and cook quickly on second side. Lower the heat and cook more slowly until tender. Allow a total cooking time of 12–15 minutes, unless the joints are very small when you should allow 10–12 minutes. Drain on absorbent paper and serve.

USUAL ACCOMPANIMENTS—fried tomatoes, fried mushrooms, fried potatoes and a green salad.

DEEP FRYING—coat the chicken joints very thoroughly with seasoned flour, egg and crumbs, or coat with seasoned flour and the batter on page 160. Test the temperature of the fat as directed on page 70. Put in the chicken joints, lower the heat so they do not become over-brown, and fry for approximately 10–12 minutes. Drain on absorbent paper and serve.

USUAL ACCOMPANIMENTS—as shallow frying above.

Paprika Fried Chicken

Divide 2 spring chickens into halves, or, if larger, divide 1 young chicken into four joints, i.e. 2 breast and wing joints and 2 legs. Put 2–3 tablespoons oil and 2–3 teaspoons paprika on a plate, add pinch cayenne pepper and pinch celery salt. Stir together until the paprika, etc., blends with the oil. Put this mixture into the frying pan and fry as usual. Serve with a green salad.

Devilled Poultry

There are a number of ways of cooking devilled poultry, and some of these are given below. Choose large thick pieces of cooked chicken, duck, turkey or goose. With leg joints, remove bones, if wished, and the skin, so coating 'sticks' better. Quantities are for 4 portions.

TO FRY: spread each piece of poultry with a little chutney, dip in 1 tablespoon seasoned flour blended with 1 teaspoon curry powder; coat with beaten egg, blended with 1 teaspoon Worcestershire sauce, and crisp breadcrumbs blended with another teaspoon curry powder; fry as usual.

TO GRILL OR BAKE: blend 50 grammes (2 oz.) butter with 1 tablespoon chutney, 1–2 teaspoons curry powder—coat poultry in this, roll in crumbs. Grill or bake in hot oven until tender.

Automatic Oven

Although not really 'frying', the chicken joints could be 'oven-fried'. Put the coated joints on to a well greased baking tray; brush lightly with oil or melted butter (be careful not to brush the crumb-coating off); set the oven for 30 minutes cooking at a moderately hot temperature. A batter coating is quite unsuitable for this method of cooking.

Speedy Meal

You can reheat ready-cooked chicken joints in a little fat or oil. Get the fat or oil hot so the chicken crisps quickly then lower the heat so joints are heated through completely.

Home Freezing

You can freeze uncooked chicken joints coated with egg and crumbs (not batter); or cook the coated joints, and freeze these. Allow them to thaw out for a cold meal. It is essential to use the egg and crumb coating.

Home Freezing

This is an excellent way of cooking frozen chicken joints, for the paprika gives a very pleasant colour to the skin. Let the joints thaw out, then dry well before frying.

Speedy Meal

This is an ideal way of heating chicken or turkey bought ready-cooked. Ask for *thick* slices or pieces if you intend to use this recipe.

Home Freezing

It is an excellent idea to prepare the cooked poultry with the coating and freeze this, ready to use a little later. Store for only 3-4 weeks though, and defrost before cooking.

Stuffed Fried Poultry

Cooked poultry can be stuffed and fried or reheated; either boil chicken as page 91, or use roasted poultry. Remove legs from body, and divide each leg into 2 joints. Skin, make a slit in each joint, then remove bones without breaking the flesh. Press stuffing in the centre of each piece of poultry in place of the bone. This can be any stuffing you prefer, but the Sausage and raisin stuffing, page 142, is particularly good for chicken and turkey; or use the Mushroom and parsley stuffing, page 140, for all poultry. Coat leg joints in seasoned flour, then in egg and crumbs, and fry steadily until the outside is crisp and brown, and the flesh inside very hot; this takes approximately 10–15 minutes, depending upon thickness of the leg.

If preferred you could use uncooked frying joints and fill boned legs as above, or split and fill breast. Coat and fry for about 15–20 minutes. After frying, drain well and serve.

Chicken Maryland

Serves 4
Cooking time 15 minutes

Ingredients	Metric	Imperial
young frying chicken *or* 4 chicken frying joints	1¼–1½ kilos	2½–3 lb.
egg	1	1
crisp breadcrumbs	50–75 grammes	2–3 oz.
TO FRY:		
deep or shallow fat	see page 94	see page 94
TO GARNISH:		
watercress	bunch	bunch
fried bananas	see below	see below
corn fritters	see page 116	see page 116
bacon rolls	see below	see below

1 Cut chicken into 4 to 6 joints, coat each joint with egg and breadcrumbs.
2 Fry joints quickly until golden brown in a depth of 1 cm (½ inch) hot fat, turning once, or use deep fat.
3 Reduce heat, cook gently until tender on both sides.
4 Drain and serve on a hot dish with watercress, fried bananas, corn fritters and bacon rolls.

Bacon Rolls

1 Remove rind from 4 rashers streaky bacon, 'stretch' the bacon with a knife; this means pulling it out firmly and it makes it easier to roll.
2 Divide each rasher in half, roll firmly and secure with wooden cocktail sticks.
3 Either fry in the frying pan, turning as necessary, or lower into deep fat, or cook under a hot grill, turning as necessary.
4 The bacon rolls will take about 5–8 minutes if fried or grilled. If preferred, cook in a moderate to moderately hot oven for about 25 minutes. Serves 4.

Fried Bananas

1 Cut 2 large bananas into halves, or quarters.
2 Coat with 1 level tablespoon flour, and fry for a few minutes as Chicken Maryland. Serves 4.

Automatic Oven

Coat chicken or turkey joints and turn carefully in 1-2 oz. hot fat until the outside becomes crisp. Cool, then put on to a baking tin or dish. (Duck or goose does not need this initial frying.) Set the oven to moderately hot and allow 25–30 minutes to heat pre-cooked chicken or duck; 35–40 minutes for uncooked young chicken; and 40–45 minutes for pre-cooked turkey or goose (or even a little longer if the legs are very large).

Home Freezing

If using pre-cooked poultry you cannot cook it *again* and freeze it, but you can prepare the poultry joints and freeze them. Thaw out when required, and cook as directions opposite. Use the stuffed joints within 1 month to 6 weeks.

Speedy Meal

Use ready-cooked jointed chicken for this dish, remove the skin so you can produce a very smooth crumb coating, and fry until crisp and brown. Fry the bananas and bacon rolls as the recipes, but do not make corn fritters; simply heat canned corn and serve as a garnish.

Home Freezing

To hasten defrosting put the wrapped chicken into cold water until thawed out. This is an ideal way of making a fairly quick meal using frozen chicken joints.

Home Freezing

Bacon does *not* freeze as well as most meats or keep in prime condition for as long a period, see page 59, but Bacon rolls are useful to put in the freezer if you are preparing a week or so ahead for a special meal.
Roll, secure with cocktail stick, and wrap, then freeze. Thaw out before cooking, or cook from frozen stage.

TO GRILL POULTRY

Grilling is very suitable for young chicken and for heating through ready-cooked poultry, as Devilled turkey, see page 94. Make sure the grill is thoroughly heated through before cooking or reheating the poultry. If grilling young chicken joints or cooked poultry, keep these well basted with oil or melted butter so that they will not dry.

Slimming Tips

Make full use of herbs, spices and seasoning when grilling chicken, etc., for these give interest without adding extra calories. Be careful in your choice of vegetables to serve with poultry; tomatoes and mushrooms are ideal, particularly if you grill these with little, if any, fat. Crisp green salads are a good accompaniment to grilled poultry.

Cooking times, etc., for grilling poultry

The cooking time for grilling chicken is the same as shallow frying, see page 94. It is difficult to give the exact time for reheating the cooked poultry since the thickness of the meat varies so much. It will be approximately 10–12 minutes. Serve grilled poultry with a crisp salad and grilled tomatoes and mushrooms, which may be cooked at the same time as the poultry, see under 'Vegetables to serve with grilled meat', page 74.

Home Freezing

Freezing tends to give a less moist and a slightly tougher texture to chicken joints; particularly to the breast, so that a marinade as suggested opposite, and on page 72, can help to counteract this.

Flavourings to add to grilled poultry

SEASONING–this can play a part in making the poultry more interesting. Add celery salt to the fat in basting chicken or turkey pieces. Cayenne pepper, paprika or crushed peppercorns may also be used.

PEPPERED BUTTER FOR GRILLING POULTRY–crush 1–2 teaspoons of peppercorns with the back of a wooden spoon or a rolling pin, (remember these are very hot and it is better to add too little rather than too much). Add to the butter, see recipe below, and cook under hot grill, or heat thoroughly. Towards the end of the cooking time turn uppermost the side of poultry that looks most attractive, and carefully spoon any remaining peppercorns and butter over the top. Replace under the grill.

HERBS OR SPICES–chopped parsley, chives or a mixture of fresh herbs, or a pinch of dried herbs, can be added to the butter and used as seasoning above. One of the most famous spiced toppings for poultry is given in the recipe for Devilled turkey, see page 94.

MARINATING–choose marinades as for meat, page 72, but remember that chicken and turkey have a very delicate flavour and too much flavouring in a marinade could be overwhelming. Duck and goose, on the other hand, are themselves very fat, and while a short time in a marinade gives a moist texture to ready-cooked poultry, it is advisable to reduce the amount of oil for either of these two birds.

VEGETABLES–details as page 74, or use fruit to flavour, see picture opposite, and page 103.

Tomato and Pepper Chicken

Serves 4
Cooking time 15–20 minutes

Ingredients	Metric	Imperial
good-sized frying chicken	1–1½ kilos	2–2½ lb.
butter *or* oil	50 grammes	2 oz.
tomato purée	1 tablespoon	1 tablespoon
black peppercorns	1½ teaspoons	1½ teaspoons

1 Divide chicken into 4 joints, brush with melted butter or oil, blended with tomato purée.
2 Put crushed peppercorns evenly over the joints and grill.

Speedy Meal

This recipe can be followed for ready-cooked chicken. Joint this and brush with the melted butter or oil (use only half the quantity in the recipe); press the peppercorns on the joints and grill for 5–7 minutes only. Pieces of cooked turkey and other poultry could be heated in the same way.

18. Oranged chicken, see page 103

TO ROAST POULTRY

This is one of the best ways to cook frozen or fresh poultry providing it is reasonably young and tender. You can roast on a spit although with the richer duck and goose this would give a great deal of fat splashing–follow cooking time as for quick roasting. There are two speeds for roasting: quick roasting is ideal for fresh poultry and can be used for defrosted frozen poultry, but in my opinion the slower method of roasting is better for defrosted frozen poultry. Here are the two temperatures you should use:
QUICK–425–450°F. (220–230°C.), Gas Mark 7 (reduce heat to 375–400°F. (190–200°C.), Gas Mark 5–6 after first 15 minutes, or see under Automatic Oven opposite);
SLOW–350°F. (180°C.), Gas Mark 3–4.
Mention has been made of defrosting frozen poultry before cooking, and it must be stressed that this will take a considerable time. For example, a 20 lb. turkey will take up to 48 hours before it is thoroughly thawed out, and unless the meat has thawed out roasting is unsatisfactory.

Home Freezing
You are wise if you store frozen *uncooked* poultry ready for cooking at a convenient time, but you cannot use this for emergency meals as the poultry takes a considerable time to thaw out, see opposite. *Cooked* roast poultry is always useful for meals, this too needs time to thaw out. Freeze the stuffings and sauces that go with roast poultry.

Mixer
The liquidiser plays an important part in preparing bread and other sauces and stuffings to serve with poultry. See the information in the relevant chapters.

Using fat when roasting poultry

Both chicken and turkey are dry and unpalatable if not kept very well basted with fat during roasting. Either cover the breast with fat bacon, or spread with clarified fat or butter, or margarine. If you are generous with the fat, you need not baste during cooking, and of course, you cannot do this if leaving poultry in an automatic oven. Duck and goose on the other hand require *no* extra fat; I find it makes the birds greasy rather than crisp. You will find recommendations for pricking duck and goose under the methods of roasting, etc., which follow.

Using a covered roasting tin or foil

You will find details of using some kind of covering when roasting on page 66, but this is not entirely satisfactory for poultry. Most people like poultry to be crisp and brown and it is important, therefore, if you are roasting chicken or turkey that you take the lid off a covered roaster (or remove the foil) at least half an hour before serving. See picture of Roast chicken facing page 89.
I would never recommend any form of covering for duck or goose as the same degree of crispness is never achieved even if you cover for part of the cooking time, and uncover for the remainder of the period. See pictures opposite, and between pages 120/121.
Guinea fowl, because of its very dry texture, is extremely satisfactory if roasted in a covered tin.

To give a crisp skin to poultry

Both chicken and turkey will have a reasonably crisp skin if you use fat or fat bacon over them when cooking. It is quite a good idea to remove the pieces of bacon towards the end of the cooking time so that the skin will brown and crisp evenly. Duck and goose, on the other hand, need slightly different treatment. Allow the birds to cook for at least half an hour, then prick the skin *gently* with a fine skewer; be absolutely certain the skewer does not penetrate the flesh. You will find that the fat begins to spurt out in little fountains. Repeat this several times when cooking a goose, and at least once more with a large duck. In this way you both crisp the skin and allow the fat to run out.
An exceptionally crisp skin and pleasantly sweet texture is given to roast duck or goose if towards the end of cooking time the flesh is brushed with a very thin layer of honey.

19. Gosling and spring vegetables

To stuff poultry

Most poultry when roasted is stuffed, but naturally this is a matter of personal opinion, and if you do not like stuffing it is a very good idea to put a good knob of butter inside chicken or turkey, for stuffing not only imparts flavour to the poultry but also helps to keep moist this rather dry flesh. Another suggestion you may care to follow is to put 1 or 2 raw potatoes and the butter, plus a sprig of fresh rosemary, inside the bird. If you intend to stuff chicken or turkey with one flavoured mixture only, this should be put at the neck end; the poulterer should always leave a good 'flap' of skin so the stuffing may be pressed against the bird and the skin brought over the stuffing as a protection. If you intend to use two stuffings, the second one is pushed into the bird at the tail end.

Duck and goose should be stuffed in the same way, but these birds generally contain so much fat that a stuffing cooked *in* the bird tends to be greasy. That is why I generally cook stuffings quite separately, to serve with either of these birds.

Cooking times, etc., for roasting poultry

To calculate cooking time, always weigh the bird after stuffing, or if you have no scales, ask the poulterer to give you the trussed weight, then add the approximate weight of the stuffing. (1 lb. weight is equivalent to just under ½ kilo.)

CHICKEN
CHOOSE–a plump young roasting fowl; you can judge whether it is sufficiently young for roasting by the flexible breastbone, and the fact that any fat is *not* too dark a yellow, which denotes an older bird.

COOK FOR:

QUICK ROASTING–15 minutes per lb., and 15 minutes over.

SLOW ROASTING–25–30 minutes per lb., 25–30 minutes over.

USUAL ACCOMPANIMENTS–Parsley and thyme (veal) stuffing, page 139, Chestnut stuffing, page 141, or any of the other stuffings recommended for poultry, Bread sauce, page 153, Cranberry sauce, page 149, Bacon rolls, page 95, cooked sausages and thickened gravy.

DUCK *or* GOOSE
CHOOSE–young birds or frozen birds; the latter should be defrosted at room temperature, and in the case of a large goose this could take up to 24 hours.

COOK FOR:

QUICK ROASTING–15 minutes per lb., and 15 minutes over.

SLOW ROASTING–25–30 minutes per lb., 30 minutes over.

USUAL ACCOMPANIMENTS–Sage and onion stuffing, page 139 or other stuffings, Apple sauce, page 148, thickened gravy, Orange salad, page 125, Bigarade sauce, page 149.

TURKEY
CHOOSE–good quality bird or frozen bird.

COOK FOR:

QUICK ROASTING–15 minutes per lb., and 15 minutes over, up to a total of 12 lb. (including stuffing); for every extra lb. over this weight, allow 12 minutes only.

SLOW ROASTING–25–30 minutes per lb., and 30 minutes over, up to a total of 12 lb. (including stuffing); for every extra lb. over this weight, allow 20–25 minutes per lb.

USUAL ACCOMPANIMENTS–as chicken.

GUINEA FOWL
This is so scarce today that many people have little opportunity to cook it. You can either cook stuffed as chicken, with the same accompaniments, or unstuffed, and serve accompaniments as game. Whichever you do, it is important to keep the breast very well covered with fat, and to baste it with fat, if possible, during cooking.

Automatic Oven
Poultry, prepared for roasting, may be left in the cold oven and the oven pre-set for the correct cooking time and temperature. If you decide to use the quick method of roasting, see page 97, you cannot reduce the temperature after the first 15 minutes, so use the lower temperature and allow a little extra cooking time.

The slower method of roasting is very satisfactory when cooking in an automatic oven: should you be delayed the oven will switch or turn off automatically, and the heat left at the lower setting is less likely to dry the poultry or cause a slight over-cooking.

It is difficult to suggest a complete menu without knowing the weight and therefore the total cooking time of the bird, but the following suggestions for chicken and duck may act as a guide.

In each case it is assumed that the cooking time is $1\frac{1}{4}$–$1\frac{1}{2}$ hours at 375–400°F. (190–200°C.) Gas Mark 5–6.

Menu 1 With stuffed roast chicken. Put the chicken with potatoes (coated in melted fat to prevent turning brown) in the hottest part of the oven.

Put Bacon rolls covered with foil in the coolest part of the oven together with a Casserole of mixed diced vegetables. Cook an upside-down pudding (with the sides of the dish protected with foil and a piece of foil lightly placed over top of container to prevent scorching) in the centre of the oven. Bread sauce could be prepared and put into a tightly covered container in the warming drawer of the cooker. The oven would prove too hot for this.

Menu 2 With roast duck and stuffing. Put duck in the hottest part of the oven. It is not possible to prick the skin as suggested on page 97. Place the stuffing in a well covered dish; protect the sides of the dish against scorching by wrapping in foil–cook in the coolest part of the oven. If you wish roast potatoes (which are *not* an ideal dish with duck as they are too rich); cook in a separate tin on the same shelf as the duck or if you have bought 2 small ducklings to serve 4 people, immediately *above* the duck. If you have 1 really large duck then put the potatoes on the shelf immediately *under* this. Naturally you will turn them in melted fat to prevent their discolouring. It is better to choose a Casserole of potatoes, see page 114, or Potatoes Anna, see page 120, and cook these and a Casserole of mixed vegetables in the centre of the oven. The orange and/or apple sauces could be heated in the warming drawer. The giblets of duck or chicken could be cooked low down in the oven in a covered casserole in water, with seasoning to give a good stock for making gravy.

STEWS AND CASSEROLES OF POULTRY

The following recipes are examples of the type of stews and casseroles that could be made with poultry. There are, however, a number of adaptations that could be used:

In the *Bordeaux chicken*, which comes below, you could use an older duck instead of the roasting chicken, proceed as stages 1 and 2, brown the duck in its own fat as stage 3. Continue as recipe, but prepare this dish one day, then allow it to cool and remove any surplus fat before reheating.

The *Coq au vin* on page 100 is a classic dish which could be prepared with pieces of breast of turkey rather than chicken, or with a very young duckling. Again it is advisable to cook, then cool and remove the surplus fat.

The *Goose cassoulet* on page 100 can be made equally as well with duckling, and the haricot beans will absorb extra fat.

The *Chicken chasseur* on page 101 is an excellent 'basic' stew for any poultry. Use red wine for goose or duck.

Bordeaux Chicken

Serves 4
Cooking time 2 hours 20–30 minutes
Oven temperature 325–350° F. (170–180°C.), Gas Mark 3–4

Ingredients	Metric	Imperial
1 roasting chicken	1½ kilos	3 lb.
and giblets	approximately	approximately
seasoning	to taste	to taste
tiny onions *or* shallots	12	12
button mushrooms	150–200 grammes	6–8 oz.
fresh *or* canned red pepper	1	1
butter	75 grammes	3 oz.
flour	25 grammes	1 oz.
white Bordeaux	284 ml	½ pint
chicken stock	see stage 1	see stage 1
TO SERVE:		
cooked rice (see page 169)	as desired	as desired
TO GARNISH:		
mushrooms	from weight above	from weight above
chopped parsley	1 tablespoon	1 tablespoon
red pepper	from above	from above

1 Cut the chicken into 4 joints; simmer giblets in water and seasoning for 1 hour to give 142 ml (¼ pint) stock.
2 Prepare onions and mushrooms, and cut the pepper into thin strips.
3 Heat the butter and brown the chicken joints in this, then put into a casserole.
4 Toss the peeled onions and mushrooms in the butter for a few minutes until the onions are just pale golden in colour.
5 Add to the chicken in the casserole, but save a few mushrooms for garnish.
6 Toss the pepper in the butter, put most of the pepper on one side for garnish, but add a little to the casserole.
7 Stir the flour into the butter remaining in the pan, then gradually blend in the wine and stock. Bring to the boil, cook until thickened, season well; pour over the chicken.
8 Cover the casserole with a lid and cook for 1 hour in the centre of a very moderate to moderate oven until the chicken is tender.
9 Meanwhile, cook the rice and heat the garnish on an ovenproof plate for a short time.
10 Place the cooked rice in a ring on the dish, lift the chicken and vegetables from the sauce, arrange on the dish. Top with the garnish; serve the sauce separately.

Automatic Oven
This chicken dish would be excellent for a dinner party. Prepare to stage 7, then put the casserole in the oven. You could cook Scalloped potatoes and Peas à la française at the same time. The rice should be cooked earlier, rinsed in cold water, then just reheated in hot butter or brought to the boil in salted water. It would be wise to serve a cold dessert.

Speedy Meal
Use ready-cooked Barbecued chicken and avoid stage 4; simply put into the casserole. Use cocktail onions (stage 2) and water and ½ chicken stock cube, instead of making stock at stage 1. Otherwise other ingredients are the same as recipe. Cook dish for 35 minutes only, at stage 8. Choose quick-cooking rice.

Home Freezing
This dish freezes excellently. Cook the chicken for 35–40 minutes only at stage 8, to avoid over-cooking when reheating. There is no need to defrost before cooking.

Coq au Vin

Serves 4–6
Cooking time 1–1¼ hours

Ingredients	Metric	Imperial
mushrooms	100 grammes	4 oz.
small onions *or* shallots	4–8	4–8
butter *or* oil	50–75 grammes	2–3 oz.
fat bacon *or* pork	100 grammes	4 oz.
joints young chicken	4–6	4–6
clove garlic*	1	1
flour	25 grammes	1 oz.
red wine	568 ml	1 pint
seasoning	to taste	to taste

*more garlic can be used if wished.

1 Slice mushrooms and fry with onions in the butter until tender and the onions golden brown. Then fry diced bacon.
2 Lift out, add chicken joints and cook steadily for about 10 minutes until golden on the outside. Remove from butter.
3 Stir crushed clove of garlic and flour into the butter remaining in the pan, cook for about 3–4 minutes then gradually add the wine, bringing just to the boil and simmering until a smooth sauce.
4 Return the chicken, mushrooms, etc., to the sauce, season well, simmer for approximately 30 minutes until the chicken is tender.

Speedy Meal
Buy ready-jointed cooked chicken. Heat well drained cocktail onions at stage 1, with canned or fresh mushrooms (they need little preparation). Fry the cooked joints of chicken at stage 2, then continue as stages 3 and 4, but simmer for about 10 minutes only, not 50 minutes as in the recipe. Because the cooking time is short, use just over half the amount of wine.

Home Freezing
This is a chicken recipe that is rather disappointing when frozen. It is better to make use of thawed frozen chicken joints, then make and serve this dish.

Goose Cassoulet

Serves 5–6
Cooking time minimum 3 hours, see stages 5 and 6

Ingredients	Metric	Imperial
haricot beans	200–225 grammes	8 oz.
ham stock*	1 litre	2 pints
brown sugar	2 teaspoons	2 teaspoons
seasoning	to taste	to taste
fat	50 grammes	2 oz.
onions	3–4	3–4
bouquet garni	spray	spray
goose meat**	1 kilo	2 lb.
Frankfurter sausages	3 large	3 large
soft breadcrumbs	50–75 grammes	2–3 oz.

*or chicken stock.
**cooked or uncooked, see stages 5 and 6.

1 Soak the haricot beans overnight in cold water to cover; drain off the water.
2 Put beans into a saucepan with half the stock, the sugar and a *little* seasoning; add a *little* extra water to cover the beans if necessary, and simmer for about 2 hours.
3 Meanwhile, heat the fat in a large saucepan, add sliced onions and fry until pale golden.
4 Pour into the rest of the ham stock, bring to the boil, add herbs.
5 Put in the pieces of diced goose; if using uncooked goose it is a good idea to have just the leg joint (or joints) and roast the breast for an entirely different meal.
6 Add the strained haricot beans (keep the liquid) to the goose, etc., and simmer very gently; for ¾ hour if using cooked goose, or 1½ hours with raw poultry. If necessary, towards the end of the cooking time, add a little of the stock used in cooking the beans.
7 Put the sliced sausages and crumbs into the pan 15–20 minutes before serving, and season well.
8 Serve with a green salad or vegetables; this dish is even better if made one day, cooled and reheated the next.

Speedy Meal
Leave out stages 1 and 2 in which the haricot beans are cooked, and begin at stage 3. Add a large can of strained haricot beans, or haricot beans in tomato sauce, at stage 7.

Mixer
The liquidiser will be useful for making the crumbs for this recipe. Although it is traditional to have the meat in the sauce, you may like to make a complete change for a second meal by lifting the pieces of goose out of the sauce, emulsifying this (with beans) in the liquidiser, pouring over the goose, and reheating.

Home Freezing
This dish should not be frozen; the haricot beans become very soft and really rather unpleasant. If you wish you can prepare the raw goose as stages 3–6 without beans, then freeze that particular part of the dish. Cook the haricot beans separately and continue as the basic recipe. On the other hand, you can reheat the frozen goose with the liquid and onions, and then add canned beans as suggested under Speedy Meal above.

Chicken Chasseur

Serves 4–6
Cooking time 1½–2 hours

Ingredients	Metric	Imperial
young roasting *or*	1½–2 kilos	3–4 lb.
boiling fowl (weight when	approximately	approximately
trussed) plus giblets		
onion	1	1
bay leaf	1	1
bouquet garni	spray	spray
seasoning	to taste	to taste
flour	50 grammes	2 oz.
streaky bacon	100–150 grammes	4–6 oz.
(cut in 1 piece)		
butter	50–75 grammes	2–3 oz.
mushrooms	50–100 grammes	2–4 oz.
skinned tomatoes	150–200 grammes	6–8 oz.
dry white wine	3 tablespoons	3 tablespoons
TO GARNISH:		
parsley	few sprigs	few sprigs

1 Make stock by simmering giblets for 1 hour in water with onion, bay leaf, *bouquet garni*; measure off 1 pint.
2 Divide chicken into 6 to 8 joints (2 thighs, 2 drumsticks, 2 pieces breast, 2 wings; if small bird, breast and wing should be kept together), dust with seasoned flour.
3 Cut bacon into fingers, fry for several minutes, lift out of pan.
4 Add butter to any bacon fat left and heat; fry pieces of chicken until golden brown, then remove from pan.
5 Fry the mushrooms and sliced tomatoes until just soft, then gradually add wine and stock blended with remainder of flour.
6 Bring to the boil, cook until thickened, season well and either replace the chicken joints and bacon in the pan, or put into a casserole.
7 If cooking in the saucepan, cover tightly, simmer until tender (30 minutes for young chicken or 1 hour for older bird). If using a casserole transfer all the ingredients and cook in a very moderate oven for slightly longer. If the sauce has become a little thick, then thin down with a little extra white wine.
8 Top with chopped parsley and serve.

Speedy Meal

This roast can be made by a much simpler method than given opposite, although of course the flavour will not be as good. Use canned tomato soup in place of the tomatoes—dilute this with a little water and a chicken stock cube. Fry mushrooms and bacon as stages 3–5, put in the diluted tomato soup, add a little wine if required and cooked chicken joints. Heat for a short time and serve.

Home Freezing

This dish freezes extremely well, although it is better if you replace the flour with 25 grammes (1 oz.) cornflour, or omit the thickening altogether and freeze as an unthickened stew. Reheat, and just before serving thicken with the quantity of flour in the recipe, or the amount of cornflour given above. You will find there is a slight loss of flavour as wine seems to lose a great deal in freezing. You may, therefore, prefer to add the wine towards the end of the reheating period.

COLD DISHES WITH POULTRY

There are a number of ways in which interesting dishes may be made with poultry. Here are one or two suggestions:

GALANTINE OF POULTRY–follow the directions for making the Beef galantine on page 87, but adapt this according to the poultry being used. If selecting chicken or turkey, use thin cream rather than stock; if using goose or duck, substitute beef sausagemeat for the pork, and use a good brown stock as the recipe on page 87. Omit the mushrooms and add 1 large grated dessert apple.

LEMON CHICKEN BRAWN–put a boiling chicken, thinly pared rind 1–2 lemons and 2 pig's trotters or calf's feet into a pan, add water to cover, seasoning and a *bouquet garni*. Simmer until the chicken is tender, remove, dice the meat from the chicken. Boil the stock as stage 6 in the Pork Brawn on page 88; when sufficiently reduced, dice the meat from the trotters, add to the chicken meat in a large basin, strain the stock over the top and allow to set.

ASPIC MOULD OF POULTRY–either follow the recipe for the Aspic meat mould on page 88, substituting poultry for veal, or dice some cooked poultry neatly and put into cold aspic jelly (made with poultry stock rather than water). Add vegetables as required–sliced raw mushrooms, cooked peas, etc.

Slimming Tips

The chicken brawn is relatively low in calories, particularly if you use the pig's trotter or calf's foot to give the jelly, but do not include this in the final mould. Both of these contain rather a lot of 'fatty' meat and are therefore high in calories. The aspic mould is a very good dish for slimmers.

Home Freezing

The 3 recipes given opposite freeze splendidly. You will find very little loss in flavour after freezing. Use all of these within about 2 months and allow to thaw out steadily at room temperature.

POULTRY WITH FRUIT

Fruit is a very pleasant accompaniment to poultry:

CHICKEN WITH APRICOT STUFFING: make or buy parsley and thyme (veal) stuffing, but add 6–7 tablespoons chopped canned or cooked apricots, bind with apricot syrup instead of an egg.

DUCK: blends well with fruit—serve with an orange (Bigarade) sauce, see page 149, or the familiar Apple sauce. There are many other ways to incorporate fruit when roasting a duck:

DUCK AND BLACK CHERRIES: roast the duck until nearly tender, then baste in some syrup from canned or cooked black cherries. Arrange duck on a dish with the cherries, make a sauce by thickening the syrup, flavour with cherry brandy, and serve with the poultry. Prunes also blend well with *duck* or *goose*. Or use canned or cooked apricots and flavour sauce with apricot brandy; use pineapple rings and flavour the sauce with a little lemon juice and/or brandy.

TURKEY OR GOOSE: blend well with a thick damson, gooseberry or sharp plum purée, instead of the more familiar sauces.

Home Freezing

The accompaniments to poultry make such an appreciable difference to the taste of the meat that it is worthwhile having supplies of frozen fruit available throughout the year. All you will need to do is to reheat the fruit adding some alcoholic drink to flavour, as suggestions opposite.

Chicken in Lemon Glaze

Serves 4
Cooking time approximately 1½–1¾ hours, plus 1 hour for simmering of giblets
Oven temperature 350–375° F. (180–190° C.), Gas Mark 4–5

Ingredients	Metric	Imperial
giblets from chicken		
water	568 ml (generous measure)	1 pint
seasoning	to taste	to taste
lemons	3	3
bouquet garni	spray	spray
roasting chicken	1¾–2 kilos (poor weight)	3½–4 lb.
cornflour	1½ *level* tablespoons	1½ *level* tablespoons
butter	25 grammes	1 oz.
sugar	to taste	to taste
TO GARNISH:		
cooked peas	50–75 grammes	2–3 oz.

1 Simmer giblets with water and seasoning until tender; this takes about 1 hour and gives an excellent stock–use the giblets as the Rillette on page 31.
2 Remove rind from 1 lemon, halve and cut out the flesh, discard pips and pith, use flesh for garnish.
3 Add the rind to the stock with the *bouquet garni*.
4 Put the chicken and lemon flavoured stock into a casserole, cover, cook for 20 minutes per lb. and 20 minutes over in the centre of a moderate oven; spoon stock over chicken once or twice during cooking.
5 Halve and squeeze juice from other 2 lemons, keeping cases intact.
6 When chicken is cooked, put on to a hot dish, keep hot, covering breast with foil so that it does not dry.
7 Measure just under 284 ml (½ pint) stock, strain and mix with the lemon juice.
8 Blend with cornflour, put into a saucepan with the butter. Cook until thickened, taste, adjust seasoning and add pinch sugar, or see below.
9 Coat chicken with this, garnish with the tiny pieces of fresh lemon. Fill halved lemon cases with cooked peas.

Note: lemons are so sharp in flavour, and vary so much in the amount of juice they contain, it may be worth while to add the juice gradually at stage 7, tasting as you do so (any left over juice can be frozen). If you reduce the amount of lemon juice you will need a little more stock.

Automatic Oven

Excellent for an oven meal, but has to be completed by thickening sauce. To complete meal, serve Vichy carrots, page 114, Fondant potatoes, page 116, Chocolate sponge, page 202.

Speedy Meal

Use bottled lemon juice; joint the chicken instead of cooking it whole.

Slimming Tips

An excellent dish, for chicken is a very good protein food and yet low in calories. If the diet is very strict, omit the sauce (stages 6–9). The chicken has a good flavour from cooking in the lemon flavoured stock.

Home Freezing

Freezes excellently in sauce, see casseroles page 76.
It may be advisable to joint the chicken after cooking, to fit into a neater shape in the freezer, and also heat through more quickly.

Oranged Chicken

Serves 4
Cooking time 13–15 minutes

Ingredients	Metric	Imperial
tiny spring chickens	2	2
butter	75–100 grammes	3–5 oz.
oranges	2	2
seasoning	to taste	to taste
TO GARNISH:		
orange	1	1
lime *or*	1	1
mint leaves	few	few

1 Either cut chickens into joints, or split down the stomachs so that the whole chickens open out flat.
2 Heat the butter in 2 large frying pans and fry quickly on either side until golden brown, then lower the heat and cook gently through until chickens are tender. If you have only one frying pan, you must cook the first chicken in half the fat, then keep this hot while you fry the second one.
3 When the chickens are brown, lift on to hot serving dishes.
4 If necessary, add a little extra butter to the pans with the juice from the 2 oranges and seasoning, heat until golden brown, pour over the chicken.
5 Garnish with slices of orange, peel of lime or mint leaves as picture facing page 96.

Speedy Meal

This is one of the quickest ways of cooking young chicken. If you do not care for the flavour of oranges, you could prepare and cook the chicken as stages 1 and 2, then allow the butter to go slightly brown and add chopped parsley, instead of oranges, to flavour.
If you split the chickens down the centre and open them out flat, the correct name to give this dish is Spatchcock of chicken.

Slimming Tips

This recipe can be adapted very easily for a slimming dish. Prepare as stage 1, leave out stage 2 where the chickens are fried in the butter, and instead put the juice of the oranges and seasoning into a pan, together with a little stock or water, and poach the chickens in this liquid until tender. If you wish the liquid to evaporate, do not cover the pan; if on the other hand you wish to retain some of the juices, put a saucepan lid or piece of foil over the frying pan.

Home Freezing

Frozen young chicken, when defrosted, can be similarly quickly cooked.

Curried Poultry

Most poultry can be served in a curried sauce, but the richer duck and goose should be skinned and any surplus fat removed before putting into the sauce. The following recipe is an excellent basic curry that may be used with any poultry; add additional sweetener with duck or goose to make a pleasing contrast to the richness of the flesh.

Serves 4–5
Cooking time 1½–2 hours

Ingredients	Metric	Imperial
onion	1 large	1 large
clove garlic	1–2	1–2
butter *or* fat	25–50 grammes	1–2 oz.
curry powder	1 tablespoon	1 tablespoon
cornflour	1 tablespoon	1 tablespoon
poultry stock	568 ml	1 pint
sugar	1–3 teaspoons	1–3 teaspoons
chutney	1 tablespoon	1 tablespoon
seasoning	to taste	to taste
sultanas	25–50 grammes	1–2 oz.
cooked poultry	½–¾ kilo	1–1½ lb.
TO SERVE:		
cooked rice	see page 76	see page 76

1 Chop the onion finely and crush the clove of garlic.
2 Fry these in the hot fat, then stir in curry powder and cornflour, cook for several minutes; gradually add stock.
3 Bring to the boil and cook until slightly thickened; add all the other ingredients, except the poultry, and simmer gently for about 30 minutes.
4 Put in the cooked poultry and continue cooking very slowly.
5 Serve on a bed of rice with the accompaniments as listed.

SERVE ALL OR SOME OF THESE: chutney; rings of raw onion or tiny onions; sliced green or red pepper; grated carrots; grated fresh or desiccated coconut; dried fruit (sultanas etc.) and sliced bananas or other fresh fruit; salted or fresh nuts; gherkins or sliced cucumber in yoghourt; fried Chapatis or Poppadums and Bombay duck.

Slimming Tips

A curry is not particularly high in calories if you use the minimum of fat and do not thicken the liquid. Simply let the curry sauce cook until much of the liquid has evaporated and serve by itself rather than on a bed of rice. It is also advisable to be sparing with the sweet ingredients, i.e. chutney, sultanas etc.

Home Freezing

Curries are one of the most successful of all stews to freeze. The flavour of a curry is so pronounced that freezing does not impair this in any way. It is advisable to thicken the sauce with cornflour rather than with flour (use half the quantity of cornflour). You may find that the curried sauce becomes a little thicker with freezing and this is why it may taste a little hotter and stronger than before it was frozen. Dilute with fresh stock or a little water before reheating—this will remedy both the points above.

Cooking Game

Many people can obtain a variety of game, but for most town-dwellers this is not easy. For this reason I have concentrated on the easily bought game–rabbit, hare, pheasant–and mentioned other game rather more briefly.

In order to enjoy game at its best, it is important that it is well hung before cooking; this does not mean it is necessarily 'high' (strong flavoured). This is a matter of personal taste–some people do not enjoy game (particularly pheasant, grouse, etc.) unless it is very strong in flavour; others dislike this intensely–so you must check with the poulterer as to the length of time the game should be hung. If game is cooked too soon after killing when it is very fresh, it is inclined to be tough. This applies even when the birds are young.

Comments about metrication calculations and automatic cooking of game are included under the poultry section, for they pose the same problems and need the same treatment.

Drinks to serve with game

Most people would agree that as all game, with the exception of rabbit, has a very definite and strong flavour it does blend better with red wines. Everyone will have their own favourite wine, but a good claret is superb. Used also in cooking game, red wine, port wine and cider or beer, all help to give a more tender texture to the flesh and a very interesting flavour.

Home freezing of game

Although game is mentioned under freezing of poultry because the method of freezing, etc., is the same, it is worth while adding that most game freezes extremely well. Make sure it has been hung for the length of time you would normally allow before cooking; it is *not* satisfactory to hang *after* freezing.

You will often find that the accompaniments (such as fried crumbs, bread sauce or other sauces) can be frozen with the game, so it is a very simple matter to produce the complete meal.

Always allow the game to thaw out completely before cooking. This will take some hours in the ordinary storage compartment of a refrigerator.

Accompaniments to game

Game is a food that depends very much on good accompaniments; it can be uninteresting without them. Roast game is served with Redcurrant jelly or Bread sauce, page 153. In addition, prepare the following:

FRIED CRUMBS–make soft breadcrumbs; most recipes state *fine* crumbs, but I prefer them to be a little coarse, as this gives a more interesting texture. Allow 1–2 tablespoons per person. Heat 50 grammes (2 oz.) butter or margarine in a pan and fry 6–8 tablespoons breadcrumbs until golden brown, turn over and fry on the second side. *If you are in a hurry*, fry packet crumbs.

YOU CAN FREEZE fried crumbs–cook, cool, drain well on absorbent paper, put into containers and freeze. To heat, simply remove quantity required from container and heat on a flat tray in a moderate oven.

GAME CHIPS–peel and cut old potatoes into wafer-thin slices, dry well with a cloth then fry as page 115, for chipped potatoes, giving either one or two fryings as desired. Drain on absorbent paper before serving.
If you are in a hurry, use packet potato crisps. Remove from box or packet, spread out on a baking tray, heat for a few minutes only. *Game chips are so brittle* they are not worth freezing.
If your mixer has a 'shredder and slicer' attachment, use this for preparing the potato slices.

TO REHEAT–both fried crumbs and chips may be fried earlier in the day and reheated in the oven on flat baking trays as required, but they scorch very easily.

FORCEMEAT BALLS (to serve with casseroled game) –prepare the Parsley and thyme (veal) stuffing as page 139, roll mixture into small balls and cook until golden brown.

Quite often one puts a piece of toast underneath the game while cooking; the purpose is to make certain no meat juices are wasted. This is traditional with the game mentioned on page 105, but can be included with all game (not venison, leveret or rabbit). Serve with watercress and a thickened or thin gravy as preferred. Occasionally a stuffing is suggested for game as page 138.

TO ROAST GAME

Although the various types of game vary a great deal in flavour, there are certain things to remember when roasting:

a) the game should be 'well-hung'–this is already mentioned in the introduction on page 104, but this makes a great deal of difference to the tenderness of the meat.

b) choose really young game to roast; this is plump and has flexible legs–not tough and 'sinewy'; old game is better in a casserole.

c) all game has a tendency to be dry, so cover with plenty of fat (a covered roaster or foil is very good) and do not over-cook. Details for extra cooking time when using a covered roasting tin are on page 66.

Choose *quick roasting* for game, i.e. 425–450°F. (220–240°C.), Gas Mark 7 (reduce heat to 375–400°F. (190–200°C.), Gas Mark 5–6 after first 15 minutes, or see under Automatic Oven, opposite).

GRAVY FOR ROAST GAME–if you have the liver from the game, it can be simmered in stock for a flavoured gravy, and the liver mashed with a little butter and spread over the toast that goes under game. There is a recipe for Game sauce on page 153.

Slimming Tips

Game is another meat that can be included in a slimming diet that is not too strict. Unfortunately, the accompaniments, fried crumbs etc., are very fattening, so these must be omitted as well as Redcurrant jelly or Bread sauce. You could serve wedges of lemon with game which gives a pleasing 'bite'.

Home Freezing

Details of freezing game are given on page 104. Roasted game can be frozen but do watch this very well indeed, otherwise it tends to be extremely dry. Use within 6 weeks to 2 months.

Usual game to roast

There are other kinds of game, but those listed below are the most readily available:

GOLDEN PLOVER	roast for 45 minutes	Do not 'draw'–roast with intestines in. Serve as pages 104, 105.
GROUSE	allow about 1 hour	Serve as pages 104, 105.
LEVERET (young hare)	allow 15–20 minutes per ½ kilo–poor weight (1 lb.) and 15–20 minutes over	Fill body with Sage and onion, page 139, or Chestnut stuffing, page 141. Serve with Bacon rolls, page 95.
PARTRIDGE	roast for 45 minutes	Serve as pages 104, 105.
PHEASANT	this can be stuffed with a) cream cheese, b) sliced fried mushrooms, c) piece herb flavoured butter. Roast for 1–1¼ hours	Serve as pages 104, 105.
PIGEON	make sure they are 'meaty' and young; allow 50 minutes–1 hour.	Serve as page 104, or with braised chestnuts.
RABBIT	see Leveret above	see Leveret above
TEAL (type of wild duck)	30–35 minutes if small and young	Accompaniments as game or duck.
VENISON (young deer)	allow 20–25 minutes per ½ kilo–poor weight (1 lb.) and 20–25 minutes over	Marinate if possible and serve with game sauce and accompaniments as pages 104, 105 or with peppered coating, page 106.
WIDGEON (another wild duck)	20–30 minutes if small and young	Accompaniments as game or duck.
WOODCOCK	allow 25–30 minutes	Do not 'draw'–roast with intestines in. Always cooked on toast. Serve as pages 104, 105.

Automatic Oven

Game can be left in an automatic oven and the choice of menu would of course depend upon the cooking time of the particular game.

Be very generous with the amount of fat spread over the game so there is no possibility of it drying as it cooks. Set the oven carefully to prevent the meat over-cooking. If you leave the oven on automatic setting you cannot alter the temperature as suggested opposite, so use the lower setting throughout the cooking time, and leave the meal in the oven for a slightly longer period.

TO ROAST VENISON

Although venison is difficult to obtain in some areas, when available do cook it, for the flavour is excellent.

Venison is rather like veal in that it is rather dry and very lean; the very best treatment is to marinate this before roasting, to provide extra fat and to tenderise the meat. The marinades on page 72 are very good, or blend equal quantities of oil and brown ale, or for a more luxurious marinade use port wine or claret. Flavour with seasoning, grated nutmeg and 1–2 crushed cloves of garlic. Lift the meat from the marinade and roast at the temperature on page 105, allowing 20–25 minutes per ½ kilo–poor weight (or 1 lb.) and 20–25 minutes over.

A very interesting coating on venison (which is equally good on veal) is during roasting to coat the outside of the meat with the following:

PEPPERED CRUMB COATING–to coat a joint for 6–8 people–melt 75 grammes (3 oz.) butter, or use dripping from roasting tin, add 150 grammes (6 oz.) soft brown breadcrumbs, ½–1 tablespoon crushed peppercorns and a good shake of salt. Spread over the outside of the joint 1–1¼ hours before the end of the cooking time, removing any skin if necessary. Continue roasting; the coating becomes crisp and a dark brown, see picture pages between 120/121.

Home Freezing
Uncooked venison freezes extremely well. It is so difficult to procure that if you can obtain this particular game it is very worthwhile freezing any spare joints.

TO BRAISE GAME

This method of cooking game is very successful, for it imparts a moist texture to the meat and the long cooking gives a tenderness to older birds, etc. Follow the directions for Braised beef on page 63, but you can add a few raisins or sultanas and shelled chestnuts to the 'mirepoix', as these give a slightly sweet flavour which blends well with game. Either serve the halved or jointed game on top of the unsieved 'mirepoix' or sieve this as suggested on page 63.

COOKING TIMES for braising game will be about twice the time given for roasting as page 105.

Home Freezing
Braised game freezes extremely well. Take care that it is not completely cooked so that it will not get dry. Although you can reheat from the frozen state, I find it better to allow braised game to thaw out before reheating.

TO FRY OR GRILL GAME

Very few birds are sufficiently young, plump and tender to be cooked by these quick methods. If they are, then follow the suggestions for frying and grilling steak on pages 70 and 74, or chicken on pages 94 and 96. The recipe that follows is very simple and extremely successful with very young partridge or pigeon.

Pigeon Cutlets

This is an excellent way to fry really young pigeons:
1 Halve 2 plump pigeons and remove as many bones as possible with a sharp knife, trying not to tear the flesh too much.
2 Fry 50 grammes (2 oz.) sliced mushrooms in 25 grammes (1 oz.) butter, add 2 finely chopped rashers of bacon and cook lightly.
3 Blend with 150 grammes (5–6 oz.) pork sausagemeat and 1–2 chopped gherkins.
4 Press this mixture round the pieces of pigeon and mould the meat, etc., into cutlet shapes.
5 Coat in 1 tablespoon seasoned flour, then in 1 beaten egg and approximately 50 grammes (2 oz.) soft fine breadcrumbs.
6 Fry in shallow or deep fat until crisp and brown, lower heat and cook more slowly until pigeons are tender; this will take 15–18 minutes in shallow fat, or about 10–12 minutes in deep fat. Serve with watercress, Bread sauce, page 153.

Note: if you are worried that the pigeons may not be tender, simmer in salted water until soft, cool, then bone.

Speedy Meal
It is a good idea to cook one or two extra pigeons (if roasting, rather than simmering as suggested opposite, take care not to over-cook). You can then prepare the cooked pigeons with the sausagemeat, etc., ready to fry on another occasion.

Home Freezing
You can prepare and freeze this dish ready to cook, but if freezing it is advisable to use uncooked pigeons.

Dijon Partridge

Serves 4
Cooking time 15–20 minutes

Ingredients	Metric	Imperial
small partridges*	4	4
seasoning	to taste	to taste
flour	1 tablespoon	1 tablespoon
butter	75 grammes	3 oz.
FOR THE SAUCE:		
white wine	142 ml	¼ pint
Dijon mustard**	1 tablespoon	1 tablespoon
chopped parsley	1 tablespoon	1 tablespoon
thick cream	4 tablespoons	4 tablespoons

*if plump, use 2 large ones only.
**a type of French mustard.

1 Split the birds under the stomach so they can be opened out like a Spatchcock of chicken.
2 Dust lightly with seasoned flour, and either fry in hot butter until just tender, or cook under the grill, basting with the melted butter.
3 When the birds are cooked, keep hot while making the sauce.
4 If you have used a frying pan, pour the wine in and stir round with a spoon to blend in any butter that remains. If the birds have been grilled, make the sauce in a saucepan but to make a richer flavour add any butter that has dropped into the grill pan.
5 Stir the mustard and parsley into the wine, heat thoroughly and add more seasoning if necessary. Finally stir in the cream and spoon over the birds; serve at once.

Speedy Meal
If you are fortunate enough to have fairly generous supplies of game, this is an ideal way to produce a quick meal with the minimum of effort. Serve with heated packet potato crisps, redcurrant jelly and a green salad. Dijon mustard like all French mustard, is ready-prepared for use.

Home Freezing
Frozen partridge should be thawed out thoroughly before preparing this dish. Dry well as when thawed out there is a slightly moist texture on the outside of frozen game. It is a good idea to split some birds *before* freezing if you like this particular recipe; they will thaw out much more quickly than whole birds.

Devilled Fried Game

Serves 4
Cooking time 10 minutes

Ingredients	Metric	Imperial
portions cooked game (rabbit legs particularly good)	4	4
TO COAT:		
flour	1 tablespoon	1 tablespoon
seasoning	to taste	to taste
dry mustard	1 teaspoon	1 teaspoon
curry powder	pinch	pinch
egg	1	1
Worcestershire sauce	1 teaspoon	1 teaspoon
crisp breadcrumbs	50 grammes	2 oz.
TO FRY:		
fat	50 grammes	2 oz.
TO SERVE:		
watercress	1 bunch	1 bunch
tartare sauce	see page 146	see page 146

1 Remove bones from the cooked game, if possible, and remove any skin; then coat in the flour blended with the seasoning, mustard and curry powder.
2 Brush with the egg mixed with the Worcestershire sauce, and then coat in the crumbs.
3 Fry in the hot fat until crisp and brown, then drain on absorbent paper. Serve with watercress and tartare sauce.

Note: this is an excellent way to present cold game in an interesting manner. To improve the flavour, marinate for several hours in 3 tablespoons oil, ½–1 teaspoon chilli sauce, pinch cayenne pepper, pinch curry powder and 1½ tablespoons wine vinegar. Lift out, drain, then coat as stages 1 and 2 above.

Speedy Meal
This is one of the quickest ways to prepare a hot dish with ready-cooked game, for although the recipe states that this is a good way to serve game cold, it also makes a very good hot dish. Serve with creamed potatoes, peas and sprouts and a well spiced Tomato sauce, see page 150.

Home Freezing
Although cooked roasted game is less satisfactory than uncooked game, there will be occasions when you have game left over and will need to freeze this to prevent it being wasted. This is an ideal way to 'use up' the cooked game when it is thawed out.
Put it into the marinade, to give a moist texture and interesting flavour, then continue as the recipe opposite.

Salmis of Game

Serves 4
Cooking time 45 minutes–2 hours*

Ingredients	Metric	Imperial
fat *or* dripping		
from cooking game	50 grammes	2 oz.
onions	2 large	2 large
carrots (optional)	2 large	2 large
flour	25 grammes	1 oz.
brown stock	284 ml	½ pint
port wine *or* red wine	142 ml	¼ pint
grouse *or* other	½–¾ kilo	1–1½ lb.
cooked game		
bouquet garni	spray	spray
seasoning	to taste	to taste
olives	1–2 tablespoons	1–2 tablespoons
TO GARNISH:		
bread	4 slices	4 slices
fat *or* butter	25–50 grammes	1–2 oz.
watercress	few sprigs	few sprigs
TO SERVE:		
redcurrant jelly		

*a salmis is a way of reheating cooked game.

1 Heat the fat in a large saucepan and fry the sliced onions and carrots for a few minutes.
2 Stir the flour into the vegetables, cook for several minutes, then gradually blend in the stock and wine and bring the sauce to the boil.
3 Lower the heat, put in the cooked game, the herbs and seasoning.
4 Simmer for about 30 minutes.
5 Add the olives and extra seasoning towards the end of the cooking time.
6 Cut the crusts from the bread, divide the slices into squares, fingers or triangles; fry in the hot fat until crisp and brown.
7 Spoon the salmis on to a hot dish, remove the herbs and arrange the croûtons of bread and watercress round the meat; serve with redcurrant jelly.

Casseroled Game

The recipe above can be used with older uncooked game birds. Uncooked joints or small whole birds should be fried in the fat until golden brown before frying the vegetables; then cook using double the quantity of brown stock and extend the cooking time to 1½–2 hours.

Barbecued Rabbit

Uncooked joints of rabbit may be simmered in the sauce above for approximately 1½–1¾ hours. Fry a little chopped fat bacon with the onions at stage 1–it improves the flavour.
Barbecued rabbit has a sweeter type of sauce–use the same recipe as the Salmis of game above, but *omit* both carrots and olives; add ½–1 tablespoon sugar to onions at stage 1, and cook until sugared onions brown in the fat. *Blend* 2 teaspoons dry mustard with flour at stage 2; 40 minutes before end of cooking time *add* ½ tablespoon concentrated tomato purée and 2–3 cored, peeled, thinly sliced dessert apples.

Automatic Oven

This is excellent for automatic cooking. *If using cooked game* then follow the recipe to stage 3, add the game, transfer to a casserole, cover tightly and heat for about 45 minutes in a very moderate oven. Add the olives and any seasoning required just before serving. Heat Duchesse potatoes, page 120, and a casserole of frozen peas and a Compôte of fruit in the oven to complete the menu.
For *Casseroled game* allow about 2 hours cooking time in a very moderate oven, and serve with jacket potatoes, see page 76, a Casserole of carrots and medium sized onions, see page 114, and a Caramel custard (which should be cooked in the coolest part of the oven in a tin of cold water), see page 187.
The Barbecued rabbit is cooked in the same way.

Speedy Meal

To most people game is too expensive to use other than for rather special meals, but if you wish to prepare a quick stew, rather similar to the Salmis opposite, heat the cooked or uncooked game in a diluted Mulligatawny soup. Add the olives towards the end of the cooking time.

Home Freezing

Both the Salmis of game and the Barbecued rabbit can be cooked and frozen. The flavour of Casseroled game is much better after freezing than the Salmis of game. Use cornflour for thickening instead of flour, allow half the quantity.

Jugged Game

Although hare is the game usually cooked in this manner, any other may be used instead. Adjust the cooking time accordingly; small game birds will cook in just about 2 hours. If using game birds, buy about 50–75 grammes (2–3 oz.) lamb's or calf's liver and use in the recipe. The term 'jugged' originated from the fact that the ingredients were cooked in a deep 'jug' or cooking utensil in a very slow oven.

Serves 6–8
Cooking time 2½–4 hours

Ingredients	Metric	Imperial
hare liver or other liver (see above)	50–75 grammes	2–3 oz.
seasoning	to taste	to taste
hare* or rabbits or equivalent in game birds	1 medium hare	1 medium hare
vinegar	1 tablespoon	1 tablespoon
cooking fat or dripping	50 grammes	2 oz.
onions	2–3 large	2–3 large
carrots	2–3 large	2–3 large
flour	50 grammes	2 oz.
brown stock	1 litre (generous measure)	2 pints
bay leaf	1	1
bouquet garni	spray	spray
port wine	4 tablespoons	4 tablespoons
redcurrant jelly	2 tablespoons	2 tablespoons
TO GARNISH:		
forcemeat balls	see page 86	see page 86
or savoury dumplings	see page 119	see page 119
TO SERVE:		
redcurrant jelly		

*ask the poulterer to save the blood of the hare.

1 Put the liver into a small pan, add seasoning and just enough water to cover; simmer for about 30–40 minutes.
2 Meanwhile, soak jointed hare or rabbit in cold water to which is added the vinegar, for about 1 hour; this whitens the flesh, but should not be done for game birds.
3 Heat the fat and fry the sliced onions and carrots in this, then stir in the flour and cook for several minutes.
4 Gradually add the brown stock, and the blood if cooking hare.
5 Bring the sauce to the boil, add the drained and dried hare (or rabbit or jointed game) and the herbs.
6 Simmer for about 1 hour with game birds or young rabbit, or about 1½–2 hours with hare.
7 Lift the game out of the sauce on to a plate, sieve the sauce and the well drained liver (this makes a great deal of difference to the flavour of the sauce).
8 Return the sauce to the pan with the port wine and jelly; simmer for a few minutes, then return the game to the sauce and continue cooking until quite tender.
9 While the game cooks, prepare and cook either the forcemeat balls or savoury dumplings.
10 Dish the hare or other game on to a large plate and top with the balls or dumplings.

Note: another garnish that is often used is fried croûtons of bread, and the traditional shape for these is a heart. Braised chestnuts and sprouts are both in season when game is at its best, and are the usual accompaniments. If you do not wish to serve redcurrant jelly, an Apple sauce, see page 148, or even a Bread sauce, see page 153, blend very well with the richness of jugged game, and this dish needs a really good claret as an accompaniment. Jugged game tastes almost better if cooked one day and reheated the next.

Automatic Oven

This dish may be left in an automatic oven to complete cooking. Follow the recipe to stage 8, then transfer to a tightly covered casserole and complete cooking in a slow to very moderate oven. Allow an extra 1¼ hours cooking time for *small birds* instead of the extra 45 minutes one would allow in a saucepan at stage 8. Allow an extra 2½ hours for *hare* instead of the 1½–2 hours one would allow in a saucepan at stage 8.

Jacket potatoes (very small with the shorter cooking time, or really large with the longer period, see page 76) and a casserole of suitable vegetables could be cooked in the same oven, together with baked fruit (if using shorter cooking period) or a milk pudding (for the longer cooking period).

The forcemeat balls should be covered if using the longer cooking period, and put into the coolest part of the oven, or browned earlier and put in the warming drawer so that they do not harden.

Mixer

The liquidiser of the mixer is invaluable for making the stuffing to form into forcemeat balls, or 'chopping' the herbs for the savoury dumplings. Read the instructions for making the stuffings, etc. on page 138.

Home Freezing

Jugged game freezes splendidly. Shorten the cooking time slightly if possible, so that game will not be over-cooked when reheated. There is no need to let this recipe thaw out completely before re-heating. Use cornflour rather than flour to thicken the liquid at stage 3, and use half the quantity given in the recipe. If wished the port wine could be added during the reheating period, as it tends to loose flavour in freezing.

Cooking Vegetables

There are so many vegetables available that one can prepare an endless variety of dishes. To make sure of enjoying vegetables at their best:
a) be critical when buying them; see they are fresh; use as soon as possible after buying;
b) cook as quickly as possible to retain flavour, colour and vitamins (except where stated to the contrary) or use uncooked where possible;
c) remember dried peas, beans and lentils (the pulses) can be used for main meals as they are a source of protein.

Metric Conversions

Completely accurate calculations are rarely necessary when making vegetable dishes, so the conversion to the metric system is no problem, except when shopping, to calculate whether the price offered is a reasonable one.

Drinks to serve with vegetables

When vegetables are part of the main course, the wine is generally chosen to blend with the fish or meat, etc. Choose a dry white wine to serve with a vegetable main dish.

New ways to serve vegetables

Vegetables are not just additions to a meal; they can provide a main meal in themselves. Peas, beans, lentils all provide protein and can take the place of meat or fish. For a vegetable meal choose a good selection, a green vegetable, a root vegetable, a protein vegetable and add any others you like. When cooked they can be topped with melted butter or served:
a) with a Cheese or Chopped hard-boiled egg sauce, recipes on page 146.
b) in a Curry sauce or Spiced barbecued sauce or a Tomato sauce, recipes on pages 147–151.
c) as a vegetable pie; put the cooked vegetables in a pie dish, coat with some kind of sauce, see above, then top with pastry or creamed potatoes and cook or brown in the oven.
d) in flans topped with a Cheese sauce, or as a Vegetable quiche, page 169.
You could also mix cooked vegetables with cooked macaroni shapes or spaghetti, and serve the dish topped with grated cheese or with a Tomato or Cheese sauce.

Cooking vegetables in the automatic oven

When planning a complete meal to be cooked in an automatic oven naturally one wants to include the vegetables, if possible.
Most vegetables *can* be cooked in the oven with the exception of green vegetables, which lose both colour and vitamins. Fortunately if cut into small pieces, or shredded finely, they cook so quickly in boiling water on top of the cooker that their cooking can be left until the meal is almost ready to dish up.

To use the automatic oven for most methods of cooking vegetables this is what you do:

TO 'BOIL' VEGETABLES–suitable for all root vegetables, peas or beans:
Put vegetables into a casserole, cover with water, add salt and a knob of margarine or butter. Cover casserole tightly; few lids are sufficiently airtight so it is better to use well-greased foil. If you do not have a suitable casserole, then use cake tins (without loose bases) and cover these with foil. As a general guidance to timing, you must allow about twice the cooking time (in a moderate oven) to the time allowed in a saucepan.

TO ROAST VEGETABLES–suitable for parsnips, potatoes, onions, swedes:
Melt a little fat in a saucepan, coat the vegetables in this; this makes sure they become evenly brown in a moderately hot to hot oven. Parsnips are more tender and have a better flavour if boiled for about 15 minutes in salted water before being drained, dried, then coated with fat. Potatoes should be treated in the same way; this prevents their discolouring during the waiting period in the oven. The colour should be quite all right if you take care to coat thoroughly in the melted fat, or even cook for a few minutes in fat before placing in the oven. Cooking time and temperature as usual; you could allow a little extra cooking time to compensate for the heating up period.

TO COOK VEGETABLES IN SAUCES, ETC.,–there are recipes for vegetables cooked in milk, tomato sauce, etc. Take care the vegetables and liquid are placed in a sufficiently deep container so that they do not boil over during cooking.

Home freezing of vegetables

The majority of vegetables can be frozen; the exceptions are lettuce, other salad greens and radishes (unless used instead of diced turnips as a cooking vegetable). Onions and courgettes (small marrow) and other vegetables are not satisfactory if treated as the table below, but information on preparing these will be found in the next column.

VEGETABLES PREPARED BY BLANCHING–the following are prepared for freezing by a process known as 'blanching'. The most usual way to do this is to immerse the vegetables in boiling water–*it is important to use sufficient water so that they move freely in the boiling water.* You need 3½–4 litres-generous measure (7–8 pints) to each ½ kilo–poor weight (1 lb.) vegetables, but it does not matter if you use less weight of vegetables to this amount of water; it is wrong though, to exceed this weight. Do not buy a special container until you are sure you are going to freeze large quantities of vegetables; make do with a preserving pan or saucepan and simply prepare small amounts at one time.

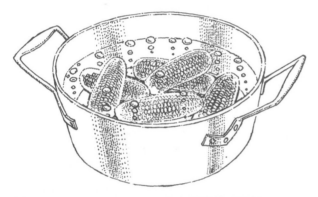

METHOD OF PREPARATION FOR BLANCHING

1. Choose really young vegetables, but mature enough to have a definite flavour.
2. Prepare as the table.
3. Lower into boiling water–do this steadily rather than all at once, so the water does not go off the boil for more than a few seconds.
4. Lift out of the boiling water; this is easier to do if the vegetables are put into a fine wire basket (do not buy a special one to begin with, use a fish fryer) or where they are small–such as peas–into several layers of muslin, which is lowered into the boiling water. Keep the ends of the muslin outside the pan so you can lift the vegetables out easily.
5. Plunge the hot vegetables into a bowl of cold water to which ice cubes are added; this cools them down quickly. Leave in the iced water for the same time as for blanching, i.e. if you blanch for 2 minutes you also cool for 2 minutes.
6. Drain on flat trays on clean folded tea cloths or several thicknesses of kitchen paper.
7. Pack and freeze as manufacturer's instructions.

Note: it is possible to blanch vegetables in a steamer *over* boiling water, not in water. I find no advantages in this method and would never use it for leaf vegetables such as spinach. To blanch in a steamer allow exactly 50 per cent longer, i.e. if blanching time in boiling water is 2 minutes allow 3 minutes in a steamer, and count the time from when you see steam coming through the holes, *not* from the time you place the vegetables in the steamer.

Times for blanching–preparation means virtually preparing as though cooking; hints under this column are peculiar to freezing:

Vegetable:	Preparation:	Blanching:
Asparagus	Do not tie in bunches; make sure length is not too deep for container.	Thin–2 minutes Thick–4 minutes
Beans, broad	If pods are very young, break into pieces, treat like French or runner beans.	3 minutes
Beans, French	If very small, just string and leave whole; if larger treat as runner beans.	2 minutes
Beans, runner	Prepare, cut in 1 inch lengths.	2 minutes
	Sliced (flavour not retained as much as in pieces).	1 minute
Broccoli	Try to choose tight heads and trim.	
	Small heads	3 minutes
	Large heads	4 minutes
Carrots	Young carrots only.	
	Diced–	2 minutes
	Whole small–	5 minutes
Cauliflower	Cut into even-sized pieces, retain 1 or 2 small leaves.	3 minutes
Corn	Must be very young. Remove outside husk.	
	Small–	4 minutes
	Large–	6 minutes
	To freeze corn off the cob blanch for 4–5 minutes, remove kernels. You do not reblanch, just cool for 1 minute and freeze.	
Mixed vegetables (Macedoine)	Turnips, swedes, peas, carrots, beans, corn, can form part of mixed vegetables. Turnips and swedes tend to soften but make a good flavour. Prepare as diced carrots. It is better to blanch each vegetable separately, cool, drain, mix before freezing.	
Peas	Choose about same size, small but large enough to have flavour.	1 minute
Spinach	Wash as usual, blanch 200 grammes (8 oz.) at a time only.	2 minutes
Sprouts	Choose young, small– prepare as usual.	2 minutes

Celery should not be frozen if it is to be eaten raw or in a salad. It can be blanched and frozen if it is to be cooked before eating.

FREEZING VEGETABLES BY METHODS OTHER THAN BLANCHING

ARTICHOKES (JERUSALEM)–cook, form into a purée (as potatoes) and freeze.

ARTICHOKES (GLOBE)–cook in usual way, remove tender base, pack and freeze.

AUBERGINES (EGG PLANT)–prepare by slicing, sprinkling with salt (this prevents bitter flavour) then allowing to stand for 15 minutes. Coat in seasoned flour, fry until tender. Drain, pack and freeze.

BEETROOT–cook young beetroot, cool, dice or slice thinly, then pack.

CABBAGE–stuff, see page 120, and freeze; or you can blanch as spinach (shred fairly finely) but allow 1½ minutes in boiling water–the flavour is disappointing, though.

CELERY AND CELERIAC–braise, cool and pack.

COURGETTES AND MARROW–use in Ratatouille or other vegetable dishes, see pages 121, or fry as aubergines, or cook, mash and freeze.

MUSHROOMS–wash and fry in butter. Cool and freeze; this gives better results than blanching.

ONIONS AND LEEKS–cook by boiling or frying; cool and freeze.

PEPPERS–although slices of pepper may be frozen by blanching for 1 minute, the best result is obtained if you wash, dry and freeze quickly without wrapping. After 24 hours, wrap. Use in salads when barely defrosted.

POTATOES–cook, cream; freeze either as plain mashed vegetable, as Duchesse potatoes, page 120 Potato croquettes, page 115–or make into chips or slices, fry until tender but not brown; spread out flat on trays covered with absorbent paper to drain away surplus fat. Freeze on flat trays, so they do not stick together, then pack. Really young new potatoes should be completely cooked, cooled, frozen.

TOMATOES–skin if wished, simmer to make pulp, season, adding pinch of sugar, then pack.

In addition most vegetables can be frozen as a purée to make stews, sauces, etc. Cool rapidly after sieving.

Note: vegetable purées tend to expand during freezing, so allow about 1–1½ cm (½–¾ inch) space (head-room) in container.

FREEZING HERBS

Herbs freeze well and retain their flavour. Pick freshly, wash and dry, then chop and–

a) put into small containers, cover, freeze. Mint can be frozen *with* sugar for mint sauce.

b) freeze a mixture of herbs in cubes of water or stock in ice making trays, remove, pack into polythene bags, use as *bouquet garni.*

c) freeze unwrapped small bunches of parsley; when brittle (straight from freezer) they can be crumbled over salads or other dishes.

Saving time when cooking vegetables

Modern methods of freezing, drying and canning all mean that vegetables may be prepared and served within the minimum of time.

Cut vegetables into smallest possible pieces; this means shredding cabbage and other greens; dividing cauliflower into small flowerets, etc. This not only shortens cooking time but makes sure you retain the maximum of flavour and a firm texture.

USE A PRESSURE COOKER for those vegetables that take a long time (all vegetables *can* be cooked in a pressure cooker, but it does mean the most careful timing for greens, etc.).

To use the pressure cooker, put vegetables on the rack with a little salt and the amount of water recommended by the manufacturer, usually this is 142 ml (¼ pint). Put on the weight, bring to 15 lb. pressure and time from then. Some of the most successful are:

BEANS–both broad and sliced runner, and whole French–about 3 minutes.

BRUSSELS SPROUTS, SHREDDED CABBAGE, SPINACH AND OTHER GREENS–1½ minutes, until cooked but firm.

CARROTS, TURNIPS, SWEDES–if very young or cut into slices, allow about 3 minutes; if larger pieces and old, and you want them soft enough to mash, allow about 8 minutes.

CAULIFLOWER–if cut into small sprigs (flowerets) allow 2 minutes; for larger flowerets up to 4 minutes–*Broccoli* takes the same time.

CORN ON THE COB–use more water than usual, about double the quantity–allow 4 minutes and be sparing with the salt.

ONIONS AND LEEKS–about 4 minutes if sliced or small; up to 6 minutes if larger.

PEAS–fresh, about 1 minute only.

POTATOES–either peeled, scraped or with jackets left on, take 8–15 minutes depending on size. The flavour is less good than when cooked in an ordinary saucepan.

Always reduce the pressure speedily by putting the cooker under cold water; this prevents the vegetables being over-cooked and spoiled.

DRIED VEGETABLES

Modern A.F.D. (Accelerated Freeze Drying) vegetables need neither soaking nor long cooking, the latest developments mean that some vegetables and soups need only a few minutes cooking. Ordinary dried peas, beans and lentils cook much more quickly in a pressure cooker. Either, cover with cold water, soak overnight, cook lentils, peas for 15 minutes, beans for 30 minutes, at 15 lb. pressure (never fill pan more than half full): or, *do not soak,* cover with cold water, cook for 1 hour at 15 lb. pressure. Allow pressure to drop at room temperature; it is unwise to cool the pan down quickly in this case.

20. Mixed grill, see page 74

SOME BASIC WAYS TO COOK VEGETABLES

There are many and varied ways to cook vegetables and the most usual are given on this page. When cooking vegetables it is essential to cook them in such a way as to retain:

a) THE MAXIMUM OF VITAMINS–green vegetables in particular contain valuable vitamins and these are retained if by careful buying you make sure the vegetables are fresh and then cook as soon as possible after buying–cooking as quickly as possible, and serving immediately.

b) THE MAXIMUM OF FLAVOUR–this is also achieved by cooking as quickly as possible, and when boiling, by using the minimum of water.

Home Freezing

By freezing vegetables you have an excellent selection throughout the year: they can be quickly and easily prepared. 'Blanching' vegetables for freezing helps to tenderise them, and therefore the cooking time for frozen vegetables can be kept to a minimum so that they retain the maximum flavour.

Frozen vegetables can be cooked in most of the ways given on these pages.

TO BAKE VEGETABLES

Potatoes are the vegetable baked more often than any other. Scrub them well, but do not peel, then bake in the oven until tender. Prick the skin so the potatoes will not 'burst' during cooking and put on to a baking tray. Ideally a large potato should take about 2 hours in the centre of a very moderate oven, but you will find deviations of cooking time and temperatures in some automatic meals in order that the potatoes will be cooked within the time given for the main dish.

Tomatoes should be baked whole or halved. Season lightly and top with a very little margarine or butter if wished. Whole tomatoes take about 20 minutes in the centre of a moderate oven.

Mushrooms are baked by washing, removing stalks if wished, then topping each with a very little margarine or butter, and seasoning. Cover the dish, bake for approximately 25 minutes in a moderate oven. Mushrooms may also be covered with milk and baked like this for the same period.

Automatic Oven

One of the easiest vegetables to cook is a potato in its skin. If you wish to cook the potatoes within a short period choose small ones and place them in the hottest part of the oven. If you wish the potatoes to bake for a very long period, buy very large ones and cook in the coolest part of the oven.

It is a wise precaution to cook potatoes on foil or a baking tin in case the skin should break (in spite of pricking them).

TO BRAISE VEGETABLES

The instructions given for braising meat and poultry are generally too complex for cooking vegetables, so a much more simple method of cooking is generally employed to 'braise' onions, celery hearts, etc. Prepare the vegetables and turn in a little hot margarine or butter until they are pale golden brown. Cover with a thin Brown sauce, or with a Brown sauce flavoured with tomato, page 147, then simmer until the vegetables are tender. Celery hearts take about 1¼ hours or medium onions about the same time.

Automatic Oven

Braising is another way of preparing vegetables that permits them to be put into a casserole and left in the automatic oven. Allow approximately the same cooking time as for 'boiling' in the oven, see above, and page 110.

TO BOIL VEGETABLES

Green vegetables should be shredded, put gradually (so the water still boils) into the minimum of salted water and cooked as quickly as possible (this varies from 2–3 minutes for shredded cabbage).

Root vegetables also should be put into boiling salted water, but since they take longer to cook you will need more water.

Dried vegetables–haricot beans, peas, etc., vary. It is possible to buy Accelerated Freeze Dried vegetables that do not need soaking or prolonged cooking; but other dried vegetables should be soaked overnight in water to cover, then cooked in fresh water, with salt to taste, until tender. This takes approximately 2 hours.

When vegetables are cooked they should be strained, tossed in a little margarine or butter and served at once. The vegetable water retains some vitamins and mineral salts so can be usefully put into gravy, sauces or soups.

Automatic Oven

It is a great asset to be able to 'boil' vegetables in a covered casserole in the oven as part of an automatic meal. You can 'adjust' the cooking period of the vegetables to fit in with the main dish by the position of the casserole in the oven, and the size of the vegetables; e.g. keep carrots whole if the cooking time is long, dice or slice them if they must be tender within a relatively short time.

A small knob of butter or margarine in the cooking water helps to retain the flavour of the vegetables, see the comments about timing on page 110.

Some interesting ways to vary boiled vegetables

To make boiled vegetables more interesting, try the following—cooking time, of course, as boiled vegetables:

CREAMED VEGETABLES: cook potatoes, carrots, etc., in salted water until nearly tender; strain, return to the pan with thin cream, or top of the milk, and continue cooking until the liquid has evaporated and the vegetables are cooked.

MACEDOINE OF VEGETABLES: cook diced mixed root vegetables and fresh peas, chopped beans, etc., in boiling salted water; drain and toss in melted margarine and chopped parsley.

TOMATO VEGETABLES: cook celery hearts or whole onions, in tomato juice instead of salted water.

VICHY CARROTS: cook young carrots in stock instead of salted water. Do not cover the pan, this allows stock to evaporate as the carrots cook and become tender; they not only then have a good flavour but a glazed appearance.

Automatic Oven

The Creamed vegetables are not practical for an automatic oven.

The Macedoine of vegetables and Tomato vegetables may be cooked in a covered casserole in the oven, allow about twice the cooking time in a covered casserole. The Vichy carrots may be cooked in an automatic oven, but it is difficult to allow the stock to evaporate without over-drying the vegetables. The best way is to cook in a covered casserole until the carrots are tender, then to tip into a saucepan and boil rapidly until the liiquid evaporates.

TO CASSEROLE VEGETABLES

Put the vegetables you would normally boil, with the exception of green vegetables, into a casserole and cover with salted water, then cook in the oven. Allow about twice the cooking time you would give the vegetables in a saucepan; see also page 110 for more details.

The more interesting ways of boiling vegetables, immediately above, are also suitable for cooking in a casserole.

One of the most suitable is to cook vegetables in tomato juice in a covered casserole. The liquid may be thickened with a little corn-flour at the end of cooking, if wished, to make a thicker sauce, which is then poured over the vegetables.

Automatic Oven

Mention has been made on several occasions about cooking vegetables in a covered casserole in an automatic oven; read the preceding pages and page 110. *Always* make sure the vegetables are well covered with liquid if they are the type that discolour easily, also that the casserole lid fits well, or the container is covered with foil.

Creamed Scalloped Potatoes

Serves 4–5
Cooking time 1–1¼ hours
Oven temperature 325–350° F. (170–180° C.), Gas Mark 3–4

Ingredients	Metric	Imperial
peeled or scraped old *or* new potatoes (weight when prepared)	½ kilo (good weight)	1¼ lb.
milk	284 ml	just under ½ pint
thin cream	4 tablespoons	4 tablespoons
butter	40 grammes	1½ oz.
seasoning	good amount	good amount

1 Cut the potatoes into very thin slices or use mixer attachment.
2 Put into an ovenproof dish—the more shallow the dish the quicker the potatoes will cook. Never over-fill any dish though, otherwise the milk boils over.
3 Heat the milk and cream in a saucepan with most of the butter, add plenty of salt and pepper.
4 Pour over the potatoes and top with the rest of the butter.
5 Bake in the centre of a very moderate oven until tender and golden brown.

Automatic Oven

Make sure the milk covers the potatoes when standing. To complete the menu, choose a meat casserole dish, as page 76, Macedoine of vegetables and Golden fruit pudding, page 202.

Speedy Meal

Use canned potatoes and half the amount of milk. Cook for 30 minutes only in a moderate to moderately hot oven, or use a coarse grater to shred raw potatoes.

Home Freezing

Freezes well after cooking, but use a little more cream when reheating to give a tender texture. Store for 4–5 weeks only.

Scalloped Potatoes

This dish is cooked in the same way as the recipe above, but use all milk instead of the mixture of milk and thin cream. To give a more piquant flavour to scalloped potatoes you can flavour the dish as follows:

ONION SCALLOPED POTATOES: mix very thinly sliced onions with the sliced potatoes.

HAM OR BACON SCALLOPED POTATOES: chop and fry a few rashers of bacon or chopped lean ham and mix with the potatoes.

Home Freezing

Both the Creamed scalloped potatoes, and the variations, can be frozen for a short time. Cook sufficiently lightly so that a little liquid remains, otherwise it tends to be over-dry when reheated. Wrap well and allow to defrost before reheating. Use within 1 month.

TO FRY VEGETABLES

Vegetables are fried in two basic ways; in shallow or deep fat. Drain *most* fried vegetables on absorbent paper.

SHALLOW FRYING

Use only a small amount of fat as indicated in the various suggestions.

AUBERGINES : slice thinly, do not peel, coat in seasoned flour (allow to stand sprinkled *very lightly* with salt if you dislike the bitter taste, then flour); heat fat to give 1 cm ($\frac{1}{2}$ inch) in pan, fry until golden brown, turn and fry on second side. Drain well.

COURGETTES : slice thinly, do not peel, coat in seasoned flour, or in batter as page 122. Fry as aubergines.

MUSHROOMS : do not peel if perfect : wash well, remove stalks if wished, slice if large, then fry steadily in hot dripping, butter or margarine until tender. Do not drain on paper.

ONIONS : peel, cut into rings, then separate these and coat in a very little milk, then seasoned flour for a crisp onion, or just dry and season for soft onion rings. Fry as aubergines and drain very well.

PEPPERS (CAPSICUMS) : cut in rings, coat in flour if wished, fry in very little fat; only drain if coated.

POTATOES : prepare as for deep frying, below. If frying raw slices or chips then you will need a minimum of $1\frac{1}{2}$ cm ($\frac{1}{2}$–$\frac{3}{4}$ inch) fat in the pan. Fry steadily until golden brown on one side, then turn and fry on the second side until golden brown and tender. You could remove and fry twice, as under deep frying, but this is not essential. Drain very well. See also recipes below.

TOMATOES : halve or slice (skin if wished) and fry steadily in a *little* hot fat, season well (add a pinch of sugar too). There is no need to drain these before serving.

Cooked potatoes can be fried in various ways, some of the popular fried dishes with cooked potatoes are:

LYONNAISE POTATOES

Boil potatoes until nearly cooked, then cool. Slice raw onions thinly, and potatoes fairly thickly. Use half amount of onions as potatoes. Heat fat to give a depth of 1 cm ($\frac{1}{2}$ inch), fry seasoned potato and onion mixture until tender; turn during frying, so the vegetables cook evenly. Top with chopped parsley. Do not drain.

POTATO CAKES

Mash cooked potatoes, season, add enough flour to give a firm consistency. Form into cakes with your hands. Fry in the same amount of fat as above, drain on paper.

POTATO CROQUETTES

As potato cakes, the mixture can be bound with an egg yolk or egg, but do not use milk when mashing the potatoes–just a little margarine or butter. Form into finger shapes, coat with seasoned flour, egg and breadcrumbs. Use as much fat as you can in the pan to brown both the sides and surface of the croquettes, turn carefully; when cooked drain thoroughly on absorbent paper.

SAUTÉ POTATOES

Slice cooked potatoes fairly thickly, fry as Lyonnaise potatoes until brown, turn during cooking. Drain on absorbent paper and top with chopped parsley before serving.

PAPER TO USE WHEN DRAINING VEGETABLES

Use either crumpled tissue paper, kitchen paper or kitchen roll. Do not use greaseproof paper–it retains fat and does not allow this to drain from food as with absorbent papers.

CLEANING FAT

When frying in shallow fat one rarely has any surplus; wipe out the pan with kitchen paper and wash. Strain deep fat or oil and keep this to use again.

Automatic Oven

Mention is made in some recipes of 'oven frying' potatoes. This is quite easily done. Brush a baking tray with melted fat or with oil. If using the oven manually it is a good idea to heat the tray then put the prepared vegetables on it. Brush sliced potatoes liberally with melted fat or oil, and cook until crisp and brown in a moderately hot to hot oven.

Naturally, if using the automatic oven, you cannot pre-heat the tin, but make sure the sliced potatoes are well coated with the oil or fat to prevent their becoming black while standing.

Speedy Meal

Ready-frozen potato croquettes and chips enable you to produce fried vegetables very easily and quickly. Frozen potatoes having been given a first frying before freezing, you need fry once only. Use ready-cooked potatoes or dehydrated potatoes for potato cakes, etc.

Canned potatoes are extremely good for Lyonnaise potatoes and Sauté potatoes.

Mixer

If you have a slicing attachment use this for cutting aubergines, and for thinly sliced potatoes for game chips. Use the whisk or beater to give very smooth creamed potatoes for potato cakes, etc.

Home Freezing

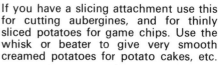

The methods of preparing many vegetables for freezing are mentioned on pages 111 and 112. Potato cakes and Potato croquettes can be prepared and frozen, ready to fry from the frozen state, or you can fry these (if wished) cool, then freeze. Reheat in the oven to save the bother (and smell) of frying. Wrap the cakes, or croquettes, after freezing so that the soft coating does not stick to the wrapping.

Corn Fritters

Serves 4
Cooking time 4–5 minutes

Ingredients	Metric	Imperial
egg	1	1
self-raising flour	2 level tablespoons	2 level tablespoons
salt	pinch	pinch
cayenne pepper	pinch	pinch
Worcestershire sauce	1 teaspoon	1 teaspoon
can corn kernels	1 large	1 large
or packet frozen cooked corn	1 large	1 large
TO FRY: deep or shallow fat*		

*see Chicken Maryland.

1 Make a batter with beaten egg, flour and seasonings.
2 Beat well, mix in the sauce and the drained corn.
3 Fry tablespoons of the mixture in a little hot fat until golden brown, turning once–4–5 minutes. You may need to add a little extra fat to the pan after frying the first batch, or drop the fritters into deep fat if using these for the Chicken Maryland, as page 95.

DEEP FRYING
Check the temperature of the fat or oil as under frying fish, page 46. Drain carefully after frying. The most suitable vegetables for deep frying are aubergines, onions and potatoes; you could also fry sliced carrots (as potatoes) and any vegetable fritters.
AUBERGINES: prepare as above, fry until crisp, drain well.
ONIONS: either coat in flour or in batter, see page 46, fry until crisp and brown, drain well.
POTATOES: cut into desired shapes, dry very well, then fry steadily in the hot fat until soft and very pale in colour. Lift out of the fat, reheat this, then fry the potatoes for the second time until crisp and golden brown, this will take only 2 minutes, approximately. Drain well. *Potato croquettes* can be fried in deep fat, and brown more evenly than in shallow fat. Check temperature of fat carefully when frying these as they will 'burst' their coating if the fat is too hot; drain well before serving.

TO ROAST VEGETABLES

Many vegetables may be roasted in hot fat in the oven; where possible put round the meat as this gives additional flavour as well as providing the fat to crisp them.
The most suitable vegetables for roasting are:
ONIONS: skin, turn in the hot fat, allow about 1¼ hours for medium sized onions in a moderate to moderately hot oven.
PARSNIPS: these tend to be better if you parboil for about 20 minutes in salted water, drain then roast. Allow 50–60 minutes for *medium* sized parboiled parsnips or up to 1½ hours if uncooked parsnips; temperature as onions.
POTATOES: many people prefer the taste of roast potatoes if they are first parboiled for about 10 minutes then drained and roasted. *Medium sized* potatoes then take about 35–45 minutes; if not partially cooked, allow about 1 hour; temperature as for onions. Old potatoes should be peeled before cooking; new potatoes may be scrubbed and roasted with their skins on, these are *not* parboiled first.
SWEDES, TURNIPS: as parsnips; they are very good roasted.

Speedy Meal
If you have no time to make fritters, then just blend the drained corn with 2 beaten seasoned eggs and fry tiny spoonfuls as a kind of corn omelette.

Mixer
This is useful for making the batter for the fritters, use either the mixer on a low speed to prevent splashing, or the liquidiser, read comments about batters on page 160.

Home Freezing
These freeze very well when cooked. Reheat in the oven to save frying again; they regain their crispness.

Mixer
Prepare the batter for coating onions in the liquidiser goblet.

Home Freezing
Ready-frozen fried chips or fried sliced potatoes may be either deep fried or fried in shallow fat. If you wish you can fry chips, etc. in deep fat, drain well, freeze and then reheat in the oven as required. This would enable you to incorporate them into complete meals in the freezer. Rissoles with fried tomatoes and fried chips—reheat in the oven on an uncovered dish to give a crisp texture. Fried chicken with fried mushrooms and potato croquettes; reheat in an uncovered dish in the oven so they regain their crispness.

Automatic Oven
Roast vegetables are ideal for an automatic meal. Sometimes the joint or main dish may need longer cooking than the vegetables, in this case choose very large ones and coat well in the melted fat before placing in the oven to cook in a cooler part. You cannot roast vegetables in a cool oven, they would be very 'soggy' and unpalatable, but **Fondant potatoes** are an ideal way of cooking the vegetable when the heat of the oven is too low for proper roasting. Brush the raw potatoes with melted fat (so they do not discolour) then put them in a roasting tin with about ¼ cm (½ inch) stock in it. This gives a combination of steaming and roasting. Cover the tin and cook for about twice the roasting time, in a very moderate to moderate oven.

Home Freezing
Roast vegetables freeze quite well for a very limited period of about 5–6 weeks.

LIGHT MEALS WITH VEGETABLES

Many light meals may be made entirely from vegetables, particularly if you include those rich in protein–peas, beans, lentils–or serve vegetables with a cheese or egg sauce. You can adapt other recipes, e.g.

LENTIL OR NUT RISSOLES: follow the recipe for rissoles, page 91; use cooked lentils or minced nuts instead of meat.

LENTIL CROQUETTES: cook 200 grammes (8 oz.) lentils and use instead of raw chicken in the recipe on page 134.

Speedy Meal
Use the excellent canned, frozen or Accelerated Freeze Dried vegetables for quick meals. The food value of many vegetables remains unimpaired by preserving, but also serve uncooked tomatoes with these meals to provide valuable Vitamin C.

Speedy Spinach Soufflé

Serves 4–6
Cooking time 35–40 minutes
Oven temperature 375–400° F. (190–200° C.), Gas Mark 5–6

Ingredients	Metric	Imperial
packet frozen chopped spinach	large	large
or fresh spinach	½ kilo (poor weight)	1 lb.
seasoning	to taste	to taste
thick cream	3 tablespoons	3 tablespoons
egg yolks	2	2
egg whites	3	3
butter	small knob	small knob

1 Cook the spinach until tender. It is a good idea if using frozen spinach to allow this to defrost before cooking, when extra water need not be added.
2 Season the spinach as it cooks then strain. Sieve fresh spinach.
3 Add the cream, egg yolks and finally the stiffly beaten egg whites.
4 Put into a lightly greased 15–18-cm (6–7-inch) soufflé dish and bake in the centre of a moderate to moderately hot oven for approximately 25 minutes.

Mixer
Put the cooked spinach, cream, egg yolks into the liquidiser to give a smooth purée, tip back into pan or bowl, fold in egg whites–whisk these stiffly in a bowl with the electric mixer.

Slimming Tips
Omit the cream and use 2 tablespoons skimmed milk instead. This is an excellent supper dish served with cottage cheese, or put a layer of cottage cheese in the soufflé dish and top with the spinach mixture. Bake for an additional 8–10 minutes.

Home freezing
While one can use frozen spinach for this recipe, it is *not* possible to freeze either a cooked or uncooked soufflé mixture, and the spinach and cream mixture does not freeze well.

Cheese and Spinach Soufflé

1 Ingredients as above, but add 75–100 grammes (3–4 oz.) grated cheese to the purée.
2 As this makes a heavier mixture, if you add 4 egg whites instead of 3 you will have a soufflé that will rise better.

Mixer
If the cheese is diced finely it may be put into the liquidiser with the ingredients.

Piquant Spinach Soufflé

1 Ingredients as main recipe, but omit the cream and use 2 large skinned tomatoes instead, and add 1 medium onion.
2 Chop the onion very finely (or grate this). Add to the spinach during cooking.
3 Mix the chopped tomatoes with spinach and onions and sieve together, then proceed as from stage 3 (omitting cream).

Mixer
Put the raw quartered tomatoes, cooked onion and spinach into the liquidiser to give a smooth purée.

Home Freezing
The exact amount of sieved or emulsified spinach, plus tomatoes and onion, may be frozen, ready to make this soufflé.

Creamy Spinach Soufflé

1 Ingredients as above, but use half the amount of spinach only–this gives a more delicately flavoured mixture. Cook as stages 1 and 2.
2 Make a thick sauce with 25 grammes (1 oz.) butter and 25 grammes (1 oz.) flour, the spinach and 142 ml (¼ pint) thick cream.
3 Add the egg yolks, season well, then fold in the stiffly beaten egg whites, or emulsify in liquidiser, and continue as main recipe.

Home Freezing
This is *not* a satisfactory mixture to freeze.

Vegetable Pancakes

Pancakes can be filled with a variety of vegetable mixtures to give interesting meals, here are some suggestions:

First make the pancake batter on page 160, cook pancakes and keep hot, either on an uncovered dish in the oven or over a pan of boiling water while you prepare the vegetable mixture. Quantities for fillings are enough for 4 as a main dish or 8 as an hors d'oeuvre or light supper dish.

a) MUSHROOM AND COTTAGE CHEESE PANCAKES WITH CREAM SAUCE: fry approximately 150 grammes (6 oz.) mushrooms in 50 grammes (2 oz.) margarine or butter, blend with 150 grammes (6 oz.) cottage cheese, chopped parsley and seasoning. Fill pancakes with mixture, top with 284 ml (½ pint) soured cream blended with seasoning and mixed herbs. Heat under grill.

b) SPINACH PANCAKES AU GRATIN: cook approximately ½ kilo (1 lb.) seasoned spinach, drain, sieve or chop and blend with about 25 grammes (1 oz.) butter and 75 grammes (3 oz.) grated cheese. Fill pancakes and put into an ovenproof dish; top with cheese sauce, crisp breadcrumbs and a little grated cheese. Brown under the grill or in oven.

c) TOMATO AND BACON PANCAKES: cook 2–3 chopped rashers of bacon for 5 minutes with 1 grated onion, add good knob of fat and fry approximately ½ kilo (1 lb.) seasoned skinned tomatoes until a thick purée. Fill pancakes with this mixture, top with fried Bacon rolls, see picture facing page 57.

Automatic Oven

The filled pancakes can be put into the oven and covered with foil to prevent drying, then reheated as part of an automatic meal that needs only about 30 minutes in a moderate heat. Cook mushrooms in either soured cream or butter in a covered casserole to serve with b) or c); bake tomatoes to serve with a) or b). Heat Duchesse potatoes, page 120, and a Compote of fruit page 135 for a complete menu.

Mixer

As stated on page 160, either the whisk or the liquidiser may be used for making pancake batters. The liquidiser would be ideal for making a smooth purée of the spinach (recipe b)) although it does make it rather soft.

Home Freezing

Pancakes freeze excellently, see page 161, and the fillings given opposite all freeze well. Make the Cheese sauce, recipe b), with cornflour rather than flour; do not over-cook the cheese mixture when reheating the pancakes. There is no need to defrost pancakes to reheat. Use within 5–6 weeks.

Mushroom Risotto

Serves 4–5
Cooking time 30 minutes

Ingredients	Metric	Imperial
oil	2 tablespoons	2 tablespoons
onion	1	1
garlic	1 clove	1 clove
mushrooms	200 or 225 grammes	8 oz.
long grain *or* Italian rice	200 or 225 grammes	8 oz.
beef *or* chicken stock, *or* water and 1–2 stock cubes	568 ml	1 pint
seasoning	to taste	to taste
sultanas	50 grammes	2 oz.
TO GARNISH:		
mushrooms	4–5	4–5
tomatoes	2–3	2–3
butter	50 grammes	2 oz.
TO SERVE:		
grated Parmesan cheese	50 grammes	2 oz.

1 Heat oil and fry finely chopped onion and crushed clove garlic for a few minutes.
2 Add sliced or whole mushrooms (depending on size) but save a few for garnish. Turn in the onion mixture for a short time.
3 Add rice and blend with oil, etc., (this helps to keep every grain separate).
4 Add stock or water and stock cubes, bring to the boil, season well and cook steadily in an uncovered pan for about 15 minutes.
5 Add sultanas; continue cooking for a further 5–8 minutes or until rice is tender and has absorbed all the liquid. Stir gently as mixture thickens, to prevent it sticking to the base of the pan.
6 Pile on a hot dish, garnish with mushrooms and tomatoes fried in the butter; serve with Parmesan cheese.

Automatic Oven

Although savoury rice dishes are normally cooked in a saucepan, it is possible to cook this in a very moderate oven. Proceed as stages 1–4. When rice has cooked for 3–4 minutes, stir well, transfer to a large casserole, cover *lightly* with foil so the liquid will evaporate but the top will not dry out. Cook for about 45 minutes in the centre of a very moderate oven; add the sultanas and cook as basic recipe.

Speedy Meal

Dilute a can of French onion soup (not concentrated) with an equal quantity of water, or use dehydrated onion soup with about 500 ml (1 pint) water. Cook the rice in this, adding canned or fresh mushrooms.

Home Freezing

Rice is *not* satisfactory to freeze, but you could use frozen cooked onions and frozen cooked mushrooms as a basis for this dish.

Vegetable Stew with Savoury Dumplings

Serves 4–5
Cooking time 45–50 minutes

Ingredients	Metric	Imperial
carrots	8–10 medium	8–10 medium
turnips	4–5 small	4–5 small
onions	4–5 small	4–5 small
peas	200 grammes	8 oz.
tomato juice	568 ml	1 pint
seasoning	to taste	to taste
FOR THE DUMPLINGS:		
self-raising flour	100 grammes	4 oz.
salt	to taste	to taste
shredded suet	50 grammes	2 oz.
chopped fresh mixed herbs	1–2 tablespoons	1–2 tablespoons
water	to bind	to bind

1 Prepare the vegetables and put into the tomato juice with plenty of seasoning.
2 Simmer for about 30 minutes (if using frozen peas, add during cooking so they are not over-cooked).
3 Sieve flour and salt, add suet, herbs and water to bind.
4 Form into little balls and drop into the liquid and cook for approximately 15–20 minutes until light and fluffy.
5 Serve as a light main course (add a topping of cheese if wished). Vary the vegetables according to the season.

Note: for a richer stew, fry vegetables in oil or fat, add some unusual ones as in Ratatouille, etc.

Speedy Meal

Heat canned vegetables in tomato juice: top with cubes of bread, dipped in seasoned beaten egg—allow to 'cook' for a few minutes only in the hot liquid. The cubes taste very much like freshly made 'dumplings'.

Mixer

Use the liquidiser to 'chop' the suet and the herbs. It is advisable to put a little flour into the goblet to stop the suet sticking to the sides.

Home Freezing

This stew freezes well, although the vegetables do become rather softened after a period of several weeks. The dumplings, like all suet pastry, are excellent when frozen. Heat gently to allow dumplings time to thaw out and reheat simultaneously.

Gammon and Vegetable Risotto

Serves 5–6
Cooking time 30 minutes

Ingredients	Metric	Imperial
butter	75 grammes	3 oz.
onion	1 large	1 large
crushed garlic	1 clove	1 clove
long grain *or* Italian rice	200 grammes	8 oz.
stock *or* water and chicken stock cube	just over 852 ml	1½ pints
nutmeg	pinch	pinch
seasoning	to taste	to taste
cooked peas	4–5 tablespoons	4–5 tablespoons
red pepper	1	1
can sweet corn kernels	1 medium	1 medium
cooked gammon bacon, diced	200 grammes	8 oz.
grated Cheddar *or* Gruyère cheese	75 grammes	3 oz.
TO GARNISH:		
parsley	few sprigs	few sprigs

1 Melt 50 grammes (2 oz.) of the butter in a pan and add finely chopped onion and crushed garlic.
2 Fry until onion is soft, but not coloured.
3 Add rice and continue to stir for 4–5 minutes until rice is opaque; take the saucepan off the heat and add stock, nutmeg and seasoning.
4 Bring slowly to the boil, stirring all the time.
5 Cover and allow to simmer gently in an uncovered pan for about 20 minutes, or until the liquid has been absorbed.
6 Add peas, chopped pepper, corn and diced bacon and cook gently for a further 5–10 minutes.
7 Mix in remaining butter, add cheese and pile on hot dish to serve. Garnish with parsley, see picture facing page 57.

Automatic Oven

This can be cooked in the oven, see page 114. Allow 45 minutes in the centre of a very moderate oven then add the peas, etc., as stage 6.

Speedy Meal

This recipe can be made with canned French onion soup, diluted with 2 cans of water or stock, or use dehydrated onion soup and 1½ pints water. If this does not give quite as strong an onion flavour as wished, add about 1 tablespoon dehydrated onion; or use 2–3 tablespoons dehydrated onion with 1½ pints water and a stock cube.

FAMOUS VEGETABLE DISHES

Most countries have special vegetable dishes that have become famous, and the following selection give a variety of interesting dishes.

Pois (Peas) à la Française

Serves 4–5
Cooking time 1 hour

Ingredients	Metric	Imperial
lettuce leaves	8–9 large	8–9 large
peas (weight shelled)	½ kilo	1 lb.
spring onions	6–8	6–8
butter	25 grammes	1 oz.
seasoning	to taste	to taste

1 Wash the lettuce leaves well, do not dry (you need the moisture round these), then wash the peas, drain, but still allow a certain amount of water round these.
2 Put a layer of lettuce leaves at the bottom of a saucepan.
3 Add the peas, the spring onions (sliced onions can be used when these are out of season), the butter and seasoning.
4 Cover with the remaining lettuce leaves and a tightly fitting lid.
5 Simmer very slowly indeed for about 1 hour; the peas turn rather yellow in colour, but their flavour is excellent.
6 Either remove the lettuce leaves and drain the peas before serving, or serve in the juice from the pan.

Automatic Oven
This method of cooking peas is excellent in an automatic oven; providing you make sure the dish is tightly covered and cook in the coolest part of the oven, the cooking time can be adjusted to suit the particular menu. If the oven temperature is fairly hot wrap the sides of the container with foil so the peas, etc. do not scorch and dry. It is also advisable to add 1–2 tablespoons water to keep them moist.

Speedy Meal
Use frozen peas, in which case the lettuce leaves can be fairly dry; shorten the cooking time to 30 minutes.

Home Freezing
You cannot freeze the lettuce leaves etc.

Pommes (Potatoes) Anna

This dish is ideal for using either old or new potatoes in an interesting way.
Cut a generous ½ kilo (1¼ lb.) peeled or skinned potatoes into wafer thin slices. Grease a cake tin, or round soufflé dish, very generously with melted butter or dripping; use a tin or dish about 14 cm (7 inches) in diameter. Pack the potatoes in layers (fitting these into a neat design) seasoning each layer well, and brushing each layer with melted butter or dripping. Cook for approximately 1¾ hours in the centre of a very cool oven; 1¼–1½ hours in a very moderate oven; or 1 hour in a moderate to moderately hot oven. Either serve in the dish or turn out rather like a cake and cut in slices. Sprinkle with a little parsley and paprika. Serves 4–5.

Automatic Oven
The cooking time can be adjusted to fit into the particular menu you are cooking. If you think that the top layer of potatoes might become too brown, cover lightly; but the crisp top layer is really very pleasant.

Mixer
The slicer attachment is ideal for cutting the very thin slices of potato needed.

Home Freezing
You cannot freeze the uncooked Potatoes Anna, but when cooked the dish freezes well; reheat from the frozen state.

Duchesse Potatoes

Mash potatoes until very smooth, sieve if necessary, or use mixer Add 25 grammes (1 oz.) butter and 1–2 egg yolks to each ½ kilo (1 lb.) cooked potatoes; do not add milk, this makes the potatoes lose their shape. Season very well, then pipe into shapes and brown in the oven. The egg whites can be saved for meringues, see page 193. or you can use a little egg white to brush over the potatoes to glaze these. Serves 4–5.

Automatic Oven
This dish is ideal for a menu that needs just a short cooking period; adjust the position in oven to the cooking time.

Home Freezing
Duchesse potatoes freeze perfectly. Do not wrap until well frozen.

Stuffed Cabbage

Many continental countries serve stuffed cabbage leaves as a light main dish. To prepare take 8–10 outer leaves and boil in salted water for a few minutes only. Drain and fill with any of the meat stuffings on page 143, or rice stuffings on page 142, roll, put into a dish; cover with a Brown sauce as page 147, or Tomato sauce as page 150, and cook in a covered casserole for approximately 1 hour in the centre of a very moderate to moderate oven. Serves 4–5.

Automatic Oven
Can be left in an automatic oven to cook.

Home Freezing
Can be frozen either for a short time, 3–4 weeks, *after* cooking, or when ready for cooking.

22. Stuffed red peppers, see page 127

23. Roast venison, see page 106
24. Duck and salads, see pages 97 and 124

Ratatouille

Serves 6–8
Cooking time 1¼–1½ hours

Ingredients	Metric	Imperial
tomatoes	4–5 large	4–5 large
onions	2 large	2 large
garlic	1–3 cloves	1–3 cloves
aubergines	2 medium	2 medium
courgettes	4–5 medium	4–5 medium
red pepper (optional)	1 medium	1 medium
green pepper	1 large	1 large
olive *or* cooking oil	3–5 tablespoons	3–5 tablespoons
seasoning	to taste	to taste
TO GARNISH:		
chopped parsley	2 tablespoons	2 tablespoons

1 Skin the tomatoes, slice on to a plate, so that no juice is wasted, then peel and chop the onions.
2 Crush the clove or cloves of garlic; the larger amount is not unduly strong; if you wish to have a very mild garlic taste then use garlic salt and omit the fresh herb.
3 Wipe the aubergines (but do not peel) and either slice or cut into small dice; if you dislike the slightly bitter taste given by the skin, then sprinkle with salt and leave for at least 10 minutes before using.
4 Wipe, and dice or slice the unpeeled courgettes; when not in season use diced marrow (peeled or not, as wished).
5 Dice the peppers, discard the centre cores and seeds.
6 Heat the oil (the amount depends upon personal taste, but the vegetables absorb this well, and the dish is not greasy).
7 Heat the onion and garlic first in the oil, then add the tomatoes, this makes sure that the juice flows from these and prevents the mixture becoming dry, with the possibility of it 'sticking' to the pan. Stir during cooking.
8 Add all the other vegetables and simmer in a very tightly covered pan, over a gentle heat, until tender. Season well.
9 Sprinkle generously with chopped parsley and serve hot or cold as a separate course or as part of the main course.

Automatic Oven

Ratatouille is an ideal dish to cook in the oven, either as part of a menu or to serve on another occasion.
Prepare the vegetables as the recipe opposite, then proceed as stages 1–8. When the vegetables start to cook, stir well to mix and put into a casserole with a tightly fitting lid. Allow about 2 hours in the coolest part of a very moderate oven: this dish takes a surprisingly long time to cook.

Speedy Meal

Use canned tomatoes, dehydrated onions, canned peppers; dice other vegetables very finely to shorten the cooking time.

Slimming Tips

Omit the oil if you are on a low fat diet, add a few more tomatoes or tomato juice so vegetables do not dry, then cook as basic recipe, flavouring very well to compensate for the lack of oil.

Home Freezing

This is one of the best cooked dishes to freeze. Simply cook as the recipe, then transfer to cartons or freeze in the cooking container (providing it is heatproof). To reheat allow to defrost slightly, so the juices flow, then heat; or defrost and serve cold.

Courgettes Provençal

Serves 5–6
Cooking time 20–30 minutes

Ingredients	Metric	Imperial
courgettes (often called zucchini)	½–¾ kilo	1–1½ lb.
onions	2 large	2 large
garlic	1–2 cloves	1–2 cloves
olive oil	3 tablespoons	3 tablespoons
tomatoes	½ kilo	1 lb.
seasoning	to taste	to taste
chopped parsley	2 tablespoons	2 tablespoons
chopped thyme	good pinch	good pinch

1 Wipe, slice thinly but do not peel the courgettes; peel and slice the onions very thinly, or chop neatly. Crush the garlic, see comments in Ratatouille, stage 2.
2 Heat the oil, then toss the onions and garlic in this (do not brown), then add the sliced skinned tomatoes.
3 Heat for a short time until the tomato juice flows, add the courgettes, seasoning and the herbs.
4 Cover the pan tightly, simmer until vegetables are tender, stir 2 or 3 times. Serve as a separate course or as part of a main dish; it is delicious hot or cold.

Note: diced peeled *marrow* can be cooked this way, or substitute sliced *aubergines* for courgettes.

Automatic Oven

This dish can be cooked in an automatic oven very successfully. Follow directions up to stage 4, transfer to a tightly covered casserole or other ovenproof dish, cook for about 1 hour, as Ratatouille.

Speedy Meal

To shorten the cooking time, use canned tomatoes, dehydrated onions, garlic salt and wafer thin slices of courgettes.

Slimming Tips

An excellent slimming vegetable dish; omit the oil and use rather more tomatoes or tomato juice and extra herbs to give more flavour.

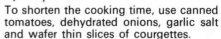

Home Freezing

This dish freezes spendidly, whether made with courgettes, marrow or aubergines. See the comments about defrosting under Home Freezing of Ratatouille, above.

Vegetables à la Grecque

Serves 4–8*
Cooking time 1½ hours

Ingredients	Metric	Imperial
onions	½ kilo	1 lb.
(as small as possible)		
garlic	1–2 cloves	1–2 cloves
courgettes	½ kilo	1 lb.
green pepper	1 large	1 large
red pepper	1 large	1 large
French *or* runner beans	200 grammes	8 oz.
olive oil	3 tablespoons	3 tablespoons
white wine	142 ml	¼ pint
chicken stock	142 ml	¼ pint
lemons (see stages 5 and 7)	1 or 3	1 or 3
seasoning	to taste	to taste
TO GARNISH:		
chopped parsley	1–2 tablespoons	1–2 tablespoons

*4 for light main dish, 8 as hors d'oeuvre.

1 Peel the onions (if small keep whole) and crush the cloves of garlic.
2 Wash the courgettes, remove each end and cut into thin slices.
3 Dice the flesh of the peppers and the beans.
4 Heat the oil in a large pan, toss the onions and garlic in this for about 5 minutes; do not allow to brown.
5 Add the wine and stock, together with the juice of 1 lemon.
6 Put in the other vegetables, season well.
7 Simmer for about 30 minutes, turning the vegetables in the liquid so they all keep moist. Slice the remaining 2 lemons and remove all pips (these can be omitted, if wished, but the lemon flavour is typical of this dish): place the sliced lemons into the pan then continue simmering for another 45 minutes. Taste and season again.
8 Either serve hot or cold. If the mixture is a little moist, lift the vegetables out with a perforated spoon into the serving dish.
9 The lemon slices can be removed before serving, if wished; top with chopped parsley.

Automatic Oven

Although the cooking instructions state simmer on the top of the cooker, this dish can be cooked in an automatic oven. Proceed to stage 7, add the lemons if wished, put into a tightly covered casserole and cook for 1 hour in a very moderate oven.

Slimming Tips

Many diets include oil, and this is a very pleasant vegetable dish if you are following a not too strict slimming diet. If you wish you can reduce the amount of oil, and the beans can be replaced by low calorie mushrooms.

Home Freezing

This dish freezes admirably. Cook completely, cool and either transfer into normal packaging or cover the dish and freeze.

Vegetable Fritters

Vegetable fritters are an excellent way of serving a variety of different vegetables. The fritter batter can be made as page 160, or you can use the slightly lighter batter, below.

FLUFFY FRITTER BATTER: blend 100 grammes (4 oz.) self-raising flour, with a generous pinch salt, shake pepper, the yolks of 2 eggs, 2 teaspoons olive oil and 4 tablespoons milk. Add 6 tablespoons water and the stiffly beaten egg whites. Coat the vegetables in this (as suggested below) and fry in deep fat until crisp and golden brown. Drain well on absorbent paper before serving.

AUBERGINES AND COURGETTES: if sliced very thinly these do not need cooking first, they can be peeled or the peel left on, see page 115. If you wish thicker slices then simmer in boiling salted water for a short time, drain, coat then fry, drain well and serve at once.
CARROTS, POTATOES, TURNIPS: slice thickly, cook in boiling salted water until just tender, then drain, coat and fry.
CAULIFLOWER: divide into neat sprigs, simmer until just soft but unbroken; drain, coat and fry.
ONIONS: prepare as page 115, dip in flour, batter and fry.

Speedy Meal

Use well drained canned carrots and coat these, or cook carefully extra vegetables (so they do not break), save to coat and fry later.

Home Freezing

Any of the vegetable fritters mentioned will freeze well. Freeze until very firm before wrapping. Use within about 5–6 weeks.

Salads

Salads are so colourful and consist of so many different ingredients that one should be able to have great variety throughout the year–for example:

WINTER SALADS–when lettuce is expensive or lacking in flavour, use shredded white cabbage or Brussels sprouts, include tiny flowerets (sprigs) raw cauliflower, grated raw carrot, swede, and a very little turnip. Include fruit such as oranges, apples, bananas, canned fruit, dried fruit and nuts.

SPRING SALADS–young lettuce are often expensive but so tender you can use every leaf. Make use of young cooked French beans and early broad beans, include red and green peppers as well as the more usual salad ingredients–tomatoes, cucumber, etc.

SUMMER SALADS–there is almost an embarrassing selection here; include fruit such as cherries, red and blackcurrants, strawberries, flavour with most fresh herbs. There will be a good supply of usual salad ingredients to blend with the more unusual foods.

AUTUMN SALADS–celery, chicory are usually at their best at this time and make excellent salad ingredients with chopped apple and/or chopped beetroot. Lettuces are sometimes getting old and tough at this time and you may do better with the heart of a green vegetable.

Some of the unusual ingredients that may go into salads *at any time of the year* are–a sweet fennel (which has a slight aniseed flavour), celeriac (celery root) which has the flavour of celery, and diced cooked sweet potatoes. Celeriac must be peeled, then grated or cut into matchstick lengths; fennel should be washed, the outer skin layer removed and then the rest chopped neatly.
Both celeriac and fennel may be cooked lightly, then blended with mayonnaise in a salad.

Metric Conversions

This is really completely unimportant in a salad when preparing the food, but it is important when you are shopping so that you can assess the prices being asked for tomatoes and other foods sold by weight. This is just a reminder, therefore, that 1 kilo is equivalent to 2·2 lb. and ½ kilo to 1·1 lb.

Drinks to serve with salads

Salads are served throughout the year and, therefore, drinks will vary according to the time of the year and other food being served with the salad. Long cool drinks of lager, cider or fruit juices blend well with summer salads or any salads to serve in hot weather.

Saving time when making salads

APPLES–these tend to go rather brown and soft if you grate them for a salad, so either shred or cut into fairly thick slices. Toss in mayonnaise, French dressing or lemon juice to prevent turning brown.

BEETROOT–this is easier and less 'messy' to prepare if you rub it against the shredding attachment, see below, or a coarse grater. If you have no time to cook beetroot or cannot obtain it, remember finely grated raw beetroot is very pleasant in a salad if used in small quantities.

CABBAGE–if you are using this in coleslaw, see page 124, or other salads; it can either be shredded with a sharp knife or rubbed against a mandolin, see below.

CARROTS–these are easily grated raw to put into salads, and grating makes them less indigestible.

CUCUMBER–if you have to slice a large quantity of cucumber for a party, rub against the shredder that is part of most graters, or use the shredder of an electric mixer. There is, however, a wonderful gadget known as a mandolin and inexpensive versions of this are becoming more plentiful. You can within a very short time cut a whole cucumber into thin perfect slices by rubbing it against this. If you let cucumber stand for a while and then pour off excess liquid, it is much more easily digested. It is also extremely pleasant if sprinkled with a very little sugar as well as seasoning, and left for a time.

EGGS–hard-boiled eggs are very difficult to slice neatly unless you use a proper egg slicer, and it is worth buying one of these. Take care in storing the slicer so that there is no pressure on the wires, as these can easily become broken.

TOMATOES–these must be sliced with a really sharp knife. If you wish to skin them see page 34.

WATERCRESS AND PARSLEY–your kitchen scissors are ideal for cutting sprigs, or chopping.

Home freezing of salad ingredients

These are often served raw; many of them–tomatoes, onions, radishes, celery, lettuce, have a high percentage of water and a crisp texture. This is spoilt by freezing, and it is quite unsatisfactory to freeze salad ingredients and expect them to thaw out and be pleasant to eat; they will have lost their firmness, texture and most of their taste. You can, however, make use of cooked vegetables in salads and when preparing root vegetables, it is wise to have extra quantities that may be cooked and put into a salad, as Russian Salad, this page.

Slimming

There should be no difficulty in choosing salads that are interesting and yet low in calories. Plan your salads to include plenty of greens–lettuce, watercress, etc., citrus fruits, tomatoes, cucumber, etc., and avoid rich mayonnaise; sweeten dressing with sugar substitute rather than sugar itself. You may find that on some diets salads are very restricted, this is because the particular diet is restricting the liquid intake, and most salad ingredients are high on water content; most diets however include almost unrestricted amounts of the *right* salad ingredients, and these help to make you feel 'well fed' when cutting down on other foods.

SALAD DRESSINGS
1. Sprinkle a little lemon juice over the salad; or mix orange and lemon juice, season well, and add sugar substitute if wished.

2. Blend 1 teaspoon French or mild mustard with 1 tablespoon lemon juice, seasoning, the equivalent of 1 teaspoon sugar in some form of sugar substitute, and 8 tablespoons natural yoghourt. Add chopped fresh herbs–this is excellent with most salads.
3. Blend 1–2 teaspoons French or English made-mustard with 6 tablespoons canned tomato juice or purée. Season well and serve over vegetable salads such as a Russian salad, in place of mayonnaise or an oil and vinegar dressing.

Using a mixer

Use the slicing and shredding attachment for shredding cabbage and cucumber, for 'grating' cheese, raw carrots, etc. The whisk and the liquidiser are both excellent for making dressings of all kinds, see page 155.

Basic salads

These basic salads are those used as accompaniments to hot and cold dishes.

COLESLAW–use the heart of white cabbage for this, or the whole cabbage if the outer leaves are not too old and tough. Shred the cabbage very finely; this is most important for it makes the salad easier to eat and more interesting. Toss the cabbage in mayonnaise or in French dressing, or a mixture of these two dressings.
Coleslaw can be varied in many ways:
a) Add finely grated carrot, chopped parsley.
b) Add chopped celery, chopped apple, nuts and raisins.
c) Mix a generous amount of made-mustard with mayonnaise, toss the cabbage in this and add chopped parsley, green pepper, celery and seedless raisins.
A small cabbage makes enough Coleslaw for about 8 people.

GREEN SALAD–mix lettuce, watercress, chopped celery, green pepper, but omit all other colours in the salad. Toss in well seasoned oil and vinegar.

MIXED SALAD–in this salad mix as many salad ingredients as are available–green salad ingredients as above, tomatoes, radishes, sliced hard-boiled egg, etc. Toss in seasoned oil and vinegar or serve with mayonnaise.

ONION SALAD–cut thin rings of onion, toss in dressing, garnish with chopped herbs; excellent with cheese. Blend rings of *Orange and onion* see picture between pages 120/121. You can also use rings of grapefruit with orange and onion.

POTATO SALAD–always try and make this while the potatoes are warm, for they then absorb the dressing well. Dice cooked old or new potatoes, blend with mayonnaise or half mayonnaise and half French dressing, add chopped parsley, chopped chives or grated onion or chopped spring onions. Allow to cool. There are many more interesting versions of potato salad such as *Apple and potato,* shown in picture between pages 120/121. Dice eating apples (do not remove skin), mix with the diced potato, add dressing as wished, garnish with sliced radish; this is good with duckling or pork.

RUSSIAN SALAD–blend diced cooked vegetables while warm with mayonnaise; season, top with chopped parsley.

TOMATO SALAD–slice tomatoes thinly, skin if wished, then put on a flat dish topped with French dressing, chopped parsley and chopped chives; leave for an hour.
When available, chicory can be included in many green or mixed salads. Known as endive in France, it requires very little preparation and the sharp flavour blends well with citrus fruits, cooked potatoes or cold meats.

SIMPLE SALADS

APPLE AND BEETROOT–dice and coarsely grate a medium sized cooked beetroot and 2 peeled dessert apples. Toss in a small amount of French or vinaigrette dressing immediately fruit is prepared, leave to stand for about 1 hour. Excellent with pork, or any dishes including pork, duck, goose or cold game. Serves 4–6.

BEETROOT AND ORANGE–dice a medium sized cooked beetroot; cut away peel from 2 large oranges and remove outer pith, cut between skin of each segment to leave flesh only, cut this into small pieces. Mix beetroot and orange together and season well. This is an excellent alternative to Orange salad, see below. Serves 4–6.

CARROT AND RAISIN–peel and grate 2 large perfect carrots, or 4–5 smaller ones. Mix with 2 tablespoons seedless raisins, previously soaked in orange juice or in a French dressing so that they are moist. The raisins should be left soaking for 1 hour before you make the salad and any surplus liquid poured away. Arrange the carrot mixture on a bed of crisp lettuce.
Children generally love this salad and it is very good with ham or cheese. Serves 4–6.

DATE AND APPLE–core 3 dessert apples, but do not peel. Cut each apple into about 4 slices, arrange on a bed of lettuce, coat apple slices with a little mayonnaise (this prevents them discolouring), top with stoned dates. Very good with most cold meats and with cheese. Serves 4.

EGG–remember that scrambled egg is a very good alternative to hard-boiled eggs in a salad, particularly if you blend the eggs with cream when cooking rather than milk. Mix the lightly scrambled eggs (do not forget they will stiffen as they cool) with a little mayonnaise, and chopped herbs if required. Serve on a bed of lettuce, and garnish with sliced tomatoes and cucumber, etc. If serving as a main dish, allow 2 eggs per person; if serving as an accompaniment to cheese, cold meat, etc., allow 1 egg for 2 people.
Stuff hard-boiled eggs with a) a little curry powder blended with mayonnaise and the egg yolk–this flavouring is very good with a cheese salad. Allow ½–1 egg per person; or b) blend the egg yolks with a little yoghourt and chopped herbs. Pile back into the white cases and top with grated Parmesan cheese. Allow 1–2 eggs per person as a main dish or ½ egg per person as an accompaniment to cold ham or other cold meats; or c) blend the egg yolk with enough tomato ketchup or skinned chopped fresh tomato to give a soft consistency. This is often a way to get children to eat eggs. If using fresh tomatoes, season before putting the egg yolk mixture back into the white cases. Serve with most meats, fish or cheese. Allow ½ egg per person, or if being served as a complete salad, 1–2 eggs per person. Arrange the tomato stuffed eggs on finely chopped lettuce, blend with a little chopped celery when in season.

ORANGE–cut away peel from 2–3 large oranges, divide in segments as Beetroot and orange salad above, or if the oranges are seedless they look more attractive if cut into rings. Toss in a small amount of French dressing, serve on a bed of lettuce. This is the classic accompaniment to duck, but it is equally good with other rather fat meats. Serves 4.

PRUNE–soak and cook prunes or use well-drained canned ones. Stone and fill with cream cheese, serve with cooked pork, ham or veal, or as a salad by itself. If serving as an accompaniment allow 2–3 prunes per person; if serving as a light dish allow 5–6 prunes. If you feel the amount of cheese is inadequate, pile a little cream cheese (topped with chopped parsley or chives) in the centre of the dish.

Slimming Tips

Avoid beetroot in the first salad; add chopped celery instead.

Substitute chopped celery or celeriac or chicory for beetroot; all of these blend well with orange.

Both carrots and raisins are high in calories, so avoid this salad.

Dates are very high in calories, so omit these and garnish the apple slices with grapes or other fresh fruit.

Egg salads are excellent on a slimming diet. Scramble the eggs in a 'non-stick' pan with very little fat and milk. Use natural yoghourt in place of mayonnaise when you stuff hard-boiled eggs in recipe a). The other suggestions, b) and c) are low calorie.

Orange salads are ideal for you; have them with most cold meats, as well as those suggested.

Prunes. like all dried fruit, are high in calories, so you may like to 'miss' this recipe. If you do decide to have this salad, use cottage rather than cream cheese.

MAIN DISH SALADS

To be satisfying as a main dish a salad must include a generous amount of protein. If you are short of meat or fish include cheese, eggs, peas or beans in the salad ingredients.

The Chef's salad that follows is an indication of the way in which small amounts of meat may be mixed to give a most appetising and economical salad. Try mixed fish salad platters–include all kinds of cooked or canned fish; offer a variety of cheeses and interesting salads.

Chef's Salad

This is a splendid salad for 'using up' rather untidy portions of left over chicken, etc.

Cut about 100 grammes (4 oz.) each of cooked chicken, cooked ham, cooked tongue, salami or any other fairly strongly flavoured meat into match-stick lengths. Mix together in a bowl, then add about the same amount of Cheddar or Gruyère cheese, also cut into narrow strips. Toss in mayonnaise, well flavoured with mustard. Serve on a bed of green salad and garnish with rings of green pepper, chopped walnuts and sliced cucumber. Serves 4–5.

Speedy Meal

Buy small quantities of the cooked meats suggested for an interesting salad.

Home Freezing

Freeze normal sized portions; cut them up when thawed.

Chicken and Almond Salad

Serves 4–8*
Cooking time 5 minutes

Ingredients	Metric	Imperial
almonds	50–75 grammes	2–3 oz.
cooked chicken	½ kilo	1 lb.
(use white and dark meat)		
green pepper	1	1
celery	few sticks	few sticks
avocado pear (optional)	1	1
black olives	2 tablespoons	2 tablespoons
lemon	1	1
mayonnaise	4–6 tablespoons	4–6 tablespoons
lettuce	1	1

*4 for light main meal, 8 as an hors d'oeuvre.

1 Blanch the almonds by putting into boiling water, then remove the skins, dry and brown under the grill.
2 Cut the chicken into narrow strips, and the pepper and celery into small pieces.
3 Halve and peel the avocado and cut into thin strips; chop flesh from the olives.
4 Mix enough finely grated lemon rind and juice to give the mayonnaise a real 'bite'. Toss the chicken, vegetables and pear in this.
5 Arrange mayonnaise mixture on the lettuce, top with the nuts and olives.

Speedy Meal

This is an ideal way to turn a ready-cooked chicken into a more interesting salad meal. If the chicken seems a little dry then 'marinate' in the lemon juice for a time, or in a little white wine, then add this to the mayonnaise as stage 4 in the recipe opposite.

Slimming Tips

Unfortunately an avocado pear is high in calories; it is, however, a fruit rich in protein and oil, so you may decide you can include this on your diet if you are not 'counting calories' but omitting only carbohydrates.

Home Freezing

You cannot freeze the mixed salad because of the mayonnaise, but you can freeze a) cooked chicken, b) avocado pears, c) both lemon juice and grated rind (it is a good idea to do this in ice trays, then take out one small 'lemon ice cube' as and when needed).

Chicken and Apricot Salad

Prepare about ½ kilo (1 lb.) cooked chicken; use both light and dark meat if possible. Cut into fairly thin strips and put into a dish. Add about 12 neatly sliced canned or cooked apricot halves. Blend 6 tablespoons mayonnaise or salad dressing with 2 teaspoons curry paste or powder (use a little less if wished), then mix with the chicken and apricots. Arrange on a bed of crisp lettuce and top with segments of apricot and 50 grammes (2 oz.) shredded browned almonds. Serves 4–5.

Slimming Tips

This salad can be adapted to become a low calorie dish. Use apricots cooked in a sugar substitute, not in sugar and water, and not canned.

Instead of mayonnaise flavour natural yoghourt with the curry powder and a little apricot syrup. The nuts can be included as they are a protein food, but they are high in calories.

Home Freezing

Unfortunately you cannot freeze this salad to thaw out and serve later.

Savoury Cheese Log

Serves 4–6
Cooking time 10 minutes

Ingredients	Metric	Imperial
eggs	4	4
Cheddar cheese	200–250 grammes	8 oz.
stuffed olives	6–8	6–8
gherkins	6–8	6–8
chopped chives	2 tablespoons	2 tablespoons
or spring onions		
made-mustard	1 teaspoon	1 teaspoon
mayonnaise	2 tablespoons	2 tablespoons
single cream	2 tablespoons	2 tablespoons
seasoning	to taste	to taste
TO GARNISH :		
sliced olives	3–4	3–4
tomato	1	1
gherkin	1	1
TO SERVE :		
lettuce	1	1
tomatoes	3–4	3–4

1 Put the eggs on to hard boil, when cooked crack the shells and plunge into cold water so you do not get a dark line round yolks.
2 Grate the cheese finely, slice the olives and gherkins, mix with the chopped eggs, cheese, chives or onions.
3 Blend with the mustard, mayonnaise and cream, taste the mixture and season very well.
4 Form into a roll with damp hands, wrap in foil and leave in the refrigerator for about 1 hour to chill.
5 Garnish with a design of olives, tomato 'petals' and gherkin 'leaves'. Serve on lettuce and sliced tomatoes.

CURRIED CHEESE LOG–use the recipe above, but blend 2–3 teaspoons curry powder with the mustard and mayonnaise.

Slimming Tips
This log is very good on a fairly 'lenient' slimming diet if you substitute 4 tablespoons natural yoghourt and a squeeze lemon juice for the mayonnaise and cream. It is also an excellent standby for a special party where your guests are 'figure conscious', for it *looks* good and can be made well ahead.

Home Freezing
Unfortunately the inclusion of hard-boiled eggs and mayonnaise mean you cannot freeze this mixture well.

Stuffed Red Peppers

Serves 4
Cooking time – none

Ingredients	Metric	Imperial
ripe red peppers	2	2
FOR THE FILLING :		
cooked *or* canned	4–6 tablespoons	4–6 tablespoons
corn kernels		
chopped spring onions	2 tablespoons	2 tablespoons
or chives		
cream cheese	100–150 grammes	4–6 oz.
mayonnaise	2 tablespoons	2 tablespoons
lemon juice	to taste	to taste
TO GARNISH :		
lettuce	few leaves	few leaves
chopped spring onions	1 tablespoon	1 tablespoon
or chives		

1 Cut each red pepper into halves, scoop out core and seeds.
2 Blend all ingredients for the stuffing together, put into the red peppers.
3 Place stuffed peppers on lettuce leaves, top with the spring onions or chives.
4 Serve with more spring onions, pickled gherkins, see picture between pages 120/121, or other mixed salad.

Note: many people do not like the very firm texture of a completely uncooked pepper; in this case, 'blanch' the pepper by boiling in salted water for 5 minutes.

Slimming Tips
Red or green peppers are excellent for people wishing to lose weight; they are sufficiently filling to give the feeling of being 'well fed'.
Adjust the recipe opposite though, by using either cottage cheese or grated Cheddar cheese, and yoghourt in place of mayonnaise. The corn kernels could be omitted since corn is a fairly 'high calorie' vegetable.

Home Freezing
As stated on page 112 raw peppers freeze well, but they *must* be used the moment they thaw out. This dish may therefore be frozen, but it is important to serve it as soon as the peppers and filling are defrosted; otherwise the pepper pulp becomes very wrinkled and 'perspires' excessively.

MOULDED SALADS

It is practical as well as attractive to set salad ingredients in a mould, as they keep moist for quite a period.

ASPIC MOULD: make up aspic jelly as directed, use slightly less water if including tomatoes and cucumber. Cool, add diced cooked and raw vegetables, sliced hard-boiled egg, cooked meat or fish, etc. Allow to set.

CHAUDFROID MOULD: make up aspic jelly with half usual amount of water, when cold add equal amount of Béchamel sauce or *thin* mayonnaise and salad ingredients. Allow to set.

LEMON MOULD: make up an ordinary lemon jelly, use 2 tablespoons less water and replace this with vinegar; season well. Cool and add salad ingredients. Allow to set.

TOMATO MOULD: make a jelly with tomato juice and recommended amount gelatine; cool, add salad ingredients. Allow to set.

Slimming Tips

The aspic mould, lemon mould (although this has some sweetening in the jelly) and tomato mould are all very suitable for a slimming diet. Use cucumber, tomatoes, lean meat, chicken, fish and eggs as well, to turn the mould into a complete meal. If you really have to watch calories very seriously then make a fresh lemon jelly using lemon juice, water and gelatine; season this well and add a little sugar substitute to take away the 'bite' of lemon.

Home Freezing

The Chaudfroid mould does not freeze well, but the others *could* freeze. *Do not freeze hard-boiled eggs, raw cucumber or tomatoes:* they will be spoiled.

Pear and Cheese Mousse

Serves 6–8
Cooking time few minutes

Ingredients	Metric	Imperial
FOR THE RING MOULD:		
cottage cheese	100 grammes	4 oz.
cream cheese	100 grammes	4 oz.
lemon	1	1
powdered gelatine	1 level tablespoon	1 level tablespoon
cold water	284 ml	½ pint
ripe pears	2	2
chopped chives *or*		
spring onions	2 tablespoons	2 tablespoons
seasoning	to taste	to taste
egg whites	2	2
FOR THE FILLING:		
oranges	2	2
pears	2	2
lemon	1	1
TO GARNISH:		
watercress	few sprigs	few sprigs

Slimming Tips

This can be made with all cottage cheese, rather than half cottage and half cream cheese. To give additional flavour use mostly skimmed milk rather than water, but to prevent any possibility of the gelatine mixture curdling it is best to dissolve the gelatine in the few tablespoons water, then add this to the cold skimmed milk and continue as the recipe.

Home Freezing

This does *not* freeze at all well, but it could be refrigerated for 2–3 days.

1 Sieve the two cheeses together, or beat until smoothly blended.
2 Add the finely grated lemon rind and blend well.
3 Soften the gelatine in 2–3 tablespoons cold water in a basin and stand this in a saucepan of very hot water; when the gelatine has quite dissolved add to the rest of the water and make sure it is mixed.
4 Spoon this into the cheese and lemon rind, beat well as you do so; allow to cool but not set.
5 Peel and dice the pears; sprinkle with all the juice of the lemon (this could be done while preparing stages 1–4 so that the pears absorb the lemon flavour).
6 When the cheese mixture begins to stiffen slightly add the pears (drain off any surplus lemon juice), the chopped chives and seasoning.
7 Finally, fold in the stiffly beaten egg whites.
8 Rinse out a 20–23-cm (8–9-inch) plain ring mould or brush lightly with oil.
9 Spoon in the mixture and leave to set.
10 Turn out on to a damp serving plate (this enables you to slide the mould into the centre of the plate if by some chance it has been turned out to one side).
11 Fill the centre with segments of orange and pear (dipped in the lemon juice to keep it white) and garnish with watercress.
12 Serve well chilled, either as an interesting supper dish or instead of a dessert. See picture opposite.

26. Pear and cheese mousse

27. Open sandwiches, see page 136

Ham Salad Mould

Serves 5–6
Cooking time few minutes

Ingredients	Metric	Imperial
aspic jelly	1 packet to give 568 ml	1 packet to give 1 pint
water	284 ml	½ pint
thin cream	6 tablespoons	6 tablespoons
made-mustard	2 teaspoons	2 teaspoons
tomatoes	4 large	4 large
green pepper	1 small	1 small
spring onions	2–3	2–3
cooked ham	300–340 grammes	12 oz.
TO GARNISH:		
lettuce	1	1
cucumber	small piece	small piece

1 Dissolve the aspic jelly in the 284 ml (½ pint) very hot water, allow to cool, then *whisk* in the thin cream and the mustard.
2 Rub the tomatoes through a sieve, blend with the aspic mixture, then add the diced pepper, spring onions and ham.
3 Put into a mould (rinsed in cold water or brushed lightly with oil) and allow to set. Turn out and garnish.

Note: mayonnaise could be used for cream, cheese for ham.

Speedy Meal
If you wish to 'hurry up' the freezing of any jellied mixture, sweet or savoury, then dissolve the jelly in a very little boiling or very hot water and make up the correct quantity of liquid with crushed ice. You will find the jelly sets almost at once.

Home Freezing
See the comments on page 128.

Stuffed Herring Salad

Serves 4
Cooking time see stage 2

Ingredients	Metric	Imperial
herrings	4 large	4 large
seasoning	to taste	to taste
FOR THE STUFFING:		
cooked potatoes (weight when cooked)	100 grammes	4 oz.
cooked cauliflower	2–3 tablespoons	2–3 tablespoons
chopped parsley	2 teaspoons	2 teaspoons
very finely chopped gherkins	2–3	2–3
chopped dill (if available)	½–1 teaspoon	½–1 teaspoon
mayonnaise*	1 tablespoon	1 tablespoon
lemon juice *or* vinegar	1 teaspoon	1 teaspoon
TO GARNISH:		
lettuce	1 small	1 small
tomatoes	2–3	2–3
lemon	1	1

*do not exceed this amount.

1 Split herrings, take out backbone; in order to do this remove head and intestines, cut along belly of fish, with cut side downwards, put on to a chopping board. Run your thumb firmly down the back of each fish and turn over again–you will then find the backbone can be removed very easily.
2 Season fish, bake or grill, taking care it keeps a good shape. Instructions for baking are on page 44, and for grilling on page 49. It is better not to fry the herrings for this particular recipe.
3 While herrings are cooking, prepare stuffing–dice the potatoes and cauliflower neatly, mix together with other ingredients and insert some of this into the herrings as they cool (this keeps the fish very moist).
4 Arrange lettuce on a flat dish, put fish on top, garnish with remaining stuffing, sliced tomatoes and wedges of lemon.

Speedy Meal
To save time in cooking potatoes, use either canned potato salad or canned potatoes. Tiny raw cauliflower sprigs give a different texture and flavour to the dish, which is extremely good.

Slimming Tips
Substitute raw chopped celery for the cooked potatoes. Herrings, as an oily fish, may not be allowed on your particular diet, so use cooked whiting instead. As whiting has less flavour than herrings, increase the seasoning of the fish *and* in the salad filling.

Home Freezing
The herrings, cooked or uncooked, freeze excellently, but the salad filling becomes too soft and mayonnaise does not freeze.

Eating Out-of-Doors

There are so many occasions when one can enjoy a meal out-of-doors, whether an informal meal in the garden, a rather special picnic or a barbecue. There are a variety of dishes in this chapter which will enable you to plan many out-door meals. Home Freezing is of particular interest for often a picnic is planned at a 'moment's notice', and a variety of suitable dishes could be available in the freezer.

Metric Conversions

The importance of this will depend upon the kind of food you are preparing. When it is a dish where you need pastry or correct proportions of fat, etc. then you will need to change from Imperial to Metric measurements with a degree of accuracy.

Drinks to choose for eating out-of-doors

The drinks you choose depend upon the special occasion. Chilled wines–white and rosé are ideal for warm sunny days, or chilled beer, fruit juice or cider. In winter, have hot drinks plus a red wine for a special occasion.

Saving time when planning picnics, etc.

Make full use of the freezer or refrigerator to plan for picnics; you will find notes about this on all pages in this section. Take fresh simple food when short of time; fresh crusty bread or rolls, butter, cheese, tomatoes, fruit, etc.

Slimming dishes for picnics, etc.

Beware of lots of patties, sandwiches, etc. for these are the most popular picnic food. If you *must* take sandwiches, then take open sandwiches, see page 136, and have plenty of salad, grilled chicken joints and fresh fruit. Sweetened cordials are high in calories so have fresh fruit drinks also.

Carry food for out-door meals

One of the secrets of a good picnic of any kind is to pack food so it is easily carried and remains in perfect condition throughout the journey.

WRAPPING PAPERS ETC: there are many very good wrappings today–
aluminium foil–can be used to keep sandwiches moist and for wrapping lettuce and other salad ingredients, for wrapping pies and cakes, too.
foil dishes–bake patties, etc., in the foil dishes and carry them on the picnic in the baking dish.
polythene bags or wrappings–these are invaluable for sandwiches, cakes, salads, etc., for they keep the food even more moist than foil. Secure with elastic bands or the special closures.
polythene boxes–these can be purchased in various sizes and shapes, so keep a selection available for carrying ready-made desserts, salads, sandwiches, cooked dishes, etc., for they keep the food very moist.
vacuum flasks–ideal for drinks, or a variety of cooked dishes and foods, see below.

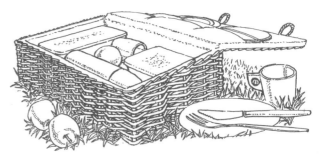

KEEPING FOODS HOT: there are many occasions when you will enjoy hot food or hot drinks on a picnic. If you take a small portable stove, or are spending time in a caravan, you will be able to cook interesting dishes and eat them freshly cooked, but on most occasions you will want to carry prepared food with you. There are *insulated bags* today that will enable you to carry food and to keep it *hot* for some hours. Soups, stews, hot fruits, may be carried in wide-necked *vacuum flasks*. *Warm the flask first*: remember food tends to continue cooking *after* it is put into the flask or insulated bag, so *never over-cook* the food you intend to carry.
KEEPING FOODS COLD: the *insulated bags* mentioned above are as effective for keeping food *cold* as they are for keeping food hot. Pack in salads, cold dishes, sweet and savoury; *chill* these before they go into the bag. Ice cream, ice cold drinks, chilled soups, can be carried in wide-necked vacuum flasks. *Ice cubes must be crushed* before they go into the flask. Carry crushed ice to chill drinks.

FOOD FOR A PICNIC

The kind of food naturally depends on the occasion for which the picnic is planned. Below you will find ideas for various kinds of picnics.

MENU 1–A LUXURY PICNIC
MELON IN SHERRY–make melon balls, or dice ripe melons, then put in a wide-necked vacuum flask, flavour with dry sherry and add sugar.
PATÉ–page 30–carry this in the container in which it was cooked or left to set; take brown crispbread or sliced rye bread, butter and lemon wedges in a polythene box.
SALMON CREAM–prepare the dish as recipe on page 134, carry in its dish, preferably in an insulated bag.
CHICKEN CROQUETTES AND SALADS–make the croquettes as recipe, page 134, wrap in foil or put in polythene boxes; serve with a variety of salads.
MOCHA ICE CREAM–carry in a wide-necked vacuum flask, or in an insulated bag.
CHEESE AND BISCUITS–carry in polythene boxes.
Vin rosé and/or white wine, coffee.

MENU 2–FOR A SUMMER PICNIC
GAZPACHO–page 41–carry this in a very well chilled wide-necked vacuum flask, and have the various garnishes in small sealed polythene boxes.
HAM SALAD MOULD–page 129–carry this in the mould–with rice salad–prepare as recipe on page 134 carry in a polythene box or tightly sealed bag.
BANANA ORANGE FOOL–page 135–take in small waxed containers preferably in an insulated bag.
White wine, cider, fruit drinks.
ICED COFFEE–page 243–carry this in a vacuum flask.

MENU 3–FOR A WINTER PICNIC
CURRY SOUP–page 37–carry in a wide-necked vacuum flask.
CORNISH PASTIES AND/OR QUICHE LORRAINE–pages 180 and 181–wrap the pasties and quiche while warm and carry the latter in the cooking dish. Serve with salad.
BANANAS AU RHUM–page 135–with cream (carry this in its carton). Half cook the bananas as the recipe, then transfer to the container or flask while hot, they will continue cooking.
CHEESE AND ROLLS–carry in polythene boxes or bags.
Red wine, hot coffee.

MENU 4–A SIMPLE PICNIC
SELECTION OF SANDWICHES–see page 136–wrapped and carried in foil or polythene bags; fresh fruit, coffee.

Speedy Meal
Instead of making your own soups as suggested in two menus opposite, choose a canned consommé and flavour this with a little lemon juice and curry powder (curry flavours are most refreshing on hot days). Or chill tomato juice, flavour this with garlic salt, lemon juice and sherry and turn into an instant Gazpacho. You could carry the same accompaniments if wished.
Instead of making the chicken croquettes, bone cooked chicken and fill the cavity with soft cream cheese blended with chopped chives, capers and gherkins; this gives a luxury touch with little trouble.

Mixer
The liquidiser can be used in preparing various dishes in the menus opposite, e.g. the Gazpacho, see page 41. The mincing attachment can be used for the chicken croquettes.

Slimming Tips
You will need to substitute quite a number of dishes in the menus opposite. Choose a clear soup; you can enjoy Gazpacho or have fruit instead; have 'plain' cooked salmon and salad and/or chicken and salad, rather than the 'made up dishes'; take cheese or cooked meats instead of the pastries or Quiche, and fresh fruit instead of the sweetened desserts. Compensate for this by having plenty of salad and interesting fruit. Choose *open* sandwiches.

Home Freezing
Many of the recipes given in the menus are dealt with elsewhere in the book, so you will see that the following will freeze, ready for a picnic:
a) the soups given, and the melon
b) the pasties, quiche and croquettes
c) the sandwiches
d) the ice cream and the fool
e) iced coffee–see page 243.

FOOD FOR 'ON-THE-SPOT'

If you intend to carry a portable stove and pans to cook food 'on-the-spot', you can choose the kind of foods mentioned under barbecues, page 132. Carry also: canned soup, canned steak, and other canned meats that can be heated easily; or if you wish to make this a gourmet occasion then carry ingredients to make dishes such as Steak Diane, recipe page 133. Be very careful when you carry raw meat, etc, that you either have this in an insulated bag, or you cook it very soon after buying, or removing from the refrigerator. It is better to buy or use frozen meats, etc, if you are travelling any distance and to put these in water-proof containers, so they will thaw out during the journey.

FOOD FOR THE BARBECUE

A barbecue is a delightful way of eating 'out-of-doors'. The barbecue equipment itself can be home-made or the more elaborate type you can buy ready-made; but the important factor is that the food is cooked over very hot coals or charcoal, or wood. This gives a new and interesting taste. In many cases the food is placed on the barbecue itself (see the picture of barbecued steak between pages 88/89), and kept 'basted' with melted fat or butter, or a well-flavoured barbecue sauce, see below.

FOODS TO CHOOSE FOR A BARBECUE

Not all foods are suitable for barbecue cooking, here are some of the best:

FISH—herrings or other oily fish. (White and other fish are not suitable).

MEATS—steaks (fairly thick or minute steaks)—keep well basted with fat or sauce so they do not dry: chops and cutlets—less fat required here but the barbecue sauce gives an excellent flavour; include sausages and kebabs—turn frequently so they do not burn; made up dishes like Hamburgers and rissoles can be heated over the fire—remember to turn over as these cook very quickly. You can of course cook steak, etc., in a frying pan over the fire, see Steak Diane, page 133, which makes a luxury meal. Jointed young chicken; this must be kept moist by basting thoroughly.

VEGETABLES—mushrooms and tomatoes can be cooked over the barbecue; place them on thick foil and brush with melted butter or oil. One of the most suitable vegetables is a *Jacket potato*; medium sized potatoes take 50–60 minutes. Cook in foil over the barbecue, serve topped with butter, cottage or cream cheese.

Barbecue Sauces

The object of a barbecue sauce is to give flavour to the meat, etc. (traditionally the sauce is rather sweet, hot and 'spicy'), and also to keep the food moist as it cooks over the fierce barbecue fire; that is why you should 'baste' with the sauce during the process of cooking.

TOMATO BASED BARBECUE SAUCE: this is enough to 'baste' about 1 kilo (2 lb.) meat, or 8 chicken joints.
Blend together 3 tablespoons concentrated tomato purée (from a can or tube), *or* tomato ketchup (if you prefer very sweet flavours) with 1 tablespoon Worcestershire sauce, 2 tablespoons oil, plenty of seasoning; including cayenne pepper, 2 teaspoons made-mustard, 1–2 tablespoons brown sugar, and about 8 tablespoons stock or water. Heat together in a small pan over the fire and brush over the meat, etc., as it cooks.
VEGETABLE BARBECUE SAUCE: this 'bastes' the same quantity of food as above, but gives sufficient to serve as a 'dip' for the meat or chicken as well.
Fry 2 finely chopped large onions in 2 tablespoons oil (do this earlier if wished, as they need turning well to prevent becoming too brown), add 2–3 crushed cloves garlic (if everyone likes this) and cook with the onion, then add 2 tablespoons brown vinegar, 2 tablespoons brown sugar, 2 tablespoons Worcestershire sauce, seasoning, including cayenne pepper, 2–3 teaspoons made-mustard, 2 chopped peppers (1 red and 1 green if possible), and either 2 tablespoons tomato or mushroom sauce and 284 ml (½ pint) brown stock. Baste meat with this, serve any remaining as a sauce or dip.

Speedy Meal
Have the meat, fish or vegetables all ready prepared, cut to size, etc., beforehand. See comments alongside each recipe.

Mixer
See comments alongside each recipe.

Home Freezing
See comments alongside each recipe.

Mediterranean Style Stuffed Herrings

Serves 2–4
Cooking time 35 minutes
Oven temperature 350–375° F. (180–190° C.), Gas Mark 4–5

Ingredients	Metric	Imperial
herrings	4	4
FOR THE STUFFING :		
porridge oats	40 grammes	1½ oz.
milk	2 tablespoons	2 tablespoons
eggs	2	2
onion	1	1
garlic	1 clove	1 clove
butter	50 grammes	2 oz.
parsley	1 teaspoon	1 teaspoon
thyme	½ teaspoon	½ teaspoon
lemon	1	1
seasoning	to taste	to taste
TO GARNISH :		
lettuce	1 small	1 small
tomatoes	2–3	2–3
lemon	1	1

1 Prepare the herrings as recipe page 129, stage 1.
2 Add the oats to the cold milk, set aside for approximately 30 minutes: meanwhile hard boil the eggs, shell and chop.
3 Chop and fry onion and crushed garlic in half the butter; do not brown.
4 Combine all ingredients with the oats, adding herbs, lemon rind and seasoning.
5 Fill herrings with the mixture; *if serving at home* dot with remaining butter, cover with greased paper, and bake in the centre of a very moderate to moderate oven.
6 *If serving for a barbecue* cut 4 pieces of foil each large enough to cover one fish–spread with the remaining butter and wrap round the fish.
7 Cook over the barbecue for about 30 minutes. Unwrap carefully.
8 Serve hot as shown in the picture facing page 48, with the salad garnish.

Speedy Meal
Scramble the eggs if you are in a hurry to prepare the stuffing.
Omit the onion, and flavour the oats with more seasoning and garlic salt. Use pinch dried herbs in place of fresh herbs.

Mixer
Use the liquidiser to chop fresh herbs.

Home Freezing
This particular filling with hard-boiled eggs is not suitable for freezing, as the white of the eggs, even when finely chopped, becomes very hard and tough.

Steak Diane

Serves 4
Cooking time few minutes

Ingredients	Metric	Imperial
onion *or* shallot	1	1
butter	50–75 grammes	2–3 oz.
very thin slices of sirloin *or* rump steak*	4	4
Worcestershire sauce	little	little
brandy (optional)	little	little
TO GARNISH :		
chopped parsley	1 tablespoon	1 tablespoon

*fillet steak is rarely used because it is not quite big enough.

1 Fry the very finely chopped onion or shallot in the butter for a minute or two.
2 Add the steak and cook on either side; lift on to plates or hot dishes; use foil plates at a barbecue.
3 Add Worcestershire sauce and brandy to the butter, ignite if wished, and pour over the steaks.
4 Garnish with chopped parsley.
5 *If serving for a barbecue* and you do not wish to use a frying pan, cook the meat with all the flavourings, etc., in squares of foil, sealed tightly, placed over the grid of the fire.

Speedy Meal
Steak Diane is an ideal dish to cook when you need a special meal in a short time. Grate the onion rather than chop for speedier preparation *and* cooking. Thick slices of cooked salted beef, cooked ham or cooked beef can be heated in the same mixture for 2/3 minutes. This is a spectacular dish for a barbecue; if you ignite the brandy at stage 3, take care not to cause too high a flame over the barbecue fire.

Home Freezing
This is an excellent dish in which to use frozen steaks.

Salmon Cream

Make up 568 ml (1 pint) aspic jelly with half usual amount of liquid; cool, blend with 6 tablespoons mayonnaise, 2 tablespoons dry sherry, 6 tablespoons whipped cream, ½ kilo (1 lb.) flaked cooked salmon, season well. Allow to set.

Home Freezing

Salmon cream will freeze well if you use Hollandaise sauce instead of mayonnaise. Do not attempt to use mayonnaise and freeze the mixture, for it will separate and be most unpleasant.

Chicken Croquettes

Serves 6–8
Cooking time 15 minutes

Ingredients	Metric	Imperial
uncooked young chicken	1¼–1½ kilos	2½–3 lb.
butter	50 grammes	2 oz.
onions	2 medium	2 medium
flour	50 grammes	2 oz.
chicken stock *or* thin cream	250 ml	½ pint
soft breadcrumbs	75 grammes	3 oz.
cooked ham cut in 1 slice	100 grammes	4 oz.
gherkins	4–6	4–6
seasoning	to taste	to taste
Worcestershire sauce	1 tablespoon	1 tablespoon
TO COAT:		
eggs	2 medium	2 medium
soft breadcrumbs	50–75 grammes	2–3 oz.
TO FRY:		
deep fat or oil		

1 Cut the meat away from the chicken with a sharp knife; put the bones and the giblets to simmer, to make stock for this recipe or to make soup.
2 Mince the meat, making sure the light and dark meats are well mixed.
3 Heat the butter and fry the very finely chopped onions until soft; add the flour, cook well.
4 Gradually blend in the liquid, you can use half stock and half cream if preferred.
5 Bring to the boil, cook until thickened, then add the minced chicken and breadcrumbs, and mix well.
6 Allow mixture to cool, add the ham, cut into small dice, the diced gherkins, seasoning and sauce.
7 Form into finger shapes, coat in beaten egg and roll in the fine soft crumbs.
8 Lower into hot oil or fat, brown quickly, then lower the heat to make sure the croquettes are cooked through to the centre.
9 Drain on absorbent paper, then put in small pieces of foil, or on small individual savoury doyleys to carry on a picnic. They can also be served hot with Tomato or Mushroom sauce, see pages 150, 146: ideal for parties.

Note: sherry can be used to flavour, instead of the Worcestershire sauce.

Automatic Oven

These croquettes can be baked in the oven if wished. It is advisable to turn them in hot fat to brown, then drain, cool, put on flat trays and bake for about 30 minutes in a moderately hot oven. Cook mushrooms in a covered casserole in soured cream, flavoured with paprika; make a purée of sliced tomatoes in a covered casserole to serve as a sauce; brown Duchesse potatoes. Baked bananas in orange juice or Bananas au rhum, page 135, would complete the menu.

Speedy Meal

Use cooked chicken instead of raw chicken, this is quicker to mince and the croquettes need browning only. Omit the sauce, and bind with 284 ml (½ pint) condensed Cream of chicken, mushroom or other suitable soup. Use crisp breadcrumbs to coat.

Mixer

The mincer attachment will prepare chicken meat quickly, and the liquidiser can be used to make the crumbs for the croquettes and the coating.

Home Freezing

These croquettes freeze excellently, although if you have this intention it is better to omit the gherkins. Either cream or stock, or a mixture, can be used to provide the liquid. The croquettes can be prepared and frozen, then cooked from the frozen state, or they can be cooked, frozen and wrapped, then stored to reheat.

Rice Salads

Choose long grain or Italian rice; boil until *just* soft, blend with mayonnaise while warm and add the various ingredients, for example:
a) cooked peas, grated raw carrot, chopped herbs, diced green pepper and diced cucumber.
b) seedless raisins, chopped dessert apple, chopped celery, chopped walnuts.
c) diced ham, diced tongue, cooked diced carrots, peas, chopped cooked beans, cooked corn, sliced radishes, sliced gherkins, a few capers.

Speedy Meal

To make the basis for the salads quickly, use the quick cooking type of rice, or choose 'boil in the bag' rice to save washing up a saucepan.

Home Freezing

It is *very unsatisfactory* to freeze these rice salads.

DESSERTS FOR OUT-DOOR EATING

There are many desserts that can be taken on picnics, carried either in wide-necked vacuum flasks, waxed or foil containers. If you have the dessert very cold before packing, it should keep cool in the container. If you have bought ice cream and do not possess an insulated bag or vacuum flask in which to carry this, then wrap in a very thick layer of newspaper–this keeps it from melting for quite a time.

FRUIT SALAD: this is one of the most pleasant and easy desserts for a picnic. Either slice all fresh fruit, moisten it with orange juice; or make a syrup of sugar and water, flavoured with pieces of orange or lemon rind and a little lemon juice; or combine canned or frozen fruit and fresh fruit, and use the syrup from the defrosted fruit or canned fruit to blend with the fresh fruits.

COMPÔTE OF FRUIT: most fruits cook well and you can make this with all fresh fruit, or dried fruits, or a mixture. If using fresh fruits, make a syrup before you put in the fruit, as this helps to keep it whole. With soft fruits allow about 75 grammes (3 oz.) sugar with 2–3 tablespoons water only; with firm fruits allow up to 284 ml (½ pint) water to ½ kilo (1 lb.) fruit. Put the prepared fruit into the hot syrup and cook very gently until soft. With dried fruits soak overnight in 568 ml (1 pint) water, then cook in this syrup until tender.
Hot compôte of fruit for a picnic can be cooked until nearly tender, then put into a *warmed* vacuum flask or container.

Automatic Oven
The fruit may be cooked in a covered container in the oven; obviously you must choose the kind of fruit according to the total cooking time of the automatic menu—soft fruits for a short cooking time, etc. Choose a deep container, so that syrup may come over the fruit. If you are worried about any fruits discolouring then flavour the syrup with lemon juice and turn in this before it is put into the container.

Slimming Tips
Modern developments in sugar substitutes, both in tablet, liquid or powder form, mean that you may cook fruit with a sugar substitute rather than sugar. Unless stated to the contrary, one has a better flavour to the fruit if one cooks it in water and then stirs in the sugar substitute.

Home Freezing
There are many details about freezing cooked fruits on pages 208/209.

Bananas au Rhum

Serves 4
Cooking time 15–20 minutes

Ingredients	Metric	Imperial
butter	50 grammes	2 oz.
brown sugar	50 grammes	2 oz.
lemon juice	1 tablespoon	1 tablespoon
orange juice	1 tablespoon	1 tablespoon
rum	3 tablespoons	3 tablespoons
bananas	8 small *firm*	8 small *firm*

1 Put the butter and brown sugar into a frying pan, stir over a low heat until the butter has melted, then allow to cook until the mixture turns golden brown.
2 Stir in the fruit juices and 1 tablespoon of rum.
3 Add the bananas, turn in the mixture: allow to simmer *gently* for 10 minutes approximately; cover the frying pan with foil or a lid to prevent evaporation.
4 Add the rest of the rum and ignite if wished.

Note: if taking on a picnic add all the rum after 5 minutes simmering, then put into the container and cover at once.

BANANAS IN ORANGE: follow recipe for Bananas au rhum, but use 4 tablespoons orange juice instead of rum and the *finely* grated rind of 2 oranges. Add a tablespoon curaçao if wished.

BANANA ORANGE FOOL: mash 4–5 firm bananas with the finely grated rind of ½ orange and 1 tablespoon orange juice. Blend with either 284 ml (½ pint) sweetened thick custard or the same amount of sweetened whipped cream. Chill, serve in glasses, top with cream and glacé cherries and angelica, or put in waxed containers.

Automatic Oven
The two suggestions for cooking bananas, i.e. in a rum flavoured or orange flavoured sauce, enable you to produce a hot dessert in an automatic oven within a relatively short cooking time. Prepare the bananas, make sure they are well coated with the sauce (to keep them a good colour), put into a casserole with the sauce, cover and bake for 20–45 minutes, time depends upon oven temperature and position.

Mixer
Banana orange fool may be prepared in the liquidiser. Put into the goblet all the bananas, tiny pieces of pared orange rind, and the thick custard or cream, switch on and emulsify. You will find the rind becomes even finer than when grated. Add the sugar towards the end of the time so as to blend well with the cream, etc.

Home Freezing
a) Bananas au rhum, etc.—cooked whole bananas, like raw bananas, do not freeze well, they lose texture and flavour.
b) Banana orange fool—this freezes excellently; store for 2–3 months, thaw out well before serving.

SANDWICHES

When making sandwiches remember:

a) use white, brown, wholemeal, rye, or fancy breads as well as crispbreads;

b) try a new presentation, e.g. toasted sandwiches; rolled sandwiches (where filling is spread on fresh crustless slices of buttered bread and rolled like a Swiss roll); ribbon sandwiches (with alternate slices of white and brown bread), etc;

c) serve the colourful open sandwiches that are so popular in Denmark. The picture facing page 129 gives some examples.

TOASTED SANDWICHES: use white or brown bread; have the fillings ready and hot where necessary, to put on to hot freshly toasted bread, serve at once. You cannot take toasted sandwiches for a picnic, but you can toast the bread over a barbecue fire and serve them as a change from meat, etc. Here are a few examples:

a) blend cream cheese with chopped canned pineapple, put between slices of hot buttered toast, top with cream cheese and pineapple or plain cream cheese. Heat for 1 minute under the grill or over the fire, top with a ring of canned pineapple and a glacé cherry, return to the grill or fire for 1 minute, see picture facing page 129;

b) sandwich brown or white toasted buttered bread with slices of cheese, ham and chutney. Top with a layer of cheese and heat until cheese melts, top with sliced tomato;

c) sandwich slices of buttered white or brown toast either with slices of cheese or with the Welsh rarebit mixture on page 163, spread a final layer of cheese or Welsh rarebit over the top, return to the grill for 1–2 minutes to brown this, then top with grilled bacon rolls and segments of dessert apple (dip these in lemon juice to keep them white), see the picture facing page 129;

d) grill or fry rashers of bacon, or use cooked ham, fry eggs. Toast the bread, do not butter. Sandwich the toast with the bacon or ham and eggs, top with bacon or ham and serve.

OPEN SANDWICHES: butter bread or crispbread lavishly, choose gay toppings. To carry the sandwiches for a picnic, lay squares of waxed paper over the topping (instead of a slice of bread as in an ordinary sandwich); here are some examples, seen in the picture facing page 129:

a) cover the bread or crispbread with mayonnaise, top with sliced hard-boiled egg and shelled prawns, garnish with paprika; top with more mayonnaise if wished;

b) roll cooked ham slices round asparagus, garnish with a prawn. Serve on lettuce if wished and spread ham with cream cheese before rolling round asparagus;

c) serve shelled prawns and sweet chutney together;

d) top bread with mayonnaise, curls of salami, tomato wedges and asparagus tips;

e) combine chopped parsley, mayonnaise and prawns;

f) sandwich brown bread with cream cheese, top with piped cream cheese, cucumber and prawns;

g) top cream cheese with chopped chives and paprika or with a design of asparagus tips;

h) cover bread and butter with salami, sliced hard-boiled egg and spring onions, or you could use tomatoes;

i) flavour mayonnaise with lemon, pipe or spread over crispbread and top with sardines and cress;

j) spread crispbread with cream cheese, top with chutney and chopped chives (or use salmon roe instead of chutney);

k) mix a pinch curry powder with the butter, spread over slices of bread, top with sardines, sliced tomato and parsley.

Speedy Meal

When you wish to cut bread for sandwiches in a hurry, cut *lengthways* instead of across the loaf. Blend butter with a little warmed milk to make it easier to spread (and more economical too). Remember that wrapped sandwiches keep fresh overnight in the refrigerator (store in the salad container if you have one) or wrap well in foil or polythene bags.

Slimming Tips

There are a number of 'starch reduced' breads on the market. Use these, and try *open* sandwiches, covered with low calorie foods. If you cut pieces of waxed or greaseproof paper to fit over the top of the open sandwiches (instead of the normal slice of bread) you will find they remain fresh-looking when carried on a picnic.

Home Freezing

Sandwiches freeze excellently. Obviously the choice of filling determines the keeping time, if you use fish then store as suggested in the fish chapter, page 42, or if the filling is meat then consult page 59. Cheese fillings keep well, although some delicate cream cheeses tend to lose flavour after several weeks, but store perfectly up to that time.

Egg fillings are less successful—the frozen white of an egg is inedible for it becomes 'like rubber', so hard-boiled or soft-boiled egg sandwiches are *not* to be frozen. Scrambled egg, providing the eggs are well beaten so there are no tiny pieces of egg white in the mixture, freeze quite well. Use within 2—3 weeks, though. Do *not* freeze sandwiches where the filling has been blended with mayonnaise, for this separates during freezing and gives a most unpleasant texture to the sandwich filling. If freezing 'open' sandwiches then freeze *before* wrapping so the topping is not harmed. Allow sandwiches to thaw out gradually, they take several hours at room temperature or if taken from the freezer at night time and placed in the cabinet of the refrigerator they will be perfect in the morning. On a picnic if the weather is warm, it is a good idea to carry still-frozen sandwiches, so they defrost *just* in time to serve.

Stuffings and Relishes

Stuffings not only give a much more interesting flavour to a variety of dishes, but are often an economy, for a piece of meat or fish, if stuffed, goes very much further and is more sustaining than when served plain. It is important to choose stuffings with care–in many recipes in this book you will find a stuffing specially chosen to go with that particular food, but in this section there are basic stuffings that will blend with a great many foods; meat, fish and poultry. An indication of the foods with which they are most satisfactory is given by each recipe.

Here are some important facts to remember about stuffings:

a) if you are stuffing meat that is inclined to be dry, for example veal, choose a stuffing with a fairly high amount of fat;
b) if you are stuffing meat or other food with a very delicate flavour, for example veal or white fish (such as sole) choose a stuffing which is not so strong that it spoils the taste of the main food;
c) if you are stuffing foods that are rather rich and full of fat, for example pork, duck or herrings, the stuffing should counteract this, i.e. it should either be sharp with a fruit flavour, like a lemon stuffing, or it should be able to absorb fat, such as oatmeal stuffing.

TO COOK STUFFINGS

Quite often stuffings are cooked inside the meat, poultry or fish, and it is important that the *total* weight of the stuffed food is calculated and you base your cooking time on this, i.e. if you are told to cook a chicken at 15 minutes per lb. and 15 minutes over, do not calculate the cooking time of the chicken without the stuffing, but put the stuffing into the chicken, weigh together and then calculate.

RELISHES are a little different from stuffings in that they are often served with food, rather than inside food. The same basic rules apply as given above, and there are a very wide variety of interesting relishes to choose from. Since these are generally cooked separately and in some cases served uncooked, all directions on the preparation and cooking are given as necessary.
Some relishes can be prepared within a matter of minutes, and can turn a hastily prepared meal into an interesting one.

Metric Conversions

The metric conversions are given in this chapter to enable you to buy and calculate. It is not particularly important to be absolutely accurate when making either a stuffing or relish, for this kind of dish depends on a good balance of flavour and this is very much a matter of personal taste. It is, therefore, relatively unimportant as to whether the amount of food in grammes is exactly the same as in ounces. The only point to consider is the amount of finished stuffing you will produce, for example in the veal stuffing the recipe gives 4 oz. breadcrumbs etc., but when you work on the metric system in this recipe the total amount is a little less. This may cause no inconvenience at all, but on the other hand your family may feel they are having slightly small and inadequate portions. It might be wise, therefore, to be a little more generous with every ingredient as you make the stuffing.

Drinks to serve with stuffed foods

Although naturally one will choose the wine with the main dish in mind, a stuffing can direct one's choice. For example if you have pork with a very sweet stuffing, a really dry wine is probably a good contrast.

Cooking stuffings in the automatic oven

Stuffed meat, fish or poultry can be cooked in a pre-set oven, as very few stuffings contain ingredients that cannot be left to stand for a while. The opening paragraph stresses that cooking time of joints, poultry, etc., must be calculated *after* stuffing has been put in the meat, etc. If stuffing is baked separately it has no effect on the timing of the meat. It can dry easily if baked separately, so cover with well-greased foil, and if you think the outside could dry, wrap foil round the dish or stand this in another dish or tin containing cold water. Do not make rice stuffings as dry as usual, for if they stand for a long period the rice has to absorb extra liquid; it is wise also to under-cook rice slightly so the texture is not spoiled.

Saving time when making stuffings

There are a range of good packet stuffings available, which give adequate flavours, but they may often be improved by adding egg in place of water; extra herbs, dried fruit such as raisins; by blending with other ingredients such as chopped green pepper or chopped celery. There are no rules about what to put in a stuffing; the remarks in the first part of this introduction may help. If you make a packet stuffing, taste it and then find it a little dull, you have the pleasure of improving it with very little effort.

Often stuffing recipes talk about breadcrumbs. As you will see, the mixer is splendid for producing these, and indeed many other ingredients required, but if you do not have a mixer there is no need to make crumbs, if in a hurry. Put required amount of bread (generally without crusts) in a basin, pour over a little boiling water or milk, leave for a short time then pour off any surplus liquid, beat bread until smooth and continue as basic stuffing. Remember to omit some of the liquid in the recipe, as bread will absorb some moisture while standing in boiling water. It is important to prevent stuffing being either too stiff (as it becomes dry in cooking) or too soft, as it can have a rather 'slimy' texture and is difficult to serve.

Slimming

True stuffings and relishes are rarely sensible for slimming diets, but *some* of the following ideas may add extra flavour though *not* extra calories:

WITH CHICKEN-if you have no time to prepare a complete stuffing, try the following: put raw potatoes (well-seasoned) inside a boiling fowl before cooking-remove them when the bird is cooked (they will help to tenderise chicken), mash and serve with the fowl; put halved lemon (with pips removed) inside chicken, this gives a delicious flavour; put a sprig of fresh rosemary in a chicken; do not use too much, it has a strong flavour.

WITH DUCK OR GOOSE-put peeled raw onions, sprinkling of sage and seasoning in the bird; place soaked, dried prunes or apricots in the bird-they become soft as the bird cooks.

WITH GAME-small squares of rump steak give a good flavour and help to tenderise the flesh. Soft cream cheese, blended with a little butter and seasoning, provides a creamy taste to pheasant, etc., without detracting from the game flavour.

WITH LAMB-slit skin at intervals; press into these pockets a 'sliver' of skinned garlic. This produces a delicious flavour.

Using a mixer when making stuffings and relishes

A mixer is admirable in preparing the ingredients for stuffings and relishes, for so often you need to chop them and this takes a great deal of time, whereas by feeding them into a liquidiser you complete the chopping within a matter of minutes. Instructions are given by each particular recipe, but the general rules to remember are:
a) do not add too large a quantity of ingredients at one time, otherwise the mixer is unable to deal with this, see the introduction page.
b) if you wish the ingredients to be *coarsely* chopped it is better to add them either with the lid tilted or through the cap in the lid while the blades revolve;
c) if on the other hand you want the ingredients *finely* chopped, it is better to put them into the goblet before you switch on.

Home freezing of stuffings and relishes

Stuffings and relishes can take a considerable time to prepare, and it is wise to make extra quantities so you can freeze the surplus. As you will see, most of the recipes in this section freeze well, although stuffed chicken etc., should be used within a shorter time than non-stuffed chicken. Here are points to remember:

FRUIT STUFFINGS AND RELISHES-do not over-cook the fruit mixture before freezing as the defrosting, then the second cooking tends to destroy some of the fruit flavour. Where a recipe needs to be thickened, use cornflour or arrowroot, or leave the process of thickening until *after* reheating.

VEGETABLE STUFFINGS AND RELISHES-many vegetables freeze extremely well, but the crisp textured vegetables (celery, peppers, etc.) lose their crispness. This means stuffings that contain these ingredients if frozen, are disappointing. Stuffings with cooked vegetables-sage and onion etc., are very good though.

HERB AND CRUMB STUFFINGS-many stuffings are based on breadcrumbs, and all of these freeze well. The stuffing may either be frozen in its dry stage and the moisture (egg, etc.) added before cooking, or it may be completely made and frozen. Bread sauce is excellent when reheated after freezing, in fact the flavour seems improved by freezing. You may find stuffing becomes a little drier with freezing, so be reasonably generous with the moisture.

HERB AND VEGETABLE STUFFINGS

The recipes below and on page 141, give some stuffings made with herbs and vegetables. Use herbs carefully, for if too strong they can spoil the flavour of the main dish. If you have to substitute *dried* herbs for fresh. then remember they are much more concentrated; use only *about one half* of the amount recommended for *fresh* herbs.

Parsley and Thyme (or Veal) Stuffing

Serves 4–5
Cooking time see stage 3

Ingredients	Metric	Imperial
shredded suet *or* melted butter	50 grammes	2 oz.
dried thyme	½ teaspoon*	½ teaspoon*
fresh thyme	1 teaspoon*	1 teaspoon*
lemon	½	½
soft breadcrumbs	100 grammes	4 oz.
egg	1	1
seasoning	to taste	to taste
chopped parsley	½–1 tablespoon	½–1 tablespoon

*or use mixed thyme and sage.

1 Mix all ingredients together thoroughly, grating the rind and extracting the juice from the lemon.
2 Cooked meat from chicken or turkey giblets can be added to make a meatier stuffing, if wished.
3 Either cook in the chicken or turkey, or separately; for approximately 45 minutes in a covered dish, or about 20–30 minutes if rolled in balls, to serve with poultry or casserole of hare, page 109.

Note: use 2–3 times the quantities for a large turkey. This is probably the most usual and useful of all stuffings as it blends with meat, fish or poultry, etc.

Speedy Meal
Use packet stuffing, and to improve this add extra herbs, a little butter or extra suet, and bind with an egg.

Mixer
If you possess a liquidiser use this for making the stuffing opposite.
You can put the bread, parsley, fresh thyme (or thyme and sage) plus small pieces of lemon rind into the goblet. Do not over-fill.

Home Freezing
This stuffing can be frozen as,
a) a dry crumb mixture. Add the lemon juice and egg before cooking,
b) a completely made but uncooked stuffing,
c) stuffing that has been cooked.

Sage and Onion Stuffing

Serves 4–5
Cooking time 15–20 minutes and see Note

Ingredients	Metric	Imperial
onions	2 large	2 large
water	142 ml	¼ pint
soft breadcrumbs	100 grammes	4 oz.
suet	25 grammes	1 oz.
dried sage	1 teaspoon	1 teaspoon
or chopped fresh sage (optional)	2–3 teaspoons	2–3 teaspoons
egg	1	1
seasoning	to taste	to taste

1 Peel and chop the onions coarsely, put into a saucepan with the water.
2 Simmer steadily for about 15–20 minutes, when the onions will be partly cooked.
3 Remove from the water on to a chopping board, or into a basin, and chop into small pieces.
4 Mix with all other ingredients–you can use onion stock instead of egg to bind.

Note: for a goose use three times the quantities given above. When putting the stuffing into a fairly fat bird or pork, it can be over-greasy. It is, therefore, a good idea to bake it (in a separate container covered with buttered foil or greaseproof paper) for approximately 45 minutes.

Speedy Meal
Use the packet sage and onion stuffing, and give this extra flavour by adding an egg, and/or extra seasoning. Instead of packet stuffing use dehydrated onions; follow directions on packet.

Mixer
Use the liquidiser for making the breadcrumbs. If using fresh sage, then put the sage leaves in with the bread. You retain all the sage flavour so do not exceed the suggested amount.

Home Freezing
This stuffing freezes excellently either when made and *not* cooked any further, or when cooked thoroughly.

CHIVE STUFFING: use recipe for Parsley and thyme stuffing, page 139; add chopped chives (or stems of spring onions) instead of parsley, with a pinch of garlic salt. This is particularly good with fish, as well as poultry. Serves 4–5.

MINT STUFFING: use recipe for Parsley and thyme stuffing, page 139; add chopped mint instead of parsley, omit thyme, add 2–3 teaspoons chopped chives or spring onions instead. Season well. This is excellent with lamb. Serves 4–5.

Note: this stuffing may also be varied by adding 75 grammes (3 oz.) 'plumped' raisins. Serves 5–6.

Mixer

Both the chive and mint stuffings may be prepared in the liquidiser goblet. Make sure the herbs are well dried, so they do not stick to the sides of the goblet, and 'feed in' gradually.

Home Freezing

These are two stuffings that freeze well in a variety of ways, see page 139 under freezing of Parsley and thyme stuffing.

Mushroom and Parsley Stuffing

Serves 8–10
Cooking time as recipe

Ingredients	Metric	Imperial
mushrooms*	up to 250 grammes	8 oz.
grated onion	½ tablespoon	½ tablespoon
chopped parsley	2–3 tablespoons	2–3 tablespoons
butter *or* margarine	50 grammes	2 oz.
yeast extract	1 teaspoon	1 teaspoon
milk *or* stock	1 tablespoon	1 tablespoon
soft breadcrumbs, white *or* brown	100 grammes	4 oz.
eggs	2	2
seasoning	to taste	to taste

*buy mushroom stalks for economy or half mushrooms and half stalks.

1 Chop mushrooms and mix with the onion and parsley.
2 Melt the butter or margarine and stir together with the yeast extract and milk or stock, until the extract is well blended.
3 Add this mixture and all the other ingredients to the mushrooms, onion, etc.
4 This is a very 'useful' stuffing for it blends equally well with fish, meat or poultry.

ONION AND HAM STUFFING: chop 2 onions very finely, toss in 50 grammes (2 oz.) melted margarine, cooking fat or poultry fat then mix with crumbs, parsley, etc., as the Parsley and thyme stuffing on page 139 (omit the suet or other fat and use only that for cooking the onions). When stuffing is mixed at stage 1, add 100 grammes (4 oz.) cooked diced ham. This is a very good stuffing for veal, chicken or turkey. Serves 6–7.

Speedy Meal

There are 'gadgets' to chop parsley and other herbs on the market. One of these could be used to chop both the parsley and the mushrooms.
The quickest way to chop parsley and other herbs, etc., is with a sharp knife— the handle in the right hand and tip between forefinger and thumb of left hand—then move blade in a clockwise movement over the parsley on the board.

Mixer

This stuffing may be 'chopped' in the liquidiser goblet, see page 138.

Home Freezing

This stuffing freezes very well and can be kept for some months.

Mixer

Use the liquidiser to prepare the crumb mixture for this stuffing, but not to chop the ham or the onions, for they need to remain in recognisable pieces, and if put into the liquidiser would 'blend in'.

Home Freezing

This freezers very well, but as the ham loses a certain amount of flavour, use within 6–8 weeks.

Vegetable Relish

Serves 5–6
Cooking time 35 minutes

Ingredients	Metric	Imperial
onions	2 large	2 large
butter	50 grammes	2 oz.
tomatoes	3 large	3 large
carrot	1 large	1 large
green peppers	1 large, 2 small	1 large, 2 small
red pepper	1 small	1 small
celery	few sticks	few sticks
seasoning	to taste	to taste

1 Chop the onions finely, toss in the hot butter for a few minutes until nearly soft, but not brown.
2 Chop all the vegetables finely and simmer in a covered pan until soft, season very well. Serve hot or cold with meat.

Mixer

Although most relishes are not smooth you can save a great deal of preparation time if you cut the vegetables quite coarsely, then tip the cooked relish into a warmed liquidiser goblet and emulsify. Reheat, and to give texture add freshly chopped tomato and a few raisins, also re-season well.

Home Freezing

This freezes excellently and will keep for months.

FRUIT RELISHES AND STUFFINGS

Fruit plays a large part in making many dishes more appetising, and a fruit stuffing is excellent with most meats. As pointed out on page 90, if poultry or meat is stuffed it keeps for a shorter time in a freezer, so you may prefer to cook and freeze the stuffing separately, or make a relish as on this page, and page 142.

Chestnut and Celery Stuffing

Serves 10–12
Cooking time 1½ hours or see stage 6

Ingredients	Metric	Imperial
chestnuts	1 kilo	2 lb.
ham stock	568 ml	1 pint
butter *or*		
poultry fat	100 grammes	4 oz.
onions	2 large	2 large
celery	200 grammes	8 oz.
chopped bacon	100 grammes	4 oz.
soft breadcrumbs	100 grammes	4 oz.
seasoning	to taste	to taste
chopped thyme	to taste	to taste

1 Slit the skins of the chestnuts and cook in boiling water for 5–10 minutes until the skins can be removed without breaking the nuts; remove both outer and inner skins.
2 Return the nuts to the saucepan with the stock (or fresh water) and cook steadily in an open pan for 20 minutes.
3 Strain the nuts and discard any stock left; sieve or chop the nuts finely.
4 Heat the fat and toss the finely chopped onions and celery in this.
5 Add to the chestnuts with the rest of the ingredients.
6 Either use this to stuff a medium sized turkey or 2 chickens, or bake separately in a moderately hot oven for about 1 hour; cover the dish well.

Automatic Oven
The stuffed turkey may be left in an automatic oven with the stuffing. When dealing with a turkey which needs long cooking, it is difficult to plan a complete menu, since vegetable dishes, etc. would be over-cooked if put into the oven at the same time as the turkey.

Speedy Meal
Use canned unsweetened chestnut purée, as this is much more smooth than fresh chestnuts; increase the amount of celery slightly.

Home Freezing
While an ordinary chestnut stuffing freezes well, you cannot freeze this recipe *with* the celery unless it has been thoroughly cooked.

Chestnut and Raisin Relish

Serves 9–10
Cooking time 40 minutes

Ingredients	Metric	Imperial
chestnuts	1 kilo	2 lb.
giblet stock	568 ml	1 pint
seasoning	to taste	to taste
raisins	150 grammes	6 oz.
sherry	6 tablespoons	6 tablespoons
flour	50 grammes	2 oz.
fat	25 grammes	1 oz.
sugar	to taste	to taste

1 Slit chestnut skins, cook, and skin as stage 1 above.
2 Put the skinned chestnuts back into the saucepan with most of the stock (made by cooking poultry giblets, or use brown stock); season well, simmer for 20 minutes.
3 Add the raisins, cook for 5 minutes until plump.
4 Blend the sherry and rest of stock with the flour, and stir into the chestnut liquid, cook until thickened, then add the fat from the cooking of the poultry or meat.
5 Taste and season again, add a little sugar.
6 Drain the chestnuts and raisins from the sauce and serve as a relish round cooked poultry. Serve the sauce as a gravy. This can take the place of a stuffing.

Automatic Oven
Prepare the chestnuts, but thicken the sauce at stage 2, and add all the ingredients *before* the chestnuts are soft. Put into a casserole, cover tightly, then cook for about 1 hour in the centre of a moderate oven.

Slimming Tips
This relish and the vegetable relish on page 140 are both ideal for 'slimmers', instead of eating a stuffing that contains bread. Chestnuts are high in calories. Strain well and do not have the thickened gravy sauce.

Home Freezing
This will freeze well for a very limited time only, for while chestnut stuffing (where the chestnuts are a purée) freezes excellently, the whole nuts tend to lose a certain amount of texture. Use within 2–3 weeks.

Lemon Stuffing

Use for all kinds of fish (see page 55); chicken (see page 98) and for veal.

Serves 4
Cooking time 4–5 minutes then as recipe.

Ingredients	Metric	Imperial
onion	1 medium	1 medium
butter *or* margarine	50 grammes	2 oz.
chopped parsley	1–1½ tablespoons	1–1½ tablespoons
soft white breadcrumbs	50 grammes	2 oz.
lemon	1 small	1 small
egg	1	1
seasoning	to taste	to taste

1 Skin and chop the onion finely, toss in the hot butter or margarine for several minutes.
2 Add to the parsley and crumbs.
3 Grate the rind finely from the lemon, stir into the crumb mixture.
4 Bind with the lemon juice, egg, and season well.

Automatic Oven
An excellent stuffing when cooking fish, etc., in an automatic oven.

Speedy Meal
Omit onion, crumbs and parsley. Bind a packet of sage and onion stuffing with fresh or bottled lemon juice and an egg.

Mixer
The crumbs, parsley and lemon can all be prepared in the liquidiser.

Slimming Tips
No stuffing containing bread is very slimming.

Home Freezing
Excellent—see comments on page 138.

Lemon Mushroom Stuffing

Slice 50–75 grammes (2–3 oz.) mushrooms (or use mushroom stalks for economy), and toss in the butter or margarine at stage 1.

Orange Rice Stuffing

Serves 5–6
Cooking time 25 minutes

Ingredients	Metric	Imperial
oranges	2 large	2 large
white stock	568 ml	1 pint
long grain rice	100 grammes	4 oz.
seasoning	to taste	to taste

1 Put grated orange rind and stock into a saucepan, bring to the boil, add the rice, season very well, add other flavourings if wished, e.g. crushed garlic, chopped herbs, etc.
2 Cook in the open pan until the rice is nearly tender, add the orange juice or diced orange pulp then cook until rice is done. Serve with duck, pork or chicken.

Speedy Meal
Use canned or frozen concentrated (this need not be diluted) orange juice instead of fresh juice.

Mixer
The orange rind may be 'chopped' in the liquidiser goblet rather than grated; be careful not to use too much white pith.

Home Freezing
Due to the rice content this is not a good stuffing to freeze. You can, however, freeze tiny containers of orange juice and grated rind when oranges are cheap.

Sausage and Raisin Stuffing

Serves 8
Cooking time as recipe

Ingredients	Metric	Imperial
seedless raisins	100–150 grammes	4–6 oz.
poultry stock	2 tablespoons	2 tablespoons
sausagemeat	½ kilo	1 lb.
soft brown breadcrumbs	50 grammes	2 oz.
chopped parsley	1 tablespoon	1 tablespoon
chopped walnuts (optional)	50 grammes	2 oz.
egg	1	1

1 Put the raisins into a basin, add the very hot stock and leave for 10 minutes so the raisins become 'plump'.
2 Add the rest of the ingredients (seasoning is not really necessary but could be added).
3 Use this stuffing with chicken, turkey, lamb, etc.

Note: if wished, you can add the finely chopped cooked liver of any poultry to make a more piquant stuffing.

Speedy Meal
This is a very quickly prepared stuffing. If in a hurry omit the parsley and use a pinch dried parsley. Remember though, parsley can be 'chopped' in a liquidiser if you possess one, and so can the walnuts. To hasten cooking, form into small balls, and bake for about 15 minutes only in a hot oven.

Home Freezing
This freezes well for a maximum of 2 months, whether cooked or uncooked.

MEAT STUFFINGS

Extra meat in a stuffing can give more nourishment to the main dish as well as additional flavour, for example:
Giblet stuffing: take any of the herb stuffings on pages 139 or 140 and add the chopped cooked giblets of poultry.
Liver stuffing: chop a small quantity of calf's or lamb's liver or use poultry liver, toss in hot butter, then add to any herb stuffing. This stuffing and the giblet stuffing are excellent with poultry or with veal.

Home Freezing
When meat is introduced into stuffings the storage time should be adjusted according to the recommendation under the particular meat.

Giblet and Nut Stuffing

Serves 10–12
Cooking time see stage 4

Ingredients	Metric	Imperial
cooked turkey giblets*		
crisp breadcrumbs	100–125 grammes	4–5 oz.
salted peanuts	100–125 grammes	4–5 oz.
butter	50 grammes	2 oz.
onions	2 medium	2 medium
seedless raisins	75 grammes	3 oz.
seasoning	to taste	to taste
sherry	3–4 tablespoons	3–4 tablespoons

*if using chicken giblets, reduce all other ingredients by half.

1 Chop or mince the meat from the giblets, mix with the crumbs and nuts.
2 Heat butter and fry the very finely chopped onions.
3 Mix with giblets and all other ingredients; use just enough sherry to make a soft mixture.
4 Put in the turkey and cook with this.

Speedy Meal
A pressure cooker is excellent for cooking giblets, either to produce a good stock for gravy, sauces, etc., or to cook the giblets for the stuffing, opposite.
If cooking the giblets to produce stock, allow a minimum of 30 minutes at 15 lb. pressure, and allow pressure to drop at room temperature.
If cooking for stuffing, it is important that the giblets retain a fairly firm texture, otherwise the stuffing is tasteless. Allow 15 minutes at 15 lb. pressure; cool the cooker down rapidly by either standing in cold water or allowing water to run over the top.

Home Freezing
This freezes excellently, both as an uncooked stuffing or when cooked.

Savoury Sausagemeat

Sausagemeat is a favourite stuffing for chicken, or turkey, and can be used for boned lamb, etc. There are various ways of adding extra flavour to the sausagemeat:
WITH POULTRY–add chopped cooked giblets, chopped parsley, thyme, savory or sage to taste.
WITH POULTRY OR MEAT–add chopped walnuts (use 3 parts sausagemeat to 1 part nuts), chopped herbs or a few seedless raisins if wished; mix 2 parts sausagemeat with 1 part finely chopped liver, fried in a little butter, blend well and add a little chopped fried onion, flavour with grated nutmeg, chopped thyme and seasoning.

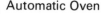

Mixer
The liquidiser is excellent for making a purée of *boned* giblets. This is very smooth, so gives a very easily carved stuffing when blended with the sausagemeat.

Home Freezing
The sausagemeat stuffings freeze well, either cooked or uncooked, and lose no flavour.

Sausage and Kidney Stuffing

Serves 4
Cooking time as recipe

Ingredients	Metric	Imperial
lamb's kidneys	4	4
sausagemeat	½ kilo	1 lb.
seedless raisins	75 grammes	3 oz.
white wine	4 tablespoons	4 tablespoons
chopped mixed herbs	2 teaspoons	2 teaspoons

1 Dice the kidneys and blend with the sausagemeat.
2 Add the seedless raisins which have been soaked in the wine, and the herbs, mix all ingredients together.

Automatic Oven
This is an excellent stuffing for lamb as well as other meats and poultry (particularly turkey and chicken). It is a solid 'meaty' stuffing, so always calculate the weight of this *with* the meat or poultry to make sure it is thoroughly cooked.

Home Freezing
Freeze either cooked or uncooked, but do not prolong the storage time: both kidney and sausagemeat or sausages mixed together deteriorate in flavour if stored in a freezer longer than 6–8 weeks.

Savoury Sauces

A good sauce makes an enormous difference to many dishes. You can heat left-over cooked meat or fish in sauces and turn them into another interesting meal, and many vegetables are improved by adding a sauce. On the following pages you will find well known sauces, together with some less usual recipes. Here are the things to remember:

1. A *coating* sauce means that the mixture gives a fairly thick coating over the back of a wooden spoon. Proportions used are 25 grammes (1 oz.) butter or other fat, 25 grammes (1 oz.) flour–or half this quantity of cornflour–to 284 ml (½ pint) liquid (this can be milk, stock or any other liquid).
2. A *thin* sauce uses the same proportions of fat and flour, but twice as much liquid.
3. A *binding* sauce (often called a panada) uses the same quantity of fat and flour but only half the amount of liquid as a coating sauce.
4. You will find hints by the recipes on giving a smooth sauce without continual stirring, but the reasons sauces are often lumpy are:
a) insufficient cooking of the flour or cornflour;
b) insufficient stirring when liquid is added, or when the sauce is boiling;
c) when the sauce has been allowed to stand a skin has formed, and this gives the appearance of lumps. To avoid skin forming on the top of sauce, either put a round of really damp greaseproof paper over the cooked sauce immediately it has thickened, or make the sauce with nearly all the liquid. When the sauce has thickened, pour the remaining cold liquid over the top–this forms a clear layer which prevents skin forming. When reheating the sauce, stir in the liquid.
d) sometimes a sauce looks lumpy because it has curdled. Many sauces have egg and lemon or wine included, and if the mixture is allowed to boil too rapidly then you will get this curdled or lumpy effect. Whisk sharply, or read the comments under mixer, page 145.
5. If a sauce has the taste of uncooked flour or cornflour, this is due either to a) inadequate cooking–sauces must cook for several minutes after boiling and thickening–or b) inefficient stirring of the 'roux' or sauce.

Metric Conversions

Exact quantities are very important to give a good consistency to a sauce, but this can easily be adjusted when the sauce is cooked. If you find

it rather thinner than you had expected, let it simmer gently in an open pan until it becomes thicker. If, on the other hand, you find it a little thicker than you would have wished, simply dilute with more liquid. You will find comments on the metric conversion under White sauce on page 146, so this way of calculating amounts should not prove a problem in any sauce.

Drinks to serve with sauces

Although sauces are only part of any dish or meal, they can influence one's selection of a drink. If the sauce is strongly flavoured, like a curry, then you need a cool refreshing wine with a certain 'bite' to go with it. If, on the other hand, it is a rather sweet flavoured sauce, a dry wine will taste even drier, and you may prefer a medium dry wine. If the sauce is rather cloying and creamy, a sharp really dry wine is an ideal choice.

Saving time when making sauces

Most recipes that follow carry suggestions on how that particular sauce may be made in a quicker manner. There are also a wide variety of packet sauces, canned sauces and concentrated soups which could be used as sauces. The following, however, may be of interest:

1. Use the blending method of making sauces, described on page 146, or use the 'roux' method in the basic white sauce but add all the liquid at stage 3, bring to the boil, *without stirring*, then whisk sharply.
2. Although this would alter the flavour considerably, a speedy sauce (not unlike a very savoury white sauce) is produced by heating ready-made mayonnaise (use a double saucepan or basin over hot water). Use this as a basis for the other sauces on page 146.
3. Use the liquidiser for 'chopping' herbs, etc.

144

28. Party quiche, see page 169

Using a mixer when making sauces

MAKING SAUCES SMOOTH–the liquidiser is a great asset when making sauces, for if you find a sauce is slightly lumpy, has formed a fairly thick skin, or looks slightly curdled, all you need to do is to pour it into the *warmed* liquidiser goblet and emulsify it for a very short time. You may find the sauce looks a little thinner when it comes from the liquidiser, but all that is necessary is to reheat and simmer gently until it returns to its original consistency. The smoothness when it comes from the liquidiser is almost unbelievable, and therefore it is worth while using the liquidiser even if the sauce is quite perfect.

CHOPPING INGREDIENTS–in a sauce where chopped parsley or grated cheese need to be added, this can be done in the liquidiser. Have the parsley washed, dried and divided into sprigs; cut the cheese into neat cubes, pour the sauce into the *warmed* liquidiser then add the parsley or cheese, switch on until the parsley is as fine as required or the cheese well blended. You may like to reheat parsley sauce to take away the slightly under-cooked flavour of the herb, but this is not essential. If the white sauce is really hot, you will find it effectively melts the cheese as it blends this into the liquid, and reheating is not necessary. If you do reheat, do not over-cook as the sauce could curdle slightly and have the familiar 'stringy' texture one always finds with over-cooked cheese. If this does happen to cheese sauce, you can sometimes 'put it right' by using the liquidiser. Other herbs or anchovies, may be added to sauces in exactly the same way. Vegetables may be emulsified for a sauce such as Espagnole, see page 147, and if you do not mind tiny particles of skin and seeds, you can use the liquidiser for making a Tomato sauce, and save the bother of sieving.

FOR WHISKED AND COLD SAUCES

Many people avoid making Hollandaise and similar sauces because of the 'hard work' of whisking the egg yolks until they are thick and fluffy. If you have a portable whisk, use this to beat the egg yolks, etc., see recipe page 152. Keep the whisk moving briskly, so the egg yolks do not set against the sides of the pan, but do make sure the egg mixture becomes thoroughly warmed, otherwise the sauce will 'collapse' when left to stand.

A mayonnaise, and sauces based on this, can be made either with the whisk or in the liquidiser; follow the directions given on page 154.

Home freezing of sauces

As many sauces take a considerable time to prepare, it is worth while making a larger amount and freezing a quantity in practical sized containers. There are, however, important things to remember:

1. Some people feel flavours are enhanced with freezing, and become stronger. I find that on the whole flavours do not become stronger, in fact in many cases the food loses a little flavour. This may be why people feel that too much seasoning was used originally, before the food was frozen, but I am sure this is not the case, the seasoning just appears more pronounced. It is, however, wise to be sparing with seasoning, and add any extra when you reheat or use the sauce.

2. There is the problem (mentioned on page 33) of sauces, like the liquid in soups and stews, becoming thinner when frozen and reheated. This happens very often with flour, and even sometimes if you use cornflour. The most satisfactory result is obtained by using cornflour or potato flour (you will use the same amount of potato flour as flour, but only half the amount of cornflour, i.e. if recipe uses 50 grammes (2 oz.) flour you need only 25 grammes (1 oz.) cornflour to have the same result). Make the sauce in the usual way, but instead of letting the thickened sauce cook for some minutes, take it off the heat the moment it begins to thicken, allow to cool, put into containers and freeze. In this way, you have the maximum chance of the sauce retaining its original consistency. If you are unlucky, and the sauce does become thin, then you must re-thicken as you reheat. Sometimes sauces containing cheese become thin as they are defrosting and thawing–this is frequently because the cheese has been cooked for too long a time in the sauce. I find the best method is to make the sauce as above, taking care it is not cooked for too long a period, add the cheese when the sauce is warm, then cool, pack and freeze.

3. Sauces will contain an appreciable amount of water whatever liquid is used, so when you pack a sauce in a container allow nearly 2 cm (¾ inch) head-room.

4. Sauces that freeze well are:
a) fruit sauces;
b) Bread sauce and any based on this;
c) Hollandaise sauce and any sauces based on this;
d) vegetable sauces, e.g. Tomato sauce etc.

5. *To defrost*–fruit and vegetable sauces can be thawed out gradually, or heated from the frozen state. Bread sauce should be thawed out and heated slowly, then stirred hard. Hollandaise sauce, etc., must thaw out slowly.

White Sauce – coating consistency

Serves 4
Cooking time 5–8 minutes

Ingredients	Metric	Imperial
butter *or* margarine	25 grammes	1 oz.
flour	25 grammes	1 oz.
milk	generous ¼ litre (284 ml)*	½ pint
seasoning	to taste	to taste

*¼ litre is slightly less than ½ pint, but since 25 grammes is less than 1 oz., this will give you the *same consistency as usual*, but slightly *less* quantity of sauce. If this bothers you, then increase *all* amounts slightly.

1 Heat the butter or margarine gently, remove from the heat and stir in the flour.
2 Return to the heat, cook gently for a few minutes so the 'roux', as the butter and flour mixture is called, does not brown.
3 Again remove the pan from the heat and gradually blend in the cold milk.
4 Bring to the boil and cook, stirring with a wooden spoon, until smooth. Season well.
5 If any lumps form, whisk sharply, or see under *Mixer tips* opposite.

BLENDING METHOD – use exactly the same ingredients as the recipe above (or use half the amount of cornflour and omit the flour). Blend the flour or cornflour with the milk, put into the pan with the butter and proceed as stages 4 and 5.

Speedy Meal
Use the same ingredients as this recipe, but blend the flour or cornflour with the milk. Put into a saucepan with the butter or margarine, bring to the boil, then whisk hard until smooth, adding seasoning. If preferred, use the roux method as given in the recipe, but add all the milk to the fat and flour or cornflour, do not stir, but bring to the boil and whisk hard as it boils until thick and smooth.

Mixer
Excellent to make a slightly lumpy sauce smooth; tip into the blender, switch on until smooth, and then return to the pan.

Home Freezing
Read the comments on page 145 on freezing all types of sauces.

Variations on White Sauce

ANCHOVY – stir in chopped anchovies or 1 teaspoon anchovy essence.
BÉCHAMEL – simmer pieces of very finely chopped onion, carrot and celery in milk; strain and make as white sauce.
CAPER – use 142 ml (¼ pint) milk and 142 ml (¼ pint) stock, add 2 teaspoons capers or a little caper vinegar.
CHEESE – stir in 75–150 grammes (3–6 oz.) grated cheese when sauce has thickened, and add a little mustard.
CREAMED TOMATO – whisk a thick tomato purée (which should be hot but not boiling) into hot white sauce. Do not boil.
ECONOMICAL HOLLANDAISE – make white sauce, remove from heat, whisk in 1 egg, 1 dessertspoon lemon juice or vinegar. Cook gently without boiling for a few minutes.
HORSERADISH (hot) – whisk about 1 dessertspoon vinegar and 2 tablespoons grated horseradish into white sauce. Add a small amount of cream and pinch sugar.
MAÎTRE D'HÔTEL – as white sauce, but use half fish stock, add 2 teaspoons chopped parsley and 3 tablespoons thick cream just before serving.
MUSHROOM – cook 50 grammes (2 oz.) chopped mushrooms in the milk, then use milk to make white sauce. Add cooked mushrooms and reheat.
MUSTARD CREAM – blend ½–1 tablespoon dry mustard with the flour, proceed as white sauce, stirring in a little extra milk or cream.
ONION – boil 3 onions, chop or slice and add to sauce – use a little onion stock.
PARSLEY – add 1–2 teaspoons chopped parsley and a squeeze lemon juice.
TARTARE (hot) – make white sauce, then whisk in 2 egg yolks, 1 tablespoon cream, 1 tablespoon chopped gherkins, 1 teaspoon chopped parsley and a squeeze lemon juice. Cook gently for a few minutes without boiling.

Speedy Meal
A quick *cheese sauce* can be made by heating the grated cheese in 284 ml (½ pint) full cream evaporated milk in a double saucepan, season very well.
Creamed tomato sauce may be made quickly by whisking 1–2 tablespoons concentrated tomato purée into a can of concentrated Cream of chicken soup; if using ordinary consistency simmer soup for a while to thicken then add the tomato purée.
Mushroom soup makes a good sauce, season well, add a little yeast extract for extra flavour.
Mustard cream sauce: flavour full cream evaporated milk with plenty of mustard, heat in a double saucepan or for a cold sauce see page 155.

Mixer
Many vegetables, herbs, etc. can be put into the liquidiser when making sauce, see page 145.

Slimming Tips
Most sauces are 'forbidden' on slimming diets, for they contain foods that are high in calories. You can thicken the sauce though, with 1 egg (or 2 egg yolks) rather than flour or cornflour. Simmer very gently to prevent 'curdling', add flavourings as suggested opposite.

Brown Sauce

Serves 4
Cooking time 5–8 minutes

Ingredients	Metric	Imperial
fat *or* dripping	25 grammes	1 oz.
flour	25 grammes	1 oz.
brown stock *or* water and stock cube	284 ml	½ pint
seasoning	to taste	to taste

1 This sauce is often referred to in savoury dishes and the method of making is the same as for white sauce by the 'roux' method, see page 146, but cook the 'roux' until light golden brown.
2 A sauce with more flavour is made by frying a finely chopped onion and carrot in the fat, then adding flour, etc. If frying vegetables, use nearly 50 grammes (2 oz.) fat and allow 15 minutes cooking time. The sauce should be strained before using.
3 Brown sauce may also be made by the blending method, and the quantities are the same as above.
4 Blend the flour with the stock, put into a saucepan with seasoning, add fat or dripping, cook until thickened.
5 If you wish to add vegetables in this method, the chopped vegetables, stage 2, can be sieved with the sauce.

GRAVY: is made in a similar way; blend the flour with fat and meat residue in roasting tin (or put in saucepan), add stock, cook until thickened, then strain before serving.

Variations on Brown Sauce

BROWN MUSHROOM–simmer 50–75 grammes (2–3 oz.) mushrooms in the sauce for 5 minutes, do not sieve.
ESPAGNOLE 2–simmer 4–6 sliced mushrooms, 2 sliced tomatoes, 1 sliced onion in stock, then make brown sauce in usual way; sieve and reheat.
MADEIRA–use half stock and half Madeira wine.
PEPPER–either infuse 12 black peppercorns in stock *then* in the sauce, strain; or crush these and cook *with* the sauce (this is very hot), add brandy to taste.
TOMATO BROWN–add 1–2 tablespoons tomato purée (from a tube or can), or 2–3 tomatoes, to sauce; sieve if wished.

Espagnole Sauce

Serves 4
Cooking time 50 minutes

Ingredients	Metric	Imperial
butter	25 grammes	1 oz.
onion	small piece	small piece
mushrooms	2 large	2 large
tomatoes	2 large	2 large
rasher bacon	1	1
flour	25 grammes	1 oz.
brown stock	generous ¼ litre	½ pint
bouquet garni	spray	spray
seasoning	to taste	to taste
sherry	2 tablespoons	2 tablespoons

1 Melt the butter in a pan.
2 Chop the onion and mushrooms; slice the tomatoes.
3 Fry in the butter for 5 minutes with chopped bacon, stirring well, then mix in flour and cook again for 5 minutes or until golden brown.
4 Gradually blend in the cold stock, add herbs, bring to the boil, simmer for 40 minutes.
5 Season well, sieve and reheat with the sherry.

Automatic Oven

Often one needs a sauce to serve with the meal, and brown sauce or any of the variations may be left to heat through, either in the warming compartment of the cooker or in the coolest part of the oven.

Speedy Meal

Stock cubes mean a good flavoured stock can be produced very quickly.

Mixer

The liquidiser will be found invaluable in emulsifying ingredients, particularly in the simplified Espagnole sauce, Tomato brown sauce, etc.

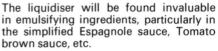

Slimming Tips

To give a moist flavour to dishes use well seasoned stock without any thickening as a sauce, or any juice that comes from the meat, etc.
Some of the variations on brown sauce will give a more interesting clear liquid to serve instead of a thickened sauce, in particular try the simplified Espagnole sauce, sieving the vegetables (or putting them into a liquidiser) to provide a thickening instead of flour or cornflour.

Home Freezing

See complications described in Home Freezing, page 145, but brown stock freezes excellently.

Automatic Oven

This sauce could be cooked for about 1½ hours in a very moderate oven in a container with tightly fitting cover. Prepare as stages 1–4, bring to the boil, then put into the container, sieve as stage 5.

Speedy Meal

Use a can of tomatoes and add dehydrated onion and mushrooms to taste; simmer with seasoning, thicken with flour or cornflour, sieve and reheat with the sherry.

Slimming Tips

An excellent sauce for slimmers: use double amount of vegetables.

Home Freezing

This sauce freezes well. You can freeze without thickening, then thicken when reheating, with the sherry.

147

FRUIT SAUCES

Fruit sauces are excellent with a number of savoury dishes.
A *Gooseberry sauce*, made as Apple sauce, below, is excellent with cooked mackerel or with ham or pork.
Apple sauce is equally good with cooked ham, pork or grilled herrings as it is with duck.
A *Black cherry sauce* is a luxurious accompaniment to duck, but equally good with lamb or turkey dishes.

Apple Sauce

Serves 4
Cooking time 20 minutes

Ingredients	Metric	Imperial
apples	¼ kilo (poor weight)	1 lb.
water	142 ml	¼ pint
sugar	1 tablespoon	1 tablespoon
butter *or* margarine	15 grammes	½ oz.

1 Peel, core and thinly slice the apples.
2 Put into a saucepan with the water, sugar and butter or margarine.
3 Cook gently until soft, then rub through a sieve or beat with a wooden spoon until smooth.

 Automatic Oven
Any of the fruit sauces can be cooked in a covered casserole in a *very moderate oven.*
Apple sauce: put the sliced fruit into the casserole and cook for about 40 minutes, remove and sieve or beat.
Apricot brandy sauce: proceed as stages 1–3, leaving the apricots in the liquid. Cook for about 30–40 minutes, remove, proceed as stages 4–5.
Apricot curry sauce: may be prepared in the oven in the same way.

Speedy Meal
Use canned fruits and add flavourings; thickening, etc., as recipe.

Mixer
The liquidiser is perfect to turn a fruit mixture, such as cooked apple, into a smooth sauce. It does make a thinner mixture so use a little less water.

Home Freezing
The sauces on this page freeze perfectly.

Apricot Brandy Sauce

Serves 4–6
Cooking time 10–15 minutes

Ingredients	Metric	Imperial
apricots	½ kilo (poor weight)	1 lb.
lemon	1	1
water	284 ml	½ pint
sugar	50 grammes	2 oz.
apricot jam	1–2 tablespoons	1–2 tablespoons
arrowroot *or* cornflour	2 teaspoons	2 teaspoons
apricot brandy	2 tablespoons	2 tablespoons

1 Halve the apricots if sufficiently ripe and remove stones, but if under-ripe cook whole.
2 Put into the pan with thinly pared lemon rind, water and sugar, and simmer steadily until *just* tender.
3 If wished the apricots can then be removed, halved if necessary, the stones discarded and the pulp cut into neat pieces; they can, however, remain in the pan.
4 Blend the apricot jam, the arrowroot or cornflour and the lemon juice with the syrup in the pan.
5 Cook steadily, stirring well until thickened, then replace the apricots if these had been removed, and add the brandy; heat if wished or serve cold.

Note: this is a most useful sauce, it is delicious on ice cream but equally good with duck. Use a smaller quantity of sugar for a sauce to serve with duck.

APRICOT CURRY SAUCE: the recipe above may be adapted to form a most delicious sauce to serve with hot or cold chicken or turkey. Use chicken stock in place of water at stage 2, blend this with 2–3 teaspoons curry powder. Cook as above, but use sherry, not brandy, at stage 5.

 Automatic Oven
Simmer the fruit, etc. at stages 1 and 2, in a covered casserole, when you have space in a very moderate oven. Then complete the sauce later.

Speedy Meal
Use canned fruit and omit the sugar.

Home Freezing
This, like all fruit sauces, freezes well; do not add the brandy until defrosted. Brandy is inclined to lose its potency in freezing so add to the sauce when thawed out and reheating.
Either defrost at room temperature for several hours, or tip into a pan and heat from the frozen state. Can be kept for a year.

Black Cherry Sauce

Serves 4–8
Cooking time 15–20 minutes

Ingredients	Metric	Imperial
ripe black cherries	½ kilo	1 lb.
raisins	50 grammes	2 oz.
water	142 ml	¼ pint
sugar	1 tablespoon	1 tablespoon
mixed spice	good pinch	good pinch

1 Simmer the ingredients together for approximately 10–15 minutes.
2 Rub through a sieve and reheat.
3 You can serve unsieved if wished, in which case the cherries should be stoned beforehand, see picture facing page 97.

Note: this is a very rich sauce, and a small portion is often sufficient. Use Morello cherries if wished.

Cranberry Sauce

Serves 4–6
Cooking time 10–12 minutes

Ingredients	Metric	Imperial
cranberries	200–300 grammes	8–12 oz.
water	142 ml	¼ pint
sugar	50–75 grammes	2–3 oz.
butter	small knob	small knob
port wine	2 tablespoons	2 tablespoons

1 Simmer the cranberries in the water, and when soft rub through a sieve.
2 Add sugar to taste and the butter, or *for an unsieved sauce*, make a syrup of the water and sugar, drop in the cranberries and cook until a thick mixture, then add the butter.
3 If wished, a little port wine can be added to this sauce, in which case use slightly less water.

Automatic Oven

The fruit sauces on this page may be heated in a very moderate oven instead of a saucepan; cranberries should be put into a *very tightly* covered container, as they are inclined to push the lid up as they cook.

Speedy Meal

Use a can of black cherries for the sauce, strain off the syrup and simmer the raisins and spice in this. Add the cherries then either heat, or sieve and heat.
It is possible to buy jars of cranberry sauce, add a little port wine if wished to improve the flavour.

Slimming Tips

All the fruit sauces in this section may be adapted for slimming diets, e.g.
a) omit thickening where mentioned; simply sieve the fruit and simmer until a *thick* purée.
b) add sugar substitute *just before* serving instead of sugar in cooking.

Home Freezing

These sauces freeze very well. Add a little lemon juice to black cherry sauce to compensate for the loss of flavour in cooking and freezing. Cranberries may be frozen whole, or as a sauce, and the flavour is extremely good. The sauces will keep for up to 1 year.

Orange Sauce (Bigarade sauce)

Serves 4–6
Cooking time 35 minutes

Ingredients	Metric	Imperial
Seville *or* sweet oranges	2 large	2 large
water	8 tablespoons	8 tablespoons
brown stock	284 ml	½ pint
port wine	2 tablespoons	2 tablespoons
sugar	1–2 tablespoons	1–2 tablespoons
cornflour	½ tablespoon	½ tablespoon
seasoning	to taste	to taste

1 Cut the rind from the oranges, remove the bitter white pith; cut the rind into very thin strips, simmer in a covered saucepan in the water for 20 minutes.
2 Put orange juice into a pan with stock, wine and sugar.
3 Blend the cornflour with the liquid from the orange rind, add to the stock mixture, bring to the boil, simmer until thickened then add the orange rind and seasoning.

Note: this sauce is excellent with duck, ham, pork, etc. To make a more savoury sauce add a little fat from meat tin; for sweeter sauce, 2 tablespoons redcurrant jelly, at stage 2.

Speedy Meal

Use a can of mandarin oranges for a quick sauce. Blend equal quantities of syrup from the can and brown stock. Thicken as in the recipe opposite, add seasoning, a little port wine and meat fat, if wished. Put in the orange segments just before serving. If you wish to have pieces of orange peel add 1–2 tablespoons jelly or fine shred (not chunky) marmalade.

Home Freezing

This sauce also freezes very well. Thicken before, or preferably *after* freezing, so there is no possibility of it becoming thinner due to storage. If you include meat stock in the sauce use within 3 months.

Cumberland Sauce

Serves 4
Cooking time 25 minutes

Ingredients	Metric	Imperial
orange	1 large	1 large
water	142 ml	¼ pint
arrowroot *or*	½–1 level	½–1 level
cornflour	teaspoon	teaspoon
lemon	1	1
seasoning	to taste	to taste
made-mustard	1–2 teaspoons	1–2 teaspoons
port wine	3 tablespoons	3 tablespoons
redcurrant *or* apple jelly	6–8 tablespoons	6–8 tablespoons

1 Cut thin match-sticks of peel from the orange; remove the white pith as this would give a bitter taste.
2 Soak in the water for 1 hour then simmer gently for 15 minutes until tender. The water should now be reduced to about 3–4 tablespoons.
3 Blend the arrowroot or cornflour with the orange and lemon juices (use the larger quantity if serving the sauce hot, for it thickens as it cools).
4 Stir into the orange peel and liquid with the other ingredients, bring slowly to the boil.
5 Simmer until the jelly has dissolved. Serve hot or cold.

TO VARY–omit stages 1–2 if no peel is required, and add an extra 3–4 tablespoons water or stock if a more savoury flavour is wished.

Speedy Meal

Heat 2 tablespoons concentrated orange squash (or frozen orange juice) and 1 tablespoon concentrated lemon squash, with 1–2 teaspoons ready-made mustard, seasoning and 4–5 tablespoons red-currant jelly. Flavour with a little port wine if required.

Mixer

If you put the hot mixture (up to stage 4) into the warmed liquidiser goblet with the jelly and emulsify, you blend the jelly without further heating; naturally the orange peel strips become very fine.

Home Freezing

Freezes splendidly; cool, then pack. Keeps for 3–4 months.

Fresh Tomato Sauce

Serves 4
Cooking time 40 minutes

Ingredients	Metric	Imperial
onion	1 small	1 small
bacon	1 rasher	1 rasher
garlic (optional)	1–2 cloves	1–2 cloves
butter	25 grammes	1 oz.
fresh tomatoes	5 large	5 large
flour	1 level tablespoon	1 level tablespoon
or cornflour	½ level tablespoon	½ level tablespoon
white stock	284 ml (generous ¼ litre)	½ pint
seasoning	to taste	to taste
brown sugar	good pinch	good pinch
bay leaf	1	1

1 Chop or grate the onion, bacon and crushed clove of garlic.
2 Heat butter and toss onion, etc., in this.
3 Add the chopped tomatoes and simmer for a few minutes.
4 Blend the flour or cornflour with the stock, add to tomatoes, etc., put in seasoning, sugar, bay leaf.
5 Simmer gently for about 30 minutes, stir from time to time; sieve, if wished, and reheat.

Note: there are many ways of varying this sauce; add a finely chopped sweet apple to the onion and/or a carrot; omit the garlic; use canned tomatoes and the liquid from the can, in place of fresh tomatoes and some of the stock. Flavour with chilli sauce or powder (this is very hot), or with a little curry powder.

Automatic Oven

Prepare the sauce to the end of stage 4, but use 2 tablespoons extra stock. Put into a *deep* casserole (so the sauce cannot boil out) and heat for 45 minutes to 1 hour in a very moderate oven.

Speedy Meal

Either flavour canned tomatoes with garlic or garlic salt, chopped bacon and a bay leaf, then simmer until a purée and sieve; or flavour condensed Vegetable soup to turn this into a sauce.

Mixer

Use the liquidiser goblet to emulsify the sauce at stage 5 instead of sieving. This tends to give a slightly thinner sauce so either use 50 per cent more flour, or decrease the liquid by 2–3 tablespoons.

Slimming Tips

Adapt the recipe opposite: omit the flour or cornflour, sugar, bacon and butter. Simmer the flavourings in the tomatoes and stock until soft; sieve or emulsify to give a smooth sauce. It is very 'useful' to serve over meat, fish, etc.

Home Freezing

This sauce freezes excellently and it is advisable to freeze containers of it when tomatoes are cheap and plentiful. Heat from the frozen state, or allow to defrost slowly.

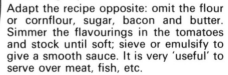

HOT SAUCES

The most famous 'hot sauce' is undoubtedly a curry; on page 25 is a typical curry and the sauce ingredients given there can be used as a basis for similar sauces for meat, fish, hard-boiled eggs, etc.

CREAMED CURRY SAUCE: fry 1 chopped onion in 50 grammes (2 oz.) butter, add 1 level tablespoon cornflour, 1 tablespoon curry powder (or to taste), cook for 3 minutes, gradually blend in 142 ml ($\frac{1}{4}$ pint) white stock and an equal amount of thin cream. Bring to the boil, season, cover and simmer for 30 minutes. Add diced cooked fish, shell fish, diced chicken, hard-boiled eggs; heat with extra stock or cream if the sauce is too thick. Serve with the usual accompaniments.

COLD CURRY SAUCE: blend 2 teaspoons curry powder, 2 tablespoons vinegar, 1–2 teaspoons sugar and 142 ml ($\frac{1}{4}$ pint) thin cream. Blend; use as a sauce over hard-boiled eggs, cold chicken, etc. Serve with sliced orange, raisins, green pepper, cucumber, but *not* chutney, this spoils the delicate flavour of the sauce.

MEXICAN SAUCE (OR CHILLI SAUCE): simmer a medium can of tomatoes with from 1 teaspoon to 1 tablespoon chilli sauce, 1–3 teaspoons dry mustard, good pinch cayenne pepper, 1–2 crushed cloves garlic, pinch curry powder, seasoning and 1 teaspoon sugar. When soft, sieve and reheat. Excellent over hard-boiled eggs, haricot beans, etc., or put cooked diced beef into this to reheat.

Speedy Meal
Use a can of Cream of chicken soup in the first recipe and flavour this with a little curry powder blended to a smooth paste with top of the milk or thin cream. Naturally this is more suitable for chicken, meat and eggs than for fish.
The second and third sauces *are* very quick to make.

Mixer
The liquidiser can be used very successfully to blend the ingredients in all three sauces; it is less essential in the first.

Slimming Tips
Adapt the second sauce; make it lower in calories by substituting natural yoghourt for the thin cream. As yoghourt has more 'bite' than cream use half the amount of vinegar.

Home Freezing
The first sauce can be frozen but it is not always as thick when thawed out as when made. The second sauce will not be successful unless you substitute *thick* for *thin* cream (thin cream does not freeze well).
The Mexican sauce freezes excellently and keeps for some months.

Horseradish Cream

Serves 3–4
Cooking time–none

Ingredients	Metric	Imperial
grated horseradish	1 tablespoon	1 tablespoon
vinegar *or* lemon juice	$\frac{1}{2}$–1 teaspoon	$\frac{1}{2}$–1 teaspoon
thick cream	2–3 tablespoons	2–3 tablespoons
seasoning	to taste	to taste

1 Mix all the ingredients together. This cream is very strong.

Speedy Meal
Use some of the very good bottled horseradish cream, and give extra flavour with vinegar and cream.

Home Freezing
Not very successful; the grated horseradish becomes slightly 'slimy' if stored more than 2–3 weeks.

Horseradish Sauce

Serves 4
Cooking time 20 minutes

Ingredients	Metric	Imperial
freshly grated horseradish	3 level tablespoons	3 level tablespoons
white sauce, page 146	284 ml	$\frac{1}{2}$ pint
vinegar	1 dessertspoon	1 dessertspoon
seasoning	to taste	to taste
sugar	good pinch	good pinch

1 Stir the grated horseradish into the hot sauce, simmer for 10 minutes.
2 Cool slightly, whisk in vinegar, seasoning and sugar.
3 Any grated horseradish left over can be stored in jars for a limited period, as naturally you often cannot buy a sufficiently small horseradish root to give 3 level tablespoons.

Mixer
You make a very good horseradish sauce if the white sauce is put into the liquidiser goblet. Add the pieces of horseradish and the other ingredients. Switch on for a short time only, so the horseradish does not become too fine.

WHISKED SAUCES

HOLLANDAISE SAUCE: is the most famous and can be adapted in several ways. *The water must not boil too hard under the eggs, etc.,* otherwise the mixture will curdle, and the butter should be added *gradually* to prevent the sauce separating.

Hollandaise sauce can be served hot or cold with fish; also with vegetables (it is particularly good over broccoli and asparagus).

BÉARNAISE SAUCE: choose white wine vinegar, add a chopped shallot (or small onion), little tarragon, bay leaf, thyme; heat for 3 minutes, strain and proceed as Hollandaise sauce. Serve hot with steaks.

MALTESE SAUCE: add the grated rind of 1–2 oranges to the egg yolks, etc. at stage 1 in the Hollandaise sauce, below. Whisk until the sauce begins to thicken, then add 1 tablespoon orange juice and whisk again before adding the butter. Serve over hot or cold asparagus and over white fish.

MOUSSELINE SAUCE: make the Hollandaise sauce and when cold fold in about 6 tablespoons whipped cream, season again if wished. Serve with cold asparagus and cold fish.

TARTARE SAUCE: add chopped gherkins, etc., as page 139, to Hollandaise sauce, instead of mayonnaise.

Hollandaise Sauce

Serves 4
Cooking time 10–15 minutes

Ingredients	Metric	Imperial
egg yolks	2	2
cayenne pepper	pinch	pinch
seasoning	to taste	to taste
lemon juice *or*	1–2 tablespoons	1–2 tablespoons
white wine vinegar		
butter	50–100 grammes	2–4 oz.

1 Use a double saucepan if possible; if not, a basin over a saucepan. Put the egg yolks, seasonings and lemon juice or vinegar into the top of the pan or basin.
2 Whisk over hot water until sauce begins to thicken.
3 Add butter in very small pieces, whisking in each piece until completely melted before adding the next.
4 *Do not allow to boil* or it will curdle–if too thick add a little cream.

Wine and Cream Sauce

Serves 4
Cooking time 20 minutes

Ingredients	Metric	Imperial
butter	25 grammes	1 oz.
flour	25 grammes	1 oz.
fish stock	142 ml	¼ pint
white wine	142 ml	¼ pint
seasoning	to taste	to taste
thick cream	4 tablespoons	4 tablespoons

1 Make a 'roux' of the butter and flour, as white sauce, page 146.
2 Gradually blend in the very well strained fish stock and white wine.
3 Bring to the boil, cook until thickened and add seasoning to taste.
4 Just before serving with cooked fish, stir in the cream and heat, without boiling.

Mussels, shrimps, cockles, flaked crab or lobster meat may be added to this sauce.

Speedy Meal

There is a quicker way of making Hollandaise sauce thicken, and variations on this if you have no electric mixer. Warm the lemon juice or vinegar with the butter, then cool slightly. Whisk the egg yolks and seasonings with 1 tablespoon very hot water; when they begin to thicken (do not wait for them to become very thick) gradually whisk in the warmed lemon juice or vinegar and butter.

You can also save undue beating if you melt the butter, allow it to cool, and add as a liquid fat, rather than in small pieces.

Mixer

There are two ways of using a mixer to make this sauce. If you have a small portable electric mixer then use this instead of a hand whisk to make the sauce; be careful though that the eggs *are* thickening over the hot water, for the electric mixer is so efficient that you whip up the eggs very quickly and if they are insufficiently heated, when you leave the sauce to stand for even a short time you will find it 'flops'.

You can also use the liquidiser to help in making the sauce.

If you have a large liquidiser then double the quantities for you must cover the blades in the goblet.

Put the eggs, seasonings, lemon juice or vinegar into the goblet and switch on until they are very light and fluffy looking. Heat the butter then add this, *while very hot,* through the 'hole' left by the cap in the lid or through a 'hole' made in a foil lid (see mayonnaise). The butter should be added gradually, with the motor on full speed. The Hollandaise sauce is *not* as light and fluffy as usual.

Home Freezing

Hollandaise sauce, and all sauces based on this, freeze perfectly. Always allow them to thaw out slowly at room temperature. Use within 2 months.

Mixer

This is the type of sauce that could curdle if it becomes too hot at stage 4. If this happens, tip the sauce into the warmed liquidiser and emulsify until smooth. Reheat if necessary.

Home Freezing

This sauce freezes well, especially if you use 15 grammes (½ oz.) cornflour rather than 25 grammes (1 oz.) flour. As this contains fish stock use within 4–5 weeks.

30. Peach meringue, see page 205

31. Golden orange pudding, see page 203
32. Chocolate choux, see page 192

Bread Sauce

Serves 4
Cooking time—few minutes

Ingredients	Metric	Imperial
onion	1 small	1 small
cloves (optional)	2 or 3	2 or 3
milk	284 ml	½ pint
	(generous ¼ litre)	
breadcrumbs	50 grammes	2 oz.
seasoning	to taste	to taste
butter	25 grammes	1 oz.

1 Peel the onion and if using cloves, stick these firmly into the onion.
2 Put into the milk together with the other ingredients.
3 Slowly bring milk to the boil, remove from heat and leave in a warm place for as long as possible.
4 Before serving, gently heat sauce, beating with a wooden spoon—remove the onion.

Automatic Oven
Bread sauce can be prepared, put into a tightly covered dish and warmed in the coolest part of oven or warming drawer.

Speedy Meal
Put a slice of crustless bread into the warmed milk, leave for 10 minutes, beat well to blend.

Mixer
The liquidiser is excellent for making breadcrumbs.

Home Freezing
This sauce freezes excellently for quite a long period (up to 3–4 months). Defrost slightly before reheating.

Mint Sauce

Serves 4
Cooking time—none

Ingredients	Metric	Imperial
mint leaves	4 tablespoons	4 tablespoons
vinegar	about 3–4 tablespoons	about 3–4 tablespoons
sugar	1–2 tablespoons	1–2 tablespoons

1 Chop the mint and put into a basin.
2 Add the vinegar and sugar. If you add a little boiling water to the mint and sugar before adding the vinegar it dissolves the sugar more readily.

Speedy Meal
Bottled mint sauce can be improved in flavour if you add a small quantity of *boiling* water and *then* stir in plenty of sugar.

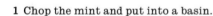
Mixer
Put vinegar and sugar into the liquidiser goblet, switch on and then drop the mint leaves through the 'hole' left by the cap —this gives a less 'fine-cut'. You can also 'chop' the mint in the dry liquidiser goblet.

Home Freezing
Mint sauce, or mint and sugar, or chopped mint freeze very well. Hasten defrosting by adding hot vinegar.

Sweet and Sour Sauces

This combination of flavours is becoming increasingly popular with the growth of interest in Chinese food. On page 132 are also ideas for some sweet and sour mixtures.

APPLE SWEET AND SOUR: blend 8 tablespoons smooth apple purée, sweetened to taste, with 1 tablespoon brown sugar, 1 tablespoon brown vinegar, seasoning, 1–2 teaspoons soy sauce, and a few raisins or sultanas. This is delicious hot or cold with ham or pork. Serves 4–5.

MUSTARD SWEET AND SOUR: use the apple mixture above, but blend in about 1 teaspoon English made-mustard; this is good with meat or oily fish. Serves 4–5.

BRANDY SWEET AND SOUR: mix 6 tablespoons mango chutney (cut the pieces of mango into fine strips), 2 tablespoons vinegar or lemon juice, seasoning, with 1 teaspoon cornflour, blended with 3 tablespoons water; simmer in a pan for a few minutes, then add 2 tablespoons brandy. Serve with game or poultry. Serves 4.

PINEAPPLE SWEET AND SOUR: use finely chopped canned pineapple in place of apple purée in the first recipe.

GAME SAUCE: although this is an adaptation of a well known British sauce it has a sweet and sour flavour. Use recipe for brandy sauce above, but substitute redcurrant jelly for chutney. Serve with any game. Serves 4.

Speedy Meal
Most of these sauces are made very quickly, use canned apple pulp or sauce for the first recipe.

Mixer
Put the cooked apples, etc., into the liquidiser goblet and emulsify. The raisins or sultanas become a pleasant purée instead of whole dried fruit.

Home Freezing
All these sauces freeze, but since they are so quickly made with ingredients in most store cupboards, this is really not necessary.

33. Golden fruit pudding, see page 202

Mayonnaise

Serves 5–6
Cooking time–none

Ingredients	Metric	Imperial
egg yolks	2	2
pepper	good shake	good shake
salt (to taste)	½ teaspoon	½ teaspoon
sugar (to taste)	½–1 teaspoon	½–1 teaspoon
dry mustard	½–1 teaspoon	½–1 teaspoon
olive *or* salad oil	8–12 tablespoons	8–12 tablespoons
lemon juice *or* vinegar	1–2 tablespoons	1–2 tablespoons
boiling water (optional)	1–2 tablespoons	1–2 tablespoons

1 Put the egg yolks into a dry bowl (make sure they are not too cold); if they come from the refrigerator then keep in the room for about 1 hour.
2 Beat in the seasonings with a wooden spoon or hand whisk.
3 Gradually beat in the oil, drop by drop; do not hurry this otherwise the mixture may curdle; the amount of oil used is purely a matter of personal taste, the more oil the richer the mayonnaise and the thicker it becomes.
4 When mayonnaise has thickened add the lemon juice or vinegar (wine vinegar is a good choice, or you can use white vinegar or a mixture of wine and tarragon vinegars–this is excellent with fish salads).
5 Lastly add the boiling water *very gradually* (this is not essential but it gives a particularly light 'fluffy' texture to the sauce), taste and adjust seasonings, add cayenne pepper, paprika and little grated lemon rind, if wished.

Note: this is one method of making the mayonnaise, you may prefer to add the lemon juice or vinegar to the egg yolks *before* the oil, in which case beat very well with the egg yolks and seasonings.

SAUCES BASED ON MAYONNAISE

CREAM CHEESE MAYONNAISE: blend 50 grammes (2 oz.) cream cheese with sauce.

CURRY MAYONNAISE: add 1–2 teaspoons curry powder (or to taste) with the other seasonings.

HARD-BOILED EGG MAYONNAISE: sieve 2 hard-boiled egg yolks, blend with the egg yolks (in mayonnaise) and continue as mayonnaise. If wished you can omit 1 of the fresh egg yolks in the basic mayonnaise, above. This is a less rich mayonnaise and very pleasant with vegetable salads. It can be turned into the classic *Sauce Remoulade* if you increase the amount of mustard to ½–1 tablespoon. The lemon juice or vinegar in this sauce is then 1 tablespoon only.

HERB MAYONNAISE: add chopped fresh herbs, chives, parsley, thyme, savory, mint, sage, etc. (adjust these according to the food with which the mayonnaise is being served).

LEMON MAYONNAISE: add up to 2 teaspoons very finely grated lemon rind with 2 tablespoons lemon juice.

TARTARE SAUCE: add ½–1 tablespoon chopped gherkins, ½–1 tablespoon chopped capers and ½–1 tablespoon chopped parsley.

TOMATO MAYONNAISE: sieve 2 large ripe tomatoes and blend with the mayonnaise, or use tomato ketchup to taste. If to serve over fish salads, give more flavour by adding a few drops either Worcestershire, chilli, Tabasco, or soy sauce.

Speedy Meal

Make use of bottled mayonnaise, adding little lemon juice or extra seasonings to give added interest.

Mixer

There are two ways of preparing mayonnaise in a mixer:
a) *in the bowl with a whisk*
Put the egg yolks in a basin if using a hand mixer; or the proper mixer bowl with a standing model. Continue as recipe opposite taking equal care to add the oil gradually, but when the sauce begins to thicken you can add oil slightly more quickly than when hand mixing, then beat in lemon juice or vinegar and boiling water. Use a low speed throughout initial stages to prevent splashing.
b) *in the liquidiser*
Either remove the cap from the lid or prepare to tilt the lid slightly to prevent splashing, or put a layer of foil over the top of the goblet and make a hole in this through which to pour the oil. Use the same recipe as opposite, but a slightly different order of mixing. Put egg yolks (or use 1 whole egg in place of 2 yolks for a less rich mayonnaise) with vinegar or lemon juice and flavourings, into the goblet. Switch on until blended, then gradually add the oil. Add boiling water if wished. Use a high speed when mixing the egg yolks, etc., but reduce this when adding oil.

Home Freezing

This mayonnaise, and any recipes based on the basic recipe, *do not* freeze, for the egg yolks and oil separate during freezing and cannot be blended together again when the mayonnaise thaws out.

Speedy Meal

All the variations opposite may be incorporated into bottled mayonnaise or salad dressing.

Mixer

If you have used the liquidiser to make the mayonnaise, you can also use this to incorporate the various flavourings.
Prepare the mayonnaise, see liquidiser instructions above, *before* adding the flavourings.

Slimming Tips

A true mayonnaise and the sauces based on this, opposite, are *not* slimming, but you can flavour natural yoghourt (which is low in calories) with the various spices, herbs, etc., as given opposite. This will then make a very pleasant dressing which blends well with most salads; it is even smoother if blended in the liquidiser.

Blue Cheese Dressing

Serves 4–6
Cooking time–none

Ingredients	Metric	Imperial
mayonnaise	142 ml	¼ pint
lemon juice	2 teaspoons	2 teaspoons
Danish Blue cheese	50 grammes	2 oz.
cayenne pepper	shake	shake

1 Blend all ingredients together.
2 Serve with a hard-boiled egg, or egg and potato salad.

Mixer

Blend the ingredients for this dressing in the liquidiser goblet. It becomes very smooth in texture.

French Dressing

Serves 4–6
Cooking time–none

Ingredients	Metric	Imperial
made-mustard– English *or* French	½–1 teaspoon	½–1 teaspoon
pepper	good shake	good shake
salt	good pinch	good pinch
sugar	good pinch	good pinch
oil*	3–4 tablespoons	3–4 tablespoons
vinegar**	1½–2 tablespoons	1½–2 tablespoons

*olive, salad or corn oil.
**white, brown or wine, or a mixture of vinegars, or use lemon juice if preferred.

1 Put the seasonings into a basin, then gradually blend in the oil, then add the vinegar to taste.

Note: the proportions of oil and vinegar above are those generally accepted as ideal, but this does depend upon personal taste.

VINAIGRETTE DRESSING: is another word for French dressing; although to be correct, it is French dressing to which is added about 2 teaspoons chopped mixed herbs. Crushed garlic may also be added.

Speedy Meal

Keep a supply ready to use: prepare a large quantity of dressing; store in screw topped bottles (where it keeps perfectly). Shake well before using.

Mixer

The ingredients may be blended in the liquidiser. The result is *not* exactly the same as when blended by hand, for the dressing becomes more 'cloudy' and slightly thicker.

More Salad Dressings

Here are some interesting salad dressings:

COOKED SALAD DRESSING: Make a white or béchamel sauce as page 146, but use 2 tablespoons less milk. When the sauce has thickened, remove from the heat, so it is no longer boiling. Whisk an egg yolk and 1–2 tablespoons vinegar together with extra seasoning and ½–1 teaspoon made-mustard. Add this to the warm sauce, then cook *gently*, without boiling, until thickened again. Stir as it cools then put into a bottle. Serves 6–8.

POTATO MAYONNAISE: sieve 200 grammes (8 oz.) boiled old potatoes, blend with salt, pepper, little made-mustard, pinch sugar and slowly add approximately 3 tablespoons vinegar (less if wished) and 2 tablespoons thick cream. Add chopped parsley and chopped gherkins (optional).
This mayonnaise is very good with cheese salads or over mixed vegetable salads. Serves 5–6.

SOURED CREAM DRESSING: blend about 8 tablespoons soured cream (or sour the same amount of thick cream with 1 tablespoon lemon juice) with cayenne pepper, mustard, then add 2 tablespoons vinegar. Serves 4–5.

Speedy Meal

Use dehydrated potatoes for the potato mayonnaise, instead of cooking fresh ones: but make into a purée with milk.

Mixer

A hand mixer can be used to blend the ingredients, except when adding herbs; or emulsify in the liquidiser.

Home Freezing

The first recipe freezes reasonably well if cornflour is used instead of flour.
The second recipe for the potato mayonnaise freezes well; the purée tends to separate slightly as it thaws out, but this is easily overcome by sharp whisking.
The third recipe freezes well for 2–3 weeks; after that time it tends to lose its smoothness. All should be slowly thawed.

Egg and Cheese Dishes

These two basic foods can provide a whole variety of interesting dishes, both for a main meal and for quick and easy snacks. Egg dishes are given throughout this book, for eggs are capable of being served in so many different ways.

Although recipes vary, there are certain basic rules to follow:
1. Never over-cook egg dishes, otherwise they become dry and uninteresting.
2. Try to cook and serve at the last minute, as egg dishes tend to spoil easily if kept waiting.

With cheese dishes it is very important to choose the kind of cheese that cooks well. Many cheeses are delicious to eat uncooked, but are spoiled by cooking and also unsuccessful in the particular dish. An indication of the kind of cheese giving the best flavour is in the recipes in this section, but if you do not have that particular cheese you can substitute Cheddar, Gruyère or Emmenthal, in most cases. Cheese counters are becoming more and more interesting with the great variety of cheeses to choose from, and on page 163 you will find brief notes about some of the most popular.

The basic rules for cheese cookery are:
1. Never over-cook the cheese, otherwise it can become tough and could cause sauces to curdle.
2. It is unwise to exceed the amount mentioned in the particular recipe, for sometimes too much cheese can spoil a dish, not only by producing too strong a flavour, but by becoming over-greasy and making the whole dish somewhat unpleasant to look at, and to eat.
3. Where cheese is used as a topping you will sometimes see that breadcrumbs are given as well; this is because a generous amount of cheese has been used and it is important to absorb the fat and to make a crisp and not a greasy topping.

Metric Conversions

Fortunately an egg is an easy commodity to deal with, and in most egg recipes the amount of butter and other ingredients are fairly elastic so the conversion to the metric system is not difficult in any way.
The comments above often apply to cheese, except in sauces, of course, where the correct proportions are important. Sauces are dealt with in greater detail on pages 144 to 155.

Drinks to serve with egg and cheese dishes

It is difficult to generalise about the choice of drinks to serve with these two foods, for they are so often combined with other flavourings which would dictate one's choice of wine or other drink.

Here are one or two points to consider: unless eggs are combined with a strong flavouring such as a curry sauce, a rather delicate white wine or vin rosé are probably the best to choose.
Cheese in itself has a very definite flavour, with perhaps the exception of cottage and cream cheeses, and it is, therefore, wise to choose a drink that has a definite flavour itself. Beers and lagers blend well with cheese, and so does cider; dry white wines are excellent with many cheese dishes, but the really full-flavoured red wines are perhaps the best accompaniment of all.

Cooking egg and cheese dishes in the automatic oven

It is often convenient to prepare an egg dish for breakfast and leave it in the oven overnight. This does mean you must cover very carefully, for an uncooked egg, if exposed to the air, develops a rather hard skin which will spoil the cooked dish.

Many cheese dishes are ideal for putting into an automatic oven, but timing must be watched most carefully so the cheese does not become over-cooked and spoiled. In timing one should also allow for the possibility of people being late and the dish continuing to cook in the heat left in the oven, even though the gas or electricity has been switched off.

Home freezing of egg and cheese dishes

Some dishes containing eggs freeze well, but do not try and freeze any dish containing boiled or poached eggs. You will find that where the egg is hard- or soft-boiled the white becomes extremely 'rubbery' and unappetising.

Cheeses of all kinds and cheese dishes, on the whole, freeze extremely well. Where cheese is used in a sauce it is wise to follow the directions given on page 145 for freezing.

SIMPLE EGG DISHES

Eggs are an ideal protein food for they are comparatively inexpensive, quick to cook and very versatile. The following are *based on boiled eggs*.

Allow 3½–4 minutes in boiling water for a soft-boiled egg and 10 minutes for a hard-boiled egg. Always crack the shell when the egg is cooked; plunge hard-boiled eggs into cold water to prevent overcooking (which gives a dark line round the yolk). Soft *or* hard-boiled eggs can be used in:

EGGS AU GRATIN: cover the shelled eggs with cheese sauce, page 146, then a layer of grated cheese and crumbs, and brown under the grill or in the oven. *Eggs Mornay* are similar except the topping is omitted.

EGGS FLORENTINE: put the eggs on a bed of spinach and cover with White or Cheese sauce, page 146.

SCOTCH EGGS: coat 4 shelled hard-boiled eggs with about 300–325 grammes (12 oz.) sausagemeat, dip in flour, brush with beaten egg and coat in crumbs then fry until crisp and brown, drain, halve and serve hot or cold.

CHEESE SCOTCH EGGS: substitute the same amount of very firm mashed potato for sausagemeat, blend with 100 grammes (4 oz.) grated cheese; coat and cook as Scotch eggs.

Baked Eggs

Eggs may be baked in small individual dishes, or several baked together in one shallow dish. The dish or dishes should be well buttered, the eggs broken into the dish, seasoned lightly, then baked in the oven for about 12–15 minutes until set. To make a more interesting dish, cover with cream, with grated cheese, or with a sauce. Naturally the additional ingredients mean longer cooking.

Fried Eggs

Break eggs on to a saucer then slide into hot fat in the pan, cook until set. Fried eggs may be varied by cooking them in butter, then allowing this to turn dark brown (beurre noir); flavour this with chopped parsley and capers. The eggs may be coated with Cheese sauce, page 146 or a hot tomato purée.

Dishes based on poached eggs

Lower the eggs into heated greased egg-poacher cups or boiling salted water, cook *steadily* for 3½–4 minutes. Serve on buttered toast, cooked spinach, etc.

EGGS BENEDICT: poach 1–2 eggs per person, put slices of cooked bacon or ham on hot buttered toast, top with the eggs, coat with Hollandaise sauce, page 152.

MEXICAN EGGS: make a tomato purée by cooking ½ kilo (1 lb.) skinned chopped tomatoes (or heating canned tomatoes) in a frying pan, season well and flavour with a little chilli powder, then dilute with about 142 ml (¼ pint) water or stock. Poach 8 eggs in this sauce, serve with cooked rice or hot toast. To make a more elaborate sauce, fry 2 chopped onions and a chopped green pepper in a little oil, then add the tomatoes and cook as above. Serves 8 as an hors d'oeuvre, or 4 as a light main dish.

Automatic Oven

It is possible to 'roast' eggs in the oven instead of boiling them, and this is ideal for a party. Prick egg-shells at 'pointed' end with a fine hat pin, stand on the racks with the rounded-end downwards and bake for about 15 minutes in a moderately hot oven.

The baked egg dishes may be left in the oven, make sure to protect the top of the egg with foil or with a thick layer of sauce or cream (or both sauce or cream and foil) so the egg does not dry while waiting to be cooked.

Speedy Meal

All egg dishes are quick and easy to prepare, that is why they are so good for breakfast dishes, for quick supper dishes, etc.

Slimming Tips

An egg is one of the lowest calorie protein foods. At the same time it gives an adequate supply of iron, and is easy to digest. Boiled eggs are ideal, for no fat is used in cooking; choose the method of poaching eggs where they are cooked in a pan of water rather than buttered egg-poacher cups, or cook them as Mexican eggs (without using oil).

Home Freezing

As stated throughout this book, eggs in the form of egg dishes (as opposite) are not satisfactory to freeze. If you have a surplus of uncooked eggs though, they can be frozen. *Separate* the eggs or freeze whole. Whole eggs *should be beaten* before freezing to stop coagulation, and add *either* ½ teaspoon salt or 2 tablespoons sugar to about 8–10 eggs (this also improves colour). If more convenient, freeze yolks and whites separately, add the salt or sugar to the beaten egg yolks—label carefully. Do not beat or flavour egg whites. Pack eggs in small convenient containers.

Dishes based on scrambled eggs

Allow 2 eggs per person, beat slightly and season well. Heat a knob of butter in the saucepan and blend a little milk or cream with the eggs, if wished. Pour into the hot butter and cook very slowly, stirring well, until lightly set. Serve on hot buttered toast, fried bread, etc.

CHEESE AND EGGS: blend 1–2 tablespoons grated Cheddar, or other cheese that cooks well, with the beaten eggs and cook gently, or add the cheese when the eggs are nearly set.

HAM AND EGGS: add finely chopped cooked ham when the eggs are nearly set. Other cooked meats may be added.

PIPERADE: this classic French dish is based on scrambled eggs–fry a chopped onion and a crushed clove of garlic in hot butter or oil, add several chopped skinned tomatoes and a diced green pepper. Beat 6–8 eggs, season well, *do not* add milk or cream, pour over the cooked vegetables; scramble in the usual way. Serve with hot toast or French bread and butter. Serves 3–4 as a main dish.

Speedy Meal
Heat the butter and milk in the pan, while cracking, beating and seasoning the eggs; you will find the eggs begin to set much more quickly when put into the butter and *hot* milk. Lower the heat though, the moment the eggs are poured into the pan.

Slimming Tips
You can reduce the calories in scrambled egg if you habitually use a non-stick pan, and omit the butter and milk; or use skimmed milk. Obviously this makes a less rich and creamy egg mixture, so season well to compensate by giving extra flavour.

Plain Omelette

Serves 1
Cooking time–few minutes

Ingredients	Metric	Imperial
eggs	2–3	2–3
seasoning	to taste	to taste
butter	25 grammes	1 oz.

1 Beat the eggs lightly (do not over-beat), season, add about 1 tablespoon water, if wished, although this is not essential.
2 Heat the butter in a small omelette pan (about 13-cm-5-inch), pour in the eggs and allow the mixture to set lightly on the bottom.
3 Loosen the omelette from the sides of the pan, then tilt the pan so the liquid egg on top runs underneath.
4 Continue like this until just set, then fold or roll (away from the handle) and tip on to a hot plate. If using a filling, put this in before folding.
5 Wipe out the pan with soft tissue or kitchen paper as soon as possible after cooking: it is better not to wash an omelette pan for continual washing encourages eggs to stick to the pan.

SOME FLAVOURINGS AND FILLINGS FOR OMELETTES

CHEESE: fill the nearly cooked omelette with grated, cream or cottage cheese, before folding.

AUX FINES HERBES: this describes an omelette flavoured with chopped fresh herbs; add to the eggs before cooking.

FISH FILLINGS: add chopped shell fish to the eggs; heat other fish in a sauce and put into the omelette before folding.

MEAT FILLINGS: ham can be added to the eggs, cooked meat and poultry blended with cream and heated or put into a sauce and heated.

VEGETABLE FILLINGS: fill the omelette with cooked vegetable purée; or mushrooms in a sauce; or add sliced fried mushrooms to the eggs before cooking.

SWEET FILLINGS: these may be put into a basic omelette but are more usual in a soufflé type omelette, page 159. Choose hot jam, fruit purée or ice cream and put into omelette; serve as soon as possible. Dust the top of the omelette with sieved icing sugar; brown under the grill if wished.

Speedy Meal
The hotter the butter (providing it does not brown, then burn) and the more quickly you cook an omelette, the better it will be; so this is an ideal dish when you are in a hurry. Use ready-prepared fillings to save extra preparation, i.e. canned tomatoes, ready-grated Parmesan cheese, cooked ham, etc.

Mixer
The mixer is of little value in blending the eggs and seasoning in a plain omelette, for it is not a good idea to over-beat.

Other types of omelettes

The omelette on page 158 is the most usual kind, but below you will find variations on this.

SOUFFLÉ OMELETTE: the ingredients for this are similar to those for a plain omelette but it is necessary to separate the egg yolks and whites. Beat the yolks with seasoning, or add a little sugar for a sweet omelette, and fold in the water, or add the same quantity of milk or thin cream for a richer flavour. Whisk the egg whites until very stiff, then fold into the yolks. Heat the butter in the omelette pan, pour in the egg mixture, then allow omelette to set as stage 2. Since the mixture is much stiffer it does not run down the sides of the pan, so it is advisable to put the pan under a very moderate grill to set the eggs on top. Fold the omelette; to do this make a fairly deep incision across the centre of the egg mixture, and turn out of the pan. The filling naturally is put in *before* folding.

TO GLAZE A SWEET OMELETTE: sprinkle sieved icing sugar over the top of the folded omelette and brown under the grill before serving.

Tortilla or Spanish type Omelette

Serves 2
Cooking time 10–15 minutes

Ingredients	Metric	Imperial
onions	1–2 medium	1–2 medium
green pepper	½	½
tomatoes	2	2
garlic (optional)	1 clove	1 clove
oil	2 tablespoons	2 tablespoons
stock	1 tablespoon	1 tablespoon
seasoning	to taste	to taste
eggs	4–5	4–5
butter	25 grammes	1 oz.

1 Chop or slice the onions very thinly, dice the pulp of the pepper (discarding core, seeds and skin), chop the tomatoes, crush the clove of garlic.
2 Simmer in half the oil and with the stock and seasoning.
3 Beat the eggs, add the vegetables, season again if wished.
4 Heat the rest of the oil and the butter in the omelette pan, pour in the mixture and cook until set.
5 Slide on to a hot dish; this omelette is not folded.

Note: instead of the vegetables you can use sliced cooked sausages and meat or cooked fish. Choose as colourful and interesting a selection of ingredients as possible.

OVEN-BAKED OMELETTE
Many types of omelettes can be baked in the oven, thus avoiding the trouble of 'working' the omelette.

OVEN-BAKED SPANISH OMELETTE: use ingredients as recipe above, but omit 1 tablespoon oil. Heat the butter in a shallow ovenproof dish, then pour in the egg and vegetable mixture as stage 4. Bake for about 20 minutes just above the centre of a moderate to moderately hot oven.

SWISS OMELETTE: mix 4 eggs with 2 tablespoons thin cream, seasoning and 100 grammes (4 oz.) grated Gruyère or Cheddar cheese. Heat 25 grammes (1 oz.) butter in the dish, pour in mixture and bake as above, garnish with chopped parsley.

Automatic Oven
The oven-baked omelettes can be placed in the oven, left for a limited time only, and then allowed to cook. The vegetables must be cold before being added to the Spanish type omelette at stage 3, otherwise the eggs would start to set and be very unpleasant.

Slimming Tips
If you use a non-stick pan for these and other omelettes you can reduce the amount of butter to half or even a quarter of that given. Make sure the pan and the very small amount of butter are very hot before adding the beaten eggs, etc. Choose low calorie vegetables for the Tortilla: onions, garlic, peppers and tomatoes are excellent, but cook in stock without the oil.

Home Freezing
It takes time to prepare vegetables for omelettes, etc., so small containers with enough cooked frozen vegetables to fill one or two omelettes are useful.

159

MAKING BATTERS

A batter is one of the most versatile mixtures; it can be used for pancakes of all kinds–small pancakes are a very good alternative to the pasta form of Cannelloni, page 169. The batter is used to make *Yorkshire puddings, Toad-in-the-Hole* and similar dishes, and with slight adjustments can form the basis of sweet or savoury fritters. *To give a richer mixture* than the one below, use 2 eggs instead of 1, and omit 2 tablespoons liquid.

METRIC CONVERSION: you will note that the grammes in the recipe below state 'generous measure', for the consistency of a batter is very important; a more accurate conversion of 4 oz. would be 115 grammes, not 100 grammes.

Pancake or Yorkshire Pudding Batter

Serves 4–5
Cooking time as recipe

Ingredients	Metric	Imperial
plain flour	100 grammes (generous measure)	4 oz.
salt	good pinch	good pinch
egg	1	1
liquid (⅔ milk, ⅓ water)	284 ml	½ pint

1 Sieve the flour and salt together into a basin, drop in the egg, then beat mixture well.
2 Gradually beat in just enough liquid to make a stiff batter. Beat until smooth, leave for about 5 minutes, then gradually beat in the rest of the liquid. A batter like this can be left for some time before being cooked.

Mixer
Use the liquidiser for making a batter. Pour the liquid into the goblet first, add the egg, then the flour. If the flour is put in first it tends to stick round the sides of the goblet.

Home Freezing
The uncooked batter can be frozen. It is wise to freeze this in the kind of container you would use for cooking a Yorkshire pudding, see below.
Cooked batters (pancakes) can be frozen, see below.

To cook pancakes

Makes 8–12 pancakes
Cooking time 3–4 minutes (each pancake)

Ingredients	Metric	Imperial
pancake batter as recipe above		
TO FRY:		
oil *or*	3 tablespoons	3 tablespoons
fat	75 grammes	3 oz.
TO SERVE:		
see below		

1 Make the batter; if it has been allowed to stand, whisk sharply before cooking.
2 Put just under a dessertspoon oil or about one eighth of the fat into a medium sized pan, heat this thoroughly.
3 Either pour the batter from a jug or spoon into the hot pan, tilting this as you do so in order to give a paper-thin layer of batter over the whole pan.
4 Cook for about 1½–2 minutes until golden brown, turn or toss and brown on second side. Add extra oil or fat before cooking each pancake (a non-stick pan needs less fat).
5 If filling the pancakes at once, lift these from the pan, put in the filling and roll–see next page.
6 If making pancakes to use later, pile on to a plate as they cook, and cover each pancake with a piece of greaseproof or waxed paper or foil, so they do not stick together. Reheat, as instructed on page 161.
7 Wipe out pan with paper after use, try not to wash–see page 158.

Automatic Oven
Filled cooked pancakes may be left in oven to heat through later, cover with foil so they do not dry.

Speedy Meal
It is possible to buy packets of batter or pancake mix, but the basic mixture is very quickly prepared–as you see opposite.
You can prepare the batter ahead and keep it for some days in a refrigerator, whisk well before using.

Home Freezing
You can either freeze the uncooked batter, see above, or you can freeze the cooked pancakes, ready to heat or fill, or you can freeze filled and rolled pancakes–see page 161.
If freezing the batter then allow time for it to defrost to make the pancakes.
If freezing cooked pancakes, sandwich pieces of paper between the pancakes and simply 'peel off' the number required then heat through.

34. Strawberry milk shake, see page 244

TO STORE AND REHEAT PANCAKES

Pancakes may be stored in the refrigerator for several days, or for a much longer period in the freezer, see opposite and on the previous page under *home freezing*.

When wishing to heat pancakes (that have *not* been frozen) either heat for about 1 minute in a hot greased pan, or, if filled, cover with foil (so they do not dry) and heat in the oven. The more sophisticated type of pancakes, such as Crêpes Suzettes, are easily heated. Fold these and heat in the prepared syrup.

FILLINGS AND FLAVOURINGS FOR PANCAKES

SWEET FLAVOURINGS: roll the pancakes on sugared paper, then serve with segments of orange or lemon; or mix grated nutmeg or powdered cinnamon with the sugar.

SWEET FILLINGS: fill with hot fruit purée, hot jam, with ice cream (then top with chocolate sauce, page 192).

CRÊPES SUZETTES: spread each pancake with the filling below, fold into four then heat in the sauce:

FILLING: cream together 100 grammes (4 oz.) butter and the same amount of sugar and the grated rind of 2 oranges (or 3 tangerines) and a little curaçao.

SAUCE: heat the juice of 2–3 oranges (or 4–5 tangerines), with sugar to taste and curaçao to flavour (some recipes add 1–2 tablespoons redcurrant jelly to the sauce).

SAVOURY FILLINGS–fill the pancakes with vegetable mixtures, these are described on page 158; or with fish, chicken, meat, in various sauces. See picture between pages 88/89.

Speedy Meal

Make use of canned fruit pie mixtures as easy fillings, or use cooked left over vegetables, meat and fish.

Home Freezing

It is a good idea to freeze small, clearly labelled, containers of fillings suitable for pancakes or omelettes.
Some of the fillings that can be frozen are: *fruit purées; the Crêpes Suzettes filling and sauce and ice cream; vegetable purées; sauces of various kinds; minced meat, cooked fish, cooked poultry.*
If freezing filled pancakes it is quite a good idea to freeze these in a dish that can be used for reheating; then heat through, from the frozen state, in the oven. The batter of pancakes keeps in the freezer for several months: the choice of filling, however, will also determine the ideal storage time.

Yorkshire Pudding

Serves 4–5
Cooking time 15–40 minutes, see stage 3
Oven temperature 450–475° F. (230–240° C.), Gas Mark 8, then 350–375° F. (180–190° C.), Gas Mark 4–5

Ingredients	Metric	Imperial
batter	as page 160	as page 160
fat	25 grammes	1 oz.

1 Make the batter, allow it to stand if wished.
2 Put the fat into either one Yorkshire pudding tin or divide between about 8–10 small deep patty tins.
3 Heat fat for 4–5 minutes at the top of very hot oven, then pour or spoon the mixture into tin, or tins; allow 10–15 minutes to cook a large pudding at the higher temperature, or 5–8 minutes for smaller puddings. After this time, reduce the heat and continue cooking until the pudding is firm and golden brown. Serve at once.

DISHES BASED ON YORKSHIRE PUDDING

TOAD-IN-THE-HOLE: heat about 8 sausages in the hot fat for 10 minutes in the Yorkshire pudding tin, pour over the batter, then continue as Yorkshire pudding. Chops, halved kidneys or other meat, may be used instead.

CHEESE YORKSHIRE PUDDING: add about 75 grammes (3 oz.) grated cheese to the batter. Bake in either one tin or the small tins; when cooked top with cooked vegetables.

NORFOLK PUDDING: heat butter or margarine in the tin in place of fat. Add about 3 sliced cooking apples, a little sugar and few sultanas, then the batter; bake as before.

Automatic Oven

The Yorkshire pudding, or dishes based on this, may be left in the oven and the oven set to automatic timing. Naturally the fat cannot be heated *just* before cooking the pudding, so grease the tin very well (and if you have time, warm the tin *and* fat so that you have an even distribution of fat). *Do not* pour the pudding mixture in while the tin is very hot though, or you will have a limited cooking period which would spoil the pudding. Choose a moderately hot to hot oven and select the type of tin and position in the oven according to the *total* cooking time of the whole menu–the deeper the mixture the longer it takes to cook.
When preparing *Toad-in-the-Hole* and similar dishes, cook the sausages for about 10 minutes, cool, then add the batter and put into the oven.

Speedy Meal

Use individual tins, cook in a short time.

Home Freezing

Freeze the batter in fairly deep foil dishes. Uncover these, but do not allow the batter to defrost; cook as instructions opposite–allow a little longer cooking time for the batter to thaw out as it cooks.

MAKING SAVOURY SOUFFLES

A hot soufflé is not only a nutritious light dish, but it can form part of a formal meal; the Liver soufflé on this page is delicious instead of pâté; the Cheese soufflé makes an excellent savoury at the end of a meal. On page 117 are recipes for vegetable soufflés.

Cheese Soufflé

Serves 4–6
Cooking time 40–45 minutes
Oven temperature 375–400° F. (190–200° C.), Gas Mark 5–6

Ingredients	Metric	Imperial
butter	25 grammes	1 oz.
flour	25 grammes*	1 oz.*
milk	142 ml**	¼ pint**
seasoning	to taste	to taste
made-mustard	½–1 teaspoon	½–1 teaspoon
cheese***	100 grammes	4 oz.
eggs	3–4	3–4

*this may be reduced to half quantity if you prefer a very soft texture.
**increase by several tablespoons if you prefer a lightly set soufflé.
***Cheddar, Gruyère or Parmesan.

1 Make a thick sauce of the butter, flour and milk, then season well and add mustard.
2 Grate the cheese finely and add to the sauce, then stir in the egg yolks and lastly the stiffly beaten egg whites.
3 Put into a 15-cm (6-inch) greased soufflé dish; bake in the centre of a moderate to moderately hot oven until lightly set and firm. Serve at once.

 Automatic Oven
See remarks below under Liver soufflé.

 Speedy Meal
Omit the White sauce, stage 1, and use 5–6 tablespoons very smooth mashed potato (this can be dehydrated potato), add 2 tablespoons milk and the rest of the ingredients as the recipe opposite. You will have a lighter soufflé, which sinks less readily, if you use 3 yolks and 4 whites.

 Slimming Tips
Although flour, butter and milk are all included in this dish, it makes such a nutritious meal that it could occasionally be served on a slimming diet. You could, of course, use *skimmed* milk, or substitute tomato juice or purée for milk, and choose low calorie cottage cheese to flavour.

 Home Freezing
See comments under recipe below.

Liver Soufflé

This makes a delicious change from pâté.

*Serves 4–6**
Cooking time 40–45 minutes
Oven temperature 350–375° F. (180–190° C.), Gas Mark 4–5

Ingredients	Metric	Imperial
butter	40 grammes	1½ oz.
flour	25 grammes	1 oz.
milk	142 ml	¼ pint
onion	1 small	1 small
seasoning	to taste	to taste
thin cream *or* top of milk	3 tablespoons	3 tablespoons
calf's *or* lamb's liver	150 grammes	6 oz.
eggs	3	3

*4 as light main dish, 6 as hors d'oeuvre.

1 Make a thick sauce with 25 grammes (1 oz.) of the butter, flour and milk, add the halved onion while the sauce is thickening to give a delicate flavour.
2 Add seasoning and the cream, then remove the onion.
3 Mince the liver finely, add to the sauce with the beaten egg yolks, taste and add more seasoning.
4 Whip the egg whites until very stiff, fold into the liver mixture and spoon into the buttered 15-cm (6-inch) soufflé dish.
5 Bake in the middle of a very moderate to moderate oven until firm and golden. Serve at once.

 Automatic Oven
A soufflé cannot stand in a cold oven but you can place it into a pre-heated oven and set the time to switch off at the end of the cooking time so as not to over-cook. A soufflé falls though, if left standing in the oven for any length of time, so serve as soon as possible.

Speedy Meal
This can be made by using finely diced ready-made liver sausage (not pâté—that is too soft). The cooking time can be shortened by 5–8 minutes.

Slimming Tips
Use skimmed milk in the recipe or clear consommé in place of liquid given. Although there is fat and flour in this dish the quantities per person are very small.

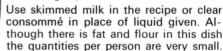 **Home Freezing**
One cannot freeze either uncooked soufflé mixture or the cooked soufflé, but you could mince liver and freeze this, ready to make soufflé or a pâté when required. Do not keep *minced* liver more than 4–5 weeks.

CHOOSING CHEESES WISELY

There is an almost bewildering number of cheeses available today. Obviously it is wise to try as many varieties as possible to give an interesting cheese board, and it is sensible to have a well balanced selection of cheeses.

CHEESES TO BUY FOR COOKING: Parmesan (which is not considered a cheese to eat uncooked), Cheddar, Gruyère, Emmenthal, Dutch Edam and Gouda and Port Salut are just some of the cheeses that are good for cooking, and to serve uncooked.

HARD CHEESES: choose Cheddar, Cheshire, Double Gloucester, Derby, etc.

VEINED CHEESES (all fairly strong); choose Danish Blue, Stilton, Gorgonzola, etc.

SOFT TEXTURED CHEESES: Camembert, Brie (definite in flavour).

CREAM CHEESES, ETC.: Bel Paese; in most stores there is a selection of cream cheeses and cream cheese spreads; cottage cheese (low in fat and calories); and a variety of processed cheeses (some of which cook quite well).

Home Freezing
One is always instructed to keep most cheeses at room temperature or away from the freezing compartment in the refrigerator. This is correct if you intend to use them within a few hours. To avoid wastage I have experimented with refrigeration and freezing of all the cheeses one can buy. A refrigerator 'halts' ripening of cheese, and if you store cheeses such as Camembert for too long a period in the refrigerator, the cheese dries out and *never* reaches a degree of maturity; but it is quite successful to keep this and most cheeses in the refrigerator for several days, *providing* you bring it out two or three hours before you wish to serve it—except when serving lightly iced.
All cheeses freeze, so if you are going away—freeze those that do not keep well. Allow plenty of time to thaw out; there is a *little* loss of flavour, particularly in soft cream cheeses, but not much. Use frozen cheese within about 6–8 weeks.

Cheese Aigrettes

Makes 20–24
Cooking time—few minutes

Ingredients	Metric	Imperial
Choux pastry	as page 176	as page 176
seasoning	to taste	to taste
Parmesan cheese	40 grammes	1½ oz.
deep fat *or* oil		
TO GARNISH:		
Parmesan cheese	25–50 grammes	1–2 oz.
parsley	few sprigs	few sprigs

1 Make the choux pastry as page 176, but add the seasoning and grated cheese after beating in the eggs.
2 Heat the fat or oil until hot enough to turn a day-old cube of bread golden brown in under 1 minute.
3 Drop small spoonfuls of the choux mixture into the hot fat; fry for several minutes until golden brown and well risen.
4 Drain on absorbent paper, then top with grated cheese and garnish with parsley.

Speedy Meal
Use drums of ready-grated Parmesan cheese.

Mixer
The liquidiser could be used for 'grating' the cheese—add very gradually. If very hard, then use a grater.

Home Freezing
Freeze before wrapping. To serve, defrost, crisp in a hot oven, then toss in the grated cheese.

Welsh Rarebit

The original Welsh Rarebit (or rabbit) mixture was soft, rather like a sauce, and very easily made.

Beat 150 grammes (6 oz.) grated Cheddar, or Cheshire, or Double Gloucester (not usually associated with cooking but excellent in this), with 2 teaspoons made-mustard, salt and pepper to taste, 25 grammes (1 oz.) butter and 3 tablespoons old ale; blend well, then add either 1–2 tablespoons extra ale or ale and Worcestershire sauce, or milk, to give a mixture like soft cream. Spread on buttered toast and grill until golden brown. Serves 4 as light dish, 8 as savoury.

A more 'solid' mixture is made by using the ingredients above, plus 1 level tablespoon cornflour. Blend the cornflour and ale (or ale *and* milk or Worcestershire sauce), and cook *with* the butter over a slow heat until thick and smooth. Add the rest of the ingredients. Servings as before.

Speedy Meal
Cover toast with a slice of Cheddar, brown under grill. The butter for the toast could be blended with a little mustard.

Slimming Tips
Cottage cheese can be spread over starch-reduced toast and grilled for a few minutes.

Home Freezing
Mixture keeps for 1–2 weeks in a tightly covered container in the refrigerator, but for about 2 months in the freezer.

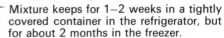

Croque Monsieur

Serves 4*
Cooking time 5 minutes

Ingredients	Metric	Imperial
slices of bread	8 medium	8 medium
butter	to spread	to spread
made-mustard	1 teaspoon	1 teaspoon
cooked ham	4 slices	4 slices
	(size of bread)	(size of bread)
Gruyère *or* Emmenthal	4 slices	4 slices
cheese	(size of bread)	(size of bread)
TO DIP:		
egg	1	1
milk	2 tablespoons	2 tablespoons
TO FRY:		
butter	50 grammes	2 oz.

*or 12–16 fingers for cocktail snacks.

1 Remove crusts from bread and spread with butter and mustard.
2 Sandwich together with the ham and cheese.
3 Beat the egg and milk and dip the sandwiches quickly in this; do not allow to become 'soggy'.
4 Heat the butter, fry until crisp and brown on either side and serve at once.

Automatic Oven

This fried sandwich, famous in France, is nicer when cooked and eaten at once from the pan but, if you wish to leave a light 'snack' ready you can fry, drain, put on a flat dish, leave in the oven and set this to give about 15 minutes heating at a moderate temperature. To turn a snack into a more complete meal, put halved seasoned tomatoes on another dish.

Speedy Meal

This is a quick way to turn an 'ordinary' sandwich into a very delicious snack; use up left-over sandwiches (made up with other foods) in the same way.

Home Freezing

It is better to use frozen sandwiches to make this, rather than freeze the completed dish. Allow the sandwiches to defrost if possible, before coating; this makes sure that the coating does not become too brown before the bread and filling are hot.

Bacon Toasts

Serves 4
Cooking time 10 minutes

Ingredients	Metric	Imperial
large slices white bread	4	4
butter	25 grammes	1 oz.
tomatoes	4	4
large slices Cheddar		
or Gruyère cheese	4	4
rashers, back *or*		
streaky bacon	4	4
TO GARNISH:		
parsley	few sprigs	few sprigs
lemon	1	1

1 Toast bread lightly on both sides.
2 Remove crusts and spread lightly with butter.
3 Cover with a layer of sliced tomatoes and top with a slice of cheese.
4 Cut bacon rashers in half (remove rinds) and arrange on top.
5 Grill slowly until cheese melts and turns golden brown and bacon is crispy.
6 Garnish with parsley and lemon, as picture facing page 57.

Lemon is not usually served with this dish, but squeezed wedges of lemon give a very good flavour.

Automatic Oven

There is no reason why this cannot be cooked in the oven. Either toast the bread as stage 1, or fry this and drain well. Continue as stages 2–4, arrange on an ovenproof dish and cook for about 20–25 minutes towards the top of a moderate to moderately hot oven.

Slimming Tips

Omit the bread and arrange halved tomatoes in a shallow dish, top with seasoning (do not use too much salt), the layer of sliced cheese and the rashers of bacon; then cook in the oven as directions under Automatic Oven. Serve with hot French bread or toast for members of the family who are *not* dieting.

Home Freezing

This is not the type of dish that is worth freezing, but remember you can take slices of frozen bread (from a sliced loaf) and toast them without waiting for them to defrost.

CHEESE MAKES A MEAL

There are many ways in which cheese can be used to make a complete meal, here are a few easy suggestions:
CAULIFLOWER CHEESE: cook cauliflower, coat with Cheese sauce, page 146. Other vegetables can be used in the same way.
CHEESE RICE: blend lots of grated cheese with boiled rice.
MACARONI CHEESE: cook approximately 75 grammes (3 oz.) macaroni and blend with Cheese sauce, top with grated cheese and crumbs, and brown in the oven or under the grill.

Mixer

Sometimes a cheese sauce becomes a little 'stringy' through leaving to heat too long, if so tip into the warmed liquidiser goblet to give a smooth sauce, see also pages 145 and 146, under *using a mixer*.

Home Freezing

None of these dishes are as good when frozen. Macaroni and rice lose their texture, and so does cooked cauliflower.

Cocktail Savouries

While many people decry a cocktail party as being too impersonal and feel they would rather invite fewer people for a meal, there are many occasions when this kind of entertaining is ideal. You can offer hospitality to a relatively large number of guests in a small space; you can make the food as simple or imaginative as you wish, so that the preparation *need not* be too time-consuming. It is important though that the food should be plentiful, for people are often quite happy to drink relatively little, but on the other hand they do like something to 'nibble'. Obviously food at a cocktail party must be in small portions so people need not bother with a plate, but you will find that many recipes are equally suitable for a buffet party, if you make them somewhat larger, and not bite-sized. Hot savouries are on pages 168 to 170.

Metric Conversions

This depends on the type of dish. If you are using one with pastry the conversion must be accurate, see page 171, but if you are having a less complicated dish the conversion is not particularly important.

Using a mixer for cocktail savouries

Use the mixer to make savoury butters, page 166, to make the pastry, as page 171 and for blending the ingredients for some of the 'dips', page 166. Keep a supply of chopped parsley beside you as you garnish the tiny canapés; the *dry* liquidiser goblet is excellent for chopping this finely, and it stores well in an air-tight container in the refrigerator.

Cooking savouries in the automatic oven

If you include hot savouries when you plan a cocktail or buffet party you will find the automatic oven invaluable for keeping these warm, without spoiling, or for cooking at a pre-set time. Hints for using the oven are found by the savouries, on pages 168, 169, 170.

Drinks to serve

This is purely a matter of personal taste; the greater the selection of drinks, the more difficult they are to serve, so you will need someone to be a 'full-time' bar-man. You may therefore decide it is better to have a more limited selection–sherry (dry and less dry), gin (with tonic, bitter lemon, orange), vermouth (sweet and dry) plus whisky (with iced water and soda) and tomato juice cocktail, soft drinks, etc.

Wine is becoming so popular you may decide to offer wine rather than a variety of drinks, and if the party is to celebrate a very special occasion, champagne (choose non-vintage for economy) or champagne cocktail is the drink to offer. In summer well chilled wine cups are economical and interesting; in winter hot punch–see recipes page 245. These may not be real cocktails but will be popular.

Home freezing of cocktail savouries

Many savouries can be frozen completely, i.e. pastry cases *and* the fillings (freeze separately in most cases, so that pastry base does not become over-soft in defrosting); some dips freeze well, see page 166; all savoury butters, page 166, can be frozen. Aspic covered canapés freeze well; it is a good idea to arrange these on the serving trays, freeze, *then* wrap. When proposing to serve: unwrap *then* allow the food to thaw out on the same tray, so saving time in re-arranging, and any possibility of spoiling the garnishes.

WELL-CHOSEN SAVOURIES–try to include the following flavours:

ASPIC–not essential but a good 'covering' for ingredients, see page 167.
CHEESE–in various hot or cold savouries. Some suggestions are given on page 168.
FISH–sardines, anchovies, shell fish, etc.
MEAT–pâté, ham, salami, tiny sausages.

SLIMMERS–you are 'safe' to eat olives and nuts, see special hints by recipes.

SPEEDY SAVOURIES–crisps and nuts, diced cheese and orange segments, sliced Frankfurters; put on cocktail sticks and arrange round a dip of mustard blended with tomato ketchup.

PLANNING A COCKTAIL PARTY

One of the secrets of any party is to plan well ahead; most well chosen cocktail savouries can be prepared in part, if not entirely, in advance, for example:

SAVOURY BUTTERS: these can be used to spread over the base or for piping on top of the canapés. They are simply well flavoured butter, and they can be varied in many ways. Some of the most useful are:
ANCHOVY BUTTER–to serve with fish or egg.
Cream 75 grammes (3 oz.) butter with shake pepper, few drops anchovy essence; a squeeze lemon juice may also be added.
CAVIARE BUTTER–to serve with fish, egg or by itself.
Blend about 2 tablespoons caviare (there are inexpensive Danish varieties) with 75 grammes (3 oz.) butter and a shake pepper. Use cod's roe in the same way.
LIVER BUTTER–to serve with ham or by itself.
Blend 50 grammes (2 oz.) smooth liver sausage with 75 grammes (3 oz.) butter, 1 teaspoon made-mustard.
SHELL FISH BUTTER–to serve with fish, egg or by itself.
Use pounded prawns, lobster, coral (roe) in place of caviare.
WATERCRESS BUTTER–as a general garnish.
Blend 2 tablespoons finely chopped watercress, 2 teaspoons lemon juice with 75 grammes (3 oz.) butter.

Speedy Meal

Use the quick-creaming margarine in place of butter, or soften butter with 1–2 teaspoons boiling water to cream quickly.

Mixer

Use the whisk to cream the butter as for cakes, etc., add the flavouring and beat by whisk, or by hand. One might waste a little of the caviare, etc., round the blades. If preferred use the liquidiser and soften the butter; put into the liquidiser with the flavourings and emulsify. The mixture would be too soft to use at once so put on one side.

Home Freezing

Put the flavoured butters into containers, cover tightly, and freeze. Use within 3–4 weeks to retain the full flavour.

Bases for canapés

Have a selection of 'bases' to add interest to the food, for example:
BREAD AND BUTTER–cut moderately thickly and choose brown, white, rye, *fresh* bread. Ideal for soft toppings (moist liver pâté, etc.) that would make pastry or toast soft.
TOAST–one of the 'bases' that do become soft easily, but is usual for aspic canapés; cut into fancy shapes, warm through in the oven, cool then top.
PASTRY–choose various kinds of pastry (cheese being the most suitable); these can be made ahead and stored.
FRIED BREAD–one of the best bases, since it is crisp and can be fried ahead then reheated just before using. Drain well on absorbent paper after frying and *reheating*.

Automatic Oven

If toast is used as the base for canapés, heat through separately where possible, then top with the mixture. Obviously in the case of hot canapés the completed canapés will be heated.
Fried bread does brown more in reheating; so take care it is only a light brown when fried the first time.

Home Freezing

All these bases freeze well, but toast and fried bread must be re-crisped in the oven.

DIPS

This is a comparatively modern innovation and 'dips' range from the sophisticated Swiss fondue, page 168, to the easy and very good packet 'dips' that are reconstituted with cream or soured cream, etc. Here are two recipes:

CHEESE DIP: make a *thick* strongly flavoured cheese sauce as page 146, using 50 grammes (2 oz.) butter, 284 ml (½ pint) milk, etc. Flavour this either with a little sherry, flaked crab-meat and chopped gherkins *or* with curry powder and a little thick cream, and add very finely chopped chives or spring onions *or* with mayonnaise and tomato ketchup. Stir as it cools to prevent skin forming. The 'dip' must be stiff enough to cling firmly to the crisps, etc. Arrange in a bowl with–around it–potato crisps, small biscuits, pieces of celery and carrot. Serves 4–5.

CRAB-MEAT DIP: hard boil 4 eggs, then sieve or chop very finely, add the contents of a small can of crab-meat, together with enough mayonnaise to make the consistency of a thick cream. Season very well, flavour with lemon juice and a good shake of cayenne pepper to give a slightly hot flavour. You can also add a few drops chilli sauce, if wished. Put into a bowl and have crisps, etc., as described above, round the bowl. Serves 6–8.

Mixer

The liquidiser is ideal to blend the cheese sauce with the other ingredients.
The crab-meat dip can be emulsified within a very short time in the liquidiser. Put all the ingredients in together, otherwise the hard-boiled eggs will 'stick' to the base.

Home Freezing

If you wish to freeze this cheese sauce use 25 grammes (1 oz.) cornflour instead of 50 grammes (2 oz.) flour. Use within a month, but preferably within 2–3 weeks. The crab-meat dip, if emulsified, will freeze, but if there are any particles of egg white *do not* freeze.

Aspic canapés

Aspic serves a very useful purpose on canapés; it makes them look more professional and also keeps the food quite moist under the jelly coating.

To use the aspic over canapés: dissolve the jelly in the amount of water stated on the packet; one packet and 568 ml (1 pint) water will coat about 40–50 tiny cocktail sized canapés. Let the jelly cool and just *begin to stiffen* and *then* make the canapés all ready to cover.

Suggestions for toppings are below; this is the method of coating:

1 Put the coated toast, etc. on a wire cooling tray with a large dish or tray underneath; in this way any jelly that 'drips' through the holes may be 'caught' and used again.
2 Either spread a thin layer of jelly over the food with a broad-bladed knife, dipped in hot water, or brush the jelly very carefully over the food.
3 Let this layer set, pipe designs on top with flavoured butter, if wished (this is not essential). Melt any remaining jelly, then cool and pour a *very thin* layer over the top again. This second coating is not essential, but it protects the savoury butter and keeps that moist; it also gives a thicker and better coating to the food. Allow to set.
4 When quite firm cut into tiny fingers, or other shapes, using a sharp knife dipped in hot water.

Speedy Meal
To set the jelly in a shorter time dissolve in about a quarter quantity of very hot or boiling water, then crush enough ice to give remaining quantity of water. Stir into the very hot jelly and it will set almost at once. In cold weather it will probably set *too* quickly, so use half very hot water and half ice.

Slimming Tips
Aspic jelly adds no calories to any canapés and because the finished result does look so much more interesting, it can be used to turn very simple savouries into more interesting ones. Coat quatered hard-boiled eggs with aspic and put on to fingers of crispbread; dip large prawns in aspic (so they do not dry), allow to set then put on cocktail sticks.

Home Freezing
There is little point in freezing made-up packet aspic jelly, it is so simple to make. The aspic coated canapés can, as stated, be frozen very successfully.

Some simple cocktail canapés

WITH EGG: coat slices of toast, or bread and butter, or biscuits, with savoury butter; top with scrambled or sliced hard-boiled egg; garnish with a) caviare, b) asparagus tips, c) savoury butter, d) prawns, e) pieces of sardine, f) anchovy fillets. Top with aspic jelly, if wished.

WITH CHEESE: coat cheese biscuits, or toast, with cream cheese or with Blue or other veined cheese, blended with butter. Top with a) shredded almonds, b) slices of radish, c) tiny strips of salami or cooked ham. Top with aspic jelly and piped cream cheese, if wished.

WITH FISH: spread toast, bread, biscuits, pastry with savoury butter or thick mayonnaise. Top with a) prawns, b) smoked salmon, c) flaked fish blended with mayonnaise, d) tiny pieces of crab or lobster (garnished with butter made from the coral). Top with aspic jelly if possible, and piped savoury butter; garnish the dish with lemons cut in a Van-Dyke design. To do this, with a sharp knife make a cut (reaching to the middle) in the centre of a lemon, cut downwards, then make an upward cut; continue round the lemon like this until the two halves part. This enables each guest to squeeze lemon over the canapés if wished.

WITH MEAT: spread bread, or toast, with liver pâté, with watercress or liver butter or butter. Top with fingers of a) salami, b) ham, c) cooked tongue, d) liver pâté.
Garnish with slices of cooked carrot, peas, asparagus tips. Top with aspic jelly, if possible, and garnish with watercress leaves, chopped parsley or sprigs of parsley.

WITH VEGETABLES: fill tiny pieces of celery with Danish blue cheese, blended with a little mayonnaise; with cottage cheese and chopped nuts; with caviare or liver butter, etc.; have radish 'roses' as garnish. To make these, either cut as lemon above, or make 8 cuts from the tip almost to the base; leave in ice cold water for 1 hour to open out before using.

Speedy Meal
Cut the loaf lengthways whether using it as a bread, toast, or fried bread base. It is far less difficult to cover a large surface and then cut it into tiny pieces afterwards than it is to try and make each tiny canapé separately.

Slimming Tips
Obviously when one is a guest it is difficult to choose particular canapés; if you can make a selection, then have those made with egg, shell fish or ham, avoid the richer sardines, pâté, etc.
If you are a hostess then it is quite an idea to have specially low calorie canapés, for so many people *are* slimming today. Have lots of radishes, filled pieces of celery (use cottage cheese), have cubes of ham, cheese, put on cocktail sticks and pressed into a melon.

Home Freezing
I have selected cocktail canapés that freeze without any problems at all. If you are *not* coating them with aspic, freeze as soon as they are prepared so there is no possibility of their becoming dry on top; canapés *must* look fresh to be appetising. Cover *lightly* with foil, or damp kitchen paper, or polythene, as they thaw out, so the food is kept moist without the possibility of the topping being harmed by any pressure of the covering.

More savouries for parties

CHEESE STRAWS : prepare the cheese pastry as page 174 then cut into narrow fingers. Put on greased baking trays, brush lightly with beaten egg and bake for about 7–10 minutes, towards the top of a hot oven. Cool, lift carefully off baking trays, store in tins.

CHOUX : make tiny shapes of choux pastry, page 176, bake as directed; when cold fill with a) cream cheese mixed with chopped gherkins, b) mashed sardines flavoured with lemon juice and cayenne pepper, c) pounded fish or chicken blended with a thick sauce or well seasoned cream.

PIZZA : either make a large Pizza, as page 170, then cut into fingers, or make individual ones; reheat if wished.

QUICHE : make one of the savoury flans (see next page and page 181) then cut into small portions, or make these in cocktail sized tartlet cases, bake for about 15–20 minutes only.

SAVOURY BOATS : line boat-shaped patty tins with short or cheese pastry, bake 'blind' (see page 172) and cool. Fill with a) scrambled eggs, top with prawns, b) fish in mayonnaise, c) cream cheese, top with tiny rolls of smoked salmon.

STUFFED MUSHROOMS : fry mushrooms, put on rounds of well drained fried bread. Fill mushroom caps with cream cheese, top with paprika. Reheat gently for 20 minutes.

STUFFED PRUNES : fill stoned cooked prunes, some with liver pâté, others with cream cheese, wrap rashers of bacon round the prunes; grill until bacon is lightly cooked, drain. Put on fingers of toast or well drained fried bread, stand on dish and reheat gently for about 20 minutes.

VOL-AU-VENTS : make small cases as described on page 172, fill with cooked fish, cooked poultry, cooked mushrooms, etc., bound with thick sauce or mayonnaise. Serve hot or cold; if serving hot put *hot* filling into *hot* cases at the last minute, to keep the pastry crisp.

WELSH RAREBIT : make the mixture as page 163; use the stiffer consistency (second recipe). Put on to fingers of toast but do *not* brown under the grill, instead heat for about 10 minutes towards the top of a moderately hot oven.

HOT DISHES FOR PARTIES

Often it is more convenient to offer one or two hot dishes instead of cocktail savouries, here are some suggestions:

FONDUE : this is possibly the most delicious of all 'dips'. Grate ½ kilo (1 lb.) Gruyère cheese (or mix Gruyère and Emmenthal) into the buttered top of a double saucepan or fondue pan, add seasoning, 250 ml (½ pint) dry white wine, 1 tablespoon brandy, heat *gently* until the cheese melts. Dip squares of fresh bread in this.

BEEF FONDUE : cut small squares or cubes of fillet steak and cook on forks in hot oil in the fondue pan. Dip in a tartare or tomato sauce and serve with vegetable side dishes.

BARBECUED FISH : make one of the barbecue sauces on page 132, put in a bowl, have fried scampi or fingers of fried fish to dip in this.

CUCUMBER PRAWNS : make a cucumber sauce–add grated cucumber to hot Hollandaise sauce, page 152. Serve with fried prawns.

Automatic Oven
Several of the recipes opposite are suitable for reheating. Choose a *very moderate heat* only to prevent any drying or over-browning.
The Pizza takes about 20–30 minutes to reheat, or tiny ones take about 7–8 minutes, see page 170.
The Quiche takes about 20–25 minutes if large, about 7–8 minutes if small.
The mushrooms would take about 20 minutes.
The stuffed prunes would take about the same time.
The vol-au-vent pastry cases *without* filling would take about 15–20 minutes, (heat the filling in the top of a double saucepan, so it does not burn), then put together and serve.

Speedy Meal
There are several ways in which less classic recipes could be used for the dishes opposite:
Cheese straws: coat thin fingers of bread with melted butter, roll in grated Parmesan cheese and brown in a hot oven for about 8–10 minutes.
Pizza: cut tiny rounds of bread, top with thick tomato purée, anchovies, grated cheese, and brown.
Savoury boats: cut wafer thin slices of very fresh bread, press into the greased boat shapes, brush the bread with melted butter and heat for about 8 minutes in a hot oven, until crisp and brown.
Vol-au-vents: cut rounds of bread, pull out the centre (to make a shape like a vol-au-vent), either fry until crisp and brown, or brush with melted butter and bake, then fill as the pastry cases.

Speedy Meal
To make a speedy Fondue make an ordinary cheese sauce, but use less milk than usual, whisk in a little brandy and wine and use this instead.

Mixer
A hand electric mixer can be used to whisk a Fondue mixture if it shows a slight inclination to 'curdle'.

Home Freezing
The *fried* fish can be frozen, ready to re-heat as required, so saving the bother of frying at the last minute. The Hollandaise and Barbecue sauce can be frozen, see notes by these on pages 152 and 132.

Party Quiche

Serves 4–8*
Cooking time 1–1¼ hours
Oven temperature 425° F. (220° C.), Gas Mark 7, then 350° F. (180° C.),
Gas Mark 3–4

Ingredients	Metric	Imperial
shortcrust pastry, see page 173	175–200 grammes	7–8 oz.
eggs	3	3
milk *or* half milk and half thin cream	284 ml	½ pint
Gruyère *or* Cheddar cheese	100 grammes	4 oz.
celery from heart	3 sticks	3 sticks
canned corn	6 tablespoons	6 tablespoons
green pepper	1 large	1 large
cooked ham	150 grammes	6 oz.
seasoning	to taste	to taste

*or small portions for more at a party.

1 Roll out pastry, line a really deep 20-cm (8-inch) flan ring, or tin or ovenproof serving dish, and continue as page 181, stages 3 and 4.
2 Beat the eggs, add the warmed milk (or milk and cream) the grated cheese, diced vegetables, ham and seasoning.
3 Spoon into the partially baked flan case, lower the heat and bake for approximately 45 minutes to 1 hour.
4 Serve hot or cold, or bake and heat gently as suggested on page 168. See picture of this dish, facing page 144.

Automatic Oven
Bake this flan and reheat as suggested on page 168; it is not satisfactory to leave the half-cooked flan standing in the oven waiting for cooking to start. If preferred you could bake the flan lightly, then add the filling and cook just before the party, setting the oven to switch 'off'.

Speedy Meal
Use bought frozen pastry.

Mixer
Use the mixer to prepare the pastry, see page 172. The liquidiser can be used to blend the eggs, milk and cheese.

Slimming Tips
There is a good depth of custard mixture; eat as little pastry as possible.

Home Freezing
See page 181. This filling freezes well, but substitute cooked onions for celery.

Pasta recipes

Most pasta dishes are ideal for a buffet party – the popular spaghetti is the least suitable since it is difficult to eat when standing at a buffet. Use short-cut pasta instead of the long strands of spaghetti (to cook, see page 85).

CANNELLONI (either the tubes of pasta that you buy ready-made) or tiny pancakes, filled, as a home-made dish are excellent – they are sufficiently soft to handle with just a fork. When not available use cooked *lasagne* or noodles, top with a) the 'filling', then b) with a cheese sauce.

STUFFED CANNELLONI: fill the cooked pasta type cannelloni or the cooked pancakes with a thick meat mixture (make as Bolognese sauce, page 85, but use half the liquid), top with a Cheese sauce, page 146, and brown under the grill; or fill with a thick Cheese sauce, mixed with fried mushrooms, or fish in a thick White or Cheese sauce, top with the Cheese sauce and brown.

Other sauces to use with pasta are, a Tomato sauce, page 150, or an Espagnole sauce, page 147; always serve with bowls of grated Parmesan cheese.

Automatic Oven
Most pasta dishes can be heated through in the oven; under-cook the pasta though, as it continues to soften in the oven heat. When boiled it is a good idea to rinse under boiling water to 'get rid of' the sticky starch on the outside.

Speedy Meal
Use canned pasta for 'emergency meals'. Put into a dish, top with a sauce and heat. To make a speedy *meat sauce* for cannelloni or other pasta, use canned stewed steak, flavour with wine, garlic salt, etc.

Home Freezing
It is a good idea to freeze sauces to blend with pasta, but pasta itself is not the most successful of dishes to freeze. The one exception perhaps is cannelloni.

Rice recipes

Savoury rice dishes are ideal for buffet parties; take care the rice is not over-cooked; it continues softening while being kept warm. Try the *risottos* on pages 118 and 119; add diced liver to make them more substantial and traditional.
Use the risottos as a basis for the most famous of rice dishes, i.e. *Paella* – add tiny pieces of raw chicken to the rice as it cooks, then stir in as great a variety of shell fish as possible, i.e. cooked mussels, flaked crab or lobster, prawns, etc. This gives a 'meal in a dish'.

Home Freezing
Rice does not freeze well, so it is not worthwhile freezing completed rice dishes.

Pizzas

This Italian savoury tart (there are a number of different toppings), is usually made with a base of a yeast bread mixture. If you are making bread therefore, as page 227, it is quite easy to take a small amount and use this instead of the baking powder dough suggested below. The method of preparation for the toppings would be the same, but you will need to allow the Pizza *with* the topping to 'prove', as stage 4, before it is baked. The baking time and temperature is exactly as given in the recipe below.

Serves 4–6
Cooking time 45 minutes
Oven temperature 425–450° F. (220–230° C.), Gas Mark 6–7

Ingredients	Metric	Imperial
FOR THE DOUGH:		
self-raising flour	325–340 grammes*	12 oz.
salt	good pinch	good pinch
margarine	50 grammes	2 oz.
milk	to bind	to bind
FOR THE TOPPING:		
olive oil	1 tablespoon	1 tablespoon
onions	2 large	2 large
garlic	1–2 cloves	1–2 cloves
tomatoes	1 kilo	2 lb.
seasoning	to taste	to taste
Mozzarella *or* Gruyère		
cheese	150 grammes	6 oz.
can anchovy fillets	1	1
black olives	8–10	8–10
Parmesan cheese	25 grammes	1 oz.

*it gives a larger layer of dough than the strict conversion, i.e. 300 grammes.

1 Sieve or mix the flour and salt, rub in the margarine, then blend to a soft rolling consistency with the milk.
2 Roll out and make into a large thin round about 25 cm (10 inches), put on a baking tray, or make an oblong shape; keep in a cool place while making the topping.
3 Put olive oil into a saucepan, fry the finely chopped onions, crushed cloves of garlic (optional) and the skinned tomatoes until soft. Season well, use while warm.
4 Spread over the dough, then cover with the thinly sliced cheese and the anchovy fillets and olives. Sprinkle the grated Parmesan cheese over the top and bake just above the centre of a hot oven, for about 20–25 minutes. If the filling has cooled, increase baking time to 35 minutes.
5 Serve hot or cold; or bake completely, cool and reheat.

MORE PIZZAS

BACON PIZZA: chop several rashers of bacon and fry with the tomatoes at stage 3, above. Continue as the basic recipe but omit anchovy fillets and olives. Beat 2 eggs, season well, then pour over the mixture at stage 4. This makes a softer topping and you need to bake for about 35 minutes; lower the heat after the first 15–20 minutes.

PASTRY PIZZA: omit either a baking powder dough, as above, or the bread dough as suggested; bake a large flan 'blind', see page 172 for information on this. When golden, fill with the basic or Bacon pizza mixture and continue baking until the filling is hot.

INDIVIDUAL PIZZAS: make the dough into small shapes, top with the mixture and bake for about 10 minutes, or use tiny lightly cooked tartlet cases, fill with the mixture and heat through.

Automatic Oven

If you make a pizza with either baking powder dough or the pastry pizza, you can leave it in the oven and set this for the correct cooking time. The Bacon pizza poses more problems as the oven temperature should be adjusted during baking. To overcome this, use a moderate to moderately hot oven, and bake for about 45 minutes. (The results are *not* as good, since the egg topping tends to toughen.) For a party it is better to bake the pizzas completely, cool, put on ovenproof serving dishes then reheat gently when required, or serve cold.

Speedy Meal

A very quick pizza or tiny pizzas can be made by cutting 1 large or many small rounds of fresh bread; put these on to a greased baking tray, brush with a little melted margarine or butter, then top with the mixture as the recipes opposite, and bake for 10–15 minutes for the first recipe, and 20–25 minutes for the Bacon pizza.

Home Freezing

Pizzas freeze very well indeed, particularly the first and best known recipe. Either cook and freeze; or prepare, freeze, then defrost and cook for the time given in the recipe; or cook from the frozen state for about 50 minutes in a moderate oven. The Bacon pizza with the egg topping is less successful, as the eggs tend to harden.

Pastry Making

Pastry is the basis of many recipes in this book, and good pastry is always appreciated. The most essential rules for pastry making are:
1. Use correct proportions of flour and fat.
2. Keep everything as cool as possible.
3. Handle the dough firmly but lightly.
4. Bake at the correct temperature.
5. Store away from cakes, bread or biscuits.

Metric Conversions

In order to convert proportions from ounces to grammes in this section, I have given you a choice of the amount of flour and fat to use. The reason for this is that often one makes *just enough* pastry to fit a certain dish, or to cut out the *required number* of tartlet cases, pasties, etc. If you convert strictly according to the approximate equivalent used in this book, i.e. 25 grammes instead of 1 oz., you would not produce as much made pastry, e.g. Shortcrust pastry (all versions need water to bind):

Imperial		Accepted conversion at 25 g.	Accurate conversion at 28·35 g	Practical conversion
flour	8 oz.	200 g.	226·8 g.	225 g.
salt	pinch	pinch	pinch	pinch
fat	4 oz.	100 g.	113·4 g.	115 g.
Total weight of rubbed-in mixture:				
	12 oz.	300 g.	340·2 g.	340 g.

This means that:
1. *In each case the proportions are correct*, i.e. half fat to flour (with flaky pastry use two-thirds fat to flour; with puff pastry equal quantities fat and flour).
2. If pastry made with 8 oz. flour etc., is *just the amount you need* you will have too little pastry if you use 200 grammes flour, etc. It would, therefore, be better to use 225 grammes, etc. (see table above) and you will then produce about the same amount of pastry as from 8 oz. flour etc.
3. If on the other hand you have always wasted a little pastry in the past, it may well be that 200 grammes etc., (instead of 8 oz. etc.) is *just the right amount*. In some recipes I have indicated which you should select, in others I have left the choice to you.
4. Recipes that refer to 8 oz. pastry etc. – this means pastry made with 8 oz. flour plus the fat etc., *not* the total amount. *In the same way* 200 *grammes pastry* means pastry made with 200 grammes flour, plus the fat, etc.

Cooking pastry in the automatic oven

With the exception of puff pastry, all pastry may be put into a cold oven, allowed to stand and then cooked later. Obviously, sometimes the filling of a pie or tart could make it unsatisfactory, but the pastry itself is not harmed by this method of cooking. If you feel that the pastry in a pie *could* overbrown, place a sheet of foil or greaseproof paper lightly over the top when putting into the oven *or* bake in a slightly cooler position than usual, or choose a few degrees (or half to one mark) cooler setting for oven temperature. If you think fruit juice, gravy etc., could boil out of a sweet or savoury pie, stand the pie dish on a baking tray–but make quite certain this is not so large that it will stop the heat circulating round the oven, so preventing the rest of the food cooking in a satisfactory manner.

Home freezing of pastry

Pastry freezes well. Details are given by individual recipes; you can freeze pastry–
a) *When made but not baked*–form pastry into a neat square or oblong. Wrap tightly in polythene or heavy foil. Label with type of pastry, weight and date. Defrost enough to handle.
b) *When rolled out and cut into vol-au-vents, tartlets, or shapes to fit on pie dishes, etc.*–freeze, wrap, label carefully. Bake from frozen state.
c) *With filling as in pies, sausage rolls, Cornish pasties, etc.*–prepare, freeze, then wrap. Bake from frozen state, except where pastry would be cooked and browned *before* the filling has thawed out properly, e.g. Cornish pasties, Steak and kidney pie etc.–it is then better to defrost and bake *when* defrosted.
d) *Baked pastry cases* (with no fillings, etc.)
TO SERVE COLD–allow to defrost (warm for a few minutes if pastry has become a little soft), cool, fill and serve.
TO SERVE HOT–put into moderately hot oven for a short time, then add hot filling.
e) *Baked completed pies, etc.*–do not overcook before freezing; you can then warm through and complete cooking in a gentle heat for a fairly long time; see Steak and kidney pudding etc., page 84, and fruit pies on page 185.

Note: if you find your shortcrust pastry is inclined to crack after freezing read page 173.

Using a mixer for making pastry

A whisk or beater can be used for blending fat into flour for 'rubbed-in' pastries, i.e. shortcrust or sweet shortcrust, and for creaming fat and sugar in flour or flan pastry. A whisk or beater has the advantage that metal is cooler than hands when making pastry; do not allow the mixer to over-handle pastry dough, otherwise it becomes too difficult to handle. Make sure the bowl is always cool.

Slimming

Pastry cannot be included in any genuine slimming diet, so in the case of pies, etc., it is wiser to eat just the filling, unless this is very rich, when the complete dish is unsuitable.

Terms used in pastry making

TO BAKE 'BLIND'–this expression means the pastry is baked without a filling. Flan and tartlet cases are often baked this way and filled when cooked. In order to prevent the pastry at the bottom rising, it is advisable to put greased greaseproof paper (greasy side downwards) into a flan case, and cover with crusts of bread or dried haricot beans. Bake the flan case for about 15 minutes then remove the paper, etc., and continue until the pastry is golden coloured. The beans may be stored and used over and over again. Small tartlet cases are not easy to fill like this, so prick the bottoms thoroughly with a fork before baking.
TO 'FLAKE'–means cutting into the edges of the pastry round the rim of a pie or tart with a knife. This is done a) to encourage the pastry to rise, and b) to become more crisp round the edges. It is particularly important when using flaky, rough-puff or puff pastry.
TO 'FLUTE'–means pinching the edges of the pastry with your forefinger and thumb or pressing this in at regular intervals to give a scalloped effect.
TO 'LINE'–means to fill a dish with pastry. It is wise to support the pastry with the rolling pin as you lift it from the table or board, also as you lower it into the dish or tin. Gently slip the rolling pin away and press the pastry down with your fingers.
TO 'ROLL AWAY EDGE'–one often cuts away the pastry, but when lining a flan ring or tin, you can pass the rolling pin firmly over the top, and the pressure will 'cut' the pastry evenly.

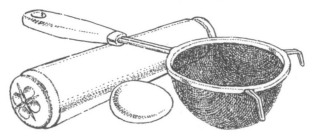

Saving time when making pastry

There are two ways of buying ready-prepared pastry, i.e., as a packet mix, or frozen pastry. Remember to check on quantities; where a recipe states 200 grammes or 8 oz. shortcrust pastry, you need to buy 300–325 grammes (12–13 oz.), i.e. total weight of flour and fat, pre-packed or frozen pastry. For 200 grammes (8 oz.) puff pastry you need to buy at least 450 grammes (1 lb) frozen pastry. Allow extra weight for frozen pastry, due to the water used in mixing. There is a quick-mix method of making shortcrust and similar pastries, see page 173.

Some familiar pastry shapes

The most usual shapes made with pastry are:

FLANS: make with fleur pastry, short or sweet shortcrust (if a sweet flan), or shortcrust, or cheese pastry (for a savoury flan)–the less rich Cheese pastry 1 is best, it is not so inclined to crack in rolling. *To fill a flan:* place the flan ring on an upturned baking tray; this makes it easy to slide off when cooked. Roll out the pastry–this should be the diameter of the ring plus 4 cm (1½ inches) all round; support this over the rolling pin and lower it into the flan ring (or tin). Slide rolling pin away, then press the pastry down firmly to the base. Either cut away any surplus pastry, or roll firmly over top of the ring so surplus pastry will fall away. Bake 'blind' as described opposite.

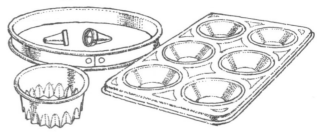

PIES: the British interpretation of a pie is that the fruit, meat, etc., is put into a deep dish and the pastry used to cover the top; this is not always true, for sometimes desserts are called 'pies' when there is a pastry base and a meringue topping.

TARTS: these can either be a pastry base and a pastry cover (sometimes called a plate tart), or a flat pastry base topped with jam, etc. Tartlets are smaller versions of tarts.

PASTIES: these are the semi-circular shapes as Cornish pasties, see picture facing page 57.

VOL-AU-VENTS: roll puff pastry or a similar light pastry to 1 cm (½ inch) in thickness, or even a little thicker. Cut into rounds or squares. Take a smaller cutter, press through pastry to a depth of about ½ cm (¼ inch). Bake in a very hot oven until well risen, lower heat to cook well, then remove centre 'lid', return case to oven to 'dry out'.

Shortcrust Pastry

Serves–as individual recipe
Cooking time as individual recipe

Ingredients	Metric	Imperial
flour*	200 *or* 225 grammes**	8 oz.
salt	pinch	pinch
fat*	100 *or* 115 grammes**	4 oz.
water	to mix	to mix

*the flour can be plain or self-raising (the former was considered correct, but today many people prefer to use self-raising). The fat can be all margarine; all lard or all cooking fat (both of these give a very short crumbly texture, and you may find the pastry easier to manage if you use slightly *under* the full quantity); all butter; or half lard and half margarine.
**see introduction, page 171.

1 Sieve the flour and salt into a mixing bowl.
2 Rub in the fat until the mixture is like fine crumbs.
3 Add the water gradually using a palette knife. You need approximately 2 tablespoons water to bind 200 or 225 grammes (8 oz.) flour and 100 or 115 grammes (4 oz.) fat. The mixture is the right consistency when it can be gathered into a ball, leaving the bowl quite clean; do not use hard pressure.
4 Put the pastry on to a lightly floured pastry board, and roll to required shape with lightly floured rolling pin.

Speedy Method of Making Pastry

The development of quick creaming margarines and cooking fat enables pastry to be made in a very short time. Choose the type of fat that softens very readily and weigh out ingredients as recipe; if using cooking fat use slightly under amount *given* in the recipe as the full amount makes a pastry dough that is difficult to handle. Put all the ingredients into the mixing bowl (allow 2 tablespoons of water) and mix firmly with a fork until blended together. Add a little more water if necessary. Use as shortcrust.

Home Freezing

The details on freezing pastry are on page 171 and on the following pages.

Sweet Shortcrust

Use the shortcrust pastry recipe above, but add 1–2 tablespoons icing or castor sugar to the flour, etc. This pastry can be mixed with water as shortcrust; with milk; or with the yolk of an egg, as fleur pastry, below.

Mixer

Use the mixer for this pastry, as shortcrust, but follow the directions carefully on page 171.

Home Freezing

This pastry freezes well; especially if mixed with milk or egg yolk.

Fleur Pastry

Serves–as individual recipe
Cooking time–as individual recipe

Ingredients	Metric	Imperial
butter	125 *or* 140 grammes*	5 oz.
castor sugar	25–50 grammes	1–2 oz.
plain flour	200 *or* 225 grammes*	8 oz.
salt	pinch	pinch
egg yolk	1	1
water	if required	if required

*see introduction, page 171.

1 Cream together the butter and sugar until soft and light in colour.
2 Sieve the flour and salt, add to the butter mixture; blend well with a flat-bladed knife.
3 Add the egg yolk, then if required stir in enough water to make a firm rolling consistency.
4 Gather the mixture together with the tips of your fingers and knead lightly but firmly.
5 Roll out; this is enough for a 22–25-cm (9–10-inch) flan.

Note: this pastry is sometimes called biscuit crust, not to be confused with the biscuit crumb crust (on the right).

TO VARY FLAN PASTRY: omit 25 grammes (1 oz.) flour and use the same amount of cornflour, to give more crisp pastry.

Another speedy way of making pastry.

Biscuit crumb pastry

This is particularly suitable for sweet flans instead of fleur pastry; cream together 100 grammes (4 oz.) butter or margarine with 50 grammes (2 oz.) sugar. Add 200 grammes (8 oz.) crushed biscuit crumbs—choose ginger nuts; digestive; semi-sweet biscuits, etc. To make a more 'pliable' dough, add 1 tablespoon golden syrup. Either form into a flan shape and allow to set for several hours, or bake for about 15 minutes in a moderate oven; cool, then use as flan pastry. You can also use the 'one mix method'.

Mixer

Fleur pastry can be mixed entirely with an electric whisk.

Home Freezing

Is inclined to be 'brittle' when thawed out. It is better to freeze the complete shape.

Cheese Pastry 1

Follow the directions for shortcrust pastry on page 173, but omit 25 grammes (1 oz.) fat. Add a generous pinch of dry mustard and a shake of pepper as well as the salt, at stage 1. Rub in the fat, then add 50 grammes (2 oz.) finely grated cheese. Either blend with water as shortcrust, or with an egg yolk and water.

Mixer

If making this in the mixer, take great care that you do not over-handle. The cheese can be 'grated' in the liquidiser goblet.

Home Freezing

This freezes well; it is inclined to crack slightly so, if intending to freeze, make a little more moist than usual.

Cheese Pastry 2

Serves—as individual recipe
Cooking time—as individual recipe

Ingredients	Metric	Imperial
plain flour	200 grammes*	8 oz.
seasoning	to taste	to taste
butter	150 grammes	6 oz.
Parmesan *or* Cheddar cheese	150 grammes	6 oz.
egg yolks	2	2
TO GLAZE:		
egg whites	1 *or* 2	1 *or* 2

*see introduction, page 171, but as this pastry is not used to cover pies, etc., one can use the 25 grammes to 1 oz.

1 Sieve the flour and seasonings—include a good pinch of mustard.
2 Rub in the butter, add finely grated cheese, bind with the egg yolks.
3 Roll out and make cheese straws, page 168, or round biscuits, etc., brush with the egg white to glaze.
4 Bake for time given in the recipe in a hot oven.
5 Although called a pastry, this is so crisp that the cooked biscuits should be stored in a separate tin.
6 These biscuits are excellent by themselves, for cocktail parties, or as a base for other foods, see page 168.

Automatic Oven

Be very careful if you ever leave this pastry in the oven for the heat to switch or turn 'on' and 'off' automatically; it is such a rich pastry that it does burn very easily.

Mixer

Over-handling of this dough makes it almost impossible to roll out and handle. If using a mixer, give the mixture the minimum of kneading.

Home Freezing

This pastry should be frozen when cut into the shapes, rather than as a piece of dough. As the cooked biscuits keep so well in tins, it is rather pointless to freeze them, unless they have been used as a base for cocktail canapés; they are extremely good for this purpose.

Suet Crust Pastry

Serves—as individual recipe
Cooking time—as individual recipe

Ingredients	Metric	Imperial
flour*	200 *or* 225 grammes***	8 oz.
salt	pinch	pinch
suet**	100 *or* 115 grammes***	4 oz.
cold water	to mix	to mix

*you can use plain flour in suet crust pastry without any raising agent, but most people prefer a suet crust to rise slightly and use self-raising, or add 2 level teaspoons of baking powder to each 200 or 225 grammes (8 oz.) plain flour.
**if you buy butcher's suet, remove the skin and chop or grate it finely. It is easier to chop if a small amount of flour is put on to the chopping board. If preferred, suet can be bought in a packet, and this has been mixed with a very small amount of flour which helps it to keep.
***see introduction page 171.

1 Sieve the flour and salt into a mixing bowl.
2 Add the suet and mix into the flour with a knife.
3 Gradually add enough water to the flour and suet mixture until it is soft enough to form into a ball but firm enough to roll out.

Note: when using suet crust for a fruit pudding (made as Steak and kidney pudding, page 83) add a little sugar to the flour, if wished.

Automatic Oven

Suet crust pastry, while often used for steamed puddings, is also a good basis for baked dishes and can be left to stand in the oven before baking.

Speedy Meal

Today, packet shredded suet saves a great deal of time in preparation.

Mixer

This is better mixed by hand, since a good suet crust should be slightly 'tacky', and would, therefore, stick to the blades of the whisk.

Home Freezing

Freezes excellently whether uncooked or cooked; there is no change in texture or flavour.

Flaky Pastry

Serves–as individual recipe
Cooking time–as individual recipe

Ingredients	Metric	Imperial
plain flour	200 *or* 225 grammes*	8 oz.
salt	pinch	pinch
fat**	150 *or* 175 grammes	6 oz.
water	to mix	to mix

*see introduction, page 171.
**the fat in this recipe can be two-thirds butter or margarine and one-third cooking fat, or all butter.

1 Sieve the flour with the salt into a mixing bowl.
2 Divide the fat into 3 portions; rub 1 portion into flour.
3 Mix to a rolling consistency with cold water and roll out to an oblong shape.
4 Cut second portion of fat into small pieces and lay on two-thirds of dough, leaving remaining third without fat.
5 Take two corners, fold over remaining third to make an 'envelope' with its flap open. Fold over top end of pastry, so closing the 'envelope'.
6 Turn pastry at right angles and seal ends.
7 'Rib' at intervals with a rolling pin to give a corrugated effect, thus equalising the pressure of air and making sure the pastry will rise evenly.
8 Repeat the process using the remaining fat and turning the pastry in the same way.
9 Roll out once more and put into a cold place for 30 minutes if it feels very soft and sticky.
10 Fold pastry as before, turn, seal edges and 'rib' again.
11 Altogether the pastry should have 3 foldings and 3 rollings.
12 Stand in a cold place for a little while before baking; this makes the pastry rise better.

Automatic Oven
Flaky pastry can stand in the cold oven, ready to be cooked at a later time. If the weather is very hot though, the results could be disappointing since, if the delay in cooking is long, the pastry could become slightly greasy in the oven.

Speedy Meal
Cut the fat into the flour at stage 2, rather than 'rubbing-in'.

Mixer
Of no use when making flaky pastry.

Home Freezing
Freezes extremely well; in fact one of the best pastries to freeze either cooked or uncooked–the same comments apply as under puff pastry, below.

Puff Pastry

Serves–as individual recipe
Cooking time–as individual recipe

Ingredients	Metric	Imperial
plain flour	200 *or* 225 grammes*	8 oz.
salt	good pinch	good pinch
cold water	to mix	to mix
lemon juice	few drops	few drops
fat (preferably butter)	200 *or* 225 grammes*	8 oz.

*see introduction, page 171.

1 Sieve flour and salt; mix to a rolling consistency with water and lemon juice.
2 Roll to an oblong shape and place neat block of fat in the centre of the pastry.
3 Fold over bottom section of pastry, and then the top, so that the fat is covered.
4 Turn dough at right angles, seal edges and 'rib' (as fiaky pastry, above).
5 Roll out and fold dough into an 'envelope' shape. Turn, seal edges and 'rib' again.
6 Repeat 5 times, so making 7 rollings and 7 foldings in all.
7 Put pastry in a cold place once or twice between rollings to prevent it becoming sticky and soft.
8 Always leave in a cold place before rolling for the last time, and before baking. Puff pastry should rise to 4–5 times its original thickness; this is due to incorporation of air in the pastry in rolling plus the high heat used in baking.

Automatic Oven
Do not leave puff pastry in a cold oven and wait for the heat to turn or switch on. Puff pastry needs *immediate* heat for a good result.

Speedy Meal
The frozen puff pastry one can buy is excellent; remember where a recipe states 200 grammes (8 oz.) puff pastry it does not mean completed pastry, but the amount of flour used, so when buying puff pastry you must allow at least double this quantity, see page 171.

Mixer
Puff pastry should be made by hand.

Home Freezing
This is also a completely satisfactory pastry to freeze, either cooked or uncooked. Complete *all* the rollings of this, flaky, or rough puff pastry before freezing. To use, thaw just enough to handle. The pastry when made into vol-au-vent cases, etc., may be cooked from the frozen state; there is no need to let it thaw.

Rough Puff Pastry

Proportions for this as flaky pastry on page 175.
1 Sieve the flour and salt into a basin.
2 With two knives, cut fat into flour until it is fairly fine.
3 Blend with cold water to an elastic paste, and roll out to a neat oblong on a floured board.
4 Fold and roll as puff pastry, page 175, allowing only five rollings and foldings.

Note: this pastry can be used in place of puff pastry, and is much quicker to make.

Automatic Oven
Not very successful—see comments about puff pastry on page 175.

Speedy Meal
If you are short of time and a recipe states flaky or puff pastry, make rough puff pastry, opposite.

Home Freezing
All comments used about freezing apply to rough puff pastry.

Choux Pastry

Serves 6–8
Cooking time—as individual recipe

Ingredients	Metric	Imperial
water	142 ml	¼ pint
butter	25 grammes	1 oz.
plain *or* self-raising flour	75 or better still 85 grammes	3 oz.
eggs	2	2
egg yolk	1	1

1 Put water and butter into a saucepan and heat until the butter has melted and liquid is *just* boiling.
2 Remove the pan from the heat, and beat in the flour.
3 Return to the heat and cook very gently, stirring all the time, until you have a smooth dry ball which leaves the sides of the pan clean.
4 Away from the heat, beat in first one egg and then the second, and lastly as much of the egg yolk as needed to produce a smooth slightly sticky texture that can be piped if wished. For baking times, etc., see recipe page 192.

Automatic Oven
Choux pastry needs immediate heat to make it 'puff', so never leave in a cold oven.

Mixer
If you have a portable hand mixer that can be used near the cooker, then stage 4 can be done with an electric mixer, rather than by hand.

Home Freezing
Choux pastry freezes very well, but only when baked. The uncooked choux pastry does not rise as well when defrosted and baked, or when formed into shapes, frozen and baked from the frozen state. Choux buns or éclairs may be filled before freezing, and iced too if wished; or the pastry shapes may be frozen, thawed out and filled just before serving.

Rolled Oat Pastry

Serves—as individual recipe
Cooking time—as individual recipe

Ingredients	Metric	Imperial
porridge (rolled) oats	150 grammes	6 oz.
soft brown sugar	50 grammes	2 oz.
butter	75 grammes	3 oz.
honey	2 tablespoons	2 tablespoons

1 Mix the oats and sugar together in a mixing bowl.
2 Heat the butter and honey gently until butter has melted; do not boil or allow to simmer for too long, otherwise it will burn. Mix with the oats and sugar; knead well. See picture facing page 192.

Automatic Oven
This 'pastry' is shown in the picture facing page 192. It needs just 25 minutes baking in a very moderate temperature (the high sugar and honey content would make it burn if left longer). It is quite suitable to leave in the cold oven, ready to be filled later; or it can be baked as a flat round or square base to cut into fingers or to top with fruit.

Home Freezing
Freezes extremely well, either uncooked or cooked and cooled; thaw out slowly.

Hot Water Crust Pastry

This pastry is often called 'raised pastry' since pies made from this are moulded (or raised) by hand, see page 179. It is made quite differently from other pastries in that the water and fat are heated together, and the pastry kept warm during handling.

For a good sized raised pie, such as that shown facing page 177, with the recipe page 178 you need: 300 or, to give a more accurate conversion, 340 grammes plain flour (read page 171) sieved with a pinch salt. Heat 125 or 140 grammes fat with 142 ml (¼ pint) water just to the boil, pour over the flour, knead well; while you roll out part of the dough, keep rest warm.

Automatic Oven
The completed pie may be put into a cold oven and cooked as the particular recipe.

Home Freezing
The completed pie is better frozen when cooked. Store for only about 6 weeks, defrost and use as soon as possible after thawing.

36. Swiss roll, see page 214

Savoury Pastry Dishes

Savoury tarts and pies are ideal for so many occasions; you will find here simple pies, tarts and patties that are very suitable for packed meals or family occasions, and unusual pastry dishes for parties.

Types of pastry

CHEESE PASTRY: use the rich cheese pastry, page 174, for cheese straws, etc., but you may find this difficult to handle in making flan cases for it is inclined to break. Use the less rich mixture, for this purpose.

FLAKY PASTRY: an excellent topping for pies, or use for some tarts, too. It is less usual for flans as it rises too much. It can be used for vol-au-vent cases, although puff or rough puff are better.

PUFF PASTRY: the richest of all pastries and the most time-consuming to prepare. You can, however, always substitute frozen puff pastry, and many bakers sell their own prepared puff pastry. Use puff pastry for pies; the type of patties where you wish the pastry to rise; in vol-au-vent cases.

RAISED PASTRY: often called *hot water* crust pastry. This is *not* an adaptable pastry, it is used only for raised pies such as veal and ham pie, etc.

ROUGH PUFF PASTRY: this is lighter in texture than flaky pastry but not quite as rich as puff pastry: it is quicker and easier to prepare. Use as puff pastry.

SCONE PASTRY: although scone dough cannot be called a true pastry, some of the most interesting dishes generally known as 'cobblers' are made with it. A scone dough is rolled out, cut into rounds or triangles and placed on meat, etc., in place of a true pastry, see page 225.

SHORTCRUST PASTRY: the most usual and practical pastry. This is suitable for most pies and tarts but *not* for vol-au-vents where the pastry needs to puff.

SUET CRUST PASTRY: this is generally used for steamed puddings, rather than pies, but it can be used in a baked savoury (or sweet) roll, as on page 180.

Decorating savoury pies

It is traditional that a savoury pie generally has some kind of decoration.

TO MAKE LEAVES: cut strips of the pastry, then cut diagonally *across* the strip to give a leaf shape. Mark lightly to look like 'veins' and press each leaf on the pie.

TO MAKE A 'ROSE': cut a long strip of pastry, turn it round at one end to make the centre of the 'rose'. Twist the band of pastry round this centre, depressing it at intervals to form the 'petals'. Press on top of the pie. One generally makes a slit in a savoury pie (either for the steam to escape or to fill with jelly), so place the rose in such a manner that it does not cover this.

TO MAKE A 'TASSEL': cut a long strip of pastry, lay it flat on the pastry board, make cuts at close intervals to come about half way down the depth of the band. Turn the band of pastry to form a round and, as you do so, gently pull the cut parts slightly apart to look like a proper 'tassel'. Press to stand upright over the 'slit' in the pie, then put the tip of a knife into the slit to open it a little more.

Filling a pie with jelly

Many cold pies, such as a Veal and ham pie on page 179, are filled with jelly. Make the jelly as the recipe, allow to cool and just stiffen very slightly. When the cooked pie is cold use a small funnel (or a cone of double greaseproof paper or foil; cut off the bottom end so the jelly runs through) and put into the slit in the top of the pie; spoon the jelly through this. By following this procedure the jelly does not soak into the pastry, but gives a clear layer on top of the filling.

To glaze savoury pies

Brush the uncooked pastry with beaten egg (diluted with water, if wished) or with egg yolk and water or milk, or with milk alone. This gives a shine to the pastry when cooked. Be sparing with water, otherwise you will make the pastry too wet.

37. Pigeon and mushroom pie, see page 178

Pigeon and Mushroom Pie

Serves 7–8
Cooking time 2½ hours
Oven temperature 350–375° F. (180–190° C.), Gas Mark 4–5

Ingredients	Metric	Imperial
FOR THE FILLING:		
pigeons	3	3
rump steak	½ kilo	1 lb.
mushrooms	200 grammes	8 oz.
seasoning	to taste	to taste
onion	1	1
bouquet garni	spray	spray
FOR THE PASTRY:		
hot water or short crust made with 300 *or* 340 grammes (12 oz.) flour, etc., see pages 177, 174		
TO GLAZE:		
egg	1	1

1 Cut meat from pigeon bones, dice meat neatly, put bones into a saucepan with water to cover.
2 Dice the steak and mix with the pigeon, the sliced mushrooms and seasoning.
3 Meanwhile, simmer pigeon bones with onion, *bouquet garni* and plenty of seasoning for about 30 minutes.
4 Make the pastry and use about two-thirds to line the bottom and sides of a 1-litre (2-pint) dish, as shown in the picture facing page 145.
5 Put in pigeon mixture, moisten with 3 tablespoons of the stock; you can also flavour with chopped herbs.
6 Cover with rest of the pastry, seal edges, make a slit on the top to allow steam to escape and keep the pastry crisp. Glaze with egg and water.
7 Bake for approximately 2 hours in the centre of a very moderate to moderate oven; if you find the pastry becoming over-brown, then lower the heat after the first hour. Serve hot and use the rest of the pigeon stock to make a gravy; or serve cold and stiffen about 12 tablespoons of the liquid with 2 teaspoons gelatine, and fill the pie as described on page 177. See illustration facing page 177.

Automatic Oven

This pie may be left and baked in the oven; have casseroles of whole onions (cooked in well seasoned stock) and carrots, (flavoured with chopped fresh herbs and cooked in well seasoned water) and Jacket potatoes. If you can, put a Caramel custard, made with 6 eggs etc., see page 187, in a deep dish (to delay cooking) in coolest part of the oven; this would complete the menu. You cannot reduce the heat, as suggested in stage 7, so use a very moderate heat for 2¼ hours.

Speedy Meal

Use a pressure cooker, cook diced meat, and pigeon meat in water to cover, with *bouquet garni*, seasoning and onion, for approximately 12 minutes at 15 lb. pressure; cool rapidly under cold water, drain. Put in pie dish, add mushrooms and stock as stage 5, cover with pastry. Bake for about 40 minutes in the middle of a moderately hot oven.

Home Freezing

This pie freezes very well. Cook as directed and heat through gently as it is then possible to heat from the frozen state. If preferred, thaw out first—you can then heat through more quickly, or the cooked pie can be defrosted and eaten cold. If you freeze the uncooked pie, I would suggest using shortcrust, rather than hot water crust pastry.

Variations on Pigeon and Mushroom Pie

This recipe is an excellent basis for many savoury pies:

CHICKEN PIE: use a small roasting chicken instead of pigeons. Simmer the bones of the chicken and the giblets to give a good stock, and dice the chicken meat. Mix either with diced steak, as recipe, or a better contrast to the delicate flavour of chicken is to use lean bacon. Use about 300 grammes (12 oz.) bacon–cut thickly–dice this and mix with the chicken meat, seasoning and mushrooms. I prefer this made with shortcrust pastry instead of hot water crust.

GAME PIE: use 2 good sized grouse or 1 large pheasant instead of the pigeons. Use steak mixed with bacon (to give a more moist texture) rather than all steak as in the Pigeon pie. Mushrooms are a very good flavouring, or substitute thinly sliced uncooked onions, or a mixture of onions and mushrooms. Use either shortcrust or hot water crust, or even flaky pastry (in which case bake for about 30 minutes in a hot oven, then reduce the heat). If using flaky pastry the pie is better hot; with hot water crust pastry, serve cold.

Automatic Oven

The variations on Pigeon pie are equally good for cooking in the automatic oven. A very good dish to serve with chicken or with game is Braised celery, see page 113, and another casserole could be filled with chestnuts cooked in a brown stock. Obviously you cannot deal with the variations in temperature, so see advice above, under Pigeon pie.

Speedy Meal

See the hints for Pigeon pie above.

Slimming Tips

The filling of any of these pies is not unduly fattening, since there is no thickened stock or extra fat used in preparation; avoid the pastry if possible, and simply eat the pigeon, chicken or game mixture with a green vegetable and/or a crisp green salad.

Home Freezing

See comments under Pigeon pie above.

Veal and Ham Pie

Serves 5–6
Cooking time 2¼–2½ hours
Oven temperature 350–375° F. (180–190° C.), Gas Mark 4–5

Ingredients	Metric	Imperial
fillet of veal	¾ kilo	1¼–1½ lb.
		(poor
cooked ham	150–200 grammes	6–8 oz.
grated lemon rind	½ teaspoon	½ teaspoon
seasoning	to taste	to taste
eggs	2–4	2–4
white stock	7–8 tablespoons	7–8 tablespoons

FOR THE PASTRY:
hot water crust, page 176, with 300–340 grammes (12 oz.) flour, etc.
TO GLAZE:

egg	1	1

FOR THE JELLY:

powder gelatine	1 teaspoon	1 teaspoon

1 Dice the veal and ham and mix with the lemon rind and a generous amount of seasoning.
2 Hard boil the eggs, crack the shells, cool in cold water and shell. Meanwhile strain the stock (made from veal bones if possible, or use water and half a stock cube).
3 Make the pastry as directions on page 176.
4 If you intend to mould or 'raise' the pie, use about two-thirds of the pastry to form the base and sides–start with a ball of dough and mould it round a 15–18-cm (6–7-inch) cake tin; remove the tin when neatly shaped. To support the pie, secure a band of greaseproof paper round the shape.
5 Keep the remaining pastry warm–if you would rather line a tin and bake in this, see opposite.
6 Moisten the meat with half the stock, put half the meat mixture into the pastry case then cover with the halved or whole hard-boiled eggs, finally add the rest of the meat.
7 Roll out remaining pastry and cover the top of the pie. Seal the edges, but do not press the 'lid' of the pastry down too firmly, as you need space for the jelly after cooking.
8 Make a slit on top of the pastry and use any pieces of pastry left over to make 'leaves', etc. Glaze with beaten egg and water.
9 Bake in the centre of a very moderate to moderate oven for about 2–2¼ hours, lowering the heat if necessary after the first hour.
10 Allow the pie to cool, then dissolve the gelatine in the remaining stock and fill the pie as described on page 177. Allow the jelly to set, but eat the pie when freshly made.

Automatic Oven
Since this pie is invariably served cold, one would rarely cook this entirely in the automatic oven; but it could be put in the oven at the right temperature and the timer set to 'switch off' or 'turn off' at the correct time. The pie would then cool down in the oven, and the jelly filling could be added when convenient.

Speedy Meal
The meat should cook fairly slowly in this to give a good moist texture; it is spoiled if the meat is pre-cooked. To line a tin, instead of raising pie: roll out pastry, cut two rounds for base and lid and a band for sides of the tin. Put in base then side band of pastry; seal together firmly, then continue as stage 6 to end of recipe.

Home Freezing
A raised pie takes time to make and it is, therefore, a pity that Veal and ham pie is not the best dish to freeze. You can freeze it, if wished, when quite cold and filled with jelly etc., but I think you will be very disappointed with the lack of flavour and moist texture in the veal when the pie has thawed out–see the variations, which freeze better.

Variations on Veal and Ham Pie

The Veal and ham pie above is the basis for a number of similar raised pies. The shape of the pies can be varied; you may like to make them as the Pigeon pie, on page 178, i.e. in a shallow wide dish–this means a slightly shorter cooking time, and you will need to use about double the amount of stock for the jelly. If you have used veal bones, the 1 teaspoon gelatine will be enough.

CHICKEN AND HAM PIE: use diced raw chicken (breast and dark meat) instead of veal, include the hard-boiled eggs.

PORK PIE: use nearly 1 kilo (2 lb.) lean fillet pork instead of veal and ham; omit the eggs, flavour stock with sage instead of a *bouquet garni*. The traditional Melton Mowbray (pork) pie recipe uses a small amount of salt and the meat is flavoured with chopped anchovy fillets.

Automatic Oven
See comments above. If the Chicken and ham pie is made with shortcrust pastry rather than hot water crust, it does make a very good hot pie–so could be part of an automatic menu.

Home Freezing
Both the Chicken and ham and the Pork pies freeze well, but the latter must be used within 4–5 weeks, for pork keeps less well than other meats in the freezer. Defrost slowly at room temperature; you will find that all these raised pies take several hours to defrost. If taking them on a picnic, therefore, it is wise to pack them while still slightly frozen to thaw out on the journey.

Cornish Bacon Pasties

Serves 6
Cooking time 1 hour
Oven temperature 425° F. (220° C.), Gas Mark 6–7, then 325–350° F. (170–180° C.), Gas Mark 3–4

Ingredients	Metric	Imperial
shortcrust pastry page 173	300 grammes flour etc. or use 325 grammes etc. see page 171	12 oz. flour etc. see page 173
streaky bacon rashers	150 grammes	6 oz.
rump steak	200 grammes	8 oz.
lamb's kidney	100 grammes	4 oz.
onion	1 large	1 large
seasoning	to taste	to taste
Worcestershire sauce	½ teaspoon	½ teaspoon
TO GLAZE:		
beaten egg	1	1
TO GARNISH:		
watercress	several sprigs	several sprigs
tomatoes	as required	as required

1 Roll out pastry and cut into six 18-cm (7-inch) rounds.
2 Mix the chopped bacon, minced or chopped steak, chopped kidney, finely chopped onion, seasoning and Worcestershire sauce.
3 Divide into six portions and place across the middle of each piece of pastry; damp edges of pastry with water, bring together, seal tightly and flute edges.
4 Glaze with the beaten egg and place on a baking tray.
5 Bake in centre of hot oven for 15 minutes, then reduce to very moderate for a further 40–45 minutes till golden brown and cooked through.
6 Serve hot or cold, garnished with watercress and tomatoes as picture facing page 57.

Note: the traditional *Cornish pasties* use diced raw potatoes in place of bacon.

Automatic Oven

The only problem about leaving these pasties in an automatic oven is the two temperatures at stage 5. To overcome this (although the pastry will not be quite as light and crisp), use a moderate heat throughout and allow just over the hour cooking time.

Speedy Meal

Buy frozen or packet shortcrust pastry.

Mixer

The mixer can be used to prepare the pastry, see page 172.

Home Freezing

Both the Bacon pasties and the traditional Cornish pasties freeze well, but the amount of potato in the latter should be reduced for freezing (it becomes somewhat soft and loses its flavour too). Use within 6 weeks. The pasties may be defrosted slowly and eaten cold, or can be reheated preferably from the defrosted state.

Baked Savoury Roll

Serves 5–6
Cooking time 1½ hours
Oven temperature 375–400° F. (190–200° C.), Gas Mark 5–6

Ingredients	Metric	Imperial
suet crust pastry page 174, made with 200 *or* 225 grammes (8 oz.) flour, etc.		
FOR THE FILLING:		
onions	2	2
fat	25 grammes	1 oz.
sausagemeat	½ kilo	1¼ lb.
chopped parsley	1 tablespoon	1 tablespoon
chopped sage	1 teaspoon	1 teaspoon
egg	1	1
TO GLAZE:		
milk	2–3 tablespoons	2–3 tablespoons

1 Make the suet crust to give a soft rolling consistency.
2 Chop onions finely, toss in the hot fat for a few minutes, blend with sausagemeat, herbs and egg.
3 Roll out the pastry to a neat oblong, press out sausagemeat to a similar size, lay on top of the pastry and roll like a Swiss Roll.
4 Lift on to a baking tray, brush with milk, bake in the centre of a moderate to moderately hot oven for 1½ hours. Reduce the heat slightly after 1 hour if necessary.

Automatic Oven

This roll can be left in the cold oven for a short time only, for suet crust used like this is better if baked fairly soon after making. Have large roast potatoes in the hottest part of the oven, see page 116 and a casserole of medium sized carrots, or carrots and sliced turnips, in the coolest part. Very large apples could also be baked, as page 199, in the coolest part of the oven.

Home Freezing

This roll freezes very well, although sausagemeat has a limited storage period in the freezer. You *could* use minced raw meat or chicken, if preferred, in place of the sausagemeat. To reheat the cooked roll, allow to defrost; otherwise the outside of this roll is over-baked before the filling is heated. If preferred, make the roll and freeze uncooked—you can then cook it from the frozen state, but allow a slightly longer cooking time, and lower the temperature after 1 hour.

Cheese and Onion Flan

Serves 4–8*
Cooking time 1–1¼ hours
Oven temperature 425° F. (220° C.), Gas Mark 6–7, then 350° F. (180°C.)
Gas Mark 3–4

Ingredients	Metric	Imperial
onions	4 medium	4 medium
seasoning	to taste	to taste
shortcrust pastry see page 173	150–175 grammes	6 oz.
eggs	3	3
milk *or* half milk and half thin cream	284 ml	½ pint
Cheddar *or* Gruyère cheese	75–100 grammes	3–4 oz.

*you can serve the smaller portions as an hors d'oeuvre

1 Peel and slice the onions thinly, put into a saucepan, season, and add just enough water to cover.
2 Cover the pan and simmer steadily until just tender; do not over-cook.
3 Meanwhile, roll out the pastry and line a 20-cm (8-inch) *deep* flan ring on an upturned baking tray, or a sandwich tin (one with a loose base enables you to lift the cooked flan out easily).
4 Bake the flan case 'blind', see page 172, in the centre of a hot oven for 15 minutes until the pastry is just set and pale golden–do not over-cook.
5 Beat the eggs, warm the milk, add to the eggs with the well drained onions, seasoning, grated cheese; spoon into flan.
6 Lower the oven heat to very moderate and bake for approximately 45 minutes to 1 hour; serve hot or cold.

Prawn Quiche

1 An excellent flan is made with prawns instead of onions. Buy either 50–75 grammes (2–3 oz.) shelled frozen prawns or generous ½ litre–568 ml (1 pint) prawns (or shrimps) in their shells.
2 Allow the prawns to thaw out before using; dry well on kitchen paper, or shell ordinary prawns. You will find the shells are removed easily if the prawns are dropped into very hot water and left for one minute.
3 Prepare the flan, as in recipe at the top of this page, as stage 3, then continue to the end of stage 4.
4 Continue as stage 5 above, but add the prawns in place of the onions, then complete the recipe.
5 Garnish with slices of lemon.

Quiche Lorraine

1 This classic Cheese and bacon flan is made like the Cheese and onion flan above, but omit onions and use 2–3 rashers of lean bacon instead.
2 Chop the bacon and fry lightly.
3 Prepare pastry as stage 3 above, and continue to the end of stage 4.
4 Continue as stage 5, but add well drained bacon in place of onions, then complete the recipe.
5 Serve hot or cold.

Note: if anyone does not like cheese, then it may be omitted from any one of the flans on this page. Naturally, the flan will be lacking in flavour, so compensate by adding extra seasoning, a little grated lemon rind, and freshly chopped herbs.

Automatic Oven

If the flan case is set, but not over-cooked, you can place this in the oven, switch or turn on immediately. If the filled flan stands without cooking, the moist egg mixture would make the pastry over-soft.

Speedy Meal

Use 225 grammes (9 oz.) frozen short-crust pastry, and dehydrated onions instead of fresh ones. Follow the directions to soften and cook these.

Mixer

Use the mixer to prepare the pastry; read the comments on page 172, regarding over-handling of pastry dough if made in a mixer. The liquidiser is excellent for grating cheese, or you could put the eggs, the milk, or milk and cream, plus the cheese into the liquidiser and emulsify these together, see remarks about egg custards on page 184.

Slimming Tips

The filling is not particularly high in calories, especially if all milk is used. You could, therefore, eat the filling and leave the pastry; or simply bake the filling as a savoury custard–in which case, follow the directions for baking time and temperature in the recipe above, stage 6. The custard looks most attractive baked in an ovenproof serving dish.

Home Freezing

Every flan of this type freezes excellently. In order that the wrapping does not stick to the filling, freeze *before* removing from the flan ring or tin, then wrap. Used cake boxes are ideal for storing flans–put each into a polythene bag when frozen, then store several flans in a cake box. In this way they are easy to remove. Results are better if half milk and half cream are used. Can be stored for 4–6 months. Thaw out, if possible, before reheating gently.

Sweet Pastry Dishes

Good pastry and puddings made with pastry will always be popular; here are the pastries to use:

CHOUX PASTRY: use for éclairs, choux (cream) puffs, etc.

FLAKY PASTRY: an excellent topping for sweet pies or use for some tarts too. It is less usual for fruit flans as it rises too much. It can be used for sweet vol-au-vent cases, although puff or rough puff are better.

FLEUR PASTRY (often called flan or biscuit crust): the correct pastry for fruit flans.

PUFF PASTRY: the richest of all pastries and the most time-consuming to prepare. You can, however, always substitute frozen puff pastry and many bakers sell their own prepared puff pastry. Use puff pastry for sweet pies, sweet vol-au-vent cases, etc.

ROUGH PUFF PASTRY: this is lighter in texture than flaky pastry but not quite as rich as puff pastry; it is quicker and easier to prepare. Use as puff pastry.

SCONE PASTRY: although scone dough cannot be called a true pastry, some of the most interesting dishes, generally known as sweet 'cobblers' are made with it—see Kent cherry cobbler, page 206.

SHORTCRUST PASTRY: the most usual and practical pastry. This is suitable for most sweet pies and tarts but *not* for sweet vol-au-vent cases, where the pastry needs to puff.

SUET CRUST PASTRY: this is generally used for steamed fruit puddings, jam roly-poly, etc.

SWEET SHORTCRUST PASTRY: use as shortcrust pastry.

GENOESE PASTRY: is so like a sponge that it is rarely included with pastry. It is also used for the same purpose as a sponge, i.e. for gâteaux, tiny petits fours, etc.

GLAZING SWEET PASTRY: it is traditional that sweet pies are not glazed with egg, but there is no reason why this should not be done; or glaze with egg white, or dust with sugar when cooked.

Decorating sweet pies, etc.

The edges of sweet pies and flans are usually 'flaked', see page 172 for the definition of this. Often the glaze on top of a flan, see below, gives the colour and decoration needed to the dessert. Choux buns are either decorated with a sauce, as the picture between pages 152/153, or dusted with icing sugar, or covered with icing.

Sweet pies can be dusted with castor or icing sugar before serving, see the Blackberry and apple pie facing page 121, and a similar decoration is added to Fruit cobblers, recipe page 206.

Filling fruit flans

A fruit flan looks most professional when filled with fruit and given a thickened glaze (made from the syrup) or the fruit is covered with jelly. A Peach or other fruit flan made from the rolled oat pastry, on page 176 and filled with fruit covered with a thickened glaze, is also a little 'different'.

GLAZE MADE FROM FRUIT SYRUP
The quantities given are enough to fill an 18–20-cm (7–8-inch) flan.
Drain off 142 ml (¼ pint) syrup from canned, defrosted frozen or cooked fruit. If using fresh fruit such as strawberries, etc., you can make the syrup with sugar, water and a little redcurrant jelly to give a good colour. Blend 1 level teaspoon arrowroot (cornflour could be used as a substitute) with the syrup. Put into a saucepan and cook very gently, stirring well, until thickened. Add a few drops of colour, if wished, or a squeeze of lemon juice for flavour. Put the cold, well drained fruit into the baked cold flan case. Brush or spread the cool glaze over the top.

GLAZE MADE FROM FRUIT JELLY
One usually has a thicker layer of jelly, so use half a packet of a suitable fruit flavoured jelly and dissolve this in 284 ml (½ pint) liquid (water, or water and fruit syrup if available). Make the jelly in the usual way; cool and when just beginning to thicken fill the flan, as instructed above, then spoon the jelly over the top. Allow to set.

Lemon Raisin Pie

Serves 4
Cooking time 45 minutes or 1 hour 50 minutes, see method
Oven temperature 325–350° F. (170–180° C.), Gas Mark 3–4 or 225–250° F. (110–130° C.), Gas Mark 0–½

Ingredients	Metric	Imperial
short *or* sweet	150 *or* 170	6 oz.
shortcrust pastry	grammes	
FOR THE FILLING:		
lemons	2	2
water	as required	as required
cornflour	25 grammes	1 oz.
sugar	50–60 grammes	2 oz.
butter	25 grammes	1 oz.
seedless raisins	75–100 grammes	3–4 oz.
egg yolks	2	2
FOR THE MERINGUE:		
egg whites	2	2
sugar	50–100 grammes	2–4 oz.
TO DECORATE:		
lemon	1	1

1 Roll out the pastry, line a deep 18–20-cm (7–8-inch) flan ring, and bake 'blind' until crisp and golden brown.
2 Grate the rind from the 2 lemons, squeeze out the juice, add enough water to give a generous ¼ litre, 568 ml (½ pint).
3 Blend the cornflour with this.
4 Put into a saucepan with the lemon rind and sugar, and cook steadily until thickened.
5 Beat in the butter and raisins, cook for another 1–2 minutes.
6 Remove from the heat, add the beaten egg yolks and put into the pastry case.
7 Whisk the egg whites until very stiff. Gradually beat in half the sugar, fold in the rest.
8 Pile in a ring round the edge of the lemon raisin filling, leaving a space in the centre.
9 If wishing to serve hot; brown for approximately 20 minutes in the centre of a very moderate oven.
10 If wishing to serve cold; use the maximum amount of sugar and set for a least 1¼ hours in a slow oven.
11 Top with the finely grated lemon rind just before serving, or scatter over the meringue before browning.

TO VARY:
TANGERINE AND SULTANA PIE
Use the grated rind and juice of 3 tangerines and 1 tablespoon lemon juice in place of lemons; sultanas instead of raisins.
LEMON MERINGUE PIE
Use the first recipe, and omit the raisins at stage 5.

Speedy Meal
Use packet lemon meringue pie mixture, but add the raisins to this, when mixed as direction on the packet.

Mixer
See hints on making meringues in a mixer, page 193, and for making pastry with the help of a mixer.

Home Freezing
Freezes well for a limited period – see comments on freezing meringues, page 193 if intending to freeze this. Freeze well before wrapping. Keep for 3–4 weeks only, for best result.

Fruit Tart

To make a fruit tart for 4–6 servings you will need a good ½ kilo (1¼ lb.) prepared fruit and pastry made with 225–250 grammes (see metric conversion on page 171) or 9 oz. flour, etc. The most usual pastries are short or sweet shortcrust, although fleur pastry could be used. Roll out pastry, line an 18-cm (7-inch) pie plate. Sprinkle a dusting of semolina, cornflour or flour over this, and a little sugar, so the fruit juices do not make the pastry 'damp'. Add fruit and sugar to taste, and the covering of pastry; cut away edges, flute to decorate. Bake as Fruit pie on next page, but lower heat a little earlier and bake a little longer, as you have two layers of pastry to cook, and you do not want the top layer to be over-cooked before the bottom layer is firm.

To make sweet bread 'cases': cut wafer-thin slices of fresh bread, remove the crusts. Grease deep patty tins very well, press the slices of bread into the tins, brush with melted butter or margarine and sprinkle very lightly with sugar. Bake for about 10 minutes in a hot oven until crisp; serve hot or cold filled with hot or cold fruit.

Automatic Oven
See comments about baking a Fruit pie.

Speedy Meal
Either use ready-made pastry, or make small tarts of bread slices as described opposite, and fill them with cooked fruit.

Home Freezing
The type of Fruit tart given opposite can be frozen cooked or uncooked; either gives a reasonably good result. If cooked, reheat through fairly slowly while still frozen as the bottom pastry does sometimes become soft with freezing, and long cooking will 'dry this out'.

Fruit Pies

One of the nicest things about a fruit pie is that it is never monotonous as the pastry and fruit may be varied. The picture facing page 121 shows a typical late summer pie of blackberries and apples.

To make a pie for 4–6 people you need pastry made with 150 grammes (or a little more, see the metric conversion on page 171) i.e. 6 oz. of flour etc. It can be short, sweet shortcrust or flaky or puff pastry according to personal taste. You need a good kilo (1¼ lb.) prepared fruit. Put the fruit in the pie dish with *very little* water with soft fruit, more with hard fruit, and add sugar to taste. Roll out the pastry, cut a band to go round the rim of the dish and moisten this lightly with water. Cover the pie dish with the rest of the pastry, seal the edges firmly, cut away any surplus pastry, 'flute' the edges and 'flake' the pastry if flaky or puff. Cook for 20–25 minutes in the middle of a hot to very hot oven (use the higher temperature for the richer pastry); lower the heat to very moderate for a further 15–20 minutes to make sure the pie is cooked. Dust with sieved icing sugar, or castor sugar, before serving.

Automatic Oven

A fruit pie can form part of an automatic menu; you can adjust cooking time and temperature by the position in the oven, although pastry *cannot* be baked too slowly. If you think that the pastry could become over-cooked, then lay a sheet of foil or greaseproof paper lightly over the pie.
It is not possible to reduce heat if the oven is on automatic setting, so use a moderate to moderately hot temperature, and allow 1 hour or 1¼ hours cooking.

Home Freezing

A fruit pie freezes well, whether cooked or uncooked, but a better idea is to freeze the fruit in the pie dish (line this with strong foil) then you can remove the pie dish and freeze the pastry case to fit the pie dish separately. See page 171.

Custard Tart

In this recipe you are combining two recipes which really do not 'belong' together; for the pastry needs a hot oven and the egg custard a slow oven; the best answer is as the following recipe:

Serves 4–6
Cooking time 45 minutes minimum, see stage 3
Oven temperature 425–450° F. (220–230° C.), Gas Mark 7, then 350–375° F. (180–190° C.), Gas Mark 4–5

Ingredients	Metric	Imperial
short *or* sweet crust pastry	125–150 grammes flour etc.	5–6 oz. flour etc.
eggs *or* egg yolks	2	2
sugar	25 grammes	1 oz.
milk	284 ml	½ pint
TO DECORATE: grated nutmeg		

1 Roll out the pastry and line an 18-cm (7-inch) flan ring or tin. Neaten the edges and bake 'blind' until crisp, but only pale golden, (about 12 minutes) in a hot oven.
2 Meanwhile, beat the eggs or egg yolks with the sugar, add the very hot milk, strain the hot custard into the hot pastry; grate nutmeg over the top before baking.
3 Lower the heat to very moderate to moderate, and continue cooking until the custard is set; this will be about 35 minutes, but could be a little longer.

Automatic Oven

In an automatic oven, you cannot have the two temperatures. Also it is not wise to leave the very 'wet' filling in the pastry for it could make this so 'soggy' that it would never set. You can, however, put a custard tart into the pre-heated oven and set the timer to 'switch' or 'turn' off.

Speedy Meal

Make and bake a flan case 'blind' until crisp. Meanwhile, make an egg custard in a saucepan, and when thickened, spoon into the flan; or make custard with custard powder, when thickened add the eggs and cook for 2–3 minutes only.

Mixer

Do not use the mixer for blending the custard, it incorporates too much air.

Home Freezing

This does not freeze well at all.

Crunchy Peach Flan

Line a 20-cm (8-inch) lightly greased flan ring with the rolled oat pastry, recipe page 176, as directed on page 182, and bake 'blind' for 25 minutes in a very moderate to moderate oven; allow to cool. *Fleur pastry* would take 20–25 minutes in a moderate to moderately hot oven. Fill with well drained peach slices, and then make a glaze, as page 182, with the syrup from the can and arrowroot,–142 ml (¼ pint) syrup and 1 teaspoon arrowroot gives a *thin* coating–increase this if wished. Decorate with glacé cherries.

Automatic Oven

As pointed out on page 176, this pastry can be left in an automatic oven, since it does not hurt with standing.

Speedy Meal

Omit the glaze as given, just melt a little apricot jam with the syrup and use this as a glaze.

Home Freezing

This flan freezes well.

38. Apricot and walnut bread, and Mixed fruit bread, see page 226

39. Plaited loaf and rolls, Crown loaf, see pages 227/8
40. Spice cake, see page 218
41. Danish cornets, see page 222

Cold and Iced Desserts

The recipes in this chapter are varied, for they include simple jellies and moulds and more sophisticated soufflés and iced desserts. Hints on making *slimming* adaptations are given where possible, although many sweets are not feasible on any type of weight reducing diet. The *mixer* is of great value in making many desserts, so read the side columns before you begin preparations. Most desserts in this section can be made well ahead.

Choose a refreshing fruit flavoured dessert if the main course is fairly rich, a creamy dessert after a more simple main course. Fruit looks attractive in clear glass containers; use interesting shaped moulds for jellies.

Metric Conversions

In many desserts it is not necessary to convert the Imperial measures accurately, but when using gelatine this is very important; too much gelatine gives a mixture that is unpleasantly stiff; if you use too little then it is over-soft and will not hold its shape. Recipes that need sugar for sweetening often depend upon personal taste, so here again the small difference between the Metric amount and the Imperial is unimportant.

Drinks to serve with desserts

The very formal meals, where a different wine was produced as one course followed another, are rarely given today, but if you wish to serve a special wine with a dessert then choose a fairly sweet white wine; the most famous one being Sauternes. Remember there are some very excellent Sauternes as well as rather over-sweet wines of this kind.

Using your refrigerator

The freezing compartment of the refrigerator is excellent for making ice creams, sorbets and other iced desserts. Refrigerators vary in the speed of freezing – with an old model with no star marking, or one with 1 star marking, turn indicator to coldest position at least ½ hour before you start to freeze ice cream, but this is not necessary when freezing water ices or sorbets. Always return to normal setting as soon as possible. With a refrigerator with 2 or 3 star markings there is no need to alter the setting.

Home freezing of cold desserts

Beside each recipe you will find information on freezing that particular dessert, but here are some general principles to follow:

1. You are 'safe' to freeze any moulds and creams that contain from about 30 per cent to 50 per cent cream. If made entirely of milk then the chances of the sweet being successful are small, particularly if you store for a long period. You will find the dessert forms tiny 'splinters' of ice and loses its texture. It must, however, be pointed out that if you intend to freeze custards (on trifles, etc.) for 1–2 weeks only, then they are generally quite satisfactory.

2. Jellies, whether made from jelly tablets or with fresh fruit, are very successful. If filled with fruit make quite certain the particular fruit will freeze, for example bananas only freeze well when made into a purée – see Banana ice cream page 196, and Banana orange fool on page 135. Fresh pineapple prevents a jelly setting under any circumstances, and while the liquid jelly filled with fresh pineapple will freeze, the moment you allow it to thaw out the jelly will return to a liquid once again.

3. For cold desserts made with pastry see also the comments about freezing on page 171.

4. Desserts topped with whipped cream freeze excellently; naturally you must freeze *before* wrapping so that you do not spoil the piping or decoration of the cream.

5. Dessert gâteaux are generally most successful when frozen, and the more moist the filling the better the texture when they are defrosted. I find it best to fill most gâteaux before freezing, rather than freezing the plain cake mixture then filling afterwards; there are more comments about this on page 215. The one exception is that ice cream filled gâteaux should be filled before serving, otherwise you will find that by the time the cake part has defrosted the ice cream has become far too soft.

6. When freezing ice creams or any iced desserts, they may be frozen in any position in the cabinet and there is no need to alter the setting. Ice creams, etc., freeze so quickly you can always use half thick and half thin cream, even when adding fruit. Allow time for the dessert to soften slightly before serving.

The size of the item affects the time required to thaw out at room temperature: a large block will take much longer than several smaller shapes.

Jellied sweets

Jellied sweets range from simple fruit jellies, made from packets, to the more elaborate moulds and soufflés given in this chapter. Follow directions about water temperature and *exact* amount to use to dissolve the jelly or gelatine. When using gelatine with very little liquid, follow the directions in stage 5 of the Pineapple cheesecake on this page.

FRUIT FILLED JELLY: make up the jelly with the required amount of liquid (either water or the juice from cooked fruit, etc.), but remember most fruit is very moist, so do not use as much water as for a plain jelly. Either blend the fruit with the *cold* jelly or pour a little jelly into a mould (rinsed in cold water), then arrange a layer of fruit on the jelly when it just begins to stiffen, add more jelly, more fruit, etc. You then have a definite design when finished.

FRUIT MOULDS: make a purée of fresh berry fruit or cooked fruit, and use this instead of water to set the jelly. If the fruit purée is fairly thick, then allow about 25 per cent extra liquid content in setting the jelly.

Speedy Meal
To make a jelly in a very short time either increase the amount of gelatine or use less water or dissolve the jelly in very little hot water and stir in crushed ice to make up the required amount.

Mixer
The liquidiser is excellent for emulsifying the fruit to give a purée; add jelly to hot purée to dissolve.

Slimming Tips
The jellies one buys are sweetened. Make fresh fruit jellies with fruit juice, sugar substitute and powder gelatine.

Home Freezing
I have always been most successful in freezing jellies whether made with fresh fruit, filled with fruit (not bananas or pineapple), or in the form of a fruit mould. A cloudy effect when thawed could be due to too slow freezing; *freeze very quickly*; thaw out slowly.

Pineapple Cheesecake

Serves 8
Cooking time few minutes heating

Ingredients	Metric	Imperial
FOR THE BISCUIT CRUST:		
digestive biscuits	50 grammes	2 oz.
castor sugar	1 level tablespoon	1 level tablespoon
butter	25 grammes	1 oz.
FOR THE FILLING:		
cottage cheese	½ kilo (poor weight)	1 lb. approx.
pineapple rings	medium can (200–225 grammes)	medium can (8 oz.)
powdered gelatine	1 level tablespoon (*or* 1 envelope)	1 level tablespoon (*or* 1 envelope)
lemon	1	1
castor sugar	100 grammes	4 oz.
eggs	2 large	2 large
thick cream	142 ml	¼ pint
TO DECORATE:		
pineapple	1 ring	1 ring
mint leaves	6–8	6–8

1 Crush biscuits, add the sugar, melt the butter slightly and blend ingredients together.
2 Sprinkle and press down over the base of a 18–20-cm (7–8-inch) glass flan dish, or cake tin with a loose base.
3 Sieve cottage cheese; drain pineapple juice into a basin, sprinkle in the gelatine.
4 Reserve 1 pineapple ring for decoration, chop the rest finely, add to cottage cheese with juice and grated lemon rind.
5 Place the basin containing juice and gelatine over a pan of hot water and allow the gelatine to dissolve.
6 Add sugar and egg yolks and whisk over the heat until the consistency of pouring cream; cool.
7 When thick, but not set, blend into the cheese mixture.
8 Lastly, fold in the stiffly beaten egg whites and lightly whipped cream.
9 Turn into prepared dish and chill until set.
10 Decorate with wedges of pineapple and mint leaves.

Speedy Meal
Use bottled lemon juice instead of fresh; crisp packet breadcrumbs with double sugar, instead of crushing biscuits. Do not bother to sieve cheese (gives a less smooth mixture).

Mixer
This is invaluable in this recipe; use the liquidiser to—
a) crush biscuit crumbs,
b) emulsify cottage cheese instead of sieving—add a little pineapple syrup to make mixture soft so no cheese is wasted,
c) add thinly pared lemon rind at stage b) to save sieving.
Use the whisk for—
a) cream,
b) egg whites,
c) beating cottage cheese smoother instead of sieving.

Home Freezing
Freeze, then lift out of tin and wrap. Defrost at room temperature for 2–3 hours. Keeps for 3 months.

EGG CUSTARD DESSERTS

The range of puddings made from a basis of egg and milk, or milk and cream, are very varied; from the plain custard to more very elaborate desserts.

There is little technique in preparing the sweet, but great care must be taken in cooking, for if the egg mixture boils it will 'curdle' i.e. separate, and could be spoiled. When 'boiling' custards, therefore, make sure the water under the basin or top of the double saucepan is hot, but never boiling. If a 'boiled' custard does curdle, a liquidiser (blender) can help—see page 198.

When baking custards, stand the dish in another containing cold water. If using the oven manually, it is an excellent idea to bake the custard for about 20–30 minutes *then* remove from the oven and stand in the container of cold water (make sure there is not too much water so it could flow into the pudding); in this way the water will tend to keep the custard cooler. When a custard-type pudding is put into an automatic oven, obviously both custard and water go in together. Check that the oven setting, timing and oven position ensure slow cooking. As an added precaution, wrap foil round the outside of both the dish containing the pudding *and* that containing the water.

Automatic Oven

An egg custard is an excellent dessert for an automatic menu being cooked in a slow to very moderate oven.
Choose the coolest part of the oven—see also Caramel crumb pudding, page 188.

Speedy Meal

Quick cooking will curdle mixture. The strange thing is that you can cook an egg custard in the great heat of a pressure cooker with no ill effect. Choose 5 lb. pressure if possible, and allow time given beside Caramel custard for a thick custard, or 5–6 minutes for a thinner custard.

Mixer

If the custard does curdle slightly, either whisk very sharply, or emulsify in the liquidiser to give a smooth texture.

Home Freezing

See below.

Orange Floating Islands

Serves 4
Cooking time 35–45 minutes

Ingredients	Metric	Imperial
eggs	2	2
milk	good ½ litre (568 ml)	1 pint
sugar	100 grammes	4 oz.
grated orange rind	2 teaspoons	2 teaspoons
TO DECORATE:		
oranges	1 or 2	1 or 2

1 Separate the yolks from the whites of the eggs, add a little milk to the yolks and cover to prevent a skin forming.
2 Put the milk with 25 grammes (1 oz.) sugar and the grated orange rind, into a large shallow saucepan, or frying pan.
3 Whisk the egg whites until they are very stiff. Gradually beat in half the sugar, then fold in the rest.
4 Drop balls of this meringue on top of the hot milk and poach for 1½–2 minutes; turn with a perforated spoon and poach on the second side. Never let the milk boil too quickly, otherwise the meringue will be tough, see page 188.
5 Lift the meringue balls off the hot milk and drain on a sieve.
6 Strain the milk over the beaten yolks, then in a double saucepan cook until a thickened custard.
7 Pour into a shallow glass bowl and top with the meringue balls.
8 Decorate with skinned segments of fresh orange.

Speedy Meal

a) use orange essence instead of grated orange rind, and continue as stages 1–5.
b) make a custard sauce with custard-powder, whisk in the egg yolks when thickened, so eliminating the long slow cooking of stage 6.

Mixer

Use whisk on high speed for preparing egg white and the meringue. The liquidiser is excellent for emulsifying the custard mixture, see page 198.

Home Freezing

Not suitable unless you use 250 ml (½ pint) milk and 250 ml (½ pint) thick cream. The custard will then keep 6–8 weeks. The ordinary version would keep a week only.

Caramel Custard

This famous dessert is easily prepared:
make the caramel sauce as recipe on page 188, then coat the mould with this. When cool, strain or pour in the custard, made by blending 4 eggs (or 4–5 egg yolks), ½–1 tablespoon sugar and 568 ml (1 pint) milk, or milk and thin cream. Stand in a dish of cold water; bake in a slow to very moderate oven or steam as page 188. The time varies according to depth of mould, etc.; allow about 1½–2 hours.

Automatic Oven

An excellent dessert for the automatic oven. Cover with foil or paper over the top so a thick skin will not form during the long cooking. To make a less firm custard, use only 2 eggs (or 2–3 yolks) with the amount of milk given.

Home Freezing

See comments above.

Caramel Crumb Pudding

Serves 4–5
Cooking time 1¾–2 hours

Ingredients	Metric	Imperial
FOR THE CARAMEL:		
loaf or granulated sugar	75 grammes good measure	3 oz.
water	6 tablespoons	6 tablespoons
FOR THE PUDDING:		
milk	generous ½ litre (568 ml)	1 pint
sugar	½–1 tablespoon	½–1 tablespoon
dried fruit	75 grammes	3 oz.
breadcrumbs	75 grammes	3 oz.
eggs or egg yolks	3	3

1 Put the sugar and half the water into a strong saucepan, stir until the sugar has melted, then boil without stirring until golden brown caramel, stir in the rest of the water.
2 Let the caramel cool slightly, then add the cold milk and heat gently until well blended, add sugar, fruit and crumbs.
3 Stir on to the beaten eggs or yolks, then pour into a greased basin and cover tightly.
4 Steam over very hot *but not boiling* water until just set, turn out carefully; or cool and turn out and serve cold.

Note: stale cake or macaroon crumbs could be used instead of breadcrumbs.

Toffee Snow Eggs

Serves 4–6
Cooking time 20–30 minutes

Ingredients	Metric	Imperial
eggs	2 large	2 large
milk	568 ml*	1 pint*
castor sugar	75 grammes	3 oz.
vanilla essence	few drops	few drops
brown sugar, (preferably Demerara)	50–75 grammes	2–3 oz.

*for a thicker custard use slightly less–remember though some milk evaporates in cooking the meringue.

1 Separate the whites from the yolks of the eggs; it is a good idea to pour a little cold water (or some of the cold milk) over the egg yolks to prevent them becoming dry.
2 Pour the milk into a very large shallow saucepan or frying pan.
3 Whisk the egg whites until very stiff; you should be able to turn the bowl upside down without the egg whites falling out.
4 Gradually whisk in 25 grammes (1 oz.) sugar, then fold in another 25 grammes (1 oz.) of sugar.
5 Meanwhile, heat the milk to about 88°C. (190°F.), *do not let it boil*, then drop heaped teaspoonfuls meringue (the balls must be small) on to the hot milk, and continue as Orange floating islands, page 187, points 4 and 5.
6 Beat the egg yolks and remainder of the sugar together, add the milk from the pan and any on the plate, strain into the top of a double saucepan, or into a large basin.
7 Add vanilla essence and cook over very hot (but not boiling) water, until custard just coats the back of a wooden spoon. In this version of the famous Snow egg (or Floating island) recipe it is important that the custard is fairly thin.
8 Pour the custard into shallow flame-resistant serving dish, allow to cool, then put the small balls on top–keep these fairly carefully spread on top to ensure even browning.
9 Sprinkle brown sugar over the top, crisp under a hot grill *for 1 minute only*; chopped almonds could be added too.

Automatic Oven

This pudding can be cooked in the oven; allow about the same time in a slow to very moderate oven. Even if the automatic oven menu is being cooked at a *slightly* higher temperature you may still be able to cook this pudding in the coolest part of the oven. Stand in a dish of cold water, and cover both the dish and the pudding with foil so the water does not evaporate.

Speedy Meal

Make the caramel; this is quicker to make if you use 3–4 tablespoons golden syrup instead of sugar. Add *no* water, but let this brown and then dilute with an equal amount of water. Make an ordinary custard-powder custard; blend with the caramel.

Mixer

Should the caramel and milk curdle, then emulsify in warmed goblet.
Use goblet for making the breadcrumbs.

Home Freezing

This freezes well if you use half milk and half thin cream.

Speedy Meal

Instead of browning the meringues at stage 9 opposite, crush some French almond rock or brittle toffee and sprinkle over the meringue balls.
To avoid the very slow thickening of the custard in this and the Orange snow eggs, make an ordinary pouring custard with custard-powder and beat in the egg yolks. Simmer for 2–3 minutes only.

Mixer

The mixer is invaluable for making the meringues, and if you have a hand electric whisk use this to whisk the custard from time to time at stage 7; do not overwhisk though for you 'slow-up' thickening.

Slimming Tips

This particular recipe, is *not* at all suitable for any slimming diet; but egg custards can be included, providing you use skimmed milk or use part of the daily milk ration recommended on most diets, and sweeten with sugar substitute.

Home Freezing

See comments under the Orange floating islands. If you do freeze this dessert do not put on the sugar topping, for it becomes very 'watery' in defrosting; instead freeze without this, add the topping when thawed out, and brown as stage 9.

Sherry Trifle

Serves 5–6
Cooking time–see stages 2 and 3

Ingredients	Metric	Imperial
small sponge cakes	4	4
jam	2–3 tablespoons	2–3 tablespoons
sweet sherry	4–5 tablespoons	4–5 tablespoons
water	3 tablespoons	3 tablespoons
sugar	1 tablespoon	1 tablespoon
thick pouring custard*	568 ml	1 pint
ratafias (optional)	to taste	to taste
blanched almonds	to taste	to taste
TO DECORATE:		
thick cream	125 ml	¼ pint
glacé cherries	to taste	to taste
angelica	small piece	small piece

*either made with custard-powder *or* 2–3 eggs or egg yolks, 1–2 tablespoons sugar and 568 ml (1 pint) milk.

1 Split the sponge cakes and spread with jam, then put in the serving dish or dishes.
2 Heat the sherry, water and sugar, spoon or pour over the sponge cakes to moisten (use more sherry if wished).
3 Make the custard and pour over the sponge cakes while still warm, add a few ratafias and almonds to the custard layer, or sprinkle over the sponge cakes if preferred.
4 Cover with a plate or foil to prevent a firm skin forming on the trifle. Leave for some hours.
5 When cold decorate with whipped cream, glacé cherries, etc.

WHITE WINE TRIFLE: a more delicate flavour is given if the cakes are moistened with a sweet wine instead of sherry, do not use any water.

JELLY TRIFLE: omit sherry if wished; make a fruit jelly, pour over sponge cakes, add fresh or canned fruit, if wished.

Speedy Meal

Use the custard-powder custard, make this with half the amount of hot milk, thicken, then whisk in cold milk to cool the custard more quickly.

Mixer

Whisk the custard to keep it very smooth, or, better still, pour the custard-powder custard into the liquidiser goblet just before pouring on to the trifle; this 'gets rid' of any skin and gives a wonderfully smooth texture. You could add a little thick cream to enrich this if wished.

Home Freezing

Although, according to 'the rules', a trifle topped with an ordinary custard should not freeze, I habitually do this. I leave it for about 1 week or a maximum of 2 weeks; the custard is perfect and the flavour is excellent.

Using fruit purées

A thick fruit purée can be used for many desserts or sauces.

FRUIT FOULE: blend together equal quantities of very thick sweetened fruit purée and either a thick sweetened egg custard, or one made with custard-powder. A richer flavour is given if half custard and half whipped cream are used, or all whipped cream. Chill well and top with cream if wished.

FRUIT SNOW: blend from 284–568 ml (½–1 pint) *cold* thick sweetened fruit purée with 2 stiffly beaten egg whites (the less fruit the lighter the dessert). Serve very cold with cream. Serves 3–4.

APRICOT CREAM DIPLOMAT: the very exotic sweet facing page 161, is very simple, if rather costly.

1 Make or buy a deep sponge cake, about 18–20 cm (7–8 inches) in diameter, cut 4 layers–or use plain sponge sandwiches instead. Moisten the layers with apricot brandy.
2 Whip a good ½ litre, 568 ml (1 pint) thick cream until it holds its shape. Put half on one side to coat the gâteau.
3 Add a little sugar to the rest of the cream and blend with 284 ml (½ pint) thick apricot purée, and 50 grammes (2 oz.) blanched shredded almonds.
4 Sandwich the layers with the apricot cream; flavour most of the remaining cream with apricot brandy. Spread over the shape, decorate with piped plain cream, glacé cherries, crystallised violet petals and grated chocolate. Serves 7–8

Speedy Meal

Use canned fruit pie fillings and canned creamed rice, instead of making custard.

Mixer

Use the liquidiser to blend the fruit and custard for the foule, but not to blend the fruit and cream; it does not whip cream. Use the mixer to whip the cream where needed, but take great care not to over-beat the cream and make it solid. If that does happen *fold* a little milk or water in at once and this could remedy the 'buttery' texture.

Home Freezing

The Fruit foule freezes very well if it has at least 25 per cent thick cream in ingredients; indeed it is like ice cream, so read instructions on page 196.
The Fruit snow freezes well too. There is no need to alter settings on either a refrigerator or freezer.
The Diplomat freezes wonderfully for 3–4 weeks, if coated (the cream coating does seem to lose flavour over a longer period), or 6 weeks if left uncoated.

MAKING A COLD SOUFFLE

A cold soufflé is a combination of cream, or an egg custard or whipped evaporated milk (for economy), gelatine, flavouring and eggs. The important point to remember is that the jellied mixture must be sufficiently thick to hold the stiffly beaten egg whites in position, otherwise they will float to the top. On the other hand if you allow the mixture to become too stiff it is impossible to fold the egg whites in evenly.

TO PREPARE A DISH FOR COLD SOUFFLÉS

1 Always choose a small dish so the mixture will stand above the top of the dish.
2 Cut a double band of greaseproof paper, brush about 5 cm (2 inches) very lightly with melted butter.
3 Tie or pin *very firmly* round the dish so the buttered part is just above the top of the dish.
4 Spoon in the mixture; allow to set.

TO REMOVE THE PAPER

1 Untie or unpin the paper.
2 Dip a palette knife in hot water, shake fairly dry, insert between the light soufflé mixture and the paper, and ease the paper away very slowly and carefully.

Raspberry Soufflé

Serves 5–6
Cooking time–few minutes

Ingredients	Metric	Imperial
powder gelatine	15 grammes	½ oz.
raspberries	300 grammes	12 oz.
eggs	3 large	3 large
castor sugar	50–75 grammes	2–3 oz.
thick cream*	284 ml	½ pint
TO DECORATE:		
thick cream	142 ml	¼ pint
raspberries		

*it is important to use *all* thick cream with the amount of fruit purée in this recipe.

1 Put the gelatine into a basin.
2 Sieve nearly all the raspberries (save some for decoration) and add to the gelatine. Stand the basin in a saucepan of boiling water and leave until the gelatine has melted.
3 Continue from stage 3 to stage 9 in the Chocolate cream soufflé recipe, adding the raspberry and gelatine mixture to the whisked egg yolks and sugar.
4 To decorate the soufflé, pipe whipped cream around the top and arrange the whole raspberries on this.

TO VARY:
Strawberries, loganberries, or ripe blackcurrants can all be used in the same way.
If wishing to make a soufflé with fruit that needs cooking before sieving, i.e. apricots, etc., then cook sufficient (*with the minimum of water* and very little sugar) to give about 8 tablespoons thick pulp.

Note: always keep the decoration on any cold soufflé rather light and delicate.

Home Freezing

Make wise use of your freezer, or refrigerator, to set the mixture sufficiently to incorporate the egg whites, as given opposite.

Mixer

The mixer can be used at various stages:
a) for whipping egg yolks and sugar; if using a large mixer and bowl which cannot stand over hot water, melt chocolate in a separate basin, whisk egg yolks and sugar in an ordinary bowl, then add melted chocolate and whip again,
b) for whipping the cream or evaporated milk,
c) for whisking egg whites.
The liquidiser can be used to chop the nuts—add to the goblet while the blades are revolving to prevent nuts being chopped too finely.

Home Freezing

This rich soufflé mixture is ideal for freezing—freeze before decorating if wished, and leave paper in position; when frozen solid cover top with foil or allow to set, remove paper, decorate, then freeze; when solid, wrap carefully. To serve—unwrap before defrosting (this saves spoiling the decoration). Defrost at room temperature for about 2–3 hours, or refrigerator temperature for 4–5 hours, or serve as a frozen soufflé, bringing from the home freezer 1 hour before serving so it is not too cold.

Chocolate Cream Soufflé

Serves 5–6
Cooking time–few minutes

Ingredients	Metric	Imperial
powder gelatine	15 grammes	½ oz.
	(1 envelope)	(1 envelope)
water	4 tablespoons	4 tablespoons
plain chocolate *or*	75–80 grammes	3 oz.
chocolate couverture		
eggs	3 large	3 large
castor sugar	50 grammes	2 oz.
vanilla essence	few drops	few drops
thick cream	142 ml	¼ pint
thin cream	142 ml	¼ pint
TO DECORATE:		
thick cream	up to 142 ml	up to ¼ pint
blanched almonds	25 grammes	1 oz.

1 Put the gelatine into a basin, add the cold water, then stand the basin in a pan of boiling water so that gelatine dissolves.
2 Break the chocolate in pieces, melt in a basin over hot, but not boiling, water.
3 Separate the whites from the yolks; put yolks, sugar and essence with the chocolate, and whisk over the hot water until light and fluffy.
4 Add the dissolved gelatine and stir together.
5 Allow this mixture to cool and begin to stiffen.
6 Whisk thick cream until it begins to hold its shape, then whisk in thin cream steadily until the mark of the whisk shows.
7 Whisk the egg whites in a separate basin.
8 Fold the cream, then egg whites into the chocolate mixture.
9 Spoon into the prepared 13-cm (5-inch) soufflé dish, see page 190, and leave to set.
10 Meanwhile, whip the cream and chop the almonds.
11 Remove the paper from round the soufflé dish very carefully, see page 190.
12 Press the chopped almonds against the side of the mixture, and pipe or spoon a border of whipped cream round the top.

Speedy Meal

To hasten the partial setting of the Chocolate cream soufflé, and recipes based upon this, stand the mixture in a bowl of ice cubes at stage 5, or put into the freezing compartment of the refrigerator or the freezer for a very short time.
Mention has been made of using whipped evaporated milk instead of cream to make more economical soufflés. To speed the whipping of evaporated milk: boil cans in a pan of boiling water for 15 minutes (make sure the cans are covered with water during boiling). Open the cans carefully while warm, tip the warm milk into a basin, add 1 teaspoon gelatine, dissolved in 1–2 tablespoons very hot water. Cool and chill thoroughly, measure amount required, then whip.
Use concentrated orange or lemon syrups instead of fresh fruit juices in these soufflés.

Mixer

Use the whisk for whipping evaporated milk. Many brands will whip quite thickly without the gelatine; a teaspoon lemon juice helps this, and so does the vigorous action of a mixer.

Home Freezing

This soufflé, and the various flavours based on it, freezes very well indeed. If decorated, freeze before covering, then cover tightly and store for several weeks. To serve: unwrap as soon as it comes from the freezer, allow 2–3 hours to thaw out. The fruit flavours take longer than the Chocolate soufflé.

Lemon Soufflé

1 Method as Chocolate cream soufflé, but omit the chocolate and vanilla essence.
2 Dissolve 15 grammes (½ oz.) gelatine in 5 tablespoons lemon juice.
3 Beat 3 egg yolks, the finely grated rind of 2 lemons, and 100 grammes (4 oz.) castor sugar, until thick and creamy; do this over hot water, if wished.
4 Continue as stage 4 in Chocolate cream soufflé to the end of the recipe.

ORANGE SOUFFLÉ is made as the Lemon soufflé above, but use 4 tablespoons orange juice *and* 1 tablespoon lemon juice at stage 2; add the grated rind of 2 oranges and ½ lemon at stage 3. The lemon rind enhances the orange flavour.

LIQUEUR SOUFFLÉ: method as Chocolate cream soufflé, but omit the chocolate and vanilla essence.
Dissolve gelatine in 3 tablespoons liqueur instead of water, add 2 tablespoons milk. Choose either crême de menthe; cherry brandy (serve the soufflé with Black cherry sauce, see page 149); orange curaçao (add ½ teaspoon grated orange rind to egg yolks and sugar); or any other favourite liqueur.

Danish Apricot Crumble

Serves 4
Cooking time 15 minutes

Ingredients	Metric	Imperial
fresh apricots	½ kilo (poor weight)	1 lb.
sugar	to taste	to taste
water	few tablespoons	few tablespoons
FOR THE TOPPING:		
margarine *or* butter	50 grammes	2 oz.
coarse white breadcrumbs	100 grammes	4 oz.
sugar	50–75 grammes	2–3 oz.
TO DECORATE:		
whipped cream	as required	as required

1 Cook apricots very carefully with the sugar and water.
2 Turn the fruit in the syrup so that it does not become discoloured when cooked. Put into a serving dish.
3 While the fruit is cooking, prepare the crumble.
4 Heat margarine or butter in a frying pan, add crumbs, turn in the hot fat until pale golden–remove from heat the moment they begin to brown–and add the sugar.
5 Top fruit with the cold crumble mixture.
6 When quite cold, decorate with cream, or as picture, opposite, with cream and some of the fruit.

Speedy Meal
Use the crisp breadcrumbs (raspings) instead of making your own, or, better still, crumble crispbread and use this instead.
Use canned fruit or fruit pie fillings; other fruits are just as successful as apricots.

Mixer
The mixture could be used to make the crumbs, but it does make them rather smooth and this can give a less interesting texture.

Home Freezing
This pudding freezes excellently, but it is also a very good idea to have containers of breadcrumbs to use as and when wished. You can take out as few or as many crumbs as you require, and the defrosted crumbs can be thawed out as they heat, at stage 4.

USING CHOUX PASTRY

The delicious sweet shown between pages 152/153, pictures the recipe below.

Chocolate Choux

Serves 6–8
Cooking time 35 minutes
Oven temperature 400–425° F. (200–220° C.), Gas Mark 5–6, then 375–400° F. (190–200° C.), Gas Mark 4–5

Ingredients	Metric	Imperial
choux pastry as page 176		
FOR THE FILLING:		
ice cream as page 195		
CHOCOLATE SAUCE:		
plain chocolate	150–200 grammes	6–8 oz.
butter	small knob	small knob
water	2 tablespoons	2 tablespoons
golden syrup	1 tablespoon	1 tablespoon

1 Make the choux pastry as recipe on page 176, and pipe, or spoon into rounds on a greased and floured baking tin.
2 Bake in the centre (or just above) of a moderately hot to hot oven for 15 minutes; lower the heat for 15–20 minutes.
3 Cool away from a draught, split, and remove any uncooked dough and 'dry out' the buns for a short time.
4 To serve: fill with ice cream (or whipped cream instead) and coat with hot or cold chocolate sauce (made by heating all the ingredients in a basin over hot water).

TINY CHOUX OR PROFITEROLES: make buns about the size of a hazel nut and bake for 10 minutes only in the hot oven. Fill sweet choux (known as profiteroles) with whipped cream and serve with chocolate sauce. Serve savoury choux as recipe page 163.

ÉCLAIRS: bake finger-shapes of choux pastry for 15–20 minutes; split, fill with whipped cream, cover with icing.

Speedy Meal
One can buy ready-made or frozen Choux or Cream buns and add ice cream to the cream filling, and coat with hot chocolate sauce.
Naturally if the buns you buy have a chocolate icing then you do not need additional chocolate in the form of a sauce.

Mixer
Do not over-beat any melting chocolate; indeed it should not be stirred too much, otherwise it loses its shine.

Home Freezing
As stated under Choux pastry on page 176, one can freeze the buns very well. You could not freeze ice cream filled buns though, as the ice cream would melt by the time the choux pastry had thawed out. The chocolate sauce could be frozen, but there is little point in doing this as it takes a short time to make.
Icing on choux pastry buns or éclairs freezes well, and chocolate icing does not lose its gloss.

43. Danish apricot crumble

44. Meringue gâteau, see page 194

Method of preparing meringue mixture

There are 3 basic ways of adding sugar to the egg whites:
1 Gradually fold in all the sugar (for a rather soft topping on a pudding).
2 Gradually whisk in half the sugar, then fold in the rest (the method usually preferred).
3 Gradually whisk in all the sugar (particularly suitable with an electric mixer).

In order to have a perfect meringue, remember:

a) egg whites will not whisk if they are too fresh; they must be at least 24 hours old;
b) the bowl should be scrupulously clean – a slight speck of flour or smear of grease will prevent whites being whisked;
c) whisk until whites are so stiff that the bowl can be turned upside down without fear of them falling out. In order to do this, a really good egg whisk is necessary (although before the development of whisks, the egg whites were whipped on a flat dish with a palette knife);
d) the amount of sugar used is very important, this is why metric equivalent gives a slightly more generous amount than if using a strict conversion counting – 25 grammes equals 1 oz.

The points above apply whether you are making a meringue topping, or meringues to store.

Automatic Oven

Providing you are certain that your oven setting or temperature is completely accurate, you can put the meringues into the *heated* oven and leave the oven to switch off as set. You *cannot* put the egg white and sugar mixture into a cold oven and allow it to stand for even a limited period.

Mixer

Use the beater attachment to whisk the egg whites until stiff. You can use a high speed where possible. Do not leave too long, otherwise the egg whites become too dry and you will have a meringue that crumbles badly when you try to take off the baking trays after cooking. When the egg whites are stiff use a low speed and add the sugar steadily until it is all blended in *or* add half by mixer, then switch off and fold in the remainder by hand (this gives a softer centred meringue).

Home Freezing

Meringues freeze perfectly. The high percentage of sugar means they will *never* become iced. Normally there is no point in freezing meringues because they store well in an air-tight tin; but if you have filled the meringues with cream or ice cream, or if they form part of a gateau, as page 194, then this is the perfect way to store any left.

Meringues

Makes 16–20 medium; 6–8 large shapes
Cooking time 1½–3 hours (according to size)
Oven temperature 225–250° F. (110–120° C.), Gas Mark 0–½

Ingredients	Metric	Imperial
egg whites	2	2
castor sugar	110 grammes*	4 oz.
or castor and	60 grammes	2 oz.
icing sugar	50 grammes	2 oz.
TO FILL:		
thick cream	142–284 ml	¼–½ pint

*for a better result than accurate conversion

1 Whisk egg whites until very stiff and add the sugar, see above.
2 Brush the baking tin or sheet with a *very little* oil or melted butter.
3 Either put spoonfuls of the mixture on to the tray or insert ½–1-cm (¼–½-inch) plain or rose shaped meringue pipe into a cloth bag, and pipe the desired shape on to the tin.
4 Bake the meringues according to size in a very cool oven. They should be dry but still uncoloured.
5 If there are several trays of meringues, the oven position cannot be determined, but the ideal position is below centre.
6 Remove meringues from baking tin while warm; lift with a warm palette knife which has been dipped in very hot water, then dried on a tea towel.
7 When cold, store in an airtight tin; they keep for weeks if desired.

TO FILL MERINGUES

MERINGUES CHANTILLY: whip thick cream until it holds its shape, flavour with vanilla essence and sweeten; sandwich the meringues with this, pipe a border of cream if wished.
MERINGUES GLACÉS: sandwich the meringues together with ice cream and decorate with whipped cream.

FLAVOURINGS FOR MERINGUES

CHOCOLATE–sieve 1 teaspoon cocoa or 2 teaspoons chocolate powder with every 25 grammes* (1 oz.) sugar before adding egg whites.

COCONUT–allow 25 grammes* (1 oz.) desiccated coconut to each egg white, blend with sugar.

COFFEE–use ½ teaspoon powdered coffee to each 25 grammes (1 oz.) sugar, blend with the sugar.

CORNFLAKES–allow 25 grammes* (1 oz.) crushed cornflakes to each egg white, blend with sugar.

ESSENCES–blend a few drops flavouring essence with egg whites when stiff.

*as you will see on page 193 it is recommended that a very generous 25 grammes is used instead of 1 oz. of sugar (i.e. 110 grammes in place of 4 oz. sugar).

Home Freezing

The flavourings of meringues make no difference to the freezing, or indeed to any points given about making, baking or storing.

Meringue Gâteau

Serves 9–10
Cooking time–about 3 hours
Oven temperature 225–250° F. (110–120° C.), Gas Mark 0–½

Ingredients	Metric	Imperial
egg whites	5	5
sugar*	275 grammes	10 oz.
ice cream	to serve 9–10	to serve 9–10
TO DECORATE:		
thick cream	284 ml	½ pint
instant coffee powder	½ teaspoon	½ teaspoon
glacé cherries	9–10	9–10

*see recipe for meringues

1 Prepare meringue mixture as page 193 using two-thirds to make 9–10 large oval meringues–use remainder to make a round base, see below for all information. Store carefully until ready to assemble the gâteau.
2 Put the round meringue on to the serving dish, place ice cream on top of this.
3 Spread flat side of each meringue with a little whipped cream, gently press them against the ice cream until you form a complete circle.
4 Put a small amount of whipped cream on one side, flavour this with the coffee powder.
5 Put the rest of the plain cream into a piping bag, pipe cream between each meringue and over top of ice cream.
6 Put coffee cream into piping bag, pipe rosettes on top of the gâteau.
7 Decorate top with whole glacé cherries, and as liked round the base. see picture facing page 193. This recipe will serve 9–10 people for a special party.

Speedy Meal

There are ready-made meringues (sold in packets or from the bakers) that could be used for this dessert. They are inclined to be much more solid than the home-made variety, so crush the underside very gently with the handle of a teaspoon and press the cream well into the shell, so giving a more generous filling of cream. You may find difficulty in obtaining the round of meringue, so make a round of small meringues on the serving dish instead; or have a round of sponge cake moistened with liqueur.

Mixer

See information on page 193.

Home Freezing

See information on page 193; this gâteau can be stored in the freezer and will thaw out very quickly.

Pavlova

This is the famous Australian dessert made of meringue. Use a minimum of 4 egg whites and the proportion of sugar given on page 193. Most recipes suggest adding 1 teaspoon vinegar (brown or white) to the meringue, just before using. If you add 1 teaspoon cornflour to the sugar it gives a slightly crisper outside. Make the meringue as the recipe on page 193. Make two rounds of greaseproof paper about 18–20 cm (7–8 inches), oil lightly, and cover with the meringue. Bake as meringues, until firm. Lift off the paper and store until required. Sandwich and top with whipped cream, ice cream and fruit.

Mixer

Take particular care that you do not over-beat the egg whites, this would make meringues so dry and 'crumbly' that the cake could break.

Home Freezing

See the comments under meringues, on page 193.

TO MAKE ICED CREAM DESSERTS

Home-made ice cream and iced desserts are a wonderful standby in the freezer, or refrigerator, and they are not difficult to make. Freeze ice creams quickly; the temperature in a 3-star refrigerator does not need adjusting; or that in a home freezer; but if you have a refrigerator with no star, or one-star marking, then turn to the coldest position *at least half an hour* before freezing the mixture. Return to the normal setting when firm.

The Orange Bavarian cream given below makes a wonderful iced pudding; that is why I have included it in this section. Either freeze with the jelly, as the recipe, or omit this and freeze the orange flavoured cream mixture (stages 6–9) alone; either in a mould or small containers.

Speedy Meal
Add various ingredients to bought ice cream to make it more interesting, i.e. chopped fruits, diced chocolate, etc.; or press the ice cream into chilled moulds to freeze as iced puddings.

Mixer
Some ice cream recipes and sorbets are better if they are beaten during freezing; the electric whisk is ideal for this purpose.

Home Freezing
It is wise to have a good supply of home-made ice cream as well as commercial ice cream in the freezer for emergency desserts. Use within 2 months if home-made.

Orange Bavarian Cream

Serves 4
Cooking time 10 minutes

Ingredients	Metric	Imperial
FOR THE CLEAR ORANGE JELLY:		
powder gelatine	1 level tablespoon	1 level tablespoon
water	see method	see method
	stages 1 to 3	stages 1 to 3
oranges	2	2
sugar	50 grammes	2 oz.
orange colouring (optional)		
FOR THE CREAM LAYER:		
powder gelatine	1 level tablespoon	1 level tablespoon
water	4 tablespoons	4 tablespoons
grated rind	1 orange	1 orange
juice	2 oranges	2 oranges
sugar	50 grammes	2 oz.
thick cream	284 ml	½ pint
glacé cherries	50 grammes	2 oz.
angelica	1 piece	1 piece
orange	1	1

1 Soak and soften the powder gelatine in 4 tablespoons of cold water.
2 Squeeze the juice from the oranges, measure and add enough water to give 284 ml (½ pint).
3 Simmer the pieces of orange rind for 5 minutes only in another 8 tablespoons water, strain, add the sugar, the orange juice and the softened gelatine.
4 Stir until gelatine has dissolved – add a few drops of orange colouring, if desired.
5 Pour half into a plain cake tin or mould and allow to set. Keep rest in a warm place, so that it does not set, but only cools.
6 For the cream layer – soften the powder gelatine in 4 tablespoons cold water. Stand the basin over hot water, stir until gelatine is dissolved.
7 Add the grated orange rind, 4 tablespoons orange juice, and sugar.
8 Cool, then fold in the whipped cream – save a little.
9 Allow this mixture to begin to stiffen a little, then fold in the chopped glacé cherries, diced angelica and the pieces of pulp from 1 orange.
10 Pour on to the set orange jelly, cover with the unset portion of cool clear orange liquid.
11 Allow to set, turn out and decorate with a little cream.

Note: for a more economical filling, use whipped evaporated milk rather than whipped cream – you will need the same quantity of evaporated milk. To whip, see directions on page 191.

Speedy Meal
Use orange squash instead of orange juice at stages 2 and 7, and add chopped canned mandarin oranges at stage 9. The syrup from the can could be used in place of some of the water at stages 2 and 6. Omit stage 3 if using canned mandarin oranges, and reduce sugar slightly.

Mixer
Use for whipping the cream, and for extracting the orange juice if you have an attachment for this purpose.

Home Freezing
Freezes excellently, see comments on moulds, etc., page 185. When set turn out on to flat container, freeze and wrap, or set and freeze in waxed container. Keeps 3 months. Defrost at room temperature.

Basic ice creams

Ice cream can be made from all cream, Recipe 1, lightened with egg whites, or it can be made with half thick custard and half cream plus egg whites (see variations) or you can use a marshmallow base as in first recipe, and the variations on the next page. One needs a reasonable amount of fat content in ice cream frozen in a refrigerator or home freezer.

Cream Ice

Serves 4–5
Freezing time 1½–2 hours

Ingredients	Metric	Imperial
thick cream *or* thick and thin cream	284 ml (generous ¼ litre)	½ pint
icing sugar	50 grammes	2 oz.
flavouring	see below	see below
egg whites	2	2

1 Whip the cream, or whip first the thick cream then whip in the single cream; add the sieved sugar and flavouring.
2 Whisk the egg whites until very stiff, fold into the cream mixture and freeze until firm: there is no need to beat this ice cream during freezing. If wished the egg yolks could be beaten with the sugar, and added to the whipped cream at stage 1.

Mixer

A delicious ice cream, rather like the 'old-fashioned' Italian ices, is made if you beat the egg yolks and sugar with the whisk until very thick, then add the whipped cream, flavouring, etc.

It is very important that cream is not over-beaten in an ice cream; it gives a very solid almost 'buttery' texture to the dessert. If you have made the cream too solid; dilute with a little milk or top of the milk and blend very gently.

Home Freezing

Ice cream from a freezer is very hard, so it needs longer than ice cream made in the freezing compartment of most refrigerators, to become the right consistency to serve.

Take out of the freezer about 1 hour before needed. Watch rather carefully, then put into freezing compartment of the refrigerator when 'just right'.

Some variations on Cream Ice

CUSTARD CREAM ICE: use 284 ml (½ pint) thick sweetened custard and the same amount of cream. If making the custard with eggs use 2 egg yolks, but not the whites. Add the sugar to the cream and flavouring, blend with the *cold* custard, then freeze until *beginning* to thicken. Remove from the trays or freezing utensils, beat well, and fold in the stiffly beaten egg whites, then return to freezer.

ECONOMY ICE CREAM: use whipped evaporated milk, see page 191, instead of cream, in the cream or custard cream ice.

FLAVOURINGS FOR ICE CREAM: blend melted chocolate or chocolate powder with the ingredients; or flavour with instant coffee powder or coffee syrup (not liquid coffee, which is too 'watery')–amount depends on personal taste.
Add various essences to flavour.
Add various sweetened fruit purées (use twice the amount of cream, or custard and cream, as fruit purée).
Add pieces of chocolate; delicious in a coffee ice cream.
Add chopped nuts; raisins, etc., soaked in rum; liqueurs, etc.

Mixer

Whisk the custard, or, emulsify in the liquidiser before adding to the cream. The whisk is ideal for beating the lightly frozen custard and cream mixture, then for whisking the egg whites, but fold egg whites into the custard gently by hand.

Home Freezing

Ice trays give a very small depth of ice cream, so use deep ovenproof casseroles, etc., for either the freezing compartment or the freezer.

Note: when adding fruit purée, liqueurs, etc., to ice cream, make sure the mixture is not over-sweet. Too much sugar also hinders freezing; an 'over-dose' of sugar completely prevents freezing.

To make Sorbets

These delicious iced mixtures were once served in between various courses at banquets as they were so refreshing. Today, when eating habits are more abstemious, they are generally served as a dessert. To make a Sorbet to serve 4–6 people, you need:

1 A *thin* fruit purée made by cooking about ½ kilo (1 lb.) fruit (gooseberries, loganberries or other fruits) with about 284 ml (½ pint) water and sugar to taste, or use approximately 568 ml (1 pint) sweetened orange, lemon or other fruit juices.
2 Dissolve 1 teaspoon powder gelatine in a little hot purée or liquid blend in–this helps to keep the Sorbet smooth.
3 Freeze until slightly thickened, remove and beat, then fold in 2 stiffly beaten egg whites and freeze again.

WATER ICES are made as Sorbets, but use only 1 egg white instead of 2.

Mixer

The liquidiser gives a very smooth fruit purée. Also whisk egg whites until very stiff, and beat the partially frozen fruit.

Home Freezing

See the comments about bringing ice creams out of a freezer some little while before serving, for this applies to sorbets too. One very attractive way to freeze and serve sorbets (lemon and orange) is to freeze in hollowed out cases of fresh orange or lemon.

Marshmallow Cherry Ice Cream

Serves 6–8
Freezing time–see method

Ingredients	Metric	Imperial
marshmallows	150 grammes	6 oz.
milk	142 ml	¼ pint
cream (you can use	284 ml	½ pint
½ single and ½ double)	(generous ¼ litre)	
chopped cherries,		
(Maraschino are best)	50 grammes	2 oz.
chopped walnuts	50 grammes	2 oz.
sugar	25 grammes	1 oz.

Mixer
The mixer is necessary only for whipping the cream; this must be done carefully, so it is not too thick; see comments on previous page.

Home Freezing
This is a very 'good-tempered' ice cream that never becomes too solid. There are no complications about freezing this.

1 Melt half the marshmallows with the milk; allow to cool.
2 Chop the rest of the marshmallows (damp kitchen scissors are ideal for this).
3 Whip the cream until it just holds its shape–if using a mixture of cream, whip the double cream until nearly firm then gradually whip in the single cream.
4 Add rest of ingredients, put into the freezing dish/tray.
5 If using an old refrigerator without star marking, set as page 196. Put into freezing compartment of the refrigerator or the home freezer.
6 The freezing time in a refrigerator will probably be 2–3 hours; in the coldest position in a home freezer approximately 1½–2 hours.

Variations on Marshmallow Cherry Ice Cream

BLACK CHERRY ICE CREAM : use canned or fresh stoned black cherries, dissolve marshmallows in liquid from can instead of milk, add little cherry brandy, if wished.
MOCHA ICE CREAM : dissolve the marshmallows in *very* strong coffee; omit cherries, add chopped *plain* chocolate instead.
ORANGE ICE CREAM : dissolve the marshmallows in concentrated orange juice (frozen type) instead of milk; flavour with a little curaçao if wished.
PINEAPPLE OR APRICOT : add 150 grammes (6 oz.) chopped fresh or drained canned pineapple, or apricots, at stage 4.

Home Freezing
Remember marshmallows are very sweet, so when adding other ingredients, particularly sweetened liqueurs, you must not be too generous otherwise the sugar content is too high.

Melon Supreme

Serves 6–8
Cooking time–none

Ingredients	Metric	Imperial
ripe melon	1 large	1 large
sherry	1–2 tablespoons	1–2 tablespoons
ice cream	portions for	portions for
see page 196	6–8	6–8
Maraschino, fresh *or*		
canned cherries	3–4 tablespoons	3–4 tablespoons

Mixer
The mixer is valuable when making the ice cream, see page 196.

Slimming Tips
Melon is very low in calories so is an ideal dessert as well as an excellent hors d'oeuvre. This dessert is equally good topped with a sorbet rather than a cream ice, and these are very much less fattening. Another suggestion for 'slimmers' is to top the balls of melon or diced melon with fresh orange and tangerine segments.

1 Insert the tip of a sharp knife into the centre of the melon and make a downwards cut; now make one upwards.
2 Continue like this until the melon has been cut in two halves, see picture facing page 185.
3 Remove the seeds from the centre of the melon, then cut the pulp away either making neat balls with a vegetable scoop or dicing this.
4 Replace the melon pulp into one half of the melon, flavour with sherry and chill thoroughly.
5 Take full scoops or spoons of ice cream and arrange over the fruit.
6 Top with the cherries, then arrange the melon lid lightly on top and serve.

Home Freezing
See the comments about freezing melon on page 209.

Hot Puddings and Sauces

There are a variety of puddings in this section, ranging from rich fruit puddings, to light steamed sponges, milk puddings and custards. Many of the 'old-fashioned' puddings take a considerable time to make: this is why I have concentrated on hints as to how they can be made more easily and quickly.

Metric Conversions

The importance of an *accurate* conversion from Imperial to Metric measurements will vary according to the *type* of recipe. In sponge and other steamed puddings it is nearly as important as for cakes, so read the comments on page 171.

Using a mixer for hot puddings

A mixer is invaluable for making many types of puddings. You will use the whisk or beater for creaming the fat and sugar in sponge mixtures, or for blending all the ingredients together in the 'quick-mix' type of pudding on page 202. An electric whisk produces a splendid meringue mixture for topping puddings, or adding to the mixture as the soufflé type mixture on page 190. Use the liquidiser for making crumbs, 'chopping' suet, lemon rind, etc., in rich puddings such as the Golden orange pudding on page 203. An egg custard sauce, or a pudding based on an egg custard, curdles very easily if cooked too quickly. Should this happen tip the mixture into the warmed liquidiser goblet, add another egg and emulsify together. You will have a very smooth custard again, which just needs heating *gently*. The reason for adding the extra egg is that the liquidiser tends to make the custard thinner in consistency and you need the fresh egg to compensate for this. Other hints on using the mixer are given by each recipe.

Cooking hot puddings in the automatic oven

In several menus in this book it has been suggested that a pudding one normally 'steams' should be cooked in the oven, as part of an automatic meal.

Oven-cooking of sponge, fruit puddings, etc., is quite possible. Make the pudding in the usual way; put into the basin and cover this. Stand the basin in a deep tin (a cake tin without a loose base is ideal), and fill the space between the basin and the tin with cold water. Cover both the basin and the tin with a tightly sealed layer of foil so the water does not evaporate, then cook as directed. See details by each recipe.

When making milk puddings and custards it is less difficult, for one so often *measures* the rice or other cereal, and custards are based on the *number* of eggs. The ½ litre (500 ml) is, as you know, less than 1 pint (568 ml), so you would have slightly less custard mixture, and it would tend to thicken more, since you have a slightly more generous proportion of eggs to liquid.

In the baked and steamed puddings, where the proportions of flour, sugar, etc., are given in the form of the accepted conversion, i.e. 25 grammes as 1 oz., you will make a slightly smaller pudding when following the metric calculations.

If you do not mind this, then use the conversion in the recipe, but if you feel you need a slightly bigger pudding, then add a few extra grammes to each ingredient. The difference in the cooking time will be relatively negligible.

Home freezing of hot puddings

Information is given by each recipe, for in this section there are such variations in recipes one cannot give general advice.

Saving time when making hot puddings

Many standard type puddings can be prepared or cooked in a very short time, so see the comments by each recipe.

Drinks to serve with hot puddings

Wines that are suitable to serve with hot puddings are similar to those suggested under Cold desserts on page 185.

Apple Fritters

Serves 4–5
Cooking time 7–8 minutes

Ingredients	Metric	Imperial
FOR THE BATTER:		
self-raising flour	100 grammes	4 oz.
salt	pinch	pinch
egg	1	1
milk *or* milk and water	142 ml	¼ pint
cooking apples	2–3 large	2–3 large
flour	1 tablespoon	1 tablespoon
TO FRY:		
deep or shallow oil *or* fat		
TO COAT:		
castor sugar	25–50 grammes	1–2 oz.

1 Make the batter by blending all the ingredients together.
2 Peel, core and cut the apples into ½-cm (¼-inch) slices (or slightly thicker), dust with flour so the batter 'sticks'. Dip in batter.
3 Heat the oil or fat, test as page 47, put in the fritters, cook until golden on outside; then lower heat to make sure they are cooked. If using shallow fat, turn during cooking.
4 Bring out, drain on absorbent paper and coat in sugar.

Note: it is important to lower the heat at stage 3, after setting the batter, so the apple cooks.

Variations on Apple Fritters

BANANA FRITTERS: use halved bananas; the cooking time can be a little less, since bananas cook quicker.
PINEAPPLE FRITTERS: use well drained rings of canned or fresh pineapple, dust lavishly with flour, then dip in batter.

Baked Apples

Serves 4
Cooking time see stage 3
Oven temperature see stage 3

Ingredients	Metric	Imperial
cooking apples	4	4
sugar	to taste	to taste

1 Core the apples, then slit the skin round the centre so they will not 'burst' during cooking, and to make the skin easier to remove.
2 Put into an ovenproof dish–a little water can be added to make sure they do not stick.
3 Fill the centres with sugar and bake in the centre of the oven. Cooking times naturally depend upon the *size* of the apple, and the cooking temperature can be adjusted *slightly* to fit into automatic menus, see opposite, but a medium sized apple takes approximately 50–60 minutes in the centre of a moderate oven. Serve with custard sauce, page 207.

Variations on Baked Apples

TO STUFF BAKED APPLES: fill with dried fruit, nuts, jam, crushed blackberries, or golden syrup and crumbs.
MERINGUE APPLES: bake apples, remove skins, coat 4 apples with a meringue made of 3 egg whites, 75 grammes (3 oz.) sugar. Set for about 20 minutes in a very moderate oven.

Speedy Meal

The fruit could be dusted in flour, then fried, without making the batter; obviously the dessert is not the same, but if served with cream or a custard sauce, page 207, they are delicious.
Bread fritters: cut rounds of bread, then dip in sweetened egg, diluted with a very little milk. Fry in hot butter or margarine until brown and crisp on both sides. Serve with hot jam or marmalade sauce, page 207, or custard sauce.

Mixer

This could be used for making the batter, see page 160.

Home Freezing

The cooked fritters could be frozen for a few days, then heated through on ovenproof plates in the oven, to restore crispness.

Automatic Oven

The cooking times of apples may be adjusted so that a medium apple will bake in 40–50 minutes in a moderately hot oven (do not exceed this temperature, otherwise the outside of the apple will be cooked too much, and the inside will be raw). If more convenient, allow about 1¼ hours in a very moderate oven. Remember you can also adjust the cooking time slightly by the position in the oven.

Speedy Meal

One can 'bake' an apple in a pressure cooker; allow about 10 minutes at 5 lb. pressure.

Slimming Tips

A baked apple can be served on a slimming diet. Choose an apple that is both a dessert and cooking apple so it is not too sharp in flavour. Serve with nutmeg flavoured natural yoghourt.

Home Freezing

A very good cooking apple can be frozen whole for a limited time, but this is rather pointless since perfect cooking apples store for some months under the correct conditions.

Hot Fruit Soufflé

Serves 4–5
Cooking time 40 minutes
Oven temperature 350–375° F. (180–190° C.), Gas Mark 4–5

Ingredients	Metric	Imperial
thick fruit purée	142 ml	¼ pint
cornflour	1 tablespoon	1 tablespoon
sugar	to taste	to taste
eggs	4	4
TO COAT :		
icing sugar	1 tablespoon	1 tablespoon

1 Blend the fruit purée with the cornflour and enough sugar to sweeten; cook until smooth, stir well.
2 Separate egg yolks and whites; stir beaten yolks into the mixture, then fold in the stiffly whisked whites.
3 Put into a greased 13–15-cm (5–6-inch) soufflé dish; bake in the centre of a very moderate to moderate oven, until firm and golden coloured.
4 Dust with sieved icing sugar and serve at once with cream.

Automatic Oven
Unfortunately you cannot cook the soufflés in an automatic oven; they must be cooked as soon as prepared.

Speedy Meal
Blend the egg whites with a thick fruit purée, and bake for about 15–20 minutes in a hot oven, then serve. Use the yolks for custards, etc.

Mixer
The liquidiser will give a very smooth fruit purée, and you can incorporate the egg yolks, stage 2. You can also emulsify the cornflour mixture and egg yolks in the liquidiser, if wished. Tip back into a pan or basin, then add the egg whites. Use the whisk, not the liquidiser, for whisking the egg whites.

Home Freezing
The mixture will not freeze well.

Soufflés based on Hot Fruit Soufflé

LIQUEUR SOUFFLÉ NO. 1: use the recipe for the fruit soufflé above, add 1–2 tablespoons liqueur with the sugar. I would suggest apricot brandy with an apricot purée; cherry brandy with a cherry or apple or redcurrant purée; brandy with an orange purée, etc. Proceed as the recipe above. The mixture is slightly softer, but this is very pleasant. Serve with cream or with the hot creamy liqueur sauce on page 207.

LIQUEUR SOUFFLÉ NO. 2: omit the fruit purée and use the same amount of milk, i.e. 142 ml (¼ pint). Blend the cornflour with this and thicken, then add 25 grammes (1 oz.) butter to give a creamier taste, 2 tablespoons of any liqueur–crème de menthe is delicious–and about 25 grammes (1 oz.) sugar. Add the egg yolks and mix well, then proceed as the Hot fruit soufflé, stage 3, above. Serve with clear liqueur sauce on page 207.

PINEAPPLE SOUFFLÉ: use canned pineapple and dice about 100 grammes (4 oz.). Measure the syrup from the can and if necessary add enough water or lemon juice to give 142 ml (¼ pint). Blend the cornflour with this and thicken as stage 1 in the first recipe on this page. Add the diced pineapple and a very little sugar if required. Proceed as stage 2 onwards in the recipe. Serve with ice cream or cream.

VANILLA SOUFFLÉ: infuse a vanilla pod for about 10 minutes in 142 ml (¼ pint) warm milk, or flavour this with ½ teaspoon vanilla essence. Blend the milk with the cornflour, remove the pod first, add 25 grammes (1 oz.) butter and 50 grammes (2 oz.) sugar, then proceed as the Hot fruit soufflé, above. Serve with cream or a hot jam sauce, page 207.

TO USE VANILLA POD
Mention is often made of a vanilla pod. You can buy these from a good grocer or store, and there are generally several in a polythene tube. To use in liquids, put the pod in the milk, or other liquid, and let it infuse with the warm liquid for as long as possible. Remove, rinse in cold water, leave to dry, store, then use again.

Speedy Meal
If you keep one or two cut vanilla pods, with the cut ends downwards, in a jar of sugar, you give a definite and very delicious vanilla flavour to the sugar, which can then be used in all recipes.

French Rice Pudding

Serves 4–6
Cooking time 1¼–2 hours
Oven temperature see stage 6

Ingredients	Metric	Imperial
FOR THE CARAMEL:		
sugar	75 grammes	3 oz.
water	6 tablespoons	6 tablespoons
FOR THE PUDDING:		
short grain (Carolina) rice	2 tablespoons	2 tablespoons
milk	568 ml (generous ½ litre)	1 pint
sugar	25 grammes	1 oz.
glacé cherries	25–50 grammes	1–2 oz.
sultanas	25–50 grammes	1–2 oz.

1 Put the sugar and 3 tablespoons of the water into a strong saucepan, stir until the sugar has dissolved, then boil, without stirring, until golden brown.
2 Stir in the rest of the water; the caramel forms a firm ball, but soon dissolves in the rest of the water over a gentle heat.
3 Put the caramel into the bottom of an ovenproof pie dish; leave this to cool slightly.
4 Heat the rice with the milk for 10 minutes until it begins to stiffen slightly, then add the sugar and the rest of the ingredients.
5 Spoon carefully into the dish, so you leave the caramel undisturbed as much as possible.
6 Bake for about an hour in a very moderate oven, or for nearly two hours in a cool oven, until the rice mixture is creamy. Serve hot, or allow to cool and top with cream.

Note: to make a rich pudding, use half milk and half thin cream.

Automatic Oven
The milk puddings can either be cooked more slowly than the time given (the slower the cooking the creamier the texture), or slightly quicker if it fits in with particular automatic menu. Keep the dish in the coolest part of the oven so the top does not become over-cooked. The Soufflé rice pudding is not suitable for an automatic menu.

Speedy Meal
Use the very excellent canned creamed rice for all these recipes:
a) *French rice pudding:* make and use the caramel, then blend the cherries and sultanas with the creamed rice and heat for about 30 minutes;
b) *Family rice pudding:* simply heat and serve;
c) *Soufflé rice pudding:* add the egg yolks and whites as stated, and bake for the time given.

Note: other cereals could be used instead.

Home Freezing
Rice puddings do not freeze well.

Family Rice Pudding

Serves 4
Cooking time 1½–2 hours
Oven temperature 300° F. (150° C.), Gas Mark 2

Ingredients	Metric	Imperial
short grain (Carolina) rice	2 tablespoons	2 tablespoons
sugar	25 grammes	1 oz.
milk	568 ml (generous ½ litre)	1 pint
butter *or* suet	small knob	small knob

1 Put the rice in a pie dish with the other ingredients.
2 Cook in a slow to very moderate oven until creamy. Stir once or twice, if possible, during cooking.

Soufflé Rice Pudding

1 Use proportions of rice, sugar and milk as in the French rice pudding above.
2 Simmer gently in a saucepan on a low heat, or in the top of a double saucepan, stirring well until a thickened mixture.
3 Cool slightly, beat in 2–3 egg yolks, 2–3 *stiffly* beaten egg whites blended with another 25 grammes (1 oz.) sugar.
4 Spoon carefully into a deep pie dish, bake for about 30–40 minutes, depending upon the depth of the mixture.
5 Serve at once, topped with sieved icing sugar and with a hot jam sauce, page 207. Serves 5–6.

Steamed Puddings

Whatever type of pudding is steamed, with the exception of an egg custard pudding, it is important that the water boils *rapidly* during the first hour of cooking. This is to make sure the pudding rises well, or sets well. In the case of a pudding based on an egg custard, as page 187, it is important that the water *never* boils, but just remains very hot.

Golden Fruit Pudding

Serves 4–6
Cooking time 1¼–1¾ hours

Ingredients	Metric	Imperial
FOR THE PUDDING:		
self-raising flour	75 grammes	3 oz.
breadcrumbs	75 grammes	3 oz.
shredded suet *or*	75 grammes	3 oz.
melted margarine		
sugar	75 grammes	3 oz.
mixed dried fruit	125 grammes	5 oz.
milk	to bind	to bind
TO COAT BASIN:		
margarine	small knob	small knob
golden syrup	2 tablespoons	2 tablespoons

1 Mix all the pudding ingredients together, add enough milk to give a sticky consistency; do not make this too dry.
2 Rub margarine round inside of a 1½–2-pint (1-litre) basin, add golden syrup then the pudding mixture; leave enough room in the basin to rise.
3 Cover with greased greaseproof paper (it is a good idea to grease the paper on both sides to keep the top of the pudding dry), then cover with foil.
4 Steam over boiling water for the longer period if using suet, or the shorter time with melted margarine.
5 Serve hot with custard sauce, page 207, or with more syrup, see picture facing page 153.

Puddings based on the Golden Fruit Pudding

APRICOT PUDDING: put whole or halved fresh apricots with sugar to sweeten, or well drained soaked, dried, or canned apricots, at the bottom of the basin. Mix the pudding with apricot syrup if you have used dried or canned fruit. Many other fruits–fresh and canned or dried–can be used.

FRUIT PUDDING: omit the golden syrup coating round the basin.

RED CAP PUDDING: use red jam at the bottom of the pudding, and omit the dried fruit in the pudding itself.

SPONGE PUDDINGS

Follow the directions on page 212 for the Victoria sandwich mixture, for this makes an excellent steamed pudding. To make a more economical mixture, omit 25 grammes (1 oz.) each of margarine and of sugar, bind with 1 egg instead of 2, plus 3 tablespoons milk or fruit juice, etc.
TO COOK THE SPONGE PUDDING: put into a greased basin, cover the top with greased paper, see previous page, and steam for about 1¼–1½ hours.
TO FLAVOUR THE SPONGE PUDDING: omit 25 grammes (1 oz.) flour and use same amount of cocoa; mix with 3 tablespoons strong coffee and 1 egg; put jam, golden syrup, etc., at bottom of basin as in Golden fruit pudding; add grated lemon rind, etc.

Automatic Oven

Read the instructions on page 198 about 'oven-steaming' of puddings; for this is typical of the kind of pudding that can be cooked in a moderate oven for about the same time as in a steamer. Be careful that the water in the tin, etc., does not boil into the pudding; cover well and do not have too much water.
The golden syrup coating on the outside could scorch in the oven; either omit this and heat the syrup separately, or protect the outside of the basin with foil.

Speedy Meal

There are many canned or ready-prepared fruit and plain puddings available. For a new taste, put in the basin the margarine and syrup, or the fruit as recipes opposite, add pudding, steam for 30 minutes only.

Mixer

The liquidiser can 'shred' the type of suet you buy from the butcher. Put this in with the bread when making breadcrumbs.

Home Freezing

Any of these puddings would freeze after cooking, and could be heated through for a further 1 hour–be careful (if you freeze in a breakable basin) that you allow this to stand for a while in the room before heating. Can also be frozen uncooked; would take same cooking time after defrosting. Use within about 3 months.

Automatic Oven

Use a moderate heat; if *too low* the pudding would be heavy; if *too high*, it would scorch.

Speedy Meal

Use the one stage mix method for making sponge puddings. Add 1 level teaspoon baking powder to give extra lightness.

Mixer

The whisk is excellent for creaming the 'proper' sponge pudding, or as above.

Golden Orange Pudding

Serves 6–8
Cooking time 2–2½ hours

Ingredients	Metric	Imperial
white bread–	150 grammes	6 oz.
without crusts		
oranges	2 large	2 large
orange marmalade	5 tablespoons	5 tablespoons
butter	75 grammes	3 oz.
light brown sugar	75 grammes	3 oz.
self-raising flour	75 grammes	3 oz.
egg yolks	4	4
glacé cherries	50 grammes	2 oz.
seedless raisins	75–100 grammes	3–4 oz.
sultanas	75–100 grammes	3–4 oz.
currants (optional)	25 grammes	1 oz.

1 Cut the bread into small cubes, put into a basin.
2 Grate the orange rind finely, put on one side, squeeze out the juice, if necessary add water to give 8 tablespoons.
3 Heat the orange juice and marmalade, pour over the cubes of bread and leave for about 10 minutes; this is what gives the pudding the 'sticky' look in the picture, between pages 152/153.
4 Cream butter, orange rind and sugar until soft and light, then stir in the remaining ingredients.
5 Lastly, add the bread and marmalade mixture; mix gently, put into a greased tin, as in the picture, or basin.
6 Although this pudding does have flour, etc., it is very light in texture and better steamed *gently*; allow 2 hours over water that does not boil too quickly, if using the more shallow tin, or 2½ hours in a basin.
7 Turn out carefully, serve with Marmalade sauce, page 207.

Automatic Oven

This pudding can be cooked in the oven as part of a menu that needs fairly slow cooking. As you will see from the picture, it is a large pudding, so for a smaller family use half quantities, and cook for about 1¼–1½ hours.

Speedy Meal

Omit stages 1 and 2 and mix everything together. You have a very delicious light but more 'ordinary' pudding.
Cook for 15–20 minutes at 5 lb. pressure in a pressure cooker.

Mixer

Use this for creaming butter, etc., at stage 4, but do *not* mix the pudding at stage 5 with an electric mixer as this would break the bread completely.

Home Freezing

This pudding can be frozen before or after cooking; either way it is excellent. If freezing before cooking, thaw out and then cook as the recipe. If freezing after cooking, defrost slightly, then steam gently for 1 hour.

Cabinet Pudding

Cut the crusts from 2 large slices of white bread, dice the bread. Heat 284 ml (½ pint) milk, pour over the bread and allow to stand for about 10 minutes. Beat 4 egg yolks with 50 grammes (2 oz.) sugar, add another 284 ml (½ pint) warm milk flavoured with vanilla, see page 200. Pour over the bread. Grease a basin well, cover base with dried fruit, spoon in the bread mixture and steam as Golden orange pudding, above, for 2 hours. Turn out and decorate with castor sugar.

Automatic Oven

Can be baked in a container of water.

Speedy Meal

Make custard with powder, beat in 2 eggs, pour over cubes of bread, put into basin lined with fruit, steam for 45 minutes.

Home Freezing

See comments above.

Christmas Pudding

Read page 198, for the amount of mixture will be appreciably less with metric measurements, and this is a case when you may like to weigh 110 grammes of each item (instead of 100 grammes) to give an amount nearer the Imperial measure.

Mix together 100 grammes (4 oz.) of each of the following: breadcrumbs, flour, shredded suet, brown sugar, currants, sultanas, grated cooking apple, grated raw carrot, chopped candied peel, chopped blanched almonds. Then add 225–250 grammes (9–10 oz.) seedless or chopped stoned raisins, 50 grammes (2 oz.) chopped glacé cherries, 1 teaspoon each mixed spice, cinnamon, and 1 tablespoon black treacle or golden syrup. Bind with 2 eggs and 142 ml (¼ pint) ale, milk or fruit juice. Put into the basin, or basins, and cover very well. Steam or boil for 4–6 hours, remove wet covers and put on fresh ones. Store in a cool dry place. Serves 10–12.

On Christmas Day, re-steam for another 2–3 hours. Serve with sherry or custard sauce, or brandy butter.

Automatic Oven

The pudding can be cooked entirely in a slow oven, allow about 6 hours and cook in a container of water, see page 198. On Christmas Day it can be reheated in the same way. This saves any problem of water 'boiling dry' under the steamer.

Speedy Meal

Cook in a pressure cooker for 1½–2 hours at 15 lb. pressure. This does slightly alter the flavour, though; the great heat causes the sugar to caramel, and the pudding is less sweet.
Moisten the Christmas puddings you buy with brandy, ale, etc., to give a better flavour before heating.

Mixer

For a very smooth texture, put all the fruit through the mincer. Make crumbs in liquidiser.

Apricot and Prune Upside Down Pudding

Serves 4–6
Cooking time 2¼ hours
Oven temperature 375° F. (190° C.), Gas Mark 4–5

Ingredients	Metric	Imperial
FOR THE BASE OF THE PUDDING:		
dried apricots	100–150 grammes	4–6 oz.
dried prunes	100–150 grammes	4–6 oz.
water	to cover fruit	to cover fruit
butter	25 grammes	1 oz.
sugar–brown or white	25 grammes	1 oz.
FOR THE PUDDING:		
margarine or butter	generous 100 grammes	4 oz.
castor sugar	generous 100 grammes	4 oz.
large eggs	2	2
self-raising flour	150–175 grammes*	6 oz.
milk	to mix	to mix

*this gives a better result than the accepted conversion.

1 Put the apricots and prunes into a basin, cover with cold water and leave overnight.
2 Simmer gently for about 1¼–1½ hours, then drain well; any liquid left can be used in a jelly or thickened to serve as a sauce with this sweet.
3 Grease the bottom of a 23–25-cm (9–10-inch) square tin with most of the butter, then grease and flour the sides of the tin.
4 Sprinkle the sugar over the butter at the bottom and arrange the dried fruit in lines or squares.
5 Cream the margarine and sugar until soft and light.
6 Gradually beat in the eggs, then add the sieved flour.
7 Finally add enough milk to mix; do not make too soft as the fruit at the base of the tin produces considerable moisture; it should be a slow dropping consistency.
8 Spread over the fruit and bake in the centre of a moderate oven for approximately 45 minutes, or until firm to the touch; reduce the heat to very moderate after 25 minutes if becoming too brown.
9 Turn out and serve hot or cold as a dessert, or for tea.

Automatic Oven

Upside down puddings are a favourite to leave in an automatic oven. As you will see from the examples opposite, the cooking time can be adjusted by the depth of the mixture used. To ensure that the outside of the pudding does not become too brown wrap foil around the outside of the tin or dish, and lay a piece lightly over the top of the container. Allow room for the pudding to rise.

Speedy Meal

Use quick creaming margarine. Put all the ingredients into a basin (allow about 2 tablespoons milk) then cream together. When well blended test the consistency; see stage 7, opposite.
You can use a pressure cooker for cooking dried apricots and prunes. Allow about 10 minutes cooking at 15 lb. pressure, then allow pressure to drop gradually.

Home Freezing

This is the type of pudding that freezes perfectly. You may either freeze the mixture before or after cooking. If freezing *before* cooking, use about 2½ tablespoons milk, as the freezing tends to dry it a little. Defrost before cooking. If freezing after cooking: cool, freeze then turn out of the tin (if more convenient) and wrap. To reheat allow to thaw out and heat gently in the greased tin. This should be used within 1–2 months if uncooked, or 3–4 months if cooked.

Ginger Pear Upside Down Pudding

1 Ingredients for the pudding as above, but sieve 1–2 teaspoons powdered ginger with flour; use about 8 halved well drained canned pears, instead of the apricots and prunes and put tiny pieces of preserved ginger *with* the pears at the bottom of the pudding.
2 This pudding is suggested as part of an automatic meal taking 1¼–1½ hours, see page 58. Naturally you must use a deeper container to slow up the cooking so choose an 18–20-cm (7–8-inch) tin or ovenproof glass dish, and bake more slowly, i.e. 1¼–1½ hours in a very moderate to moderate oven.
If *your* particular oven is fierce, read the comments opposite.

Spiced Pineapple Upside Down Pudding

Use the Apricot and prune recipe above, but substitute drained rings of pineapple, and arrange on the butter and sugar at stage 4. Blend 1 tablespoon golden syrup and 1 tablespoon canned pineapple syrup; spoon over the fruit. Use the ingredients for the pudding, but sieve 1 teaspoon mixed spice with the flour and omit the milk, to give a more crumbly texture; bake as above.

Peach Meringue

Serves 4–5
Cooking time–see stage 6
Oven temperature–see stage 6

Ingredients	Metric	Imperial
canned peach halves	8–10*	8–10*
FOR THE TOPPING:		
almonds	75 grammes	3 oz.
egg whites	3 large	3 large
castor sugar	75 grammes**	3 oz.**

*if serving these with ice cream you can allow 1 per person.
**see note at end of recipe.

1 Open the can of peaches and lift out the fruit.
2 Put into an ovenproof or heatproof dish with 2–3 tablespoons of syrup from the can.
3 Blanch almonds–to do this, put into a basin and pour over boiling water, or put into a saucepan and bring just to the boil; do not over-heat otherwise the almonds lose their firm texture. The skins then come away easily.
4 While making the meringue, brown almonds for a few minutes under the grill or in the oven.
5 Whisk egg whites until very stiff, gradually beat in sugar, and add coarsely chopped almonds.
6 Pile on top of each peach; either bake for approximately 15 minutes in a very moderate oven, or brown for 2–3 minutes only, under the grill.

Note: as canned peaches are very sweet, it would spoil this recipe if the sugar was increased, but it means that the meringue will tend to become rather wrinkled if served cold. So it is better to serve it hot, see picture facing page 152.

Speedy Meal

Put a few marshmallows in each peach half instead of making the meringue, and brown for about 1 minute under a hot grill.

Mixer

Use the whisk for beating the egg whites until stiff, see comments on meringues page 193.

Home Freezing

Unfortunately, frozen peach halves are disappointing. As you see in the information at the end of this chapter, it is recommended that peaches are sliced before freezing. If you care to freeze just a few skinned peach halves in a heavy lemon flavoured sugar syrup you can–use minimum of 200–225 grammes (8 oz.) sugar to each 500 ml (1 pint) liquid–but use the peaches fairly soon after freezing, since the pulp becomes soft and loses a lot of flavour when frozen in large pieces such as whole or halved.

Ratafia Pudding

Prepare a custard by whisking 2 large eggs with 25 grammes (1 oz.) sugar and 426 ml (¾ pint) milk. Put 4–5 tablespoons ratafias, recipe below, in a dish with 25 grammes (1 oz.) sultanas, 25 grammes (1 oz.) glacé cherries and 25 grammes (1 oz.) chopped blanched almonds. Pour the custard over, bake in the centre of a very moderate oven for 1 hour.

Automatic Oven

Ratafia pudding can be baked as part of an automatic menu. If ratafias are too costly, use slices of bread and butter, with a little more dried fruit and grated nutmeg or spice to flavour.

Home Freezing
This does not freeze well.

Ratafias

Makes about 36
Cooking time 12 minutes
Oven temperature 350–375° F. (180–190° C.), Gas Mark 4–5

Ingredients	Metric	Imperial
egg whites	2	2
almond essence	few drops	few drops
castor sugar	150 grammes	6 oz.
ground almonds	approx. 125 grammes	approx. 5 oz.
rice paper	as required	as required
glacé cherries	approx. 18	approx. 18
almonds	approx. 18	approx. 18

1 Whisk the egg whites lightly. Add the almond essence, then sugar and ground almonds. If the egg whites are exceptionally large, then work in a little more ground almonds.
2 Roll the mixture into rounds about the size of a walnut, and put, well spaced out, on rice paper. Put a cherry or almond on top of each biscuit.
3 Bake for approximately 12 minutes in the centre of a very moderate to moderate oven. Cut round rice paper when cold.

Fruit Crumble

Serves 4
Cooking time 35–40 minutes
Oven temperature 375° F. (190° C.), Gas Mark 4–5

Ingredients	Metric	Imperial
prepared fruit	½ kilo	1 lb.
sugar	to taste	to taste
water	if required, see stage 1	if required, see stage 1
FOR THE TOPPING:		
margarine	50 grammes	2 oz.
flour	100 grammes (generous measure)	4 oz.
sugar	75 grammes	3 oz.

1 Put the prepared fruit with sugar and any water required into a pie dish; use no water with soft fruits.
2 Heat for about 10–15 minutes in a fairly hot oven.
3 Meanwhile, rub margarine into flour, or use mixer, add the sugar.
4 Sprinkle over the hot fruit, spread flat with a knife.
5 Bake for about 25 minutes until golden brown.

TO VARY A CRUMBLE TOPPING:
ORANGE CRUMBLE: add grated orange rind at stage 4.
COCONUT CRUMBLE: use generous 75 grammes (3 oz.) flour plus 25 grammes (1 oz.) desiccated coconut; this is very good with apples.

Automatic Oven
This is an excellent pudding to include in an automatic oven. If you wish the cooking time in the oven to be extended, do not cook the fruit first, but put in the dish with sugar and water, if required, and cook at a moderate temperature for at least an hour (longer in a cooler oven).

Speedy Meal
There are crumble mixtures on the market; they can often be improved by adding fresh fruit juice to fruit mixture, grated lemon or orange rind to topping.

Home Freezing
There are no problems about freezing this dessert, either cooked or uncooked. If cooked, defrost before heating, if possible. If uncooked, defrost slightly and bake rather more slowly until crisp and brown.

Kent Cherry Cobbler

This pudding is a complete change from a fruit pie:
1 Tip canned cherries into a pie dish, or use about ½ kilo (1 lb.) cherries with a little water and sugar; heat for about 15 minutes until nearly tender.
2 Make scone mixture, page 225, use 100 grammes (4 oz.) flour only. Cut into rounds, as recipe, place these on the hot fruit, sprinkle with little sugar to give a glazed topping.
3 Bake the Cobbler for 10–15 minutes just above centre in a hot oven. Serve hot, dusted with more sugar, and cream.

Note: other fruits may be used in the same way with the scone topping. Vary the scone flavouring; add dried fruit, if wished, to serve on apples, for example. A well-seasoned scone dough instead of a sweetened scone can be used over cooked stewed meat, instead of making pastry.

Automatic Oven
Make sure fruit is nearly tender; cool, then place scone mixture on top. The fruit mixture should be fairly dry, as juice could soak into the scones during standing. Bake for 25 minutes in moderate oven, to heat fruit again and cook scones.

Speedy Meal
Buy scones, split into halves, brush with a little melted butter, sprinkle with sugar.

Home Freezing
Better to freeze separately, fruit and cooked or uncooked scone mixture.

Fruit Charlotte

Serves 4–5
Cooking time 50 minutes
Oven temperature 375° F. (190° C.), Gas Mark 4–5

Ingredients	Metric	Imperial
prepared fruit	½ kilo	1 lb.
sugar	to taste	to taste
water	as required	as required
bread	4 large slices	4 large slices
butter *or* margarine	75 grammes	3 oz.
brown sugar	50 grammes	2 oz.

1 Cook the fruit with sugar to taste and the minimum of water, to give a thick purée.
2 Make bread into coarse crumbs, toss in hot butter or margarine until golden, add the brown sugar.
3 Pack a layer of crumbs and then fruit in a dish, continue like this, ending with crumbs. Bake for 35–40 minutes in a moderate oven. Serve hot with cream.

Automatic Oven
This may be left for a short time in oven ready to cook later. If left too long the crumb mixture tends to become soft; so it is a good idea to turn into a *Brown Betty pudding* (which *should* have a softer crumb mixture), preparing fruit as opposite, with crumbs at base and top of dish only, then before cooking pour over a sauce made of 2 tablespoons golden syrup and 1 tablespoon water. If sliced fruit and sugar are used instead of cooked fruit, for either Charlotte or Brown Betty, cook for about 1¼ hours.

Clear Liqueur Sauce

Serves 4–5
Cooking time 10 minutes

Ingredients	Metric	Imperial
white wine	142 ml	¼ pint
sugar	50 grammes	2 oz.
arrowroot	2 teaspoons	2 teaspoons
water	4 tablespoons	4 tablespoons
liqueur	4 tablespoons	4 tablespoons

1 Put the white wine and sugar into the saucepan, heat gently until the sugar has dissolved.
2 Blend the arrowroot with the water, add to the wine and stir until the mixture begins to thicken and become clear.
3 Stir in the liqueur and serve hot or cold.
4 This is excellent with hot soufflés, or, as a contrast, serve very hot over ice cream.

Some whole fruit can be added at stage 3, if wished:
a) black cherries with cherry brandy;
b) orange segments with curaçao;
c) halved apricots or sliced peaches with apricot brandy.
Instead of white wine, use fresh or canned fruit juice.

Speedy Meal
Simply heat your chosen liqueur with a little orange or lemon juice and use: expensive, but delicious.

Home Freezing
Does not freeze very well and loses flavour.

Creamy Liqueur Sauce

1 Blend 1 level tablespoon cornflour with nearly 284 ml (½ pint) milk, add 1 tablespoon sugar, stir gently until liquid has thickened.
2 Stir in 2–3 tablespoons any liqueur, remove from heat, add 2 tablespoons thick cream. Serves 4–5.

Mixer
The sauce has a velvet-like texture if emulsified for a short time before serving.

Home Freezing
Only freezes well if you use half milk and half thin cream.

Egg Custard Sauce

1 Blend 1 egg or 2 yolks with 1 tablespoon sugar; if you beat these well, you need not strain the custard.
2 Flavour with vanilla, sherry or lemon rind.
3 Add 284 ml (½ pint) warmed milk.
4 Cook in a basin over hot water, or double saucepan, stirring until the mixture coats the back of a wooden spoon.
5 For a change of flavour, add 25–50 grammes (1–2 oz.) chocolate at stage 4; or half milk, half strong coffee at stage 3.

Mixer
See page 198 for advice on using the liquidiser *should* the custard curdle.

Home Freezing
This may be frozen for a very limited period of one week only.

Jam Sauce

1 Blend 1 teaspoon cornflour with 142 ml (¼ pint) water (or use a mixture of water and lemon juice).
2 Put in pan with 5–6 tablespoons jam or jelly, heat gently, stirring well, until smooth and thickened, or emulsify. Serves 4–5.

Many other sauces can be made in the same way:
FRUIT SAUCES: use fruit purée in place of jam.
GOLDEN SYRUP SAUCE: use golden syrup in place of jam.
MARMALADE SAUCE: use marmalade and fresh fruit juice in place of most of the water in the jam sauce recipe.

Speedy Meal
Simply heat diluted jam, or any of the alternatives, with a little water and squeeze of lemon juice.

Home Freezing
The fruit sauce can be frozen; whisk sharply as it heats, or emulsify.

Tutti-Fruitti Sauce

1 Blend 142 ml (¼ pint) orange juice with 2 teaspoons arrowroot or cornflour; cook until thickened.
2 Cool slightly, add 4 tablespoons chopped pineapple, 2 tablespoons sultanas, 2 tablespoons nuts, 8 tablespoons *thin* cream; serve over sponge puddings. Serves 4–5.

Home Freezing
Not a good sauce to freeze.

Home freezing of fruit

Most fresh fruit freezes well in some form or another, and as many desserts can be made from fruit it is wise to have stocks in the freezer. Choose the fruit carefully; it must not be damaged –if parts are bruised cut these away before freezing. Discard over-ripe fruit for it will be very soft when defrosted; and under-ripe fruit which often lacks good flavour and is hard.

There are five ways in which fruit may be frozen, see below. Some fruits (e.g. cooking apples) can be frozen by every one of the five methods; other fruits (e.g. cherries) are better frozen in one way only.

Fruits that are not good when frozen

Bananas should not be frozen by themselves, but they can be frozen as part of desserts and ice cream.

Pears seem to lose much of their flavour. Pineapple is disappointing by itself, but excellent in desserts and ice cream, see page 196.

Most fruit may be stored in the freezer for up to 1 year without appreciable loss of flavour or texture.

Methods of freezing

AS A PURÉE

This is an excellent method of preparing fruit for freezing as you have a concentration of fruit in a comparatively small container. If you are planning to prepare and freeze a generous 568 ml (1 pint) fruit purée for a special container or recipe then you will need to buy just over ½ kilo (a good 1¼ lb.) fruit. This weight refers to the fruit when peeled, etc.

To prepare the purée you either mash or sieve, or liquidise the fruit (with or without sugar as desired); or you cook the fruit, again adding sugar if desired, and turn this into a purée by beating hard or putting through a sieve or into a liquidiser. Put the cold purée into containers, fill these to within 2 cm (approximately ¾ inch) of the top; this allows for expansion as the purée freezes, cover and freeze quickly. If you wish to freeze fruit for someone who cannot have sugar (a diabetic for example) then add sugar substitute when defrosting the fruit. Sugar seems to cause fruit to retain slightly more flavour, but note the amount used so you can work out if any extra is needed in a particular recipe. Unsweetened purée, on the other hand, is more versatile, as you can use it in recipes that require little sugar or for 'slimmers'.

TO DEFROST FRUIT PURÉE: allow to thaw out; to hasten this put the container into cold or warm water. Naturally when the purée is sufficiently defrosted to remove from the container it can be tipped into a pan and heated to hasten defrosting, but this does give the fruit a 'cooked' flavour which you may not like.

TO USE A FRUIT PURÉE: in fruit moulds, page 186, Fruit snow, and Fruit foule, page 189, in various sauces to serve with ice cream, etc., page 196; to turn into jam.

FRUIT JUICE

With citrus fruit you simply squeeze out the juice and sweeten if wished. With soft fruit put through a sieve or into the liquidiser then allow to drip through a jelly bag; sweeten if wished. With hard fruit, simmer with enough water to give a purée, add sugar to taste, if desired, then allow to drip through a jelly bag. Put into suitable containers and proceed as fruit purée.

TO DEFROST FRUIT JUICE: as a purée.

TO USE FRUIT JUICES: lemon juice is always required in recipes, so freeze the juice of lemons when the fruit is cheap. Try to choose very tiny containers so you have only the juice of 1 or 2 lemons in each.

Other fruit juices can be used in desserts and savoury dishes, and to turn into jelly when convenient.

AS UNCOOKED FRUIT IN SUGAR

Prepare the fruit, i.e. cut grapefruit and oranges in segments discarding all pips, pith and skin; halve dessert plums if wished, slice skinned peaches, remove stalks from loganberries, etc. Put a layer of fruit into a container then a sprinkling of sugar.

Continue to put fruit, etc. into container, but fill only to within 2 cm (¾ inch approximately) of the top of the container. Cover and freeze.

TO DEFROST FRUIT: allow plenty of time (several hours) for the fruit to thaw out naturally, but use fairly soon after defrosting as the fruit tends to 'collapse'.

TO USE SWEETENED FRUIT: in any recipe or on any occasion where you would use sweetened fresh fruit.

AS UNCOOKED UNSWEETENED FRUIT

Follow exactly the directions for fruit in sugar. Whereas one *needs* sugar to preserve fruit in jam making, this is not necessary in freezing. I give my own opinion about the value of sugar, etc. by the individual fruits, but this is purely personal taste.

Defrost and use as sweetened fruit.

IN A SUGAR SYRUP

Fruit that is normally cooked, for example, cooking plums, damsons, etc., should be *lightly* cooked in sugar (or honey or golden syrup) and water, cooled, put into containers and frozen. Pack as a purée, but if the fruit is inclined to turn a bad colour if exposed to air above the syrup, place a thick piece of aluminium foil over it, then press down so the foil keeps the fruit *under* the

45. Marmalade, see page 240

syrup. You can freeze the fruit in pie dishes to make a pie later. Do not over-cook the fruit before freezing.

TO DEFROST COOKED FRUIT: as a purée.

TO USE THE COOKED FRUIT: in pies, puddings or as Compôte of fruit, see page 135.

How to freeze fruits

APPLE: choose good cooking apples, peel and drop into salted water (4 level teaspoons to 2 pints cold water). When ready to prepare, rinse and dry. Freeze as a purée; fruit juice (to add to drinks, etc., or make apple jelly when convenient); as unsweetened or sweetened uncooked fruit, or as cooked fruit in a sugar and water syrup.

APRICOT: wash dry then halve and remove stones or keep whole; freeze as apples, except a fruit juice is rather extravagant.

AVOCADO PEAR: freeze as whole fruit though they will become discoloured if over-ripe.

BANANA: only freeze in ice cream or desserts.

BLACKBERRY: wash, and dry. Freeze in all ways, as wished, by themselves or with apples.

BLACKCURRANT: wash, top and tail if wished; freezing allows you to rub off the ends when still frozen. Freeze as purée; a fruit juice (wonderful for drinks); in sugar or without sugar–blackcurrant skins tend to become somewhat hard and tough when frozen raw.
You may need to sieve blackcurrants after defrosting. (Blackcurrants are better simmered in a little water and sugar until skins are tender then frozen.)

BILBERRY: (blueberry) as blackcurrants, but no 'topping and tailing' is necessary and the skins are never hard.

CHERRY: choose cooking cherries or black cherries. Simmer in sugar and water syrup, then freeze.

CRANBERRY: in every way (see apples), most convenient method is a purée for Cranberry sauce.

FIG: Simmer until tender in sugar and water syrup, and freeze.

GOOSEBERRY: see blackcurrants. Can be frozen in all ways but the skins can be tough if not cooked.

GRAPEFRUIT: in segments with or without sugar, see page 208.

GRAPE: skinned if wished and frozen with no sugar, or as part of a fruit salad–loses flavour rather.

GREENGAGE: as apricot.

LEMON: As juice or whole fruit. Freeze, then wrap. A frozen lemon grates very easily for grated lemon rind.

LIME: as lemon.

LOGANBERRY: wash and dry. Can be frozen in every way, depending upon need when thawed out–see apple.

MANGO: as a smooth purée only.

MELON: cut into tiny cubes or balls and freeze in a flavoured sugar and water syrup, see this page.

NECTARINE: best as a purée (sweetened and flavoured with a little lemon juice), or sliced, sprinkled with sugar and frozen.

ORANGE: as lemon. Also freeze orange segments with or without sugar. Freeze whole Seville or bitter oranges for making marmalade when convenient.

PASSION FRUIT: as a purée.

PAW-PAW: as melon.

PEACH: as nectarine.

PEAR: poor in flavour and texture. Only way is to cook in a lemon flavoured syrup, then freeze.

PINEAPPLE: freeze in ice cream or desserts.

PLUM: as apple. They freeze in any way, the skins tend to toughen though, so the best methods are as a sieved purée, a fruit juice, or cooked until tender.

POMEGRANATE: as a sieved purée. Very good as a sauce for ice cream.

QUINCE: as apple.

RASPBERRY: as loganberry but I prefer them frozen whole *without* sugar.

REDCURRANT: as blackcurrant, but no problems about tough skin.

RHUBARB: as apple–can be frozen in all ways.

ROSEHIP: simmer, strain juice, sweeten and freeze. Excellent for drinks.

STRAWBERRY: the 'problem' fruit. Pick or buy when just ripe, wash only if soiled. Arrange on flat trays *without* sugar. Freeze until hard, then pack. Even so, much flavour is lost.

TO EAT FROZEN FRUITS–always serve frozen dessert fruits–raspberries, strawberries, etc., the moment they are defrosted.

Tea-time Recipes

In this chapter you will find the traditional cakes, including a rich fruit cake and Victoria sandwich –with a method for preparing this in minutes– and a wide selection of other tea-time recipes: biscuits and breads, favourite sponges and unusual gâteaux–plus suggestions for freezing these.

Metric Conversions

Before weighing out the ingredients, read through the notes on metric conversion under pastry making, page 171. The same rules apply when making cakes, biscuits and breads of all kinds. The accepted conversion for 1 oz. is 25 grammes not the mathematically correct 28·35 grammes. As *all* ingredients are calculated by this system *All proportions* are correct, and your cakes and other recipes will look and taste the same as usual–your only problem may be in the total amount made, for (as pointed out under pastry) when you multiply 25 grammes by 8 you have considerably less food than 8 oz. (200 grammes instead of the correct 226·80). This may not matter at all, but it does mean you will make a slightly smaller cake than usual, so *watch* the baking time carefully. If more convenient increase the proportions slightly, or follow the directions under Victoria sandwich on page 212, i.e. return to weighing eggs on one side of the scales and the fat, sugar and flour on the other.

Using a mixer for making cakes, etc.

A mixer is a wonderful help in making a great many cakes, biscuits, etc., for it can deal with the 'hard-work' of creaming and beating. But a mixer must be used with thought and care, for cake making (or any form of baking) entails careful preparation of the ingredients; see next page for a definition of the various methods of handling ingredients, and the way in which a mixer can be used to 'copy' hand actions. There is often a mistaken idea that the *more* you beat a cake mixture the better and lighter it will be; that is far from true, many cakes (particularly sponges) are spoiled if the mixture is over-handled. This is why one must regulate the use and speed of a mixer.

Drinks to serve with cakes, etc.

Although this chapter is headed 'Tea-time recipes', there may be occasions when you wish to offer friends a drink. If you have no savoury canapés, etc., to accompany the drinks a finger of rich fruit cake goes well with sherry or champagne, etc.

Speedy ways of preparing tea-time recipes

Most people would like to make their own cakes, biscuits and breads if they had time, but unfortunately most of such recipes do need a fair amount of preparation. So you will find many 'short cuts' or easy alternatives given beside each recipe. Modern quick creaming margarine and fats mean that you can use the 'quick mix' or 'one-stage' method for many cakes, and information about this is given where it is applicable.

Home freezing of cakes and bread

Each recipe in this section mentions the method of freezing; baked foods such as cakes, bread, etc. are highly successful. This means you can always have a supply of cakes and bread available.
In addition to freezing loaves of bread as described on pages 228 onwards, have wrapped sliced bread in the freezer.
You can take out the number of slices required and toast them while still frozen; they will brown and crisp very quickly.

Cooking cakes and bread, etc., in the automatic oven

The automatic cooking of cakes is quite safe if you are *sure* of the baking time. It is probably better to control the oven manually so you can turn down as and when wished. What is so interesting though, is that many kinds of cakes, bread, etc., can be put into a cold oven, so there is no need to switch or turn on the heat before cooking. The exceptions are the 'real' sponge, page 213, Genoese pastry, page 211, scones, page 225.

The correct technique for baking and cake making

It is important to use right method of handling ingredients.
a) BEATING : a brisk blending with a wooden spoon, incorporating air.
b) CREAMING : beating fat and sugar until light in texture.
c) FOLDING : a gentle lift or 'flick' to blend ingredients or mixtures together; use a metal spoon or knife.
d) KNEADING : pushing and stretching dough with heel of hand and fingers to make smooth texture.
e) STIRRING : a brisk circular movement with spoon to mix ingredients.
f) WHISKING : a quick movement with fork or whisk to incorporate air and give light texture.

To test cakes

It is very important to test cakes carefully before removing from the oven or tins, to prevent any possibility of their being undercooked.
a) TO TEST A LIGHT SPONGE TYPE CAKE : press gently but firmly on the top; if no impression is left and the sponge has shrunk *slightly* away from the sides of tin, it is cooked.
b) TO TEST A FAMILY TYPE FRUIT CAKE–as above; if still doubtful, you can insert a very fine warmed plain skewer into the cake; if it comes out 'clean' the cake is cooked.
c) TO TEST A RICH FRUIT CAKE–as a) above; bring the cake out of the oven and listen carefully, if there is no 'humming' sound, the cake is cooked.

Genoese pastry

This pastry is French in origin, and used as the basis of many gâteaux. It has the advantage that it is light in texture (indeed it could be mistaken for a sponge), but the butter content makes it keep moist for several days. Careful handling of the ingredients is the secret of success.

Servings depend on fillings, etc.
Cooking time 15 minutes, or see method
Oven temperature 350–375° F. (180–190 C.), Gas Mark 4–5 or 325–350° F. (170–180°C.), Gas Mark 3–4

Ingredients	Metric	Imperial
eggs	3 large	3 large
castor sugar	100 grammes	4 oz.
butter	75 grammes	3 oz.
self-raising flour*	75 grammes	3 oz.

*the whisking of eggs and sugar incorporates so much air you could use plain flour if wished, but the addition of a small amount of raising agent makes sure the mixture will rise well. If using plain flour, add ½ level teaspoon baking powder.

1 Whisk eggs and sugar until thick, see sponge, page 213.
2 Melt the butter, allow to become cool but not set in any way.
3 Sieve the flour once, or better still, sieve it twice.
4 Carefully fold the flour, then butter into the whisked eggs, using a metal spoon or palette knife.
5 Line one oblong tin, about 25 cm (10 inches) by 20 cm (8 inches) with greased paper, or line the bottom of two 16–18-cm (7-inch) sandwich tins with greased paper.
6 Put in the mixture and bake towards the top of a moderate oven, for approximately 15 minutes, or until just firm to the touch (as the metric measurements give slightly less mixture, test after 12–13 minutes). If in doubt, choose the lower temperature, and if necessary bake for a longer period.
7 If preferred, put into one lined 16–18-cm (7-inch) cake tin, and bake for approximately 40 minutes in the centre of a very moderate oven. Cool away from a draught.

 Mixer
The mixer used correctly, can be employed for most of the techniques opposite: i.e.
a) use the beater or whisk on a medium speed.
b) use the beater or whisk for small quantities; use a slow speed until well softened, then you can use a medium speed.
c) this is better done by hand.
d) only a dough hook really handles the dough well.
e) use the beater or whisk at a slow then medium speed.
f) use the whisk on high speed.

 Automatic Oven
Genoese pastry must be cooked immediately after being mixed. The mixture loses its light texture if kept waiting.

Speedy Meal
There is no quick way to make this pastry, and no real alternative method.

 Mixer
Use the whisk for stage 1, *but not* for the later stages.

Home Freezing
This mixture can be frozen; it does tend to become a little less moist after storage – that is why I think it is better if turned into a gâteau with a moist filling before freezing. Allow 2–3 hours for thawing out at room temperature.

Victoria Sandwich

Serves: see below
Cooking time see below
Oven temperature see below

Ingredients	Metric	Imperial
butter *or* margarine	100 grammes	4 oz.
castor sugar	100 grammes	4 oz.
eggs	2 medium	2 large
self-raising flour	100 grammes	4 oz.
TO FILL:		
little jam		
TO DECORATE:		
castor *or* icing sugar		

Note: the old method of weighing out ingredients for a Victoria sandwich was to place the eggs required in the recipe on one side of the scales, instead of weights, then weigh out an equal amount of fat, sugar and flour. You can use this method again if metric measurements bother you, take a *large* egg as your weight.

TO BAKE: USE–

6–8 portions (above quantities): two 16–18-cm (6–7-inch) sandwich tins; 15–20 minutes in a moderate oven, 350–375°F. (180–190°C.), Gas Mark 4–5 **'A'**. As the metric conversion gives a smaller quantity, test after 14 minutes.
One 20-cm (8-inch) sandwich tin; 20–25 minutes as above.
One 16–18-cm (6–7-inch) cake tin; 40–45 minutes in a very moderate oven, 325–350°F. (170–180°C.), Gas Mark 3–4 **'B'**. Test early if using metric quantity.
8–12 portions (use 150 grammes (6 oz.) butter etc.): two 18–20-cm (7–8-inch) sandwich tins; 20–23 minutes, temperature **'A'**.
One 22-cm (8½-inch) sandwich tin; 25–30 minutes, temperature **'A'**.
One 18–20-cm (7–8-inch) cake tin; 45–50 minutes, temperature **'B'**. Test early if using metric quantity.
12–16 portions (use 200 grammes (8 oz.) butter etc.): two 20–22-cm (8–9-inch) sandwich tins; 20–25 minutes, temperature **'A'**.
One 25-cm (10-inch) sandwich tin; 30–35 minutes, temperature **'A'**, turn down if necessary.
One 20–22-cm (8–9-inch) cake tin; 55–60 minutes, temperature **'B'**. Test early if using metric quantity.
16–20 portions (use 250 grammes (10 oz.) butter etc.): two 22–25-cm (9–10-inch) sandwich tins; 25–30 minutes, temperature **'A'**.
One 27-cm (11-inch) sandwich tin; 35–40 minutes, temperature **'A'**, turn down if necessary.
One 22–25-cm (9–10-inch) cake tin; 60–65 minutes, temperature **'B'**. Test early if using metric quantity.

1 Cream butter, or margarine, and sugar until soft and light.
2 Whisk the eggs well and gradually beat into the mixture, adding a little sieved flour if it shows signs of curdling.
3 Lastly, fold in the sieved flour, see page 211.
4 The mixture should be a soft consistency, so if necessary add a very little water.
5 Put into the greased and floured tins or tin, and bake as above. Test as page 211.
6 Turn out carefully on to a folded cloth on the palm of the hand, and reverse on to a cooling tray to prevent wire marking top of cake.
7 When cold, sandwich or split and fill with jam, top with sugar.

Automatic Oven

This type of mixture is not harmed in any way by being kept in an oven for a limited period before being baked; if it stands for too long the raising agent in the mixture loses its effectiveness when the cake starts to cook. Most people, however, would rather watch a cake like this, to make sure it does not over-cook.

Speedy Meal

The quickest way to make this type of cake is by the *'one stage' or 'quick mix' method;* put *all* ingredients in the mixing bowl and beat together for 2 minutes.
In order to use this method you must purchase the type of margarine or cooking fat that creams instantly. As the creaming of the fat and sugar normally incorporates air (and lightness) into the mixture, you will have a less well-risen cake by this method, unless you add 1 *extra* level teaspoon baking powder to each 100 grammes (4 oz.) of self-raising flour.

Mixer

Use the beater or whisk for creaming the fat and sugar. Add the beaten eggs *gradually* by mixer, for if put in too quickly the mixture will curdle, just as it would if the eggs were added too speedily by hand. *Do not* use the mixer for adding the flour, do this by hand.
You can use the mixer for the 'quick mix' method above; cream for about 1–1½ minutes on medium speed.

Home Freezing

This cake freezes excellently, but see the comments on the previous page regarding Genoese pastry. It takes a little longer to thaw out, allow 3–4 hours.

Sponge Cake

Serves: see below
Cooking time see below
Oven temperature see below

Ingredients	Metric	Imperial
large eggs	2	2
castor sugar	75 *or*	
	85 grammes*	3 oz.*
self-raising flour	50 grammes*	2 oz.

TO FILL:
little jam
TO DECORATE:
castor *or* icing sugar

*see introduction page 210.

TO BAKE: USE—
4–6 portions (above quantities) two 16–18-cm (6–7-inch) sandwich tins;
9–10 minutes in a moderate to moderately hot oven, 375–400°F.
(190–200°C.), Gas Mark 5–6 '**A**'.
One 20-cm (8-inch) sandwich tin; 12–14 minutes as above.
One 16–18-cm (6–7-inch) cake tin; 25–30 minutes in a moderate oven
350–375°F. (180–190°C.), Gas Mark 4 '**B**'.
6–8 portions (use 3 eggs and increase sugar and flour proportionately):
two 18–20-cm (7–8-inch) sandwich tins; 10–12 minutes, temperature
'**A**'.
One 22-cm (9-inch) sandwich tin; 14–16 minutes, temperature '**A**'.
One 18–20-cm (7–8-inch) cake tin; 30–35 minutes, temperature '**B**'.
8–10 portions (use 4 eggs etc.): two 20–22-cm (8–9-inch) sandwich
tins; 12–14 minutes, temperature '**A**'.
One 25-cm (10-inch) (or *deep* 22-cm (9-inch) sandwich tin; 16–18
minutes, temperature '**A**'.
One 20–22-cm (8–9-inch) cake tin; 35–40 minutes, temperature '**B**',
lower heat if necessary.

1 Whisk the eggs and sugar until thick, see below. If the eggs are small
   add ½–¾ tablespoon hot water.
2 Fold in the sieved flour as described.
3 Divide mixture between the greased and floured (or floured and
   sugared) tins, or in one tin, and bake as above. Test as page 211.
4 Turn out carefully; when cold, sandwich (or split and sandwich)
   with jam, and top with sugar.

Note: an even lighter texture is given if the egg yolks and sugar are
whisked first, then the whisked egg whites added to them.

Coating–this type of sponge is improved by coating tins with equal
quantities of flour *and* sugar to give crisp outside.

Automatic Oven
This sponge cake must be baked immediately after mixing, otherwise it loses
its light texture.

Speedy Meal
There are many sponge mixes on the
market which need little, if any, whisking.
Use these when in a hurry.

Mixer
The whisk is excellent for beating eggs
and sugar until they are thick. There is no
need to put the bowl over hot water. Do
not use the mixer for incorporating flour
into the egg and sugar mixture though.

Home Freezing
This sponge is particularly suitable for
freezing, especially if filled with cream,
fruit, etc.
Allow to thaw out gradually at room
temperature, or in the refrigerator. It takes
a good 2 hours to thaw out at room
temperature. Use within 3 months.

Technique of whisking eggs and sugar

Mention is made in Genoese pastry, and in the sponge above, of
whisking the eggs and sugar until thick. The best way to do this is to
put them into the mixing bowl and whisk with a rotary or flat whisk.
You should be able to see the trail of the whisk in the mixture.
It is quicker if this is done over hot water; stand the basin over a
saucepan of hot water (do not allow the water to boil too rapidly),
and whisk until thick. Take great care that the egg mixture does
not set around the sides of the basin; when thick, remove and continue whisking until cool. Use castor sugar in making this and all
sponges and fine textured cakes, for this gives a better consistency.
It is very important to sieve the flour; self-raising flour is given in
the recipe, but plain (and no baking powder) could be used if you
beat the eggs and sugar well.

Swiss Roll

The sponge mixture on page 213 is ideal for making a light Swiss roll pictured facing page 176

For a small Swiss roll use 2 eggs, etc., but since the mixture needs to flow readily add a little hot water (even with large eggs) or melt 15–25 grammes (½–1 oz.) butter, allow this to cool slightly, then fold into the sponge mixture *after* adding the flour.

Line a Swiss roll tin measuring 18 by 28 cm (7 by 11 inches) with greased greaseproof paper. Bake for 7–9 minutes towards the top of a hot oven. While the cake is baking sprinkle a sheet of greaseproof paper with castor sugar and *warm* the jam; do not over-heat this. Turn the cake out on to the paper, trim away the edges if crisp, spread with jam and roll firmly as shown in the picture facing page 176. Cream-filled Swiss roll is mentioned opposite.

Home Freezing

A Swiss roll is a particularly good cake to freeze, especially if filled with cream or cream and fruit.

Make the roll as instructed opposite; but instead of spreading with jam lay another sheet of greaseproof paper over the top and roll with this inside; or fold the sugared paper into the sponge as you roll.

When cold unroll gently, so you do not crack the sponge. Spread with whipped cream and with fruit or jam and re-roll. If wished the Swiss roll may be frozen without a filling, then defrosted, unrolled and filled.

Macaroon Cherry Gâteau

Serves 8
Cooking time–see Genoese pastry, page 211
Oven temperature–see Genoese pastry, page 211

Ingredients	Metric	Imperial
as Genoese pastry		
TO FILL AND DECORATE:		
thick cream	426 ml*	¾ pint*
macaroon biscuits	100 grammes	4 oz.
can black cherries	1 large	1 large
cherry brandy	1 tablespoon	1 tablespoon
sugar	to taste	to taste
blanched almonds, (coarsely chopped)	25 grammes	1 oz.
blanched almonds, (whole)	50 grammes	1½–2 oz.

*this is a very generous amount which could be reduced, or see note at bottom of recipe.

1 Make and cool the Genoese pastry. For this gâteau it is advisable to make it either in two sandwich tins or a cake tin, not in an oblong tin. Split to give 4 layers in all.
2 Whip the cream until it just holds its shape.
3 Crumble the biscuits into coarse crumbs; it is better to do this by hand rather than in a liquidiser.
4 Drain the cherries, stone half and add to the crumbs with half the cream, the brandy, sugar to taste and the coarsely chopped, blanched almonds.
5 Sandwich the layers of cake with this mixture.
6 Brown the rest of the almonds under the grill or in the oven.
7 Decorate the top of the gâteau with piped cream, the almonds and cherries.

FOR ECONOMY: use 284 ml (½ pint) thick and 142 ml (¼ pint) thin cream, which whip together well–particularly if you have an electric mixer.

Speedy Meal

The interesting filling can be used for a bought sponge cake, or one made with a cake mix.

Mixer

A mixer is invaluable for preparing this recipe, both for the Genoese pastry, see page 211, and for whipping the cream. The liquidiser can be used to chop the almonds–drop in while the blades revolve slowly, so nuts are not chopped too finely.

Home Freezing

This is the type of gâteau which freezes well. Complete the recipe, freeze without covering so the cream is not spoilt, wrap after 24 hours. This keeps for approximately 2–3 months. To serve–unwrap before thawing and allow several hours in a refrigerator.

Chocolate Pear Gâteau

1 Ingredients as basic recipe, but use coarsely grated or chopped plain chocolate in place of nuts; sliced pears instead of cherries and sherry instead of cherry brandy.
2 Gingernut crumbs could be used in place of macaroon, if wished.

Turning sponges into gâteaux

The three basic recipes on pages 211–213 are ideal for making gâteaux. The true sponge mixture is best if eaten fresh, and ideal for filling with cream and fruit. Both the Genoese pastry and Victoria sandwich mixtures can be made several days ahead.

To coat top and sides of a 18–20-cm (7–8-inch) cake, and give a filling through the middle of the cake and a little simple piping on top, make butter icing with 200–225 grammes (8 oz.) butter, etc. Make a little more for elaborate piping.

CHOCOLATE WALNUT GÂTEAU: add chopped walnuts to chocolate filling, coat sides with chocolate butter icing and roll in chopped nuts. Top with icing, piping and walnuts.

COFFEE WALNUT OR ALMOND GÂTEAUX: use almonds or walnuts with a coffee flavoured butter icing.

DOBOZ TORTE: cover the top layer with caramel as page 188, using only the 3 tablespoons water. When firm, sandwich the cake together with chocolate butter icing and spread the sides with this. Press chopped nuts against the sides and mark the top caramel into segments, so the cake is easy to slice, then pipe with chocolate butter icing.

LEMON GÂTEAU: make a lemon flavoured sponge (see below) filled and coated with lemon flavoured butter icing. Make the cake with 200 grammes (8 oz.) butter, etc.; bake in a 20–22-cm (8–9-inch) deep cake tin; see page 212 for full instructions and baking times. Use lemon butter icing made with $\frac{1}{2}$ kilo (1 lb.) butter, etc., as above. To decorate, spread the cake with the butter icing, then take a very fine skewer or metal knitting needle and 'draw' lines round, or pipe as wished.

Speedy Meal
The quick creaming margarines are useful for making fillings with the minimum of blending.
Other fillings you can use are:
Jam blended with coconut to make a thick layer; marzipan (you can buy this ready made) mixed with chopped nuts and cherries.
Boil cans of condensed milk for 2 hours (make sure they are covered with water while they boil). When cold the condensed milk forms a fudge-like filling; see also the fudge recipe on page 235.

Mixer
Use this for creaming the mixture for fillings; the icing sugar must be sieved, otherwise you will still have tiny lumps which the mixer does not break.

Home Freezing
Either freeze the completed gâteaux, or freeze the cakes, ready to fill. You can freeze containers of flavoured butter icing too. Use this within 2–3 months.

Some flavourings for sponges, etc.

All the three basic recipes, i.e. Genoese pastry, Victoria sandwich and the sponge can be flavoured. The amounts suggested below are for the Genoese pastry and sponge made with 3 eggs, etc., and for the Victoria sandwich made with 100 grammes (4 oz.) butter or margarine, etc. Obviously when making larger cakes the flavouring will be increased in proportion. Flavouring essences can be added without altering any proportions of ingredients.

CHOCOLATE: omit 25 grammes (1 oz.) flour and use the same amount of chocolate powder. If you need a stronger flavour for the Victoria sandwich, use sieved cocoa instead.

COFFEE: omit 2–3 teaspoons flour and use the same amount of instant powdered coffee.

LEMON OR ORANGE: add the finely grated rind of 1–2 lemons or oranges to the eggs and sugar, or creamed butter and sugar. Add fruit juice instead of water where suggested in recipe.

Butter Icing

Cream 50 grammes (2 oz.) butter or margarine with 75–100 grammes (3–4 oz.) sieved icing sugar; the amount of icing sugar depends upon how firm you like the icing. Flavour with: essences; a little chocolate powder; sweetened coffee essence; grated lemon and orange rinds, and juice to taste.

Roasted Almond Gâteau

Serves 6–8
Cooking time 45–50 minutes
Oven temperature 350–375° F. (180–190°C), Gas Mark 4–5 (see stage 4)

Ingredients	Metric	Imperial
ground almonds	100 grammes (generous weight)	4 oz.
large egg whites	4	4
castor sugar	250 grammes*	9 oz.
malt vinegar	1 teaspoon	1 teaspoon
vanilla essence	½–1 teaspoon	½–1 teaspoon
TO GREASE TINS :		
olive oil	1–2 teaspoons	1–2 teaspoons
TO FILL :		
thick cream	142–284 ml	¼–½ pint
plain chocolate	100–150 grammes	4–6 oz.
blanched almonds	25 grammes	1 oz.

*it is important to use enough sugar in this recipe so the conversion has been given to make sure of this.

1 Spread the ground almonds on to a flat baking tray and brown for 7–8 minutes in a very moderate to moderate oven until slightly brown; allow to cool.
2 Whisk the egg whites until *very* stiff, gradually whisk in the sugar. Fold in almonds, vinegar and vanilla essence.
3 Line the base of two 18–20-cm (7–8-inch) sandwich tins with rounds of greaseproof paper; oil base and sides.
4 Spoon in mixture, spread flat on top. Bake for approximately 40 minutes just above the centre of the oven, until firm to the touch; look after 15–20 minutes and if browning too quickly lower heat to 325° F. (170°C.), Gas Mark 2–3. Cool slightly, turn out.
5 When cool remove paper and sandwich with whipped cream; do not sweeten this, for the cake is sufficiently sweet.
6 Melt chocolate over hot but *not* boiling water, spread over the top of the cake; decorate with blanched almonds.

Mixer

The whisk is ideal for whisking the egg whites—watch carefully as they become stiff so they do not become too dry in texture; add the sugar as for meringues, page 193, fold in the rest of the ingredients with a metal spoon.

Home Freezing

This cake freezes perfectly; the high sugar content prevents it from becoming too hard. The cream becomes solid with freezing, but the whole cake will thaw out within about 1–1½ hours if left at room temperature.

Chocolate Almond Gâteau

Serves 8–12
Cooking time 40–45 minutes
Oven temperature 350–375° F. (180–190°C.), Gas Mark 4–5

Ingredients	Metric	Imperial
FOR THE CAKE :		
as Victoria sandwich, page 212, using 3 eggs, etc.; but allow 100 grammes (4 oz.) flour, plus 25 grammes (1 oz.) ground almonds, plus 25 grammes (1 oz.) crushed biscuit crumbs.		
FOR THE FILLING, ETC :		
butter	150 grammes	6 oz.
sieved icing sugar	150 grammes	6 oz.
plain chocolate	150 grammes	6 oz.
sultanas	50 grammes	2 oz.
rum	2 tablespoons	2 tablespoons
blanched almonds	50 grammes	2 oz.

1 Make as Victoria sandwich, keeping the mixture fairly firm.
2 Put into a well greased and floured 1 kilo (2 lb.) loaf tin or a long shape, as in the picture facing page 160, and bake in the centre of a moderate to very moderate oven; reduce heat after 30 minutes, if necessary.
3 When cold split the cake into layers and sandwich with some of the chocolate butter icing made by creaming the butter, icing sugar and melted chocolate.
4 Soak the sultanas in half the rum, mix with the almonds and 1 tablespoon icing (made as stage 3), spread on top of the cake.
5 Gradually add the rest of the rum to the icing left over and pour over the top of the cake. Allow to set.

Speedy Meal

See comments under Victoria sandwich, page 212, for 'one stage' mixing, for this is just as successful with this mixture, although it can be rather 'hard work', as the crumbs make a stiffer mixture.

Mixer

Use the mixer for creaming butter and sugar and adding the eggs, but add flour, etc., by hand. Use the mixer also for making the butter icing.

Home Freezing

This gâteau freezes perfectly. As you will see in the picture, the icing on top is so soft it is almost like a sauce; if you feel this is difficult to freeze then freeze an amount of stiffer icing separately; blend with rum when the cake is thawed out and before serving. Naturally you will freeze before wrapping this gâteau, then wrap afterwards.

48. Overlanders' punch, see page 243
49. Birthday cake, see page 217

TO MAKE LARGE CAKES

The recipe that follows is an excellent rich fruit cake that is ideal for special occasions. It needs time to mature, as mentioned in stage 10.

METRIC CONVERSIONS—because you are dealing with rather large quantities, the conversion becomes more apparent. If you do not mind a more shallow cake, *which will cook in a rather shorter time*, follow the recipe. If you prefer a deeper cake, then follow the amounts given at the bottom of ingredients, which will then correspond to the Imperial measurements. If you do this, use 4 large eggs and bake for the full time.

Rich Dark Cake

Makes 24–30 slices
Cooking time approximately 3 hours
Oven temperature 325–350° F. (170–180° C.), Gas Mark 3, then 275–300° F. (140–150° C.), Gas Mark 2

Ingredients	Metric	Imperial
flour	300 grammes*	12 oz.
mixed spice	½–1 teaspoon	½–1 teaspoon
butter	200 grammes**	8 oz.
sugar, preferably moist brown	200 grammes**	8 oz.
black treacle *or* golden syrup	1 level tablespoon	1 level tablespoon
eggs	4 medium	4 large
milk, sherry *or* brandy	4 tablespoons	4 tablespoons
mixed dried fruit	¾–1 kilo	1¾–2 lb.
chopped glacé cherries	50–100 grammes	2–4 oz.
chopped candied peel	50–100 grammes	2–4 oz.
chopped blanched almonds (optional)	50–100 grammes	2–4 oz.

*or use 340 grammes.
**or 225 grammes.

1 Sieve the flour with the spice.
2 Cream the butter, sugar and treacle, until soft and light.
3 Whisk eggs with milk, sherry or brandy and gradually beat into butter mixture; if showing signs of curdling add a little sieved flour.
4 Fold flour gently into mixture with a metal spoon, add prepared fruit (make certain this is dried for 48 hours after washing), cherries, peel and almonds.
5 Line bottom of a tin, 20 cm (8 inch) square, or 23 cm (9 inch) round with double round of brown paper, then greased greaseproof paper, line sides with deep band of greaseproof; put in mixture, flatten on top, tie band of brown paper round outside of tin.
6 Bake for 1–1½ hours in the middle of the oven at higher temperature, then reduce heat for the rest of cooking time.†
7 Test cake; if shrunk away from sides of tin, listen carefully–if cooked the cake is silent, if uncooked there is a distinct 'humming noise'.
8 Cool in tin; if you try to turn out a cake as rich as this the weight of the fruit may cause it to crack.
9 When quite cold, store in airtight tin or wrapped in foil.
10 To give a very moist texture make this cake some 5–6 weeks before required (or even longer), and every week prick the cake, spoon over sherry, rum or brandy. This soaks into the cake and gives a wonderful flavour.

†If following metric measurements you will produce a much shallower cake, which will not require so long baking.

Automatic Oven

If you are completely confident that your oven is accurate, you could cook this cake automatically. If in any doubt, use 1 mark lower on gas and 10°C. (25°F.) lower on an electric cooker, for slower cooking does not harm this type of cake. Obviously though, the only way to feel completely confident is to bake a cake once while you check the oven, and then to trust the oven.
If you are baking automatically you cannot alter settings, so use the lower setting throughout and set the oven for 4 hours rather than 3.

Speedy Meal

The 'quick mix' method of incorporating the ingredients may be used if you substitute margarine for butter, but butter is richer for a good cake like this.

Mixer

Use the mixer for creaming the butter and sugar and adding the eggs, but do not over-beat, for if you do the cake mixture can be too light for the weight of the fruit and this could contribute to fruit 'falling' in a cake. Do not beat in the flour with the mixer.

Home Freezing

There is no need to freeze a cake like this, it keeps perfectly.

x

Decorating large cakes

A large cake, as page 217, is often iced for a celebration.

FIRST COAT THE CAKE WITH MARZIPAN; recipe on page 232; use ½ kilo (1 lb.) ground almonds, etc., to coat the top and sides of the cake given on page 217.

TO COAT WITH MARZIPAN: brush away surplus crumbs, then brush with egg white or sieved apricot jam. Roll marzipan on sugared board, either to coat the whole cake or cut out a round for the top and band for the sides. Press on cake; 'tidy' top using rolling pin, and round the sides with a jam jar.

TOP WITH ROYAL ICING: to make enough to give 2 layers over the whole cake, plus some for piping, use 2 kilo (4 lb.) sieved icing sugar, 8 egg whites and lemon juice to flavour. Method of making is on page 232; spread over the cake as water icing, next page.

Speedy Meal
Marzipan can be bought ready-made, and this is excellent to use for coating cakes. It tends to be stiffer than home-made so handle a little (but not over-much as it becomes oily). If you have handled the marzipan quite a lot in rolling, etc. then leave to dry out for 48 hours before coating. If, on the other hand, you handle quickly, you can put on the icing at once.

Mixer
The mixer should be used to blend Royal icing, *but do not over-beat for you incorporate air bubbles in the mixture which you cannot get out.*

Home Freezing
Royal icing tends to crack with freezing but it keeps perfectly in a tin, so do not freeze.

Spice Cake

Makes approximately 10–12 slices
Cooking time 1–1¼ hours
Oven temperature 325–350° F. (170–180° C.), Gas Mark 3–4

Ingredients	Metric	Imperial
large eggs	3	3
castor sugar	170 grammes*	6 oz.
butter	75 grammes	3 oz.
full cream evaporated milk**	3 tablespoons	3 tablespoons
lemon rind	½ teaspoon	½ teaspoon
plain flour	150 grammes*	5½ oz.
baking powder	2 level teaspoons	2 level teaspoons
mixed spice	1–2 level teaspoons	1–2 level teaspoons
powdered cinnamon	1–2 level teaspoons	1–2 level teaspoons
TO DECORATE:		
sieved icing sugar	100–150 grammes	4–6 oz.
water	to mix	to mix

*this is not the 'literal' translation of amount, but gives the best result.
**the Danish golden evaporated milk was used.

1 Whisk eggs and sugar until light and fluffy as for a sponge, see page 213.
2 Melt the butter, do *not* have it too hot, then add to the egg mixture with the evaporated milk; fold both butter and milk into the eggs with a metal spoon.
3 Next add the lemon rind and the sieved dry ingredients; do not over-beat when adding these.
4 Grease and flour a loaf tin approximately 22 cm (9 inches) long, and put in the mixture.
5 Bake until firm to the touch in the centre of a very moderate oven.
6 Turn out and cool; when quite cold blend the icing sugar with enough water to give a fairly soft consistency.
7 Spoon on top of cake and allow to flow slightly down sides; leave until set, then slice, see picture between pages 184/185.

Note: if preferred this cake can be left plain, and it is then delicious spread with butter and served with cheese.

VARIATION ON SPICE CAKE
FAMILY FRUIT CAKE: use the spice cake above; add an extra 50 grammes (2 oz.) flour and 100–150 grammes (4–6 oz.) mixed dried fruit.

Mixer

The mixer is ideal for whisking the eggs and sugar at stage 1; then could be used on a slow speed to incorporate the melted butter, but *not* for adding the flour.

Home Freezing
This is the type of cake where it is worth freezing, for it becomes stale very quickly and might well be wasted—or be less enjoyable if stored in a tin. Wrap and freeze the whole cake or part left, then use when required. The whole cake takes about 3–4 hours to thaw out at room temperature.

SMALL CAKES

The Victoria sandwich mixture on page 212 can be used to make small cakes.

BUTTERFLY CAKES: shown in picture facing page 209: follow the Victoria sandwich recipe, page 212, but as small cakes should rise to a good 'peak', use small eggs only to mix: this is particularly important when following metric measurements, which give a smaller quantity than the Imperial measurements (explained more fully on page 210). If preferred you can make more economical cakes by using 75 grammes (3 oz.) margarine, 75 grammes (3 oz.) sugar to the 100 grammes (4 oz.) flour and 2 eggs. Mix the cakes as for Victoria sandwich, put into about 12–15 patty tins or paper cases (supported in patty tins or on a baking tray). Bake for about 12–15 minutes towards the top of a hot oven. When cold, cut a slice from top of each cake, spread or pipe butter icing, recipe page 215, or whipped cream on the top. Cut the slice removed into two portions; press these into the cream or butter icing to look like 'wings'. Sprinkle sieved icing sugar over them. The cake mixture can be flavoured with chocolate. Omit 25 grammes (1 oz.) flour and use same amount of chocolate powder; or omit 1 tablespoon only flour, and substitute cocoa. See picture facing page 209.

CUP CAKES: use the Victoria sandwich mixture, keep this soft. Fill paper cases, bake as Butterfly cakes above. When cold coat with glacé icing, see recipe below, decorate with halved glacé cherries, or nuts, etc.

FAIRY CAKES: use the Victoria sandwich mixture, but omit 25 grammes (1 oz.) flour and substitute the same amount of cornflour. Add 50 grammes (2 oz.) currants. Bake as Butterfly cakes.

Automatic Oven
Use the automatic timer to switch off or turn off the oven when baking small cakes; it is so easy to be 'caught' on the telephone and forget them.

Speedy Meal
Use the 'quick mix' method for small cakes.
Omit the extra baking powder recommended under Victoria sandwich, for these do not need to rise so high as a sandwich cake.
If preferred, the fat could be rubbed into the flour, particularly if you are 'cutting down' on the amount used.

Mixer
Use the mixer for blending the cake mixture together, and if you use a very low speed you could incorporate the flour, as the texture with small cakes is not quite so important.

Home Freezing
Small cakes dry out and become stale very quickly, and any left should be frozen the day of making so they retain their freshness when thawed out.

Chocolate Almond Buns

Makes about 15 buns
Cooking time 12–15 minutes
Oven temperature 400° F. (200° C.), Gas Mark 6

Ingredients	Metric	Imperial
margarine	75 grammes	3 oz.
self-raising flour	100 grammes	4 oz.
castor sugar	75 grammes	3 oz.
eggs	2 small	2 medium
blanched almonds	25 grammes	1 oz.
plain chocolate	75 grammes	3 oz.
TO DECORATE:		
icing sugar	100 grammes	4 oz.
water	3 teaspoons	3 teaspoons
blanched almonds	25 grammes	1 oz.
plain chocolate	25 grammes	1 oz.

1 Rub the margarine into the flour, add the sugar and eggs, chopped almonds and chopped chocolate.
2 Bake as the Butterfly cakes, above, using a slightly lower heat, as the chocolate could scorch; cool.
3 Blend icing sugar and water, spread over cakes; top with blanched almonds, shredded chocolate, just before icing sets.

Glacé or water icing

Blend icing sugar with warm or cold water, or fruit juice: for a stiff icing allow barely a tablespoon water with 200–225 grammes (8 oz.) icing sugar, and spread with a damp knife. For a flowing icing allow 3–4 tablespoons water to this amount of icing sugar, see picture between pages 184/185.

Mixer
Use this to blend glacé or water icing, for it gives a good shine and smoothness.

Lemon Cheese Cake

Serves 5–6
Cooking time 1–1¼ hours
Oven temperature 300–325° F. (150–170° C.), Gas Mark 2–3

Ingredients	Metric	Imperial
FOR LINING DISH:		
biscuit crumbs	50 grammes	2 oz.
butter	25 grammes	1 oz.
FOR THE FILLING:		
butter	75 grammes	3 oz.
castor sugar	75–85 grammes	3 oz.
lemons	2	2
eggs	3 small *or* 2 large	3 small *or* 2 large
cream cheese	300 grammes	12 oz.
thick cream	2 tablespoons	2 tablespoons

1 Crush the biscuit crumbs finely.
2 Spread the butter over the bottom and sides of the dish. This is a fragile cheese cake and is better cooked in an ovenproof serving dish–it should measure approximately 23 cm (9 inches) in diameter and be about 5 cm (2 inches) in depth.
3 Sprinkle the crumbs over the bottom and sides of the dish to make a light coating, and press firmly with a knife.
4 Cream the butter and sugar for the filling with the *very finely* grated lemon rind, until soft and light.
5 Add the egg yolks gradually, beating well, then the cream cheese.
6 Stir in a *full* tablespoon lemon juice and the unwhipped cream.
7 Finally, fold in the stiffly beaten egg whites.
8 Spoon into the crumb-lined dish, and bake in the centre of a very cool to cool oven until firm to the touch.
9 *It is an advantage if this is allowed to cool in the oven rather than being brought out into a cold room*, but if using electricity allow for the fact that there will be some further cooking as the oven cools down, and time the initial cooking accordingly.

MORE CHEESE CAKES BASED ON THE RECIPE ABOVE

1 PARTY CHEESE CAKE: top Lemon cheese cake with piped cream, crystallised lemon slices and chopped nuts.
2 CHEDDAR CHEESE CAKE: use 300 grammes (12 oz.) finely grated Cheddar cheese with 3 tablespoons thick cream.
3 COTTAGE CHEESE CAKE: use sieved cottage, not cream cheese, and thick cream instead of lemon juice.
4 FRUIT CHEESE CAKES: most fruits blend with Cheese cake.
IF USING CANNED FRUIT: add lemon rind; use syrup from the can of fruit instead of lemon juice. Put a layer of well drained fruit over the biscuit crumbs (which should be thicker than usual), cover with the Cheese cake and bake. Decorate with canned fruit and whipped cream. This freezes less well than the Lemon cheese cake.
IF USING FRESH BERRY FRUITS: omit lemon rind and juice, blend the cheese mixture with 3 tablespoons thick cream. Top with fresh berries and cream just before serving. Freeze the plain Cheese cake and top with the fruit, etc., before serving.
5 SPICED CHEESE CAKE: add ½–1 teaspoon any spice (cinnamon, allspice, etc.) to any version you prefer.
6 SULTANA CHEESE CAKE: omit lemon rind and juice, add 15 grammes (½ oz.) cornflour to mixture. Use the eggs whole, do not whisk whites. Stir 75 grammes (3 oz.) sultanas (which can be soaked for about 30 minutes in 1 tablespoon dry sherry or fruit juice) into mixture. If you do not wish to soak the sultanas, use 3 tablespoons cream instead of 2.

Automatic Oven

This cheese cake is better cooked s● after making–can be put into the ● oven providing cooking will comme● within about 15 minutes.

Speedy Meal

Use quick creaming margarine instead● butter and add all ingredients, except ● whites, to mixing bowl; beat well u● very smooth, then continue as stage●

Mixer

Use the blender for making the crum● the mixer for
a) creaming the butter and sugar at st● 4, and
b) whisking both the cream and the ● whites.

Slimming Tips

The version No. 3 with cottage chees● *less* fattening, of course, than with ● cream cheese, especially if lemon juic● used and sugar substitute. Choose v● plain biscuits to make the base of ● cheese cake.

Home Freezing

Freezes excellently. Freeze then w● well, and keep for maximum of 3 mon● Defrost at room temperature; takes ab● 2–3 hours.

Shortbread

Makes 8 triangles
Cooking time 50–60 minutes
Oven temperature 325° F. (170° C.), Gas Mark 3

Ingredients	Metric	Imperial
plain flour	150 grammes*	6 oz.
or plain flour and rice flour, ground	100 grammes*	4 oz.
rice *or* cornflour	50 grammes*	2 oz.
butter	100 grammes*	4 oz.
castor sugar	50 grammes*	2 oz.
cornflour *or* rice flour	a little	a little

*when calculating weights for shortbread on metric system remember you need one-third amount of sugar to flour or flour and rice flour; two-thirds amount of butter to flour or flour and rice flour.

1 The perfect shape of a shortbread is made by a shortbread mould made of wood.
2 Sieve the flour into a mixing bowl; add the butter and sugar and rub in with the fingertips. Knead until a smooth dough is obtained.
3 Lightly dust the inside of the shortbread mould with cornflour or rice flour and press the dough into it.
4 Allow to set for a short time. (Alternatively roll out to 7-inch round and flute edge.)
5 Brush a baking sheet with melted butter, and turn the shortbread out of the mould very carefully on to this.
6 Bake in the centre of a very moderate oven for 50–60 minutes.
7 Remove and mark into 8 pieces. Cool on a wire tray.

Speedy Meal

It is possible to melt the butter (but not to an oil) which makes the mixture blend together much more easily.

Mixer

Use the mixer to 'rub-in' the butter, or cream the butter and half the sugar, add the flour and reduce the speed to 'knead'; use the dough hook if you have one, *then* add the rest of the sugar.

Home Freezing

Do not freeze these biscuits, they keep perfectly in a tin.

Melting Moments

Makes 12 biscuits
Cooking time 15–20 minutes
Oven temperature 350° F. (180° C.), Gas Mark 4

Ingredients	Metric	Imperial
butter	75 grammes	3 oz.
icing sugar	50 grammes	2 oz.
vanilla essence	few drops	few drops
cornflour	50 grammes	2 oz.
plain flour	50 grammes	2 oz.

1 These very short, crisp biscuits are piped into fancy shapes. Recipes vary a little in the proportion of ingredients, but in order that the biscuits should keep a good shape and have the very short, crisp texture, it is important to use icing sugar and a mixture of cornflour and flour.
2 Cream the butter, icing sugar and essence until soft and light.
3 Work in the cornflour and flour.
4 Put into a piping bag with a ½-cm (¼-inch) rose pipe and force shell shapes on to a well greased and floured tin or into greaseproof paper cases (supported in patty tins).
5 Bake for approximately 15–20 minutes in the centre of a very moderate to moderate oven.
6 Either serve the biscuits plain or sandwich two together with butter icing, page 215, or top with a teaspoon of glacé icing, page 219, or jam.

Note: keep butter icing stiff for putting into biscuits.

Speedy Meal

Sandwich bought shortcake biscuits together with butter icing, and top with jam or glacé icing.

Mixer

Use the mixer to cream the butter and icing sugar (which must be well sieved as the mixer does not take out lumps); do not use the mixer for adding the flour, as the dough becomes too 'firm' to pipe. Use the mixer also for butter icing.

Scandinavian Biscuits

Makes approx. 40 biscuits
Cooking time 7–15 minutes
Oven temperature 375° F. (190° C.), Gas Mark 4–5

Ingredients	Metric	Imperial
plain flour	200 grammes	8 oz.
baking powder	½ level teaspoon	½ level teaspoon
butter	125 grammes	5 oz.
castor sugar	75 grammes	3 oz.
beaten egg	about 2 tablespoons	about 2 tablespoons

1 In Scandinavia small biscuits are made as part of Christmas fare, or for any festivity. They vary quite a lot in the basic recipe but the above ingredients are used for many shapes in Denmark.
2 Sift the flour and baking powder; rub in the butter until you have fine crumbs.
3 Stir in the sugar and add egg to make a soft smooth dough; if you wish to make The Jodekager and Finskbrod biscuits, below, divide the dough into two.

JODEKAGER: the biscuits are made into wafer-thin rounds and topped with beaten egg, cinnamon, sugar and chopped, blanched almonds. They need only about 7 minutes baking, on a well greased baking tin in the centre of a moderate oven.

FINSKBROD: the dough is made into a slightly flattened sausage shape, cut into 1-cm (½-inch) thick slices, slantwise, and baked for 15 minutes, as above.

VANILJEKRANSE: the dough is made richer by using equal quantities of butter and flour and adding 50–75 grammes (2–3 oz.) finely chopped, blanched almonds and vanilla essence to flavour, then piped (using a small tube) into rings and baked for 10 minutes, as above.

Speedy Meal
Use the 'quick mix method of incorporating all the ingredients together. Chill slightly, then form into a long roll. Chill this for some hours, then cut off wafer thin slices for the first recipe.

Mixer
This may be used either for the normal method of mixing, as the recipe, or for the 'quick mix' recipe above.
Use the liquidiser to 'chop' the almonds.

Home Freezing
Not suitable.

Krammerhuse – Danish Cornets

Makes 12–16 cornets
Cooking time 5 minutes
Oven temperature 450–475° F. (230–240° C.), Gas Mark 8–9

Ingredients	Metric	Imperial
large egg	1	1
castor sugar	40 grammes	1½ oz.
flour, perferably plain	40 grammes	1½ oz.
vanilla essence	½–1 teaspoon	½–1 teaspoon
water	1 teaspoon	1 teaspoon
thick *or* canned cream	150 grammes *or* about 142 ml	6 oz. *or* ¼ pint
red jam *or* jelly	2 tablespoons	2 tablespoons

Mixer
Use this for whisking the eggs and sugar for they must be very thick in this recipe, but do *not* use the mixer for incorporating the flour, etc.
If whipping cream with an electric mixer use a slow speed and be very careful that it is not over-whipped.

Home Freezing
Not suitable for freezing.

1 Whisk egg and sugar well, until thick.
2 Fold in sieved flour, vanilla essence and water.
3 Spread the mixture thinly on the baking tray with a teaspoon to make oval shapes, 10 cm (4 inch) by 6 cm (2½ inch)–say 4 per tray to allow room to spread out.
4 Bake for 5 minutes, towards top of a hot to very hot oven.
5 Remove one at a time with a palette knife; keep the rest in a warm place if possible.
6 Shape to a cornet in the hand and place on a clean bottle neck until cool and firm (a few seconds).
7 If the other rounds of mixture become rather hard on the tin, warm through for about ½ minute, this is why it is essential not to over-cook at stage 4.
8 Store until needed in an airtight tin.
9 Before serving, fill each cornet with thick canned cream or whipped cream and top with a little jam or jelly.
10 Serve, in the Danish way, standing upright in a bowl of sugar, see picture pages between 184/185.

Anzacs

Makes 36 biscuits
Cooking time 15 minutes
Oven temperature 300° F. (150° C.), Gas Mark 2

Ingredients	Metric	Imperial
butter	125 grammes	5 oz.
golden syrup	1 level tablespoon	1 level tablespoon
bicarbonate of soda	1 level teaspoon	1 level teaspoon
boiling water	2 tablespoons	2 tablespoons
plain flour	100 grammes	4 oz.
rolled oats	100 grammes	4 oz.
sugar	100–150 grammes	4–6 oz.
raisins	100 grammes	4 oz.

1 Melt butter and syrup.
2 Dissolve soda in water and add.
3 Mix flour, oats, sugar and raisins and pour liquid on to them. Mix well.
4 Place in teaspoonfuls on greased baking tray, allowing quite a lot of room for spreading.
5 Bake in slow oven for approximately 15 minutes.
6 Do not remove from baking tray until slightly cool and set.
7 Store in airtight tins when quite cold.

Note: many traditional recipes from Australia or New Zealand omit the raisins and add 100 grammes (4 oz.) desiccated coconut instead. This may mean adding a very little extra water.

Speedy Meal
These are a very quick biscuit, but you save a few moments 'clearing up' if you use a large saucepan for stage 1, then mix all ingredients in this.

Home Freezing
These biscuits can become soft unless the tin is completely air-tight; you may prefer to freeze them in polythene bags instead. Allow about 2 hours thawing out period at room temperature.

Piped Petits Fours

Makes about 40 biscuits
Cooking time 12–15 minutes
Oven temperature 325° F. (170° C.), Gas Mark 3

Ingredients	Metric	Imperial
butter	50 grammes	2 oz.
castor sugar	150 grammes	6 oz.
almond essence	few drops	few drops
ground almonds	100 grammes	4 oz.
cornflour	25 grammes	1 oz.
egg yolk	1	1
TO GLAZE:		
glacé cherries	approx. 20	approx. 20
egg white	1	1

1 Cream the butter with the sugar and essence.
2 Add the ground almonds and the cornflour then enough of the egg yolk to make a consistency that you can pipe.
3 Pipe (marble size) on to lightly greased baking tray.
4 Press half a glacé cherry on each biscuit then brush with egg white.
5 Bake for 12–15 minutes in the centre of a very moderate oven; cool on baking tray.

Mixer
It is important that the butter and sugar are well creamed in this recipe, so a mixer is ideal, but do not overbeat as it would become too sticky to pipe.

Home Freezing
These can be stored in the freezer either in polythene bags or as part of a dessert. Allow about 1 hour to thaw out.
Petits fours made with Genoese pastry can be frozen so they keep fresh for some weeks. Allow about 1 hour to thaw out.

MORE PETITS FOURS
There are many other small cakes that may be offered as part of a selection of petits fours. Make the Genoese pastry on page 211, cut into minute shapes, decorate with glacé and butter icings, pages 219 and 215, with tiny pieces of cherry, angelica, nuts and crystallised petals.
Make meringues about the size of hazel nuts; when cold top with a small amount of cool melted chocolate and allow to set.
Ratafias on page 205, can be included in petits fours.

Sables au Citron

Makes 36–48 biscuits
Cooking time 15–20 minutes
Oven temperature 350–375° F. (180–190° C.), Gas Mark 4–5

Ingredients	Metric	Imperial
butter	100 grammes	4 oz.
plain flour	200 grammes	8 oz.
castor sugar	75 grammes	3 oz.
finely grated lemon rind	1	1
egg	1	1

1 These French biscuits can also be made as recipe for Melting moments, flavoured either with a little lemon essence or finely grated lemon rind; do not use lemon juice otherwise the mixture is too 'watery'. Pipe into rose shapes, decorate with a small piece of cherry, if wished, and then bake as Melting moments, page 221. (There is, however, an easier method of making tiny sables–crisp biscuits–see opposite.)
2 Rub the butter into the flour, add the sugar, lemon rind and enough egg to bind.
3 Roll out until about ⅓ cm (⅛ inch) in thickness, and cut into required shapes or 5-inch rounds divided into 4 wedges.
4 Bake on an ungreased baking tin for 15–20 minutes, in the centre of a very moderate to moderate oven, until very crisp but still golden coloured.

Speedy Meal

Chill the mixture very well in the form of a small 'sausage shape' roll. Cut into wafer thin slices and bake for about 6–7 minutes, or place on rice paper if wished.

Mixer

Use the mixer on a low speed to 'rub-in' the butter, or cream butter and sugar and add the egg yolks. If you continue to use the mixer (if following a creaming method) to incorporate the flour, then use a very low speed, so the mixture does not become unduly sticky.

Home Freezing

Not particularly suitable for freezing or necessary since they, like most biscuits, keep in an air-tight tin.

Honey Twists

Makes 16–18 twists
Cooking time 8–12 minutes each batch
Oven temperature 325–350° F. (170–180° C.), Gas Mark 3

Ingredients	Metric	Imperial
flour	exactly 50 grammes	2 oz.
butter	55 grammes	2 oz.
sugar	55 grammes	2 oz.
thin honey	2 level tablespoons	2 level tablespoons
grated lemon rind	½ teaspoon	½ teaspoon

1 If using Imperial measure take 1 teaspoon of flour away, so scales no longer give quite 2 oz.
2 Put butter, sugar and honey into a saucepan.
3 Mix flour and lemon rind.
4 Allow butter to melt slowly, then take pan off heat and stir in flour.
5 Grease two or three baking tins very well indeed, do not flour.
6 Put teaspoons of the mixture on the trays, allowing 8 cm (3 inches) all round, since they spread out a great deal.
7 As rolling takes several minutes, put one tray into the oven to begin with, setting it at a very moderate heat.
8 Put the second tin into the oven after about 5 minutes, then the third after about 10 minutes.
9 Keep trays as near middle of oven as possible.
10 Allow to cool for 2 minutes after the biscuits come from the oven, then roll as cornets on page 222, stage 6, or round the handle of a greased wooden spoon.
11 Hold in position for a few seconds to give biscuit a chance to set, then put the biscuit on a wire sieve.
12 Do the same with the next biscuit, trying to work quickly with each tray, as when biscuits start to harden they cannot be removed from tin.
13 If this happens to last few, put tin back in oven for a minute and start testing again when you bring it out.
14 Store away from all other biscuits and cakes, in air-tight jar or tin; fill with lemon curd before serving, if wished.

Speedy Meal

The biscuit dough is easy and quick to make, it is the rolling that takes the time, so if preferred keep these biscuits flat as a 'honey-wafer'. You can sandwich two wafers together with thick cream (flavoured with a little grated lemon rind) before serving, if wished.

Home Freezing

These store well and would spoil with freezing.

Plain Scones

Makes 8–12
Cooking time 10 minutes
Oven temperature 450–475° F. (230–240° C.), Gas Mark 7–8

Ingredients	Metric	Imperial
self-raising flour*	200 grammes	8 oz.
salt	good pinch	good pinch
margarine *or* butter	25–30 grammes	1–2 oz.
sugar, optional	25 grammes	1 oz.
milk	to mix	to mix

*to give a lighter scone you *could* add 1 teaspoon baking powder, or
¼ teaspoon bicarbonate of soda and ½ teaspoon cream of tartar (this
is not essential).
With plain flour, use exactly double these amounts *or* 4 *level* teaspoons baking powder.

1 Sieve the flour and salt; if using extra baking powder or other raising
agents sieve very well indeed.
2 Rub the margarine or butter into the flour, add the sugar and
enough milk to give a soft rolling consistency; never make a scone
dough too firm.
3 Roll out on a lightly floured board until about 1 cm (½ inch) in thickness.
4 Cut into rounds or triangles, lift on to an ungreased baking tray,
and bake towards the top of a hot to very hot oven until golden
brown. To test if cooked, press the sides firmly and your fingers
should leave no impression. See picture facing page 145.

Note: the difference in the amounts between metric and Imperial
measurements does not matter with scones, except that you will
probably make one less.

RECIPES BASED ON PLAIN SCONES

BUTTERMILK SCONES: if you blend the dough with soured milk or
butter milk you can leave out the cream of tartar and just use ½
teaspoon bicarbonate of soda to each 200 grammes (8 oz.) plain flour.
CHEESE SCONES: omit the sugar, sieve a generous amount of seasoning with the flour. Rub in the margarine or butter, add 75 grammes
(3 oz.) finely grated Cheddar or other cooking cheese to the mixture,
bind with milk. Roll out the scone dough, cut into required shapes
and put on to greased trays (cheese scones are inclined to 'stick'),
then brush the tops with milk or beaten egg and sprinkle a little
grated cheese over the top, if wished. Bake as plain scones, but
reduce the heat after 5 minutes, if necessary.
FRUIT SCONES: add 25–75 grammes (1–3 oz.) dried fruit to the scone
dough, see picture facing page 145.
SAVOURY SCONES: use well seasoned scone dough: very good when
split and filled with cheese mixtures, or as a savoury Cobbler.

Automatic Oven

See remarks under small cakes for they
apply to scones too. Scones need to be
put into a hot oven where possible, to
help the dough to rise quickly.

Speedy Meal

If you cut fairly thick rounds of fresh
bread, brush them with melted butter on
top, sprinkle them with sugar and heat for
about 5 minutes in a very hot oven, you
can split these and serve as scones, topped
with butter, jam, or jam and cream.

Mixer

The mixer should not be used for a scone
dough, since it would handle this too
much; the less you handle the better.

Home Freezing

Scones are one of the very successful
baked foods to freeze. There is no
difference between a scone that has been
frozen for some weeks, then defrosted,
and a freshly baked scone. The baked
scones must be frozen while fresh though.
Allow 1–2 hours at room temperature to
thaw out; if in a hurry warm in the oven,
but this is not as good, the texture seems
less light. Use within 6 months.

Scotch Pancakes or Drop Scones

1 Weigh out a generous 100 grammes–important to keep correct
consistency–(4 oz.) self-raising or plain flour. To plain flour add
2 level teaspoons baking powder.
2 Sieve flour with a good pinch salt, add 1 egg and 142 ml (¼ pint) milk,
plus 25 grammes (1 oz.) melted butter or margarine. Blend well.
3 Drop spoonfuls on to a hot greased solid hotplate, or into a hot
greased frying pan, cook for about 2 minutes on *either* side. Cool,
wrapped in a tea-cloth, serve with butter. Makes about 18.

Speedy Meal

If you have any smooth mashed potato
left, use this to make a *Potato drop scone*.
Add a teaspoon baking powder to about
6–8 tablespoons mashed potato, then
25 grammes (1 oz.) self-raising flour, an
egg and enough milk (about 5 tablespoons) to make a thick batter. Cook as
Scotch pancakes.

Home Freezing

These freeze very well indeed; wrap well.
They thaw out in an hour.

Apricot and Walnut Bread

Makes 20 thin slices
Cooking time 1¼–1½ hours
Oven temperature 325° F. (170°C.), Gas Mark 3

Ingredients	Metric	Imperial
dried apricots	200–225 grammes*	8 oz.
water	4 tablespoons	4 tablespoons
milk	142 ml	¼ pint
self-raising flour	300–340 grammes*	12 oz.
salt	good pinch	good pinch
sugar	100 grammes	4 oz.
walnuts	100 grammes	4 oz.
butter *or* margarine *or* cooking fat	75 grammes	3 oz.
eggs	2	2
TO DECORATE (OPTIONAL):		
walnuts	25 grammes	1 oz.

*you need the larger amount here to give same result.

1 Cut the apricots into pieces with kitchen scissors, put in a basin and pour the water and milk over these.
2 Leave standing for 30 minutes if the apricots are moist, or an hour if rather firm and dry; this makes a lot of difference to the loaf, for the apricots should be tender.
3 Sieve flour and salt, add sugar and coarsely chopped nuts.
4 Melt the butter (or margarine or fat), cool slightly.
5 Pour into the flour, add the apricots and all the liquid and finally the eggs; beat well together.
6 Put into 1-kilo (2-lb.) loaf tin, lined with greased paper.
7 Press the walnuts on top to decorate, bake in the centre of a very moderate oven until firm to the touch; lower the heat if necessary after 1 hour.
8 Keep the paper on this loaf until ready to serve, for this helps to keep it moist, see picture facing page 184.

Automatic Oven

This may be prepared and left in the oven to cook, providing you have tested it to see that the oven temperature is suitable to leave without turning down, at stage 7.

Speedy Meal

Make the mixture into small rolls instead of a loaf. Omit 2 tablespoons water from the recipe, and put into well greased deep patty tins. Bake for about 20 minutes, just above the centre of a moderate oven.

Mixer

If the apricots are somewhat hard then put through the mincer, rather than chop. The mixer could be used on a low speed at stage 5, for a very short time.

Home Freezing

This loaf, like all baking powder breads, freezes well. Allow 3–4 hours at room temperature (or even longer) to thaw out, well before using. Keeps some months.

Mixed Fruit Bread

Makes 12–15 thin slices
Cooking time 1–1¼ hours
Oven temperature 350° F. (180°C.), Gas Mark 4

Ingredients	Metric	Imperial
self-raising flour	300–340 grammes*	12 oz.
salt	½ teaspoon	½ teaspoon
allspice	½–1 teaspoon	½–1 teaspoon
sugar	75 grammes	3 oz.
mixed dried fruit	150–175 grammes	6–7 oz.
glacé cherries	25–50 grammes	1–2 oz.
margarine	75 grammes	3 oz.
milk	12 tablespoons	12 tablespoons
eggs	2	2
FOR THE ICING:		
icing sugar	150–200 grammes	6–8 oz.
water	to mix	to mix
glacé cherries	7–8	7–8

*you need the larger amount here to give same result.

1 Sieve or mix the dry ingredients together, then add dried fruit, and halved cherries.
2 Melt margarine in milk; do not heat for too long a period, otherwise the liquid evaporates and the mixture is too dry.
3 Beat into the fruit and flour, then add the eggs.
4 Bake in centre of a moderate oven, in a well greased and floured or lined 1-kilo (2-lb.) loaf tin, until firm to touch.
5 Turn out and cool, then coat with the glacé icing, make a soft consistency so it pours easily, see picture facing page 184, and top with the cherries. Eat while fresh.

Automatic Oven

This is very suitable for leaving in the oven, since it is the type of fairly plain bread that will not scorch easily. Check though, the first time of baking, that the time is exactly right for your oven. Ovens vary so much and cooking times and settings can be a guide only.

Speedy Meal

Bake in small patty tins as suggested above, the consistency should be just slightly stiffer so use 11 tablespoons milk.

Mixer

Rather stiff for the mixer to handle.

Home Freezing

See comments under bread, above.

MAKING BREAD

There are few cookery processes which give greater satisfaction than making bread. The smell of the yeast dough rising (generally called 'proving'), then being baked is most inviting. Remember when you cook with yeast:

a) fresh yeast deteriorates at room temperature; so store in the refrigerator or freeze it; use thawed out frozen yeast within 3–4 months to preserve quality; if wished use dried yeast instead—method of using this is given in the basic recipe, stage 2.

b) do not 'prove' too quickly over too high a heat.

c) *bake* the dough quickly to give a good result; the effect of this is to kill the yeast during the early stages of baking.

Rich White Bread Dough

Makes 1 loaf
Cooking time–see separate recipes, page 228
Oven temperature 425–450° F. (220–230° C.), Gas Mark 7 (see recipes)

Ingredients	Metric	Imperial
DRY MIXTURE:		
plain white flour	½ kilo	1 lb.
salt	2 level teaspoons	2 level teaspoons
margarine	50 grammes	2 oz.
YEAST LIQUID:		
fresh yeast*	14–15 grammes	½ oz.
milk and water, mixed	284 ml	½ pint
EGG WASH:		
egg	1	1
sugar	1 teaspoon	1 teaspoon
water	1 tablespoon	1 tablespoon

*for dried yeast, see below, stage 2.

1 Sieve or mix the flour and salt; rub in the margarine.

2 Blend the fresh yeast with the warm milk and water (110° F. or 43° C.), or if using dried yeast dissolve 1 teaspoon sugar in the warm liquid, then sprinkle on 2 teaspoons dried yeast. Allow to stand for 10 minutes until frothy, then continue as below.

3 Blend the yeast liquid with the flour and margarine with a spoon or fork, then work with your hands into a firm dough. Makes of flour vary slightly in the amount of liquid they absorb (also remember that ½ kilo is slightly more than 1 lb.), so if the dough is too moist work in a little extra flour; if too dry then add a *very little* more warm liquid.

4 Turn the dough on to a lightly floured board or table, knead thoroughly, pulling the dough with the 'heel' of your hand until quite firm and elastic; this takes about 10 minutes. To test if sufficiently kneaded press with a floured finger; if the impression comes out, then the dough is ready for the next stage.

5 Shape the dough into a ball and put this to 'prove'. This can be done in a covered bowl, or a lightly greased polythene bag (tie the bag loosely) but allow space in the bowl or bag for the dough to rise until double its original size.

6 To 'prove' allow 45–60 minutes in a warm place, this can be the airing cupboard or warming drawer of the cooker; or allow 2 hours at average room temperature, or up to 12 hours in a really cold room, or 24 hours in the cabinet of the refrigerator. Slow 'proving' gives a particularly good result, but always allow dough that has been allowed to rise in the refrigerator to stand for a minimum of 30 minutes in room temperature before kneading and shaping.

7 Knead the risen dough again (this is called 'knocking back' the dough), then shape as wished, see next page.

Speedy Meal

Choose the method of making rolls on page 228 when short of time.

Mixer

Use a dough hook attachment and a slow speed; so you 'imitate' the steady process of hand kneading.

Home Freezing

Bread you buy: if pre-wrapped keep in this wrapping, put into a polythene bag as well, and seal tightly. To use: allow to thaw out at room temperature (this takes 5–7 hours) or overnight in the cabinet of the refrigerator; either method gives the best result for a whole loaf. If time does not permit, heat the frozen loaf steadily, wrapped in foil, so the outside does not scorch.

Store sliced loaves, for you can 'peel off' as many slices as required; allow these to thaw out steadily, or toast them.

Really crusty long loaves such as French bread are excellent for freezing. Sometimes you will find that if the bread is kept longer than a week/10 days the very crisp crust falls off. To avoid this cut a very thin slice from either end before wrapping. Advice varies as to whether you should unwrap cooked bread before or after thawing out. I find the crust is better if I unwrap while still frozen (except if heating through in the oven—when I remove the polythene wrappings and put into foil).

Home made dough: if you are baking to freeze, the enriched dough opposite, i.e. with margarine or other fat added, freezes rather better *for a longer period* than a completely plain dough. Yeast dough mixed with milk, or with egg and milk, freezes splendidly.

You can freeze home-made bread in various ways:

1. Cook until firm but pale. Cool, wrap tightly, label and freeze. Unwrap to thaw, then bake until crusty—15–50 minutes. Store 4–6 weeks.

2. Bake completely, cool and freeze. Defrost as above: if crust is soft, crisp in oven. Store as 1.

3. Prepare yeast dough, knead, but do not 'prove'. Brush lightly with olive oil or melted butter. Lightly grease inside of a polythene bag, put dough in this, wrap fairly tightly, but allow a little space for expansion until frozen, then fasten tightly. To extract air, put a straw into bag and suck out air. Thaw as bread. Untie bag, loosen, allow to 'prove'. Keeps 4–5 weeks.

4. Prepare and allow to 'prove'. Knead again, continue to wrap and freeze as 3. Thaw, shape, etc., but use within 2–3 weeks.

Using the rich white bread dough

To make a tin loaf: grease and warm a 1-kilo (2-lb.) loaf tin. Form the dough into an oblong the width of the tin length, fold the dough into three so it just fits the tin, leave plenty of depth for the loaf to rise. Brush with the egg wash, see previous page; cover the top of the tin lightly with greased polythene or a cloth then allow to 'prove' until well risen in the tin (about 30 minutes at room temperature); bake for about 25–30 minutes in the centre of a hot oven, then lower the heat to moderate and bake for about 20 minutes, until the bread is golden brown and firm. A less rich loaf is made by mixing with all water, and using about 15 grammes (½ oz.) fat to the flour.

To make twists or plaits as in the picture between pages 184/185. Cut off two-thirds of the dough and divide into two equal pieces for a twist, or three pieces for a plait. Roll the pieces into strands 30–36 cm (12–14 inches) long. Either cross the two strands, or plait the three, loosely until a neat loaf, put on a greased baking tray and brush with the egg wash, sprinkle with poppy seeds if wished. Slip carefully into a large lightly greased polythene bag and allow to 'prove' for 30 minutes at room temperature, then bake for 30 minutes in the centre of a hot oven. The remaining dough can be made into small plaited rolls.

Plaited rolls as in the picture between pages 184/185. Divide dough into small pieces about 50 grammes (2 oz.) in weight, then divide each piece of dough into three strands and plait these. Proceed as the plaited or twisted loaf, 'proving' for the same time; bake for 15–20 minutes.

CROWN LOAF: the amount of dough given in the recipe on the previous page will make two loaves as picture between pages 184/185. Divide the dough for each loaf into 6 equal sized pieces. Shape each piece into a smooth ball. Place 5 balls to form a ring in a greased 15-cm (6-inch) sandwich tin, and put the sixth ball in the centre. Brush with the egg wash, sprinkle with poppy seeds, if wished, then 'prove' and bake as the twists above.

TO INCREASE THE AMOUNT OF DOUGH
If you wish to make a larger quantity of dough at one time, all ingredients are increased in exact proportion except the yeast. For 1½ kilo (3 lb.) flour you still need only 25 grammes (1 oz.) fresh yeast.

Automatic Oven
Obviously the uncooked yeast dough would rise (prove) in the oven during the waiting period before the heat was turned or switched on; it is however possible to put the loaf in the *cold* oven, then set the oven to the right temperature or gas thermostat and the bread cooks perfectly.

Speedy Meal
This is a quick recipe for as you will see the dough does not need 'proving' in bulk, but just when shaped into the rolls. If forming into loaves you can omit the bulk proving too, if wished.

Mixer
See comments on previous page, but this is a dough that should not be over-kneaded.

Slimming Tips
Carbohydrates are one of the foods to be avoided or limited when on a slimming diet; even so, most well balanced slimming diets do advise a limited amount of bread, since this is a most valuable food.

Wheatmeal Bread Dough

1 To make wheatmeal rolls (or various loaves), sieve or mix 200–225 grammes (8–9 oz.) white plain flour and 200–225 grammes (8–9 oz.) brown flour with 2 level teaspoons salt.
2 Rub in knob, about 6–7 grammes (¼ oz.) lard; this is a piece the size of a hazel nut.
3 *If you use fresh yeast* add 2 teaspoons sugar to the flour, etc., blend 14–15 grammes (½ oz.) fresh yeast with 284 ml (½ pint) warm (110°F. or 43°C.) water.
   If you use dried yeast mix 1 teaspoon of sugar with the flour, etc., dissolve a second teaspoon sugar in 284 ml (½ pint) hand-hot water, add 2 level teaspoons dried yeast; leave until frothy, proceed as below.
4 Add the yeast liquid to the flour, etc., and knead for only about 3 minutes until a soft scone like consistency. Divide into 12 small pieces, roll in balls with floured palm, brush with salted water, sprinkle with poppy seeds or cracked wheat or cornflakes, allow to 'prove' as white rolls, etc., above; bake for about 20–25 minutes in the centre of a very hot oven.

Home Freezing
This dough can be frozen if wished. If you wish to freeze before cooking then form into rolls, put on warmed greased baking tray, allowing plenty of room to 'prove'. Slip into greased polythene bag, allow little space for 'proving' before freezing, although with small rolls this is not very likely. Freeze. If wished remove from the tray when hard, and separate with squares of greaseproof paper, put into a polythene bag and seal tightly.
To use: put back on to greased tray, put into a polythene bag, allow to thaw out, this takes about 2–3 hours at room temperature, then to 'prove' and bake as instructed opposite. If preferred bake, cool, then freeze.

Making Sweets

Sweets and Candies are not difficult to make, you just need to follow the directions for heating to the correct temperature, and the simple 'rules' below.

Firstly, remember you are heating the ingredients to a dangerously high temperature, so make sure that children are not left alone in the kitchen. and ensure the handle of the saucepan is put in such a way that it cannot be knocked with the possibility of tipping the pan.

These are the most important points when producing boiled sweets:

1. Choose a strong saucepan, for you will be heating the ingredients to a very high temperature and they are likely to burn if a thin pan is chosen.

2. If you are following a recipe where a definite cooking time is given, test a little early, so that you are sure you have not over-cooked.

3. *Cooking times are NOT given in these recipes:* this depends upon the heat of the boiling ring or plate, and thickness and diameter of the pan (the smaller the pan; the greater the depth of mixture and the longer the cooking time).

4. As well as a strong pan, choose a sufficiently large pan. In many recipes the mixture is likely to rise considerably as it boils, and you do not want the possibility of it boiling over.

5. Keep a bowl or jug of cold water and a pastry brush beside you. This is to brush down the sides of the pan as the sugar mixture boils up. If you do not do this, the mixture tends to harden during cooking. Keep brushing repeatedly for good results.

6. Stir until the sugar is dissolved.

7. When the sugar has dissolved, stir as little as possible. In some recipes, like fudge, where you have a high percentage of milk or cream, you will need to stir from time to time, but continual stirring does slow up the cooking of the mixture and it can mean it is almost impossible for the sweets to reach the right temperature. In boiled sweets it is less necessary to stir where just sugar, water and flavouring are used.

8. Test early, see points 2 and 3, and take pan off the heat as you test.

9. The directions for stirring or not stirring *when* the mixture reaches the right temperature are important where included in the recipe, for this alters the texture of the sweet.

10. Use oil or butter to grease tins to set sweets. When firm, wrap, if recommended, to prevent the mixture becoming sticky.

Metric Conversions

Although you should *try* to use the accurate conversion of ingredients, the most important point is to reach the right temperature, or stage, so read the directions given for this.

To test for stages of sweet making

As stressed in the introduction, it is important to test early for sweetmeats, for if you pass a certain stage you cannot cool the mixture and expect it to be successful. Here are the points to remember when testing cooked sweets or candies:

IF YOU HAVE NO SUGAR THERMOMETER: have a basin or cup of cold water available, and drop in a small quantity of the mixture to see which stage has been reached.

IF YOU HAVE A SUGAR THERMOMETER: allow the mixture to boil for a minute or two after the sugar mixture has been stirred and the sugar is thoroughly dissolved. Put in the thermometer and gently stir the mixture for a moment. This gives you an accurate reading. Try to read the thermometer without lifting it out too far from the sugar mixture. Do *not* put the thermometer into cold or even hot water, or on a cold surface, when it comes out of the pan of hot ingredients. Whether you are testing with or without a thermometer, remove pan from heat as you test or take the reading.

Stages of sugar boiling

1st stage–known as Thread

Appearance	°F.	°C.
At this stage the syrup is so thin that it will run off the spoon into the cold water when testing, but if you keep some on the spoon for a moment you can pinch it to feel a hot substance. This is a stage not often used in sweet making but it does give a sticky coating on some sweets. A firmer coating is given if the sugar is boiled to 228°F. (108·8°C.).	225	107·2

2nd stage-known as Pearl

Appearance	°F.	°C.
At this stage you find the syrup forming tiny pearl-like balls in cold water. Here again the mixture is too soft to form a sweetmeat by itself, but occasionally this stage is needed for binding ingredients or for coating.	230–233	110–111·6

3rd stage-known as Blow

Appearance	°F.	°C.
The bubbles float when tested in cold water. A continuation of the pearl stage, again not hard enough for a sweetmeat by itself.	235	112·7

4th stage-known as Soft Ball

Appearance	°F.	°C.
The sugar mixture drops into the water and can then be gathered up between your finger and thumb and formed into a soft ball. 238°F. (114·4°C.) will give you a rather soft fudge, for this is one of the main sweet recipes in which this temperature is used, but since fudge tends to harden a little on keeping, many people prefer this temperature to a slightly higher one.	238–240	114·4–115·5

5th stage-known as Firm Ball

Appearance	°F.	°C.
At this temperature the ball is still soft and pliable when tested in your fingers, but you can certainly mould it more readily. It gives a firmer, harder fudge. In the higher temperatures, i.e. 245–250°F. (115·5–121·1°C.) it is a very firm ball which will produce, from a fudge recipe, a sweet that is crisp enough to be called a candy. *Between the temperatures of 250–280°F. (121·1–137·7°C.) there is a stage where you do not produce any particular result. That is why it is important to test continually, since if you pass the ball stage the fudge will not be successful.*	240–250	115·5–121·1

6th stage-known as Crack

Appearance	°F.	°C.
In the crack stage the sugar mixture will break quite easily between your fingers. This temperature is used for certain toffees or caramels, or sweets like butterscotch.	280	137·7

7th stage-known as Caramel

Appearance	°F.	°C.
At this stage the sugar begins to change colour drastically and turns into caramel (dark brown). Care must be taken not to exceed this too much, for if the caramel-coloured sugar becomes very dark, it also becomes completely unpalatable.	312	155·5

To test sweetmeat mixture without a thermometer

Have ready a small basin of cold water—
SOFT BALL mixture forms a soft, pliable mixture that can be rolled into a ball.
FIRM BALL the ball formed is very solid.
BRITTLE the mixture is hard and breaks when handled firmly.
HARD CRACK as the mixture is put into the cold water it makes a distinct 'crack' sound and breaks off very easily when handled.

Uncooked sweets

Some sweets may be prepared without cooking:

CHOCOLATE CLUSTERS: melt 100 grammes (4 oz.) plain chocolate in a basin over hot but not boiling water, cool slightly, add 50 grammes (2 oz.) nuts or nuts and raisins, stir well. Put tiny heaps on to a plate or tin to set.
COCONUT TRUFFLES: blend small can of full cream evaporated milk with approximately 125 grammes (5 oz.) desiccated coconut, add about 50 grammes (2 oz.) chopped glacé cherries. Roll into small balls, then roll in equal amounts of chocolate powder and sieved icing sugar.
MARZIPAN DATES: make marzipan as recipe page 232. Remove stones from dessert dates, fill with pieces of marzipan, decorate with halved walnuts or other nuts.
PEPPERMINT CREAMS: whisk 1 egg white lightly and beat in little peppermint essence, 200 grammes (8 oz.) sieved icing sugar. Roll out on a board coated with icing sugar, cut into tiny rounds, leave to set.

Butterscotch

Makes ⅝ kilo (560 grammes–good 1¼ lb.)
Cooking time–see stage 2

Ingredients	Metric	Imperial
Demerara sugar	½ kilo	1 lb.
milk	142 ml	¼ pint
water	3 tablespoons	3 tablespoons
butter	75 grammes	3 oz.
cream of tartar	pinch	pinch

1 Put all the ingredients into a pan. Stir until sugar has dissolved.
2 Boil steadily, stirring once or twice as the mixture thickens, until it reaches 280°F. (137·7°C.), forming a very 'brittle' thread.
3 Put into an oiled or buttered tin. A smaller tin gives a thicker Butterscotch.
4 When nearly set, mark into squares.
5 Break when cold. Always wrap in paper.

Uses of Butterscotch

Butterscotch can be made as a sweet by itself, or to coat brazils and other nuts. It is not possible to get the crisp texture of butterscotch without well cooking. If using butterscotch to coat nuts, drop them into the sweetmeat at stage 2 opposite, turn until thinly coated, lift out with a spoon, put on to an oiled or buttered tin.

Speedy Way to Use Nuts

When you have no time to coat nuts in butterscotch, roll them
a) in marzipan,
b) salt them; this will please people who have a less sweet palate–heat a little butter in a frying pan, put the nuts in this and turn until evenly coated and slightly browned, drain on absorbent paper, toss in a little salt.

Coconut Ice

Makes generous ¼ kilo (500 grammes–good 1 lb.)
Cooking time–see stage 3

Ingredients	Metric	Imperial
water	284 ml	½ pint
loaf sugar	½ kilo	1 lb.
powdered glucose *or*	25 grammes	1 oz.
cream of tartar	pinch	pinch
desiccated coconut	100 grammes	4 oz.
thick cream	1 good tablespoon	1 good tablespoon
pink colouring	few drops	few drops

1 Put water and sugar into a strong pan.
2 Stir until sugar has dissolved and add glucose or cream of tartar.
3 Boil steadily until mixture reaches 'soft ball' stage, 238°F. (114·4°C.), when tested in cold water.
4 Add coconut and cream.
5 Beat until cloudy. Pour half into buttered tin.
6 Colour the remainder pale pink, and pour on top.
7 Cut into slices when cold.

Uses of Coconut Ice

Coconut ice can also be used as a filling in tartlet cases or in a sponge. Continue as stages 3 and 4, but increase the amount of cream to 2–3 tablespoons to give a softer texture. Cool and spread in the cake with a knife dipped in hot water.

Speedy Way to Make Coconut Ice

Blend 100 grammes, generous measure, (4 oz.) desiccated coconut with 150 grammes (6 oz.) icing sugar. Add 2 tablespoons sweetened condensed milk; colour half and continue as stages 6 and 7 in recipe.

Golden Toffee

Makes a good ½ kilo (500 grammes–good 1 lb.)
Cooking time–see stage 2

Ingredients	Metric	Imperial
sugar, preferably Demerara	½ kilo	1 lb.
water	189 ml	⅓ pint
butter	40 grammes	1½ oz.
golden syrup	2 level tablespoons	2 level tablespoons
vinegar	1 teaspoon	1 teaspoon

1 Put all the ingredients into a strong saucepan and stir over a steady heat until the sugar has dissolved.
2 Bring to the boil and cook until the mixture reaches the 'hard crack' stage, 290°F. (143·3°C.).
3 Pour into oiled or buttered tin and either allow to set as a slab, or mark in squares as the toffee becomes partially set, then cut or break when completely set.

Uses of Golden Toffee

Add sultanas, nuts, a little desiccated coconut etc., to the toffee at the end of stage 2, continue as stage 3.
Make the toffee, cut into neat pieces and dip in melted chocolate.

Speedy Way to Make Toffee

There is no way to make a real toffee without cooking, but a speedy crisp toffee-like sweet is made as follows: make a caramel sauce, see page 188 with 6 tablespoons golden syrup–boiling until really brown: cool slightly, then add as many rice crispies or really crisp cornflakes as the caramel will absorb. Put in tiny heaps on a greased tin and allow to set.

French Brazil Rock

Makes nearly ⅞ kilo (875 grammes–1¾ lb.)
Cooking time–see stage 2

Ingredients	Metric	Imperial
loaf *or* brown sugar	½ kilo	1 lb.
glucose *or*	50 grammes	2 oz.
cream of tartar	¼ teaspoon	¼ teaspoon
water	scant 284 ml	scant ½ pint
butter	50 grammes	2 oz.
blanched brazils*	200 grammes	8 oz.

*blanched almonds could be used.

1 Put the sugar, glucose (or cream of tartar) and water into a strong saucepan and stir until sugar has dissolved.
2 Boil steadily, without stirring, until the mixture reaches the 'brittle' stage, 260–280° F. (126·6–137·7°C.).
3 Beat in the butter and coarsely chopped brazils. Stir together, then pour into buttered or oiled tin.
4 Either break in pieces when cold, or wait until cool enough to handle and form into neat shapes; see picture facing page 217, (brown sugar was used in this recipe).
5 Wrap in waxed paper to store.

Uses of French Brazil Rock

This sweet is excellent crushed and used over the top of desserts—particularly trifles and plain ice cream. It can also be sprinkled over the top of a sponge cake, which should be spread with a thin layer of whipped cream or butter icing.

Speedy Way to Make a Brazil Sweetmeat

Make a caramel sauce as suggested above, but instead of putting cereal in, add a few brazils and leave to set. Use this sweetmeat fairly quickly as the caramel does not become as hard and brittle as the rock or toffee.

Cooked Fondant

Makes 1 kilo (good 2 lb.)
Cooking time–see stage 1

Ingredients	Metric	Imperial
sugar, granulated *or* loaf	1 kilo	2 lb.
water	142 ml	¼ pint
glucose	75 grammes	3 oz.

1 Put sugar and water into a strong pan, stir until sugar has just dissolved. Add the glucose and boil quickly until mixture reaches 240–245°F. (115·5–118·3°C.), a 'soft ball', but a little firmer than the usual 'soft ball'. The varying temperatures enable one to have the right degree of hardness for individual tastes, and if liked, fondant can be softened for fillings and coatings.
2 Do not beat fondant in pan, otherwise it may become granular, but allow to cool and stiffen very slightly.
3 Sprinkle a little warm water on to slab, turn the sweet out and leave for a few minutes to set further before handling.
4 Work sweet up and down with a spatula or palette knife until it becomes very white and firm in texture. If wishing to use at once, knead and mould with warm hands to required shapes. If required to store, wrap in plenty of waxed paper or foil and keep in a covered tin, or cool place.

Uses of Fondant

Use as the centre of chocolates; make tiny shapes and dip in chocolate, which has been melted in a basin over a pan of hot but not boiling water—allow to dry and set. Add chopped nuts, glacé cherries etc., at stage 4; roll out on a board dusted with sieved icing sugar and cut into fancy shapes.

Speedy Way to Make Fondant

The quickest way to make Fondant is exactly the same as a *Royal icing*. Beat one egg white lightly and add 225 grammes (8 oz.) sieved icing sugar, together with a little lemon juice.
To use Royal icing, simply spread on top or over the cake with a knife dipped in hot water. This amount is sufficient for the top of only a 18–20-cm (7–8-inch) cake.

Marzipan

Makes approx. ½ kilo (500 grammes–good 1 lb.)
Cooking time–none

Ingredients	Metric	Imperial
ground almonds	200 grammes	8 oz.
castor sugar	100 grammes	4 oz.
icing sugar	100 grammes	4 oz.
almond essence	few drops	few drops
egg yolks to mix	approx. 1½–2	approx. 1½–2

1 Mix all the dry ingredients together.
2 Add enough egg yolk for a firm mixture; colour if wished.
3 Knead thoroughly, do not overhandle; cut into fancy shapes.

Note: marzipan can be adapted to give a variety of sweets. Tint various colours as suggested at stage 2. Roll on a sugared board, cut into fancy shapes and leave exposed to the air to dry. Nuts or glacé cherries may be added or used to decorate.

Uses of Marzipan

Marzipan is one of the most versatile of all sweets; it is the traditional coating of Christmas, wedding and rich fruit cakes under the icing. The amount given opposite will cover the top and sides of a 20–22-cm (8–9-inch) cake giving a fairly thin layer.
Use any marzipan left over as a stuffing for stoned dates, to roll round nuts etc.

Marshmallows

Makes ⅜ kilo (375 grammes–just over ¾ lb.)
Cooking time–see stage 2

Ingredients	Metric	Imperial
sugar, loaf *or* granulated	250 grammes	10 oz.
water	142 ml and 4 tablespoons	¼ pint and 4 tablespoons
orange flower water *or*	4 tablespoons	4 tablespoons
juice of lemon	1	1
glucose (optional)	1 dessertspoon	1 dessertspoon
powdered gelatine	3 level dessertspoons	3 level dessertspoons
egg white	1	1
icing sugar	a little	a little

1 Put the sugar with 142 ml (¼ pint) of the water, the orange flower water or lemon juice and glucose into a saucepan.
2 Stir until the sugar has dissolved, then boil steadily until it reaches 260°F. (126·6°C.) or forms a 'firm ball' when tested in cold water.
3 Dissolve the gelatine in the remaining water, then pour the sugar mixture on to the gelatine and stir together thoroughly.
4 Beat well and then pour on to the stiffly beaten egg white.
5 Continue beating until the mixture starts to stiffen, then pour into a tin lined with greaseproof paper and liberally dusted with icing sugar.
6 Dust the top of the mixture with more icing sugar and lay a piece of paper on top and a heavy weight.
7 When quite set, cut into squares (scissors are the best thing to use) and roll each piece in icing sugar.
8 Leave exposed to air for 24 hours, then put into boxes.

Uses of Marshmallows

One of the most usual uses of marshmallows is as a flavouring, sweetening and lightening ingredient in some ice creams, see page 197.
You can also add marshmallows to ordinary fruit jellies. Allow the jelly to cool but not set, and then stir in a few whole or cut marshmallows.

Mixer

The whisk is excellent for the egg whites at stage 4, and you can continue to use a hand electric mixer on a low speed at stage 5.

Nut Brittle

Makes nearly 1¼ kilo (2½ lb.)
Cooking time–see stages 3 and 5

Ingredients	Metric	Imperial
sugar	½ kilo	1 lb.
golden syrup	200 grammes	8 oz.
water	142 ml	¼ pint
blanched peanuts, almonds *or* other nuts*	250 grammes	10 oz.
salt	¼ teaspoon	¼ teaspoon
butter	15 grammes	½ oz.
bicarbonate of soda	¼ teaspoon	¼ teaspoon

*to blanch the nuts cover in boiling water, leave for a short time then remove skins; dry well.

1 Combine sugar, syrup and water in heavy pan.
2 Cook slowly, stirring till sugar dissolves.
3 Cook to 'soft ball' stage, test a few drops in cold water, 238°F. (114·4°C.).
4 Add nuts and salt.
5 Cook to the 'hard crack' stage, 280°F. (137·7°C.), stirring constantly. Remove from the heat while testing.
6 Add butter and bicarbonate of soda, stir to blend–the mixture will bubble–pour on to large buttered tins.
7 Partially cool by lifting around edges with a spatula, so it will not stick–when firm but still warm, turn over.
8 Pull to make thin brittle, break in pieces when cold, or cool enough to handle, form into ball shapes as picture facing page 217. Wrap to keep crisp in waxed paper.

Uses of Nut Brittle

This sweet is excellent crushed and used over the top of desserts–particularly trifles and plain ice cream. It can also be sprinkled over the top of a sponge cake, which should be spread with a thin layer of whipped cream and butter icing.

Speedy Way to Make Nut Brittle

Make a caramel sauce and add blanched peanuts, almonds or other nuts to this.

Nougat

Makes approx. ¾ kilo (750 grammes–1½ lb.)
Cooking time–see stages 1 and 6

Ingredients	Metric	Imperial
granulated sugar	½ kilo	1 lb.
water	142 ml	¼ pint
golden syrup	3 level tablespoons	3 level tablespoons
cream of tartar	pinch	pinch
honey	3 tablespoons	3 tablespoons
egg whites	4	4
blanched pistachio nuts	100 grammes	4 oz.
vanilla essence	few drops	few drops
rice paper *or* wafers	as required	as required

1 Put sugar, water and syrup into strong saucepan, stir quickly until sugar has dissolved, then boil steadily until the mixture reaches 270° F. (132·2° C.)–very 'firm ball'.
2 Stir in cream of tartar.
3 While syrup is boiling, stand honey over very low heat to become hot.
4 Whisk egg whites in big bowl until very stiff, stand over pan of boiling water, gradually pour on syrup mixture, stirring very well all the time.
5 When thoroughly blended, add hot honey and chopped nuts and essence.
6 Stir for a few minutes over boiling water, then test by dropping a little in cold water–it should make 'firm ball'–if a little soft, continue cooking and testing.
7 Line a 22–24-cm (9–10-inch) square tin with rice paper, or wafers, pour in mixture.
8 Cover with more wafers or paper, and leave to set then cut in pieces; or put into oiled tin without wafers or rice paper.
9 Wrap in waxed paper to prevent becoming sticky.

Uses of Nougat

Nougat is an excellent centre for chocolate. Make the Nougat to stage 8–do not use rice paper. When quite set, dip in *warm* melted chocolate, put on a tray until the chocolate is firm.

Speedy Way to Make Nougat

Whisk 2 small egg whites until very stiff, add 225 grammes (not 200 grammes) of sieved icing sugar (8 oz.) and few drops of either almond, vanilla or other essences. Add 25 grammes (1 oz.) blanched chopped almonds, 25 grammes (1 oz.) chopped glacé cherries, 25 grammes (1 oz.) seedless raisins or sultanas and mix thoroughly. Put rice paper at the bottom of the tin, spread the Nougat over this, cover with more rice paper and leave to set for a day. Cut into squares.

Mixer

Use the whisk at stage 4 to beat the egg whites until very stiff. If you have a hand mixer which can be used on a very low speed, this can be utilised to stir the syrup over the egg whites at stage 4.

Turkish Delight

Makes ½ kilo (500 grammes–good 1 lb.)
Cooking time–see stages 2, 4 and 6

Ingredients	Metric	Imperial
sugar	½ kilo	1 lb.
water	852 ml	1½ pints
tartaric acid	¼ teaspoon	¼ teaspoon
icing sugar	175 grammes	7 oz.
cornflour	75 grammes	3 oz.
lemon	1	1
honey	50 grammes	2 oz.
pink colouring	few drops	few drops
TO COAT:		
icing sugar	50–75 grammes	2–3 oz.

1 There are many recipes for this Oriental sweet, some very quick and easy, but in order to have the correct consistency, this rather longer process is advisable, for it produces a most delicious jelly sweet.
2 Boil the sugar and 142 ml (¼ pint) water until a 'soft ball', 240° F. (115·5° C.).
3 Add the tartaric acid.
4 Blend the icing sugar and cornflour with the rest of the water and bring to the boil, stirring all the time.
5 Boil and beat until thick and clear.
6 Add syrup, then gradually boil for 25–30 minutes, stirring and adding the lemon juice. The mixture will then be straw-coloured and transparent.
7 Add honey and pour half the mixture into a buttered tin.
8 Colour the rest pink and pour either into a second tin, or cool slightly and pour on top of the first layer.
9 When cold and firm, cut into squares with kitchen scissors and roll in sieved icing sugar.

Uses of Turkish Delight

Turkish delight is an excellent accompaniment to coffee at the end of a meal, so it is quite a good idea to keep stocks available for special occasions.
Turkish delight can be dipped in chocolate. Make certain it is very firm before you attempt to do this i.e. that you have made the sweetmeat at least 24 hours before coating. Melt the chocolate in a basin over hot but not boiling water–allow this to cool but not become set–turn the squares of Turkish delight in the chocolate, lift out on to a tray and leave until the chocolate is hard.

Speedy Way to Make Turkish Delight

Although this is not a true Turkish delight, it is a jellied sweet which is very pleasant: make up any fruit flavoured jelly–lemon or orange are the best–but use only 125 ml (¼ pint) water to dissolve the jelly. Add 250 ml (½ pint) very thick fruit purée; taste and add a squeeze lemon juice if necessary. Pour into a lightly oiled tin, leave to set. Cut into squares with a knife dipped in hot water, and roll in icing sugar.

Rich Vanilla Fudge

Makes nearly ¾ kilo (750 grammes–1½ lb.)
Cooking time–see stage 3

Ingredients	Metric	Imperial
granulated sugar	½ kilo	1 lb.
cream (preferably thin)	284 ml	½ pint
butter	50 grammes	2 oz.
water	3 tablespoons	3 tablespoons
milk	142 ml	¼ pint
vanilla essence *or*	1–2 teaspoons	1–2 teaspoons
use vanilla pod		

1 Put all the ingredients, including the vanilla essence or the cut vanilla pod, into a strong saucepan–this is very important because of the high cream content.
2 Stir until sugar is thoroughly dissolved.
3 Boil steadily, stirring quite frequently, until the mixture reaches the 'soft ball' stage. This is a nicer fudge if rather soft, so do not let it exceed 238°F. (114·4°C.).
4 If using vanilla pod, take out, rinse under cold water and store in a jar of sugar.
5 Beat fudge until slightly cloudy.
6 Pour into a well oiled or buttered tin.
7 Allow to set, and then cut in squares.
See picture, facing page 217.

Flavourings for fudge

BRANDY FUDGE: use this recipe but add brandy instead of water.
CHOCOLATE FUDGE: use this recipe and add 50 grammes (2 oz.) sieved cocoa to the other ingredients when the fudge has almost reached 238°F. (114·4°C.).
FRUIT AND NUT FUDGE: add 100–200 grammes (4–8 oz.) sultanas or seedless raisins alone or with the same amount of chopped nuts, when the fudge has nearly reached 238°F. (114·4°C.), or add chopped glacé cherries as picture facing page 217.
NUT FUDGE: add 100–200 grammes (4–8 oz.) chopped walnuts, almonds, or brazils, when the fudge has nearly reached 238°F. (114·4°C.).

FOR A FIRMER FUDGE: boil to 240°F. (115·5°C.), but never exceed this.

Coffee Family Fudge

Makes nearly ¾ kilo (750 grammes–1½ lb.)
Cooking time–see stage 3

Ingredients	Metric	Imperial
water	2 tablespoons	2 tablespoons
granulated sugar	½ kilo	1 lb.
coffee essence	3 tablespoons	3 tablespoons
butter	25 grammes	1 oz.
evaporated milk	284 ml	½ pint
(full cream)		

1 The method of making is exactly as the Rich vanilla fudge above.

Crisp Candy

To turn any fudge into a candy, boil to 240°F. (115·5°C.). This sweet is in the background of the picture facing page 217. In candy use ordinary milk in place of cream or evaporated milk, if wished.

Uses of Fudge

Fudge makes a delicious filling and topping for a plain Victoria sandwich. To make both filling and topping you need only half the quantity of sugar etc., in the recipe opposite. Make the Fudge to stage 5, then beat in 1–2 tablespoons thick cream to give a spreading consistency. Use half the mixture to sandwich two rounds of sponge cake together, use the rest to spread over the top of the cake, and decorate with nuts, etc.
The recipe opposite is a basic one; add nuts, sultanas or other dried fruit at the end of stage 3.
Flavour the Fudge with 50 grammes (2 oz.) cocoa at stage 3 when it is nearly set, or add 2 tablespoons coffee essence at the end of stage 2.
Rum or other essences may be used in place of vanilla.
Coat the Fudge in chocolate as suggested under other sweetmeats in this section.

Speedy Way to Make Fudge

Heat 50 grammes (2 oz.) butter, 50 grammes (2 oz.) white or brown sugar, 2 tablespoons golden syrup and a little vanilla essence in a saucepan. Take off the heat and stir in 6 generous tablespoons of dried milk powder (you will need slightly less if following the metric quantities, since these are slightly smaller than the Imperial). Press into a small buttered tin, leave to set and cut into squares.
Sultanas, nuts, etc., may be added to this before putting in the dried milk powder. This coffee fudge is excellent as a chocolate cake, see remarks above on the uses of fudge. Add walnuts or other nuts if wished.
When made into a candy (as in the back of the picture), press out rather more thinly, so you have a crisp sweetmeat.

Making Preserves

Home-made preserves are an economy, if you grow fruit or can buy it cheaply; they are also very delicious if made well.

Points to remember when making jams, jellies, etc.

1. Choose and look over fruit carefully–discard any bruised or damaged portions.
2. Be certain that the fruit is very clean, it is wise to wash it. The best way to do this is to lay the fruit on fine sieves and gently pour water over it. If you actually immerse the fruit in water, it absorbs too much and will, in consequence, make the jam watery:
a) with soft fruits, transfer to absorbent kitchen paper to dry;
b) with firm hard fruits, dry with a cloth. Never wash in hot water as this softens the fruit too early.
3. In some recipes one will need to 'top and tail' the fruit, i.e. in the case of gooseberries. The easiest way to cut off the stalk and flower end (which is what is meant by the term 'top and tail') is to use a pair of sharp kitchen scissors.

4. To remove stones from hard fruit, cut with a stainless knife, take out the stones. You may find this a little difficult if the fruit is slightly under-ripe, in which case leave the stones in and take them out after the fruit has softened.
To stone cherries, insert a fine new hairpin into the fruit with the bent end going into the cherry. Move this around until you feel it lock around the stone, then pull sharply and you will find it brings the stone with it. Do this over the preserving pan, as you tend to bring juice out with the stone and then it is not wasted.
If you are following a recipe where it says ½ kilo (1 lb.) *stoned* fruit and you have left the stones in, allow an extra 100 grammes (4 oz.) fruit.

Where the recipe says ½ kilo (poor weight), (i.e. deduct about 30 grammes for each ½ kilo) which gives the equivalent of 1 lb. *stoned* fruit, you should allow an extra 75 grammes (3 oz.) if you do not remove the stones.
5. When peeling fruit, use a stainless knife, and peel as thinly as possible so the minimum of fruit is wasted.
If you wish to skin fruits, such as peaches, immerse for a few seconds in boiling water to loosen the skin, lift out, place in cold water to cool the fruit rapidly, and then skin.
Note:
These preparations should be done just before making the jam as the moment you wash, stone or peel the fruit it is inclined to deteriorate.

6. Follow recipe exactly as amount of sugar to fruit. Where a fruit has little natural pectin (setting quality), i.e. sweet cherries–you need more fruit than sugar, and in addition it helps to add acid in the form of lemon juice, redcurrant juice, or commercial pectin. Where a fruit is rich in pectin, e.g. blackcurrants, you get a better jam if you use more sugar than fruit.
7. Select a large pan so there is plenty of room for the jam to boil hard–without splashing or boiling over.
8. Preserving sugar is ideal, but you can use loaf or granulated sugar. Warm the sugar slightly as this will make it dissolve more quickly.
9. Do stew the fruit slowly. This is very important, for it:
a) extracts pectin (natural setting substance);
b) softens skins–test most carefully for the skin must be soft before you add the sugar;
c) helps to keep jam a good colour.
10. Stir until sugar has dissolved–this is essential, for it makes certain the jam or jelly does not burn, or crystallise, during cooking. You can tell if all the sugar has dissolved by tapping your wooden spoon on base of pan, it should give a hollow sound.
11. When the sugar has dissolved boil jam *rapidly without stirring*. The quicker the jam or jelly sets, the better the yield, flavour and colour. It is essential to have plenty of room in the pan, or the jam will boil over.
12. Test early for setting. Some jams are ready within 3–5 minutes, others take 10–15 minutes, or even more. Many fruits will lose their set-qualities if boiled too long and then the jam *never* sets.

Process of making preserves

Preserves incorporate jams, jellies, chutneys, etc., and the points about choosing fruits, etc. apply to all of these. A preserve will not be satisfactory if the fruit is stale or over-ripe, but it will also be disappointing if it is under-ripe. Follow the process of making jams and jellies and chutneys, as outlined in this chapter, and when you are satisfied that the preserve has reached setting point, put into the warmed jars and cover. See advice given below.

Storing preserves

All preserves should be stored in a cool, dry place, away from steam, etc. This is not easy in modern houses, for you also need air circulation, if possible, and so many modern kitchens are over-warm. If you feel that *your* kitchen is too warm, then pour the very hot jam, or jelly or chutney, into warmed preserving jars and seal down immediately. This gives an air-tight container which is not affected by outside warmth, steam, etc. Naturally the bottling jars can be used over again, with new lids if the newer type, or new rubber rings if the older design.

Filling and covering jars

Obviously the jars must be well warmed for the hot preserve to be put into them, and the jars must be well covered.
Cellophane jam pot coverings are perfectly satisfactory for jams and jellies, providing there is a

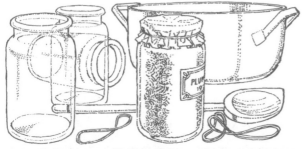

waxed circle as well. Put this on the very hot jam; or allow jam to become cold (covered with a clean tea cloth to keep away flies); but *never* cover luke-warm jam or jelly as this would encourage the growth of mould. Chutneys, on the other hand, are better covered with thick layers of brown paper as well as these other coverings, since chutney can dry out easily.
In a home with efficient central heating there is a possibility of jam drying also, so use bottling jars, where possible, to stop evaporation.

Saving time when preparing preserves

A pressure cooker is one of the best ways of saving time when making preserves, especially when making marmalade–see the comments by individual recipes.

To test when preserve is set

A. TEST BY WEIGHT, i.e. weigh first the empty pan (if scales are sufficiently strong) then when you feel jam or jelly is ready, weigh again. Deduct weight of pan from total weight and if it is more than given below, the jam needs boiling a little longer.
The ideal yield is calculated on the weight of sugar.

SUGAR USED	IDEAL YIELD
½ kilo *less* 25–30 grammes (1 lb.)	(1⅔ lb.)
1½ kilo *less* 100 grammes (3 lb.)	(5 lb.)
2 kilo *less* 125–130 grammes (4 lb.)	(6⅔ lb.) etc.

B. TEST BY TEMPERATURE
If you make a lot of jams or jellies it is worth investing in a sugar thermometer–stir round in pan; hot jam should be 220–222°F. (104–105·5°C); and jelly 220–221°F. (104–105°C.). Be careful not to put thermometer on cold surface or it will break.

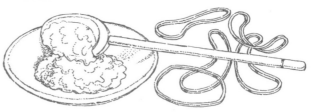

C. FORMING A SKIN
Put a little jam on an old saucer, allow to become quite cold, then see if it forms a skin and wrinkles when pushed with a spoon or finger.
Take pan off heat while waiting for jam to cool on saucer.

D. FORMING A FLAKE
Stir wooden spoon round in jam so that it becomes thoroughly coated, then allow to cool. Hold horizontally and inspect jam. If it hangs in a firm drop or flake then it has reached setting point. Take pan off heat while waiting for jam to cool on spoon.

Home freezing of fruits for preserves

The section beginning on page 208 gives more information on freezing fruit. This is an excellent idea for you can freeze the fruit when readily available, and use for making preserves at your convenience.
Seville oranges should be wrapped and frozen whole, then defrosted and used in the recipe on page 240, where the marmalade is made from fresh fruits.
Other fruits can be pulped, then frozen, see pages 208/9.
Where the fruit requires a large amount of water, i.e. blackcurrants, you can freeze with very little water; *label carefully* and add the extra water when making the jam.
Always make the preserve as soon as possible after defrosting so that no pectin is lost in storing the fruit at room temperature.

When the preserves have reached setting point

1. When you are satisfied that the jam is ready, take pan off the heat, remove the scum. If there is not much scum, most of this will disappear if stirred steadily.

2. For a jelly or jam that contains no whole fruit:
a) pour at once into hot dry, clean jars. Tap the jar as you fill, to bring air bubbles to the surface. Fill to at least ¼–½ cm (⅛–¼ inch) from top of jar. The jam or jelly will shrink a little as it cools. This also makes certain there is less air space in the jar and, therefore, less chance of it becoming mouldy. Jars filled to the brim also look more attractive;
b) for a jam containing whole fruit, allow jam to cool in pan until it stiffens slightly, then stir to distribute peel or whole fruit and pour into hot jars.

3. Put on waxed circles at once—also final transparent cover; or wait until jam is quite cold. Tie down firmly or use rubber band.

4. Store in a cool, dry dark place.

5. If jam shows signs of mould, it is due to:
a) damp fruit;
b) insufficient boiling—giving too low a proportion of sugar in the finished jam;
c) bad storage conditions (damp in particular);
d) not filling jars sufficiently or covering well.

6. If jam crystallises it is due to:
a) either using too much sugar in proportion to the amount of fruit, or too little sugar, which will necessitate over-cooking to stiffen jam;
b) not stirring thoroughly to make sure sugar has dissolved before boiling;
c) too long cooking.

7. If jam shows signs of fermenting and has a 'winy' flavour, it is due to:
a) using over-ripe fruit;
b) bottling before the jam has reached setting point;
c) using too little sugar or not boiling jam sufficiently to give the right proportion of sugar in finished jam;
d) bad storage conditions;
e) not covering jars correctly.

8. If jam or jelly is hard and dry, it is due to:
a) over-boiling.
b) bad covering, so that jam dries out in storage. Where there is central heating it is always advisable to put jam or jelly either into bottling jars, or use tightly fitting caps over waxed circles—not just paper covers.

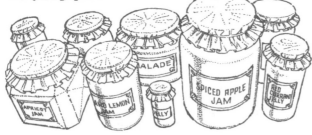

9. If jam or jelly is syrupy and not firmly set it is because:
a) the first juice was lacking in pectin (not enough natural setting quality);
b) not boiled sufficiently, or over-boiled. Jam which is boiled *passed* setting point gives sticky, syrupy texture;
c) fruit juice in jelly left too long after straining—use as soon as ready.

10. If jam or jelly is a poor colour, it is due to:
a) poor quality fruit;
b) not stewing fruit slowly enough to soften it sufficiently;
c) over-boiling, or boiling jam too slowly up to setting point;
d) storing in bright light;
e) using a poor quality preserving pan; aluminium or copper is best.

11. If jam or jelly has disappointing flavour it is because:
a) the fruit used was too ripe or under-ripe;
b) too much sugar was used, giving over-sweet taste;
c) boiling too slowly or over-boiling, takes away fresh fruit flavour;

12. If jelly is cloudy in appearance it is because:
a) it was badly strained—use proper jelly bag or several thicknesses of muslin over a hair (not wire) sieve;
b) the pulp was forced through the jelly bag or muslin—allow to drip by itself without pressing or encouraging it through with a spoon.

Grouping fruits for jams, etc.

Fruits vary in the amount of pectin (natural setting quality) they contain. The *less* pectin the *more* fruit you need in proportion to sugar. Sugar does not set jam or jelly; it is the pectin; sugar acts as the preservative in a jam or jelly.

1. FRUITS WITH LITTLE PECTIN
Fresh apricots (if ripe), *blackberries, dessert cherries, strawberries*. To ½ kilo prepared fruit use ½ kilo sugar *less* 75* grammes, or to 1 lb. fruit use 1 lb. sugar *less* 2 oz., also juice of 1 *large* lemon (see next page). Use minimum of water.

2. FRUITS THAT ARE RICH IN PECTIN
Cooking apples, blackcurrants, damsons, green gooseberries. To ½ kilo prepared fruit use ½ kilo sugar *plus* 75 grammes, or to 1 lb. fruit use 1 lb. sugar *plus* 2 oz. and approximately 8–12 tablespoons water.

3. OTHER FRUITS have an average amount of pectin, and need an equal amount of sugar and fruit with the minimum of water (see next page).
*A ½ kilo is 1·1 lb., This is why 75 grammes.

To make jam

1. Simmer the fruit *gently* with water, the amount is given on page 238. This varies according to the type of fruit. Fruits in groups 1 and 3 need *no* water, or 1–2 tablespoons only to prevent the fruit burning. Always cook the fruit *gently* to extract the pectin.
2. Always make sure the fruit is tender before adding the sugar. If skins of fruit (blackcurrants, in particular) are not tender when the sugar is added they will *never* become soft after the sugar has been added.
3. Stir in the sugar; preserving or loaf sugar is best. Make certain the sugar is thoroughly dissolved. To test, tap the wooden spoon hard on the bottom of the pan. If not dissolved, you will hear the slight noise of tapping a "gritty" layer of sugar, and feel this too.
4. When once the sugar has dissolved add lemon juice for fruits in group 1, then let the jam boil *hard* until setting point is reached (see page 237).
5. If making a jam with whole fruit, wait until the jam has stiffened slightly, then pour into warmed jars and seal as instructions on previous page.

Some interesting jams

GROUP 1–see page 238 for proportions.
APRICOT AND LEMON–add the grated rind of 2 lemons to each ½ kilo (1 lb.) fruit.
CHERRY ALMOND–when cherry jam is nearly set, add 50 grammes (2 oz.) split almonds to each ½ kilo (1 lb.) completed jam.
STRAWBERRY PRESERVE–sprinkle the sugar over the whole fruit, stand for 2 hours, then simmer until the sugar has dissolved, add lemon juice and a tablespoon brandy; boil until setting point is reached.

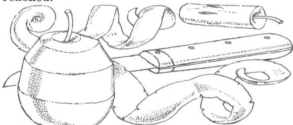

GROUP 2–see page 238 for proportions.
APPLE GINGER–cook the prepared apples with the recommended amount of water. When soft add sugar, and to each ½ kilo (1 lb.) fruit used add 50 grammes (2 oz.) sliced preserved ginger, plus a tablespoon syrup.
GOOSEBERRY RAISIN–when the jam is almost set, stir in about 25 grammes (1 oz.) seedless raisins to each ½ kilo (1 lb.) fruit used.

GROUP 3–see page 238 for proportions.
LOGANBERRY AND REDCURRANT CHEESE–allow two parts of loganberries to one part of redcurrants, and simmer with no water until tender. Sieve, to remove all the pips, then add the sugar and boil until the setting point is reached.

To make jelly

Fresh fruit jellies are delicious and quite easy to make. The amount of water used depends upon the pectin content of the fruit.
1. FRUITS SUITABLE FOR JELLY WITH LITTLE PECTIN: *blackberries, ripe dessert gooseberries, raspberries.* To 1 kilo (2 lb.) prepared fruit allow 125 ml (¼ pint) water and either 2 medium cooking apples or the juice of 2 large lemons. When the fruit has been strained through the jelly bag, measure, and to 1 litre juice allow just over ¾ kilo sugar, i.e. to 2 pints juice allow 2 lb. sugar.
2. FRUITS SUITABLE FOR JELLY THAT ARE RICH IN PECTIN:
cooking or crab apples, cranberries, damsons, green gooseberries.
To 1 kilo (2 lb.) prepared fruit allow a minimum of 375 ml (¾ pint) water. If the fruit is very hard, increase this amount slightly. If very ripe, decrease it slightly. The amount of sugar is as above.
3. OTHER FRUITS should have 250 ml (½ pint) water and sugar as above.

Method of making jelly

1. Put the washed fruit into the preserving pan. There is no need to peel or core apples, just cut into pieces. Gooseberries do not require 'topping or tailing'.
2. Add the water and simmer gently until the fruit is a pulp. In any recipes where it is suggested that cooking apples are added to give extra pectin, they should be simmered with the fruit, but lemon juice is added at next stage.
3. Put the fruit pulp into a jelly bag and allow this to drip into a bowl; do *not* press the bag to make juice drip through more rapidly–this would give a 'cloudy' liquid.
4. When all the juice has dripped through, you may care to simmer the pulp again, adding just under *half* the original amount of water.
5. Allow this second infusion to drip and mix with the first, then measure.
6. Put back into the preserving pan, add the sugar–see amount necessary above.
7. Stir until the sugar has thoroughly dissolved, see point 3 opposite–add lemon juice if recommended for group 1 fruits.
8. Boil until setting point is reached (see page 237) then pour into warmed jars and seal (see page 238).

Note: jelly bags are obtainable from good stores or ironmongers. If you do not have one, put several thicknesses of fine muslin (buy this from a chemist) on a nylon sieve over a bowl, and let the juice drip through.

To make marmalade

There are two ways of making marmalade; if you wish a fine cut fruit peel as picture facing page 208, use Method 1; if you wish a more 'chunky' marmalade use Methods 1 or 2.

FOR MARMALADE:
CHOOSE–either all Seville or bitter oranges; lemons; mixture of citrus fruit.
ALLOW–a) to ½ kilo Seville or bitter oranges a generous litre water and 1 kilo sugar for a *fairly 'bitter' marmalade* (or to 1 lb. oranges, 2 pints water and 2 lb. sugar).
b) for a *sweeter marmalade*–½ kilo Seville or bitter oranges a generous 1½ litres water, juice 2 lemons and 1½ kilo sugar (or to 1 lb. oranges, 3 pints water, juice 2 lemons and 3 lb. sugar).
c) for a *lemon marmalade*, choose proportions under a).
d) for a *mixed fruit marmalade*, choose 1 large Seville orange, 1 large sweet orange, 1 large lemon and proportions under a) or b) according to personal taste.

METHOD 1
1 Wash fruit, halve, squeeze out orange juice and put into a basin.
2 Remove pips, tie in a bag of muslin, put in a large bowl with all the water.
3 Mince or cut oranges finely. If you wish a very fine cut peel, cut away some of the white pith and put to soak with the pips. Add orange peel, etc., to the water and bag of pips and leave soaking overnight.
4 Simmer slowly until peel is quite soft. This should take about 1½ hours, but the cooking time will vary with thickness of the peel.
5 Take out bag of pips, add orange juice, the warmed sugar and lemon juice, if needed.
6 Stir until sugar has dissolved, then bring to the boil and boil rapidly until setting point is reached, see page 237.
7 Cool slightly until beginning to thicken, stir to distribute the peel, put into warmed jars and seal as page 238.

Speedy Ways to Make Marmalade
Method 2
Put whole fruit (unsoaked) in pan with water. Simmer slowly for about 1½ hours or until a blunt wooden skewer will easily pierce the skin of the fruit. Remove oranges from liquid, allow to cool. Cut up neatly. Put pips into the liquid, boil steadily for 10 minutes to extract the pectin from them. Remove pips with a perforated spoon, and replace the cut orange pulp. Bring to the boil, stir in the warmed sugar, continue stirring until sugar is dissolved. Bring to the boil, boil rapidly without stirring until setting point is reached. Continue as Method 1.

Using a pressure cooker:
1. Cut the amount of water to half.
2. Use Method 1 and cook for 10 minutes at 15 lb. pressure, or Method 2, above, and cook for 15 minutes at 15 lb. pressure. Allow pressure to drop gradually, then add sugar and use pressure pan as an ordinary saucepan.

Home Freezing
See page 237.

To make chutney

This is made by gently simmering the ingredients with the vinegar (which with the sugar acts as a preservative), and when soft adding the sugar and letting it cook steadily. The recipe below is a good basic one that can be adjusted by adding other fruits.

CHOOSE–good cooking apples and the mature rhubarb together with pure malt vinegar.
ALLOW–1 kilo (2 lb.) cooking apples (weight after peeling and coring), ½ kilo (1 lb.) rhubarb, ½ kilo (1 lb.) onions, ¼ litre–284 ml (½ pint) vinegar, 2 teaspoons mixed pickling spices, 1–2 teaspoons powdered ginger, 1 teaspoon salt, ½ kilo (1 lb.) brown sugar.

1 Chop the fruit into neat pieces and the onions very finely.
2 Simmer in about half the vinegar with the pickling spices, tied in a muslin bag, and the ginger and salt.
3 As the fruits soften, add more vinegar and when quite soft (this takes about 25 minutes), stir in the sugar.
4 Continue stirring until the sugar has dissolved. Add any remaining vinegar, then cook for about 20 minutes until like thick jam. Remove bag of spices and put the chutney into hot jars. Seal down tightly.
About 150 grammes (6 oz.) dried fruit could be added at stage 3.

Speedy Way to Make Chutney
A pressure cooker could be used to soften the fruit etc., i.e. stages 1 and 2: allow 5 minutes at 15 lb. pressure, and let pressure drop at room temperature then stir in the sugar and treat the pressure cooker as an ordinary saucepan. Do not reduce the amount of vinegar in the recipe.

Drinks for all Occasions

In this section are some interesting drinks, both alcoholic and non-alcoholic. When entertaining you often will find it is cheaper and more interesting to present a wine cup, or a really warming punch, than the usual selection of spirits, etc. Children will enjoy some of the drinks made with fruit juices, as well as the interesting milk shakes. A flavoured milk drink may persuade a child, who hitherto has disliked milk, to enjoy drinking this, and milk is a most important food for both children and adults.

Metric Conversions

Metric conversion in drinks is not unduly complicated, except you will buy liquids by the litre not the pint. Most drinks are a matter of personal taste and an exact conversion is relatively unimportant. The liquid conversion is completely accurate, i.e. 568 ml = 1 pint, but 1 litre is under 2 pints.

Using a mixer

Occasionally you will need to whisk an egg white for a 'fluffy' drink, but generally you can use the liquidiser (blender) to give a smooth shake or iced drink.

Read the manufacturer's instructions carefully about using ice cubes in *your* particular goblet, for large ice cubes could in time, damage the blades. It may be wiser to crush the ice slightly before putting this into the goblet. Never fill the goblet too full when making drinks of any kind; for the liquid rises up in the goblet very quickly. It is also very important to see the lid is placed firmly in position before switching on, and wise to hold it on for the first few seconds. Use a high speed where possible for blending the ingredients for drinks, but increase the speed *gradually* to prevent a sudden up-surge of the liquid which could dislodge the lid.

When you wish to blend the ingredients without a liquidiser, you can use a fairly tall container and your small electric mixer (kept to the lowest speed possible to prevent splashing).

Slimming

Most slimming diets limit the intake of alcohol, so I have included several interesting drinks in this chapter where alcohol is kept to a minimum or omitted altogether. If you are still allowed a limited amount of alcohol, then choose dry wines wherever possible; beers of all kinds, whisky and gin are all high in calories. As pointed out, however, in the first chapter of this book, the recipes given are to enable you to adapt family or party dishes (or drinks), so they become lower in calories and less fattening–rather than give you a complete slimming regime.

You can easily omit the sugar in some of the fruit cups and punches, and use a sugar substitute.

Every day drinks

GOOD COFFEE
Use 2 heaped or 4 level tablespoons to each 568 ml (1 pint) freshly drawn water. Make sure the coffee is freshly ground. Put the coffee into a warmed jug, pour the boiling water over, cover the top, infuse for 4 minutes; strain and use. There are many more ways of making coffee, but the basic proportions remain.

GOOD TEA
Always warm the pot with boiling water, and bring the pot to the kettle (as should be done to coffee too) so that *fresh* boiling water is added.

Tip the water out of the teapot, after making sure it is well warmed, add the tea then the boiling water. Infuse for 3–4 minutes and serve. Allow 1 teaspoon per person and 1 for the pot if you like strong tea.

HOT CHOCOLATE
For each cup of hot chocolate either blend 1–2 teaspoons cocoa with a little cold milk and pour on the very hot milk, stirring well as you do so, or one has a smoother drink if the cocoa is tipped back into the saucepan and heated for a few minutes.

If using chocolate powder, then stir or whisk into the hot milk; allow 2–3 teaspoons per cup.

Cold Drinks

Throughout the year cold refreshing drinks are ideal for parties. Cold punches and cups can be made with inexpensive wines; fruit drinks are enjoyable for adults as well as children, and iced milk shakes, etc., enable one to serve milk in a variety of ways; both sophisticated and simple. Have plentiful supplies of ice available for parties; store in the refrigerator, home freezer or insulated containers.

Raspberry Cider Cup

Gives 12 glasses
Cooking time—none

Ingredients	Metric	Imperial
lemon	1	1
bottled raspberry syrup	284 ml	½ pint
or juice from a tin of	(generous ¼ litre)	
raspberries		
raspberries	200 grammes	8 oz.
cider	1,136 ml	approx. 2 pints
soda water	568 ml	1 pint
	(generous ½ litre)	
TO DECORATE:		
mint	few sprigs	few sprigs
apples	1 *or* 2	1 *or* 2
ice cubes	568 ml	1 pint

1 Wipe the lemon and slice thinly, and place in a large jug or bowl.
2 Pour on the raspberry syrup and add the raspberries.
3 Leave to soak until ready to serve, allow at least one hour.
4 Pour in the cider and soda water.
5 Decorate with mint leaves and unpeeled apple slices, and stir well. Add ice cubes and serve in frosted glasses.

TO FROST GLASSES: lightly beat 1 egg white, dip the rim of each glass in this then into castor sugar. Leave to harden.

Home Freezing
Frozen raspberries can be used in this drink; you may not have as much syrup as from canned fruit, so either dilute slightly (since it is very strong), or add some bottled raspberry syrup as well.

West Indian Punch

Gives 16 glasses
Cooking time—none

Ingredients	Metric	Imperial
pineapple	1 medium	1 medium
castor sugar	2 tablespoons	2 tablespoons
rum	1 miniature	1 miniature
	bottle	bottle
chilled cider	2 flagons	2 flagons
soda water	284 ml	½ pint
TO DECORATE:		
cucumber	small piece	small piece
mint	several sprigs	several sprigs

1 Peel and chop three-quarters of the pineapple and put into a punch bowl or jug, with the sugar.
2 Leave until the juice of the fruit runs.
3 Add the rum with the chilled cider and soda water.
4 Decorate with cucumber slices and mint leaves; pieces of angelica could be used instead of mint leaves if wished.
5 Cut the rest of the pineapple, with the skin still on, into neat pieces and press over the edges of the glasses.

Home Freezing
Mint leaves can be frozen to use as decoration for drinks like this when fresh mint is out of season.
Have sprigs of mint in polythene bags (this gives a rather soft texture to the mint), or freeze the sprigs uncovered, when they become fairly 'crisp', but soften when put into drinks.
You can also freeze mint leaves in trays of ice cubes, to add to drinks like the one opposite.

Overlanders' Honey Punch

Gives 30 tall glasses

Ingredients	Metric	Imperial
grapefruit	1 small	1 small
pineapple pieces	1 can	1 can
brandy	284 ml	½ pint
lemons	3	3
clear honey	4 dessertspoons	4 dessertspoons
cracked ice*	as required	as required
inexpensive Chablis	4 bottles	4 bottles
fizzy lemonade	just over 2 litres	4 pints
TO DECORATE:		
mint	few sprigs	few sprigs
cherries	as required	as required
lemon slices	as required	as required

*to crack ice, lay the cubes on a folded tea cloth, cover with a second tea cloth and bang hard with either an ice cracker or a *wooden* rolling pin. The tea cloth prevents the ice 'jumping' in all directions.

1 *Cut* away the peel from the grapefruit, so removing the pith, and divide into neat segments, removing the pips and any skin.
2 Drain syrup from pineapple and dice the fruit.
3 Soak the fruit in the brandy for an hour or so.
4 Add the juice of the lemons and honey, stirring well.
5 Pour this mixture into a glass punch bowl and add the cracked ice.
6 Pour on the Chablis, stirring.
7 Half fill tall glasses, top up with lemonade.
8 Decorate with sprigs of mint, cherries and chopped lemon slices as picture between pages 216/217.

The amount of lemonade may be varied to suit your taste, and may be omitted altogether if desired; this recipe does not use the syrup from the canned pineapple, but it could be added if desired at stage 4.

Slimming Tips
Use the Chablis and grapefruit but substitute fresh pineapple or orange segments, instead of sweetened canned pineapple. Use sugar substitute instead of honey and one of the low calorie lemonades, or more lemon juice and soda water.

Home Freezing
Freeze slices of lemon (or orange too) ready for party drinks. Pack in polythene bags; there is no need to wait for the lemon slices to defrost in a drink like this, they help to chill the drink if they are added straight from the freezer.

Strawberry Punch

Gives 3–4 glasses
Cooking time–none

Ingredients	Metric	Imperial
strawberry jam	3 tablespoons	3 tablespoons
natural *or* strawberry		
yoghourt	small carton	small carton
milk	426 ml	¾ pint

1 Whisk the ingredients together sharply in a deep jug until fluffy.
2 Pour into 3–4 small tumblers and serve with a teaspoon, so the strawberries may be enjoyed.

Mixer
Put all the ingredients into the goblet. Switch on for a few seconds only. A very little ice could be added, too much dilutes the flavour.

Slimming Tips
Use fresh fruit, natural yoghourt and skimmed milk. This is an excellent low calorie food, for it provides the goodness of fatless milk and enables you to include milk quite often in the menu.

Iced Coffee

Since the coffee is generally diluted with milk or cream it should be very strong; increase the proportion of coffee therefore, see page 241.

Put a little crushed ice into each glass, add about two-thirds very cold coffee, then fill with cold milk or thin cream; or use milk, and top the glass with thick cream and a little grated plain chocolate. When topped with cream serve with a long spoon.

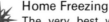

Home Freezing
The very best way to produce perfect strong iced coffee is to freeze strong coffee in ice cubes. You can then crush this slightly, fill the glass two-thirds full of the iced coffee and top up with milk, thin cream, or as opposite. This produces a superb cold drink.

Calypso Cider

Gives 8 glasses
Cooking time 5 minutes

Ingredients	Metric	Imperial
clear honey	2 tablespoons	2 tablespoons
oranges	4	4
cinnamon sticks	1–2	1–2
water	142 ml	¼ pint
cloves	12	12
brandy	2 tablespoons	2 tablespoons
chilled cider	1 flagon	1 flagon
TO DECORATE:		
maraschino cherries	as required	as required
orange slices	as required	as required
cinnamon sticks	8	8

1 Put the honey, juice from 2 of the oranges, cinnamon sticks and water into a saucepan.
2 Bring to the boil and simmer for 5 minutes.
3 Stud the other oranges with the cloves, put into a punch bowl and pour the hot liquid over them.
4 Leave until cold, then add the brandy and chilled cider.
5 Decorate with maraschino cherries on cocktail sticks if wished, and orange slices.
6 Serve in glasses with a cinnamon stick in each. These cinnamon sticks should be removed, rinsed in cold water, dried, and again stored.

Slimming Tips

This drink is still excellent if made without the honey, follow stage 1 but omit the honey and add sugar substitute at the end of stage 2.
You *could* make 1 glass only by this method, using one eighth quantities and sugar substitute instead of honey, then make remainder with honey.

Home Freezing

Maraschino cherries are expensive, and if you freeze morello cherries in a really thick sugar syrup, flavoured with a little maraschino syrup, you have a rather similar flavour.

Milk Shakes

Milk shakes are made by blending milk, flavouring, etc., to produce a light fluffy texture; ice or ice cream can be incorporated in cold shakes.
If using a hand whisk, blend in a tall, fairly wide jug to give plenty of movement; naturally the liquidiser, see opposite, is ideal for this purpose.
The liquidiser not only gives a light mixture but, because of the speed in blending, enables you to mix acid fresh fruits (such as lemon juice, blackcurrants, etc.) with hot milk, with no fear of curdling. It would be unwise to try and do this by hand.

Speedy Meal

Fruit syrups to flavour milk are available at stores and grocers. Choose also rose hip or blackcurrant syrups, which are rich in Vitamin C, this is not destroyed if you use cold, or hot, but *not* boiling milk.

Mixer

The goblet is ideal for making milk shakes. Read the instructions though about adding ice, for large ice cubes can damage the blades, and it is advisable to crush this to put in most liquidisers.
Put all ingredients into goblet together. Never fill the goblet too full, and turn to full speed (necessary to give a very fluffy drink) very gradually; emulsify for ½–1 minute. Make sure the lid is tightly in position for the liquid rises very drastically in the goblet.

Iced Fruit Milk Shake

Gives 1 glass
Cooking time—none

Ingredients	Metric	Imperial
ice *or* ice cream	as required	as required
fruit syrup *or* jam *or*	½–1 tablespoon	½–1 tablespoon
fresh fruit *or* juice	2–3 tablespoons	2–3 tablespoons
sugar	to taste	to taste
cold milk	½ tumbler	½ tumbler

1 If using ice or ice cream put into jug, add syrup (or jam, crushed or sieved fresh fruit, or fresh fruit juice and sugar).
2 Mix briskly then gradually whisk in the milk. Decorate with fresh fruit if desired, see picture facing page 160.

Home Freezing

It is worth freezing small containers of fruit pulp or juice for milk drinks.

HOT FRUIT MILK SHAKES: use hot, but not boiling milk, omit ice or ice cream.
BRANDY AND EGG: whisk 1 tablespoon brandy and 1 egg yolk (with ice for a cold shake); add milk, sugar to taste.
COFFEE OR CHOCOLATE: use instant coffee powder or syrup, cocoa or chocolate powder.
SAVOURY MILK SHAKES: use 1–2 teaspoons yeast or meat extract (these are better well iced).

Lemonade

Gives 2–3 glasses
Cooking time—none

Ingredients	Metric	Imperial
lemons	2	2
boiling water	568 ml	1 pint
	(generous ½ litre)	
sugar, glucose, etc.	to taste	to taste

1 Grate the yellow 'zest' only from the lemons, do not use any of the bitter white pith.
2 Add boiling water, lemon juice and sweetening. Leave until cool then strain, or serve hot.

Orangeade IS MADE THE SAME WAY.

Mixer
Pare the rind very thinly from the lemons, put into the liquidiser with some of the water. Switch on until emulsified. This does give a more cloudy drink, but you can dilute this with a greater quantity of water than in recipe; strain if necessary, add rest of water, juice, etc.

Home Freezing
Freeze grated lemon rind, juice, etc. in form of ice cubes for lemonade.

Hot Red Wine Punch

Gives 16 glasses
Cooking time few minutes

Ingredients	Metric	Imperial
orange juice	6 tablespoons	6 tablespoons
lemon juice	2 tablespoons	2 tablespoons
sugar	2–3 tablespoons	2–3 tablespoons
red wine*	2 bottles	2 bottles
brandy *or* rum	to taste	to taste
nutmeg	to taste	to taste

*inexpensive wine is quite good, but for special occasions choose claret.

1 Heat the fruit juices with the sugar in a large pan.
2 Add wine, bring to boiling point, pour in brandy or rum.
3 Pour into a warmed punch bowl and top with grated nutmeg.

More hot punches

RUM AND ORANGE PUNCH: heat 1 litre (2 pints) canned orange juice and ½ bottle rum, serve topped with orange slices.

CIDER BRANDY PUNCH: press cloves into several small dessert apples, bake until golden brown (this gives a very good flavour to the punch); heat 1 litre (2 pints) sweetened cider, add ½ bottle brandy pour over apples.

COFFEE RUM PUNCH: heat strong coffee, with rum to taste, together with a cinnamon stick and sugar as required, top with powdered cinnamon.

Speedy Meal
Use lemon or orange sweetened cordials instead of fresh fruit juices.

Gaelic or Irish Coffee

Gives 1 glass
Cooking time—none

Ingredients	Metric	Imperial
whisky *or* whiskey*	to taste	to taste
strong black coffee	¾ glass**	¾ glass**
sugar	to taste	to taste
thick cream	1–2 tablespoons	1–2 tablespoons
(thin could be substituted)		

*the second spelling denotes Irish whiskey.
**generally served in stemmed glasses not cups.

1 Put whisky into warmed glass, add coffee and sugar to taste.
2 Pour cream over back of spoon to give thick coating on top.
3 Sip the very hot coffee through the layer of cool cream.

Speedy Meal
Use instant coffee powder to make the coffee. Make sure it is strong.

Your questions answered

I hope your various problems on cooking today with the help of modern equipment have been answered throughout the book, but as a general 'summing-up', here are some of the most important questions and answers.

On home freezing

Q. Throughout this book ideal storage times have been given for keeping food in the freezer. Does this mean the food is unfit or dangerous to eat if stored longer than this?

A. No, the food will still be safe to eat but tends to be less satisfactory, for example a pâté kept longer than the recommended period becomes dry and 'crumbly' and loses its creamy texture and much of the flavour.

Q. Why is it so important to cover foods in a freezer, and what would happen if they were left uncovered?

A. Good wrapping is needed to conserve moisture in the food; if left unwrapped, the food would become very dry and unappetising. The cold is so intense in a freezer that it could cause a form of 'burning' in the food, rather like 'frost-bite' experienced by humans in excessively cold conditions. Wrapping prevents this, and one needs *strong* wrappers or containers, for most people handle the food quite a lot in a freezer, and fragile wrappings could break, and would at the same time offer inadequate protection against the cold conditions.

Q. Is it possible to freeze salad ingredients and so have them out of season?

A. Lettuce and similar green salad vegetables contain mostly water, so are spoiled by freezing and lose their crisp texture. Radishes, spring onions and tomatoes become soft. Root vegetables can be blanched and frozen for macedoine of vegetables or in a dressing as Russian salad. You can freeze tomato purée for tomato flavoured mayonnaise in fish salad.

Q. Can rich fruit cakes be frozen?

A. Yes, but pointless to do so as they are rich enough to keep moist in airtight tins.

Q. How are ice cubes stored in the freezer?

A. When made, pack cubes in ice trays in polythene bags or any suitable container, or just in bags, if wishing to use ice trays.

Q. What happens if there is a power failure?

A. Keep lid or door closed firmly; the food will remain frozen for some hours.

Q. Can one freeze dairy cream and desserts made with dairy cream?

A. Many of the desserts in this book contain a high percentage of cream, and so when you freeze these ice creams or cream moulds you have a smooth texture, but desserts with a low percentage of cream often do not freeze well, as they develop tiny ice particles. This is why homemade ice cream can be rather expensive as you have to use the full quantity of cream, or full cream evaporated milk.

Much of the cream sold in cartons does not freeze satisfactorily, because the fat content is too low. If you have really rich cream, with over 45 per cent butter fat, you can freeze this and still retain a smooth texture. Some cream is specifically marked with a label '*do not freeze*', and you are, of course, unwise to freeze this as you will be disappointed with the texture when thawed out. Obviously there will be occasions when you have bought too much cream, and rather than waste it, I would suggest you *do* freeze it. When it has thawed out, it will appear to have separated and look very unattractive, but I have found that if I want to use it as a liquid cream all I need to do is to put it in the liquidiser and switch on for a few seconds. If I wish to whip it, I use an electric or rotary whisk and beat very hard; it will whip quite satisfactorily although it never seems quite as smooth as one would wish for piping. Many desserts are decorated with whipped cream, and you will be pleasantly surprised to find how well this freezes.

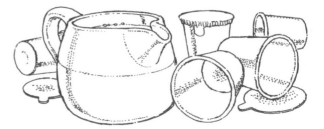

Soured cream does not freeze well by itself, and neither does cottage cheese, which is often used in dessert type cheese dishes, but both of these freeze well when combined with other ingredients. Yoghourt (so often spelt as yogurt today) does not freeze well by itself, but when combined in recipes it freezes perfectly. Because milk has such a high water content it is quite unsatisfactory to freeze bottles or cartons of milk, for they expand a great deal and could cause the bottle or carton to break, and the milk forms ice crystals which when defrosted gives a very poor texture.

However, as explained in the introduction to freezing cold desserts, milky desserts can be frozen for a short period, but would contain ice crystals if left longer.

On automatic cookers and baking

Q. If using an automatic cooker for the first time how much longer should one allow to cook a familiar menu?

A. Surprisingly little. If you are sure you will be home to eat the meal the moment the oven switches *off* then allow only about 10–15 minutes longer; or delay dishing-up as you lay the table, etc. If you are doubtful as to whether you will be present at the end of cooking time, then set the oven for about 5–10 minutes shorter period than you would normally, to allow for the fact that the food will continue cooking in the heat of the oven and that retained by cooking utensils.

Q. I cannot understand why one *can* put foods such as meat, etc., into a cold oven. I was always taught that one needs immediate heat to 'seal in' the flavour; can you tell me if automatic cooking really is satisfactory?

A. Modern cookers 'heat up' so quickly that you do get very quick heating through. There are certain foods that need 'pre-treatment' to stop their spoiling while waiting – for example potatoes *must* either be covered with water or coated with fat so they do not discolour, see below. Some foods, e.g. puff pastry or true sponges, etc., must *not* be kept waiting before cooking, but the effect upon meat is not harmful.

Q. How does one keep potatoes from going black if left in the oven?

A. By coating them very well in melted fat to exclude the air, or by completely covering with water in a casserole. If you feel the potatoes may rise above the water in cooking, put over them a thick layer of foil, or a saucer, to keep them under the salted water in the casserole.

On slimming

Q. Are there any safe between-meal 'nibbles' one can eat?

A. Eating between-meals is one of the main causes of putting on weight, so try and avoid this where possible. If very hungry eat citrus fruit (unless you are following a diet where fruit intake is controlled), raw carrot, celery or olives; it may be wise to 'keep-back' part of the fruit allowance from a meal, so you can enjoy this during mid-morning or when you are hungry.

Q. Does the amount of water you drink affect weight?

A. Some people *are* over-weight simply because their body retains surplus fluid and the Doctor will limit the amount of liquid. The question of liquid intake varies with various diets and it is often a case of 'trial and error'; follow a diet or sensible mode of eating and if you still do not lose weight then try and limit the liquid intake and see if this helps.

Q. Is it safe for everyone to follow a slimming diet without medical advice?

A. It has been stressed thoughout this book that it is *not* a book of slimming diets but there are hints to reduce the calories of certain dishes. If you are just a little over-weight and want to lose a few kilos, then a period of controlled eating, where you 'cut out' or limit carbohydrates (starches and sugars), should be sufficient to restore the weight to normal. If you have to lose a lot of weight you then need a proper slimming diet, and you should consult your Doctor before following this.

On using mixers

Q. Why does one find the fat and sugar 'thrown' to the sides of the bowl when creaming?

A. This is because the fat was probably too hard when you switched on. Warm the bowl slightly to assist in the initial creaming. Use a slow or low speed at the beginning of creaming and switch to a medium speed as the mixture becomes softer. Do *not* use high speeds though, otherwise the mixture will be pushed to the sides of the bowl.

Q. How full can one fill the liquidiser goblet?

A. This rather depends upon the food being blended, see below. Liquids rise in the goblet when the motor is switched on, so be careful that you never put too much in.

Q. Why, when making crumbs for stuffings, etc. do the blades cease to revolve in the liquidiser?

A. This is probably because you have put too much into the goblet. Use only small amounts and the moment the blades cease to revolve, switch off and remove any bread, etc., that has not formed into crumbs; tip out the crumbs and start again. It can also be because you are not 'feeding in' the food; often you can emulsify a greater quantity if you add this through the 'hole' in the lid while the blades are revolving; this is particularly true if bread is rather fresh.

Q. One reads about 'feeding in' bread, etc., and oil for mayonnaise, through the 'hole' left when removing the cap in the lid of the liquidiser, what does one do if there is no removable cap?

A. Remove the lid altogether; make a very thick layer of foil and fit this over the top of the goblet, then make a hole in this.

Index

253